教育部首批课程思政示范课程配套教材 | 全国教育科学"十三五"规划课题成果

国家文化产业资金支持媒体
融合重大项目 | 高等职业教育金融类专业富媒体智能型教材·数字化教材

岗课赛证融通教材

INTERNATIONAL FINANCIAL PRACTICE

U0648897

国际金融实务

（双语教材）

沈立君　薄文雅　主编

欧捷　副主编

东北财经大学出版社　大连
Dongbei University of Finance & Economics Press

图书在版编目（CIP）数据

国际金融实务=International Financial Practice：双语教材 / 沈立君，薄文雅主编. —大连：东北财经大学出版社，2022.12

（高等职业教育金融类专业富媒体智能型教材·数字化教材）

ISBN 978-7-5654-4505-7

Ⅰ.国…　Ⅱ.①沈…②薄…　Ⅲ.国际金融–双语教学–高等职业教育–教材–英、汉　Ⅳ.F831

中国版本图书馆CIP数据核字（2022）第 067316 号

东北财经大学出版社出版

（大连市黑石礁尖山街217号　邮政编码　116025）

网　　址：http：//www.dufep.cn

读者信箱：dufep@dufe.edu.cn

大连日升彩色印刷有限公司印刷　东北财经大学出版社发行

幅面尺寸：185mm×260mm　　　字数：1 067千字　　　印张：33.25

2022年12月第1版　　　　　　2022年12月第1次印刷

责任编辑：李丽娟　张晓鹏　吴　茜　　责任校对：李合一
　　　　　徐　群　刘晓彤

封面设计：冀贵收　　　　　　　　　　版式设计：原　皓

定价：75.00元

教学支持　售后服务　联系电话：（0411）84710309
版权所有　侵权必究　举报电话：（0411）84710523
如有印装质量问题，请联系营销部：（0411）84710711

富媒体智能型教材出版说明

"财经高等职业教育富媒体智能型教材开发系统工程"入选国家新闻出版广电总局新闻出版改革发展项目库，并获得文化产业专项资金支持，是"国家文化产业资金支持媒体融合重大项目"。项目以"融通""融合""共建""共享"为特色，是东北财经大学出版社积极落实国家推动传统媒体与新媒体融合发展的重要举措之一。

"财济书院"智能教学互动平台是该工程项目建设成果之一。该平台通过系统、合理的架构设计，将教学资源与教学应用集成于一体，具有教学内容多元呈现、课堂教学实时交互、测试考评个性设置、用户学情高效分析等核心功能，是高校开展信息化教学的有力支撑和应用保障。

富媒体智能型教材是该工程项目建设成果之二。该类教材是我社供给侧结构性改革探索性策划的创新型产品，是一种新形态立体化教材。富媒体智能型教材秉持严谨的教学设计思想和先进的教材设计理念，为财经职业教育教与学、课程与教材的融通奠定了基础，较好地避免了传统教学模式和单一纸质教材容易出现的"两张皮"现象，有助于教学质量的提高和教学效果的提升。

从教材资源的呈现形式来说，富媒体智能型教材实现了传统纸质教材与数字技术的融合，通过二维码建立链接，将VR、微课、视频、动画、音频、图文和试题库等富媒体资源丰富呈现给用户；从教材内容的选取整合来说，其实现了职业教育与产业发展的融合，不仅注重专业教学内容与职业能力培养的有效对接，而且很好地解决了部分专业课程学与训、训与评的难题；从教材的教学使用过程来说，其实现了线下自主与线上互动的融合，学生可以在有网络支持的任何地方自主完成预习、巩固、复习等，教师可以在教学中灵活使用随堂点名、作业布置及批改、自测及组卷考试、成绩统计分析等平台辅助教学工具。

富媒体智能型教材设计新颖，一书一码，使用便捷。使用富媒体智能型教材的师生首先下载"财济书院"APP或者进入"财济书院"（www.idufep.com）平台完成注册，然后登录"财济书院"输入教材封四学习卡中的激活码建立或找到班级和课程对应教材，就可以开启个性化教与学之旅。

"重塑教学空间，回归教学本源！""财济书院"平台不仅仅是出版社提供教学资源和服务的平台，更是出版社为作者和广大院校创设的一个教学空间，作者和院校师生既是这个空间的使用者和消费者，也是这个空间的创造者和建设者，在这里，出版社、作者、院校共建资源，共享回报，共创未来。

最后，感谢各位作者为支持项目建设所付出的辛劳和智慧，也欢迎广大院校在教学中积极使用富媒体智能型教材和"财济书院"平台，东北财经大学出版社愿意也必将陪伴广大职业教育工作者走向更加光明而美好的职业教育发展新阶段。

东北财经大学出版社

Publishing Notes for Rich Media Intelligent Textbook

"Finance and Economics Higher Vocational Education Rich Media Intelligent Textbook Development System Project" is selected into the Press and Publication Reform and Development Project supported by State Administration of Press, Publication, Radio, Film and Television. It also achieves the special fund support of cultural industry, and is the "Major Project Supported by National Cultural Industry Fund for Media Integration". The project is characterized by "coordination", "integration", "co - construction" and "sharing", which is one of the important measures taken by Dongbei University of Finance and Economics Press to actively implement the national promotion of integration and development of traditional media and new media.

"Caiji Academy" intelligent teaching interactive platform is one of the achievements of the project construction. The platform integrates teaching resources and teaching applications through a systematic and reasonable architecture design. It has core functions such as diversified presentation of teaching content, real - time interaction of classroom teaching, personalized setting of testing and evaluation, and efficient analysis of users' learning situation. It is a strong support and application guarantee for colleges and universities to carry out informationalized teaching.

Rich media intelligent textbook is the second achievement of this project. This kind of textbook is an innovative product of the supply-side structural reform of our press, and it is a new form of three - dimensional textbook. The rich media intelligent textbook upholds the rigorous teaching design idea and advanced textbook design concept, laying a foundation for the integration of teaching and learning, curriculum and textbook of finance and economics vocational education, and better avoiding the "two skins" phenomenon that is easy to appear in traditional teaching mode and single paper textbooks, which contributes to the improvement of teaching quality and teaching effect.

In terms of the presentation form of textbook resources, the rich media intelligent textbook realizes the integration of traditional paper teaching material and digital technology, and presents rich media resources such as VR, micro - lesson, video, animation, audio, graphics and question bank to users through the establishment of links via QR code. From the perspective of selection and integration of textbook content, it realizes the integration of vocational education and industrial development, not only pays attention to the effective docking of professional teaching content and vocational ability training, but also solves the problems of learning and training, training and evaluation of some professional courses. In terms of the teaching process of textbook, it realizes the integration of offline autonomy and online interaction, students can complete pre - study, consolidation and review with the network support, and teachers can flexibly use teaching tools such as class attendance, homework assignment and correction, self-test and paper-forming examination, and statistical analysis of grades to assist teaching.

The rich media intelligent textbook designed with innovation, each textbook comes with a code, and it is easy to use. Teachers and students using the rich media intelligent textbook can download the APP of "Caiji Academy" or access to the website of "Caiji Academy" (www.idufep.com) to complete registration. Then, they can log in to "Caiji Academy" and input the activation code in the learning card of the textbook back cover to establish or find the corresponding textbook of the class and course, and start the personalized teaching and learning journey.

"Reshape the teaching space and return to the origin of teaching!" "Caiji Academy" platform is not only a platform of the press to provide teaching resources and services, but also a teaching space created by the press for authors and majority of colleges and universities, the authors and teachers and students of colleges and universities are not only the users and consumers of this space, but also the creators and builders of this space, where the publishers, authors, institutions jointly build the resources, share the rewards, and create a better future.

Finally, thank you for the authors with the hard working and wisdom to support the construction of the project, and also welcome the majority of colleges and universities to use the rich media intelligent textbook and the "Caiji Academy" platform. Dongbei University of Finance and Economics Press is willing to and will certainly accompany our vocational educators towards to a brighter and better stage vocational education development.

Dongbei University of Finance & Economics Press

前　言

当今世界，国际金融形势风起云涌，复杂多变。在刚刚过去的几年里，国际金融体系发生了深刻变革，国际货币格局正在经历微妙调整。在中美贸易摩擦升级的情况下，我国的"一带一路"倡议和人民币国际化仍然取得了显著成绩。人民币成为主要国际货币中第一个新兴市场国家货币，这对国际货币格局变迁具有重大意义。中国向世界传递了主动开放市场的明确信息和坚定信念，成为引领第三次全球化浪潮的先锋力量。

近两年，新冠肺炎疫情冲击着世界经济，WTO争端解决机制陷入停摆，贸易保护主义、单边主义暗流涌动，多边贸易体制和经济全球化陷入危机，国际经济局势急转直下。2020年11月15日，东盟十国和中国、日本、韩国、澳大利亚及新西兰正式签署区域全面经济伙伴关系协定（RCEP），意味着全球约1/3的经济体量形成了一体化大市场，自由贸易、多边主义和区域经济一体化发展进程在亚太地区继续推进，为全球经济复苏带来了新希望。RCEP的建立必然影响和改变区域内国际贸易活动、国际结算方式、国际资金投资流向及国际资本市场格局。在此大背景下，结合国家职业教育发展规划及要求，本教材编写组在广泛进行社会调研，充分征询行业专家、相关企业和高等职业院校教学一线教师建议的基础上，按照高等职业教育金融类专业教学计划和教学规律的要求编写了本教材，以满足金融行业应用型技能人才的培养需求。

本着理论够用、实务为主的理念，教材编写组根据高等职业教育学生的认知特点，对国际金融的相关知识进行了筛选和编排。本教材主要介绍国际收支、国际储备、国际金融市场、国际货币体系等宏观基础理论，实务部分选取外汇与汇率、外汇市场与外汇业务、国际结算及融资、外汇风险管理等内容。

本教材围绕教学目标进行了形式多样的知识呈现，体例新颖，紧贴时事，特色鲜明。

1.以"项目—任务"为载体组织教学单元

本教材根据项目化教学设计的特点精心组织教学单元，内容编排科学，结构合理。每个项目开头设置"学习目标""课程导入"栏目，明确学生所要掌握的知识与技能，使学生对学习内容形成初步认识；每个项目中设计"知识链接""拓展阅读""案例探析"等栏目，一方面可以增强学生学习的兴趣，另一方面有助于对知识的延伸和运用；每个项目结尾设置"项目思维导图"以及"项目训练"环节，从"教、学、做、思"四个方面综合考察学生的知识掌握情况，帮助学生更好地巩固并掌握所学内容。

2.探索融合"岗课赛证"

本教材探索将金融行业相关岗位要求、全国职业院校金融技能大赛的最新内容以及银行业专业人员职业资格证书考试内容等自然融入教材体系中。与银行、国际金融公司等合作，探索校企合作开发教材，将教材内容与实际工作岗位需求对接，将学历教育与职业资格证书考试相结合，使教材内容更具有时效性和实用性，从而更好地满足金融行业应用型技能人才培养的需求。

3.融入课程思政元素

为了落实教育"立德树人"的根本任务，本教材设置了"思政小课堂"栏目，将专业知识与思政内容相结合，弘扬社会主义核心价值观，增强学生爱国敬业、遵纪守法的意识，培养学生精益求精、开拓创新的工匠精神。

4.配套丰富的数字化资源

本教材配套了丰富的教学视频、微课、动画等数字化资源，并以二维码的形式呈现在教材中，方便学生自主学习，更好地掌握重要知识点，了解实际操作业务。此外，本教材还配套了课件、电子教案、习题库及参考答案等教学资源，以更好地服务于教学。

本教材既可作为高等职业院校财经类专业学生的教学用书，也可作为财经或金融爱好者的学习参考书。

本教材是教材编写组集体智慧的结晶，主要成员均为广西金融职业技术学院的教育部首批课程思政示范课"国际金融实务"课程教学名师。本教材由沈立君教授和薄文雅老师担任主编，共同负责提纲的拟定和统稿；欧捷担任副主编，负责视频资源的梳理等工作。本教材内容编写分工如下：沈立君编写项目一和项目二，唐雪花编写项目三和项目八，宋福常编写项目四和项目六，薄文雅编写项目五和项目七，欧捷编写项目九和项目十。在编写过程中，本着校企共建的原则，我们得到了校企合作企业交通银行南宁分行、中国农业银行南宁分行、中国邮政储蓄银行南宁分行、广西农村信用社等金融行业领域专业人士的指导，也得到了深圳希施玛数据科技有限公司的鼎力相助。

本教材为教育部首批课程思政示范课程"国际金融实务"配套教材，也是全国教育科学"十三五"规划成果。本教材的编写得到了教育部首批课程思政示范课"国际金融实务"教学团队的大力支持，以及广西壮族自治区职业教育金融管理专业群发展研究基地项目、国际金融特色示范专业及实训基地建设项目的资助，在此谨致谢意！

由于国际金融市场复杂多变，规则及政策时有调整，书中所引数据及信息或有出入，学术观点也仍有可探讨的空间，恳请广大读者多提宝贵意见，以便编写组提供水平更高的教材回馈大家。

编 者

2022年6月

Preface

In today's world, the international financial situation is turbulent and complex. In the past few years, profound changes have taken place in the international financial system and the international monetary structure is undergoing subtle adjustments. In the situation of the escalation of trade frictions between China and the United States, China's "The Belt and Road" initiative and the internationalization of the RMB have still made remarkable achievements. The RMB has become the first emerging market currency among major international currencies, which is of great significance to the change of the international monetary structure. China has showed clear message and steadfast conviction to the world about taking the initiative to open the financial market, becoming a vanguard force in leading the third wave of globalization.

In the past two years, COVID - 19 has hit the world economy, the WTO dispute settlement mechanism has been suspended, the trade protectionism and unilateralism are surging, the multilateral trading system and economic globalization are in crisis, and the international economic situation has taken a turn for the worse. On November 15, 2020, ASEAN countries, and China, Japan, Republic of Korea, Australia and New Zealand signed the Regional Comprehensive Economic Partnership (RCEP), means that about a third of the global economic dimension to form an integrated market, and free trade, multilateralism, and regional economic integration development process continue to push forward in the Asia-Pacific region, it has brought new hope for global economic recovery. The establishment of RCEP is bound to affect and change international trade activities, international settlement methods, international capital investment flows and international capital market patterns within the region. Under this overall background, combined with the national vocational education development plan and requirements, our author team writes this textbook on the basis of the wide social investigation, the adequate consultation of industry experts and related enterprises, and the suggestion of teachers of higher vocational colleges who are teaching in the first-line, and in accordance with the requirements of teaching plan and teaching rule of financial major of higher vocational education, to meet the training demand of financial industry application-skilled talents.

In line with the concept of useful theory and sufficient practice, the textbook author team has selected and arranged the knowledge related to international finance according to the cognitive characteristics of students in higher vocational education. This textbook mainly introduces the basic theories of balance of payments, international reserve, international financial markets, international monetary system and so on, and the practical part selects the contents of foreign exchange and exchange rates, foreign exchange market and foreign exchange transactions, international settlement and international financing, foreign exchange risk management and so on.

This textbook presents various forms of knowledge around the teaching objectives, with novel style, close to current events and distinctive features.

1. Organize the teaching units with "Project-Task" as the carrier

The textbook organizes the teaching units according to the characteristics of project-based teaching design carefully, the content is arranged scientifically and the structure is reasonable. At the beginning of each project, columns of "Learning Objectives" and "Course Introduction" are set to clarify the knowledge and skills that students need to master, so that students can form a preliminary understanding of the learning content. In each project, columns such as "Knowledge Link", "Extended Reading" and "Case Analysis" are designed. On the one hand, they can enhance students' interest in learning, and on the other hand, they can help to extend and apply knowledge. At the end of each project, "Mind Map" and "Project Training" are set to comprehensively inspect students' knowledge mastery from four aspects of "teaching, learning, doing and thinking", to help students consolidate and master what they have learned.

2. Explore the integration of "Position Course Competition Certificate"

The textbook explores the natural integration of the relevant job requirements of the financial industry, the latest content of the national competition for financial skills of vocational education and the content of the qualification certificate of banking professional into the textbook system. Cooperate with banks and international finance companies to explore college-enterprise cooperation in the development of teaching materials, connect the content of teaching materials with the needs of actual jobs position, and combine academic education with vocational qualification examination to make the content of teaching materials becomes more timeliness and practicability, so as to better meet the needs of application-skilled talents training in the financial industry.

3. Arrange the Mini Case study section to encourage students to think

In order to encourage students' independent thinking and summarizing ability, this textbook set the Mini Case study column, which consists the global financial events, hot news, financial market data and so on. These mini cases will guide students to understand the real market and to form their own ideas.

4. Provide the rich digital resources

The textbook is equipped with abundant digital resources such as teaching videos, micro lessons and animations, and presented in the textbook in the form of QR code, which is convenient for students to learn independently, better master important knowledge points and understand practical operations. In addition, this textbook is equipped with teaching resources such as courseware, electronic teaching plan, question bank and reference answers, so as to better serve the teaching.

This textbook can be used not only as a teaching book for students major in finance and economics in higher vocational colleges, but also as a learning reference book for finance and economics enthusiasts.

This textbook is the crystallization of the collective wisdom of the author team. The main members are from the Guangxi Financial Vocational College. This textbook is edited by Professor Lijun Shen and Teacher Wenya Bo, who are jointly responsible for the drafting of the outline and the final compilation; Jie Ou served as associate editor, who is responsible for the sorting of the video resources and other work. The content division of the textbook is as follows: Lijun Shen writes Project One and Two, Xuehua Tang writes Project Three and Eight, Fuchang Song writes Project Four and Six, Wenya Bo writes Project Five and Seven, and Jie Ou writes Project Nine and Ten. There are eight team members take part in the translation project. Wenya Bo translates Project Five and Seven, Fuchang Song translates Project Two and Six, Jiayan Zhang translates Project One and Three, Geyu Dong translates Project Eight and Ten, Manman Lu translates Project Four and Nine. At the same time, this English version is also supported by experts from the financial industry, who are Yu He from China Development Bank Guangxi Branch, Xinyu Fan from Agricultural Bank of China Nanning Branch, Jing Huang from Guangxi GIG Energy Group.

In the preparation process, in line with the principle of college - enterprise co - construction, we have received the guidance of exports in the financial industry from college-enterprise cooperative enterprises such as Bank of Communications Nanning Branch, Agricultural Bank of China Nanning Branch, Postal Savings Bank of China Nanning Branch, Guangxi Rural Credit Union and so on, as well as the full support of Shenzhen CSMAR.

This textbook is the achievement of the thirteenth five-year plan for national education and science. The compilation of this textbook has been funded by the development and research base project of financial management professional group of vocational education in Guangxi, and the construction project of international financial characteristic demonstration major and practical training base. Thank you very much!

As the international financial market is complex and changeable, the rules and policies may be adjusted from time to time, the data and information cited in this textbook may be inconsistent, and there is still space for discussion of academic views. We sincerely invite readers to provide more valuable suggestions, so that our author team can provide higher-level textbook to feedback to you.

The Editor
In June 2022

目　录

中文篇

英文篇

中文篇

中文摘

项目一
国际收支

学习目标

知识目标

理解国际收支的概念及含义，了解国际收支平衡表的编制原理，掌握国际收支平衡表的内容及结构。

能力目标

掌握国际收支平衡表的分析方法，理解国际收支失衡的原因和影响，掌握国际收支调节的手段和措施。

操作目标

能够运用所学知识对我国国际收支状况进行初步分析。

课程导入

国家外汇管理局公布 2020 年 5 月我国国际货物和服务贸易数据

2020 年 5 月，我国国际收支口径的国际货物和服务贸易收入 15 894 亿元，支出 11 654 亿元，顺差 4 240 亿元。其中，货物贸易收入 14 592 亿元，支出 9 650 亿元，顺差 4 942 亿元；服务贸易收入 1 302 亿元，支出 2 004 亿元，逆差 702 亿元。

按美元计值，2020 年 5 月，我国国际收支口径的国际货物和服务贸易收入 2 239 亿美元，支出 1 642 亿美元，顺差 597 亿美元。其中，货物贸易收入 2 055 亿美元，支出 1 359 亿美元，顺差 696 亿美元；服务贸易收入 183 亿美元，支出 282 亿美元，逆差 99 亿美元。

资料来源：国家外汇管理局. 国家外汇管理局公布 2020 年 5 月我国国际货物和服务贸易数据 [EB/OL]. [2020-06-29]. http://www.safe.gov.cn/safe/2020/0629/16534.html. 有删减。

思考讨论：上述资料里提到的国际收支、顺差、逆差、货物贸易、服务贸易等术语如何理解？通过本项目的学习，学生在理解基本概念的基础上，能够对我国国际收支状况进行初步分析。

世界经济发展史告诉我们，国际经济交易的起源是国际贸易，而国际贸易的最初形式则是跨国的货物贸易，贸易的进行必然伴随着资源的转移、财富的流动和货币的跨国支付。全球科学技术的进步推动了社会生产力的发展，国际经济关系也日趋密切，当今的国际贸易已经不仅仅局限于最初的货物贸易，而是扩展到服务贸易、各国间的资本流动和直接投资、政府间的转移支付（如援助、捐赠等）等政治经济活动领域。

任务一　　　　　国际收支概述

一、国际收支的概念及含义

各种不同类型的国际经济交易一旦发生，就会引起各种债权债务关系以及与之相联系的货币支付。例如，一国居民出口一批商品会获得一笔对外债权，进口一批商品则会产生一笔对外债务。在国际金融贸易中，这种债权债务关系被称为国际借贷。所谓国际借贷，是指一国在一定日期（时点）对外债权债务的综合情况。

国际借贷所体现的债权债务关系需要在一定时间内清算、结算，以债权国收入货币、债务国支付货币了结。这种清算、结算或支付就形成了国际收支。国际收支在某种程度上反映了一国在一定时期内的对外收入和支付情况。

教学视频1-1

国际货币基金组织（International Monetary Fund，IMF）对国际收支的定义是：国际收支是在一定时期内，一个经济实体的居民同非居民之间所发生的全部经济来往的系统记录。

认识国际货
币基金组织

二、理解国际收支的概念

要理解国际收支的概念，需要从以下三个方面考虑：

1.国际收支是一个流量概念，不是存量概念

国际收支记录的是一定时期（季度、半年、年）内一国对外收入和支出发生的变动数。流量是指一定时期内发生变动的数量的数值，如一定时期内存款变动数、人口出生数等。

2.国际收支记录的是一国的全部经济交易

经济交易不仅包括有形贸易，如货物贸易，也包括无形贸易，如服务、技术转让。

3.国际收支记录的是居民与非居民之间的交易

居民（resident），是指在一个国家的经济领土内居住达1年或1年以上的，具有一个经济利益中心的经济单位。不满足上述条件的，为非居民（non-resident）。居民可以是自然人，也可以是政府机构或法人。居住地的不同是划分居民与非居民的依据。也就是说，以居民从事生产、消费等经济活动和交易的所在地为划分标准。

知识链接1-1

中国居民的范畴

国家外汇管理局发布的《通过银行进行国际收支统计申报业务指引（2019年版）》规定：

机构按照注册地国家或地区确定居民和非居民身份。在华国际组织、国际组织驻华机构、外国驻华领事馆不属于中国居民。

个人按照个人有效身份证件确定居民和非居民身份。

持有境外永久居留证、外国护照、港澳居民来往内地通行证、台湾居民来往大陆通行证等有效证件的个人，认定为非中国居民；持有中国居民身份证、外国人永久居留身份证或其他中国有效证件的个人，认定为中国居民；同时持有所属国籍（地区）身份证件和永久居留证件的个人，鉴于国际收支统计采用经济利益中心的居民原则，优先按照永久居留证件认定居民身份；持有中国护照的个人需同时配合其他有效证件进行认定，即同时持有中国护照和境外永久居留证的个人认定为非中国居民，不持有境外永久居留证的个人认定为中国居民。

资料来源：国家外汇管理局. 国家外汇管理局关于印发《通过银行进行国际收支统计申报业务指引（2019年版）》的通知［EB/OL］.（2019-09-18）.http://www.gov.cn/xinwen/2019-09-18/content_5430887.htm.

任务二　　　　　　　　国际收支平衡表

一、国际收支平衡表的概念

一个国家的国际收支情况只有通过具体的统计数字才能得到切实的体现，这就涉及国际收支平衡表（balance of payments）。国际收支平衡表是反映一个经济实体在一定时期（年度、半年度或季度）内以货币单位表示的全部对外经济往来的一种统计表。所以，国际收支平衡表实际上是国际收支的外在表现形式。

动画微课1-1

国际收支及
国际收支平
衡表

二、国际收支平衡表的编制原理

国际收支平衡表是按照复式记账的原理编制的，即"有借必有贷，借贷必相等"。按照这种记账原理，一切收入项目或负债增加、资产减少的项目都列为贷方，以"+"号表示；一切支出项目或资产增加、负债减少的项目都列为借方，以"-"号表示。每一笔交易都必须同时记录相应的借方和贷方，金额相等。实践中，任何导致对外国人进行支付或外汇需求的交易，即资产增加、负债减少，都记入借方；任何导致从外国人那里获得收入或外汇供给的交易，即资产减少、负债增加，都记入贷方。

因此，原则上，国际收支平衡表全部项目的借方总额与贷方总额总是相等的，其净差额为零。但是，实际上，国际收支平衡表每一具体项目的借方和贷方（即收入和支出）是经常不平衡的，收支相抵总会出现一定的差额。当收入大于支出，即贷方数额大于借方数额时，差额为正数（+），称为顺差；反之，当支出大于收入，即贷方数额小于借方数额时，差额为负数（-），称为逆差。各项目收支差额的总和，便是国际收支总差额。

三、国际收支平衡表的构成

（一）国际收支平衡表的结构

由于各国国际经济交易的内容与范围不尽相同，经济分析的需要也不完全一样，因此编制的国际收支平衡表也有所不同。为了指导成员方编制平衡表，并使各国（地区）的平衡表具有可比性，国际货币基金组织编制的《国际收支和国际投资头寸手册》（第六版）将整个国际收支划分为两大账户，即反映商品、服务进出口以及净要素支付等实际资源流动的经常账户和反映资产所有权流动的资本与金融账户。此外，还设置了人为调整平衡的账户——净误差与遗漏账户。我国国际收支平衡表的具体内容见表1-1。

表1-1　　　　　　　　　　　　我国国际收支平衡表　　　　　　　　单位：亿美元

项目	差额	贷方（+）	借方（-）
I.经常账户			
A.货物和服务			
a.货物			
1.一般商品			
2.用于加工的货物			
3.货物修理			
4.各种运输工具在港口购买的货物			
5.非货币性黄金			
b.服务			
1.加工服务			
2.维护和维修服务			
3.运输			
4.旅游			
5.建设			
6.保险和养老金服务			
7.金融服务			
8.知识产权使用费			
9.电信、计算机和信息服务			
10.其他商业服务			
11.个人、文化和娱乐服务			
12.别处未提及的政府服务			

项目	差额	贷方（+）	借方（－）
B.初次收入			
a.雇员报酬			
b.投资收益			
C.二次收入			
a.个人转移			
b.其他二次收入			
Ⅱ.资本和金融账户			
A.资本账户			
B.金融账户			
a.非储备性质的金融账户			
1.直接投资			
2.证券投资			
3.金融衍生工具			
4.其他投资			
b.储备资产账户			
1.货币黄金			
2.特别提款权			
3.在国际货币基金组织的储备头寸			
4.外汇储备			
5.其他储备资产			
Ⅲ.净误差与遗漏			

资料来源：1.国际货币基金组织. 国际收支和国际投资头寸手册［M］. 6版. 北京：中国金融出版社，2012.

2.国家外汇管理局国际收支分析小组. 2018年中国国际收支报告［R］. 北京：国家外汇管理局，2019.

（二）国际收支平衡表的内容

1.经常账户（项目）

经常账户（current account），是指实质资源的流动，包括进出口的货物、输入输出的服务、对外应收及应付的收益，以及在无同等回报的情况下，与其他国家或地区之间发生的提供或接受经济价值的经常转移。经常账户是一国国际收支平衡表中最基本、最重要的项目。以我国国际收支平衡表的项目为例，经常账户包括货物、服务、初次收入和二次收入四个子项目。

（1）货物。该账户记录一国货物的进口和出口情况。货物项目是一国经常账户中最基本的项目，也是收支规模最大的项目。进口记入借方，出口记入贷方，两者的差额称为贸易差额。货物包括一般商品、用于加工的货物、货物修理、各种运输工具在港口采购的货物、非货币性黄金等项目。

（2）服务。服务是经常项目中的第二大项目，主要记录无形贸易输入和输出产生的收支变动。服务输出记入贷方，服务输入记入借方。服务包括加工服务，维护和维修服务，运输，旅游，建设，保险和养老金服务，金融服务，知识产权使用费，电信、计算机和信息服务，其他商业服务，个人、文化和娱乐服务以及别处未提及的政府服务。

（3）初次收入。初次收入包括居民与非居民之间的两大类交易：第一类是雇员报酬，主要指付给非居民工人（如季节性的短期工人）的工资报酬；第二类是投资收益，包括直接投资、证券投资和其他投资的收入和支出。最常见的投资收入是股本收入（红利）和债务收入（利息）。

（4）二次收入。二次收入是指商品、劳务或金融资产在居民与非居民之间转移后，并未得到补偿与回报的转移，因而也被称为无偿转移或单方面转移。它涉及所有非资本项目的转移，包括政府间的无偿转移（如战争赔款、政府援助、政府向国际组织定期交纳的费用以及国际组织作为一项政策向各国政府定期提供的转移）和私人的无偿转移（如侨汇、捐赠、继承、资助性汇款、退休金等）。从本国向外国的无偿转移记入借方，从外国向本国的无偿转移则记入贷方。

2. 资本和金融账户（项目）

资本和金融账户（项目）（capital and financial account），是指对资产所有权在各国间的流动行为进行记录的账户，包括资本账户和金融账户两大部分。

（1）资本账户（capital account），反映资产在居民与非居民之间的转移。资产从居民向非居民转移会增加居民的对外债权，减少居民的对外债务。而资产从非居民向居民转移则恰恰相反。因此，此账户表明本国在一定时期内资产与负债的增减变化。

同经常账户以借方总额和贷方总额记录的方法不同，资本账户是按净额（借贷差额）记入借方和贷方的。债权或资产的净减少，以及债务或负债的净增加，记为贷方项目；债权或资产的净增加，以及债务或负债的净减少，记为借方项目。

（2）金融账户（financial account），反映居民与非居民之间投资与借贷的增减变化。同资本账户一样，金融账户也是按净额记录的。居民对非居民的投资和提供的信贷的净增加记入借方；非居民对居民的投资和提供的信贷的净增加记入贷方。

金融账户按照投资类型或功能可分为：

①非储备性质的金融账户，包括直接投资、证券投资、金融衍生工具、其他投资；

②储备资产账户，包括货币黄金、特别提款权（SDR）、在国际货币基金组织的储备头寸、外汇储备及其他储备资产。

储备资产的存在，主要是为了调节由经常账户差额和资本与金融账户差额导致的总差额的不平衡。如果总差额为顺差，官方储备增加；如果总差额为逆差，则官方储备减少。储备资产的增减是国际收支数量变化的结果。

3.净误差与遗漏

净误差与遗漏（errors and omissions account）是一种人为设置的抵销账户，用来抵销编表时出现的净的借方或贷方余额。原则上，国际收支平衡表采用复式记账法，借方与贷方总额应当是相等的，差额为零。但实际上，一国的国际收支平衡表不可避免地会出现净的借方余额或净的贷方余额，很难达到平衡。这个余额是由于统计资料有误差或遗漏而造成的。为此，需要人为地在平衡表中设立一个单独的"净误差与遗漏"项目，使差额为零。如果经常账户、资本和金融账户（包括储备资产账户）的贷方出现余额，就在净误差与遗漏项下的借方列出与余额相等的数字；如果这几个账户的借方出现余额，则在净误差与遗漏项下的贷方列出与余额相等的数字。

任务三　　　　　　　　　国际收支失衡及调节

一、国际收支的平衡与失衡

1.国际收支的平衡

国际收支平衡表从其编制原理来看，在某种程度上总是平衡的，其平衡的表现有两个方面：

（1）由于采取复式记账原理，因此国际收支平衡表的借方总额和贷方总额总是相等的。

（2）由于设立了平衡项目，因此经常项目和资本项目的合计差额最终总是可以通过官方储备的增减和净误差与遗漏项目得到平衡，使最终的账面差额即总差额（overall balance）必然为零。

因此，这种平衡成为账目上的平衡，而不是真实意义上的平衡。

2.国际收支的失衡

从另一方面看，国际收支又常常是不平衡的，不平衡的表现也有两个方面：

（1）国际收支平衡表中的各个项目一般是不平衡的，总会出现一定的差额，这就是所谓的局部差额，这些局部差额很可能会引起国际收支总差额。

（2）从国际经济性质上看，一国国际收支活动是由各种各样的对外经济交易引起的，不可能做到收支完全相抵。因此，一个国家真实的国际收支活动往往不是顺差就是逆差，只不过差额的大小不同而已。

二、判断国际收支失衡的标准

国际收支失衡分为两种情况：对外贸易的顺差和逆差。顺差通常表现为对外经济交易收入大于支出，逆差则表现为支出大于收入。一国国际收支记录的全部对外经济交易可以分为自主性交易和调节性交易。由自主性交易形成的国际收支平衡是主动平衡，而调节性交易带来的国际收支平衡是被动平衡。

1.自主性交易

自主性交易是指经济主体或居民个人，如金融机构、进出口商、国际投资者等，出于某种自主性目的，如追求利润、减少风险、资产保值、逃税避税、逃避管制或投机等进行的交易活动。从动机上看,这些交易完全没有考虑一国国际收支是否会因此出现失衡,所以称为自主性交易。自主性交易体现的是经济主体或居民的个人意志,不代表哪一个国家或政府的意志,具有事前性、自发性和分散性的特点。

2.调节性交易

调节性交易又称补偿性交易,是指中央银行或货币当局出于调节国际收支差额、维护国际收支平衡、维持货币汇率稳定的目的而进行的各种交易,包括国际资金融通、资本吸收引进、国际储备变动等。调节性交易是在自主性交易出现差额时,为了弥补或调节这种差额,由政府出面进行的交易活动,体现了一国政府的意志,具有事后性、集中性和被动性等特点。

如何判断国际收支是否平衡?主要看一国的自主性交易是否平衡。由自主性交易达成的主动平衡是各国国际收支平衡追求的目标。自主性交易的平衡与否是判断一国国际收支是否真实平衡的标准。

三、国际收支失衡的原因

国际收支的均衡是暂时的,而国际收支不平衡是长期的。造成国际收支不平衡的原因很多,主要原因可以从以下四个方面进行分析:

1.经济周期

由一国经济周期波动引起的国际收支不平衡,称为周期性不平衡。在市场经济条件下,由于经济周期的影响,一国经济会周而复始地出现繁荣、衰退、萧条、复苏四个阶段。经济周期的不同阶段会对国际收支产生不同的影响。在繁荣时期,由于国内需求旺盛,进口相应增加,出口反而减少,国际收支可能出现逆差;而在萧条时期,由于国内需求不足,进口就会下降,出口反而上升,就会出现顺差。

2.国民收入

由国民收入的变化而产生的国际收支不平衡,称为收入性不平衡。随着一国经济增长率的高低变化,其国民收入也会相应地增加或减少。国民收入的增加引起的购买力的上升会导致进口的增加,同时,服务、捐赠、旅游及投资等方面的对外支出也会因此上升,造成国际收支逆差;反之,国民收入减少将引起国际收支顺差。

3.货币价值

货币性不平衡是指货币供应量的相对变动所引起的国际收支不平衡。一国货币供应量增长过快,会使该国出现较高的通货膨胀,在汇率变动滞后的情况下,国内货币成本上升,出口商品价格相对上升而进口商品价格相对下降,从而出现国际收支逆差。货币性不平衡可能是短期的,也可能是中长期的。

4.经济结构

结构性不平衡是指一国产业结构不适应世界市场的变化而出现的国际收支不平衡。结构性失衡包括两层含义:

(1)因一国的国民经济和产业结构变动的滞后和困难引起的国际收支失衡。当国际市场发生变化,新款式、高质量产品不断淘汰旧款式、低质量产品,新的替代产品不断出现的时候,如果该国的生产结构不能及时根据形势加以调整,那么,其原有的贸易平衡就会遭到破坏,贸易逆差就会出现;反之,如果调整及时,就可能出现贸易顺差。

（2）因一国的产业结构单一、产品价格弹性较大引起的国际收支失衡。20世纪70年代以来，中东石油输出国因石油价格暴涨暴跌而导致国际收支巨额顺差和巨额逆差，就是一个典型的例子。结构性失衡具有长期的性质，扭转起来相当困难。

除以上引起国际收支不平衡的因素以外，国际政治关系、自然条件、心理预期等因素以及政府的政策等方面的变化，都会影响一国国际收支的稳定，从而导致国际收支的不平衡。

案例探析 1-1

钉住汇率制度、国际收支失衡与墨西哥金融危机

1994年12月，墨西哥金融危机爆发，并很快波及巴西、阿根廷和智利等国家，出现了震惊世界的拉美经济危机。比索钉住美元的汇率制度是此次危机的根源，国际收支失衡是此次危机的导火索。

1982年以前，墨西哥以国有经济为主体，包括商品价格、利率和汇率在内的所有价格都受政府严格管制。与许多拉美国家一样，墨西哥也选择了进口替代的工业化发展战略，希望由此快速实现经济现代化，缩小与主要发达国家的差距。随着时间的推移，墨西哥遇到了所有实行进口替代发展战略国家都很难避免的问题——国际收支失衡。最初，这一问题似乎可以通过在国际金融市场上借债来解决，但当经济放缓时，政府无力按时偿还到期的国际债务；当国内政治形势发生动荡时，国外债权人不再提供新的贷款，债务危机由此而爆发。

1982年8月，以墨西哥政府宣布无力偿还到期的国外债务为标志，第三世界的债务危机拉开序幕。债务危机宣告了政府主导型经济增长和进口替代发展战略的失败。危机之后，墨西哥政府下决心推进经济改革计划，其主要措施包括：推进私有化，引入市场机制，形成市场竞争；降低关税、取消进口许可证和进口补贴，开放国内市场；加快比索可兑换，加入由美国、加拿大和墨西哥组成的北美自由贸易协议（NAFTA）。

在快速推进经济改革的同时，墨西哥政府却依然坚守比索钉住美元的汇率制度。由于当时墨西哥的通货膨胀率远远高于美国的通货膨胀率，钉住美元的汇率制度造成了比索高估，产生了鼓励进口、抑制出口的结果，形成了庞大的贸易赤字和巨额的经常账户逆差。为了维持国际收支平衡，墨西哥政府加快开放资本市场，吸引国外资本流入。然而，大量资金并没有进入实体经济而是进入了资本市场，当国内外政治经济形势发生变动时，国际资本流向逆转，最终引发了墨西哥金融危机。

资料来源：中国人民银行研究局研究员.钉住汇率制度、国际收支失衡与墨西哥金融危机[N/OL].第一财经日报，2015-01-26 [2021-06-08]. https://www.yicai.com/news/4067360.html.

思考讨论：国际收支失衡与墨西哥危机之间的内在逻辑。

四、国际收支失衡对经济的影响

一国国际收支无论是出现持续性的巨额顺差还是逆差，都对本国经济有所不利。持续性的逆差会导致官方储备的不断流失，使国内经济活动承受紧缩压力，抑制经济增长；反之，持续性的巨额顺差，又会导致本国货币汇率上升，削弱出口竞争力，或者会

引起官方储备的过多积累，这意味着放弃实际资源的使用权，引发通货膨胀，有时还会产生并加深与其他国家之间的矛盾和冲突，形成贸易争端。

1. 国际收支持续逆差的消极影响

首先，在对外经济方面，会形成本币对外贬值的压力，影响本币汇率的稳定，降低本币的信誉，并造成贸易条件的恶化。要维持本币汇率的稳定，政府就必须在该国国际收支出现大量逆差时，动用外汇储备来干预外汇市场，从而引起本国官方储备的减少。

其次，伴随着大量国际收支逆差，出口乘数效应缩减，带来国内经济不景气和高失业率。在市场化条件下，储备的减少还可能导致国内货币供应量降低和利率水平上升，加剧通货紧缩，影响国民经济的增长速度。

最后，持续的国际收支逆差会降低一国的对外资信，造成大量资金外流，加剧国内的经济恶化。

2. 国际收支持续顺差的消极影响

过大的国际收支顺差也会给一国对外经济关系及国内经济带来一定的消极影响。

首先，在对外经济关系方面，大量的国际收支顺差会造成一国储备资产迅速增加，带来本币对外升值的压力，继而造成本国出口产品的相对价格上升、进口产品的相对价格下降，从而不利于出口，有利于进口，使国际收支转为逆差。

其次，大量国际收支顺差还会招致贸易伙伴的不满，引起贸易摩擦和国际争端，影响对外经济政治关系的正常发展。

最后，伴随国际收支顺差与储备资产增加的是国内货币供给量的增加和通货膨胀的压力。因此，可能造成一国经济在外部失衡的同时出现内部失衡，加大其宏观经济调控的难度。

五、国际收支失衡的调节

一国的国际收支如果发生暂时性的不平衡，即短期的、由非确定或偶然因素引起的不平衡，那么这种不平衡一般程度较轻，持续时间不长，带有可逆性，因而不需要采取政策调节，不久便可自行得到纠正。但是，如果一国的国际收支不平衡属于持续性不平衡，是由一些根深蒂固的原因造成的，且属巨额顺差或逆差，那么这种不平衡没有可逆性，属于基本性不平衡，就必须采取相应的对策加以纠正。

（一）国际收支的自动调节

对于短期的、突发的国际收支不平衡，市场机制内部"看不见的手"会自发调节使其恢复平衡。一国经济的市场化程度越高，国际收支的自发调节作用就越明显。在不同的货币制度下，国际收支自发调节作用的表现形式也不同。

国际金本位制度下，一国的国际贸易收支出现逆差，会迫使该国货币汇率下跌至黄金输出点而使黄金外流。黄金外流导致银行准备金降低，货币发行量减少，引起价格下跌，进而增强该国商品在国际市场上的竞争力，导致出口增加；同时，国外价格水平的相对上升也抑制了进口。最终，外来收入增加，对外支出减少，逐步消除逆差，国际收支恢复平衡。价格-现金流动机制如图1-1所示。

黄金外流	→	货币供应减少	→	价格下降	→	出口增加 进口减少
↑						↓
国际收支逆差						国际收支顺差
↑						↓
出口减少 进口增加	→	价格上升	→	货币供应增加	→	黄金内流

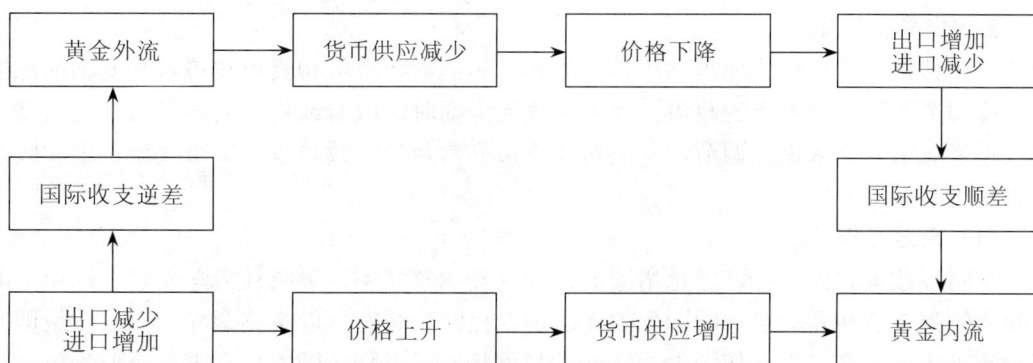

图 1-1　价格-现金流动机制

在纸币流通条件下，虽然黄金流动对国际收支平衡发挥的作用已经不复存在，但国际收支的自动调节机制仍然可以通过价格、汇率、利率、收入等经济变量发挥作用，使国际收支趋于平衡。例如，国际收支逆差会引起外汇供不应求，促使本国汇率下跌，进口商品价格上升，出口商品价格下降，导致出口增加、进口减少，国际收支改善。浮动汇率下国际收支自动调节机制如图 1-2 所示。

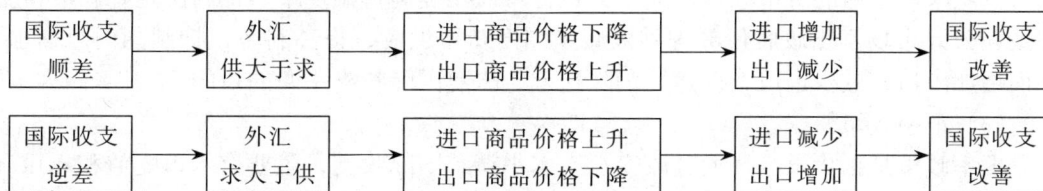

国际收支 顺差	→	外汇 供大于求	→	进口商品价格下降 出口商品价格上升	→	进口增加 出口减少	→	国际收支 改善
国际收支 逆差	→	外汇 求大于供	→	进口商品价格上升 出口商品价格下降	→	进口减少 出口增加	→	国际收支 改善

图 1-2　浮动汇率下国际收支自动调节机制

（二）国际收支的政策调节

国际收支的政策调节是指一国政府尤其是货币当局通过一定的政策措施使原有的国际收支变化趋势得以遏制甚至逆转，进而恢复平衡。

在现代不兑现纸币本位制度下，金融体系越来越复杂，各国政府对外汇市场的干预也越来越多，导致国际收支自动调节效果受到了极大的削弱。因此，当国际收支出现失衡时，一国当局不能仅依靠经济体系的自动调节机制，而是需要采取适当的政策加以调节。

1. 外汇缓冲政策

外汇缓冲政策是指政府通过外汇储备的变动或短期的对外借款来干预外汇市场，调节国际收支失衡。中央银行通过在外汇市场上买卖外汇、改变外汇供求对国际收支进行调节，或者通过从外国政府、国际金融机构或国际金融市场融通资金，以弥补国际收支逆差，主要作用是抵消国际收支失衡带来的消极影响，只用于解决暂时性的国际收支失衡。

外汇缓冲政策能使国际收支失衡产生的消极影响止于国际储备，而不至于波及国内经济和金融。但实施外汇缓冲政策仅能解决国际收支短期性逆差，而不能解决那些巨额、长期的国际收支逆差。因为一国的官方储备毕竟是有限的，央行在外汇市场上长期大量买卖外汇，将导致外汇储备过多或枯竭，进而引发新的矛盾和问题。

2.支出转换政策

支出转换政策也称管理需求政策，即通过运用财政政策和货币政策等改变国内总需求，来调节国际收支失衡的政策。当国际收支失衡时，政府或货币当局可以运用宏观经济政策来对国内需求进行调节。支出转换政策通常包括财政政策、货币政策、汇率政策和直接管制政策等。

（1）财政政策。

在财政政策方面，可以通过增减财政开支和调整税率，影响社会总需求，以调节国际收支的顺差或逆差。当一国国际收支出现逆差时，政府可以实施紧缩的财政政策即削减财政支出或提高税率，使国内经济处于紧缩状态，以降低国内总需求、降低物价，从而刺激出口、抑制进口，使国际收支恢复平衡；反之，当一国国际收支出现顺差时，则可采用扩张的财政政策，扩大政府支出、降低税率，以扩大国内总需求、提高物价，从而使进口增加、出口减少，使国际收支恢复平衡。

（2）货币政策。

货币政策是指通过利率的调整来实现对国际收支的调节。当国际收支产生逆差时，政府可以采取紧缩的货币政策，即中央银行可以用提高再贴现率、提高法定存款准备金率或在公开市场卖出政府债券等手段减少国内货币供应，提高利率，抑制国内总需求，从而增加出口、减少进口，以达到消除逆差、恢复国际收支平衡的目的。

（3）汇率政策。

汇率政策是指货币当局通过改变汇率水平调节国际收支，主要有本币贬值和本币升值两种政策。例如，若国际收支逆差，则采用本币贬值政策，使出口增加、进口减少，从而改善国际收支；反之，若国际收支顺差，则采用本币升值政策。汇率政策的优点是可以避免通货紧缩，缺点是汇率的经常波动会加剧经济的不稳定，容易引起通货膨胀。因此，汇率政策要结合紧缩性的财政或货币政策实施，主要适用于调节货币性的国际收支失衡。

（4）直接管制政策。

直接管制是政府通过强制性的行政手段如法规和条例，对进出口和外汇买卖予以规定的做法。直接管制的出发点是限制涉及对外支付的交易，如进口和购买外汇，鼓励涉及外来收入的交易，如出口和卖出外汇，从而达到改善国际收支的目的。对进出口的直接管制通常称作贸易管制，而对外汇买卖、收支、存兑的直接管制则称作外汇管制。直接管制的优点是比较灵活，可以进行结构性调整，可以提高关税或减少配额，对鼓励出口的产品可以多实行补贴或优惠，且见效快；缺点是容易引起各国的"贸易战"。直接管制主要适用于调节短期的、结构性的国际收支失衡。

3.国际经济合作政策

在全球经济一体化的背景下，在解决国际收支不平衡问题上，各国要注重加强国际经济金融合作，具体包括：

（1）协调经济政策。为避免贸易摩擦，各贸易伙伴国应加强磋商和对话，协调彼此的经济政策，这样有助于调节各国国际收支不平衡。

（2）加强国家间的信用合作。当一国国际收支出现不平衡尤其是出现严重逆差时，极易引发金融危机，需要国家间的紧急信贷来调节国际收支不平衡。

（3）充分发挥 IMF 等国际金融机构在平衡一国国际收支中的作用。

任务四　　国际收支平衡表的分析

国际收支平衡表上给出了一些简单的数字，但每一具体数字都代表特定的对外经济交易活动，分析国际收支平衡表必须采取历史的、科学的态度。

科学地分析国际收支平衡表，能全面、及时地了解本国的经济交往状况，并从中找出国际收支顺差和逆差形成的原因，以便采取相应的调节措施；使货币金融管理当局及时掌握本国外汇资金的来源和运用情况，以及国际储备的增减情况；全面掌握本国的经济地位和实力状况，以制定相应的贸易、金融、外汇政策等。

一、国际收支平衡表的分析方法

1.静态分析

静态分析是对某国在一定时期的国际收支平衡表进行逐项细致的分析。一般来说，静态分析是指分析国际收支平衡表中的各个项目及其差额、差额形成的原因以及对国际收支总差额的影响。

2.动态分析

动态分析又称纵向分析，是对某国连续的不同时期的国际收支平衡表进行分析。由于一国对外经济政策的连续性和经济结构调整的时效性，一般来说，一个时期的国际收支情况与上一时期和下一时期的国际收支情况都有着密切的联系，因此，分析国际收支平衡表也应将不同时期的国际收支情况联系起来，以掌握长期变化趋势。

3.横向比较分析

横向比较分析是对不同国家相同时期的国际收支平衡表进行分析比较，以了解一国的经济地位和实力，以及各国对外经济发展情况，以便更好地把握世界经济的发展趋势。

分析一国的国际收支平衡表时，必须对国内外的宏观经济、政治背景情况进行全面考察和分析，了解各因素对国际收支可能产生的影响，这样才能使分析得出的结论更全面、更客观、更科学。

二、我国国际收支平衡表的总体分析

1.我国国际收支平衡表的编制现状

我国由国家外汇管理局编制并公布国际收支平衡表。从 2015 年开始按《国际收支和国际投资头寸手册》（第六版）规定的标准分类。原则上，国际收支平衡表涵盖中国居民和非中国居民之间进行的全部交易；在可以得到市场价格的情况下，按市场价格对交易定值，债务工具大多按面值定值，货物出口按离岸价格定值；来自海关的进口数据是到岸价格数据，采用 5% 的调整系数，以便得到离岸价格数据。出口和进口在货物通过海关边境时记录，其他国际收支交易按权责发生制记录。

动画微课1-2

我国的国际收支

2. 我国2018年国际收支平衡表分析

2018年，我国国际收支延续基本平衡态势。经常账户保持在合理的顺差区间，全年顺差491亿美元，与GDP之比为0.4%。其中，货物和服务贸易合计顺差1 029亿美元，与GDP之比为0.8%，贸易收支更加平衡。

非储备性质的金融账户保持顺差，全年顺差1 306亿美元。其中，直接投资顺差1 070亿美元，仍是较稳定的顺差来源；证券投资顺差1 067亿美元，创历史新高，主要体现了资本市场进一步开放的效果；其他投资逆差770亿美元，在双向波动中保持基本稳定。

总体看，以中长期投资和资产配置为目的的资本流入仍占主导，我国对外投资保持理性。2018年，交易形成的外汇储备资产小幅增长、基本稳定，说明我国国际收支继续呈现自主平衡格局。

2018年年末，我国对外金融资产和负债较2017年年末分别增长2.5%和2.9%，对外净资产为2.13万亿美元，增长1.4%。2018年中国国际收支平衡表（概览表）见表1-2。

表1-2　　　　　　　　2018年中国国际收支平衡表（概览表）

项　目	行次	亿元	亿美元	亿SDR
1. 经常账户	1	3 527	491	362
贷方	2	193 053	29 136	20 601
借方	3	−189 526	−28 645	−20 239
1.A 货物和服务	4	7 054	1 029	741
贷方	5	175 694	26 510	18 747
借方	6	−168 640	−25 481	−18 006
1.A.a 货物	7	26 366	3 952	2 804
贷方	8	160 237	24 174	17 096
借方	9	−133 871	−20 223	−14 292
1.A.b 服务	10	−19 312	−2 922	−2 064
贷方	11	15 457	2 336	1 650
借方	12	−34 769	−5 258	−3 714
1.B 初次收入	13	−3 394	−514	−364
贷方	14	15 526	2 348	1 659
借方	15	−18 920	−2 862	−2 022
1.C 二次收入	16	−133	−24	−16
贷方	17	1 833	278	196

项　　目	行次	亿元	亿美元	亿SDR
借方	18	-1 966	-302	-212
2. 资本和金融账户	19	7 231	1 111	777
2.1 资本账户	20	-38	-6	-4
贷方	21	20	3	2
借方	22	-58	-9	-6
2.2 金融账户	23	7 269	1 117	781
资产	24	-24 436	-3 721	-2 621
负债	25	31 705	4 838	3 402
2.2.1 非储备性质的金融账户	26	8 306	1 306	904
2.2.1.1 直接投资	27	6 964	1 070	750
资产	28	-6 393	-965	-682
负债	29	13 357	2 035	1 432
2.2.1.2 证券投资	30	6 954	1 067	751
资产	31	-3 481	-535	-374
负债	32	10 435	1 602	1 125
2.2.1.3 金融衍生工具	33	-415	-62	-44
资产	34	-326	-48	-34
负债	35	-89	-13	-9
2.2.1.4 其他投资	36	-5 198	-770	-552
资产	37	-13 199	-1 984	-1 407
负债	38	8 002	1 214	854
2.2.2 储备资产	39	-1 037	-189	-123
3.净误差与遗漏	40	-10 758	-1 602	-1 138

数据来源：国家外汇管理局网站。

思政小课堂

　　国家外汇管理局发布的报告显示，2019年，我国国际收支总体平衡，表现出较强的稳健性和适应性。请下载2019年中国国际收支平衡表并加以分析，思考我国经济的稳健性和适应性表现在哪些方面？我国取得如此伟大的经济成就的原因有哪些？

项目思维导图

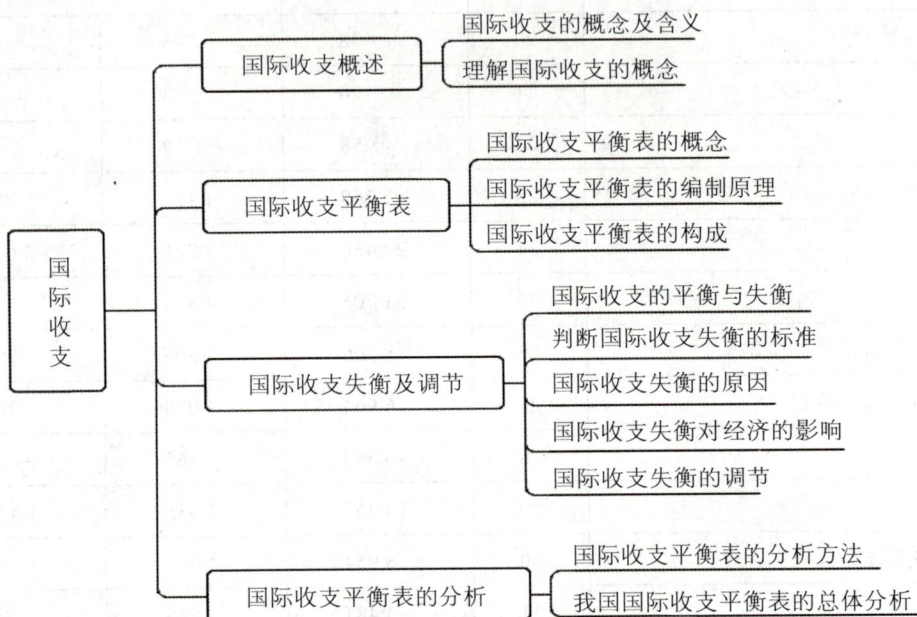

国际收支
- 国际收支概述
  - 国际收支的概念及含义
  - 理解国际收支的概念
- 国际收支平衡表
  - 国际收支平衡表的概念
  - 国际收支平衡表的编制原理
  - 国际收支平衡表的构成
- 国际收支失衡及调节
  - 国际收支的平衡与失衡
  - 判断国际收支失衡的标准
  - 国际收支失衡的原因
  - 国际收支失衡对经济的影响
  - 国际收支失衡的调节
- 国际收支平衡表的分析
  - 国际收支平衡表的分析方法
  - 我国国际收支平衡表的总体分析

项目训练

一、单选题

1.下列选项中，不可以划为本国的居民的是（　　）。

A.刚刚注册的企业

B.在该国居住了两年的自然人

C.国际货币基金组织驻该国代表

D.驻本国的外国领事馆雇用的当地人员

2.若在国际收支平衡表中，储备资产项目为1 000亿美元，则表示该国（　　）。

A.增加了1 000亿美元的储备　　　　B.减少了1 000亿美元的储备

C.人为的账面平衡，不说明问题　　　D.无法判断

3.下列选项中，能够较好地衡量国际收支对国际储备造成的压力的是（　　）。

A.贸易收支差额　　　　　　　　　　B.经常项目收支差额

C.资本和金融账户差额　　　　　　　D.综合账户差额

4.一国出现持续性的顺差，可能会导致或加剧（　　）。

A.通货膨胀　　　　　　　　　　　　B.国内资金紧张

C.经济危机　　　　　　　　　　　　　　D.货币对外贬值

5.国际收支平衡表按照（　　　）原理进行统计记录。

A.单式记账　　　　　　　　　　　　　　B.复式记账

C.增减记账　　　　　　　　　　　　　　D.收付记账

二、多选题

1.《国际收支和国际投资头寸手册》（第六版）将国际收支账户分为（　　　）。

A.经常账户　　　　　　　　　　　　　　B.资本与金融账户

C.储备账户　　　　　　　　　　　　　　D.净误差与遗漏账户

2.下列属于所在国居民的有（　　　）。

A.外国领事馆的外交人员　　　　　　　　B.外资企业

C.在外国领事馆工作的当地雇员　　　　　D.国家残疾人联合会

3.国际收支平衡表的经常项目包括（　　　）。

A.货物和服务　　　　　　　　　　　　　B.直接投资

C.初次收入　　　　　　　　　　　　　　D.二次收入

4.在国际收支平衡表中，（　　　）是通过统计数字直接得到的。

A.经常账户　　　　　　　　　　　　　　B.资本与金融账户

C.净误差与遗漏账户　　　　　　　　　　D.储备与相关项目

5.国际收支顺差出现的影响有（　　　）。

A.本币汇率升值　　　　　　　　　　　　B.本币供应量增长

C.本币汇率贬值　　　　　　　　　　　　D.通货紧缩

三、判断题

1.国际收支是一个流量、事后概念。　　　　　　　　　　　　　　　　　　（　　　）

2.综合账户差额比较综合地反映了自主性国际收支状况，对全面衡量和分析国际收支状况具有重大意义。　　　　　　　　　　　　　　　　　　　　　　　　（　　　）

3.由于一国国际收支不可能正好收支相抵，因此国际收支平衡表的最终差额绝不会为零。　　　　　　　　　　　　　　　　　　　　　　　　　　　　　　（　　　）

4.从理论上来说，国际收支不平衡是指自主性交易的不平衡，但在统计上很难做到。　　　　　　　　　　　　　　　　　　　　　　　　　　　　　（　　　）

5.资本与金融账户可以无限制地为经常账户提供融资。　　　　　　　　　（　　　）

四、实践训练

登录国家外汇管理局网站，查阅并分析我国2015—2020年国际收支平衡表数据，比较分析其中的变化和原因。

任课教师可以进行引导性讲解，将班级学生视情况分成若干小组，让学生自己查阅资料，进行讨论和分析，最后形成简要的分析报告，并制作PPT进行讲解，教师进行点评。

项目二
国际储备

课程导入

全球外汇储备中的人民币资产

外汇储备是各个国家储备的可兑换成外国货币的外国资产，通俗地说就是外国的货币。不过，并不是所有外国货币都能成为外汇储备，能作为外汇储备的货币，至少在国际上要有一定的认可度。而作为外汇储备的资产或货币占比越高，表明该货币在国际上的认可度也越高。那么，在全球外汇储备中，人民币资产占了多大比例呢？

我国有3.1万亿美元的外汇储备，是全球外汇储备最多的国家，但人民币在全球外汇储备中的占比并不高。根据国际货币基金组织公布的数据，截至2019年年底，全球的外汇储备为11.08万亿美元。在这些外汇储备中，人民币资产仅有2 177亿美元，占比1.97%左右，排在美元、欧元、日元和英镑之后。目前，人民币作为全球外汇储备资产的比例虽然还不高，但是一直都在增长，而且增长速度不慢。与2018年相比，2019年增长了约146亿美元，增速达到了7.2%，按照这个增速，到 2031 年时可超过 5 000 亿美元。

资料来源：佚名. 全球外汇储备，为什么 60% 以上都是美元资产？[EB/OL]. [2021-06-26]. https://view.inews.qq.com/w2/20200403A0O7VB00.

思考讨论：什么是外汇储备？什么是国际储备？一个国家的国际储备有哪些形式？其具体内容又是怎样的？本项目将介绍相关内容。

国际储备是一国对外经济交往的最终结果，也是一国国际金融实力及其在国际经济竞争中地位的重要标志。一国国际储备的规模适度、结构合理、管理科学，是其弥补国际收支逆差、维持对外支付能力及干预外汇市场、维持汇率稳定的前提条件，也是其对外借债和偿还外债的信用保证。

任务一　　　　　　国际储备概述

一、国际储备的概念和特征

国际储备（international reserve）是指一国货币当局为弥补国际收支差额和稳定汇率而持有的国际上普遍接受的流动性资产。

动画微课 2-1

国际储备

能够作为国际储备的资产（简称储备资产）一般具备以下典型特征：

1. 官方持有

国际储备资产必须是一国货币当局（一般是中央银行或财政部）持有的资产，非官方金融机构、企业和私人持有的黄金、外汇资产不能算作国际储备。因此，国际储备又称官方储备。

2. 普遍收受性

作为国际储备的资产，必须能够在外汇市场和政府间清算国际收支差额时得到普遍认同和接受，储备资产这一被广泛接受的特性就是普遍收受性。不能在国际上转让和兑换的金融资产不能作为储备资产。

3. 充分流动性

国际储备应有充分的变现能力，在一国出现国际收支逆差或干预外汇市场时可以随时动用。因此，储备资产的表现形式主要是存放在银行里的活期外汇存款和容易变现的有价证券（尤其是外国政府债券）等。

4. 可自由兑换性

国际储备资产必须能自由地与其他可对外支付的资产兑换。如果缺乏可兑换性，其支付能力就会受到限制，从而无法发挥其弥补国际收支差额和干预外汇市场的功能。

5. 非本币性

外汇储备不能是本币资产，因为有些国家的货币在国际上被广泛接受，如美元、欧元，这些国家有时候对外支付直接用本币，如果把本币算作外汇储备，就无法对国际储备进行数量上的统计。

二、国际储备和国际清偿能力

一国实际持有的国际储备从最终所有权来看可分为两部分：自有储备和借入储备。自有储备包括货币性黄金、外汇储备、在IMF的储备头寸和特别提款权四种形式；借入储备由备用信贷、互惠信贷协议、借款总安排和一国商业银行的对外短期可兑换货币资产组成。

与国际储备关系密切的另外一个概念是国际清偿能力。国际清偿能力（international liquidity）是指一国为弥补国际收支逆差而融通资金的能力。它不仅包括货币当局所持有的各种国际储备，还包括该国从外国政府或中央银行、国际金融组织和商业银行等筹借资金的能力，也称为借入储备。国际清偿能力是该国具有的现实的对外清偿能力和可能拥有的对外清偿能力的总和。因此，通常讲的国际储备仅指一国具有的现实的对外清偿能力，是狭义的国际储备，即自有储备。根据IMF的定义，广义的国际储备指的是国际清偿能力，即一国的自有储备和借入储备之和。

国际清偿能力和国际储备间的关系如图2-1所示。

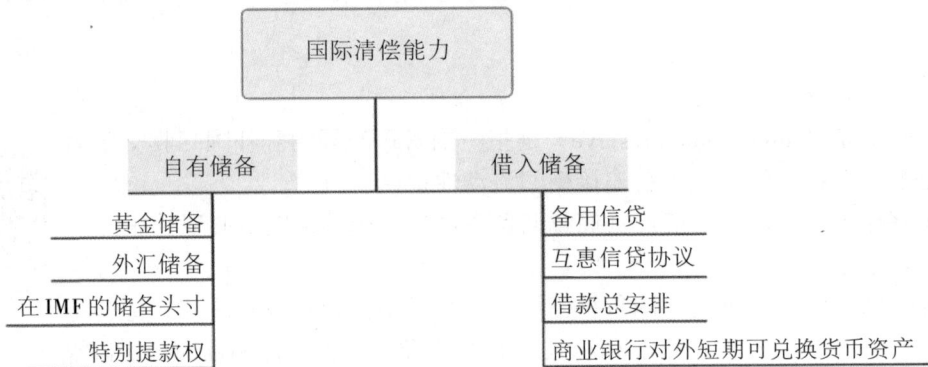

图2-1 国际清偿能力和国际储备关系图

三、国际储备的作用

（一）调节国际收支不平衡

当一国由于各种原因而发生临时性国际收支逆差时，可动用国际储备以弥补差额，防止由于采取影响宏观经济的财政政策或货币政策产生的经济衰退、失业率上升等不利影响。即使一国国际收支发生结构性不平衡，不得不采取调整措施，动用国际储备也可对政策调整的实施形成一定缓冲，从而避免政策调整所导致的国内经济波动。

（二）干预外汇市场，稳定本国货币汇率

一国国际储备的数量，在一定程度上反映出该国政府干预外汇市场能力的强弱。当本币汇率发生波动特别是投机因素造成不稳定时，政府通常会利用国际储备（主要是外汇储备）对外汇市场进行干预，使本国货币汇率稳定在与国内经济政策相适应的水平上。通过出售储备购入本币，可使本国货币汇率避免下跌；反之，通过购入储备抛出本币，可增加市场上本币的供应量，从而避免使本国货币汇率上升。

必须强调的是，外汇干预只能在短期内对汇率产生有限的影响，它无法从根本上改变汇率变动的长期趋势。而且要使国际储备充分发挥干预的作用，一国必须拥有比较发达的外汇市场且本国货币必须具有完全的可自由兑换性。

（三）增强国际清偿能力，提高对外借款的信用保证

国际储备是衡量一个国家经济实力和偿付能力的标志之一，也是国际评级机构评估国家风险的重要指标之一。充足的国际储备有助于提高一国的自信和货币稳定性的信心。国际储备多，意味着国际清偿能力增强；反过来，国际清偿能力强，该国向外借款的保证就得到加强，同时表明该国的金融实力的增强和国际地位的提高。

任务二　　国际储备的构成和来源

一、国际储备构成的演变

国际储备的构成，是指充当国际储备资产的资产种类。在不同的历史时期，充当国际储备资产的资产种类有所不同。

国际储备资产的构成是随着历史的发展而变化的。在国际金本位制度下，黄金是天然的国际货币，世界各国都接受其作为支付手段并认可其作为财富代表的地位。布雷顿森林体系时期，国际储备主要由黄金和美元组成，布雷顿森林体系崩溃后，储备货币开始多元化。发展到今天，主要有四种形式：黄金储备（gold reserves）、外汇储备（foreign exchange reserves）、在国际货币基金组织的储备头寸（IMF reserve position）、在国际货币基金组织的特别提款权（special drawing rights，SDRs）。截至 2019 年 1 月 31 日，中国官方储备资产和其他外币资产数据见表 2-1。

动画微课 2-2

我国的国际储备构成

表 2-1　　2019 年 1 月中国官方储备资产和其他外币资产（近似市场价值）

项目	（亿美元）	（亿 SDR）
A. 官方储备资产	31 863.52	22 748.33
（1）外汇储备（可兑换外币）	30 879.24	22 045.61
（a）证券	30 737.14	21 944.16
（b）货币和存款总额，存放于以下机构：	142.10	101.45
（i）其他国家的中央银行、国际清算银行和基金组织	10.68	7.63
（ii）总部设在报告国的银行	45.91	32.77
其中：办事处位于国外的银行	45.91	32.77
（iii）总部设在报告国以外的银行	85.51	61.05
（2）国际货币基金组织储备头寸	84.85	60.58
（3）特别提款权（SDRs）	107.86	77.01
（4）黄金（包括黄金存款和适用情况下的黄金掉期）	793.19	566.29
以盎司计算的纯金数量（百万盎司）	59.94	59.94
（5）其他储备资产（请列明）	-1.63	-1.16
金融衍生产品	-1.63	-1.16
B. 其他外币资产（请列明）	1 839.35	1 313.17

注：自 2016 年 4 月起，除按美元公布国际储备与外币流动性数据模版外，增加以国际货币基金组织特别提款权（SDR）公布相关数据，折算汇率来源于国际货币基金组织网站，其中 2019 年 1 月 USD/SDR=0.71393。

数据来源：国家外汇管理局网站。

二、国际储备的构成

（一）黄金储备

黄金储备是一国货币当局持有的货币化黄金（monetary gold），不包括为了满足工业用金和民间藏金需求作为商品储备的黄金。

黄金是历史最为悠久的储备资产，在国际金本位制度和布雷顿森林体系时期，黄金一直占据着重要的地位。布雷顿森林体系解体后，随着黄金非货币化，黄金不再作为直接进行对外支付的手段，但作为一种特殊的商品，可以在国际黄金市场上出售，换成可自由兑换的外汇。

1. 黄金储备增加的途径

黄金储备的增加有两种途径：

（1）货币当局在国内收购黄金，即所谓黄金的货币化。

（2）在国际黄金市场上购买黄金。但是对非储备货币发行国而言，在国际市场上购买黄金，需要动用本国的外汇，所以，不会改变本国国际储备的总量，只是黄金储备和外汇储备之间的结构转换。

2. 黄金储备的特点

黄金之所以成为国际储备构成中的重要组成部分，在于其具有其他形式的储备资产所不具备的特点：一是黄金本身是特殊商品、一种可靠的保值手段；二是黄金储备完全属于一国主权所拥有的国家财富，不受他国的支配和干预。

但是，黄金储备与外汇储备相比，流动性较差，并且黄金储备没有利息，所以黄金储备的多少取决于一国的黄金政策。

但在国际局势动荡特别是有战争爆发的危险或战争中，黄金储备是一国国际储备中最坚实的部分。西方经济学家凯恩斯曾形象地概括了黄金在货币制度中的作用，他说："黄金在我们的制度中具有重要作用，它作为最后的卫兵和紧急需要时的储备金，还没有任何其他更好的东西可以替代它。"根据世界黄金协会的统计，2018年世界各国黄金储备排名（部分）见表2-2。

表2-2　　　　2018年世界各国黄金储量排名（部分）

排名	国家（地区、组织）	吨	占国际储备的百分比
1	美国	8 133.5	73.4%
2	德国	3 369.7	68.8%
3	IMF	2 814.0	n/a
4	意大利	2 451.8	65.1%
5	法国	2 436.0	59.1%
6	俄罗斯	2 036.2	16.9%
7	中国	1 842.6	2.2%
8	瑞士	1 040.0	5.0%

排名	国家（地区、组织）	吨	占国际储备的百分比
9	日本	765.2	2.3%
10	荷兰	612.5	65.5%
11	印度	579.9	5.5%
12	欧洲央行	504.8	25.1%
13	中国台湾	423.6	3.4%
14	葡萄牙	382.5	63.1%
15	哈萨克斯坦	335.1	42.5%
16	沙特阿拉伯	323.1	2.4%
17	英国	310.3	7.7%
18	黎巴嫩	286.8	19.5%
19	西班牙	281.6	15.8%
20	奥地利	280.0	46.9%

数据来源：根据世界黄金协会公布的数据整理。

知识链接2-1

黄金作为货币的职能的历史

第二次世界大战爆发后，黄金失去了在发达经济体中作为货币的地位。第二次世界大战结束时，固定汇率机制布雷顿森林体系建立。1971年，美国单边终止其金本位制，布雷顿森林体系瓦解。美国的金本位制规定每盎司黄金可兑换35美元。

金本位制通常指历史上的两个关键时期：古典金本位制时期和布雷顿森林体系黄金挂钩汇率制度之后的时期。

古典金本位制时期

金本位制是一套体系，在该体系下，所有国家都将其货币的价值与一定黄金数量挂钩，或者是将它们的货币与另一国家已经与一定黄金数量挂钩的货币挂钩。国内货币能够以固定的价格自由兑换成黄金，黄金输入输出不受限制。金币与其他金属硬币和纸币一起作为国内货币流通，而各国的金币组成不尽相同。由于各币种的价值都以一定的黄金数量来确定，因此参与这一体系的各币种间的汇率也是确定的。

布雷顿森林体系时期

第二次世界大战后，世界需要一个全新的国际体系来取代金本位制，这一点在第二次世界大战期间就已较为明显。1944年在美国召开的布雷顿森林会议起草了该体系的蓝图。美国拥有的政治和经济地位使美元自然而然地处于该体系的核心位置。经历过两次世界大战后的混乱局面，各国都渴望稳定，因为固定的汇率被视为对贸易具有重要意义，同时也渴望拥有比传统的金本位制更好的灵活度。会议确立的体系以当时35美元1盎司的黄金平价将美元与黄金挂钩，同时，其他国家货币与美元挂钩，但是汇率可调整。与古典金本位制不同，该体系允许各国进行资本管制来刺激其经济，且无须接受金融市场惩罚。

资料来源：佚名. 黄金的历史［EB/OL］.［2021-06-20］. https：//www.gold.org/cn/page/9372.

（二）外汇储备

外汇储备是一国货币金融管理当局持有的以储备货币表示的对外流动性资产，其主要形式为现钞、国外银行存款与外国政府债券、货币市场工具、外汇衍生品合约等。

IMF对外汇储备的定义为：它是货币金融管理当局以银行存款、财政部国库券、长短期政府债券等形式所保有的在国际收支逆差时可以使用的债权。

外汇储备是目前国际储备资产的主要构成部分。储备货币是指被各国广泛用作外汇储备的货币，包括美元、欧元、英镑、日元等。自2016年年底人民币加入SDR之后，人民币在各国央行外储货币当中也占有一席之地。2018年1月IMF报告中显示，我国外汇储备规模达到3 161.50亿美元，位居全球第一。具体数据见表2-3。

表2-3　　　　　2018年1月世界外汇储备国家（地区）（前十名）

排名	国家/地区		外汇储备（十亿美元）
1	中国	China	3 161.50
2	日本	Japan	1 204.70
3	瑞士	Switzerland	785.70
4	沙特阿拉伯	Saudi Arabia	486.60
5	中国香港	Hong Kong China	437.50
6	印度	India	397.20
7	韩国	South Korea	385.30
8	巴西	Brazil	358.30
9	俄罗斯	Russia	356.50
10	新加坡	Singapore	279.80

数据来源：根据IMF数据整理。

（三）储备头寸

国际储备的第三种表现形式是成员在IMF的储备头寸，简称储备头寸，又称普通提款权（general drawing rights），是基金组织成员在IMF的普通账户中可以随时自由提取和使用的资产。储备头寸包括：

（1）以黄金、外汇或特别提款权认缴的25%的份额。

（2）IMF为满足成员借款需要而使用的本国货币。按照IMF规定，成员认缴份额的

75%可用本国货币缴纳。

（3）IMF向某成员借款的净额，也称为该成员对国际货币基金组织的债权。

普通提款权属于成员在IMF的债权，因此，IMF各成员可以无条件地提取，用于弥补国际收支逆差。一国若要使用其在IMF的储备头寸，只需向IMF提出要求，IMF便会通过提供另一国的货币予以满足。普通提款权在国际货币基金组织成员的国际储备资产总额中占的比重很小。

（四）特别提款权

特别提款权是相对于普通提款权而言的，是IMF创造的无形货币，是其分配给成员的一种用来补充现有储备资产的手段，是成员在IMF的账面资产。因为它是普通提款权即储备头寸以外的一种特别使用资金的权利，因此称为"特别提款权"，又名"纸黄金"。

1.特别提款权的功能

特别提款权是一国国际储备的重要构成部分，能用于国际货币基金组织成员政府之间的结算，可同黄金、外汇一起作为国际储备，并可用于向其他成员换取可兑换货币，支付国际收支差额，偿还IMF的贷款，但不能直接用于贸易与非贸易支付。

2.特别提款权的特征

特别提款权具有以下特征：

（1）它是一种凭信用发行的资产，其本身不具有内在价值，是国际货币基金组织人为创造的、纯粹账面上的资产。

（2）特别提款权由IMF按份额比例无偿地分配给各成员，接受者不付出任何代价。

（3）特别提款权属于国有资产，只能由成员货币当局持有，在国际货币基金组织及各国政府之间发挥作用。非官方金融机构不得持有和使用。

三、国际储备的来源

1.国际收支顺差

国际储备资产大多以国际收支顺差积聚而成。一国国际收支出现盈余，该国国际储备存量增加。国际收支中经常项目的顺差，是国际储备的主要来源；国际收支中资本和金融账户的顺差，是国际储备的重要补充。

2.国际借贷

国际借贷是指一国政府或银行直接向国外借款，如从国际金融机构或他国政府取得贷款以及中央银行间的互惠信贷等。

3.在外汇市场买入外汇

这是指一国货币管理当局为保证本国货币价值对外稳定，干预外汇市场购进外汇而增加的国际储备存量。央行干预外汇市场的手段通常是公开市场业务，抛售本币，购进外汇，进而增加本国国际储备。

4.国际货币基金组织分配的特别提款权

国际货币基金组织分配给成员的特别提款权也是各国国际储备的一个来源。由于分配的额度较小，而且分配不均衡，对发展中国家而言，特别提款权不能成为其国际储备的主要来源。

任务三　　　　国际储备的管理

一、国际储备的管理原则

国际储备管理是指一国政府及货币当局根据一定时期内本国的国际收支状况和经济发展规律的要求，对国际储备的规模、结构及储备资产的运用等进行调整、控制，以实现储备资产规模适度化、结构最优化的过程。在国际储备管理过程中应遵循以下原则：

1.安全性

安全性是指储备资产本身的价值稳定且存放可靠。首先，外汇储备要选择那些汇率稳定的货币，汇率波动较大、容易受外汇市场波动影响的货币应减少储备；其次，储备资产的存放应该选择经济发达、市场监管宽松的国家。很多国家选择把本国黄金储备存放在美国，一方面因为美国市场稳定、安全，另一方面美国有世界最大的黄金市场，存放在美国便于进行交易，减少运输成本。

2.流动性

流动性是指储备资产随时能够获得与使用。在储备资产中，不同的资产流动性是各异的。例如，现钞、活期存款、汇票等资产的流动性较高，可作为一级储备。黄金、外国中期国债等资产的流动性较弱，只能作为二级储备。在管理国际储备时，应该把流动性强弱不同的各种储备资产用于不同期限的投资，既能保值增值，又能维持流动性，不影响使用。

3.盈利性

盈利性是指储备资产在保值的基础上有较高的收益。一国在管理储备资产时，一般应在满足安全性和流动性的前提下，尽可能提高储备资产的盈利性，以降低持有储备资产的机会成本。

国际储备本质上是一种随时用于对外支付的准备金，在一国国际收支不平衡时用于弥补逆差。国际储备的这一特点决定了它必须具备流动性、安全性及盈利性三种性质。在这三种性质中，流动性是最重要的，安全性仅次于流动性。只有在流动性和安全性都得到充分保证的前提下，才考虑投资的盈利性。同时，这三种性质不是完全独立的，它们都是国际储备本质的体现，不可或缺。

二、国际储备的管理方法

国际储备管理可以分为两个方面：一是国际储备规模管理；二是国际储备结构管理。通过合理科学的管理，可以达到维持一国国际收支正常进行、提高国际储备使用效率的目的。

（一）国际储备规模管理

所谓国际储备规模管理，是指对国际储备规模进行确定和调整，使一国的国际储备数量保持在适度的水平上。一国的国际储备规模，应当既能满足国家经济增长和对外支付的需要，又不因储备过多而形成资产浪费。

确定适度的储备规模是国际储备管理的首要任务。国际上比较流行的是用比率分析法，这一方法是美国经济学家罗伯特·特里芬提出的，通过测算一国国际储备与进口额之比（用 R/M 表示）来测算一国国际储备的需求量。一国的 R/M 比例应该以 40% 为最高界限、20% 为最低界限。按全年储备对进口额的比例进行计算，约为 25%~30%。换句话说，一国的国际储备应能保证支付 3~4 个月的进口，或者说储备与进口额的比例（年度数字）不低于 25%。

但是，由于世界各国经济发展水平不一，用一个标准测算也不合理。实践中，往往是发达国家倾向于选择较低的国际储备水平，发展中国家倾向于选择较高的国际储备水平，这主要是由于发达国家有较强的借款能力，尽管其国际储备不能支付 3 个月的进口，但其国际清偿能力并不低于发展中国家，而且往往高于发展中国家。

知识链接2-2

为什么美国不需要外汇储备？

很多人都说美国没有外汇储备，作为世界上的经济大国，美国没有外汇储备是如何保证经济持续稳定发展和抵御经济风险的？

从严格意义上讲，美国也存在外汇储备，只不过规模非常小，相当于其进口额的 0.59 个月左右。德、法、英、加等发达国家，其外汇储备相当于其进口额的 1.1~1.9 个月；相比之下，日本经济发展仅次于美国、中国，又是一个金融资产大国、资本输出大国，资本极度过剩，拥有相当于 13 个月进口额的外汇储备，中国的外汇储备比日本还高。

美国之所以几乎没有外汇储备，主要原因在于美元是货币霸主，而欧元、英镑、人民币、日元等是储备货币。美元与黄金直接挂钩，各国货币与美元挂钩，使得美元成为国际货币的中心，这也导致美国几乎没有外汇储备。

美国不需要外汇储备的另一个重要原因，就是美元作为国际储备货币，在对外贸易中可以直接用于国际支付，根本不需要用外汇储备调节国际收支、外汇市场和进行国际支付。

资料来源：根据相关资料整理。

（二）国际储备结构管理

国际储备结构管理是指如何使各项储备资产实现最佳组合搭配，如何使外汇储备中的各种储备货币保持适合的比例。

国际储备的四个组成部分在流动性、安全性和盈利性方面有很大不同。它们各自所占比重不同，直接决定了整个国际储备的流动性、安全性和盈利性水平。货币当局应本着扬长避短的原则不断优化储备结构，使其发挥最大效能。由于储备头寸和特别提款权数量由国际货币基金组织分配决定，一个国家很难改变，所以国际储备的结构管理主要集中在黄金和外汇两项储备资产上。

1.黄金储备的结构管理

由于黄金价值相对稳定，各国黄金储备的数量和规模基本保持不变。但近年来由于全球经济的不景气，美元在全球储备货币中的霸主地位被动摇，各国政府在黄金储备策略上有所变化。

根据世界黄金协会的官方数据，2018年以来，世界各国购入黄金储备的数量保持着高速增长的趋势，截至2018年上半年，各国总计买入黄金的数量为193.3吨，相比2017年上半年的总采购数量，上涨幅度高达8%。俄罗斯、中国、印度、菲律宾、泰国等国家2018年也都在积极地增加本国的黄金储备。

2.外汇储备的结构管理

外汇储备在国际储备中占的比重较高，因此外汇储备的结构管理是国际储备结构管理的核心所在。外汇储备管理的确定包含两重含义：一是外汇储备与黄金储备及其他储备资产的比例的确定；二是外汇储备中各种货币构成比例的确定，即最优结构的确定。因为黄金储备的比例基本上不变，所以讨论的意义不大。外汇储备结构管理的主要内容包括币种结构的选择和资产形式的选择。

（1）外汇储备的币种结构管理。

选择外汇储备币种时，各国应该根据本国对外贸易的实际情况，基本上遵循以下原则：

①尽可能选择本国国际贸易和国际支付所需的币种，与能弥补逆差和干预市场所需的币种保持一致，这样可以在一定程度上避免汇率风险，降低交易成本；

②选择硬币、减少软币储备，从而保证储备货币的币值稳定；

③增加汇率波动幅度小的货币储量，减少汇率波动幅度大的货币的储备；

④保持货币储备多元化，做到分散风险。

图2-2反映了2018年全球范围内各国央行外汇储备中主要储备货币的占比情况。

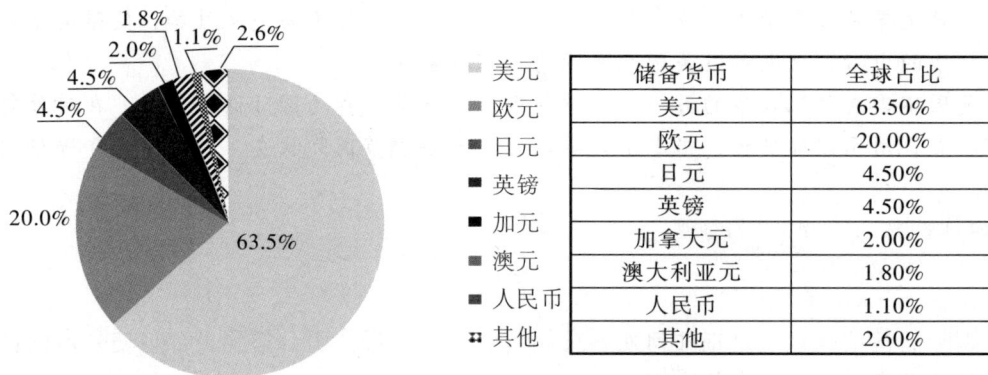

储备货币	全球占比
美元	63.50%
欧元	20.00%
日元	4.50%
英镑	4.50%
加拿大元	2.00%
澳大利亚元	1.80%
人民币	1.10%
其他	2.60%

图2-2　2018年全球储备货币占比

数据来源：根据IMF数据整理。

（2）外汇储备的资产结构管理。

由于国际储备的主要作用是弥补国际收支逆差，因而各国货币当局更加注重储备资产的流动性。按照流动性高低，可以将外汇储备分成以下三类：

①一级储备：流动性最高，但盈利性最低，包括在国外银行的活期存款、外币商业票据和外国短期政府债券等。这些流动性很高的资产的盈利性是非常低的。

②二级储备：盈利性高于一级储备，但流动性低于一级储备。各种定期存单、2年期和5年期的中期外国政府债券等都属于二级储备。这些储备主要在一国发生临时性、突发性事件时使用。

③三级储备：盈利性高于二级储备，但流动性低于二级储备。三级储备主要用于弥补一级储备收益过低的缺陷，属于长期投资，因此其收益率最高。三级储备包括长期外国政府债券、AAA级欧洲债券等。到期后可以转化成一级储备，但未到期提前变现的话，则要遭受收益上的巨大损失。

世界各国经济发展情况不同，因此外汇储备的资产形式也不同。但总体而言，国际收支呈现逆差的国家，偏重保留较大比例的一级储备，以维持其流动性；顺差国则无需过多保留一级储备，可以偏重保留盈利性较高的三级储备，因为顺差国本身借入储备的能力比较强，无需保留大量一级储备。

案例探析2-1

中国外汇储备规模占全球30%，许多国家增持黄金抛售美债

外汇储备又称为外汇存底，是指为了应付国际支付的需要，各国的中央银行及其他政府机构所集中掌握的外汇资产。中国外汇储备2005年至2014年的10年间平均收益率为3.68%，而截至2018年年末，中国的黄金储备规模达到1 852吨，位居全球第六。IMF统计数据显示，中国外汇储备规模占全球外汇储备规模的近30%。

尽管中国的黄金储备仅位居全球第六，但作为占全球外汇储备近30%的大国，中国的外汇变动自然会引起多方关注。除了中国增持黄金外，新兴市场国家正以50年来前所未有的罕见速度在囤积黄金。世界黄金协会最新数据显示，截至2019年6月底，全球央行的黄金净购买量为247.3吨，同比增长73%，俄罗斯、中国、土耳其和哈萨克斯坦成黄金四大买家。

由于越来越强烈的"去美元化"意愿，许多国家在不断增持黄金之余大幅抛售美债。美联储最新报告显示，美国金融体系的债务已达到72万亿美元，而美国国债的债务总额也已经超过22.5万亿美元。当大幅抛售美债与增持黄金相结合时，只要美国经济的债务赤字风险爆发，拥有黄金的国家将有可能成为全球金融市场重置后的主导者。

资料来源：财经新鲜事. 中国外汇储备规模占全球30%，许多国家增持黄金抛售美债［EB/OL］. ［2019-07-30］. https://baijiahao.baidu.com/s?id=1640447399684891842&wfr=spider&for=pc. 有修改。

结合上面的材料，请思考：

1.为什么中国的外汇储备规模如此巨大？

2.近年来各国黄金储备增加的原因是什么？

3.如何才能做到合理地管理一个国家的国际储备？

思政小课堂

　　1996年11月，我国的外汇储备首次突破1 000亿美元。2001年，这一数字翻了一番，达到2 000亿美元。此后，我国外汇储备增速加快。2006年2月底，我国首次超过日本，位居全球第一。同年10月，我国外汇储备首次突破1万亿美元大关。2009年6月，外汇储备突破2万亿美元，此后不到一年时间，外汇储备增长到3万亿美元，增长了50%。自此我国外汇储备一直处于3万亿美元以上高位。

　　我国高达3万亿美元的巨额外汇储备，用于投资美国国债的份额占1/3以上，黄金储备不足2 000吨，仅占中国外汇储备的2.2%。部分发达国家持有的黄金储备基本上构成了其外汇储备的大部分。

　　请思考：我国如此庞大的外汇储备规模是如何形成的？具有什么样的特点？我国如何对国际储备进行管理？

项目思维导图

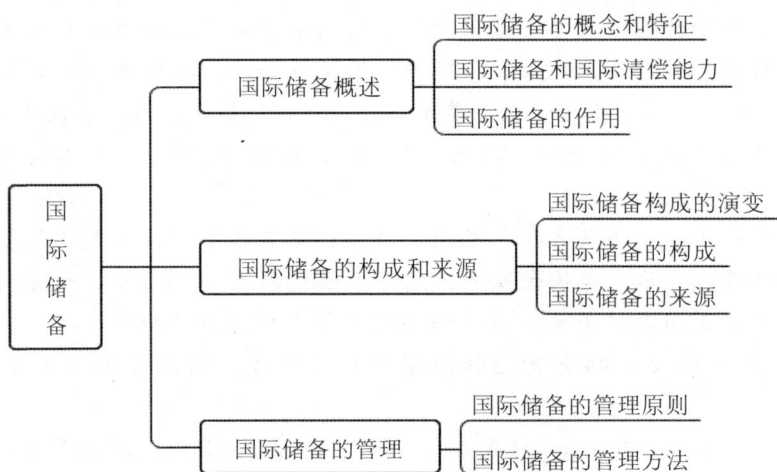

项目训练

一、单选题

1.国际储备不包括（　　　）。

A.商业银行储备　　　　　　　　　B.外汇储备

C.在IMF的储备头寸　　　　　　　D.特别提款权

2.国际储备运营管理的基本原则有（　　　）。

A.安全性、流动性、盈利性　　　　　B.安全性、固定性、保值性

C.安全性、固定性、盈利性　　　　　D.流动性、保值性、增值性

3.三级国际储备资产包括（　　　）。

A.特别提款权　　　　　　　　　　　B.普通提款权

C.长期债券　　　　　　　　　　　　D.收益性低于一级国际储备资产

4.国际储备最基本的作用是（　　　）。

A.干预外汇市场　　　　　　　　　　B.充当支付手段

C.弥补国际收支逆差　　　　　　　　D.作为偿还外债的保证

5.特别提款权（SDR）是（　　　）。

A.欧洲经济货币联盟创设的货币　　　B.欧洲货币体系的中心货币

C.IMF创设的储备资产和记账单位　　D.世界银行创设的特别使用资金的权利

6.我国国际储备管理的重点是（　　　）。

A.外汇储备　　　　　　　　　　　　B.特别提款权

C.黄金　　　　　　　　　　　　　　D.普通提款权

7.目前世界各国广泛使用（　　　）的进口额作为确定适度国际储备量的标准。

A.6个月　　　　　　　　　　　　　B.3个月

C.9个月　　　　　　　　　　　　　D.1年

8.特别提款权是一种（　　　）。

A.实际资产　　　　　　　　　　　　B.账面资产

C.流动资产　　　　　　　　　　　　D.固定资产

9.普通贷款的最高限制是成员份额的（　　　）。

A.100%　　　　　　　　　　　　　　B.25%

C.75%　　　　　　　　　　　　　　D.125%

10.在国际储备中，（　　　）曾在历史上占有极其重要的地位，但从20世纪50年代开始，它在国际储备总额中所占的比重趋于下降。

A.黄金　　　　　　　　　　　　　　B.普通提款权

C.外汇储备　　　　　　　　　　　　D.特别提款权

二、多选题

1.国际储备具有的特点有（　　　）。

A.官方持有性　　　　　　　　　　　B.自由兑换性

C.充分流动性　　　　　　　　　　　D.普遍接受性

2.国际储备主要包括（　　　）。

A.黄金储备　　　　　B.外汇储备　　　　　　　　C.土地基金

D.普通提款权　　　　E.特别提款权

3.关于特别提款权，下面说法正确的是（　　　）。

A.特别提款权是一种实际发行的货币

B.特别提款权可以充当流通手段

C.特别提款权是一种账面资产

D.特别提款权具有严格限定的用途

E.特别提款权不具有内在价值

4.下列金融资产中，可以作为国际储备的有（　　　）。

A.特别提款权　　　　　　　　　　B.自然人在境外的投资

C.居民手持外币　　　　　　　　　　D.黄金

5.国际储备管理应当遵循原则的有（　　　）。

A.适度性　　　　　　　　　　　　　B.安全性

C.流动性　　　　　　　　　　　　　D.盈利性

三、判断题

1.特别提款权主要用于弥补成员国际收支逆差或偿还国际货币基金组织的贷款，任何私人和企业均不得持有和使用，也不能用于贸易或非贸易支付。　　　（　　）

2.一国中央银行在国际黄金市场收购黄金不仅改变了国际储备的结构，而且国际储备的总量也有大幅增加。　　　（　　）

3.目前，国际储备币种结构已实现多元化，美元已不是主要的储备货币了。（　　）

4.一国持有的国际储备可以调节国际收支逆差，可以稳定本币汇率，因此国际储备越多越好。　　　（　　）

5.一般来说，国际储备大小与一国经济活动的规模大小成反比。　　（　　）

四、实践训练

1.登录国家外汇管理局网站，查阅我国近年来有关国际收支、进出口数额、外债规模及外汇储备的基本数据，选择其中某一年的数据进行分析。

2.了解我国国际储备资产的运作情况，试着撰写2020年我国外汇储备规模及适度性分析报告。

任课教师可以进行引导性讲解，然后将班级学生视情况分成若干小组，让学生自己查阅资料，进行讨论和分析，最后形成简要的分析报告，并制作PPT进行讲解，教师进行点评。

项目三
国际金融市场与金融机构

学习目标

知识目标

了解国际金融市场的含义和分类，掌握国际货币市场、国际资本市场及欧洲货币市场的概念和构成。

能力目标

掌握国际货币市场、国际资本市场及欧洲货币市场的业务及功能。

操作目标

掌握主要的国际金融机构的业务范围，为企业或组织寻找融资机会。

课程导入

中国首次负利率发行欧元主权债券

2020年11月18日，中国财政部顺利发行40亿欧元主权债券。其中，5年期7.5亿欧元，发行收益率为-0.152%；10年期20亿欧元，发行收益率为0.318%；15年期12.5亿欧元，发行收益率为0.664%。

此次发债是2019年重启欧元主权债券发行后连续第二年发行，取得了截至目前我国境外主权债券发行的最低收益率水平。其中，5年期采用溢价发行，票息为0，首次实现负利率发行。此次发行采用"三地上市、两地托管"模式，在伦敦证券交易所、卢森堡证券交易所和香港证券交易所三地上市。同时，为支持香港国际金融中心的建设，首次在香港债务工具中央结算系统（CMU）托管清算此次欧元主权债券5年期品种，以促进香港金融基础设施建设。此外，国际评级公司给予了信用评级。

从簿记情况来看，国际投资者认购踊跃，订单规模达到发行量的4.5倍，投资者涵盖央行、主权基金、超主权类及养老金、资管和银行等。欧洲投资者最终投资比例高达72%，体现出国际资本市场投资者对中国经济稳中向好的信心。欧元主权债券的顺利发行，更加体现出中国更高水平全面对外开放的决心和信心，顺应经济金融全球化的趋势，也将进一步深化中国与国际资本市场的融通以及与国际投资者的合作。

主权债券是一国政府在国际市场上以外币发行的债券。这类债券之所以被称为主权债券，是因为它是以政府为主体发行的一种债券，且以政府信用背书。出现负利率发行的原因跟目前的全球经济环境有关。近年来，为应对经济下行压力，许多国家采取了宽松的货币政策，负利率是一种非常规货币政策工具。目前，欧元区的存款基准利率已经是负值，欧洲多国长期国债收益率也在负利率期间，这次我国财政部发行的5年期欧元主权债，发行收益率虽然为-0.152%，但是与其他欧元区主权债券的收益率相比还是较高的。而且市场预期欧元区基准利率还有可能继续下降，那么债券的价格就会上升。对投资者而言，这意味着即便不持有到期，通过二级市场卖出也可以获利。

主权债券的信用依赖的是国家信用，国际资本热捧中国的主权债券，其实质是对中国经济发展投下信任票。对中国而言，发行欧元主权债券有利于进一步推进人民币国际化，对中国金融市场融入世界经济也具有重要意义。随着人民币的国际化，未来中国的国债也会走向世界，肯定会更多地发行，包括美元、欧元，甚至是日元、英镑等主权债券，这是中国国债结构优化的一个具体体现。实际上，这也是在人民币国际化大背景下的一些具体举措。人民币要国际化，就需要资金的双向流动，除了吸收很多外汇到国内外，人民币也要"走出去"。

资料来源：中华人民共和国财政部. 财政部顺利发行40亿欧元主权债券[EB/OL].（2020-11-19）. http://www.mof.gov.cn/zhengwuxinxi/caizhengxinwen/202011/t20201119_3626191.htm.

思考讨论：

（1）什么是主权债券？

（2）为什么欧洲投资者热衷于投资中国发行的负利率欧元主权债券？

任务一　　　　　国际金融市场概述

一、国际金融市场的含义

国际金融市场有狭义和广义之分。狭义的国际金融市场是指进行国际资金借贷或融通的场所。广义的国际金融市场是指从事各种国际金融交易的场所和交易网络，包括资金在国际上进行借贷、有价证券在国际上发行和买卖等国际金融业务。国际金融市场可细分为国际货币市场、国际资本市场、国际黄金市场、国际外汇市场和金融衍生品市场。由于计算机技术在银行业务中的广泛应用，各种跨境金融交易一般通过电话、电报、电传等通信工具进行。因此，国际金融市场并不局限于某一地理上的场所，更体现为一种无形的交易网络。本项目所述国际金融市场是指广义的国际金融市场。

二、国际金融市场的分类

（一）按照交易主体所属区域和金融交易受市场所在国的控制程度划分

国际金融市场按照交易主体所属区域和金融交易受市场所在国的控制程度划分，可分为在岸金融市场和离岸金融市场。

（二）按照有无固定的交易场所划分

国际金融市场按照有无固定的交易场所划分，可分为有形市场和无形市场。

有形市场是指有固定交易场所的国际金融市场，如国际股票市场。无形市场是指没有固定的有形交易场所，国际金融交易供需双方通过电话、电传、计算机等通信工具进行交易，如国际外汇市场。国际金融市场大多属于无形市场。

（三）按照经营业务的种类划分

国际金融市场按照经营业务的种类划分，可分为国际借贷市场、国际证券市场、国际外汇市场、国际黄金市场和金融衍生品市场。

（四）按照交易期限划分

国际金融市场按照交易期限划分，可分为国际货币市场和国际资本市场。

国际货币市场是指期限在一年及一年以下的金融工具的跨国交易市场，也称短期资金市场。

国际资本市场是指经营一年期以上的国际性中长期资金借贷和证券买卖业务的国际金融市场。

（五）按照金融资产交割方式划分

国际金融市场按照金融资产交割方式划分，可分为现货市场、期货市场和期权市场。

三、国际金融市场的形成与发展

国际金融市场是随着国际贸易、资本输出和生产的国际化，逐步形成和发展起来的。

第一次世界大战以前，英国工业革命及海外扩张，使其经济实力跃居世界首位，英镑成为世界上主要的国际储备和结算货币。伦敦也率先成为世界上首个国际金融市场。

微课3-1

国际金融市场的演变

第一次世界大战爆发至第二次世界大战结束，英国的经济受到严重破坏，伦敦国际金融市场的作用被削弱，英镑的地位下降。美国的纽约金融市场趁机崛起，美元成为各国的主要储备和结算货币。瑞士作为中立国，因未受战争破坏，经济、政治稳定，瑞士法郎能够自由兑换，使得苏黎世金融市场一跃而起。这一阶段，纽约、伦敦和苏黎世成为世界三大国际金融市场。

这一时期的国际金融市场，实质上都只是带有国际性业务的国内金融市场，即"传统的国际金融市场"。所从事的国际业务主要是发生在市场所在国的居民与非居民之间的国际信贷和国际债券业务，并受所在国政府的金融法律法规管制。其本质是一种资本输出。

20世纪50年代末期，欧洲货币市场产生，其信贷交易更加国际化，国外贷款人与国外借款人可以进行交易，交易货币几乎包括了西方各国的货币。从此，国际金融市场不再局限于少数几个传统的金融中心，而是迅速扩展到巴黎、法兰克福、布鲁塞尔、阿姆斯特丹、斯德哥尔摩、东京、卢森堡、新加坡、中国香港、开曼群岛等地。这一时期的国际金融交易扩展到市场所在国的非居民之间，且不受任何国家国内金融法律法规的制约和管制。

20世纪70年代以后，随着全球经济一体化的迅速发展，国际资本和产业技术输出到许多发展中国家。各国纷纷主动与国际惯例接轨，建立与之相适应的金融环境。如亚洲的马来西亚、菲律宾、泰国，中东石油输出国，以及拉丁美洲各国、非洲各国等发展中国家的金融市场逐渐兴起。

四、国际金融市场的作用

国际金融市场的形成和发展，无论对发达国家，还是对发展中国家，乃至对整个世界经济，都起着极其重要的作用。

（一）积极作用

国际金融市场加快了资本的流动，促进了全球的经济发展，具体表现在以下几个方面：

（1）促进了世界经济的发展。国际金融市场促进了国际贸易资金融通，为资本短缺国家提供外资、扩大生产规模，进而促进了世界经济的发展。

（2）调节国际收支。国际金融市场日益成为各国外汇资金的重要来源。一方面，国际收支顺差的国家将其外汇的盈余资金投放于国际金融市场；另一方面，国际收支逆差的国家从国际金融市场贷款，来弥补国际收支逆差。

（3）优化国际分工，推进了世界经济一体化。国际金融市场使各国间资金调拨的成本大大降低，促进了国际贸易的发展，也加快了国际资本的移动，使资金向优化世界经济资源配比的方向流动，促进国际分工体系的建立。

（二）消极作用

国际金融市场也有其不利的影响，主要反映在以下几个方面：

（1）国际金融交易中，投机比例过大，实体经济交易与投资占比小，导致国际市场上金融风险不断增大。

（2）国际金融市场将金融风险带到全世界。随着国际资本的流动，过度投资、经济泡沫、国际性债务也被带到世界各地。另外，金融机构之间、金融市场之间联系紧密，任何一个地方出现问题，风险就可能波及整个国际金融体系。

（3）国际金融市场成为国际走私、贩毒及其他金融犯罪活动洗钱的场所，在一定程度上削弱了有关国家在这方面的执法力度。

知识链接3-1

国际金融中心

国际金融中心（International Finance Center）是指聚集了大量金融机构和相关服务产业，全面集中地开展国际资本借贷、债券发行、外汇交易、保险等金融服务业的城市或地区。其能够提供最便捷的国际融资服务、最有效的国际支付清算系统、最活跃的国际金融交易场所。金融市场发达、服务业高度密集、对周边地区甚至全球具有辐射影响力是国际金融中心的基本特征。

国际金融中心的地位是建立在多种资源条件的综合优势之上的，是在一系列供给和需求因素的推动下形成和巩固的。根据历史经验和相关研究成果，可将这些条件概括如下：（1）强大繁荣的经济基础；（2）安定和平的政治环境；（3）高效健全的金融制度；（4）分布集中的金融机构；（5）鼓励扶持的政策取向；（6）低廉合理的税费成本；（7）完备齐全的基础设施。

2020年9月25日，由国家高端智库中国（深圳）综合开发研究院与英国智库Z/Yen集团共同编制的"第28期全球金融中心指数报告（GFCI 28）"在中国深圳和韩国首尔同时发布，从营商环境、人力资源、基础设施、金融业发展水平、声誉等方面对全球主要金融中心给予评价和排名。共有111个金融中心上榜，全球前十大金融中心为：纽约、伦敦、上海、东京、中国香港、新加坡、北京、旧金山、深圳、苏黎世。上海超过东京，首次进入全球三甲。

资料来源：佚名. 第28期全球金融中心指数：上海进入前三，深圳跻身全球前十［EB/OL］.［2020-09-25］. https://www.thepaper.cn/newsDetail_forward_9345476.

任务二　国际货币市场

一、国际货币市场的含义

国际货币市场是指期限在一年及一年以下的金融工具的跨国交易市场，也称短期资金市场。国际货币市场的参加者主要是商业银行、中央银行、各国政府的财政部门、货币机构、跨国公司、票据承兑公司、贴现公司、证券公司、跨国银行等。其中跨国银行处于市场的关键地位，是国际货币市场资金的主要供给者和需求者。

在货币市场上发行和流通的票据、证券，如国库券、商业票据、银行承兑汇票和大额可转让定期存单等都是短期的。这些票据和证券具有期限短、风险小和流动性强等特点，都具有活跃的二级市场，随时可以出售变现。

教学视频3-1
国际货币市场的构成与作用

二、国际货币市场的特点

国际货币市场一般具有以下几个方面的特点：

（1）期限较短，最短融资期限只有一天，最长的也不过一年。

（2）交易的目的是解决短期资金周转的需要。国际货币市场上的资金来源主要是资金所有者暂时闲置的资金，需求者只是为了弥补短期内流动资金的不足。

（3）金融工具具有较强的流动性。国际货币市场上交易的金融工具一般时间短、流动性强、变现快。

（4）交易者信誉高，融资规模大，借贷成本低，资金周转快，流量较大。

因为国际货币市场具有以上特点，所以要求该市场具有良好的管理监控机制，并提供相当成熟的社会经济发展环境。也就是说，国际货币市场只有在经济高度发达、中央银行体系高度健全、信用工具相当完备、市场条件十分优越、法律制度非常完善的条件下才能形成和发展起来。

三、国际货币市场的构成

国际货币市场按照业务种类可以划分为银行短期信贷市场、短期证券市场和贴现市场。

（一）短期信贷市场

短期信贷市场主要指银行间市场。该市场提供1年或1年以内的短期贷款，目的在于解决临时性的资金需要和头寸调剂。贷款的期限最短为1天，最长为1年，也提供3天、1周、1个月、3个月、半年等期限的资金；通常利率以伦敦银行同业拆放利率为基准；交易通常以批发形式进行，少则几十万英镑，多则几百万、几千万英镑；交易简便，无需担保和抵押，完全凭信誉，通过电话和电传进行交易。

（二）短期证券市场

短期证券市场是国际上进行短期证券交易的场所，期限不超过1年。交易对象有短期国库券、大额可转让定期存单、银行承兑汇票和商业承兑汇票。其中，国库券是西方各国财政部为筹集季节性资金需要，或是为了进行短期经济和金融调控而发放的短期债券，期限一般为3个月或半年，利率视情况而定，通常以票面金额打折和拍卖的方式推销。

银行存单是存户在银行的定期存款凭证，可以进行转让和流通。银行承兑汇票和商业承兑汇票都是信用支付工具，前者由银行承兑，后者由企业承兑，承兑后可背书转让，到期可持票向付款人提示要求付款。由于银行信誉较高，银行承兑汇票比商业承兑汇票的流动性强。

（三）贴现市场

贴现是指持票人将未到期的票据抵押给银行或贴现公司，由银行或贴现公司按票面金额扣除贴现利息后将剩余的资金交给持票人的一种金融交易。贴现市场是对未到期的票据按贴现方式进行融资的场所。贴现交易使得持票人提前取得票据到期时的金额（票面金额扣除贴现利息后的余额），而贴现行则向要求贴现的持票人提供信贷，取得贴现利息。贴现业务是货币市场资金融通的一种重要方式。贴现的票据主要有国库券、银行债券、公司债券、银行承兑汇票和商业承兑汇票，贴现率一般高于银行利率。贴现行可以将贴现后的票据向其他商业银行申请转贴现，也可以向中央银行申请再贴现。中央银行利用这种再贴现业务来调节信用、调节利率，进而调控宏观金融。

任务三　　　　　　　　国际资本市场

一、国际资本市场的含义

国际资本市场是指经营一年期以上的国际性中长期资金借贷和证券买卖业务的国际金融市场。

国际资本市场的资金供应者主要包括：（1）各种机构投资者，如商业银行、投资银行、保险公司、基金公司以及跨国公司等；（2）各国货币当局以及国际金融机构；（3）私人投资者。

国际资本市场的资金需求者主要包括：各国政府、国际金融机构、商业银行以及跨国公司等。

交易的内容主要包括：中长期资金的借贷、中长期证券的买卖以及国际租赁等。

二、国际资本市场的特点

因其交易对象的期限比较长，故国际资本市场具有以下特点：

（1）资金融通期限较长，一般在一年以上，甚至长达几十年；

（2）交易规模巨大，交易的目的一般是追加资本或弥补财政赤字；

（3）交易的金融工具期限较长，流动性较差，风险较大。

三、国际资本市场的构成

国际资本市场主要由中长期借贷市场、中长期证券市场和国际租赁市场构成。当前国际资本市场中最主要的业务仍然是中长期信贷业务和证券业务。

教学视频3-2

国际资本市场的构成与作用

（一）中长期信贷市场

中长期信贷市场主要是指各国政府、国际金融组织以及跨国银行向客户提供中长期资金融通的市场。

政府贷款的期限比较长、利率低，但有一定的附加条件。政府贷款的期限最长可达30年，利率最低可为零，而附加条件一般是限制贷款的使用范围，如规定贷款的用途，或规定借款国必须在其经济政策或外交政策上做出某些承诺或调整。因此，政府贷款是一种约束性贷款。

跨国银行贷款一般对贷款的用途不加约束，贷款利率按市场行情和借款人的信誉而定。对于数额比较大的贷款，一般采用联合贷款或辛迪加贷款的方式以分散风险。

联合贷款或辛迪加贷款是指几家甚至十几家银行共同向某一客户提供贷款，由一家银行做牵头行，若干家银行做管理行，其余银行做参与行。

（二）中长期证券市场

国际中长期证券市场一般由国际股票市场和国际中长期债券市场构成。

1.国际股票市场

国际股票一般是指一国工商企业在境外发行的，以市场所在国货币计值的股票。国际股票的发行者和投资者，或者发行者和股票计值货币分别属于不同的国家或地区。例如，我国在新加坡发行的 S 股，以及在纽约发行的 N 股，如中国企业网易有道于 2019 年 10 月 25 日在美国纽约证券交易所以美元为面值币种发行股票。

国际股票市场是指在国际范围内发行并交易股票的场所或交易网络。比较有名的国际股票市场，如纽约证券交易所、伦敦证券交易所、新加坡证券交易所、香港证券交易所等。

2.国际中长期债券市场

国际债券是指一国政府、企业、金融机构等为筹集资金在境外发行的以外币计值的债券，或者国际金融机构为筹集资金而在各国金融市场上发行的债券。大多数国际债券的发行由银行或证券公司承销。国际中长期债券的融资期限在 1 年以上。

国际债券分为外国债券和欧洲债券两类。

外国债券是指一国政府、企业、金融机构在境外债券市场上发行的以市场所在国货币计值的债券，或者国际金融机构在一国债券市场上发行的以该国货币计值的债券，如英国公司在美国债券市场上发行的以美元为计值货币的债券，或者国际金融公司在我国债券市场上发行的以人民币为计值货币的债券。筹资者发行外国债券，会受到市场所在国证券监管机构的监管及金融法令的约束。

规模较大的外国债券主要包括：美国的"扬基债券"（外国筹资者在美国债券市场上发行的以美元为计值货币的债券）、英国的"猛犬债券"（外国筹资者在英国债券市场上发行的以英镑为计值货币的债券）、日本的"武士债券"（外国筹资者在日本债券市场上发行的以日元为计值货币的债券）以及中国的"熊猫债券"（境外筹资者在中国大陆债券市场上发行的以人民币为计值货币的债券）。

欧洲债券是指一国政府、企业、金融机构在境外债券市场上发行的以第三国货币计值的债券，或者国际金融机构在一国债券市场上发行的以第三国货币计值的债券。这里的"欧洲"不是地理上的欧洲，指的是"境外"。比如美国公司在东京机构债券市场上发行的以英镑计值的债券。筹资者发行欧洲债券，一般较少受到市场所在国金融法令的约束。

外国债券与欧洲债券概念的比较见表 3-1。

表 3-1　　　　　　　　　　外国债券与欧洲债券概念的比较

类别	概　念
外国债券	债券发行者和发行地属于不同的国家或地区，但债券发行地和债券计值货币属于同一个国家或地区
欧洲债券	债券发行者、发行地、债券计值货币分别属于不同的国家或地区

（三）国际租赁市场

租赁是指承租人向出租人定期支付若干数额的款项以获得某种资产的使用权的一种安排。它使承租人不必购买短期或季节性需要使用的设备，只需定期支付给出租人一定数额的费用便可获得所需设备的使用权，这等于出租人变相向承租人提供了信贷。在经济生活中，许多制造业不仅出售设备，还从事设备租赁。此外，银行也大量从事租赁，此时的租赁实际上是一种资金融通的方式。当租赁跨越国界时，便成为各国间资金融通的一种方式。

任务四　　　　　　　欧洲货币市场

一、欧洲货币市场的含义

欧洲货币市场是指非居民之间，以银行为中介在某种货币发行国国境之外从事该种货币借贷的市场，又称为离岸金融市场。其中在发行国境外被交易的货币称为"欧洲货币"；经营欧洲货币业务的银行，被称为"欧洲银行"。

"欧洲银行"利用其全球性的分支机构和客户网络、现代化的通信工具，将世界各地的欧洲货币供求者联系在一起，形成以若干离岸金融中心为基础的、全球化无形市场。

对于欧洲货币市场的含义，有以下几点要注意：

（1）欧洲货币（eurocurrency）又称境外货币（off-shore currency），是指在货币发行国境外被存储和借贷各类货币的总称，并非指欧洲国家的货币。"欧洲"一词也不是地理上的概念，并不局限于欧洲，而是指"境外""离岸"的意思。例如，在美国境外存贷的美元被称为"欧洲美元"；在英国境外存贷的英镑被称为"欧洲英镑"。目前，离岸金融市场上经常使用的欧洲货币包括：美元、瑞士法郎、日元、英镑和欧元等，其中美元仍占主导地位。

动画微课3-2

人民币离岸
市场

（2）欧洲货币市场是欧洲货币的交易市场。同样的，"欧洲"一词也不是地理概念，而是指货币发行国的"境外"。例如"人民币离岸市场"就是在我国境外进行人民币存贷交易的市场，目前主要是新加坡和中国香港，而我国境内也可以设立欧洲货币市场（或称为离岸金融市场）。

知识链接3-2

离岸金融业务范围

离岸金融是金融全球化和开放的产物，能有效促进金融资源在世界范围内的优化配置，为国际资金融通和国际债务结算提供便利，并推动国际贸易的快速发展。离岸金融业务主要包括银行、保险、证券等金融业务，以及船籍注册等非金融业务。

目前比较著名的离岸金融中心有英属维京群岛、开曼群岛、巴哈马群岛、百慕大群岛、所罗门群岛等。离岸银行在离岸金融中心也得到了快速发展。比如亚洲银行就在英属维尔京群岛注册成立，利用最新的金融科技，为其全球客户提供全面的跨境金融服务。离岸银行业务范围往往包括向境外的生意伙伴（比如从事进出口贸易、咨询类业务的公司）提供付款和结算业务；用离岸账户接受境外投资的收益；接受投资人的资金，并将资金投入到被投项目中；还能为暂时不用的资金设立定期存款。

全球离岸金融市场在监管和信息透明度上也在不断取得进步，为离岸业务的进一步发展营造了良好的氛围和环境。

资料来源：佚名. 离岸金融市场下，离岸银行业务范围有哪些？[EB/OL].[2020-12-16]. http://cn.dailyeconomic.com/roll/2020/12/16/139530.html.

二、欧洲货币市场的产生与发展

（一）欧洲货币市场的产生

欧洲货币市场产生于20世纪50年代，其前身是欧洲美元市场。第二次世界大战结束后，美国对苏联及其他社会主义国家采取了敌视和遏制政策。苏联和东欧国家担心它们存放在美国的美元资金会被冻结，因此将这一部分美元资金转存到了英国的银行。当时的英国政府正需要大量资金以恢复英镑的地位、支持其国内经济的发展，所以准许伦敦的各大商业银行经营境外美元的存贷款业务。于是，欧洲美元市场应运而生。

（二）欧洲货币市场的发展

欧洲美元市场的发展是各方因素促成的结果。

1958年以后，美国的国际收支开始出现赤字，且规模越来越大。美元大量流出美国，为欧洲美元市场提供了大量资金。为了防止国际收支进一步恶化，美国采取了限制资本外流的政策，迫使美国境外居民将美元借贷业务转移到欧洲美元市场上来，美国的银行也相应地在欧洲开设了许多分支机构，这些都刺激了欧洲美元市场的发展。

从20世纪60年代开始，除了美元之外，在欧洲美元市场上交易的货币还包括德国马克和瑞士法郎等币种。此外，亚洲的新加坡、中国香港等金融市场纷纷开始经营美元、马克的借贷业务。至此，欧洲美元市场演变为欧洲货币市场。其中的"欧洲"不再是一个表示地理位置的概念，而是指"境外"。而"欧洲货币"则是指在货币发行国境外流通的货币。

20世纪70年代后，世界石油两次大幅提价，一方面使得石油输出国积累了大量石油美元，这些美元大多被投入到欧洲美元市场上；另一方面，非石油输出国中发展中国家的国际收支纷纷出现逆差，使得它们转向欧洲美元市场借入资金以弥补赤字，如此便使得该市场上的资金需求增加了。

动画微课3-3

欧洲货币市场与欧洲货币

20世纪80年代后，欧洲货币市场的意义又发生了新的变化。1981年，美国联邦储备银行（美联储）批准在纽约设立国际银行业务设施，允许美国的存款机构和外国银行在美国的分行或经理处经营外国客户的美元存款和其他外币存款，而且这一部分的美元存款及外币存款不受美国国内存款准备金和利率限制，同时还允许这些机构利用从非居民处吸收的美元和外币存款资金向外国客户提供信贷。由此可见，国际银行业务设施可以经营非居民业务，不受货币发行国的金融政策限制，属于广义的欧洲货币市场。

三、欧洲货币市场的经营特点

欧洲货币市场是完全国际化的金融市场，是国际金融市场的主体，具有以下经营特点：

（1）市场范围广，不受地理限制，交易主要通过现代通信网络达成。

（2）市场交易规模巨大，交易品种及币种繁多，金融创新极其活跃。欧洲货币市场上的单笔交易金额绝大部分超过了100万美元，交易的币种除了美元、日元、德国马克、瑞士法郎、英镑及加拿大元等币种外，还有不少发展中国家的货币，甚至还出现了以特别提款权和欧洲货币为标价币种的交易。这些交易使得欧洲货币市场与外汇市场紧密地联系在一起。

（3）独特的利率结构。欧洲货币市场利率体系以伦敦银行同业拆放利率为基础，市场上的存贷利差较小。一方面，由于欧洲货币市场不受法定存款准备金和存款利率上限的限制，银行提供的存款利率较高；另一方面，由于欧洲货币市场属于银行同业市场，而贷款客户通常是信誉较好的大银行、大公司或政府机构，交易规模巨大，贷款的风险较小，贷款的成本较低，使得贷款的利率较低。

（4）受到的管制较少，市场风险日益加剧。由于欧洲货币市场从事的是境外货币的借贷，参加的主体主要是非居民，因此一般不受任何国家国内法律的管制，使得这一市场上的风险日益加剧。

四、欧洲货币市场的类型

（一）一体型

一体型货币市场是指本国居民参加交易的在岸业务与非居民间进行的离岸业务之间没有严格的界限，境内资金与境外资金可以随时互相转换。伦敦金融市场和香港金融市场即属此类。

（二）分离型

分离型货币市场是指本国居民参加交易的在岸业务与非居民间进行的离岸业务相互分开。分离型货币市场有助于隔绝国际资金流动对本国货币存量和宏观经济的影响。美国离岸金融市场上设立的国际银行业务设施、日本东京离岸金融市场上设立的海外特别账户，以及新加坡离岸金融市场上设立的亚洲货币账户都属于此类。

（三）走账型或簿记型

这类市场没有或几乎没有实际的离岸金融业务交易，只是起到其他金融市场资金交易的记账和划账作用，目的在于逃避税收和管制。巴哈马群岛、开曼群岛和百慕大群岛等离岸金融市场即属此类。

五、欧洲货币市场的构成

按照借贷方式、借贷期限和业务性质，欧洲货币市场可分为欧洲货币信贷市场和欧洲债券市场。

（一）欧洲货币信贷市场

欧洲货币信贷市场包括欧洲货币短期信贷市场（借贷期限在一年或者一年以内）和欧洲货币中长期信贷市场（借贷期限在一年以上）。

1.欧洲货币短期信贷市场

该市场主要是银行间同业拆借市场，经营的业务主要包括一年以内的短期资金借贷，最短的期限为日拆。该市场的借贷业务主要依赖参与者的信用，无须担保，交易一般通过电话或电传达成，成交额以百万或千万美元以上为单位。该市场的存款大多数是企业、银行、机关团体和个人在短期内的闲置资金；这些资金又通过银行提供给另一些国家的企业、银行、私人和官方机构做短期资金周转。

欧洲货币短期信贷市场的特点主要包括：

（1）交易品种的期限短，一般为3个月以内；

（2）交易属于批发性质，单笔交易金额比较大；

（3）交易灵活方便，在借款期限、借款币种和借款地点等方面都有较大的选择空间；

（4）以伦敦银行同业拆放利率为基础，利率由双方协商决定。

2.欧洲货币中长期信贷市场

欧洲货币中长期信贷市场的资金借贷期限在一年以上。筹资者主要是世界各地的国有或私营企业、政府以及国际金融组织。由于贷款期限较长，流动性较差，所以风险较大。贷款利率一般以伦敦银行间拆放利率为基础来调整，并且大多采用浮动利率。该市场交易的特点主要包括：

（1）贷款期限较长，一般为2～10年，有的甚至长达20年；

（2）贷款金额大，一般在2 000万～5 000万美元，也有几十亿美元的贷款；

（3）一般以国际银团贷款或辛迪加贷款为主，以分散风险；

（4）实行浮动利率，根据市场变化，每3个月或半年调整一次；

（5）贷款必须签订协议，有的甚至需要一国政府提供担保。

（二）欧洲货币债券市场

欧洲货币债券市场即欧洲债券市场，是指非居民为筹集资金而在一国债券市场上以第三国货币发行债券所形成的市场。该市场是欧洲货币市场的重要组成部分。欧洲债券市场上的债券种类主要包括普通固定利率债券、浮动利率债券、可转换债券、授权证债券、合成债券等。

六、欧洲货币市场的作用

（一）欧洲货币市场的积极作用

欧洲货币市场对世界经济的积极作用包括以下几点：

1.促进金融全球化

欧洲货币市场打破了国际金融市场的国界限制，通过众多货币市场24小时不间断的业务活动，加强了各国之间的金融联系，形成了一个全球性的金融市场。

2.促进国际贸易发展

欧洲货币市场为国际贸易融资提供了便利，帮助一些国家解决了国际支付中外汇匮乏的问题，促进了国际贸易的发展。

3.促进一些国家的经济发展

欧洲货币市场上的巨额资金使得第二次世界大战后西欧国家和日本的经济得以快速恢复与发展。一些发展中国家，尤其是非产油国，也从欧洲货币市场筹集到发展所需的部分资金，从而促进了这些国家经济的发展。

（二）欧洲货币市场的消极影响

1.增加了经营欧洲货币存贷业务银行的经营风险

欧洲货币市场上的存贷业务，基本上是短存长贷，即银行吸收的欧洲货币存款绝大部分是短期的，而发放的欧洲货币贷款又多半是长期的，存在期限不匹配的问题，这无疑使经营这些业务的银行增加了经营风险。另外，欧洲货币贷款业务主要以辛迪加贷款为主，若贷款客户到期无力偿还，还些银行都将遭受损失。

2.加剧了外汇市场的动荡

欧洲货币市场因不受市场所在地金融法令的限制，易引起国际资本大规模流动，使得资本流入国和资本流出国外汇市场动荡不安。

　　3.削弱各国金融政策的实施效果

　　当一国实施紧缩性货币政策，提高利率以抑制通货膨胀时，国内的企业和银行却可以很方便地从欧洲货币市场获得较低利率的资金；当一国实施扩张性货币政策，降低利率以刺激国内经济时，国内的银行可能会将资金调往国外寻求更高的利息收入。这就使得国内的金融政策难以达到预期的效果。

任务五　　国际金融机构

一、国际货币基金组织

　　国际货币基金组织（International Monetary Fund，IMF），简称基金组织，根据成员方1944年7月在布雷顿森林会议上签订的《国际货币基金组织协定》，于1945年12月27日正式成立，总部设在美国首都华盛顿。该组织与世界银行集团、世界贸易组织构成第二次世界大战后国际经济的三大支柱。

动画微课3-4
国际金融机构、世界银行、国际货币基金组织

　　（一）国际货币基金组织成立的宗旨

　　国际货币基金组织成立的宗旨如下：

　　（1）促进国际货币合作，为国际货币问题的磋商和协作提供方法；

　　（2）促进国际贸易的扩大与平衡发展，以增加和维持高水平就业和实习收入，以及开发成员方的生产资源；

　　（3）稳定国际汇率，在各成员方之间操持有秩序的汇价安排，避免竞争性的汇价贬值；

　　（4）协助建立各成员方之间经常性交易的多边支付制度，消除妨碍世界贸易的外汇管制；

　　（5）向成员方提供临时性资金，帮助成员方纠正国际收支失衡。

　　（二）国际货币基金组织的组织架构

　　理事会是国际货币基金组织的最高决策机构，由各成员方指派一名理事和副理事组成，任期5年。理事通常由该成员方的财政部部长或中央银行行长担任，有投票表决权。副理事在理事缺席的情况下才有投票表决权。理事会的主要职权是批准新纳入的成员方。

　　（三）国际货币基金组织的职能

　　国际货币基金组织的职能包括：

　　（1）制定成员方间的汇率政策和经常项目的支付以及货币兑换性方面的规则，并进行监督；

　　（2）对发生国际收支困难的成员方在必要时提供紧急资金融通，避免其他国家（或地区）受其影响；

　　（3）为成员方提供有关国际货币合作与协商等会议场所；

　　（4）促进各国间金融与货币领域的合作；

（5）维护各国间的汇率秩序；

（6）协助成员方之间建立经常性多边支付体系等。

（四）国际货币基金组织的资金来源

国际货币基金组织的资金主要来源于成员方缴纳的基金份额、借款、出售黄金所得的信托基金。其中，成员方缴纳的基金份额是基金组织的主要资金来源。

1.成员方缴纳的基金份额

国际货币基金组织的资金来源主要是成员方缴纳的基金份额，并将此用于对成员方的资金融通。份额是成员方参加IMF时所要认缴的一定数额的款项。每个成员方被分配一个份额，份额大致基于成员方在世界经济中的相对规模。成员方应缴份额的多少，是综合考虑成员方的国民收入、黄金外汇储备、平均进口额、出口变化率、出口额占国民收入的比例等经济指标决定的，最后由基金组织成员方磋商确定。

2.借款

借款是IMF的另一个重要的资金来源。国际货币基金组织通过成员方或其他途径对外借款弥补份额作为资金来源的不足。对外借款对于基金组织在紧急情况下寻求临时性资金补充发挥了重要作用。

3.出售黄金

基金组织持有约9 050万盎司的黄金，是全球黄金最大官方持有者之一。《国际货币基金组织协定》严格限制黄金的使用，出售黄金是一项临时性的资金来源。

如果获得成员方总投票权85%多数同意，基金组织可以出售黄金或接受成员方以黄金支付，但基金组织不能购买黄金或参与其他黄金交易。

（五）国际货币基金组织主要的业务活动

1.向成员方提供各种贷款

国际货币基金组织主要的日常业务活动是向出现国际收支困难的成员方提供不同类型的贷款。IMF贷款类型是不断发展的。早期的基金组织只发放普通贷款，后来陆续增加了中期贷款、补偿贷款、缓冲库存贷款和一些临时性贷款。

（1）普通贷款。

普通贷款也称普通提款权，是国际货币基金组织为解决成员方暂时性国际收支困难而设立的，是IMF最基本的贷款，期限不超过5年，主要用于弥补成员方国际收支逆差。贷款最高额度为成员方所缴纳份额的125%。贷款分为储备部分贷款和信用部分贷款两个部分。前者占成员方所缴纳份额的125%，成员方提取这部分贷款是无条件的，也不需要支付利息，但须用外汇或特别提款权的份额作保证。后者占成员方所缴纳份额的100%，共分4个档次，每档占份额的25%。成员方申请第一档贷款比较容易获批，一般只需提交借款申请即可得到批准，而第二档至第四档属高档信用借款，贷款条件较严格，成员方要借取就必须提供全面的财政稳定计划，而且在使用时必须接受IMF的监督。

（2）中期贷款。

中期贷款也称扩展贷款，是1974年设立的，用于成员方因在生产、贸易等方面存在结构性问题而进行长期调整的一项专用贷款，其贷款额度要比普通贷款高。其最高贷款额度为借款成员方所缴纳份额的140%，备用期3年，提款后第4年开始偿还，10年内还清。申请国必须提出贷款期内改进的国际收支计划，以及在次年准备实行有关政策的详细说明和实现措施。IMF根据成员方实现计划目标、实行政策的实际情况，分期发放贷款。

（3）出口波动补偿贷款。

IMF于1963年2月设立出口波动补偿贷款。最初规定为，当初级产品出口成员方因自然灾害等无法控制的客观原因造成初级产品出口收入下降，从而发生国际收支，在原有的普通贷款以外，可另行申请此项专用贷款。1981年5月IMF又补充规定，当成员方粮食进口价格超过前5年的平均价格而造成国际收支困难时，也可申请补偿贷款。该贷款最高限额为成员方所缴纳份额的100%，贷款期限为3~5年。1988年8月IMF又通过了一个修改方案，将应急机制结合原来的补偿贷款，并把贷款名称更改为补偿与应急贷款。

成员方在执行IMF支持的经济调整计划中，如遇突发性、临时性的经济因素而造成经常项目收支偏离预期调整目标，可申请该项贷款。

2.汇率监督与政策协调

国际货币基金组织除了提供金融贷款之外，还开展下列活动：

（1）通过发行特别提款权来调节国际储备资产的供应和分配；

（2）通过汇率监督促进汇率稳定；

（3）协调成员方的国际收支调节活动；

（4）促进国际货币缺席改革。

3.为成员方提供培训、咨询等服务

（1）为成员方提供培训、咨询等服务；

（2）收集和交换金融信息与统计。

二、世界银行集团

世界银行集团由国际复兴开发银行、国际开发协会、国际金融公司、多边投资担保机构以及国际投资争端解决中心五个相对独立的机构组成，是一个不断发展的国际金融机构。

（一）世界银行

世界银行是根据1944年7月布雷顿森林会议通过的《国际复兴开发银行协定》于1945年12月宣告成立的，其总部设在华盛顿，并于1946年6月开始正式营业，1947年11月成为联合国的专门机构。它同IMF有紧密的联系，只有IMF的成员方才有资格申请加入世界银行。1980年，中国恢复世界银行的成员地位，次年接受了世界银行的第一笔贷款。目前，世界银行已有189个成员。

1.世界银行的宗旨

虽然世界银行是营利性组织，但不以利润最大化为经营目标，按照《国际复兴开发银行协定》的规定，世界银行的宗旨是：

（1）通过对生产事业的投资，协助成员方经济的复兴与建设，鼓励不发达国家对资源的开发；

（2）通过担保或参加私人贷款及其他私人投资的方式，促进私人对外投资。当成员方不能在合理条件下获得私人资本时，可运用该行自有资本或筹集的资金来补充私人投资的不足；

（3）鼓励国际投资，协助成员方提高生产能力，促进成员方国际贸易的平衡发展和国际收支状况的改善；

（4）在提供贷款保证时，应与其他方面的国际贷款配合。

世界银行在成立之初，主要是资助部分欧洲国家恢复被战争破坏了的经济，但在1948年后，欧洲各国主要依赖美国的"马歇尔计划"来恢复第二次世界大战后的经济，于是世界银行主要转向向发展中国家提供中长期贷款与投资，促进发展中国家经济和社会发展。

世界银行在努力缩小这种差距，把富国的资源转化为穷国经济增长的助力。作为世界上提供发展援助最多的机构之一，世界银行支持发展中国家政府建造学校和医院、供水供电、防病治病和保护环境的各项努力。

2.世界银行的组织机构

（1）理事会。

理事会是世界银行的最高权力机构，由每一成员方派理事和副理事各一人组成。理事和副理事的任期为5年且可以连任，副理事在理事缺席时才有投票权。理事一般由各成员方财政部长或中央银行行长担任。理事会每年举行一次会议，一般与国际货币基金组织的理事会联合举行。

（2）执行董事会。

执行董事会是负责组织并处理日常业务的机构，行使董事会赋予的职权。执行董事会成员有25名执行董事。世界银行行长由美国公民担任，任期5年，且可以连任。行长担任执行董事会主席，并负责世界银行的全面管理。一般情况下，行长无投票权，只有在执行董事会表决中赞成、反对票数相同时才可以投决定性的一票。在未经执行董事会明确授权的情况下，执行董事不能单独行使任何权力，也不能单独做出承诺或代表世界银行。

（3）行政管理机构。

世界银行行政管理机构由行长、若干副行长、局长、处长及其他工作人员组成。行长是行政管理机构的首脑，负责银行的日常管理工作，任免银行高级职员和工作人员。

3.世界银行的资金来源

（1）各成员方缴纳的世界银行股份。

与IMF一样，世界银行也是按股份制原则建立的，凡成员方均需认购该行股份。各国缴纳股金以其国民收入、贸易总额及在基金组织所缴纳份额而定。

世界银行建立时法定资本为100亿美元，实缴资本为20%，其中2%以黄金或美元缴纳，18%以本国货币支付；待缴资本占80%，由成员方保存，需要时以黄金、美元或所需的货币支付。经世界银行数次增资，实缴资本仅占认缴股金的6%。

（2）对外借款。

世界银行平均每年发放贷款200多亿美元，依靠成员方实缴股金远不能满足资金需要。世界银行依靠向国际金融市场借款作为信贷资金的主要来源。其中，发行国际债券借入的资金，满足了发放贷款所需资金的70%。

世界银行发行债券有两种方式：一种是直接向成员方的政府、中央银行出售中、短期债券；另一种是通过投资银行、商业银行等承销商向私人投资市场出售债券。目前，世界银行已成为世界最大的非居民借款人。

（3）转让债权。

世界银行为了加速与扩大信贷资金的周转，把贷出资金的债权转让给商业银行等私人投资者，从而收回一部分信贷资金，这也是世界银行的资金来源之一。

4.世界银行的业务活动

（1）向成员方提供贷款。世界银行向成员方和由成员方政府担保的私人企业提供长期贷款。期限最长可达30年（宽限期5年），贷款实行浮动利率，但一般低于市场利率。

贷款必须用于特定的项目，如农业、交通、能源、环境卫生等，且借款方必须有偿还能力。贷款程序严密，审批时间较长，一般要一年半到两年时间。

世界银行的贷款以美元计值，且只提供项目所需的外汇部分，占项目总额的30%～40%。

（2）向成员方提供广泛的技术援助。例如，派遣专家，提供咨询服务，帮助成员方中高级官员进行经济管理，特别是项目管理的培训。

（二）国际开发协会

国际开发协会是世界银行的一个附属机构，成立于1960年9月，1960年11月开始营业，总部设在华盛顿，现有成员方169个。

1980年，中国恢复了在世界银行的合法席位，并同时成为国际开发协会的成员方。中国在国际开发协会的投票权为344 829票表决权，占总投票权的1.88%。截至1999年7月，国际开发协会共向中国提供了102亿美元的软贷款，共执行69个项目。从1999年7月起，国际开发协会停止对中国提供贷款。2007年12月，我国向国际开发协会捐款3 000万美元。

1.国际开发协会的宗旨

国际开发协会的宗旨是帮助世界上欠发达地区的成员方促进经济发展，提高生产力和生活水平。

2.国际开发协会的组织结构

国际开发协会的理事、执行董事、经理都由世界银行的相应人员担任，可以说是"两块牌子，一套人马"，但在法律上和财务上是相互独立的。

3.国际开发协会的资金来源

（1）成员方认缴的资本。成员方按经济发展水平分为两组：

第一组：发达国家（地区）或收入较高的国家（地区），认缴股份必须以黄金或外汇支付；

第二组：发展中国家（地区），认缴股份的10%以外汇支付，90%以本币支付。

（2）成员方提供的补充资金，主要由第一组国家提供，已达100亿美元。

4.国际开发协会的业务活动

国际开发协会专门向欠发达地区的成员方，即没有能力向国际复兴开发银行借款的国家（地区），提供条件宽松、期限长、无息的贷款资金，以解决这些国家（地区）在发展方面的需要。因此，国际开发协会被称为世界银行"软贷款窗口"。

（1）贷款对象：低收入的发展中国家（人均国民生产总值低于925美元）。

（2）贷款期限：长期优惠贷款，最长50年（含10年宽限期）。第一个10年为宽限期，第二个10年每年偿还1%，后30年每年偿还3%。

（3）贷款利息：无息贷款，仅收0.75%手续费。

（4）贷款以特别提款权为计算单位，可以部分或全部用本国货币偿还。

（三）国际金融公司

国际金融公司于1956年7月24日成立，1957年2月成为联合国的一个专门机构，现有会员175个。国际金融公司是首个将推动私营企业发展作为其主要目标的政府间组织。

1.国际金融公司的宗旨

配合世界银行的业务活动，向成员方特别是其中的发展中国家（地区）的重点私人企业提供无须政府担保的贷款或投资，鼓励国际私人资本流向发展中国家（地区），以推动这些国家（地区）的私人企业的成长，促进其经济发展。

2.国际金融公司的组织结构

国际金融公司的理事、执行董事、经理也是由世界银行的相应人员担任，"两块牌子，一套人马"，但国际金融公司有自己的业务人员。

3.国际金融公司的资金来源

国际金融公司成立时，有法定资本1亿美元。其余资金主要来源于从世界银行和金融市场的借款。此外，还有投资、放贷的业务净收益。

4.国际金融公司的业务活动

国际金融公司向发展中国家（地区）会员的私营企业提供贷款，一般倾向于制造业、加工业、开采业。贷款分为A、B两种，A贷款是由国际金融公司直接提供；B贷款是由国际金融公司出面，组织商业银行提供贷款。具体贷款条件如下：

（1）生产性私人企业，而且这些企业不能以合理条件从其他渠道获得资本。

（2）期限一般是7~15年，还款时须用原借入货币进行支付。

（3）是能够获利的项目，不需要政府担保。

（4）低于市场利率，略高于世界银行的贷款利率。

此外，国际金融公司还可以直接入股，参股投资一般不超过25%，但收益率要在10%以上，对项目的选择较严格。

思政小课堂

　　2013年，习近平主席出访东南亚时提出了筹建亚洲基础设施投资银行（以下简称"亚投行"）的倡议，得到许多亚洲国家的积极响应。2015年6月，50个意向创始成员代表共同签署《亚洲基础设施投资银行协定》，另有7个国家随后签署。2015年12月，《亚洲基础设施投资银行协定》达到法定生效条件，亚投行正式宣告成立。2016年1月，亚投行正式开业运营。截至2020年7月29日，亚投行的成员数量由开业时的57个增至103个，覆盖亚洲、欧洲、非洲、北美洲、南美洲、大洋洲六大洲。成员主体为发展中国家，但也吸收了包括英国、法国、德国、加拿大等在内的发达国家。

　　亚投行是一个政府间性质的亚洲区域多边开发机构，它成立的宗旨就是促进亚洲区域基础设施互联互通，以及经济一体化的进程，并且加强中国及其他亚洲国家（地区）的合作。

　　请结合本项目所学内容，思考亚洲基础设施投资银行的成立对我国有何意义，对全球经济发展会产生什么样的影响。

项目思维导图

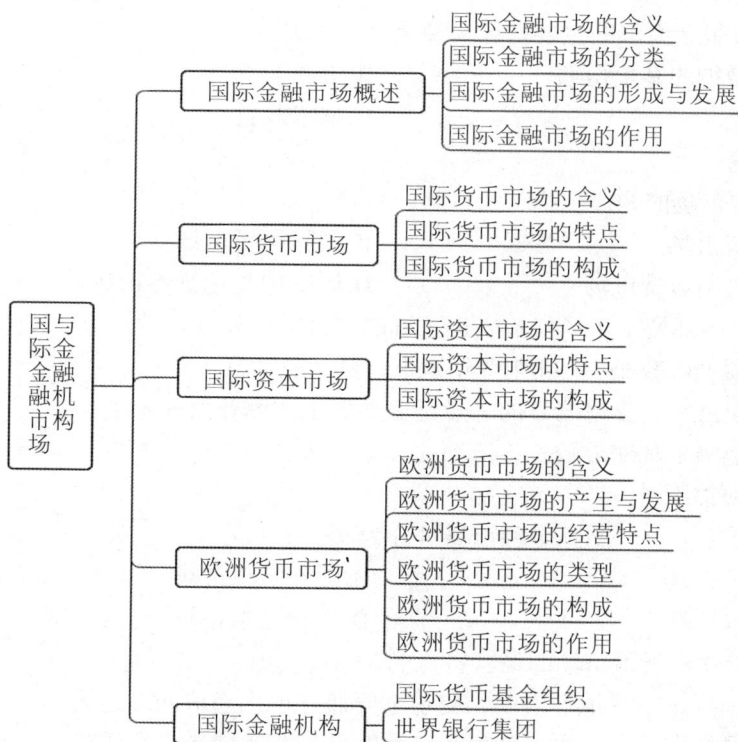

项目训练

一、单选题

1.下列不属于国际货币市场特点的是（　　　）。

A.期限较短，最短的融资期限只有1天，最长的也不超过1年

B.交易的目的是解决长期资金不足的需要

C.金融工具具有较强的流动性，国际货币市场上交易的金融工具一般时间短、流动性强、变现性高

D.交易者信誉高，融资规模大，借贷成本低，资金周转快，流量性大

2.非居民在美国金融市场上发行的以美元为面值的债券称为（　　　）。

A.猛犬债券　　　　　　　　　　　B.武士债券

C.扬基债券　　　　　　　　　　　D.熊猫债券

3.对成员方的生产性私营企业进行贷款的国际金融机构是（　　　）。

A.国际金融公司　　　　　　　　　B.世界银行

C.国际开发协会　　　　　　　　　D.国际货币基金组织

4.下列不属于国际货币市场金融工具的是（　　　）。

A.股票　　　　　　　　　　　　　B.商业票据

C.短期国库券　　　　　　　　　　D.大额可转让定期存单

5.国际货币基金组织的主要资金来源是（　　　）。

A.成员方缴纳的基金份额　　　　　B.借款

C.出售黄金　　　　　　　　　　　D.债权收益

二、多选题

1.国际资本市场的构成包括（　　　）。

A.国际信贷市场　　　　　　　　　B.国际租赁市场

C.国际中长期信贷市场　　　　　　D.国际中长期证券市场

2.下列关于国际资本市场特点表述正确的是（　　　）。

A.资金融通期限较长，一般在1年以上，甚至长达几十年

B.交易规模巨大，交易的目的一般是追加资本或弥补财政赤字

C.交易的金融工具期限较长，流动性较差，风险较大

D.以上选项都不对

3.按融资期限分类，国际金融市场可分为（　　　）。

A.国际外汇市场　　　　　　　　　B.国际货币市场

C.国际资本市场　　　　　　　　　D.离岸金融市场

4.下列属于欧洲货币市场的经营特点的是（　　　）。

A.市场范围广，不受地理限制，交易主要通过现代通信网络达成

B.市场交易规模巨大、交易品种及币种繁多，金融创新极其活跃

C.受到的管制较少，市场风险日益加剧

D.欧洲货币市场上的存贷款利差较大

5.下列属于欧洲货币市场构成的是（　　　）。

A.欧洲货币短期信贷市场

B.欧洲货币中长期信贷市场

C.欧洲货币债券市场，即欧洲债券市场

D.以上都对

三、判断题

1.按照经营的业务内容分类，国际金融市场可分为国际货币市场和国际资本市场。　　　　　　　　　　　　　　　　　　　　　　　　　　　　（　　）

2.欧洲债券的发行者、发行市场和债券面值属于不同的国家。　　　（　　）

3.欧洲货币指的是欧洲国家发行的货币。　　　　　　　　　　　　（　　）

4.欧洲货币市场的前身是欧洲美元市场。　　　　　　　　　　　　（　　）

5.国际金融公司贷款的对象是各成员方政府。　　　　　　　　　　（　　）

四、实践分析题

2003年11月起，中国人民银行在香港提供人民币清算业务。2004年，香港银行开始在中国内地以外地区试办个人人民币业务，包括存款、汇款、兑换及信用卡业务，这是离岸人民币市场发展的开端。

2010年离岸人民币市场初步形成，中国人民银行与香港金融管理局签署《香港人民币业务清算协议》并发布联合公告，人民币自2010年7月19日起可在香港交割。至此，离岸人民币市场正式启动，香港自此踏出了人民币离岸金融市场建设的第一步，经过了十几年的发展也已初具规模。

2012年4月18日，伦敦金融城人民币业务中心启动，伦敦成为继香港之后全球第二大人民币离岸交易中心。随着人民币被国际认知并接受的程度不断加深，人民币离岸市场的发展已经驶入快车道。继香港、伦敦后，越来越多的国际金融中心希望成为人民币离岸金融市场。

2013年2月，中国人民银行授权中国工商银行新加坡分行担任新加坡人民币业务清算银行，即可直接通过美元人民币市场得到人民币供给。

请根据以上材料，以小组为单位进一步收集信息，研究我国为什么要大力发展离岸人民币市场，并制作PPT汇报。

项目四
外汇与汇率

学习目标

知识目标

掌握外汇、汇率的概念和种类；能够正确识别不同类型的汇率；理解固定汇率制度和浮动汇率制度的阶段、特征、异同、优缺点；了解人民币汇率制度历史；理解影响汇率变动的因素以及汇率变动产生的影响。

能力目标

能够正确区分固定汇率和浮动汇率的特征、优缺点；能够分析各种因素如何影响汇率的变动以及汇率变动对各因素产生何种影响。

操作目标

正确识别汇率牌价中的标价方法；能够进行汇率套算。

课程导入

外汇交易员的一天

迈克尔·班博（Michael Bamber），是一名外汇交易员，我们看看他的一天：

1.早上6：00起床，6：10准时打开电脑，查看个人的订单情况，风雨无阻！

2.在查看完自己的订单和市场最新情况后，班博并不会急于开始交易，而是先进入冥想状态（注：冥想是国外很多交易员极为推崇的一种方式）。

3.在此之后，班博会开始分析目标交易标的，他是一位技术分析交易员，擅长趋势分析和K线图分析。

4.不知不觉到了午餐时间，这比方便面还要简单的午餐，既能补充足够的能量，还能保持身材。

5.到了下午3：00，正是市场交易的高峰时期，班博显得比较忙碌。时不时也会与自己的经纪商、客户经理沟通交易方面的问题。

6.交易英镑/瑞士法郎获利，总体来说今天的成绩不错，班博比较满意。

7.傍晚7：00，班博会准时驱车前往健身房做运动，作为其锻炼身体和调节心态的最佳方式。

8.晚上9：00，回到家后，班博还会回顾当天的交易策略，并寻找继续交易的机会。

9.几近凌晨，班博并不急于休息，而是在睡觉前写交易日记，养成记录每日交易重点的好习惯。

10.00：45，班博方才上床睡觉。

从班博的交易日常我们可以看出，他对于工作绝对是认真的。作为一名全职交易员，班博从来没有懈怠。极强的自律性也是他能够帮助客户赚到钱的原因。

资料来源：根据相关资料整理所得。

思考讨论：

看到上面的外汇交易员日常工作的一天，想想如果是自己，你愿意并且能够胜任这份工作吗？

任务一   外汇与汇率

一、外汇的概念

世界上大多数国家都有自己的货币，中国使用的是人民币，美国使用的是美元，英国使用的是英镑。然而，只要是对外经济交往都离不开外汇，各国之间的贸易往来会引起不同货币之间的相互交换。例如，当一个中国投资者购买外国的商品、劳务或者金融资产时，必须把人民币兑换成外国货币。在我国，随着改革开放的日益深入，对外经贸往来日益频繁，涉及外汇的业务也越来越多。因此，学习国际金融课程，掌握外汇基本知识是必不可少的环节。

（一）外汇概念的动态与静态

1.动态外汇的概念

动态外汇是指一种活动，即把一国货币兑换成另一国货币，以清偿国际债权、债务关系的一种专门性的经营活动。这种活动并不是表现为直接运送现金，而是采用委托支付或者债权转让的方式。

例如，日本一家出口商向美国出口汽车，结算时美国进口商将一张以纽约 A 银行为付款人的美元支票支付给日本出口商，而日本出口商又将这一笔外汇存入 A 银行。这样美国进口商把其在 A 银行所拥有的债权转移到日本出口商在 A 银行的账户上，日本出口商在美国 A 银行就拥有一笔外汇债权。可见，动态外汇是指国际结算活动和行为。

2.静态外汇的概念

静态外汇又可以进一步分为广义与狭义两个范畴。

广义的静态外汇指的是对国际债务清偿过程中所形成的金融资产的统称，具体可分为以外币表示的支付凭证、信用凭证和外币现钞，如以外币表示的票据、外国的国债等。

而狭义的静态外汇是指国际清偿债务过程中以外币表示的支付凭证，如外币现钞。

《中华人民共和国外汇管理条例》（2008年8月修订）则明确指出，我国的外汇是指以外币表示的可以用作国际清偿债务的各种支付手段和资产，外汇范围具体为：①外币现钞，包括纸币、铸币；②外币支付凭证或者支付工具，包括票据、银行存款凭证、银行卡等；③外币有价证券，包括债券、股票等；④特别提款权；⑤其他外汇资产。

动画微课4-1

外汇及主要外币

关于外汇的定义，需要明确以下两点：

（1）外汇必须是以外币表示的资产。以某进出口贸易为例，假设英国从美国进口一批商品，双方约定以美元进行结算。据此，英国进口商就应该向美国出口商支付美元。对英国境内的公司来说，美元是一种外国货币，因此英国进口商确实支付了以外币表示的资产，即外汇。但是，美国出口商所收到的美元，对美国境内的公司来说，只是本国货币，而不是外币，所以美国出口商所得到的美元不能称为外汇。如果当初他们商定的约定是使用欧元来进行结算，那么由于欧元对美国出口商和英国进口商来说，都是外币，于是在这种情况下这笔贸易使用的支付手段，无论对美国出口商还是英国进口商来说，都属于外汇。

（2）外汇是必须能在国际上得到偿付、被各国所接受并可以转让、可以自由兑换成其他形式的资产或支付手段的货币及外币凭证；反之，凡是不能在国际上得到偿付的各种外币凭证、空头支票或者拒付汇票等均不能被视为外汇。

（二）世界主要货币名称及符号

在进行货币兑换的过程中，当今世界上流行使用代码来表示货币名称。表4-1列出了当今世界上主要货币的简况，包括货币的使用国家或地区、标准中/英文名称、货币符号和辅币进位制。根据国际标准化组织ISO 4217标准的定义，每种货币都由三个字母的代码来表示。

表4-1　　　　　　　　　　货币名称及符号

国家或地区	货币名称		货币符号	辅币进位制
	中文	英文	标准符号	
中国	人民币元	Renminbi Yuan	CNY	1CNY=10jiao（角）=100 fen（分）
美国	美元	U.S. Dollar	USD	1USD=100 cent（分）
欧元区	欧元	Euro	EUR	1EUR=100 euro cents（欧分）

国家或地区	货币名称		货币符号	辅币进位制
	中文	英文	标准符号	
日本	日元	Japanese Yen	JPY	（无）
中国香港	港元	Hong Kong Dollar	HKD	1HKD=100 cents（分）
英国	英镑	Pound	GBP	1GBP=100 new pence（新便士）
澳大利亚	澳大利亚元	Australian Dollar	AUD	1AUD=100 cents（分）
新西兰	新西兰元	New Zealand Dollar	NZD	1NZD=100 cents（分）
新加坡	新加坡元	Singapore Dollar	SGD	1SGD=100 cents（分）
瑞士	瑞士法郎	Swiss Franc	CHF	1CHF=100 centimes（生丁）
加拿大	加元	Canadian Dollar	CAD	1CAD=100 cents（分）
马来西亚	马来西亚林吉特	Malaysian Ringgit	MYR	1MYR=100 cents（分）
泰国	泰铢	Thai Baht	THB	1THB=100 satang（萨当）

资料来源：根据相关资料整理所得。

二、汇率及标价方法

一个美国人想到意大利去旅游，但他持有的是美元，而意大利境内流通的货币是欧元。如果他要实现自己的愿望，就必须把美元换成欧元。美元与欧元之间的兑换必然有一个交换比率，这个比率就是"外汇汇率（foreign exchange rate）"，即以一定单位的一国货币与一定数量的另一国货币相交换的比例关系。例如，2019年6月30日，欧元对美元的汇率是1.15美元。这里1.15美元所表示的就是欧元兑换美元的比价，或者也可以说用1.15美元表示1欧元的价格。

汇率作为一种交换比率，反映的是不同国家货币之间的价值对比关系。在国际经济贸易中，汇率起着重要的作用。

（一）汇率的变化

通常我们用升值、贬值来表示汇率的变化。一件商品价值100元人民币，如果美元对人民币的汇率是1∶6.85，则这件商品在国际市场上的价格是14.6美元；如果美元对人民币汇率涨到1∶7，即美元升值（人民币贬值），则这件商品在国际市场上的价格是14.29美元，此时该商品在国际市场上的价格会变低，对买者有利；如果美元对人民币的汇率跌到1∶6.5，即美元贬值（人民币升值），则这件商品在国际市场上的价格是15.38美元，此时对买者有利。这就是汇率变化给国际贸易带来的影响。

知识链接4-1

汇率与利率的比较

汇率是两种货币的兑换比例；利率是使用货币的代价。虽然二者是一国货币对外、对内价值的不同表现，但是二者关系密切。

一般来说，如果一国利率水平相对高于其他国家，就会刺激国外资金流入国内，国内资金流出减少，由此会使资本账户出现顺差，促使本币汇率提高；反之，则会导致一国的本币汇率下降。

（二）汇率的标价方法

动画微课4-2

汇率及其标价方法

汇率既然是两种货币之间的兑换比率，在进行标价时，就必须确定是以本币还是以外币为标准来表示的问题。选择的标准不同，汇率的表示方法也会有所不同。目前，世界上主要有两种汇率的表示方法，即直接标价法和间接标价法。

直接标价（direct quotation）法是指用一定整数单位（通常是1或者100的倍数）的外国货币作为标准，折算成若干数额的本国货币的标价方法。也就是说，以本国货币来表示外国货币的价格。直接标价法是以一定单位的外国货币为基准来计算应付多少本国货币，即应付多少本国货币才能获得一定单位的外国货币，所以又称之为"应付标价法"。例如，我国外汇交易中心对外公布的美元牌价为USD100=CNY687.85，这里的100美元就是一定单位的外国货币，而687.85元人民币则是100美元应付人民币的价格。

间接标价（indirect quotation）法是指用一定整数单位（通常是1或者100的倍数）的本国货币为标准，折算成若干数额的外国货币的标价方法。跟直接标价法刚好相反，间接标价法是以一定单位的本国货币为基准来计算应收多少外国货币，即收入多少外国货币需要支付一定单位的本国货币，所以又称之为"应收标价法"。例如，我国外汇交易中心对外公布的泰铢牌价为1CNY=4.5005THB，这里的1元人民币就是一定单位的本国货币，而4.5005泰铢则是花费1元人民币获得的泰铢价格。

（三）两种标价方法的区别与联系

1.两种标价法的标准不同

通常情况下，我们把两种货币当中数量始终不变的那种货币，称为"基准货币"；数量随时间变化而发生变化的那种货币，称为"报价货币"。

直接标价法中，外币作为基准货币，而本币则作为报价货币；

间接标价法中，本币作为基准货币，而外币则作为报价货币。

2.两种标价法在表示外汇行情上涨或者下跌上不同

外汇汇率上涨的含义是外国货币币值上升，本国货币币值下降；外汇汇率下跌的含义是外国货币币值下降，本国货币币值上升。由于存在这两种标价方法，因此外汇汇率涨跌的表达方式不同。

在直接标价法下：外国货币数量固定不变，如果外币币值上升，就需要支付比原来数额更多的本国货币才能兑换同样数量的外国货币；反之，如果外币币值下降，为了换得与原来同样多的一定单位的外币，只需要支付比原来数额较少的本国货币。

在间接标价法下：本国货币数量不变，应收的外国货币的数量随着本国货币币值的升降而增减。如果外汇汇率上升，所获得的外币数量就比以前少；如果外汇汇率下降，所获得的外币数量就比以前多。

3.直接标价法和间接标价法互为倒数

$$\frac{1}{直接标价法}=间接标价法，\frac{1}{间接标价法}=直接标价法$$

例如，1美元兑换人民币 **6.8785** 元，这是直接标价法；反过来，则为间接标价法，即1元人民币兑换约 **0.1454** 美元（即$\frac{1}{6.8785}$）。

三、汇率的种类

根据不同划分标准，我们可以把汇率划分为以下几类：

（一）从银行买卖外汇的角度划分

从银行买卖外汇的角度划分，汇率可分为买入汇率、卖出汇率和中间汇率。

教学视频4-1

汇率的种类

1.买入汇率

买入汇率（buying rate/bid price）又称买入价，是银行买入外币时使用的价格。它包括现钞买入价和现汇买入价两种。现钞买入价是指银行用本国货币买入外汇现钞时使用的价格，而现汇买入价则是指银行用本国货币买入外汇现汇时使用的价格。通常情况下，现钞买入价要低于现汇买入价。这是因为在购买外汇现钞时，银行通常情况下是要积累到一定数额以后，再将这堆现钞存入国外的银行同业中，在中间间隔的这段时间，银行是没有利息收入的；还有，在运送外汇现钞去国外银行的过程中涉及运费和保险费，银行必须把这些成本转嫁到出卖外汇现钞的客户身上，所以银行买入外汇现钞时使用的价格通常低于现汇买入时使用的价格。

2.卖出汇率

卖出汇率（selling rate/offer price）又称卖出价，是银行卖出外币时使用的价格。它包括现钞卖出价和现汇卖出价两种。由于银行卖出外币时不存在生息和运输的过程，所以通常情况下现钞卖出价和现汇卖出价是一样的，也有些银行直接标注"卖出价"，而不注明是现钞还是现汇。

3.中间汇率

买入汇率与卖出汇率的算术平均值，即$\frac{买入汇率+卖出汇率}{2}$叫作中间汇率，也叫作中间价。

银行同业间外汇买卖均按中间价折算；电视、网络等媒体所公布的汇价也常为中间汇率；经济学家分析经济现象、外汇市场专家分析行情等所引用的汇率通常也都是中间汇率。但是，中间汇率一般不用于客户买卖。

4.银行报价的注意事项

必须强调的是，买入汇率和卖出汇率均是从报价银行的角度出发的。银行买卖外汇的目的是追求利润，即通过低买高卖赚取差价。外汇买入价和卖出价的差额即为银行买卖外汇所获得的收益，一般为所买卖外汇价格之差的 1‰～5‰。在外汇市场上，买卖差价通常以"基点"来表示，每一个基点为万分之一（即0.0001）。

外汇市场上外汇牌价通常采用双向报价的方式，即同时报出买入价和卖出价。所报出的汇率尽管都是前一个数值较小，后一个数值较大，然而，在不同标价方法下，其含义却不同。

（1）在直接标价法下，一定数额外币的前一个本币数字表示"买入价"，即银行买入外币时支付给客户的本币数；后一个本币数字表示"卖出价"，即银行卖出外币时向客户收取的本币数。

（2）在间接标价法下，一定数额本币的前一个外币数字表示"卖出价"，即银行收进一定数额本币而卖出外币时支付给客户的外币数；后一个外币数字表示"买入价"，即银行付出一定数额本币而买进外币时向客户收取的外币数。

例如，2019年7月28日，中国银行外汇报价中（采用直接标价法），美元对人民币的汇率是1USD=6.8661/6.8952CNY，前一个数字CNY6.8661/USD是美元的买入价，即银行买入1美元付给客户6.8661元人民币；后一个数字CNY6.8952/USD表示美元的卖出价，即银行卖出1美元收取客户6.8952元人民币，中间的价差0.0291元人民币（6.8952-6.8661）就是银行做这笔交易的利润。

动画微课4-3

外汇牌价

再如，2019年7月28日，中国银行外汇报价中（采用间接标价法），人民币对泰铢的汇率是1CNY=4.4841/4.4909THB，前一个数字THB4.4841/CNY是泰铢的卖出价，即银行卖出4.4841泰铢收取客户1元人民币；后一个数字THB4.4909/CNY是泰铢的买入价，即银行买入4.4909泰铢付给客户1元人民币，中间的价差是0.0068元人民币（4.4909-4.4841）。

需要指出的是，无论是直接标价法还是间接标价法，银行都是以低价买入外币，以高价卖出外币。

知识链接4-2

现钞与现汇

现钞和现汇是由于我国外汇管理体制造成的，是我国居民持有外汇资产的两种不同形式。现钞指的是国内居民手持的外汇钞票，是具体的、实在的外国纸币、硬币，如美元、日元、欧元、澳元、加元等。现汇指的是从国外银行汇到国内的外汇存款，以及外币汇票、本票、旅行支票等银行可以通过电子划算直接入账的国际结算凭证。现汇也可以理解为账面上的外汇，是客户银行账户上持有的外汇，不能取出来，取出来就成了现钞。

无论是外汇现钞还是现汇，都表示客户拥有的外汇的数量，在价值上没有本质区别。但是，在使用和管理上还是有很大的区别：在转移出境时，现汇可以直接汇入和汇出，在我国外汇管理的政策限额之内自由地转移出境或者从境外转移入境，不存在实物形式的转移，可以直接汇出或者直接汇入，只是账面上的划转。因此，外汇现汇的划转和汇款更方便。而现钞则不同，理论上账户上的现钞不能直接汇向国外，客户手中的现钞也只能采取随身携带的方式出境。当然，我国对随身携带的外汇现钞有一定的限制和要求，只要超过这个规模就要进行申报。

现钞和现汇的不同之处在于：现钞是可以存入也可以取出的，现汇只能在兑换成现钞后才能取出；现钞不能直接向国外转账汇出，只能兑换成现汇后才能汇出，而现汇可直接汇出。

资料来源：作者根据相关资料整理。

中国银行外汇牌价如表4-2所示。

表4-2　　　　　　　　　　　　　中国银行外汇牌价

序号	名称	现汇买入价	现钞买入价	现汇卖出价	现钞卖出价
1	南非兰特（ZAR）	48.0500	44.3600	48.3700	52.0600
2	美元（USD）	686.6100	681.0200	689.5200	689.5200
3	新台币（TWD）	—	21.3400	—	23.0100
4	泰铢（THB）	22.1900	21.5100	22.3700	23.0500
5	新加坡元（SGD）	500.2800	484.8500	503.8000	505.3000
6	瑞典克朗（SEK）	72.1100	69.8800	72.6900	72.8900
7	卢布（RUB）	10.8000	10.1400	10.8800	11.3000
8	新西兰元（NZD）	454.5500	440.5300	457.7500	463.3600
9	挪威克朗（NOK）	78.5300	76.1100	79.1700	79.3900
10	马来西亚林吉特（MYR）	167.3100	—	168.8200	—
11	澳门元（MOP）	85.5100	82.6400	85.8500	88.6000
12	韩元（KRW）	0.5789	0.5585	0.5835	0.6047
13	日元（JPY）	6.3065	6.1106	6.3529	6.3564
14	港元（HKD）	87.8100	87.1100	88.1600	88.1600
15	英镑（GBP）	848.6900	822.3200	854.9400	857.0100
16	欧元（EUR）	762.2300	738.5500	767.8500	769.5600
17	丹麦克朗（DKK）	101.9900	98.8400	102.8100	103.1000
18	瑞士法郎（CHF）	689.7000	668.4100	694.5400	696.8300
19	加拿大元（CAD）	519.9800	503.5600	523.8100	525.0800
20	澳大利亚元（AUD）	473.5000	458.7900	476.9800	478.1500

资料来源：作者根据相关资料整理。

（二）按照计算方法不同划分

按照计算方法不同，汇率可分为基础汇率和套算汇率。

1. 基础汇率

基础汇率是指根据一国货币与国际上某一关键货币（key currency）之间的汇率确定的比率。各国一般选定一种在本国对外经济交往中最为常用的重要货币作为关键货币，以此确定的汇率即为基础汇率。很多国家都是选择美元作为关键货币，将本国货币与美元之间的汇率作为基础汇率。各国银行之间在报出汇价时，通常只报出基础汇率，至于其他外国货币与本国货币之间的汇率，则根据各国的基础汇率进行换算。

2.套算汇率

套算汇率是指通过两种不同货币分别与关键货币的汇率间接计算出这两种货币之间的汇率。如已知A国货币兑换B国货币和A国货币兑换C国货币的汇率，想知道B国货币兑换C国货币的汇率或者C国货币兑换B国货币的汇率，其中A国货币即为关键货币。

在双向报价法下，套算汇率的计算过程如下：

例如，已知USD/HKD和EUR/USD汇率为：

USD/HKD=7.7586/7.7665，EUR/USD=1.3885/1.3975

同边相乘法：要知道EUR/HKD的汇率，可以套算如下：

EUR/HKD =（EUR/USD）×（USD/HKD）

　　　　　=（7.7586×1.3885）/（7.7665×1.3975）

　　　　　=10.773/10.854

EUR=10.773 ~ 10.854 HKD

1USD=HKD7.7586/7.7665

　　　　　　　　　　　　　　　　（同边相乘）

1EUR=USD1.3885/1.3975

例如，已知EUR/USD和GBP/USD的汇率为：

EUR/USD=1.3885/1.3975，GBP/USD=1.5695/1.5760

交叉相除法：要知道EUR/GBP的汇率，可以套算如下：

EUR/GBP =（EUR/USD）÷（GBP/USD）

　　　　　=（1.3885÷1.5760）/（1.3975÷1.5695）

　　　　　=0.8810/0.8904

EUR = 0.8810 ~ 0.8904 GBP

1EUR=USD1.3885−1.3975

　　　　　　　　　　　　　　　　（交叉相除）

1GBP=USD1.5695−1.5760

据此，套算汇率的规则和步骤可以总结如下：

（1）第一步：判断该"乘"还是"除"。

（2）第二步：判断"谁乘谁"或"谁除谁"。

若相乘，则：（小数×小数）/（大数×大数）

若相除，则：（小数÷大数）/（大数÷小数）

（三）按照外汇交易的交割期限划分

按照外汇交易的交割期限不同，汇率可分为即期汇率和远期汇率。

1.即期汇率（spot rate）

即期汇率指外汇买卖成交以后，原则上两个营业日（T+2）内即办理交割时所依据的汇率。即期汇率是外汇市场的报价基础。

2.远期汇率（forward rate）

远期汇率指外汇买卖成交以后，在未来一段时间内才进行交割（成交和交割不在同一时间进行），在成交时就约定好的汇率。远期外汇的交割期，通常为1个月至1年。与即期汇率不同的是，同一个时间点上，会有多个不同交割期限的远期汇率存在，如30

天、90天、180天、360天等。远期汇率是建立在即期汇率的基础上，反映即期汇率变化的趋势。一般来说，即期汇率与远期汇率是同方向变动的。

（四）按外汇买卖所使用的工具划分

按外汇买卖所使用的工具划分，汇率可分为电汇汇率、信汇汇率和票汇汇率。

1. 电汇汇率（telegraphic transfer rate，T/T rate）

电汇汇率是指银行用较快捷的电信方式通知其国外分行或业务往来银行付款时使用的汇率。用电汇方式交易收款的时间快，银行几乎不能占用顾客的资金，因此，电汇汇率最高。在市场经济国家，银行同业间的外汇交易使用的买卖价均为电汇汇率。每天报纸上报道的外汇行情中的现汇汇率也是电汇汇率。电汇汇率是目前市场上计算其他汇率的基础。

2. 信汇汇率（mail transfer rate，M/T rate）

信汇汇率是指银行用信函通信方式通知其国外分行或业务往来银行付款时使用的汇率。由于信函的邮程时间较电信通知时间长，银行可以在邮程期间充分占用顾客的资金，故信汇汇率较电汇汇率低。

3. 票汇汇率（demand draft transfer rate）

票汇汇率是指银行买卖外汇汇票、支票和其他票据时使用的汇率。用票汇方式，从银行售出票据到兑付款项往往要间隔一段时间，在这一段时间里银行可以占用顾客的资金，因此票汇汇率也比电汇汇率低。

（五）按外汇管制的松紧程度划分

按外汇管制的松紧程度划分，汇率可分为官方汇率和市场汇率。

1. 官方汇率（official rate）

官方汇率是国家外汇管理当局（如央行、财政部或者指定外汇管理银行）规定并予以公布的汇率。在外汇管制较严格的国家禁止外汇自由买卖，无市场汇率，所有外汇交易均按照此汇率进行。

2. 市场汇率（market rate）

市场汇率是指在自由外汇市场上买卖外汇的实际汇率。这种汇率是由外汇市场上的供求关系决定的，它随着外汇供求关系的变化而变化。

（六）从外汇银行营业时间的角度划分

从外汇银行营业时间的角度划分，汇率可分为开盘汇率和收盘汇率。

1. 开盘汇率（opening rate）

开盘汇率是指外汇银行在每个工作日开始营业时成交的第一笔外汇买卖所使用的汇率，也叫开盘价。

2. 收盘汇率（closing rate）

收盘汇率是指外汇银行在每个工作日营业结束前成交的最后一笔外汇买卖所使用的汇率，也叫收盘价。

拓展阅读4-1

外汇小白必听的外汇故事

一位有经验的外汇交易高手经常给新手讲下面一个与投资者行为非常相似的故事：

三毛的爹给了三毛一毛钱去打酱油。杂货店的老板把三毛拿去的碗装满了酱油后，为难地说："三毛啊，还有一点点酱油盛不下呢，怎么办啊？"三毛一看，傻笑道："老板，这还不容易吗？我有办法哩！"说着将装满酱油的碗一翻，说："这碗底不就可以装吗？"

三毛一回到家，他爹一看傻了眼，骂道："三毛你真是蠢得可以啦，一毛钱就买回这么点酱油啊？你被人骗了！"三毛得意地说："爹，你以为儿子真的那么蠢？这后面还有呢！"说着把碗又翻了过来，把碗底那仅有的一点酱油也倒了……

很多投资者在日常的生活工作中很聪明，但是一旦进入汇市，智商就"掉线"了。有些投资者往往把外汇卖在最低点，买在最高点。下面就是一些投资者投资失败的例子，希望大家不要再出现这种情况了：

1.任何短线波动都能够影响情绪，在最低点时情绪最坏，最高点时情绪最好

这种情况是最典型的"三无"（无实战经验、无实战信息、无实战心态）投资者的表现，在实战中要把握关键的、简单的东西，利用自己可以把握的两个关键点的价差来赚钱，而不是通过多数时间不可能猜对的短线波动来赚钱，在外汇市场中要想赚到钱必须忍受时间的煎熬和反向波动的折磨。

2.一叶障目，不见泰山

证券投资活动非常考验投资者全面分析问题的能力，既要对趋势进行分析，又要对单个外汇进行分析，还要对风险和操作手段进行分析，同时与新出现的机会进行比较。而许多投资者在投资活动中，只把目光聚焦在自己希望看到的一点上，其他的相关因素却看不到。特别是某些投资者只有分析，没有操作手段，只要汇价没有按照自己分析的那样波动，就立刻产生怀疑，在一项投资活动时机还不成熟时，就仓促应战，然后草草收场，结果不言而喻很不理想。

3.让失误的投资失去控制

由于人性的因素，在投资活动中不可避免地会出现某些失误。当出现失误的时候，你必须做好下面几件事：第一件事是分析失误后的风险，因为有大风险的操作必然是短线，小风险的操作可以尝试长线，投资分析中除了机会分析还有风险分析。第二件事是获利的关键点是否还存在，如果存在，并且远远大于风险，那么你可以利用操作手段来纠正，不要轻易结束这次投资。第三件事是如果发现机会点已经消失，并且风险较大，那么应该果断结束这个项目，否则可能出现较大的失误。

资料来源：根据相关资料整理所得。

思考题：

1."三毛"的故事给了你什么启发？

2.你认为投资外汇、股票等金融产品，对于新手来说，应该具备什么条件？

任务二　　　　　　　　　　　　汇率制度

汇率制度是指一国货币当局对本国汇率水平的确定、汇率变动方式等问题所做出的

一系列安排或规定。传统意义上，汇率制度被分为两大类：固定汇率制度和浮动汇率制度。

一、固定汇率制度（fixed rate system）

固定汇率制是指两国货币比价基本固定，或者把两国货币比价变化波动限制在一个很小的浮动范围内。从历史来看，国际金本位制和布雷顿森林体系下的汇率制度都属于固定汇率制。在此制度下，一国货币当局有义务维持货币的汇率在规定的幅度内变化，不能超出上限，也不能低于下限。

（一）典型的国际金本位制下的固定汇率制度

典型的国际金本位制是金币本位制，其特点是每一货币单位（铸币）都有法定的含金量，于是货币的含金量便成为各国货币汇率的基础。两国货币间的比价就是两种金币含金量之比。这种比价称为"铸币平价"。铸币平价便是那时国际金本位制下汇率决定的基础。

例如，英国规定1英镑金币的含金量为113.0016格令，美国规定1美元金币的含金量为23.22格令，则英镑与美元之间的比价为113.0016/23.22=4.8665，即1英镑=4.8665美元。如果英镑与美元金币的含金量发生不成比例的变动，铸币平价也随之变动。

1.黄金输送点

但是，典型的国际金本位制下，外汇市场上的现实汇率同铸币平价并不总是保持一致，而是随着外汇市场的供求关系发生波动，即汇率以铸币平价为基础，围绕着铸币平价上下波动。不论外汇的供求力量多么强大，汇率的波动总是有限的。这个界限就是黄金输入点与黄金输出点，黄金输入点和黄金输出点又合称为"黄金输送点"。

2.黄金输送点与汇率的变化

那么，汇率是如何受黄金输送点的影响的？

汇率的运行机制是这样的：在某国外汇市场上，当外汇汇率出现上升趋势并超过黄金输出点时，黄金就开始流出该国；而当该汇率出现下跌趋势并跌破黄金输入点时，黄金则开始流入。黄金的流动方向正好同外汇市场上供求关系的变化方向相反，因而具有抵消外汇市场供求力量的作用，使汇率变动不至于超出黄金输送点的界限，如图4-1所示。

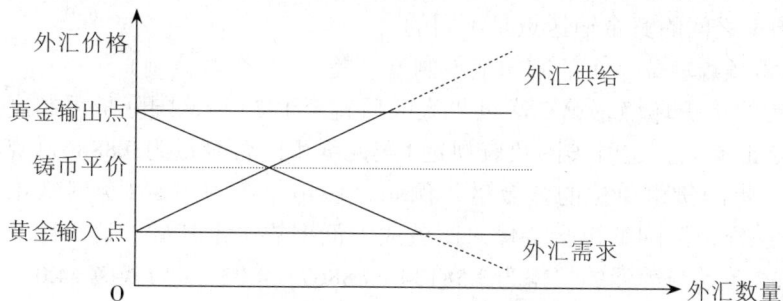

图4-1　汇率变动的黄金输送点

如图4-2所示，例如，在纽约外汇市场上，英镑与美元的铸币平价是GBP1=USD4.8665。纽约至伦敦的黄金运输成本为0.02美元。在纽约，黄金的输出点为铸币平价+黄金运输成本=4.8665+0.02=4.8865美元。假定在纽约外汇市场上由于对英镑的需求量超过英镑的供给量，迫使英镑汇率上升，铸币平价GBP1=USD4.8665上升至黄金输出

点 GBP1=USD4.8865。至此，英镑汇率不会再进一步上升，因为如果英镑汇率高于
4.8865美元，美国的进口商就不会购买英镑，而会按4.8665~4.8865美元的价格用美元
向美国货币当局购买黄金，然后运送到伦敦，把黄金卖给英国货币当局换取英镑，再用
于清偿彼此间的债权债务。这样做的结果，美国进口商所得英镑是按铸币平价加运输成
本计算的，只增加了运输成本0.02美元的支出。否则，他就要以高于黄金输出点的价格
购买英镑。所以，在英镑汇率上升至黄金输出点时美国进口商都以输出黄金来清偿债务
而不需要在纽约购买英镑，这就减少了对英镑的需求量，英镑汇率自然不能继续上升了。

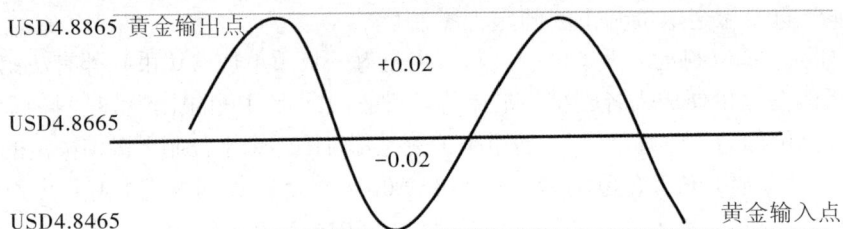

图4-2　黄金输送点=铸币平价±运费

同样，如果纽约市场上英镑的供给量超过需求量，就会迫使英镑汇率下降至黄金输
入点（4.8665-0.02），伦敦进口商就不会以GBP1=USD4.8465以下的低价出售英镑，而
宁可用英镑向英国货币当局购买黄金，再把黄金输送到美国，卖给美国货币当局换取美
元，再进行债务的清算。这时他的美元是以铸币平价减运输成本0.02美元计算获得的。
若不这样做，伦敦的进口商就必须用低于黄金输入点的价格购买美元，那么他就要支出
更多的英镑才能兑换到原来所需数额的美元。在纽约，由于黄金不断流入使英镑的供给
量减少，英镑的供求趋于平衡，英镑汇率自然不会进一步下跌，反而会回升到黄金输入点之上。

教学视频4-2

汇率形成
机制

这便是典型金本位制度下黄金输送点对汇率的自动调节机制。黄金输送
点主要取决于黄金输送成本，而黄金输送成本则主要取决于两国之间的距
离，因为地理距离决定着运费、保险费及运输途中的利息支出。所以，不同
国家之间的黄金输送点是不同的。

（二）布雷顿森林体系下的固定汇率制度（美元-黄金本位制）

由于特定的历史环境，第二次世界大战后直至1973年，国际货币制度都是以美元
为中心的固定汇率制，这时美国政府规定1美元纸币的含金量为0.888671克，其他国家
也同时规定了本国货币单位的含金量，例如，1946年英国规定1英镑纸币的含金量为
3.58134克。这样，两国纸币含金量之比就成为汇率的决定基础，这一比值叫作"黄金
平价"。例如，英镑与美元的汇率为3.58134/0.888671=4.03，即1英镑=4.03美元。

与典型国际金本位制一样，外汇市场上的实际汇率因供求关系不可能刚好等于黄金
平价。但当时国际货币基金组织（IMF）规定，汇率的波动幅度为±1%（例如，英镑对美
元的波动幅度的上限为4.03+4.03×1%=4.0703美元，下限为4.03-4.03×1%=3.9897美元）。

如果超过这个幅度，有关国家政府就应对外汇市场进行干预，使汇率回到这个幅度
之内。为了对外汇市场进行干预，各国都要建立包括本币、外汇、黄金在内的"外汇平
准基金"。当外汇汇率的变动低于平价的1%时，政府就动用基金中的本币或黄金收购

外汇，以使外汇的供给小于需求，从而使外汇汇率回升。

之后国际货币基金组织将这一变动幅度调整为±2.25%，但各国政府仍有义务干预外汇市场，以稳定外汇汇率。不仅如此，当时国际货币基金组织还规定，各国不得轻易变动其平价，只有出现国际收支基本不平衡时，即调节国际收支不平衡所采取的措施与国内经济均衡发展发生矛盾时，才可以较大幅度地变更平价；而且其变动要接受国际货币基金组织的安排与监督。

由此可见，布雷顿森林体系下的固定汇率制是种可调节的钉住制度。这种可调节的钉住制度把美元与黄金等同起来，各国货币与美元保持固定的法定比价，美元处于国际货币制度的中心地位，充当国际储备、结算和干预的国际本位货币，其他国家货币则都依附于美元。

动画微课4-4

巨无霸指数

（三）两种固定汇率制度的比较

典型金本位制度下的固定汇率制与布雷顿森林体系下的固定汇率制的共同点是：两种汇率制度都是以各国货币的含金量为基础的。但它们之间又有着明显的区别：

1.与黄金的联系不同

典型金本位制度下的固定汇率制是以两国货币的铸币平价为基础的；布雷顿森林体系下的固定汇率制则是以黄金平价为基础，以美元等同于黄金为中心的。

2.汇率的调节机制不同

典型金本位制度下的汇率是围绕着两国货币的铸币平价来波动，而波动幅度不超过黄金输送点，当超过黄金输送点时，通过黄金自由输出输入的自动调节，使汇率稳定在黄金输送点之内；布雷顿森林体系下的固定汇率制，其波动幅度是人为规定的，也是人为维持的，即超过规定幅度，可通过各国政府或中央银行的直接干预，使汇率稳定在规定的幅度之内。

3.汇率变化的影响范围不同

典型金本位制度下，当汇率发生变化时，只涉及两国的货币及贸易收支状态；在布雷顿森林体系下，若关键货币美元由于美国的国际收支恶化导致币值不稳定，对美元币值的调整会波及所有钉住它的货币，从而影响到关键货币发行国以外的其他国家的贸易收支及汇率的稳定。因此，关键货币的发行国——美国，有充足的黄金储备及良好的国际收支状况是布雷顿森林体系得以维持的基础。

4.黄金含量变化不同

典型金本位制下的货币含量一般不会变动，即使变动也无须他国同意；布雷顿森林体系下，任何一国货币黄金量的调整都必须在发生国际收支不平衡时，并应经过国际货币基金组织的同意。

（四）固定汇率制度的优缺点

1.优点

固定汇率制度的最大优势在于汇率波动风险小。由于两国货币比价基本固定，汇率相对稳定，这样国际贸易、国际信贷和投资的经济主体在进行成本、收益和利润核算的时候，就比较清晰明确了。这有效地促进了国际经济的发展。

2.缺点

（1）固定汇率基本不能发挥国际收支的经济调节作用。汇率变动对国际收支有着很深的影响，因而汇率也被称为调节国际收支的经济杠杆。固定汇率制度下货币比价基本固定，所以很难起到调节国际收支的作用。

（2）固定汇率制度无法满足一国的对内对外的同时均衡。因为在固定汇率制度下，汇率基本不能发挥调节国际收支的经济杠杆作用，当一国出现国际收支逆差时，就需要采取紧缩性货币、财政政策进行调节，这样做会使得国内经济增长受到抑制和失业扩大，从而牺牲内部均衡；相反，则采用扩张性货币、财政政策进行调节，这样做会加重国内的通货膨胀和物价上涨，从而牺牲内部均衡。

二、浮动汇率制度（floating rate system）

浮动汇率制是指各国货币当局不再公布本国货币的含金量，不再规定本币对外币汇率变化的波动幅度，也不再承担维持汇率波动在一定幅度范围内的义务，汇率完全按照外汇市场上外汇的供求关系自由波动的一种汇率制度。

在浮动汇率制度下，铸币平价、黄金平价及汇率波动的上、下限都不再存在了。既然汇率的上下波动没有了中心轴，因此，我们只能用与前一时期做比较来说明该种货币的汇率升降。如果外汇需求超过供给，那么外汇汇率上浮，这种币值趋于上升的货币叫"硬货币"（hard currency）；反之，如果外汇的供给超过需求，那么外汇汇率下降，这种币值趋于下降的货币叫"软货币"（soft currency）。

（一）浮动汇率制度的类型

1.按政府干预外汇市场的程度不同划分

按政府干预外汇市场的程度不同，可将浮动汇率分为自由浮动和管理浮动。

（1）自由浮动（free floating），又称清洁浮动，是指一国货币当局对汇率上下波动一般不采取干预措施，汇率听凭外汇市场供求变化而自由涨落、自发调节，政府不承担维持汇率波动幅度的义务。只有在汇率变动异常而又对本国经济不利时，货币当局才直接或间接对外汇市场进行干预，使其有利于本国经济的发展。美元、英镑和日元等均属于自由浮动的货币。

（2）管理浮动（managed floating），又称不清洁浮动是指一国货币当局采取的各种不同措施，不时地干预外汇市场，使汇率朝着有利于本国经济发展的方向浮动。中国的人民币就属于该类浮动的货币。

2.按汇率浮动的不同方式划分

按汇率浮动的不同方式，可将浮动汇率分为单独浮动、联合浮动和钉住浮动。

（1）单独浮动（independent floating），是指一国货币不与其他国家货币组成集团而单独实行浮动汇率制度，其汇率根据外汇市场的供求变化自行调整，而不受任何国家货币的影响。美元、英镑、日元和瑞士法郎等属于单独浮动货币。

（2）联合浮动（joint floating），是指一些国家组成货币集团，集团内部货币实行固定汇率制度，汇率波动被规定在一定的幅度内，而对外统一实行共升共降的浮动汇率制。如原欧共体国家在1979年3月建立了欧洲货币体系（EMS）后，成员的货币与欧洲货币体系内部的欧洲货币单位确立了比价，并重申成员之间维持固定比价，对非成员实行联合浮动。英国曾于1990年10月加入联合浮动，但在1992年欧洲统一大市场前，由于英镑大幅度贬值，它又退出联合浮动而实行单独浮动直至今日。

（3）钉住浮动（pegged floating），是指一国货币钉住某种储备货币或钉住一揽子货币，并与被钉住的货币保持固定的兑换比率，而对其他货币则自由浮动。如许多发展中国家使本国货币钉住美元、英镑等单一货币；沙特阿拉伯、阿拉伯联合酋长国等货币钉住特别提款权。与单独浮动和联合浮动相比，钉住浮动的汇率相对稳定，但汇率调整易受所钉住的货币的控制，缺乏自主性。

（二）浮动汇率制度的优缺点

1. 优点

（1）防止大量外汇储备的流失。在浮动汇率制度下，各国货币当局没有义务维持货币的固定比价。当本币汇率下跌时，不必动用外汇储备去购买被抛售的本币，这样可以避免外汇储备的大量流失。

（2）自动调节国际收支。在浮动汇率制度下，一国的国际收支可以通过汇率的波动进行调节，因此起到经济杠杆作用。例如，当对本国商品和劳务的需求下降时，国际收支出现逆差，浮动汇率使得本币贬值，从而使本国商品和劳务的价格下降，促进出口的增长，部分抵消了这种需求下降带来的不利影响。

（3）货币政策更具自主性。如果各国央行不再为固定汇率制而被迫干预外汇市场，各国政府就可以灵活地运用货币政策来达到国内和外部的平衡。

2. 缺点

（1）增加了国际经济交易中的风险。由于汇率变动幅度大，给国际贸易带来极大的不确定性。成本、利润的核算都难以掌握，这对跨国公司来说不好做出正确的经营决策。

（2）助长了国际投机活动。汇率无限制的波动，给国际投机者以套利、套汇的可乘之机，甚至会发生局部的、世界性的金融危机，如2008年的全球金融危机及2009年欧债危机。

三、人民币汇率制度

人民币是中华人民共和国独有的、统一的、稳定的货币。由于历史的原因，我国政府没有规定人民币的黄金平价，这就决定了人民币与其他货币汇率的确定具有其自身的特殊性。人民币汇率安排一向坚持独立自主的方针，坚持平等互利的原则，做到公平合理，既有利于我国对外经济关系的发展又能促进他国的经济贸易进步。人民币对西方国家货币汇价的演变过程大体可分为以下几个阶段：

（一）改革开放前的人民币汇率制度

1. 管理浮动制度（1949—1952年）

人民币诞生初期，计划经济体制尚未建立，人民政府宣布人民币不以黄金为基础，在实际操作中实行的是管理浮动制。人民币对美元汇率根据人民币对美元的出口商品比价、进口商品比价和华侨日用生活费比价三者加权平均来确定；这段时期，人民币汇率确定的依据是物价，其作用实际上是调节对外贸易，照顾侨汇收入。

2. 固定汇率制度（1953—1972年）

自1953年起，我国进入社会主义工业化建设和社会主义改造时期，国民经济实行计划化，物价由国家规定且基本稳定。这一时期的人民币汇率主要是用于非贸易外汇兑换的结算，按国内外消费物价对比而制定的汇率已适当照顾了侨汇和其他非贸易外汇收入，亦无调整的必要。由于在此阶段资本主义国家的货币实行固定汇率制度，汇率不常变动，因此人民币汇率亦保持稳定，实质上是固定汇率制度。

3. 人民币实行"一篮子货币"钉住汇率制度（1973—1980年）

1973年3月，西方国家货币纷纷实行浮动汇率制度，汇率波动频繁，人民币对外比价要保持相对合理，就必须根据国际市场汇率的波动，相应地上调或下调。人民币汇率在固定汇率时期已确定的汇价水平的基础上，按"一篮子货币"原则，确定对西方国家货币的汇价。

（二）改革开放后的人民币汇率制度

1. 贸易内部结算价（1981—1984年）

为了鼓励出口、限制进口，加强外贸的经济核算和适应我国对外贸易体制的改革，自1981年起，我国实行两种汇价。一种是适用于非贸易外汇收支的对外公布的汇价；另一种是适用于贸易外汇收支的贸易内部结算价。在此期间，我国实际存在着三种汇率：第一种是对外的，并适用于非贸易收支的官方牌价；第二种是适用于贸易收支的贸易内部结算价；第三种是外汇调剂市场的外汇调剂价。

2. 以美元为基准的有限弹性汇率制度（1985—1993年）

1985年1月1日，我国停止贸易内部结算价的使用，贸易收支与非贸易收支均按官方牌价结算。贸易内部结算价虽然与官方牌价并轨，但调剂外汇市场功能仍然存在，实际上除官方牌价外，仍存在一个外汇调剂价。

3. 以供求为基础的、单一的、有管理的浮动汇率制度（1994—2005年）

1994年1月1日，我国对人民币汇率制度进行重大改革，实施以市场供求为基础的、单一的、有管理的浮动汇率制度。人民币汇率一步并轨到1美元兑换8.7元人民币，国家外汇储备大幅度上升。我国实行新的外汇管理体制。在这种新的体制下，人民币汇率有以下几个特点：

①人民币汇率不再由货币当局直接制定；

②由外汇指定银行自行以市场供求为基础，制定自己的外汇牌价；

③以市场供求为基础所形成的汇率是统一的。

4. 参考"一篮子货币"进行调节的、有管理的浮动汇率制度（2005年至今）

自2005年7月21日起，我国实行以市场供求为基础的、参考"一篮子货币"进行调节的、有管理的浮动汇率制度。人民币汇率不再钉住单一美元。

汇率调节的方式：实行以市场供求为基础的、参考"一篮子货币"进行调节、有管理的浮动汇率制度。中间价的确定和日浮动区间：中国人民银行于每个工作日闭市后公布银行间外汇市场美元等几个主要交易货币对人民币的收盘价，作为下一个工作日该货币对人民币的中间价格。

2019年7月21日19时，美元对人民币交易价格调整为1美元兑换7.1158元人民币，作为次日银行间外汇市场上外汇指定银行之间交易的中间价，外汇指定银行可以自此时起调整对客户的挂牌汇价。调整主要是依据我国贸易顺差程度和结构调整的需要来决定的，同时也考虑了国内企业进行调整的适应能力。

案例探析4-1

以史为鉴——1998年港币保卫战

1998年，金融巨鳄索罗斯刚刚完成了对泰国、马来西亚、缅甸等国的碾压战，在索罗斯的攻势下，这些国家的GDP在几个月之内就遭遇断崖式下跌，尤其是泰国，国民财富一日之内就被索罗斯抢走了三分之一。索罗斯在这场"热身战"中净赚100多亿美元。

然而，他的真正目标却不在此，而是正处于命运分岔口的中国香港。彼时，中国香港经济泡沫已经形成，房价在1997年之前7年间上涨4倍。趁此机会，索罗斯在8月对港币发起狙击。8月5日，国际炒家从美国股市借出近290亿港元进行抛售。中国香港金管局利用外汇储备接起了240亿港元沽盘。8月6日、7日，索罗斯率领的对冲基金再次借出近200亿港元。8月12日，国际炒家继续疯狂做空，索罗斯与香港特别行政区政府之间的激战空前惨烈，此时，香港恒生指数一路狂跌到6600点，总市值蒸发2万亿港元。时任香港特别行政区财政司司长的曾荫权回忆说："半夜哭泣数次，唯恐输掉全港人的钱，跳楼都是百身莫赎。"

早在索罗斯掀起第一轮狙击时，香港特别行政区政府就十分清楚，以香港现有的外汇储备，根本无力单独应付可能的金融袭击。但是，香港特别行政区政府得到了中央不遗余力的支持。这也是在首轮港元阻击战中香港特别行政区政府死守港元汇率的底气来源。索罗斯在《华尔街日报》上公然叫嚣："香港必败。"时任国务院总理朱镕基强硬地说："只要香港特别行政区有要求，中央将不惜一切代价维护香港的繁荣！"

8月13日，香港特别行政区政府组织内地资金入市，展开8月期指合约争夺战。从14日开始，香港特别行政区政府开始进入股市、期市进行全面干预。香港这一役举世瞩目，如果恒生指数失守，香港特别行政区政府的数百亿港元将付之东流。反之，炒家们将损失20亿美元以上。

然而，索罗斯眼看胜利在望，却发现有一股神秘的资金，不声不响地把所有抛盘照单全收。

8月28日是期指结算日，也意味着多空双方的最后决战正式打响，这一天上午，索罗斯动用400亿美元资金疯狂抛盘打压股市，可是神秘资金还是不动声色地在低位接盘，却绝不拉高。下午，多方开始进行全面反攻，仅一个半小时就完成了390亿美元的成交量。

此时香港恒生指数被快速拉高，形势发生了剧烈翻转，面对对方的强势攻击，索罗斯"军团"内部开始出现分裂动摇，许多财团反水加入了多方，最终，当日收盘时，恒生指数和期货指数分别稳坐7829点和7851点，曾荫权也立即宣布："在打击国际炒家、保卫香港股市和货币的战斗中，香港特别行政区政府已经获胜。索罗斯大势已去，败局收场。向中国货币宣战？呵呵！"

战争从来没有真正的赢家，1997—1998年的这场"官鳄大战"几乎将香港变成了杀戮之城，据香港特区政府后来估计，香港人在这场金融危机中合计损失大约6.8万亿港元。如果按当时香港600余万人口计算，香港人平均每人损失100多万港元。在这场金融危机中，无数人倾家荡产，甚至跳楼自尽。可以说，在中央政府的强大支撑下，中国香港虽然保住了自己的经济命脉，但也只能说获得了"惨胜"，若没有中央政府这个强大的后盾，其后果就更加无法想象了，金融战争的残酷由此可见一斑。

对于这场战争，中央政府的表现获得了全世界的广泛赞誉，其角色定位之精准、策略之稳重让世界赞叹，这也成为中国政府参与世界金融战争的"首秀"。由于这场战争的胜利，朱镕基被国外杂志评为当年"世界金融三强人"之一。

而在十几年之后，有人评论道："你一定没有想到，中国曾经那么伟大过——挡住了一场全球性的金融危机，不然，2008年全球金融危机早在1998年就爆发了。"如今，索罗斯公开唱空中国，有分析认为，他是为了一雪18年前之耻。

2016年1月26日，人民日报海外版在头版刊文：《向中国货币宣战？"呵呵"》。索罗斯向亚洲货币"宣战"，还为中国创造了深化东亚财金合作乃至"一带一路"财金合作的机遇。

财经作家、媒体人黄斌汉表示，索罗斯拿什么与拥有超过3万亿美元外汇储备的中国斗？不要说中国香港的外汇储备已从当年的1 000多亿美元增长到了现在的3 000多亿美元，单看中国内地外汇储备增长就超过30倍，再斗可能索罗斯一生的荣誉都将葬身东方。

资料来源：佚名. 1998年香港金融保卫战启示录［J］. 新传奇，2016（9）.

思考题：

中央政府为什么要并且也能够帮助中国香港阻击索罗斯等国际炒家对港币的金融冲击？

任务三　　　影响汇率变动的因素

在当今的浮动汇率制度下，影响汇率变动的因素很多，各种经济的、政治的、人为的、社会的、自然的等因素都能使外汇汇率频繁波动，甚至产生大幅波动，导致金融危机。具体来说，主要有以下几个方面的因素：

一、从长期看，通货膨胀是影响汇率变动的根本因素

如果一国货币发行过多，流通中的货币超过了商品流通过程中的实际需求量，就会引起通货膨胀。

通货膨胀直接导致一国货币在国内的购买力下降，使得货币对内贬值，在其他条件不变的情况下，必然会导致货币对外贬值。因为汇率是两国货币的对比，发行货币过多的国家，其单位货币的价值量就会变小，因此在该国货币折算成同等数额外国货币时，就要付出比原来多的该国货币。

这样，本国商品和服务的价格在折算成外币时也会相应提高，这就削弱了本国商品和服务在国际市场上的竞争力，抑制出口；与此同时，也会使得国内居民转而购买相对便宜的外国商品和服务，从而促进了进口。

同时，通货膨胀还会引起实际利率下降。在名义利率保持不变的情况下，资本会向利率高的国家流动，所以最终导致该国资本外流，影响到本国货币的需求量，从而导致本币汇率下降。

总之，一国通货膨胀率很高，比其他大部分国家都高，就会导致该国货币汇率下降，从而实现货币的对内贬值传导至对外贬值。通货膨胀对汇率的影响如图4-3所示。

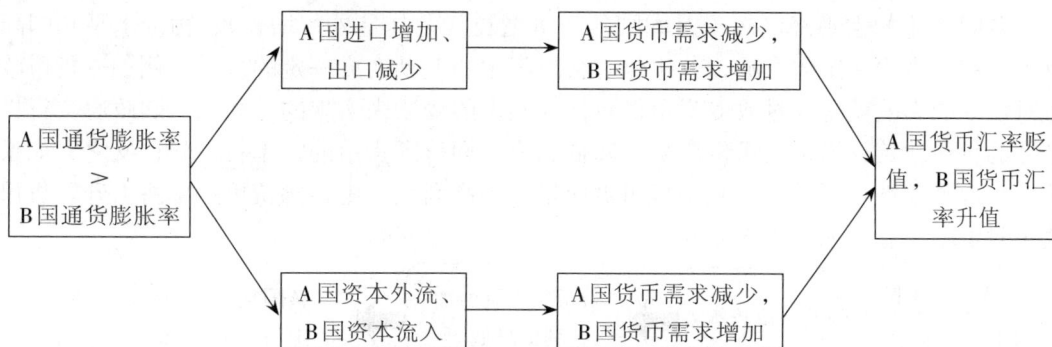

图4-3 通货膨胀对汇率的影响

二、从短期看，国际收支是影响汇率变动的直接因素

国际收支和汇率的关系十分紧密，有的时候它们之间甚至互为因果。国际收支的顺差或逆差都会直接影响汇率的变动，而汇率的变动又会反过来影响顺差或者逆差的变化。一国的国际收支若出现大量顺差，外汇收入必然大于外汇支出，则表明该国国内市场上外汇供给大于需求，而本币供不应求。因此，本币对外币就会升值；反之，本币对外币就出现贬值。国际收支对汇率的影响如图4-4所示。

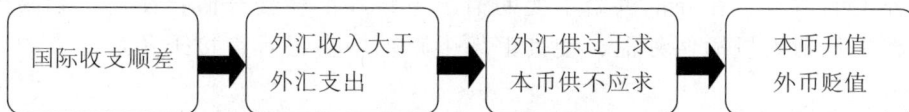

图4-4 国际收支对汇率的影响

三、利率是影响汇率变动的一个重要因素

各国利率差异是影响汇率变动的一个十分重要的因素。利率作为借贷资金的价格，其变动直接影响一国资本的输入、输出。如果一国利率水平普遍高于别国，国外资金持有者就会将资金投向该国，以追求较高的利息收入，这样做会使得该国外汇收入增加，外币供大于求，从而促使外币贬值、本币升值；反之，就会促使该国汇率下降。国际利率水平的差异对短期国际资本的流动影响尤为明显，而当今国际金融市场当中充斥着巨额的短期流动资本，这些国际游资为了投机的目的，大规模进出各国外汇、金融市场，对汇率的波动影响颇大。利率对汇率的影响如图4-5所示。

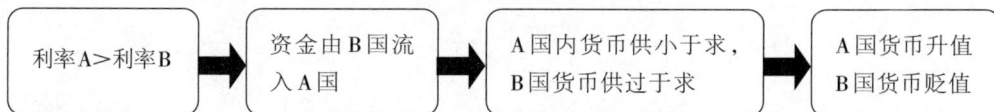

图4-5 利率对汇率的影响

四、市场预期心理是影响汇率变动的一个不容忽视的因素

市场心理预期是短期内影响汇率变动的主要因素，具有易变、捉摸不透的特点。如果外汇市场参与者预期某国的通货膨胀率比较高、国际收支将会产生不小逆差、实际利率水平比较低，或者其他对该国经济不利的因素，那么人们就会预期该国货币将会贬值。表现在行为上就是：该国货币将会在外汇市场上被大量抛售，从而使该国货币汇率成为真正的贬值货币；反之，该国货币则会真正升值。

五、各国宏观经济政策是影响汇率变动的又一重要因素

各国实施的宏观经济政策对本国的经济增长（尤其是外贸增长）、物价水平和国际收支等都会产生一定的影响，这也势必会对汇率的变动造成一定的影响。例如，货币政策对汇率的影响就是通过改变货币供应量和利率的变动来实现的。如果一国政府实行扩张性的货币政策，增加货币供应量、降低利率，则该国货币的汇率将下降；反之，如果政府采取紧缩性货币政策，减少货币供应量、提高利率，则该国货币汇率将上升。货币政策对汇率的影响如图4-6所示。

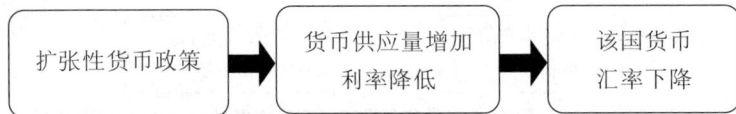

扩张性货币政策 → 货币供应量增加 利率降低 → 该国货币 汇率下降

图4-6　货币政策对汇率的影响

六、中央银行直接干预是影响汇率变动的不应忽视的因素

正如前面所介绍的那样，不论在固定汇率制度下还是在浮动汇率制度下，央行都被动或者主动地干预外汇市场，稳定本币汇率，以避免汇率波动对经济造成的不利影响。央行参与干预的主要方式是通过直接在外汇市场上买卖外汇，从而影响到外汇市场的供求关系。具体的做法是：如果外汇汇率下跌，央行则大量买进外汇，增加对外汇的需求，在外汇供给不变的情况下，外汇就会升值；反之，如果外汇汇率上升，央行则大量抛售外汇，使其汇率下降。中央银行直接干预对汇率的影响如图4-7所示。

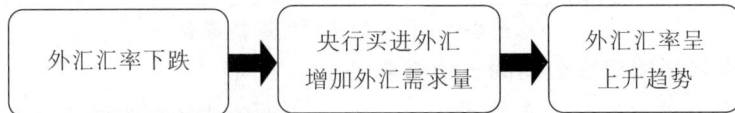

外汇汇率下跌 → 央行买进外汇 增加外汇需求量 → 外汇汇率呈 上升趋势

图4-7　中央银行直接干预对汇率的影响

除了上述所列六种因素外，影响汇率变动的因素还有很多，如重大国际政治事件、恶性投机行为、自然灾害（如2013年日本海啸）、战争等。由于影响汇率变动的因素千差万别，同时又错综复杂，而它们的作用有时又相互抵消、有时又相互促进。因此，在分析汇率变动的时候，我们要针对不同情况做到全面考察、综合分析，才能得出比较正确的判断。

任务四　　　　　　　　　汇率波动产生的影响

　　汇率是外汇市场的特殊价格，是各国货币的联系中枢。在开放的经济条件下，汇率与多种经济因素密切联系，使汇率成为各国宏观经济中的重要变量。

一、汇率变动对国际收支的影响

　　（一）对有形贸易和无形贸易收支的影响

　　这里说的有形贸易指的是一国商品的进出口，而无形贸易指的是一国服务的输入输出。汇率变动对二者产生的影响是一致的，主要通过汇率变动引起商品和服务相对价格的变动。

　　当一国货币汇率下降时，折算成外币表示的本国商品和服务的价格就会跟着下降，这就刺激外国客户对本国商品和服务的需求，从而使商品和服务的输出增加。例如，从中国进口的华为手机 P30 Pro 在德国售价为 1 024 欧元（2019 年 6 月 15 日人民币对欧元汇率为 1EUR=8CNY），至 2019 年 7 月 30 日，当人民币汇率下降时，变为人民币对欧元汇率为 1EUR=8.2CNY。对我国出口商来说，同样出售 1 024 欧元的华为手机，按人民币贬值前的汇率折算，出口商可以得到 8 192 元人民币的收入；若按人民币贬值后的汇率折算，出口商能够获得 8 396.8 元人民币的收入。与人民币贬值前相比，无形中就可以多获得 204.8 元人民币，大大刺激了出口商的积极性。

　　相反，当一国货币汇率上升时，折算成外币表示的本国商品和服务的价格就会上升，从而抑制了外国对本国商品和服务的需求，使得商品和服务的出口减少。

　　（二）对国际资本流动的影响

　　汇率的变动会对资本持有者的收益产生影响，因而会影响到资本在境内外的流动。当一国货币汇率呈下降趋势但尚未开始下降时，会引起本币汇率贬值的预期，本币资本持有者便会将资本转移到国外，造成资本外流。这种资本外流会一直持续到汇率下降结束。当人们预期本币汇率下降已经到头了，即将面临反弹（即本币汇率上升）时，转移出去的资本会重新回到国内，还可能引起更多的资本流入国内。汇率波动对短期基本流动的影响尤为明显。

二、汇率变动对外汇储备的影响

　　（一）对外汇储备数量的影响

　　一国货币汇率变动通过进出口贸易额和资本转移的多少，直接影响该国的外汇储备的增减。一般来说，一国货币汇率稳定，有利于该国吸引外资，从而促进该国外汇储备的增加；反之，则会引起资本外流，使得外汇储备减少。

　　（二）对外汇储备价值的影响

　　如果一国所持有的储备货币的汇率下降，会使持有这种储备货币国家的外汇储备实际价值降低，而储备货币国家则减少了债务负担，从中获利；反之，会使持有这种储备货币国家的外汇储备实际价值上升，而储备货币国家则将增加债务负担。例如，美元对人民币汇率这几年一直处于下降趋势，这使得我国以美元为主的外汇储备价值实际降低，美国的负债也随着降低。

同时，汇率变动导致的储备货币贬值会让该国央行考虑是否调整外汇储备的币种结构，减少美元的持有比例，增加其他储备货币的持有比例。例如，国家外汇管理局发布的《国家外汇管理局年报（2018年）》指出，从1995年到2014年的20年时间里，我国外汇储备中美元所占的比例，就从79%降到58%。

三、汇率变动对国内经济的影响

（一）对国民收入和就业的影响

经济学家常把出口、需求和投资比喻成拉动经济增长的三驾马车。由于本币汇率的贬值，有利于商品和服务的出口，因此本币贬值可以激活闲置的生产要素，扩大生产规模，提高就业和国民收入；反之，由于本币升值不利于产品和服务的出口，因此对经济的增长、国民收入的增加和就业率的提高都可能产生抑制作用。

（二）对国内物价的影响

在其他条件不变的情况下，本币汇率的变动会导致国内物价跟汇率变动呈相反方向变动。也就是说，本币汇率贬值促进了商品和服务的出口，增加了外汇收入，从而导致本国货币的需求量上升，推动国内物价水平的上涨；反之，本币汇率上升会导致国内物价水平下降。

四、汇率变动对国际贸易的影响

可以把世界市场形象地比喻为一块大蛋糕，这块蛋糕在分配时会出现不均。某些国家为了能占有更多的份额，可能会利用汇率贬值，扩大出口，从而影响到其他国家的利益。其他国家为了维护自身利益，采取同样的方式进行货币贬值（称之为"竞争性货币贬值"），或者采取贸易保护主义，从而使国与国之间发生贸易战，对国际贸易的发展产生不利的影响，进而影响国际关系，如这几年的"中美贸易争端"。

知识链接4-3

商品倾销与外汇倾销

商品倾销是指出口商以低于正常价格的出口价格，集中地或持续大量地向国外抛售商品。按照倾销的具体目的，商品倾销可以分为偶然性倾销、间歇性或掠夺性倾销和长期性倾销三种形式。

1.偶然性倾销通常是指因为本国市场销售旺季已过，或公司改营其他在国内市场上很难售出的积压库存，以较低的价格在国外市场上抛售。

2.间歇性或掠夺性倾销是指以低于国内价格或低于成本价格在国外市场销售，达到打击竞争对手、形成垄断的目的。待击败所有或大部分竞争对手之后，再利用垄断力量抬高价格，以获取高额垄断利润。

3.长期性倾销是指无期限地、持续地以低于国内市场的价格在国外市场销售商品。商品倾销的最终目的是打开市场、战胜竞争对手、扩大销售和形成垄断。

外汇倾销是指一国政府利用本国货币对外贬值的手段来达到提高出口商品的价格竞争能力和扩大出口的目的。外汇倾销不能无限制和无条件地进行，只有在具备以下条件时，外汇倾销才能起到扩大出口的作用。

1.货币贬值的幅度要大于国内物价上涨的幅度。一国货币的对外贬值必然会引起货币对内也贬值，从而导致国内物价的上涨。当国内物价上涨的幅度赶上或超过货币贬值的幅度时，出口商品的外销价格就会回升到甚至超过原先的价格，即货币贬值前的价格，因而使外汇倾销无法实行。

2.其他国家不同时实行同等幅度的货币贬值。当一国货币对外实行贬值时，如果其他国家也实行同等幅度的货币贬值，这就会使两国货币之间的汇率保持不变，从而使出口商品的外销价格也保持不变，以致外汇倾销不能实现。

3.其他国家不同时采取其他报复性措施。如果其他国家采取提高关税等报复性措施，那也会提高出口商品在国外市场的价格，从而抵消外汇倾销的作用。

资料来源：根据相关资料整理所得。

五、汇率变动促使国际金融工具不断创新

汇率的不稳定会加剧国际贸易和国际投资的汇率风险。为了防范和减少此类风险的发生，金融市场上使用的金融工具不断推陈出新，诸如货币期货、货币期权、货币互换等以货币（主要是外汇）作为标的资产的金融衍生品工具不断出现，一定程度上减缓了汇率波动带来的风险。金融产品的创新是国际金融市场进一步发展的必然产物。

思政小课堂

2020年10月29日通过的《中共中央关于制定国民经济和社会发展第十四个五年规划和二〇三五年远景目标的建议》提出"稳慎推进人民币国际化，坚持市场驱动和企业自主选择，营造以人民币自由使用为基础的新型互利合作关系"，明确了未来人民币国际化注重以市场为导向，以培育真实需求为基础的发展原则。

2020年11月15日，由东盟十国和中国、日本、韩国、澳大利亚、新西兰共15个国家正式签署《区域全面经济伙伴关系协定》（以下简称《协定》），《协定》所覆盖的人口超过35亿人，经济总量达到29万亿美元，占全球总量的30%。《协定》的签署为人民币国际化提供了广阔的市场基础。

请查阅资料并思考：

1.当前人民币国际化取得了哪些成就？

2.人民币国际化面临的机遇和挑战有哪些？

项目思维导图

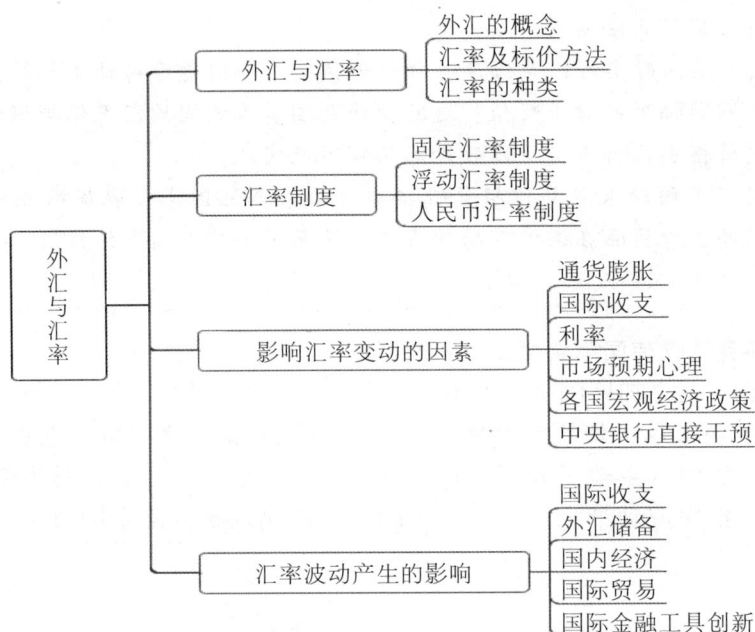

外汇与汇率
- 外汇与汇率
  - 外汇的概念
  - 汇率及标价方法
  - 汇率的种类
- 汇率制度
  - 固定汇率制度
  - 浮动汇率制度
  - 人民币汇率制度
- 影响汇率变动的因素
  - 通货膨胀
  - 国际收支
  - 利率
  - 市场预期心理
  - 各国宏观经济政策
  - 中央银行直接干预
- 汇率波动产生的影响
  - 国际收支
  - 外汇储备
  - 国内经济
  - 国际贸易
  - 国际金融工具创新

项目训练

一、单选题

1.从狭义上讲，静态的外汇是以（　　　）表示的可用于国际之间结算的支付手段。

A.本国货币　　　　B.外国货币　　　　C.外国有价证券　　　D.特别提款权

2.某日，东京外汇市场汇率为 1 美元=115.20 日元，如果前一交易日汇率为 1 美元=112.80 日元，则下列描述正确的是（　　　）。

A.与前一交易日相比，说明美元贬值、日元升值；标价方法为直接标价法

B.与前一交易日相比，说明美元升值、日元贬值；标价方法为直接标价法

C.与前一交易日相比，说明美元升值、日元贬值；标价方法为间接标价法

D.与前一交易日相比，说明美元贬值、日元升值；标价方法为间接标价法

3.在直接标价法下，本国货币数量减少，说明（　　　）。

A.本币汇率下降　　　　　　　　　　B.本币汇率上升

C.外币汇率上升　　　　　　　　　　D.外币汇率下降

4.将汇率制度分为单独浮动和联合浮动是按（　　　）进行分类的。

A.政府是否干预　　　　　　　　　　B.汇率的浮动方式

C.汇率的性质　　　　　　　　　　D.浮动管理的松紧程度

5.当外币汇率过高时，一国政府为了抑制外汇汇率的进一步升高，可以采取（　　）措施进行调节。

A.限制外汇支出　　　　　　　　　B.大量买进外汇

C.大量抛售外汇　　　　　　　　　D.限制本币流通

二、多选题

1.广义的外汇是对国际债务清偿过程中所形成的金融资产的统称，具体包括（　　）。

A.外币支付凭证　　　　　　　　　B.信用凭证

C.外国债　　　　　　　　　　　　D.外币存款

2.以下属于外汇的范畴有（　　）。

A.外币有价证券　　　　　　　　　B.外汇支付凭证

C.外国货币　　　　　　　　　　　D.外币存款凭证

3.按计算方法的不同来划分，汇率可分为（　　）。

A.套算汇率　　　　　　　　　　　B.基本汇率

C.官方汇率　　　　　　　　　　　D.市场汇率

4.影响汇率变动的因素主要有（　　）。

A.通货膨胀情况　　　　　　　　　B.国际收支情况

C.人们心理预期　　　　　　　　　D.国际政治事件

5.下列选项中，有可能引起一国货币贬值的因素有（　　）。

A.国际收支逆差　　　　　　　　　B.通货膨胀率高于其他国家

C.国内利率上升　　　　　　　　　D.紧缩性货币政策

三、判断题

1.汇率直接标价法是以本国货币作为基准货币，以外国货币作为报价货币。（　　）

2.基础汇率是指一国货币与国际上某一关键货币之间汇率的比率。（　　）

3.在固定汇率制度下，两种货币的汇率一经确定就不会发生任何改变。（　　）

4.一般来说，如果一国通货膨胀率提高，则会使本币汇率上升，外币汇率下降。（　　）

5.一国货币汇率下降，有利于该国旅游和其他服务收支的改善。（　　）

四、实践应用题

1.某中国公司欲在美国投资，得到的银行报价为1美元=6.8355/6.8366元人民币，则该公司投资1 000万美元需要花费多少元人民币？

2.汇率套算

（1）已知某日外汇市场上汇率报价为：1USD=1.2179/1.2183CHF，1USD=1.0491/1.0496CAD。试计算瑞士法郎与加元之间的套算汇率并说明其含义。

（2）已知某日外汇市场上汇率报价为：1USD=1.2179/1.2183CHF，1GBP=2.0110/2.0115USD。试计算英镑与瑞士法郎之间的套算汇率并说明其含义。

项目五
外汇市场与外汇交易

学习目标

知识目标

掌握外汇市场的含义、特征、参与者、分类等基础知识；理解并掌握即期外汇交易、远期外汇交易的含义、作用及报价规则和交易流程。

能力目标

掌握即期、远期、掉期、套汇、套利等外汇交易的原理，能灵活运用。

操作目标

能够借助不同交易工具设计外汇交易方案，进行套期保值操作。

课程导入

中国外汇交易市场

中国外汇交易市场是中国金融市场的重要组成部分，在完善汇率形成机制、推动人民币可兑换、服务金融机构、促进宏观调控方式的改变，以及促进金融市场体系的完善等各方面已经发挥不可替代的作用。自1994年后，我国外汇市场开始由外汇调剂市场过渡到以中国外汇交易中心为核心的银行间外汇市场，这无疑是我国外汇市场的重大进步。

近年来，中国外汇市场总交易额呈现稳定增长趋势。2018年中国外汇市场总交易额为1 929 748亿元，同比增长18.92%。2019年中国外汇市场总交易额为2 005 619亿元，同比增长3.93%。其中，银行对客户市场交易为额为283 791亿元，银行间外汇市场交易额为1 721 828亿元；短期交易额为783 173亿元，占比39.05%；长期交易额为26 257亿元，占比1.31%；外汇和货币掉期交易额为1 137 609亿元，占比56.72%；期权交易额为58 580亿元，占比2.92%。

表5-1为2015—2019年中国外汇市场各品种交易额情况。

表5-1　　2015—2019年中国外汇市场各品种交易额情况　　　单位：亿元

年份	短期	长期	外汇和货币掉期	期权
2015年	515 521	30 712	537 838	25 219
2016年	588 349	25 253	674 412	63 967
2017年	640 077	28 631	913 426	40 607
2018年	734 966	35 488	1 102 877	56 415
2019年	783 173	26 257	1 137 609	58 580

资料来源：根据国家外汇管理局资料整理所得。

思考讨论：

（1）我国外汇市场交易的发展呈现什么趋势？

（2）查询资料，思考未来我国外汇交易市场会有哪些变化？

通常认为，国际贸易是外汇市场建立的最主要原因。由于各国的货币制度存在差异，因此各国的货币币种不同，在国际债权债务清偿时，首先要解决各国货币之间的兑换问题，贸易中需要用一定数量的一种货币去兑换另一种货币，这个问题的解决需要依靠外汇市场交易。最初，外汇市场的产生主要是满足国际贸易结算的需要。后来，随着交易手段的现代化、全球国际贸易规模的不断扩大，外汇市场已经远远超越了最初的贸易结算的基本功能，即期交易、远期交易、掉期交易、外汇期货交易、期权交易等金融创新带来的衍生品交易进一步丰富了外汇市场产品。

任务一　　外汇市场概述

一、外汇市场的含义

外汇市场（foreign exchange market）是指进行外汇交易的场所或网络，是经营外汇业务的银行、各种金融机构、外汇需求者、外汇供给者、买卖中介机构以及个人进行外汇买卖、调剂外汇供求的交易场所。

外汇市场是国际金融市场的重要组成部分，国际贸易、国际融资以及其他国际经济活动都涉及不同货币之间的兑换，都要通过外汇买卖来实现，因而这些活动都离不开外汇市场。简而言之，外汇市场是指进行外汇买卖的场所，即各种不同货币彼此进行交换的场所。这个市场上进行买卖的是特殊商品——外国货币。

动画微课5-1

外汇市场及特征

外汇市场进行的是不同货币之间的兑换，可以是本国货币与外国货币之间的兑换，也可以是不同币种的外汇之间的买卖。例如，在中国外汇市场上，交易者可以用人民币购买美元、欧元、日元等外国货币；在国际外汇市场上，交易者可以用美元购买欧元、澳大利亚元、日元等外汇。根据交易者自身的交易意图，可以买入外汇，也可以卖出外汇。

二、外汇市场的特征

1.外汇市场是全球性市场，可以24小时连续交易

在通信及网络技术还不够发达的阶段，外汇交易主要局限于本地，辐射范围较小。随着技术的进步，使全球较为分散的外汇交易市场互相联系起来成为可能，区域性的交易逐渐转变为全球性的交易。由于时区的关系，世界上任何地方、任何时间都有外汇交易的发生，全球主要外汇市场处于不同时区，一个市场闭市、另一个市场开市在理论上是可以实现的，因此全球外汇交易是连续的，可以实现24小时不间断交易。

知识链接5-1

外汇交易是24小时不间断吗？

数字货币可以365×24小时不间断交易，而外汇并不是7×24小时随时交易。外汇交易与股票和数字货币不同，它没有集中的交易所。外汇必须通过交易商（一般是银行）完成交易和结算。本质上，外汇市场是分散的：交易地域、交易商、交易品种都是分散的。

每周一至周五，外汇交易可以24小时不间断，但周六和周日没有交易。因为外汇交易的时间是由全世界不同国家的金融市场拼接完成：每天从大洋洲到亚洲再到欧洲最后到美洲不停轮动。如下列所示（以北京时间计）：

1.周一早上凌晨五点，澳大利亚外汇市场开启全新一周的交易。

2.上午七点，日本东京外汇市场开盘标志着亚太地区开始交易，新加坡外汇市场和中国香港外汇市场一小时以后开始交易。

3.在澳大利亚和日本工作人员下班前，德国法兰克福外汇市场接棒，欧洲交易时段开启。

4.随后，全球外汇交易的霸主伦敦外汇市场于下午三点上场。

5.晚上八点，纽约外汇市场加入，与伦敦外汇市场联袂演绎一天中全球外汇最活跃的几个小时，伦敦交易时段于凌晨结束。

6.纽约交易时段一直持续到次日，恰好与澳大利亚交易时段无缝衔接。

资料来源：佚名.外汇基础之一：外汇交易是24小时不间断吗？[EB/OL].[2019-07-21].https://zhuanlan.zhihu.com/p/74506940.

2.交易方式多样性、交易规模最大的市场

外汇市场诞生的最初目的是进行贸易结算，随着全球国际贸易的规模扩大、外汇市场交易量不断增加、交易范围不断扩大，由此造成外汇市场的风险也在不断增大。为了减少和降低外汇风险，在传统的外汇交易基础上，通过金融创新，市场上产生了大量的新型外汇交易方式及产品——金融衍生工具。金融市场呈现多样化的交易格局，外汇交易活动也越来越复杂，交易规模迅速扩张。

3.外汇市场价格波动剧烈、投机活动普遍

在牙买加货币体系下，世界各国普遍实行浮动汇率制，汇率直接受到市场供求关系的影响，因而波动相对频繁、剧烈，尤其是投机性的外汇交易，更加剧了汇率的不稳定，市场风险进一步加剧。

4.无形市场比重越来越大

外汇交易是外汇买卖发生的场所。这一场所可以是有形的，也可以是无形的。当前，世界上大部分外汇交易都是通过现代化的电子通信设备进行的，不受场地和时间限制，交易速度快，市场效率高。因此，在全球外汇交易中，无形市场已经成为当代外汇市场的主要形态，这也进一步推动了外汇交易规模的扩大。

5.各国央行对外汇市场干预不断

中央银行是外汇市场重要的参与者，其参与外汇交易的目的不是规避外汇风险和投机，而是干预外汇市场，维持本国货币的汇率稳定，或者通过外汇干预使汇率向有利于本国利益的方向发展。例如，干预外汇市场促进本国国际收支平衡，达到影响或稳定国内经济发展的目标。不管是发达国家还是发展中国家，各国政府从来没有也不会停止对外汇市场的干预。

三、外汇市场的分类

根据不同的分类标准，可以把外汇市场划分成不同类型，在此介绍三类主要的分类：

（一）按组织形态划分

外汇市场按组织形态划分，可分为有形外汇市场和无形外汇市场。

1.有形外汇市场

最初的外汇交易活动是在一个具体的固定交易场所内进行的。进行交易的各方在固定交易场所和设施的外汇交易所内（通常设在证券交易所内），在规定的营业时间里进行交易，我们称之为有形外汇市场。比较著名的有形外汇市场主要集中在欧洲大陆国家，如瑞士的苏黎世、法国的巴黎、德国的法兰克福、荷兰的阿姆斯特丹等。

2.无形外汇市场

当今的外汇市场更多的时候表现为一个无形的市场。这是一个由电话、电传、传真或计算机网络等通信工具将买卖双方连接起来的庞大的外汇交易系统，交易的任何一方只要通过电信方式就可以进入这个市场进行交易，因此现在的外汇市场更多的是一种交易网络，是抽象的、无形的市场。

由于无形外汇市场使外汇交易更加便利，并且效率明显提高，因此无形外汇市场迅速发展，即使在欧洲大陆国家，大部分外汇交易也是在无形市场进行的。无形外汇市场是当今外汇市场的主导形式。

（二）按交易主体划分

外汇市场按交易主体划分，可分为外汇零售市场和外汇批发市场。

1.外汇零售市场

外汇零售市场主要是银行同客户之间买卖外汇的市场。客户可能是因为进出口需要买卖外汇，也可能因为投资于某一外汇资产而买卖外汇，无论是哪种情况，银行都在外汇终极供应者与终极需求者之间起中介作用，即一方面从客户手中买入外汇，另一方面又把外汇卖给需要的客户，从中赚取买卖差价。这一层次的外汇市场与外汇批发市场相比，每笔交易的金额相对较小，因此被称为外汇零售市场。

2.外汇批发市场

跟外汇零售市场相对应的是外汇批发市场。外汇批发市场是银行同业之间进行外汇交易的市场，因为交易的金额大、起点高，所以被称为外汇批发市场。外汇批发市场汇集了巨大的供求流量，所以外汇批发市场决定着外汇市场的即时汇率。外汇零售市场的汇率是在外汇批发市场汇率的基础上加减一定点数形成的，因此外汇零售市场汇率要高于外汇批发市场。

（三）按照交易工具划分

外汇市场按交易工具划分，可分为传统外汇市场和新型外汇市场。

传统外汇市场包括即期市场、远期市场、掉期市场等。

动画微课5-2

新型外汇市场是外汇市场创新的结果，又称外汇金融衍生市场，具体包括外汇期货市场、外汇期权市场、互换市场等。本书将在后面项目中详细介绍，在此仅做简单讲解。

外汇交易分类

四、外汇市场的参与者

外汇市场上交易的对象是各国货币，而外汇市场上的交易者则包括商业银行、外汇经纪商、商业或投资活动的企业和个人、投机者和套汇者、中央银行等，它们被统称为外汇市场的参与者。参与者参与外汇市场的目的不同，参与方式也各异。

1.商业银行

各发达国家的商业银行通常都有外汇买卖以及承办外汇存款、汇兑、贴现等业务。在一些实行外汇管制的国家中，外汇业务是由各国中央银行制定或授权经营外汇业务的银行办理。商业银行是外汇市场的主体和外汇业务的中心，外汇市场上 90% 的交易量来自银行同业间的外汇买卖。

在外汇零售市场上，商业银行可以接受进出口商的委托，办理进出口结售汇业务，充当外汇买卖的中介人赚取费用，还可以通过自行买卖外汇来获取买卖差价。在外汇批发市场上，如果银行卖出的外汇多于买进的外汇，可以使用自身的外汇账户出售自己的外汇以弥补差额，也可以和其他银行进行交易，以保持原有的外汇平衡。商业银行在外汇市场上有时也做投机交易，通过投机交易获取收益。例如，银行预计未来3个月美元将升值，就会当下买入美元，等到3个月后美元真的按照预期升值后，再卖出美元获得投机收益。但是，投机交易的前提是对外汇市场的汇率要有较为准确的判断，才能保证决策准确，否则将会亏损。

2.外汇经纪商（broker）

外汇经纪商是专门从事介绍成交或者代客户买卖外汇，从中收取手续费的中介机构。外汇经纪商本身并不是交易主体，不持有外汇，只提供服务收取佣金。外汇经纪商一般不和外汇最终供给者和需求者接触，其主要服务对象是各大经营外汇业务的商业银行，为商业银行提供合适的交易价格和合适的交易对手促成交易。一般而言，经过外汇经纪商撮合的外汇交易数额巨大。外汇经纪商之所以能够被商业银行青睐，是由于其具备收集全球外汇市场信息及掌握外汇行情的能力，能够为客户节约信息收集成本，并且为银行隐藏交易身份而获得有利的交易条件。外汇经纪商的存在，有利于外汇交易的迅速成交，提高外汇市场的效率。

3.外汇的实际供给者和需求者

从事进出口贸易的商业企业、跨国投资者、个人等都是外汇市场的最终需求者和供给者，其进行外汇交易的目的各异。例如，进口商需要购买外汇支付国外的货款；为了规避汇率波动的风险，出口商可以借助外汇远期合约来尽量减少外币贬值带来的损失。

4.外汇投机者和套汇者

投机者和套汇者的交易目的是从市场本身的交易中，借助买卖差价获取收益，他们的交易没有贸易背景，不产生任何价值，他们的获利是交易对手的损失，因此在某种意义上外汇交易被称为"零和游戏"。

5.中央银行

各国中央银行是外汇市场的间接参与者，一般不直接参与外汇市场交易，通常通过外汇经纪商进行外汇交易。交易的动机不是为了获取收益，而是为了稳定本国汇率。在外汇市场上，中央银行可以通过外汇经纪商或商业银行增加外汇储备或卖出多余的外汇资产来稳定本国货币的汇率，从而实现其货币政策，调整宏观经济的发展。

知识链接5-2

全球外汇市场

外汇市场是不分国界的，外汇交易也是跨越了时间、地域、国家概念的全球一体化交易，但是外汇交易市场有很多种，在世界的各大洲都有不同数量的外汇交易市场。其中最重要的五个外汇交易市场为：英国的伦敦、美国的纽约、澳大利亚的悉尼、亚洲的东京和香港。

英国的伦敦外汇交易市场

伦敦是全球老牌金融中心，也是开办外汇交易最早的地方。伦敦外汇交易市场的悠久传统使得各国银行习惯性地在其开盘后才开始进行大宗的外汇交易。因此，全球外汇市场一天的波动也就随着伦敦外汇交易市场的开盘而开始加剧。交易时间约为北京时间15：30至23：30。

美国的纽约外汇交易市场

纽约外汇交易市场是重要的国际外汇市场之一，其日交易量仅次于伦敦。高度的活跃性也造就了大量投资者的盈利机会。目前，占全球90%以上的美元交易最后都通过纽约的银行间清算系统进行结算，因此纽约外汇市场成为美元的国际结算中心。除美元外，各主要交易币种依次为欧元、英镑、瑞士法郎、加拿大元、日元等。交易时间约为北京时间20：00至次日4：00。

澳大利亚的悉尼外汇交易市场

从北京时间来看，悉尼外汇交易市场是每天全球最早开市的外汇交易市场之一。交易品种以澳元、新西兰元和美元为主。交易时间约为北京时间6：00至15：00。

日本的东京外汇交易市场

东京外汇交易市场是亚洲最大的外汇交易市场。在东京外汇交易所交易时段，可能仅有日元出现波动的概率大一些。此外，日本作为出口大国其进出口贸易的收付较为集中，因此具有易受干扰的特点。东京外汇市场的交易货币比较单一，主要是日元、美元和欧元的交易。交易时间约为北京时间8：00至15：30。

中国的香港外汇交易市场

香港外汇交易市场与上述其他四大交易市场有明显的不同之处，因为香港外汇交易市场是美元固定的交易场所，外汇交易者通过网络或者其他通信联络设施即可进行外汇交易，所以香港外汇交易市场是一个无形市场，但无形并不代表不活跃。香港作为国际金融中心，有大量的国际资本涌入，香港外汇交易市场的活跃度一直处于世界前列。交易货币主要以港币和美元为主。交易时间为北京时间09：00至16：00。

资料来源：佚名. 关于全球五大外汇交易市场的详解［EB/OL］.［2018-03-01］. https：//www.sohu.com/a/224621165_249239.

五、中国的外汇市场

中国外汇市场是中国金融市场的重要组成部分，在完善汇率形成机制、推动人民币可兑换、服务金融机构、促进宏观调控方式的改变以及促进金融市场体系的完善等各方面发挥着不可替代的作用。虽然中国外汇市场起步较晚，但是其发展迅速，主要利用先进的电子交易平台进行国内外的外汇交易。

从市场结构来看，中国外汇市场分为三个层次：

1.零售市场，即客户与外汇指定银行之间的市场

在中国，外汇零售市场又称客户市场，特指银行与个人及公司客户之间进行的外汇买卖行为及场所。银行在与客户的外汇交易中起着中介作用，一方面从客户手中买入外汇，另一方面又将外汇卖给客户，从中赚取外汇买卖差价，是银行对客户提供的外汇服务业务，也是外汇市场存在的基础。

外汇零售市场上，交易客户主要有企业、进出口商、个人等。由于国际贸易、国际投资以及其他方面的需要与银行进行外汇买卖，构成了外汇市场的基本业务。外汇零售业务主要包括银行与个人及公司客户之间进行的外汇交易，如货币兑换、进出口结算和外汇买卖；个人、企业通常与银行直接进行交易。外汇零售市场以零星交易为主，没有最小交易金额限制，每笔交易较为零散，交易量比较小，交易成本比较高，买卖差价大。

2.批发市场，即银行间外汇市场

凡在中国境内营业的金融机构，它们之间的外汇交易，均应通过银行间外汇市场进行。经中国人民银行、国家外汇管理局批准可以经营外汇业务的境内金融机构（包括中外资银行和非银行金融机构）之间通过中国外汇交易中心的银行间外汇交易系统进行人

民币和外汇之间交易的市场就是银行间外汇市场。

外汇指定银行在办理结售汇业务的过程中，会出现买超或卖超的现象，可以通过银行间外汇市场进行外汇交易，平衡其外汇头寸。另外，在牙买加货币体系下实行浮动汇率制，市场汇率波动大，投机性外汇买卖获利机会很多，银行出于投机目的，也会进行套汇、套利、套期保值等外汇业务。

批发市场的特点是交易规模大，主要采取整数批发交易，有最小交易金额的限制（如在欧洲外汇市场上，美元的最低交易量是100万美元）。由于交易量巨大，因此交易成本较低，买卖差价较小。批发市场是外汇市场的主流，其交易占外汇交易总额的90%以上，我们一般在新闻报道中提到的外汇市场通常是指银行间外汇市场。

3.中央银行与外汇指定银行间的市场

中央银行出于宏观调控的目标，在外汇批发市场上进行公开业务操作。中央银行可以适时地以普通会员身份入市，进行市场干预，调节外汇供求，保持汇率相对稳定，这是中国人民银行对外汇市场进行调控和管理的有效途径。

另外，在中国外汇市场上主要开展的外汇业务包括人民币外汇即期、人民币外汇远期、人民币外汇掉期、人民币外汇货币掉期、人民币外汇期权、外币对、外币利率等。以上相关内容将在后面项目中详细介绍。

知识链接5-3

中国外汇交易中心

中国外汇交易中心暨全国银行间同业拆借市场，成立于1994年4月18日，总部位于上海，分中心在北京。中国外汇交易中心旨在为银行间外汇市场、货币市场、债券市场和衍生品市场提供交易系统并组织交易，同时履行市场监测职能，保障市场平稳、健康、高效运行。中国外汇交易中心主要经营的业务和服务包括：

1.银行间外汇市场

银行间外汇市场由人民币外汇市场、外币对市场、外币拆借市场和相关衍生品市场组成，是机构之间进行外汇交易的市场，实行会员管理和做市商制度。中国外汇交易中心为银行间外汇市场提供统一、高效的电子交易系统，该系统提供竞价、询价和撮合等模式，并提供交易分析、做市接口和即时通信工具等系统服务。此外，交易中心也与上海黄金交易所合作银行间黄金询价即期、远期和掉期交易。

2.银行间本币市场

银行间本币市场由货币市场、债券市场和相关衍生品市场组成，是金融机构实施流动性管理、资产负债管理、投资交易管理及利率和信用风险管理的重要场所，也是央行货币政策传导的重要平台。

中国外汇交易中心为银行间本币市场的机构投资者提供高效、便捷的本币交易系统，覆盖多类型利率、信用等交易品种，支持询价、做市报价、请求报价、双边授信撮合等多种交易方式。同时，本币交易系统还为市场成员提供同业存单发行服务和常备借贷便利。

资料来源：根据中国外汇交易中心网站的资料整理所得。

任务二　　　　　即期外汇交易

外汇交易的类型有许多种，其中即期外汇交易、远期外汇交易和掉期交易是外汇市场上最基本的交易形式，被称为传统的外汇交易形式。随着技术的不断进步，国际金融业的不断发展，金融工具创新层出不穷，外汇市场上出现了很多外汇交易创新形式，外汇期货交易、外汇期权交易、货币互换与利率互换交易、远期利率协议等，这些都被称为外汇衍生工具。本节以与外汇银行相关的外汇交易为重点，介绍即期外汇交易、远期外汇交易、外汇掉期交易、套利交易的基本原理及应用。

一、即期外汇交易的概念

即期外汇交易（spot exchange transaction），是指买卖双方在外汇买卖成交后，在成交当日或两个营业日内办理交割手续的外汇交易。即期外汇交易又被称为现汇交易或现货交易，是外汇市场上最常见、最普遍的交易形式。

为了更好地理解即期外汇交易，必须明确以下内容：

（一）成交与交割

在外汇交易中，成交是指确定外汇买卖协议，该协议规定了外汇交易的买方、卖方，外汇买卖的币种、数量和价格以及交割标准。成交仅指确定买卖关系，并不发生实际收付行为。

交割是指成交后，买卖双方实际收付货币的行为，交易双方分别按照对方的要求将卖出的货币汇入对方指定的银行账户。交割发生的那一天称为"交割日"。

（二）交割方式

交割日又称结算日、起息日，是指买卖双方相互交换货币资金的日期，此日也是双方的货币资金划拨到指定账户银行并开始计息的日期。根据不同的市场习惯，即期外汇交易的交割日不同，主要有以下三种类型：

1.标准日交割（T+2）

标准日交割是指即期外汇交易一般采用T+2的交割方式，与欧洲账户的结算同步，即成交后的第二个营业日交割。目前，一些主要的外汇市场基本都是采用T+2的交割方式。例如，一家美国进口商从德国进口印刷机，5月10日货到验明后付款，在两日内也就是5月13日前按当日银行外汇牌价完成交割，就是即期外汇交易中的标准日交割。

2.隔日交割（T+1）

隔日交割，又称现金交割，是指即期外汇交易一般采用T+1的交割方式，即成交后的第一个营业日交割。某些国家或地区因时差的原因采用此交割方式。例如，在中国香港外汇市场上，港元对日元、新加坡元、澳大利亚元的即期交易成交后的次日为交割日；美元对加拿大元、墨西哥比索的即期交易也是成交后的次日为交割日。因为这些国家或地区基本上属于同一时区。

3.当日交割（T+0）

当日交割是指即期外汇交易一般采用T+0的交割方式，即成交当日进行交割。银行与当地客户的零星即期外汇买卖一般是当天就可以实现外汇的收付，了结该笔外汇买卖。

国际外汇交易市场上，一般是在成交后的第二个营业日进行。如果交割的那一天正逢节假日，则可顺延。即期交易采用即期汇率，通常是经办外汇业务银行的当日挂牌价，或参考当地外汇市场主要货币之间的比价加一定的手续费。

二、即期外汇交易的作用

即期外汇交易方式可适用于外汇的汇入、汇出，服务于个人客户、进出口企业客户、外汇投机者。即期外汇交易的作用有以下三点：

1.满足临时性支付需求

企业或个人在日常业务或生活中临时性的外汇需求可以通过即期外汇交易来满足。客户可以将手中的本币或外币通过即期外汇买卖兑换成另一种货币，用以对外支付。例如，居民个人出境旅游需要兑换外币时，可通过银行柜面按照当日汇率将本币兑换成外币。

2.规避外汇风险

外贸企业由于持有不同外汇，汇率的波动会导致企业面临外汇风险，通过即期外汇交易，企业可以随时调整手头的外汇头寸，避免汇率波动的风险。

3.进行外汇投机

投机者通过买卖现汇的方式进行外汇投机交易。通过"低买高卖"的操作，可以获得投机收益。外汇投机的前提是能够发现价差，准确预测未来汇率走势，否则将会出现相反结果——亏损。因此，外汇投机是有风险的。

三、即期外汇交易的报价规则与程序

（一）即期外汇交易的报价规则

即期外汇交易的报价是达成交易的基础。在即期外汇市场上，一般把提供交易价格（汇价）的机构称为报价者，通常由外汇银行充当这一角色；而把向报价者询价并在即期汇价上与报价者成交的其他外汇银行、外汇经纪商和中央银行等统称为询价者。在即期外汇交易中，外汇银行在报价时要遵循一定的惯例和规则。

1.双向报价

外汇银行的报价一般都采用双向报价方式，即银行同时报出买入价和卖出价。买入价和卖出价的差额称为差价。例如，2018年8月10日欧元对人民币的即期外汇报价为EUR/CNY=7.8561/7.9141。在此报价中，欧元是基准货币，人民币是标价货币；7.8561是银行的买入价，7.9141是银行的卖出价，即银行每买入1欧元，需要支付7.8561元人民币；银行每卖出1欧元，可收取7.9141元人民币。

2.省略报价

即期外汇交易中，银行所报的汇率一般用5位有效数字表示，由大数和小数两个部分组成。大数是汇价的基本部分，通常交易员不会报出，只有在需要证实交易时或者在变化剧烈的市场上才会报出。假设某日USD/CNY=6.8271/85，其中6.82是大数，71和

85是小数，71和85之间的差额14称为价差。一般外汇市场上汇率的小数变化比较活跃，大数相对稳定。外汇交易时每一秒汇率都会发生变动，因此报价要求简练、快速。外汇银行之间报价通常报最后两位，即报小数部分。

3.基点的概念

报价中的最小单位及小数点后最后一位数，被称为一个基点或一点。在交易中，规定1基点=0.0001。通常用点数的变化来表示货币汇率的变动。例如，美元对人民币的汇率由6.8271上升到6.8285，可以说美元汇率上涨了14个基点或点。

（二）即期外汇交易的程序

大部分外汇交易属于银行交易。银行间的即期外汇交易都有标准的一套流程。其交易程序一般经过询价、报价、成交、确认、记录交割等过程。下面是两个外汇交易员就欧元对美元的掉期交易过程：

A：HIHI FRD ANY INT TO SWAP EUR 2 MIO AG USD

B：FOR TOM/1W?

　　3.38　　3.48

A：DONE I S/B EUR

B：CFM I B/S EUR 2 MIO AG USD AT+3.48

　　REATS ARE 1.2310 N 1.231348

　　MY EUR TO DEUTDEFF

　　MY USD TO BKTRUS33

A：ALL AGREE

　　MY EUR TO DRESDEFF

　　MY USD TO CITIUS33

A：你好，朋友。欧元对美元外汇掉期的报价？金额为200万欧元。（询价）

B：即期明天交割，远期一周后交割？即期买欧元远期卖美元报掉期率在3.38，即期卖欧元远期买美元报掉期率在3.48。（报价）

A：好的，成交。我即期卖欧元远期买美元。（成交）

B：确认一下，我即期买远期卖200万欧元对美元，掉期率3.48，即期汇率1.2310，远期汇率1.231348，我的欧元汇到德意志银行账户，美元汇到美国信孚银行账户。（确认、记录交割）

A：确认成交。我的欧元汇到德累斯登银行账户，我的美元汇到花旗银行账户。（确认、记录交割）

从以上外汇交易员之间的交易对话中可以看出，外汇交易员是一个专业性非常强的岗位，银行间的即期外汇交易通常都有专门的规范术语。从事外汇交易需具备超强的综合素质、较强的承压能力，善于观察和学习，能够捕捉细节，具有风险意识和止损意识等，这些都是成为外汇交易员不可缺少的技能和素质。

四、即期外汇市场上的套汇交易

套汇交易属于典型的即期交易。套汇是指套汇者利用外汇市场上某些货币存在的汇率差异进行贱买贵卖，从中获取利润的行为。按照套汇地点的分布，套汇交易可分为直接套汇和间接套两种。

1.直接套汇

直接套汇，又称两角套汇，是指套汇者利用两个不同地点的外汇市场上两种货币之间存在的汇率差异，在汇率低的市场买入某种外汇的同时，在汇率高的市场卖出该种外汇，从中获利的行为。

【例5-1】某日，在伦敦外汇市场上GBP/USD=1.6260/70，在纽约外汇市场上GBP/USD=1.6280/90。如何进行直接套汇呢？

分析套汇操作过程如下：

由已知条件可知，同一时间，英镑在伦敦外汇市场上的价格比在纽约外汇市场上的价格低，根据贱买贵卖的原则，套汇者在伦敦外汇市场上以GBP/USD=1.6270的汇率买入英镑、卖出美元，同时在纽约外汇市场以GBP/USD=1.6280的汇率卖出英镑、买入美元。这样，套汇者在进行两地套汇买卖以后，每1英镑可以赚取0.01美元的利润（不计算套汇成本）。

套汇的结果是在伦敦外汇市场上英镑汇率上升，美元汇率下跌；在纽约外汇市场上英镑汇率下降，美元汇率上升。最终两个市场的汇率趋于一致，套汇自动终止。由于电子通信系统的发展，两地市场间的套汇机会能很快被捕捉，从而使得两地市场外汇报价差别大为缩小，套汇者直接套汇的机会大大减少。

2.间接套汇

间接套汇，又称三角套汇，是指套汇者利用三个不同地点的外汇市场上三种货币之间的汇率差异，同时在三个市场上贱买贵卖从中赚取利润的行为。

由于涉及三个市场、三种货币，因此在进行三角套汇时首要任务是识别间接套汇的机会。常用的方法是将三地的有关汇率按统一的标价方法表示，然后将其相乘。若乘积为1，则不存在机会；反之，就有机会，且乘积与1的背离越大，说明套汇的收益越高。

【例5-2】某日，纽约外汇市场上USD1=CHF0.9807，伦敦外汇市场上GBP1=USD1.6782，苏黎世外汇市场上GBP1=CHF1.6052。如何进行间接套汇呢？

分析套汇操作过程如下：

第一步：统一标价法。纽约和伦敦外汇市场上采用的是间接标价法，而苏黎世外汇市场上采用的是直接标价法。因此，首先按统一的标价方法表示，将苏黎世外汇市场上的报价转化为间接标价，即CHF1=GBP1/1.6052。然后，将三个汇率的等号右边相乘，0.9807×1.6782×1/1.6052=1.0253≠1，说明在这三个市场间存在套汇机会。

第二步：进行市场操作。从市场差价来看，英镑在伦敦外汇市场上最贵，而通过在纽约和苏黎世外汇市场套取的英镑较便宜。于是，套汇者便在纽约和苏黎世外汇市场套取英镑，然后将其在伦敦外汇市场出售，从而获利（即在纽约外汇市场以美元购买瑞士法郎，并以此瑞士法郎在苏黎世外汇市场购买英镑，最后在伦敦外汇市场出售英镑并购回美元）。若以1美元为本金，不计交易费用，则可以获利0.0253美元（1×0.9807÷1.6052×1.6782-1），利润率为2.53%。

如果采用的是双向报价，那么在计算三角套汇的收益时就要考虑交易中买卖价格的问题。三角套汇只有银行交易员才能从事，公众参与者很难进行这样的套汇交易。

任务三　　　　　　　　远期外汇交易

一、远期外汇交易概述

远期外汇交易（forward exchange transaction），又称期汇买卖，是指交易双方（至少有一方为银行）先签订外汇买卖合约，成交后并不立即交割，而是在未来的某个约定日期（成交后第三个营业日之后）进行交割的一种交易方式。

动画微课5-3

远期外汇交易

远期汇率并非未来的即期汇率。远期汇率是预先由买卖双方在合同中规定的，是不能改变的。而未来的即期汇率则是现实的市场汇率，它可能上升也可能下跌，因此可能会高于、低于或等于远期汇率。远期汇率与未来到期时的即期汇率之间的差额表现为远期交易的盈亏。

远期外汇交易是通过远期合约来完成的。合约中一般约定交易的货币种类、汇率、数量、交割期限和买卖外汇的类型五种信息。

1.远期外汇交易的交割期限

远期交易的交割期一般为1个月、3个月、6个月，也有的长达1年或1年以上，其中以3个月最为普遍，而1年以上的交易很少。这是因为，交割期限越长，交易的不确定性就越大，交易者所冒的风险就越大。

计算具体的远期交割日的办法是以即期交割日加上相应的远期月数。比如，在6月7日达成的3个月期远期交易，其交割日就是即期交割日6月9日加上3个月，为9月9日，如果这一天恰好遇到节假日，则一般情况下交割日要向后顺延，远期交易使用的汇率为远期汇率。

知识链接5-4

交割日如何计算？

交割日是买入或卖出外汇时应予交付通货的日期。买入外汇的客户，要交付本国的货币，而卖出外汇者则应交付卖出的外国货币。合格的交割日必须为交割货币发行国家的营业日，即使交易双方均为放假日，只要交割货币的国家是营业日，仍属合格交割日。

交割日可分为：现汇交割日和期汇交割日两类。

现汇交割日，通常是指成交日后两个营业日。即期外汇交易通常采用此类方法。

期汇交割日，通常是指自现汇交割日起算，再加合约约定月数而计算出来的交割日，如果这个交割日为非合格交割日，则予以顺延，假如日期顺延至下月，则惯例上不予顺延，而改为倒算。

例如，2019年11月25日（星期一）成交，现汇交割日为11月27日（星期三）；一个月期汇交割日为12月27日（星期五）；两个月期汇交割日为2020年1月27日（星期一）；三个月期汇交割日为2020年2月27日（星期四）。

2.远期外汇交易的产生

远期交易是为了避免外汇风险而产生的。相比国内贸易，国际贸易活动更复杂，从签约到结清货款要出现一段时间间隔。进出口商从签订出口合同到收付货款之间一般要隔几个月的时间，这段时间中如果用于支付货币的币值发生变化，就会给交易一方带来额外的损失。特别是在牙买加货币体系下，各国采用浮动汇率制度，汇率波动频繁，更加加剧了交易者的汇率风险。同样，在国际上进行投融资活动的金融交易者的收益与成本也会受到投资期限中汇率变动的影响。远期外汇交易可以减少或避免汇率波动给交易者带来的损失。

二、远期外汇交易的报价方法

（一）直接报价法（完整报价法）

直接报出完整的不同期限远期外汇的买入价和卖出价。银行对客户的远期外汇报价通常使用这种方法。

例如，某日美元对日元的1个月远期汇价为USD1=JPY119.77/119.83，该报价表示：1个月远期美元的银行买入价为1美元=119.77日元，银行卖出价为1美元=119.83日元。

又如，中国银行2018年12月1日报出1个月远期美元汇价为USD/CNY=6.8660/6.8770，该报价表明：1个月远期美元的银行买入价为1美元=6.8660元人民币，银行卖出价为1美元=6.8770元人民币。

（二）点数报价法（远期差价报价法）

点数报价法只标出远期汇率与即期汇率的差额，不直接标出远期汇率的买入价和卖出价。目前，国际外汇市场上通常都采用点数报价法。远期汇率与即期汇率的差额，称为汇水或远期差价。远期差价在外汇市场上是以升水、贴水和平价来表示的。

动画微课5-4

升水、贴水概念

1.升水和贴水

在外汇市场上，表示远期汇率点数的有前后两栏数字，分别代表买价和卖价。例如，升水（at premium）表示远期外汇比即期外汇贵，即当卖价大于买价时，为升水。贴水（at discount）表示远期外汇比即期外汇便宜，即当买价大于卖价时，为贴水。平价（at par）表示远期外汇和即期外汇二者相等。

升水和贴水的大小，主要取决于两种货币利率差幅的大小和期限的长短。一般而言，利率高的货币在远期市场上表现为贴水，利率较低的货币在远期市场上表现为升水。

在实际的远期外汇交易中，银行只报出即期汇率和远期汇率升水、贴水的点数，并不说明是升水还是贴水。实际的远期汇率可通过即期汇率加上或减去升水、贴水的点数得出，但报价中的数字并未标明是升水还是贴水，因此必须首先进行判断远期是升水还是贴水，然后才能对升水、贴水进行加减。

2.远期汇率的计算

由于汇率标价方法不同，因此计算远期汇率的公式也不相同。

在直接标价法下，远期汇率的计算公式为：

远期汇率=即期汇率+升水点数

远期汇率=即期汇率−贴水点数

在直接标价法下，基准货币判断远期汇率的方法为：前小后大是升水，用加法，前大后小是贴水，用减法。

在间接标价法下，远期汇率的计算公式为：

远期汇率=即期汇率−升水点数

远期汇率=即期汇率+贴水点数

【例5−3】某日，纽约银行报出的英镑买卖价为：

即期汇率GBP/USD=1.6783/93，3个月远期英镑/美元汇水为80/70。

分析：美元对英镑采用直接标价法，3个月远期英镑/美元汇水为80/70，根据上述判断方法"前大后小是贴水，用减法"，则计算出英镑的远期汇率为：

3个月远期英镑买价=1.6783−0.0080=1.6703

3个月远期英镑卖价=1.6793−0.0070=1.6723

【例5−4】某日，在纽约外汇市场上，即期汇率为GBP1=USD1.5575/81。若1个月远期英镑升水为10/20，求英镑的1个月远期汇率。

分析：在直接标价法下，即期汇率GBP1=USD1.5575/81，1个月远期英镑升水，所以远期汇率=即期汇率+升水点数，即：

1个月远期英镑买价=1.5575+0.0010=1.5585

1个月远期英镑卖价=1.5581+0.0020=1.5601

无论是哪种标价方法（直接标价法、间接标价法、美元标价法与非美元标价法），只要远期差价点数的顺序是前小后大，就用加法，只要远期差价点数的顺序是前大后小，就用减法，即"前小后大往上加，前大后小往下减"。同时，远期差价点数"前小后大"说明标准货币升水，报价货币贴水；远期差价点数"前大后小"说明标准货币贴水，报价货币升水。

三、远期外汇交易的应用

教学视频5−1

远期外汇交易

远期合约中的合同金额、到期时间、约定汇率等都可以由签约双方协商确定，所以远期合约可以说是一种为客户"量体裁衣"式的合约，受到很多进出口商的欢迎。但也因为其自身具有的"个性"，或者说非标准化的特点，使其流动性较差，合约无法中止，到期必须执行合约，在市场上难以转手。远期合约的非标准化特点，使远期外汇交易一般采用场外交易方式。

在实践过程中，进出口商一般通过跟银行签订远期外汇合约来规避风险。通过签订远期外汇合约，买方实际上把未来的汇率风险转嫁给银行，当然，银行也会及时调整自己的头寸，或者通过货币市场、外汇市场把风险转嫁给其他投资者。

（一）进出口商借助远期外汇交易套期保值规避汇率风险

【例5-5】2020年2月中旬，纽约外汇市场上的即期汇率为GBP/USD=1.6700，3个月远期贴水16。美国出口商签订向英国出口价值625 000英镑货物的协议，预计3个月后才能收到英镑，到时需要将英镑兑换成美元核算。假设美国出口商预计3个月后即期汇率将贬值为GBP/USD=1.6600。在不考虑交易成本的情况下，请问美国出口商要如何操作才能避免汇率损失，并分析其做远期交易的盈亏状况。

具体分析如下：

（1）美国出口商的操作方法。

美国出口商预计会面临远期汇率贴水导致的货款损失。为了减少损失，可以在签订出口协议之后，跟银行签订卖出3个月远期英镑合约，合约中约定好3个月后卖出625 000英镑给银行，汇率为双方协商汇率。之后不管3个月后实际汇率如何变化，都按照合约执行。

（2）美国出口商做远期交易的盈亏状况。

根据已知条件即期汇率为GBP/USD=1.6700，3个月远期贴水16，可计算出3个月远期英镑的汇率为：

GBP/USD=1.6700-0.0016=1.6684

在做远期交易的情况下，美国出口商3个月后收到625 000英镑可换回的美元为：

625 000×1.6684=1 042 750（美元）

在不做远期交易的情况下，美国出口商3个月后收到625 000英镑可换回的美元为：

625 000×1.6600=1 037 500（美元）

两种方法相比，做远期交易可多换回5 250美元（1 042 750-1 037 500）。在上述案例中，美国出口商为避免外币贬值使自己得到的本币数量减少，可以卖出远期外汇锁定未来收益。事实上，进口商为避免外币升值使自己在付款时支付的本币增加，也可以事先通过买入远期外汇确定未来支付的本币余额。同理，从事国际借贷者也可以通过远期交易进行保值避险。

【例5-6】2018年3月20日，中国进口商从美国进口一批货物，3个月后支付货款100万美元。当时美元对人民币即期汇率为6.3141/6.3409，中国银行3个月远期美元对人民币报价为6.4620/6.4822。为了避免汇率变动造成成本增加，中国进口商与本国银行签订远期合约，买入3个月期的100万美元。如果3个月后付款日的即期汇率为6.4648/6.4922。请问中国进口商不做远期外汇交易会有什么影响（不计交易费用）？

分析：中国进口商买入3个月期的100万美元，预期支付人民币为：

1 000 000×6.4822=6 482 200（元）

如果中国进口商没有进行外汇远期交易，3个月后按即期汇率买入美元支付货款，需支付的人民币为：

1 000 000×6.4922=6 492 200（元）

所以，如果中国进口商不做远期外汇交易，将多支付10 000元人民币（6 492 200-6 482 200）。

知识链接5-5

什么是套期保值

套期保值（hedging），也称对冲交易，是指当事人预计即将持有的外币资产（债权）或负债（债务）在到期时因汇率的变动而面临风险，在外汇市场卖出或买进未来日期办理交割的外汇，以达到避免经济损失的外汇交易行为。

进行套期保值操作后，如果汇率变动使原有的外汇头寸在到期时发生损失，但其在外汇市场上的交易却产生收益，便可以抵消损失。同理，如果外汇市场上的交易因汇率变动而出现亏损，但原有的外汇头寸反而获利，便可抵消损失。可见，只要外汇市场上的交易与原有外汇头寸由于汇率变动而发生相反的结果，相互间的盈亏就能够抵消。

例如，中国公司向德国出口产品，合同规定3个月后可以收到500万欧元货款。若3个月后欧元汇率急剧下跌，中国公司就会遭受损失。为此，中国公司可提前卖出3个月远期的500万欧元，3个月后，即使欧元汇率下跌，中国公司仍然可以按远期合约规定的汇率办理交割，从而回避了汇率风险。当然，如果3个月后欧元汇率出现上升，中国公司也就无法获取汇兑收益。

由此可见，套期保值的目的不是获取汇兑收益，而是回避风险。通常，持有远期外汇债券或债务者，如进口商、出口商、国际资金借贷者，通过签订远期交易合约，到期按约定汇率进行实际交割，可以获得固定的外汇收入或者提前固定外汇成本，使其避免远期市场汇率波动带来的风险，起到保值避险的效果。

资料来源：根据网络资料整理所得。

（二）银行借助远期外汇交易平衡其头寸，规避外汇风险

进出口商远期交易的对手是银行，在它们平衡了自己的远期外汇头寸，转嫁了外汇风险的同时，其交易对手银行就难免会在某种货币上出现远期头寸的不平衡，这实际上是将汇率风险转移到了银行身上。为避免风险，银行也要设法平衡其远期头寸，方法就是在外汇市场上卖出远期多头头寸，买入远期空头头寸。

（三）外汇投机者利用远期交易投机获利

远期外汇交易还可以满足投机商的需要。外汇投机者的目的是利用汇率的波动，从中获取汇价差额。外汇投机交易可分为卖空和买空两种类型。

卖空是投机者预计外汇汇率将下跌，在外汇市场上所做的"先卖后买"的行为。卖空的具体操作方式为：预计将来外汇汇率下跌，在当前汇率相对较高时先行预约卖出，日后汇价下跌再买回同样数量的外汇，从而获利。买空是预计外汇汇率将上升，在外汇市场上所做的"先买后卖"的行为，即在当前低价位买进外汇，日后汇率上升再卖出。无论是买空还是卖空，投机者仅仅是在到期日收付汇率涨落的差价，并没有十足的交割资金，而且外汇投机者的外汇买卖并不是建立在真实的贸易基础上的，具有投机性质，如果预测方向相反，则面临损失。

四、远期外汇交易的分类

1.固定交割日的远期外汇交易

固定交割日的远期外汇交易是指交易双方约定在将来某一固定日期进行外汇交割。签订这种远期合同的进出口商或债权债务人一般已经签订了合同，合同约定了何时收取外汇或者何时支付外汇，所以通过固定交割日的远期外汇交易来规避外汇风险。在实际交易中，这种交易方式较为常用，但它缺乏灵活性和机动性，如果外汇市场突发变动，固定交割日的外汇交易是无法临时变动的。

2.择期交割的远期外汇交易

择期交割的远期外汇交易是指客户可以在某一段时间内任意选择交割日的远期外汇交易。当客户在不能确定付汇（进口商）或收汇（出口商）的确切时间的情况下，选择择期交割的方式可以规避外汇风险。

对客户而言，择期交割的远期外汇交易具有更大的灵活性、便利性；对银行而言，择期交割的远期外汇交易使其风险加大，因此银行在确定择期交割的远期汇率时，会选择在择期期限内对银行有利的汇率作为交易的履约汇率。

任务四　　　　外汇掉期交易

掉期交易（swap transaction）是指交易双方约定在未来某一时期相互交换某种资产的交易形式。较为常见的是货币掉期交易和利率掉期交易。掉期交易与期货、期权交易一样，是近年来发展迅猛的金融衍生品之一，成为国际金融机构规避汇率风险和利率风险的重要工具。

一、外汇掉期交易的概念

外汇掉期（foreign exchange swap）是指在进行一笔外汇交易的同时，进行另一笔币种相同、金额相同，而方向相反、交割期限不同的交易。简单地说，外汇掉期是在买入或卖出某种货币的同时，卖出或买入期限不同的同种货币，把原来手中持有的货币进行一个掉期，即第一笔交易：卖出 A 货币，买入 B 货币；第二笔交易：买入 A 货币，卖出 B 货币。

以上两笔交易的特点是：买与卖是有意识地同时进行的；买与卖的货币种类相同，金额相等；买卖交割期限不相同。

（教学视频5-2　外汇掉期交易）

二、外汇掉期交易的分类

根据第一笔交易的交割时间，掉期可分为即期对远期、即期对即期、远期对远期三类。

1.即期对远期（spot against forward）

即期对远期的掉期交易是指买入或卖出一笔现汇的同时，卖出或买入一笔期汇。例如，某日本银行因业务需要，用日元购买 1 000 万美元存放于纽约 3 个月。为了防止 3 个月后美元汇率下跌，存放于纽约的美元不能够换回原来数额的日元，该银行采用掉期交易的方式，在即期买入 1 000 万美元现汇的同时，卖出 3 个月 1 000 万美元的期汇，这样就可以转移未来三个月美元下跌带来的风险。

2. 即期对即期（spot against spot）

即期对即期的掉期交易是指买入或卖出一笔即期外汇的同时，卖出或买入同种货币的另一笔即期外汇，但两笔即期交易的交割日不一致。这种掉期交易多用于银行同业的隔夜资金拆借。

3. 远期对远期（forward to forward）

远期对远期的掉期交易是指交易者在买入或卖出一笔期汇的同时，卖出或买入另一笔交割时间不同的期汇。在远期对远期的掉期交易中，时间相对较近的远期又可称近期，由此形成近期对远期的掉期交易。例如，美国 ABC 公司准备 3 个月后在法国债券市场投资 1 000 万欧元，6 个月后收回，ABC 公司可以在买入 3 个月远期 1 000 万欧元的同时，卖出 6 个月远期 1 000 万欧元来规避汇率风险。

知识链接 5-6

历史上著名的掉期交易

1981 年，IBM 公司和世界银行进行了一笔瑞士法郎和德国马克与美元之间的货币掉期交易。当时，世界银行在欧洲美元市场上能够以较为有利的条件筹集到美元资金，但是实际需要的却是瑞士法郎和德国马克。此时，持有瑞士法郎和德国马克资金的 IBM 公司正好希望将这两种货币形式的资金换成美元资金，以回避利率风险。

在所罗门兄弟公司的运作下，世界银行将以低息筹集到的美元资金提供给 IBM 公司，IBM 公司将自己持有的瑞士法郎和德国马克资金提供给世界银行。通过这种掉期交易，世界银行以比自己筹集资金更为有利的条件筹集到了所需的瑞士法郎和德国马克资金，IBM 公司则回避了汇率风险，以低成本筹集到美元资金。

这是迄今为止正式公布的世界上第一笔货币掉期交易。通过这项掉期交易，世界银行和 IBM 公司在没有改变与原债权人之间的法律关系的情况下，以低成本筹集到了自身所需的资金。

1982 年德意志银行进行了一项利率掉期交易。德意志银行向某企业提供了一项长期浮动利率的贷款。当时，德意志银行为了进行长期贷款需要筹集长期资金，同时判断利率将会上升，以固定利率的形式筹集长期资金可能更为有利。德意志银行用发行长期固定利率债券的方式筹集到了长期资金，通过进行利率掉期交易把固定利率变换成了浮动利率，再支付企业长期浮动利率贷款。这笔交易被认为是第一笔正式的利率掉期交易。

资料来源：佚名. 什么是掉期交易 [EB/OL]. [2006-10-20]. https://www.233.com/zq/jichu/Instructs/20061020/102020497.html.

三、外汇掉期交易的应用

掉期业务是利用远期外汇交易进行避险的一个重要工具。接下来，我们将进一步讨论如何利用掉期进行保值避险。

【例 5-7】 假设美国 ABC 公司需要 1 000 万欧元投资于法国证券市场（假定投资品种为固定收益证券），计划 3 个月后收回。已知欧元对美元的即期汇率为 EUR/USD=

1.3372/1.3374，3个月的远期差价为20/24。请问如何运用掉期业务规避 ABC 公司面临的汇率风险？

具体分析如下：

（1）计算远期汇率。

EUR/USD=1.3392/1.3398

（2）计算 ABC 公司买入即期欧元所需要的美元。

1 000×1.3374=1 337.4（万美元）（第一笔交易）

（3）计算 ABC 公司进行保值卖出远期欧元得到的美元。

1 000×1.3392=1 339.2（万美元）（第二笔交易）

这样不管3个月后的即期汇率如何变化，ABC 公司都可以确切地知道其投资成本和收益。

任务五　　　　　套利交易

套利交易，又称利息套汇，是指在两国短期利率出现差异的情况下，将资金从低利率的国家调到高利率的国家，从而赚取利息差额的行为。

例如，美国金融市场短期利率的年息为7%，而英国则为9.5%，于是短期投资者可以在美国以7%的年息借入一笔资金，购入英镑现汇，汇往英国。假如不考虑手续费等因素，在英国运用英镑资金的利润比在美国高2.5%，即英、美两国短期利率的差额。由于调往英国的资金无论是自有的还是借入的，都要承担英镑汇率波动的风险，因此在美国购进英镑现汇的同时，一般还要做一笔远期外汇买卖，即同时在英国售出与这笔美元资金等值的英镑远期外汇，以避免英镑汇率波动带来的损失，这种做法被称为抵补套利。如果套利者在将资金转移至高利率国家的同时，不做远期外汇交易，那么这种套利就是非抵补套利。

套利与套汇一样，是外汇市场上重要的交易活动。由于目前各国外汇市场联系十分密切，一有套利机会，大银行或大公司便会迅速投入大量资金，最终促使各国货币利差与货币远期贴水率趋于一致，使套利无利可图。套利活动使各国的利率和汇率形成了一种有机联系，互相影响制约，推动国际金融市场一体化。

思政小课堂

中国是最早产生纸币的国家。在北宋时期，第一张纸币性质的货币——北宋交子诞生了，当时的世界经济重心在东亚，北宋无疑是当时世界上最富裕发达的地区；今天，当人民币国际化浪潮席卷全球之时，世界经济重心再次向东方转移。正是在这样的背景下，随着"一带一路"倡议的实施和亚洲基础设施投资银行（AIIB）的诞生，一个新时代即将到来。

请思考：随着中国金融市场的全面开放，人民币国际化的纵深发展，中国外汇市场将面临哪些机遇和挑战？

项目思维导图

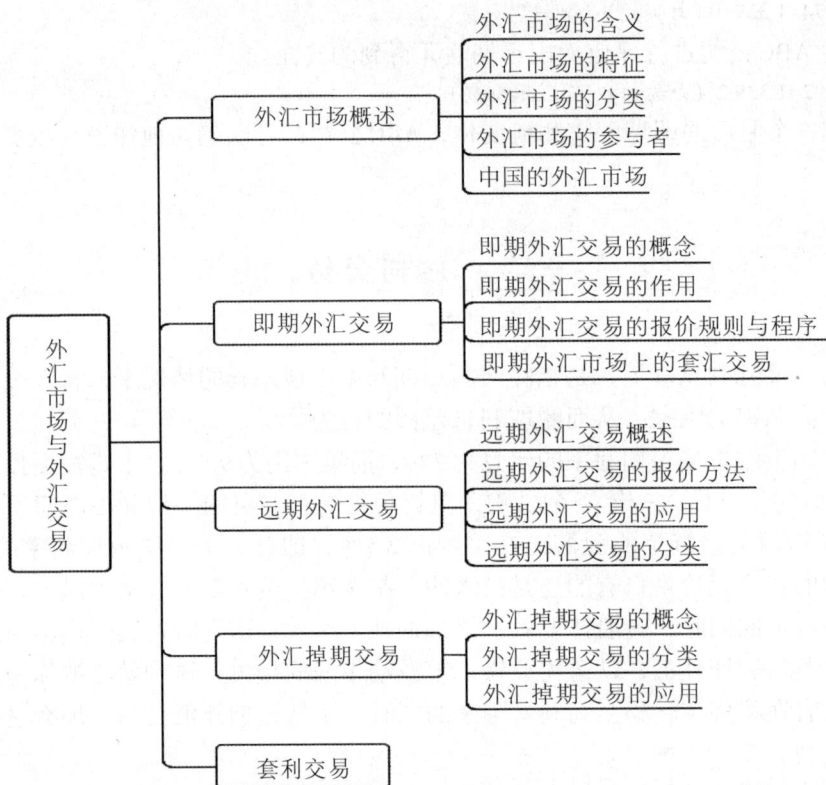

```
                                    ┌─ 外汇市场的含义
                                    ├─ 外汇市场的特征
                        外汇市场概述 ─┼─ 外汇市场的分类
                                    ├─ 外汇市场的参与者
                                    └─ 中国的外汇市场

                                    ┌─ 即期外汇交易的概念
                        即期外汇交易 ─┼─ 即期外汇交易的作用
                                    ├─ 即期外汇交易的报价规则与程序
                                    └─ 即期外汇市场上的套汇交易
   外汇市场与外汇交易 ─┤
                                    ┌─ 远期外汇交易概述
                        远期外汇交易 ─┼─ 远期外汇交易的报价方法
                                    ├─ 远期外汇交易的应用
                                    └─ 远期外汇交易的分类

                                    ┌─ 外汇掉期交易的概念
                        外汇掉期交易 ─┼─ 外汇掉期交易的分类
                                    └─ 外汇掉期交易的应用

                        套利交易
```

项目训练

一、单选题

1.银行与客户之间的外汇交易被称为（   ）。

A.外汇零售市场　　　　　　　　　B.外汇批发市场

C.无形外汇市场　　　　　　　　　D.有形外汇市场

2.即期外汇市场上，汇价通常采用的报价方式是（   ）。

A.买卖双价　　　　　　　　　　　B.买价

C.卖价　　　　　　　　　　　　　D.中间价

3.同业市场是指（   ）。

A.银行和客户之间的市场　　　　　B.银行间的市场

C.中央银行与商业银行之间的市场　　　D.商业市场

4.外汇市场的最重要参与者是（　　　）。

A.商业银行　　　　　　　　　　　　B.外汇经纪商

C.客户　　　　　　　　　　　　　　D.中央银行

5.如果两个外汇市场存在明显的汇率差异，人们就会进行（　　　）。

A.间接套汇　　　　　　　　　　　　B.直接套汇

C.抛补套利　　　　　　　　　　　　D.非抛补套利

6.即期外汇交易，又称现汇交易，是指买卖双方成交后，在（　　　）办理交割的外汇买卖。

A.两个营业日内　　　　　　　　　　B.当天

C.一个月以内　　　　　　　　　　　D.两个营业日以后

7.外汇市场的最终供给者和需求者是（　　　）。

A.外汇银行　　　　　　　　　　　　B.外汇经纪商

C.中央银行　　　　　　　　　　　　D.客户

8.假定某外汇银行对外报出即期汇率为1欧元=1.3219/49美元，1个月的汇水为20/40，则欧元对美元1个月远期汇率是（　　　）。

A.1.1219/0.9249　　　　　　　　　　B.1.3199/1.3209

C.1.3239/1.3289　　　　　　　　　　D.1.5219/1.7249

9.两种货币的利差是决定其远期汇率的基础，利率高的货币，其远期汇率会（　　　）。

A.升水　　　　　　　　　　　　　　B.贴水

C.平价　　　　　　　　　　　　　　D.不变

10.在商品的进口交易中，如果在支付外币货款时外汇汇率较合同签订时上涨，则进口商付出的本币会（　　　）。

A.更少　　　　　　　　　　　　　　B.更多

C.不变　　　　　　　　　　　　　　D.不确定

二、多选题

1.外汇市场的作用有（　　　）。

A.调节外汇供求　　　　　　　　　　B.形成外汇价格体系

C.便利资金的国际转移　　　　　　　D.提供外汇资金融通

E.防范外汇风险

2.外汇市场上的参与者有（　　　）。

A.外汇银行　　　　　　　　　　　　B.进出口商

C.外汇经纪商　　　　　　　　　　　D.中央银行

E.留学生

3.下列属于外汇零售市场的有（　　　）。

A.某中国服装公司向中国银行购买美元，用于进口西服面料

B.小李到美国大学留学，向中国银行购买2万美元的外汇

C.某公司到美国投资设立彩电生产线，向花旗银行购买5 000万美元的外汇

D.中国银行上海分行美元头寸太多，出售1亿美元给花旗银行上海分行

4.外汇银行对外报价时，一般同时报出（　　）。

A.交割价　　　　　　　　B.中间价　　　　　　　　C.买入价

D.卖出价　　　　　　　　E市场价

5.掉期交易实际上由（　　）组成。

A.两笔远期交易　　　　　　　　　　B.两笔即期交易

C.一笔即期交易，一笔远期交易　　　　D.以上都不对

三、实践应用题

1.某外汇交易员进行外汇交易，预测英镑将相对美元升值，因此在对手银行报价为GBP/USD=1.5740/60时买入500万英镑。一小时后银行报价变为1.5775/95，该交易员立刻将500万英镑卖出。请问该交易员的获利是多少？

2.某日伦敦外汇市场上即期汇率为1英镑=1.6955/1.6965美元，3个月远期贴水为50/60。请问3个月远期汇率是多少？

3.假设某日外汇市场即期汇率为GBP/USD=1.5520/1.5530，2个月远期汇率为20/10。美国出口商向英国进口商出口价值200万英镑的机器设备，合同规定2个月后以英镑付款。

请问：（1）如果现在就收款（即期收款），美国出口商可收到多少货款？

（2）若到期时市场汇率为GBP/USD=1.5115/1.5145，则美国出口商可收回多少美元？盈亏如何？

（3）若想控制风险，美国出口商该如何进行保值？到期可收回多少美元？盈亏如何？

四、实践训练

1.模拟在银行大堂场景下，银行客户经理对客户个人办理外汇换汇业务。班级学生可分客户、银行客户经理角色演练。

2.登录五家银行网站，查询其外汇理财产品情况，挑选一个外汇理财产品在班级分享。

项目六
外汇衍生品交易

学习目标

知识目标

理解外汇期货、外汇期权和货币互换的定义、分类及其特点；了解外汇期货交易的流程；掌握外汇期货、外汇期权和货币互换的应用策略。

能力目标

掌握外汇期货、外汇期权和货币互换的各种应用策略的能力。

操作目标

能够在模拟系统当中应用外汇期货、外汇期权和货币互换的应用策略进行模拟操作。

课程导入

衍生品的故事

情形一：阿松要买10斤猪肉，去猪肉铺找到老板阿荣，阿荣报价每斤猪肉50元，阿松拿出500元付款，带上10斤猪肉回家。这是现货交易，也就是基础资产。

情形二：阿松打算一个月后买10斤猪肉，怕猪肉涨价，去猪肉铺找到老板阿荣，说了他的要求。阿荣同意了，但价钱不再是50元每斤，而是每斤51元。为什么？阿荣也怕猪肉涨价，一个月后的价格他也说不准，他会先买好80斤猪肉冻在冷库里，一个月后卖给阿松。因为阿荣要先垫钱进货，还要占用冷库储存，他要收些成本。另外，阿荣还担心阿松一个月后忘了这事，先收了50元定金。这就是期货交易。

情形三：阿松打算一个月后买10斤猪肉，去猪肉铺找到老板阿荣，阿荣向他推荐了情形二的交易。但阿松存了个小心思：一个月后没准猪肉价格降下来了，我还是以51元每斤的价格购买，岂不是买贵了？于是，阿松跟阿荣说："能不能跟你商量一下，一个月后卖

课程导入

给我 10 斤猪肉，价格就是 51 元，这叫执行价。但是，到时如果我不想要了，可以放弃。"阿荣摇头不干，说好事不能都让你占了。此时阿松递上一包价值 20 元的烟，阿荣很开心地答应了。

　　资料来源：佚名. 外汇衍生产品介绍及交易［EB/OL］.［2019-12-29］. https://zhuanlan.zhihu.com/p/100041382.

　　思考讨论：如果你是故事中的阿松，你会选择哪种交易模式，为什么？

任务一　　　　　　外汇期货交易

一、外汇期货交易概述

外汇期货交易（foreign exchange futures transaction），是指外汇交易双方通过经纪人在期货交易所内以公开竞价的方式，买卖某一特定外汇，但是日期按事先约定好的，汇率也是事先约定好的，是期货合约的一种标准化的外汇交易方式。

由于现货市场存在价格波动的风险，因此许多交易者进入期货市场的目的是规避现货市场的价格风险。但是，还有很多交易者进入期货市场只是单纯地为了赚取价差，很少有人愿意进行实物交割，而是在合约到期前进行对冲。所谓对冲，是指买进（或卖出）期货合约的人在合约到期前卖掉（或买进）期货合约。在期货交易所，这些先买后卖或先卖后买的行为都是被允许的，只是规模受到限制。

（一）外汇期货交易的特点

外汇期货交易通过期货合约为交易者提供套期保值和投机机会，但是外汇期货交易又具有自己的特点：

1.合约标准化

合约标准化，即外汇期货合约标准化。外汇期货合约是交易所制定的一种法律契约，规定交易双方各自支付一定的保证金和佣金，并按照交易币种、交易数量、交割月份与地点等买卖一定数量的外汇。外汇期货合约对合约单位有严格要求，具体表现在以下方面：

（1）每份合约的交易单位是标准的。

各外汇交易所对外汇期货合约的面额都有特别规定，且不同币种的合约面额也不同。例如，在芝加哥国际货币市场上，每份外汇期货合约的标准面额为 10 万加元、1 250 万日元、12.5 万瑞士法郎、2.5 万英镑。各币种的交易数量必须等于合约面额的整数倍。

（2）每份合约的交割月份和交割日期是标准的。

所有外汇期货合约的交割月份均为每年的 3 月、6 月、9 月和 12 月。交割月份的第三个星期的星期三为该月交割日，如果这天不是营业日，则顺延到下一个营业日；交易截止日期在交割日前的第二个营业日，最后一个交易日的汇率为交易结算价。

【例6-1】某人2021年6月6日卖出一份三个月期的欧元期货合约，如果到9月6日前没有进行对冲（即在9月6日前没有买进一份相同的欧元期货合约），那么他必须在9月19日（本月第三个星期的星期三），用欧元现货按合约规定价格卖出。

2. 以美元报价

在外汇期货交易中，交易货币都以单位货币折算为多少美元进行报价。作为外汇期货合约标的货币（某种外汇）与商品期货标的物一样，它的价值应该用结算货币（通常为美元）表示出来。例如，某外汇期货交易报价为：1加元=0.7511美元、1新加坡元=0.7393美元、1瑞士法郎=0.9978美元。

3. 最小价格波动和最高限价

在国际金融市场上，各种货币的价格几乎每分每秒都在发生变化，而且有的货币价格波动幅度较大，有的货币价格波动幅度较小。基于货币价格波动幅度的差异，外汇期货交易所为了便于竞价，对外汇期货合约涉及货币的每次价格波动最小幅度给出统一规定，即最小价格波动。例如，英镑期货合约规定的最小价格波动为6.25美元，表明每份英镑合约的每次价格波动最小为6.25美元。

最高限价，也称每日价格波动的最高限度，是指在外汇期货交易中，合同约定货币的每日价格波动的最高幅度。如果外汇期货合约价格波动超过这个限度，该交易将自动停止。例如，英镑期货合约规定的最高限价为125美元，表示每份英镑合约的每日最高限价为125美元。

4. 实行保证金制度

外汇期货交易依赖标准化的期货合约，而期货合约是由外汇期货交易所制定的，所以交易所在外汇期货交易中充当第三方担保的角色。为保障交易双方的利益，交易所规定交易双方开立保证金账户，并缴纳一定数额的"初始保证金"，一般为合约价值的5%~10%。与"初始保证金"相关的一个概念是"维持保证金"。在外汇期货交易的过程中，对未平仓合约都要按当日收盘价进行清算，具体盈亏通过结算价格反映，并同时调整保证金账户金额。如果出现盈余，则保证金账户余额增加；如果出现亏损，则保证金账户余额减少。若保证金账户余额减少至低于交易所规定的最低保证金限额（即维持保证金），则交易所就会给客户发出追缴保证金的通知，如果客户在规定期限内没有追加保证金，交易所将强行平仓。

5. 每日盯市结算制度

所谓"盯市"，是指在外汇期货交易的过程中，在每日交易结束时，清算所（交易所下设的营利机构）要对每笔交易根据收市价格进行结算。结算价格，即浮动盈亏，反映在保证金账户上。这样交易双方可以清楚掌握盈亏状况。表6-1为中国金融期货交易所欧元对美元（EUR/USD）期货仿真交易合约。

（二）外汇期货交易的操作流程

外汇期货交易是在交易所内进行交易的，其参与者主要包括外汇期货交易所、外汇期货交易者、经纪商（充当中介）和清算公司。外汇期货交易通过这四类参与者完成，具体步骤包括：

表6-1　　　　中国金融期货交易所欧元对美元（EUR/USD）期货仿真交易合约

合约标的	欧元对美元即期汇率（EUR/USD）
合约面值	10 000欧元
最小变动价位	0.01美元/100欧元
合约月份	最近三个连续月份及随后三个季月，季月是指3月、6月、9月、12月
交易时间	9：00至11：30；13：00至15：15
最后交易日交易时间	9：00至11：30；13：00至15：00
每日价格最大波动限制	上一个交易日结算价的±3%
最低交易保证金	合约价值的3%
最后交易日	合约到期月份的第三个周三，遇国家法定假日顺延
交割日期	同最后交易日
交割方式	现金交割
交易代码	EF
上市交易所	中国金融期货交易所

　　资料来源：中国金融期货交易所。

　　1.选定经纪商，开立保证金账户

　　外汇期货交易所实行会员制度，只有交易所的会员才能进入交易所进行交易，且会员数量一般都是固定的，新会员只能通过递补方式获得交易席位进行交易。同时，要获得会员资格必须向有关部门申请并通过批准，会员每年都必须缴纳巨额会费。所以，个人或企业想要尽快进行外汇期货交易就要通过外汇期货经纪商。

　　各经纪商的服务条件存在或多或少的差别，外汇期货交易者根据自己意愿来选定经纪商。经纪商选定后，外汇期货交易者需要按规定在经纪商处开设保证金账户，并按交易规模缴纳"初始保证金"。

　　2.下达交易指令，委托买卖

　　下达交易指令，就是外汇期货交易者给经纪商下达订单，委托经纪商相应外汇期货交易的指令。委托订单主要包括以下内容：交易地点、交易方向（买进或卖出）、交易币种、交割月份、价格种类和有效期限。

　　（1）经纪商执行指令。

　　经纪商接到交易指令后，立刻通过电传或电话等通信手段将具体的指令内容传达给本公司驻交易所的（纯粹的）场内经纪人（也称"出市代表"或"候机人"）；场内经纪人收到指令后填写订单，并加盖时间戳记；然后将订单交给"跑手"送给交易圈内的交易员。场内交易员接到订单后，按照"价格优先、时间优先"的原则进行竞价成交；成交后在订单上记录成交价格和成交数量，随后将订单交给"跑手"，并将成交价报告"黄马甲"。如果出现新的成交价，"黄马甲"需将最新价格输入交易所的行情报价系统，通过交易所大屏幕显示出来，以随时报告场内的最新交易价格。

（2）交易登记、每日清算。

场内交易员将成交订单交给"跑手"后，"跑手"立即将成交单交给场内经纪人。场内经纪人接到成交单后，一方面，通知经纪商指令成交，经纪商进行登记并据此对客户保证金账户进行每日清算；另一方面，通知清算公司，清算公司对所有会员每日的每笔交易进行登记，收盘后进行清算。

二、外汇期货交易的应用

外汇期货交易的应用主要包括保值和投机两个方面。

（一）外汇期货交易用于保值

利用期货合约来降低或减少现汇市场汇率波动的风险，因此交易者进行的外汇期货交易属于保值目的。

利用外汇期货交易进行套期保值的具体操作是：根据外汇期货价格与现汇价格变动方向一致的特点，在外汇期货市场上进行与现汇市场方向相反的买卖，从而对所持有的外汇债权或债务进行保值。外汇期货套期保值分为多头套期保值和空头套期保值。

1.多头套期保值

多头套期保值，是指预期未来某一时间将在现汇市场上买入某种外汇时，为避免该外汇汇率上升导致成本增加，先在外汇期货市场买入相应外汇期货，处于多头地位；到规定时间在现汇市场买入现汇时，同时在外汇期货市场上把之前买的外汇期货卖出（即进行平仓）。

【例6-2】假设3月初美国某公司从英国进口了一批商品，价值500 000英镑，3个月后支付货款。为避免3个月后英镑汇率上升而增加成本，美国公司进入外汇期货市场，买入英镑期货（每份英镑期货合约的面值为62 500英镑）进行套期保值，具体操作见表6-2。

表6-2   多头套期保值的具体操作

现汇市场	外汇期货市场
3月初 预付500 000英镑 汇率：1英镑=1.5950美元 折合美元：500 000×1.5950=797 500（美元）	3月初 买进8份6月份到期的英镑期货 价格：1英镑=1.5955美元 价值：62 500×8×1.5955=797 750（美元）
6月初 买进500 000英镑 汇率：1英镑=1.6040美元 折合美元：500 000×1.6040=802 000（美元） 损失：797 500-802 000=-4 500（美元）	6月初 卖出8份6月份到期的英镑期货 价格：1英镑=1.6090美元 价值：62 500×8×1.6090=804 500（美元） 盈利：804 500-797 750=6 750（美元）

由表6-2可知，虽然3个月后英镑汇率上升导致该公司在现汇市场多支付4 500美元，但是在外汇期货市场上做了多头套期保值，盈利了6 750美元，从而弥补了现汇市场上的损失。当然，如果3个月后现汇市场汇率下跌，那么该公司在外汇期货市场就会出现损失，但是此时现汇市场可获得收益，从而弥补外汇期货市场上的损失。

2. 空头套期保值

空头套期保值，是指预期未来某一时间将在现汇市场上卖出某种外汇时，为避免该外汇汇率下跌导致收益减少，先在外汇期货市场卖出相应外汇期货，处于空头地位；到规定时间在现汇市场卖出现汇时，同时在外汇期货市场上将开始卖出的外汇期货进行平仓（即买入相应的外汇期货）。

【例6-3】假设3月10日美国某公司向英国出口了一批商品，价值50万瑞士法郎，2个月后收到货款。为避免2个月后瑞士法郎汇率下跌而遭受损失，英国公司进入外汇期货市场，卖出瑞士法郎期货（每份瑞士期货合约的面值为125 000瑞士法郎）进行套期保值，具体操作见表6-3。

表6-3   空头套期保值的具体操作

现汇市场	外汇期货市场
3月10日 预收500 000瑞士法郎 汇率：1美元=1.0105瑞士法郎 折合美元：500 000÷1.0105=494 805（美元）	3月10日 卖出4份5月份到期的瑞士法郎期货 价格：1瑞士法郎=0.9850美元 价值：125 000×4×0.9850=492 500（美元）
5月10日 卖出500 000瑞士法郎 汇率：1美元=1.0315瑞士法郎 折合美元：500 000÷1.0315=484 731（美元） 损失：484 731-494 805=-10 074（美元）	5月10日 买进4份5月份到期的瑞士法郎期货 价格：1瑞士法郎=0.9645美元 价值：125 000×4×0.9645=482 250（美元） 盈利：492 500-482 250=10 250（美元）

由表6-3可知，虽然2个月后瑞士法郎汇率下跌导致该公司在现汇市场少收入10 074美元，但是在外汇期货市场上做了空头套期保值，盈利了10 250美元，从而弥补了现汇市场上的损失。当然，如果2个月后现汇市场汇率上升，那么该公司在外汇期货

市场就会出现损失，但是此时现汇市场可获得收益，从而弥补外汇期货市场上的损失。

（二）外汇期货交易用于投机

通过对外汇期货套期保值的分析，大家应该知道外汇期货套期保值的前提是交易者拥有外币债权或承担外币债务。而投机者利用外汇期货进行投机，并不要求实际拥有外币债权或承担外币债务，只需要根据自己对汇率变化的预期，通过在外汇期货市场上低买高卖赚取差价。外汇期货交易用于投机主要包括卖空和买空两种做法。

1.卖空

卖空，是指投机者预期未来某货币汇率将下跌时，在外汇期货市场上先卖出该种货币的期货合约，然后再买进该种货币的期货合约。

【例6-4】假设3月初某投机者预期3个月后英镑对美元的汇率将下降，于是该投机者进入外汇期货市场以1英镑=1.3040美元的价格卖出10份6个月到期的英镑期货（每份英镑期货合约面额为62 500英镑）。如果3个月后英镑对美元汇率真的下跌了，该投机者以1英镑=1.2950美元的价格买入10份6个月到期的英镑期货合约，可以获得的利润为5 625美元（62 500×10×（1.3040-1.2950））。

2.买空

买空，是指投机者预期未来某货币汇率将上升时，在外汇期货市场上先买进该种货币的期货合约，然后再卖出该种货币的期货合约。

【例6-5】假设6月初某投机者预期3个月后日元对美元的汇率将上升，于是该投机者进入外汇期货市场以1日元=0.008940美元的价格买进10份9个月到期的日元期货（每份日元期货合约面额为12 500 000日元）。如果3个月后日元对美元汇率真的上升，该投机者以1日元=0.009055美元的价格卖出10份9个月到期的日元期货，可以获得的利润为14 375美元（12 500 000×10×（0.009055-0.008940））。

三、外汇期货交易与外汇远期交易的区别

外汇期货交易与外汇远期交易都是约定在未来某一确定的时间按照协议价格买卖一定数量外汇的交易活动。但是，二者借助的载体不同，外汇期货交易借助期货合约，是一种标准化的合约；而外汇远期交易借助远期合约，是一种非标准化的合约。所以，外汇期货交易与外汇远期交易属于两种不同的交易形式，它们之间存在很多区别（见表6-4）。

表6-4　　　　　　　　　　外汇期货交易与外汇远期交易的区别

区别	外汇期货交易	外汇远期交易
交易对象不同	期货合约	远期合约
交易双方关系不同	可以对对方完全不了解	必须对对方的信誉和实力等方面作充分的了解
交易场所不同	有固定场所，在交易所内进行交易，一般不允许场外交易	没有固定场所，通常在无形市场上进行交易
交易结果不同	绝大多数都通过平仓来了结	绝大多数都会在交割日交割
违约风险和管理方式不同	采取保证金制度和每日结算制度，且有清算公司介入，违约风险几乎为零	仅以双方的信誉为担保，违约风险很高
结算方式不同	每日结算，通过保证金账户反映浮动盈亏	到期才进行交割清算，期间均不进行结算

任务二　　　　　　　　　　　外汇期权交易

一、外汇期权交易概述

期权，是指赋予期权买者在未来某确定时间以约定价格买进或卖出一定数量某种商品或金融资产的权利。商品交易最早引入期权交易形式，后来才被引入金融资产交易中。

所谓外汇期权交易（foreign exchange options transaction），是指期权买方支付一定费用后，获得在约定时间内决定是否以约定价格买入或卖出约定数量的某种货币的权利的一种交易活动。简单来说，外汇期权交易中，交易双方实际上是交易"选择权"，买方买进"选择权"后，有权决定是否按照期权合约规定的价格买入或卖出某种外汇。

期权买方的基本思路是：当现汇市场行情对买方有关交易不利（如成本增加）时，买方就可以执行期权合约，即按合约规定价格向期权卖方买入或卖出某种外汇；相反，当现汇市场行情对买方有关交易有利（如成本减少）时，买方则放弃执行期权合约，即不按期权合约规定价格向期权卖方买入或卖出某种外汇，而是到现汇市场按现价（对自己有利）买入或卖出某种外汇。

（一）外汇期权交易的分类

按照不同的标准，外汇期权交易可分成很多不同种类。

1.按期权买者执行期权的有效期限划分

按期权买者执行期权的有效期限划分，外汇期权可分为欧式期权和美式期权。

（1）欧式期权是期权买者只能在期权到期日才能执行期权，这种期权在欧洲国家比较流行，所以称为欧式期权。

（2）美式期权是期权买者可以在期权到期前的任一营业日都可以执行期权。与欧式期权相比，美式期权更加灵活，买者可以在有效期内选择有利的时点执行期权；但是，对卖方来说，就很不利，即卖者的风险较大，所以美式期权的期权费比欧式期权高。

2.按期权买者的权利划分

按期权买者的权利划分，外汇期限可分为看涨期权和看跌期权。

（1）看涨期权（call option），也称买权，是指期权买者支付一定数量期权费后，有权在规定期限内按约定价格买进约定数量的某种外汇的期权。

（2）看跌期权（put option），也称卖权，是指期权买者支付一定数量期权费后，有权在规定期限内按约定价格卖出约定数量的某种外汇的期权。

3.按交易内容不同划分

按交易内容不同划分，外汇期权可分为现汇期权、外汇期货期权和期货式期权。

（1）现汇期权，也称现货期权，是指期权买者支付一定数量期权费后，有权在规定期限内按约定价格买进或卖出约定数量的某种外汇现汇的期权。

（2）外汇期货期权，是指期权买者支付一定数量期权费后，有权在规定期限内按约定价格买进或卖出约定数量的某种外汇期货的期权。

（3）期货式期权，是指期权交易双方以期货交易的方式，根据期货价格的涨跌买进或卖出该种期权。

（二）外汇期权交易的特点

与外汇期货交易相比，外汇期权交易具有以下特点。

1.权利与义务不对等

外汇期权交易借助期权合约完成交易，而在期权合约中，买方只拥有权利不承担义务，卖方则只承担义务不拥有权利。简单地说，就是当合约约定汇率与未来市场即期汇率相比，对外汇期权买方有利时，买方就有权执行合约，此时对卖方是不利的，但是卖方必须按照规定履行合约；反之，买方可以选择放弃执行期权，即放弃权利，卖方也必须接受买方的决定。

2.交易风险小，灵活性大

对期权买者来说，不管市场汇率如何变动，最大损失就是所支付的期权费，即损失额度有限，交易风险小。另外，期权交易不需要每日清算，到期前不会发生现金流动，当市场行情对买者有利时，可以选择执行期权，当市场行情对买者不利时可以放弃行权，具有很大的灵活性。

3.期权费不能追回

期权费，也称保险费，是买者为获得权利支付给卖者的费用。也就是说，期权费就是期权的价格。双方在期权合约成交时，买者一次性付清期权费，并且不管在期权有效期内买者是否行使期权，都不能追回期权费。另外，不同的期权合约期权费均不相同，期权费的高低主要与期权合约的有效期长短、汇率波动大小等有关。

二、外汇期权交易的应用

根据外汇期权交易的特点，基于外汇期权交易者的目的，外汇期权交易包括买入看涨期权和买入看跌期权。

（一）买入看涨期权

对拥有外汇债务的借款者或进口商来说，如果外汇汇率上升将导致负债增加（如进口货款增加等），通过买入外汇看涨期权，就可以锁定汇率水平，规避汇率上升的风险，达到保值目的。在看涨期权有效期内，当现汇市场即期汇率大于等于期权合约中的协议价格时，买方可执行期权；当现汇市场即期汇率小于期权合约中的协议价格时，买方应放弃执行期权。

【例6-6】假设2021年4月初某美国公司预计2个月后要支付500 000瑞士法郎的进口货款，此时外汇市场即期汇率为1美元=1.1135瑞士法郎。为了防止瑞士法郎汇率上升带来成本增加，该公司便买进4份6月份到期的瑞士法郎欧式看涨期权（每份瑞士法郎期权合约面额为125 000瑞士法郎），协议价格为1美元=1.1173瑞士法郎，期权费为1瑞士法郎=0.02美元。假定2个月后外汇市场即期汇率可能出现两种情况：（1）1美元=1.0005瑞士法郎；（2）1美元=1.1350瑞士法郎。请分别计算两种情况下该公司的进口成本。

分析：（1）当外汇市场即期汇率为1美元=1.0005瑞士法郎时，期权协议价格（1美元=1.1173瑞士法郎）低于市场即期汇率，所以该公司可以执行期权，按协议价格买入500 000瑞士法郎。

支付美元=500 000÷1.1173=447 507（美元）

支付期权费=500 000×0.02=10 000（美元）

支付美元总额=447 507+10 000=457 507（美元）

（2）如果该公司没有买进瑞士法郎看涨期权，则需要按外汇市场即期汇率买进500 000瑞士法郎（1美元=1.0005瑞士法郎）。

支付美元=500 000÷1.0005=499 750（美元）

支付美元总额=499 750+10 000=509 750（美元）

所以，当外汇市场即期汇率上升时，买进瑞士法郎看涨期权可以让该公司节省52 243美元（509 750-457 507）。

（3）当外汇市场即期汇率为1美元=1.1350瑞士法郎时，期权协议价格（1美元=1.1173瑞士法郎）高于市场即期汇率，此时该公司放弃期权，直接从市场上买进500 000瑞士法郎。

支付美元=500 000÷1.1350=440 529（美元）

支付期权费=500 000×0.02=10 000（美元）

支付美元总额=440 529+10 000=450 529（美元）

从两种情况下公司的实际支付状况可知，对于外汇看涨期权交易双方有：期权规定有效期内，当外汇市场即期汇率高于看涨期权协议价格时，对期权买方有利，应该执行期权，能获得盈利（减少成本支付），利润为市场即期汇率与期权协议价格的差额，并且外汇市场即期汇率越高，期权买方盈利越多，且可能是无限的。但是，对期权卖方来说，其盈亏状况与买方刚好相反，所以这种情况下，卖方的亏损有可能是无限的。当外汇市场即期汇率低于看涨期权协议价格时，对期权买方不利，应该放弃执行期权，买方损失仅为期权费（期权费是有限的），即有限亏损；对期权卖方来说，这种情况下可以获得有限收益，即期权费。

不考虑交易费用，外汇看涨期权的买方盈亏分布图如图6-1（a）所示，X为期权协议价格，C为期权费，E为外汇市场即期汇率。由于期权合约是零和游戏，买方盈亏与卖方盈亏刚好相反，据此可以画出外汇看涨期权卖方的盈亏分布图如图6-1（b）所示。

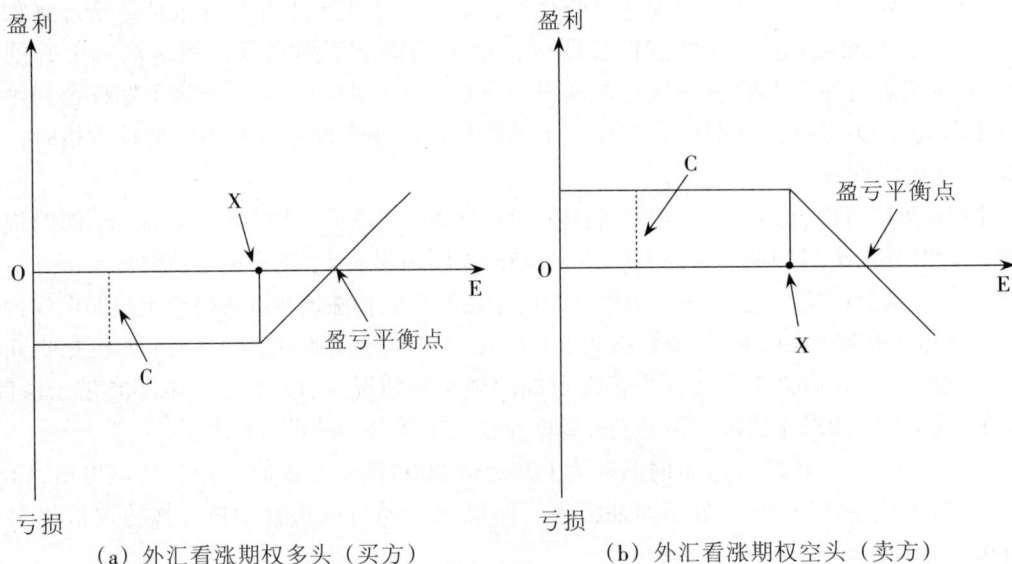

（a）外汇看涨期权多头（买方）　　　（b）外汇看涨期权空头（卖方）

图6-1　外汇看涨期权盈亏分布图

（二）买入看跌期权

对拥有外汇债权的投资者或出口商来说，如果外汇汇率下降将导致资产贬值（如出口收入减少等），通过买入外汇看跌期权，就可以锁定汇率水平，规避汇率下跌的风险，达到保值目的。在看跌期权有效期内，当现汇市场即期汇率小于或等于期权合约中的协议价格时，买方可执行期权；当现汇市场即期汇率大于期权合约中的协议价格时，买方应放弃执行期权。

【例6-7】假设2018年3月初美国某公司向英国出口一批货物，预计3个月后收到货款125 000英镑，此时外汇市场即期汇率为1英镑=1.2990美元。为了防止英镑汇率下降带来出口收入减少，该公司便买进2份6月份到期的英镑欧式看跌期权（每份英镑期权合约的面额为62 500英镑），协议价格为1英镑=1.3000美元，期权费为1英镑=0.02美元。假定3个月后外汇市场即期汇率可能出现两种情况：（1）1英镑=1.2750美元；（2）1英镑=1.4350美元。请分别计算两种情况下该公司的进出口收入。

分析：（1）当外汇市场即期汇率为1英镑=1.2750美元时，期权协议价格（1英镑=1.3000美元）大于市场即期汇率，所以该公司可以执行期权，按协议价格卖出125 000英镑（2×62 500）。

收入美元=125 000×1.3000=162 500（美元）

支付期权费=125 000×0.02=2 500（美元）

出口净收入=162 500-2 500=160 000（美元）

（2）如果该公司没有买进英镑看跌期权，3个月后则需要按外汇市场即期汇率卖出125 000英镑。

收入美元=125 000×1.2750=159 375（美元）

出口净收入=159 375-2 500=156 875（美元）

所以，当外汇市场即期汇率下跌时，买入英镑看跌期权可以让该公司避免收入减少3 125美元（160 000-156 875）。

（3）当外汇市场即期汇率为1英镑=1.4350美元时，期权协议价格（1英镑=1.3000美元）小于市场即期汇率，此时该公司应放弃期权，直接到现汇市场上卖出125 000英镑。

收入美元=125 000×1.4350=179 375（美元）

支付期权费=125 000×0.02=2 500（美元）

出口净收入=179 375-2 500=176 875（美元）

从两种情况下公司的实际支付状况可知，对于外汇看跌期权交易双方有：期权规定有效期内，当外汇市场即期汇率低于看跌期权协议价格时，对期权买方有利，应该执行期权，能获得盈利（避免收入减少），即期权协议价格与市场即期汇率的差额，并且外汇市场即期汇率越低，期权买方盈利越多，且可能是无限的。但是，对期权卖方来说，其盈亏状况与买方刚好相反，所以这种情况下，卖方的亏损有可能是无限的。当外汇市场即期汇率高于看跌期权协议价格时，对期权买方不利，应该放弃执行期权，买方损失仅为期权费（期权费是有限的），即有限亏损；对期权卖方来说，这种情况下可以获得有限收益，即期权费。

假设不考虑交易费用，外汇看跌期权的买方盈亏分布图如图6-2（a）所示，X为期权协议价格，C为期权费，E为外汇市场即期汇率。由于期权合约是零和游戏，买方盈亏与卖方盈亏刚好相反，据此可以画出外汇看跌期权卖方的盈亏分布图如图6-2（b）所示。

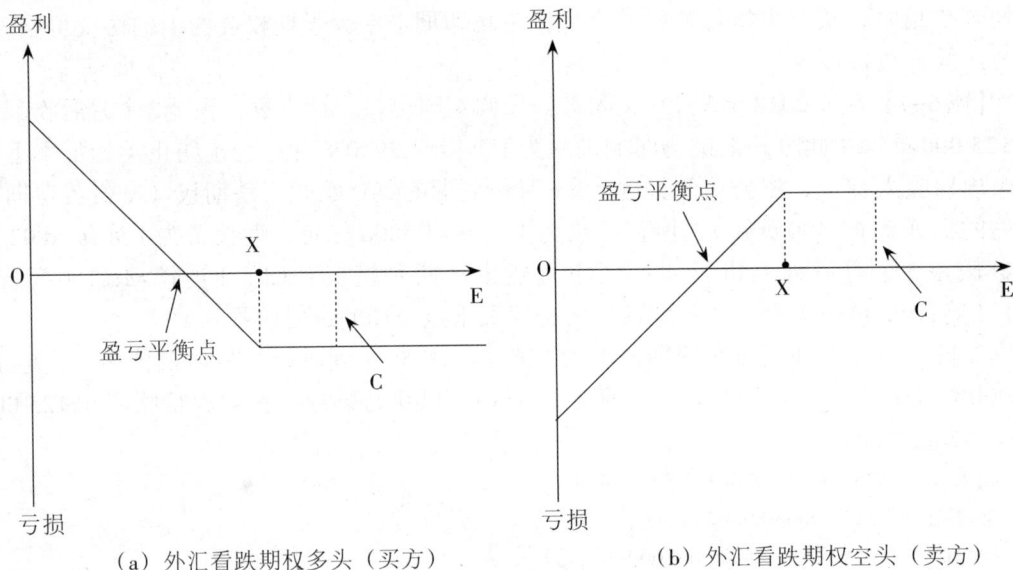

（a）外汇看跌期权多头（买方）   （b）外汇看跌期权空头（卖方）

图6-2　外汇看跌期权盈亏分布图

动画微课6-1

外汇衍生品
交易

三、外汇期权与外汇期货的区别

（一）买卖双方的权利、义务不同

外汇期权交易的买卖双方的风险收益是不对等的。期权的买方在合约的有效期内可以选择自己执行或者不执行该项权利。如果价格变动对自己有利，则执行该项权利，否则可以不执行该项权利；而期权的卖方在买方提出执行权利时，是不可以拒绝不履行的，因此买卖双方的权利、义务是不对等的。然而，外汇期货交易的买卖双方的风险收益是对等的。期货交易合同中规定，买卖双方在合同到期时都必须履行合同约定（除非到期前对冲）。

（二）交易的内容不同

外汇期权交易的是一种"权利"，即在未来某一时间点上以事先约定好的价格买卖外汇的权利；而外汇期货交易的是一定数量的外汇实物，会在合同中阐明。

（三）交易的价格不同

外汇期权交易价格在期权合约推出时就按交易所的规定确定了，写在合同中；外汇期货交易价格是由市场竞争形成的，这个价格是市场所有参与者对合约到期日价格的预期。

（四）保证金的规定不同

在外汇期权交易中，买方是不需要缴纳保证金的，只需要缴纳期权费（买期权的费用）；而在外汇期货交易中，买卖双方都需要缴纳保证金。

（五）损失的风险不同

在外汇期权交易中，买方亏损可能是有限的，亏损不会超过期权费，卖方的亏损则是无限的；在外汇期货交易中，买卖双方的风险都是无限的。

（六）获利的机会不同

在外汇期权交易中，由于期权的买方可以行使或放弃买进或者卖出标的物的权利，因此盈利的机会会相对大一些，尤其是在套期保值和投机交易中，如果使用外汇期权，更加大了获利的可能性。在外汇期货交易中，在做套期保值交易时，总会在现货市场或者期货市场中的某一个市场出现亏损，这无疑是摊薄了利润；在做投机交易时，可能会获得丰厚的回报，也可能血本无归。

案例探析6-1

中信泰富撞上法律红线，澳元外汇衍生品投资巨亏

中信泰富是投资、经营在澳大利亚的铁矿石项目的港资企业，它需要澳元资金及从欧洲进口部分设备。为对冲澳元、欧元升值的风险，锁定美元支出的成本，从2007年8月至2008年8月，中信泰富分别与汇丰银行、花旗银行等13家银行签订了24份"外汇远期合约"，做多澳元、欧元。合同约定在此后2年内，中信泰富每个月以0.87美元/澳元的平均兑换汇率，向对手方支付美元获得澳元。当时市场普遍认为，签约后澳元市场价要高于0.87美元。

然而，美国次贷危机的蔓延使得全球经济衰退风险加剧，澳大利亚央行不得不降息以刺激经济，澳元对美元汇率几乎直线回落，从2008年7月中旬到8月中旬短短一个月间，澳元对美元跌幅高达10.8%，几乎抹平了2008年以来的涨幅。同时，欧元对美元的汇率也持续下降。中信泰富所签订的外汇合约风险也充分暴露出来，终酿成巨额损失。

给中信泰富带来灭顶之灾的外汇远期合约全称为"累计目标可赎回远期合约"，它约束中信泰富以合同约定的价格在未来的特定时期内持续买入特定数量的澳元、欧元。澳元合约的平均行权价为1澳元=0.87美元，即中信泰富有权利、也有义务每月按1澳元=0.87美元的价格从对方手中买入一定数量的澳元，不论市场上澳元对美元的汇率是多少，直至达到合约中规定的累计金额。如果澳元市场汇率高于0.87美元，中信泰富就因以较便宜的价格买入澳元而获利；如果澳元市场汇率低于0.87美元，中信泰富以该行权价购入澳元就遭受了损失。

通常来说，远期合约下多空双方的权利和义务是对等的，风险承担也是相同的。但"累计目标可赎回远期合约"与此不同，其"可赎回"的特点限制了多头一方可能获得的最大收益。这是通过合同中的"敲出条款（knock-out）"来实现的，即合约在满足事先约定的条件时将被终止。例如，在中信泰富所签订的澳元合约中，每份合约都规定150万美元至700万美元不等的利润封顶线。当中信泰富因澳元汇率发生有利于自己的变化而获利，且获利水平达到封顶线时，合约就会终止。由于"敲出条款"的存在，中信泰富在这一系列澳元外汇远期合约下最多可获利5 150万美元，约4亿港元。如果中信泰富在合约下亏损，即澳元市场汇率跌至0.87美元以下，合约中却没有设定终止条款。也就是说，只要澳元对美元不断贬值，中信泰富就必须不断高位接货，并加大接货量，直到总量达到累计目标为止。由此可知，中信泰富仅获得了有限的收益，却承担了无限大的损失风险。

2009年3月25日，中信泰富公布了2008年年报，宣布亏损127亿港元，其中外汇合同所导致的变现亏损为146亿港元，成为这家著名蓝筹公司成立19年来的首次亏损。如果别除外汇合约的损失，中信泰富本可以在2008年交出一份税后盈利19亿港元的漂亮年报。然而，中信泰富外汇衍生交易巨亏事件震惊世界，被称为"美国次贷危机以来全球非金融机构遭遇的最大损失"。那么，谁应当对此承担责任呢？

中信泰富在事发后承认，外汇交易损失源于公司相关职能部门的越权操作以及未能正确估计到合约中潜在的最大风险。换句话说，中信泰富是"无知者无畏"。其中，在越权操作方面，主要是"负责集团对冲策略的财务董事张立宪没有按照既定的程序事先获得主席许可就进行外汇交易，超越了职权范围；而财务总监周至贤没有尽到监督责任，也没有提醒主席有不寻常的对冲交易"。

鉴于中信泰富外汇合约的巨大规模，一些投资者对媒体透露：中信泰富的上述解释隐瞒了外汇衍生交易决策的真实过程，由此引发了对中信泰富管理层串谋欺诈的质疑，最终导致香港警方的介入。不论关于中信泰富内部决策程序的最后调查结果如何，可以确定的一点是，中信泰富的公司治理的确存在很大缺陷。首先，管理层对于复杂的衍生品交易缺乏足够的认知；其次，在缔结规模如此巨大、风险如此之高的交易时，公司的决策程序、风险控制程序几乎完全失效。可以预见，公司股东将会追究相关高管、董事的渎职责任。

中信泰富在2008年9月7日发现外汇合同亏损。此时，澳元对美元的汇率已跌至0.84美元以下，中信泰富澳元合约的公允价值损失已经超过20亿港元，构成了重大损失，应即时披露该信息。然而，中信泰富延迟至10月20日才披露，此时损失已经达到155亿港元。延迟披露不仅导致中信泰富的股东无法及时抛出股票以减少损失，更关键的是，此时正至2008年9月华尔街风暴的前夜，数日之后，美国雷曼兄弟公司申请破产保护，推倒了华尔街风暴的第一张"多米诺骨牌"。可以设想，如果中信泰富及时披露外汇合约的重大损失，股东们甚至可能侥幸躲过华尔街风暴。因此，中信泰富的未及时披露不仅违反了公司法与证券监管法规，而且进一步造成了非常严重的损害后果。

不仅如此，9月12日中信泰富在旗下子公司大昌行的股东大会上发出了股东通函，对市场上有关公司外汇合约重大损失的传言给予了回应，称"……就董事所知，本集团自2007年12月31日以来的财务或交易状况概无出现任何重大不利变动"。这个公告覆盖的信息范围最迟可至9月9日。这意味着，中信泰富可能在发现合约损失之后两天，仍向外界宣布公司"无重大不利变动"。如果此情况最终被证实，中信泰富9月12日的公告内容就存在不实及误导成分，构成了标准的虚假陈述。

资料来源：克伟. 事件解密：中信泰富撞上了每一条法律红线？[EB/OL]. [2009-04-16]. https://business.sohu.com/20090416/n263432186_1.shtml.

思考题：

（1）中信泰富在做外汇交易决策时出现了哪些问题？这些问题是否违反了相关的法律、法规或者职业道德？

（2）在金融衍生品风险投资的过程中，企业应当注意些什么？

任务三　　　　　　　　　　外汇互换交易

一、外汇互换交易的含义

互换（swap），又称掉期，是指交易双方约定在一定期限内按照商定条件互换一系列现金流的合约。互换是比较优势理论在金融领域最典型的应用，根据比较优势理论，只要满足以下两个条件，就可以进行互换：双方对对方的资产或负债都有需求；双方在两种资产或负债上均具有比较优势。

互换的种类主要包括货币互换和利率互换。下面主要介绍货币互换。

货币互换（currency swap），即外汇互换，是指在规定期限内将一种货币的本金与另一种货币的等价本金进行交换。由于外汇市场存在汇率风险，进行货币互换，把一种外汇计价的资产或债务转换为以另一种外汇计价的资产或债务，可以规避汇率风险，降低成本，达到保值目的。

二、外汇互换交易的应用

外汇互换交易的应用主要是套期保值，一般包括三个步骤：期初的本金互换、期中的利息交换和期末的本金再交换。下面举例说明外汇互换的应用及具体操作。

【例6-8】某公司有一笔人民币贷款，金额为1 000 000万元人民币，贷款利率为固定利率4.35%，期限为5年，付息日为每年6月10日和12月10日。2015年12月10日提款，2020年12月10日到期归还。该公司提款后，将人民币兑换成美元，用于采购生产原料；生产出的产品出口收入为美元，没有人民币收入。在这种情况下，该公司的人民币贷款存在汇率风险。原因在于：该公司借的是人民币，采购时用的是美元，收入的也是美元。2020年12月10日，该公司需将美元收入换成人民币，如果到时人民币对美元升值，那么该公司需要用更多的美元来购买同样金额的人民币。这样，由于该公司的人民币贷款在借、用、还上都存在货币不统一的情况，因此存在汇率风险。

针对上述情况，该公司为控制汇率风险，可与A银行做一笔外汇互换交易。双方规定，交易于2015年12月10日生效，2020年12月10日到期，使用汇率为1美元=6.7030元人民币。

这一外汇互换的具体操作流程如下：

（1）提款日（2015年12月10日），该公司与银行互换本金：该公司从贷款银行提取贷款本金，同时支付给A银行，A银行按约定汇率向该公司支付相应数额的美元。

（2）付息日（2015—2020年期间每年的6月10日和12月10日），该公司与银行互换利息：A银行按人民币利率向该公司支付人民币利息，该公司将人民币利息支付给贷款银行，同时按约定的美元利率向A银行支付美元利息。

（3）到期日（2020年12月10日），该公司与A银行再次互换本金：A银行向该公司支付人民币本金，该公司将人民币本金归还给贷款银行，同时按约定的汇率向A银行支付相应数额的美元。

从外汇互换流程可知，互换期初和期末，该公司与A银行都按预先约定的同一汇率

（1美元=6.7030元人民币）互换本金，而且在贷款期间公司只支付美元利息，收入的人民币利息刚好用于归还人民币贷款利息，从而使公司完全规避了未来汇率变动的风险。

拓展阅读6-1

我国人民币外汇衍生品市场发展

中国现代外汇市场始于20世纪90年代初期。近年来，为更加有效地支持实施人民币经常项目可兑换、人民币汇率市场化、跨境贸易人民币结算以及跨境直接投资人民币结算等一系列重大改革举措，中国外汇交易中心相继于2005年8月、2006年4月、2007年8月和2011年4月在银行间外汇市场正式推出了人民币外汇远期、人民币外汇掉期、货币互换、外汇期权等产品，形成了我国外汇市场衍生产品结构体系。

境内外汇市场的发展，提升了人民币的国际地位和市场份额，有效加快了人民币国际化的改革步伐。不过，站在全球视野，对比国内和国际两个市场，我国境内外汇市场仍然存在一定的不足，主要表现在以下方面：

1.市场规模与我国经济的全球地位不相称。目前，我国国民生产总值占全球国民生产总值的比例接近15%，而境内外汇市场日均交易额仅为全球外汇市场的1%左右，相差悬殊。

2.人民币市场规模发展迅速，对在岸市场构成反客为主的压力。中国人民银行发布的人民币国际化报告显示，香港、新加坡、伦敦等主要离岸市场人民币外汇日均交易量是境内市场日均交易量的4倍以上。

3.目前，外汇市场的参与者结构过于单一，造成市场的活跃度不高。从2005年7月我国启动人民币汇率形成机制改革以来，银行间人民币外汇市场发展迅速，但对参与者的主体限制仍比较严格，市场主体以金融机构为主，客观上限制了市场的发展。2015年银行间交易占整个外汇市场的比重为67.7%，银行与非金融客户交易的比重为30.5%，而在国际外汇市场，银行占整个外汇市场交易金额的比重已经由20世纪90年代的70%左右下降到了30%左右。

国内和国际外汇市场对比呈现的反差，究其原因，除了人民币汇率形成机制改革尚未最终完成、境内外汇市场对外开放程度还不够等宏观因素外，也有在岸市场存在人民币衍生品交易品种不够丰富，外汇期权和外汇远期的成交不够活跃，汇率风险管理工具不够均衡等原因。

资料来源：孔军. 推动我国人民币外汇衍生品市场发展［EB/OL］.［2017-02-16］. https：//www.financialnews.com.cn/sc/wh/201702/t20170216_112731.html.

思考题：

（1）请结合材料说一说我国外汇市场发展面临什么问题？

（2）请查阅资料，讨论我国外汇市场可能面临哪些机遇？

思政小课堂

2020年4月，珠海格力电器股份有限公司发布《关于2020年开展外汇衍生品交易业务的专项报告》。报告指出：董事会同意公司使用不超过100亿美元开展外汇衍生品交易业务。公司2019年出口收汇金额约25亿美元，进口付汇金额约5亿美元，为规避上述两项业务的汇率风险，公司有必要开展外汇衍生品交易业务。公司开展外汇衍生品交易业务以进行外汇套期保值、管理进出口业务汇率风险和调剂资金余缺为目的，不存在任何投机性操作。

请进一步查询资料，结合本项目所学内容分析：

（1）该公司为什么要进行外汇衍生品交易？

（2）该公司的外汇衍生品交易主要包括哪些交易品种？

（3）结合我国"十四五"规划新目标，谈谈对我国外汇市场发展的前景展望。

资料来源：佚名. 格力电器：关于2020年开展外汇衍生品交易业务的专项报告［EB/OL］. ［2020-04-30］. https://stock.zdcj.net/f10new.php?newid=ggmx000651_6226555.html.

项目思维导图

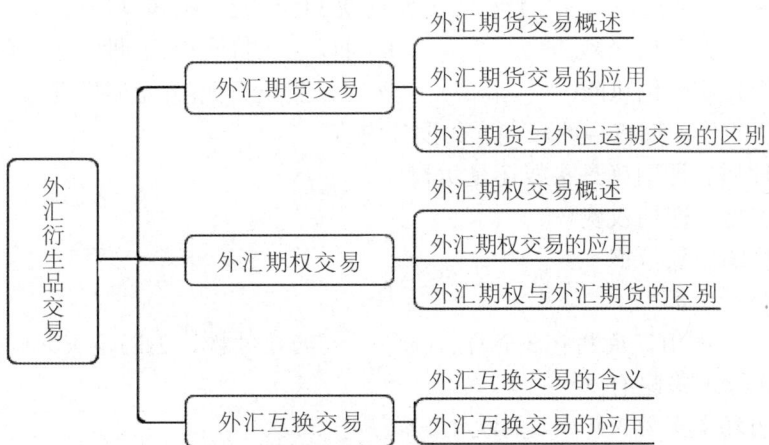

项目训练

一、单选题

1.利用（   ）可以规避由汇率波动所引起的汇率风险。

A. 利率期货　　　　B. 外汇期货　　　　C. 商品期货　　　　D. 金属期货

2. (   ) 交易中，买方向卖方支付一定费用后，在未来给定时间，有权按照一定汇率买进或者卖出一定数量的外汇资产。

A. 外汇期货　　　　　B. 外汇互换　　　　　C. 外汇掉期　　　　　D. 外汇期权

3. 投资者在外汇期货市场上进行与现汇市场方向相反的买卖，从而对所持有的外汇债权或债务进行保值。这一过程被称为 (   )。

A. 套期保值　　　　　B. 套利　　　　　C. 互换　　　　　D. 投机

4. 以下属于利率互换的特点是 (   )。

A. 交换利息差额，不交换本金　　　　　B. 既交换利息差额，又交换本金

C. 既不交换利息差额，又不交换本金　　D. 以上都不是

5. 一个投资者在国际货币市场（IMM）上以GBP1=USD1.5000的价格卖出两份英镑期货合约，持有到期。交割日的结算价为GBP1=USD1.4500，请问如果此时平仓，则该投资者的盈亏情况是 (   )。（每份英镑期货合约的面值为62 500英镑）

A. 盈利6 250美元　　B. 盈利3 125美元　　C. 亏损6 250美元　　D. 亏损3 125美元

二、多选题

1. 以下关于外汇期货的说法，正确的有 (   )。

A. 外汇期货合约的内容由买卖双方自行决定

B. 外汇期货交易需要缴纳保证金

C. 外汇期货多数以美元结算

D. 外汇期货合约到期时，一般按规定交割实物

2. 某美国机械设备进口商3个月后需支付货款3亿日元，则该进口商 (   )。

A. 可能承担日元升值风险　　　　　B. 可以买入日元/美元期货进行套期保值

C. 可能承担日元贬值风险　　　　　D. 可以卖出日元/美元期货进行套期保值

3. 一个完整的外汇期权合约应包含的要件有 (   )。

A. 期权的性质，即明确是买权还是卖权

B. 期权的价格，即期权费

C. 标的资产的协议价格

D. 期权的合约金额

4. 假设一个欧洲出口商将在3个月后收到一笔美元付款，为防范美元贬值的风险，该出口商可以采取的策略有 (   )。

A. 在期货市场上买入3个月期的欧元

B. 在期货市场上卖出3个月期的欧元

C. 买入3个月期的美元的看跌期权

D. 卖出3个月期的美元的看涨期权

5. 货币互换的进行，必须要求两笔资金 (   )。

A. 金额相同　　　　　　　　B. 期限相同

C. 计算利率方法相同　　　　D. 货币不同

三、判断题

1. 金融衍生品市场上存在大量的投机交易，投机交易的存在破坏了市场

秩序。　　　　　　　　　　　　　　　　　　　　　　　　　（　　　）

2. 外汇期货交易只能够为参与者规避风险，不能够为投机者提供获利机会。　　　　　　　　　　　　　　　　　　　　　　　　　（　　　）

3. 外汇期权产品买卖的是一种权利，所以买方即可以行使这项权利，也可以放弃这项权利。　　　　　　　　　　　　　　　　　　　　　（　　　）

4. 外汇期货买卖双方的权利、义务是对等的；而外汇期权买卖双方的权利、义务是不对等的。　　　　　　　　　　　　　　　　　　　　（　　　）

5. 货币互换的前提条件是双方对对方的货币都有需求。　　　　　（　　　）

四、实践应用题

1. 假设某投资者在9月初预测3个月后英镑对美元汇率将下跌，于是该投资者以1英镑=1.3050美元价格卖出1份12月份到期的英镑期货。请问：如果12月份英镑对美元即期汇率为1英镑=1.2950美元，该投资者能否获利？如果可以获利，请计算具体获利金额。

2. 假设2020年4月某英国公司预计2个月后要支付2 500万日元的进口货款，此时外汇市场即期汇率为1英镑=147.050日元。为了规避汇率风险，该公司买进2份6月份到期的日元期权合约（每份日元期权合约的面额为12 500 000日元），协议价格为1日元=0.0075英镑，期权费为1日元=0.0002英镑。假定2个月后外汇市场即期汇率可能出现两种情况：1英镑=146.850日元；1英镑=147.350日元。请分别计算两种情况下该公司的进口成本。

项目七
国际结算

知识目标

理解国际结算的概念及含义，了解国际结算方式的演变；掌握常见的国际结算工具的特点。

能力目标

掌握汇款、托收、信用证等传统的国际结算方式，掌握备用信用证、银行保函等新型的国际结算方式。

操作目标

能够借助模拟系统进行汇率、托收、信用证等业务的操作。

课程导入

人民币结算系统"朋友圈"不断扩大

在中国经济影响力增加的背景下，截至2020年7月底已有97个国家和地区的984家金融机构加入中国的跨境支付系统，估计在年内将突破1 000家。

当今的国际资金结算以美元为主，主要通过总部设在比利时的环球银行间金融电信协会（SWIFT）的系统来交换汇款信息，平均每天的结算额为5万亿~6万亿美元，其中美元支付约占四成，人民币支付所占比重不足2%。

人民币国际结算系统，又称人民币跨境支付系统（Cross-border Interbank Payment System，CIPS）是由中国人民银行组织开发的独立结算系统，旨在进一步整合现有人民币跨境支付结算渠道和资源，提高跨境清算效率，满足各主要时区的人民币业务发展需要，该系统于2012年4月12日开始建设，2015年10月8日正式启动。

在2015年10月启动后，加入的银行有865家，遍布89个国家和地区。对此，中国人民银行引进了"人民币跨境支付系统"。以英语办理业务，每笔交易即时结算，扩大了人民币结算的范围。由在该系统开设账户的"直接参与银行"和通过直接参与银行接入的"间接参与银行"构成，只要与任意银行完成交易，就可轻松将资金转移至中国企业的账户，根据运营母体跨境银行间支付清算（上海）有限责任公司的公告，可以看到人民币结算量正在逐渐增加。不仅是金额，从交易笔数来看，2018年为144万笔，比上年增长15%。

截至2019年4月，包括中资银行在内，有来自不同国家和地区的865家银行加入了该系统，如日本就有三菱UFJ和瑞穗两家超大型银行、21家地方性银行、7家外资银行的东京分行，总计30家银行参与，其中两家超大型银行成为直接参与银行。引人关注的是，俄罗斯有23家银行参与，俄罗斯企业在支付来自中国的进口货款方面采用人民币的比率从2014年的9%提高至2017年的15%。俄罗斯中央银行截至2018年9月，将外汇储备中人民币的比率提高至14%，与2017年9月的1%相比大幅提高，美元比率则从46%下调至23%。

加入人民币跨境支付系统的另一个很明显特点是，中国是在基础设施项目和资源开发领域加强影响力的国家，南非和肯尼亚等非洲各国有31家银行参与，多于北美。参加中国"一带一路"倡议的国家，加入人民币跨境支付系统得也越来越多，人民币结算的需求增高。但是，人民币要想成为轴心货币的道路还很遥远，人民币在SWIFT的资金结算中的份额截至2019年3月仅为1.89%，低于美元、欧元、英镑和日元，排在第五位，与每天收发3000万件以上电文的SWIFT相比，人民币跨境支付系统的规模仍然很小。

资料来源：吕栋. 日媒称中国国际结算系统存在感提高［EB/OL］.［2019-05-22］. https://www.guancha.cn/internation/2019_05_22_502562.shtml.

思考讨论：
（1）我国为什么要推出人民币跨境支付系统？
（2）人民币跨境支付系统和"一带一路"战略有何关系？

国际贸易活动最终落脚在交易资金的收回和支出，需要通过一定的工具和手段实现债权债务的清偿，完成资金的转移，银行的国际结算业务为完成这一过程提供了通道。然而，伴随着贸易活动资金的收付，进出口企业会出现资金余缺不均衡的情况，买方、卖方或者双方可能会需要融资，这就为银行带来了伴随国际结算的贸易融资。本项目主要介绍国际结算及在结算基础上的贸易融资活动。

任务一　　　　　　　国际结算概述

一、国际结算的含义

国际结算（international settlement）是指对国际债权债务进行清算的一种经济行为。处于两个不同国家或地区的当事人，因为商品买卖、提供服务、资金调拨、国际借贷等业务，运用一定的金融工具，通过银行或其他金融机构进行货币收入的行为。

从国际结算发生的原因来看，国际结算总体上可以概括为两类：具有贸易背景的贸易结算和不具备贸易背景的非贸易结算。非贸易结算以汇款为主，操作比较简单，风险小。贸易结算较为复杂，风险较大。本书主要介绍贸易结算。

从微观层面来看，国际结算属于银行的中间业务，比国内结算复杂，是以国际贸易为基础、与国际金融密不可分的。从宏观层面来看，国际结算以最科学、最有效的方法来清算国际间以货币表现的债权债务关系或跨国转移资金。国际结算的研究对象主要是支付手段、结算方式和以银行为中心的划拨方式。国际结算不一定需要贸易融资，但融资一定离不开国际结算，在此前提下，国际结算的主导地位非常明显。国际贸易融资也可以促进国际贸易结算业务的发展，有利于银行吸收存款，增强银行资金实力，改善银行资金质量。

知识链接7-1

国际结算的发展

19世纪以前的国际结算被称为传统国际结算。随着国际贸易的发展和现代商业银行的产生，传统的国际结算不断发生着变化。从现金结算发展到非现金结算，从凭货付款到凭单付款，从买卖直接结算发展到通过银行结算，进而又发展成国际结算与贸易融资相结合。

19世纪以后，国际结算进入现代阶段。国际结算的特点是以票据为基础、单据为条件、银行为中枢、结算与融资相结合且日益规范。在不断的发展中，国际结算在国际领域中有以下特点：单据标准化、以快邮处理函件、结算手段电子化、非信用证业务增加、融资期限延长。单证成为国际贸易的基本载体，也是国际结算的重要依据。

资料来源：佚名. 国际结算发展趋势［EB/OL］.［2020-05-23］. https://www.docin.com/p-2368273214.html.

二、国际结算工具

（一）结算工具

国际结算中使用的支付工具之一是票据。票据是出票人签发的无条件约定自己或要求其他人支付一定金额，经背书可以转让的书面支付凭证。票据一般包括汇票、本票和支票三类。

1.汇票（bill of exchange）

汇票是国际结算的主要支付工具，是出票人向受票人签发的要求对方于见票时或将来某一时间，对某人或持票人无条件支付一定金额的书面支付命令。汇票本质是债权人提供信用时开出的债权凭证。其流通使用要经过出票、背书、提示、承兑、付款等法定程序，若遭拒付，可依法行使追索权。

汇票可分为四类：

（1）按出票人不同，可分为银行汇票和商业汇票。银行汇票的出票人和付款人都是银行，商业汇票的签发者为企业或个人。

（2）按付款时间不同，可分为即期汇票和远期汇票。即期汇票在提示或见票时即付。远期汇票是特定期限或特定日期付款的汇票。

（3）按有无附单据，可分为光票和跟单汇票。光票不附单据，而跟单汇票附货运单据。

（4）按承兑人不同，可分为银行承兑汇票和商业承兑汇票。银行承兑汇票是由银行承兑远期汇票，商业承兑汇票是由企业或个人承兑的远期汇票。

图7-1是填写完整的汇票：

教学视频7-1

汇票的分类

图7-1　汇票

2.本票（promissory note）

本票是指由出票人签发、承诺自己于见票时或于一定时间向收款人或持票人无条件支付一定金额的书面凭证。当事人只有出票人和收款人。本票可分为商业本票、银行本票、国际小额本票、旅行支票、流通存单、中央银行本票等。图7-2是填写完整的本票：

```
                         Promissory Note

USD 8 000.00                              New York，6 Jun.，2020
   At 60 days after date we promise to pay Nanjing Import and Export Corp. or order the
sum of US dollars eight thousand only.


                                          For CITIC BANK New York
                                          Signature
```

图 7-2　本票

3. 支票（check）

支票是银行存款户对银行签发的授权其见票对某人或指定人或持票人即期无条件支付一定金额的书面支付命令。

支票必须具以下主要内容：

（1）写明"支票"字样；

（2）无条件支付命令；

（3）付款银行名称；

（4）出票人签字；

（5）出票日期和地点；

（6）付款地点；

（7）一定金额；

（8）收款人或其指示人。

图 7-3 是填写完整的支票：

```
Cheque for USD 10 000.00                    London，26th Sept. 2020
Pay to the order of ABC.Co.
the sum of TEN THOUSAND POUNDS ONLY .
To Midland Bank Ltd.

                                           For D Co. London
                                           Signature
```

图 7-3　支票

（二）国际结算中的单据

国际结算中的单据分为基本单据和附属单据。

基本单据是指出口方向进口方提供的单据，有商业单据、运输单据、保险单据。这些单据在国际贸易实务中都有详细介绍，在此不再赘述。

附属单据是指出口方为符合进口方政府法律法规而提供的特殊单据，这些单据又称官方单据或政府单据。除进出口许可证外，还有海关发票、领事发票、产地证等。

教学视频 7-2

汇票、本票和
支票的区别

任务二　传统国际结算方式

国际结算方式，又称国际支付方式，在进出口买卖合同中也称支付条件。传统的国际结算方式有汇款、托收、信用证三类，备用信用证、保函、保理、福费廷等是现代新的融合融资、担保及结算于一体的综合结算方式，也是未来的发展方向。国际结算业务主要通过银行等金融机构进行。

动画微课7-1

商业银行国际结算业务

一、汇款

（一）汇款的定义

汇款（remittance），又称汇付，是指由付款人主动向银行提出申请，把一定金额的货币通过银行或者其代理行和国外联行，汇给指定的收款人的一种结算方式。

结算方式按照资金流及结算工具传递的方向，可分为顺汇和逆汇两类。顺汇也称汇付，债务人提交申请书及款项给银行，委托银行使用具体的结算工具，交付一定金额给债权人或收款人的结算方法。顺汇的特点是结算工具和资金传递运动方向一致，从付款方到收款方。逆汇，又称出票，债权人开出汇票，委托银行向国外债务人收款。逆汇的特点是结算工具和资金传递运动方向相反。

（二）汇款的当事人

1.汇款人

汇款人（remitter）是指向银行提出申请，要求汇出款项的人。在进出口业务中通常为合同的进口商。

2.汇出行

汇出行（remitting bank）是指受到汇款人的委托并根据其指示，向其分行或代理行发出付款委托书，委托它们向收款人解付汇款的银行。在进出口业务中通常为进口商所在地的银行。

3.汇入行

汇入行（paying bank）又称付款行或解付行，是指接受汇出行的委托，把款项付给指定收款人的银行。在进出口业务中通常为出口商所在地的银行，汇入行经常是汇出行的海外分行或者代理行。

4.收款人

收款人（payee）是指收取汇款款项的人，即汇款业务的受益人。在进出口业务中通常为合同的出口商。

教学视频7-3

票汇、电汇和信汇的比较

（三）汇款的种类

1.电汇

电汇（telegraphic transfer，T/T）是汇出行应汇款人的申请，用加押电报（tested cable）、电传（telex）或SWIFT形式指示汇入行付款给指定收款人的一种汇款方式。

电汇业务在银行业务中一般为当天处理，因此具有资金转移速度快、安全可靠、效率较高的特点。但是，因为交款速度快，银行不能利用客户的资金，所以汇款人要承担较高的电汇费用。由于电信技术的飞速发展，电信业务的成本大大降低，现在国际汇款业务中大多数采用电汇方式，而且多用于急需用款和大额汇款。

电汇业务流程如图7-4所示。

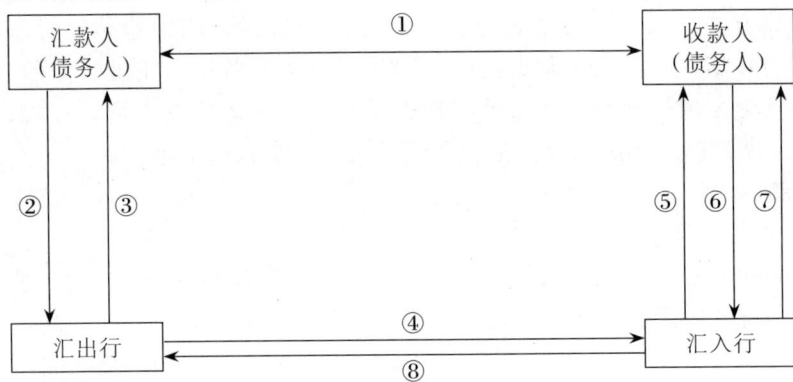

图7-4　电汇业务流程

电汇业务流程的步骤：

①汇款人和收款人双方建立贸易关系，决定采用电汇结算方式；

②汇款人填写汇款申请书，交付汇款资金及手续费；

③汇出行收妥资金及费用后，出具电汇回执给汇款人，确立汇出行与汇款人自检的业务委托关系；

④汇出行通过电报、电传、SWIFT等方式，向汇入行发出电汇委托书；

⑤汇入行收到电信指令后，核对密押无误，制作电汇通知书给收款人；

⑥收款人持电汇通知书及身份证明到汇入行取款；

⑦汇入行核对凭证并解付汇款；

⑧汇入行向汇出行发出付讫通知。

知识链接7-2

环球银行金融电信协会

环球银行金融电信协会（Society for Worldwide Interbank Financial Telecommunications, SWIFT），是国际银行同业间的国际合作组织，成立于1973年，全球大多数国家的银行已使用SWIFT系统。SWIFT系统的使用，为银行间的结算提供了安全、可靠、快捷、标准化、自动化的通信业务，从而提高了银行的结算速度。由于SWIFT系统的格式标准化，信用证的格式主要是用SWIFT电文。

SWIFT总部设在比利时的布鲁塞尔，同时在荷兰阿姆斯特丹和美国纽约分别设立了交换中心（switching center），并为各参加国开设集线中心（national concentration），为国际金融业务提供快捷、准确、优良的服务。SWIFT运营着世界级的金融电文网络，银行和其他金融机构通过它与同业交换电文（message）来完成金融交易。除此之外，SWIFT还向金融机构销售软件和服务，其中大部分的用户都在使用SWIFT网络。

1980年，SWIFT联接到香港。中国银行于1983年加入SWIFT，是SWIFT的第1 034家成员行，并于1985年5月正式开通使用，成为中国与国际金融标准接轨的重要里程碑。之后，中国的各国有银行、商业银行及上海和深圳证券交易所，也先后加入SWIFT。

资料来源：佚名. SWIFT背景知识介绍［EB/OL］.［2020-03-20］. https://www.docij.com/doc/a1100cf2ba0d4a7303763a01.html.

2.信汇

信汇（mail transfer，M/T）是指应汇款人的申请，由汇出行将信汇委托书或支付委托书通过航空邮寄发往汇入行，授权其解付一定金额给收款人的一种汇款方式。信汇汇款费用低，但速度比电汇慢，目前在发达国家市场银行间已经很少使用信汇这种支付方式。信汇业务的流程类似于电汇业务流程。

3.票汇

票汇（demand draft，D/D）是指汇出行应汇款人的申请，代其开立以汇入行为付款人的银行即期汇票，由汇款人自行寄给国外收款人，由收款人到汇入行凭票取款的一种汇款方式。需要指出的是，票汇业务中使用的支付指令是一张即期银行汇票，由汇出行作为出票人，由汇入行作为付款人，由汇款收款人作为汇票的收款人。票汇的特点是安全性相对较差，银行参与较少，因此也最便宜。

由于汇款业务的资金负担和风险集中在付款方，因此在我国大多用于支付预付款或尾款，在国际结算中所占份额不大。在发达国家之间，由于大量的贸易是跨国公司的内部交易，且外贸企业在国外也有可靠的贸易伙伴，汇款仍然是主要的结算方式之一。

在实际的国际贸易业务中，具体选择哪种结算方式通常应结合企业交易情况、市场销售状况、交易对手信用状况等综合考虑，由交易双方共同商议决定。

教学视频7-4

托收基本要素的比较

二、托收

（一）托收的定义

托收（collection）是债权人（卖方）提供汇票及有关单据委托本国银行向国外债务人（买方）收款的一种结算方式。托收是建立在商业信用基础上的结算方式。银行在办理托收业务时是出口商/卖方的代理人，仅仅代理收款，并不承担付款的责任。在托收业务中，出口商/卖方承担的风险较大。

（二）托收的当事人

1.委托人

委托人（principal），即把汇票和贸易单据等交给银行委托收款的人，一般是出口商（卖方）、债权人、受益人。由于委托人常常需要出具汇票委托银行向国外付款人收款，因此往往被称为汇票的出票人（drawer）。

2.托收行

托收行（collection bank）一方面接受委托人的委托受理托收业务，另一方面委托其国外的联行或代理行向债务人收款。托收行一般是委托人的开户行。托收行按照委托人的指示行事，负责接收单据并制作托收指示。托收行的业务要遵照国际惯例，如果委托人没有在申请书中加以指示的，一切按照常规处理。

3.代收行

代收行（collecting bank），又称受托行，指的是接受委托行的委托向债务人（买方）收款的银行，通常是托收行的海外分行或者代理行。因为是托收行的代理行，所以其一切活动均需要按照托收行的指令办事，否则责任自负。一般情况下，代收行在收到全部货款之后向进口商放单，对因交单延误导致的任何后果不负责。

4.付款人

付款人（drawee/payer）指的是汇款的付款人，即债务人、进口商，是收款的对象。在收到代收行的代收通知后，按照合同规定付款并换取单据。

除了以上四个基本当事人外，托收业务中还涉及提示行和代理人。提示行一般是负责向债务人提示汇票和单据的银行，一般情况下由代收行担任提示行。代理人，指的是在付款人拒付货款时，代替委托人在付款地处理后续事项的人。

（三）托收的分类

根据办理托收时是否附有货运单据，可分为光票托收和跟单托收。

1.光票托收（clean collection）

光票托收是指卖方开立汇票时不附带任何货运单据的托收，即卖方提交汇票，委托银行代为收款。光票托收的汇票，可分为即期和远期两种。在实际业务中，由于一般代收金额都较小，即期付款的汇票较多见。

2.跟单托收

跟单托收是卖方开立汇票连同一整套货运单据一起交给国内的托收行，再委托国外的代收行代收货款。跟单托收中单据是非常重要的，根据向进口商交单条件的不同，跟单托收可分为付款交单和承兑交单两种。

（1）付款交单（documents against payment，D/P）是指出口商的交单以进口商的付款为条件，即出口商发货后，取得货运单据，委托银行办理托收，并指示银行只有在进口商付清货款以后，才能把商业单据交给进口商。付款交单又可根据汇票的付款期限不同，分为即期付款交单和远期付款交单两种。图7-5是付款交单流程：

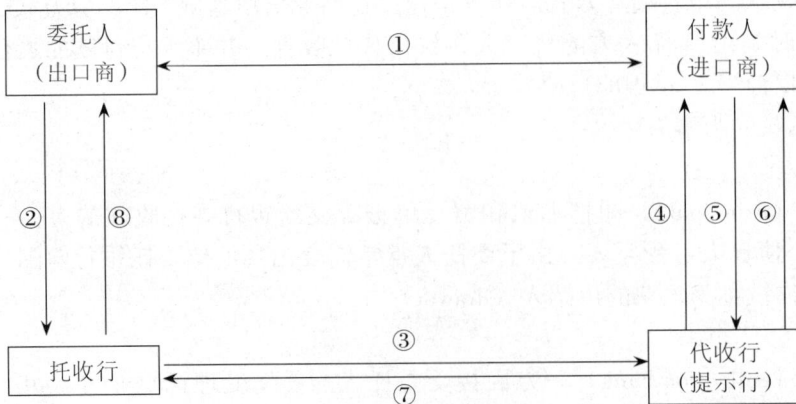

图7-5　付款交单流程

付款交单流程的步骤：

①买卖双方建立贸易关系，约定采用付款交单的结算方式；

②出口商发货备单，填写托收申请书，开立汇票（即期或远期）连同商业单据一并交给托收行；

③托收行核对单据，填写托收委托书，提交汇票及商业单据给代收行或提示行；

④代收行向付款人提示，要求付款（即期付款交单下）或者承兑（远期付款交单下）；

⑤付款人付款（即期付款交单下），付款人承兑（远期付款交单下）；

⑥代收行交单（即期付款交单下），远期汇票到期时代收行提示付款人付款，付款人付款，代收行交单（远期付款交单下）；

⑦代收行将货款交付托收行；

⑧托收行将货款交给出口商。

以上流程中，远期付款交单仅仅比即期付款交单多了一个承兑的过程，其他环节都是一样的。

（2）承兑交单（documents against acceptance，D/A）是指出口商的交单以进口商在汇票上承兑为条件，即出口商在装运货物后开具远期汇票，连同商业单据，通过银行向进口商提示，进口商承兑汇票后，代收行将商业单据交给进口商，在汇票到期时，进口商再履行付款义务。承兑交单方式只适用于远期汇票的托收。

承兑交单的流程跟远期付款交单类似，区别之处在于：远期付款交单是远期汇票到期后，买方付款之后才可以从代收行提取单据；而承兑交单是进口商承兑汇票后，代收行即可放单。承兑交单对进口商有利，因为承兑后即可取单提货，有可能在汇票到期付款时，货物已经变现，不占用自己的资金；对出口商而言，这种结算方式风险很大，因为承兑交单仅仅是对方承诺付款，但并没有真正付款，出口商能否收到货款，完全取决于进口商的信用。

三、信用证

作为现代国际贸易结算的主要方式，信用证结算属于银行信用，能在很大程度上缓解进出口双方互不信任的矛盾，大大降低交易风险，因此在国际上得以广泛应用。

（一）信用证的含义

信用证（letter of credit）是银行（开证行）根据买方（进口商）的要求和指示，向卖方（出口商）开立的在一定期限内凭规定的单据符合信用证条款，即期或一个在未来可以确定的日期支付一定金额的书面承诺。简言之，信用证是一种有条件的银行付款承诺。信用证可分为光票信用证和跟单信用证两类，在国际贸易中主要使用的是跟单信用证。

教学视频7-5

信用证的基本内容

（二）信用证的特点

（1）信用证是一种银行信用，开证行履行付款责任。对出口商而言，收汇保证较高，因此比较安全。

（2）信用证是一种独立文件，它的执行不受交易双方买卖合同的约束。

（3）信用证业务是一种单据买卖，银行凭单付款，不查验货物，因此信用证结算业务容易产生欺诈行为。

（4）信用证业务手续烦琐、成本费用高。信用证业务流程复杂，进口商要支付给银行的各项费用远远超过汇款、托收等结算方式。

信用证业务流程，如图7-6所示：

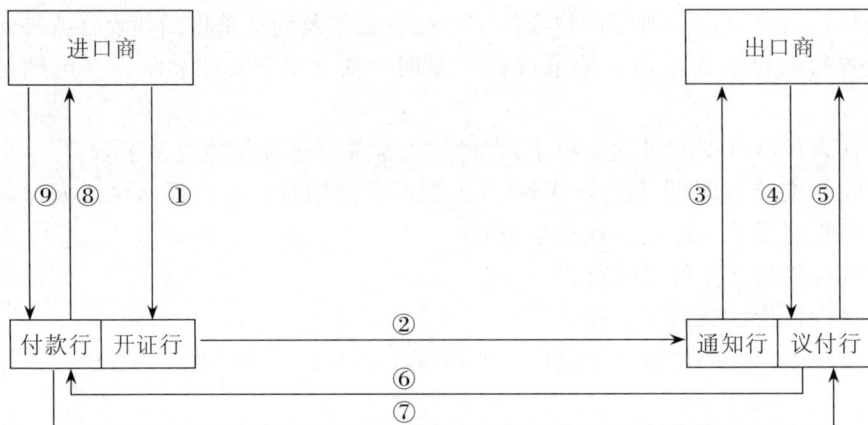

图7-6 信用证业务流程

信用证业务流程的步骤：

①进口商根据买卖合同规定，填写开证申请书，并缴纳押金或提供其他保证，向开证行申请开立信用证；

②开证行接受进口商开证申请，收取开证押金后，依据开证申请书内容开出信用证，寄往出口商所在地通知行；

③通知行鉴定信用证的真实性后，将信用证交给出口商；

④出口商审核信用证与合同相符后，按信用证规定装运货物，备齐各种货运单据并开立汇票，在信用证规定的交单期和有效期内送交当地银行（议付行）议付；

⑤议付行按信用证条款审核单证一致、单单一致后，按汇票金额扣除贴现息税和手续费，将余额垫付给出口商；

⑥议付行将汇票和货运单据寄往付款行索偿货款；

⑦付款行核对单据无误后，付款给议付行；

⑧付款行通知进口商付款赎单；

⑨进口商付款赎单。

信用证结算用银行信用代替了商业信用，曾经占据国际结算主导地位长达百年之久，对国际贸易的发展起到了很大的推动作用。自20世纪90年代以后，国际结算发生了变化，商业信用结算占比逐年上升，信用证结算比例逐渐下降，主要原因在于以下方面：

（1）成本和费用较高。申请开证的进口商要交开证押金、开征申请费、电报费用等，这些费用导致进口商资金被长期占用，增加企业成本；出口商也要缴纳通知费和议付费。

（2）信用证结算手续烦琐，操作复杂。信用证结算要经历信用证开立、审查、修改等多个环节，并且经历各种制单手续、银行单据和货运单据的收集和传递等，被认为是最复杂的结算方式。

（3）交易中的货物品质难以保证。因为信用证业务是单据的买卖，银行只负责处理单证并不查验货物，只要单据上显示"单证相符、单单一致"字样，银行就会接收单据并履行付款责任。

鉴于以上原因，采用信用证结算的贸易双方，应该互相深入了解，不能过度依赖银行。合作前要做交易对手的资信状况调查，以确保交易的顺利进行。

知识链接7-3

国际结算方式的发展趋势

虽然信用证结算是全球使用最广泛的一种国际结算方式，但并不是在所有的国家和地区都是如此。目前，在一些发达国家之间，60%以上的结算业务是赊账方式（open account，O/A）的，这是因为以这种方式处理单据业务量比较小，结算效率较高。因此，较多地采用手续比较简单的O/A、D/P（付款交单）、D/A（承兑交单）等支付方式是国际结算发展的趋势。不过，这些方式的基础是商业信用，对卖方风险较大，必须辅之以其他方式，如要求买方提供银行保函等，才能保障卖方收回货款的权益。备用信用证、保函、保理、福费廷等新兴的、带有融资性质的综合结算方式逐渐被广泛使用，这是国际结算发展的新趋势。

资料来源：根据网络资料整理所得。

任务三　　　　　　　　　　新型国际结算方式

一、银行保函

（一）银行保函的定义

银行保函，又称银行保证书，属于银行信用，是指银行应申请人或委托人的要求向受益方开出的，担保申请人一定履行某种义务，并在申请人未能按规定履行其责任和义务时，由担保行代其支付一定金额或作出一定经济赔偿的书面文件。

教学视频7-6

进口保函的种类

保函的种类很多，用途十分广泛，可适用于商品、劳务、技术贸易，工程项目承包、承建，物资进出口报关，向金融机构融资，大型成套设备租赁，诉讼保全，各种合同义务的履行等领域。银行保函在形式上无一定的格式，对有关方面的权利和义务的规定、处理手续等未形成一定的惯例。

（二）银行保函业务的当事人

银行保函业务中涉及的主要当事人有委托人、受益人和担保人。此外，银行保函业务中涉及的当事人还有通知行、保兑行和反担保人等。

1.委托人（principal）

委托人，也称申请人，是指向担保行申请开立保函的人。在具体的贸易中，委托人可以是投标人、卖方、买方、承租人等。

2.受益人（beneficiary）

受益人，是指收到保函并凭此向银行索偿的一方，一般是申请保函的委托人的交易对手。

3.担保人（guarantor）

担保人，也称担保银行，是指接受委托向受益人开立保函并承担委托人违约时付款责任的银行或金融机构。

4.通知行（advising bank）

通知行，是指接受担保行的委托将保函传递给受益人的银行，一般是委托行在海外的子机构或业务合作银行。

银行保函业务的主要参与者之间的关系是：

委托人与受益人之间基于彼此签订的合同而产生的债权债务关系或其他权利和义务关系，委托人与银行之间的法律关系是委托担保关系，双方签署的保函委托书是银行向委托人收取手续费及履行保证责任后向其追偿的凭证。因此，银行在接到委托人的担保申请后，要对委托人的资信、债务及担保的内容和经营风险进行评估审查，以最大限度降低自身风险。担保银行和受益人之间的法律关系是基于保函而产生的保证关系。在大多数情况下，保函一经开立，银行就要直接承担保证责任。

（三）银行保函的分类

随着国际贸易形式的不断发展和创新，银行保函可广泛用于货物和服务贸易，跨境工程项目承包、承建以及对外劳务合作等领域。根据保函在基础合同中的不同作用和担保人承担的不同担保职责，常见的保函有：

1.借款保函

借款保函是指银行应借款人的要求向贷款行作出的一种旨在保证借款人按照借款合约的规定按期向贷款方归还所借款项本息的付款保证承诺。

2.融资租赁保函

融资租赁保函是指承租人根据租赁协议的规定，请求银行向出租人出具的一种旨在保证承租人按期向出租人支付租金的付款保证承诺。

3.投标保函

投标保函是指银行应投标人申请向招标人作出的保证承诺，保证在投标人报价的有效期内投标人将遵守其诺言，不撤标、不改标、不更改原报价条件，并且在其一旦中标后，将按照招标文件的规定在一定时间内与招标人签订合同。

4.履约保函

履约保函是指银行应供货方或劳务承包方的请求而向买方或业主方作出的一种履约保证承诺。

5.预付款保函

预付款保函，又称还款保函或定金保函，是指银行应供货方或劳务承包方的请求向买方或业主方保证，当申请人未能履约或未能全部按合同规定使用预付款时，银行负责返还保函规定金额的预付款。

6.付款保函

付款保函是指银行应买方或业主的申请，向卖方或承包方出具的一种旨在保证贷款或承包工程进度款支付的付款保证承诺。

其他保函品种还有来料或来件加工保函、质量保函、预留金保函、延期付款保函、票据或费用保付保函、保释金保函和海关免税保函等。

（四）银行保函的作用

1.为委托人增强自身信用

开立银行保函相当于为企业提供了商业信用以外的银行信用，企业可凭此争取到比较合理的价格。

2.帮助企业扩大贸易机会

在商品贸易、服务贸易和技术贸易的过程中，交易对手常常要求企业提交银行保函来保证贸易的顺利开展。

3.减少资金占用

对使用授信额度开立保函的企业来讲，可减少自有资金的占用，减缓企业资金压力。

二、备用信用证

在国际贸易活动中，交易者出于清偿债权债务、获得融资便利、降低交易成本、规避风险的考虑，对金融服务的要求日趋综合化。备用信用证是一个集担保、融资、支付及相关服务为一体的多功能金融产品，用途广泛、运作灵活，在国际贸易活动中得以普遍应用。

（一）备用信用证的概念

备用信用证（standby letters of credit，SBLC）是开证人（一般是银行）应支付人的请求开给受益人，保证在受益人出示特定单据或文件、开证人的单证相符的条件下，必须付给受益人一笔规定的款项或承兑汇票的一种书面凭证。备用信用证在开立后便是一项不可撤销的、独立的、要求单据的、具有约束力的承诺。

教学视频7-7

备用信用证与商业信用证的比较

备用信用证起源于美国。1879年美国联邦法律禁止商业银行为客户办理担保业务，作为应对之举，一些商业银行便以商业信用证的派生形式——备用信用证变相提供担保服务。其后，备用信用证的适用范围逐步扩大，迅速演化为一种国际性的金融工具。

（二）备用信用证的分类

1.根据备用信用证的应用实践划分

根据备用信用证的应用实践，《国际备用证惯例》（ISP98）将其划分为履约备用信用证、投标备用信用证、预付款备用信用证、直接付款备用信用证、融资备用信用证、对开备用信用证、保险备用信用证、商业备用信用证等类型。

（1）履约备用信用证（performance standby/C）用于担保履行除支付金钱以外的义务，包括对由于申请人在基础交易中违约所致损失的赔偿。

（2）投标备用信用证（tender bond standby/C）用于担保申请中标后执行合同的责任和义务。

（3）预付款备用信用证（advance payment standby/C）用于担保申请人对受益人的预付款所应承担的责任和义务。

（4）直接付款备用信用证（direct payment standby/C）用于担保到期付款，尤指到期没有任何违约时支付本金和利息。

2.根据备用信用证是否可以撤销划分

根据备用信用证是否可以撤销，分为可撤销的备用信用证和不可撤销的备用信用证。

（1）可撤销的备用信用证是指附有申请人财务状况，当出现某种变化时可撤销或修改条款的信用证。这种信用证旨在保护开证行的利益，开证行是根据申请人的请求和指示开证的。如果没有申请人的指示，开证行是不会随意撤销信用证的。

（2）不可撤销的备用信用证是指开证行不可以单方面撤销或修改的信用证。对受益人来说，开证行不可撤消的付款承诺使其有了更可靠的收款保证。

（三）备用信用证的功能

1.国际结算功能

在国际范围内，发达国家的信用证的应用率已降至不足20%，赊销/记账交易（open account，O/A）、承兑交单（documents against acceptance，D/A）、保付代理（factoring）等支付技术被广泛应用。实践中，备用信用证通常不直接用于贸易货款和相关费用的支付，而是与O/A、D/A等商业性支付方式共同构成支付组合，即O/A＋备用信用证、D/A＋备用信用证等方式完成跨境支付。在利用O/A、D/A的竞争优势的同时，通过备用信用证（或出口信用保险）获得来自金融机构的风险保障，以防不测。这一操作方式可以兼顾交易双方的利益，简化支付程序，提高贸易的效率，有效降低交易成本，增加了交易者控制风险的手段，有利于减少贸易过程中的风险。

2.国际担保功能

作为一种具有双重性质的金融工具，备用信用证在国际工程承包、BOT项目、补偿贸易、加工贸易、国际信贷、融资租赁、保险与再保险等国际经济活动中被广泛应用，只要基础交易中的债权人认为商业合约对债务人的约束尚不够安全，即可要求债务人向一家银行申请开出以其（债权人）为受益人的备用信用证，用以规避风险，确保债权实现。

备用信用证的优势在于担保责任的确定性和应用的灵活性。首先，备用信用证开立之后，作为担保方的银行，其付款责任始终是肯定和明确的，这有助于减少误解和争议，提高担保服务的质量与效率。其次，备用信用证的受益人多是在对债务人履约具有基本信任的基础上，将备用信用证作为风险规避的补充手段。如果基础交易合约得以顺利履行，备用信用证通常是"备而未用"。这种"备用性"使开证人承担的独立担保责任具有了一定弹性，通过灵活的运作满足了国际经济交易对银行信用补充性支持的需求。实践中，"备而未用"者在备用信用证业务中占据多数。

3.国际融资功能

备用信用证也是一种国际通行的融资工具。合理利用其融资支持功能，对于企业拓展国际融资途径、扭转融资艰难局面，具有积极意义。

国际信贷安排中常用的融资备用信用证主要支持包括偿还借款在内的付款义务的履行，境外投资企业可以通过融资备用信用证获得东道国的信贷资金支持。直接付款备用信用证主要支持与融资备用信用证有关的基础付款义务的履行。实践中，普遍地用于商业票据融资支持。

新型的国际结算方式除了银行保函和备用信用证之外，还有国际保理、福费廷等融资特点鲜明的综合性金融工具，将在下一个项目中详细介绍。

思政小课堂

2020年中旬，中国银行业协会发布的《中国贸易金融行业发展报告（2019—2020）》显示：在国际结算方面，2019年中国商业银行国际结算业务量为6.89万亿美元，与2018年相比略有下降。其中，国有商业银行是办理国际结算业务的主力，业务量在全行业占据主要地位。在国际贸易融资方面，2019年国际贸易融资业务呈现小幅下降的趋势。在国内信用证及其项下贸易融资方面，2019年国内信用证结算业务量普遍增长较快。

请结合本项目所学内容，思考在全球贸易局势紧张、新冠疫情全球蔓延、投资大幅缩减、金融动荡的大背景下，我国国际贸易金融及结算逆势增长的原因是什么？

项目思维导图

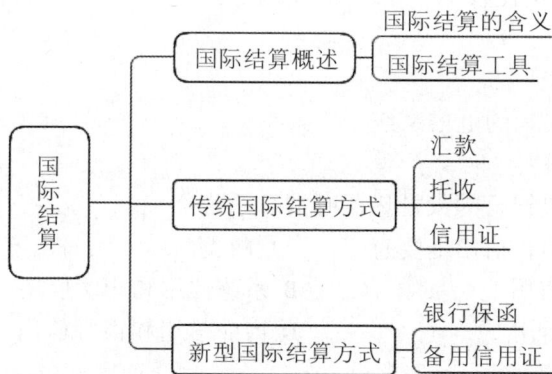

项目训练

一、单选题

1.适宜采用电汇结算的债权债务，一般是（　　　）。

A.零星的小额货款　　　　　　　　B.付款时间紧急的大额货款

C.贸易从属费用　　　　　　　　　　D.不紧急的款项

2.托收业务的结算基础是商业信用，这是因为（　　　）。

A.没有银行参与　　　　　　　　　　B.出票人开立的汇票是商业汇票

C.银行不承担保证付款的义务　　　　D.进口商可凭信托收据借单

3.信用证对出口商的作用是（　　　）。

A.不必占用资金，反而能得到开证手续费的收入

B.获得一笔数目可观的结算手续费

C.可以凭信托收据，要求开证行先交付单据，在出售货物后再交付货款

D.只要将符合信用证条款的货运单据交到出口地与其有来往的银行，便能取得货款，加速资金周转

4.审核单据的基本原则是（　　　）。

A.单据和贸易合同一致　　　　　　　B.单单一致、单证一致

C.信用证和贸易合同一致　　　　　　D.单据和开证申请书一致

5.备用信用证产生于美国，具有担保的功能，实际上属于一种（　　　）。

A.商业信用证　　　B.银行保函　　　C.融资方式　　　D以上三种都可以

二、多选题

1.传统的国际结算方式大体分为（　　　）。

A.汇款　　　　　　B.托收　　　　　　C.信用证　　　　D.银行保函

2.国际货款收付在采用非现金结算时使用的支付工具有（　　　）。

A.货币　　　　　　B.汇票　　　　　　C.本票　　　　　D.支票

3.下列属于商业信用的结算工具是（　　　）。

A.信用证　　　　　B.托收　　　　　　C.汇款　　　　　D.银行保函

4.SWIFT是一个（　　　）。

A.美元国际支付系统

B.传递银行间金融交易的电信系统

C.英镑票据清算系统

D.欧元区个成员中央银行的大批量实时清算系统

5.传统的国际结算中，信用主要有（　　　）两类。

A.系统信用和银行信用　　　　　　　B.系统信用和司法信用

C.商业信用和司法信用　　　　　　　D.商业信用和银行信用

三、判断题

1.托收是依赖银行信用的国际结算方式。　　　　　　　　　　　　　　（　　　）

2.国际贸易结算发展与支付方式的变革关系密切。　　　　　　　　　　（　　　）

3.国际结算经历了从现金结算到非现金结算，从商品买卖到单据买卖，从买卖直接结算到通过银行结算，从使用简单的贸易条件到交货与付款相结合的比较完整的贸易条件的发展过程。　　　　　　　　　　　　　　　　　　　　　　　　　　　　　（　　　）

4.侨民汇款、旅游开支、服务偿付等属于有形贸易结算。　　　　　　　（　　　）

5.进口商以电汇方式支付货款可以加速出口商资金周转，从而可以降低出口商汇率

风险。　　　　　　　　　　　　　　　　　　　　　　　　　（　　　）

四、实践训练

我国某出口商 A 出运货物一批，开出以买方 B 为付款人的 60 天远期汇票及附属全套单据，委托 H 银行以 D/P 方式向国外托收货款。单据寄到对方代收行 M 后，付款人在办理承兑手续时，货已抵埠，且行情看好，但付款期未到。付款人当即向代收行 M 出具信托收据，保证到期付款，从而从代收行 M 借到单据。货物出售后，付款人因其债务关系而倒闭，无力付款。在这种情况下，代收行 M 是否应于汇票到期之日将货款拨付给我方？

项目八
国际融资

学习目标

知识目标

了解国际贸易融资的类型、掌握短期贸易融资和中长期贸易融资的内容；掌握国际项目融资的概念及其典型方式；了解国际债券融资概念及其类型。

能力目标

利用所学国际融资知识，为进出口企业提出融资方案，能分析BOT项目融资方案。

操作目标

能够根据企业或项目实际情况设计合适的融资方案。

课程导入

以"熊猫"命名的债券已经发行逾4 000亿元

2020年6月11日，亚洲基础设施投资银行在中国银行间债券市场发行30亿元人民币熊猫债。这是亚洲基础设施投资银行首次发行熊猫债。本次发行债券为中国银行间市场交易商协会注册的新冠肺炎疫情防控债。

根据Wind数据统计，截至2020年6月11日，银行间市场和交易所市场累计发行熊猫债已超过4 000亿元。仅2020年上半年发行就超过300亿元。

熊猫债市场的发展伴随着金融改革不断深入，以及中国资本市场对外开放和人民币国际化进程而日益壮大。

"境外优质主权类机构和地方政府、国际开发机构，作为最早进入境内人民币债券市场融资的境外主体，在熊猫债发展历程中扮演着关键角色。"国际金融专家赵庆明认为，这些机构发行熊猫债，不仅丰富了我国债券市场，也展现了对中国经济和中国金融市场发展的信心。

专家认为，这将进一步提高熊猫债发行效率，降低沟通成本，增强市场对国际发行人和投资人的吸引力，提高利用熊猫债融资的示范效应，进一步推动熊猫债市场的健康发展。

市场预期，随着我国加快推动熊猫债市场改革步伐，包括"一带一路"沿线国家在内的外国中央政府发行熊猫债的进程有可能显著加快。在中国经济金融深度融入全球化的背景下，完善熊猫债发行规则，对于丰富中国债券市场的境外发行人和投资人群体，形成更加开放、更加市场化的金融体系具有重要意义。

资料来源：刘开雄. 以"熊猫"命名的债券已经发行逾4 000亿元［EB/OL］.［2020-06-16］. http://www.xinhuanet.com/fortune/2020-06/16/c_1126121417.html.

思考讨论：

（1）熊猫债券属于哪一种国际债券？

（2）外国债券和欧洲债券有什么区别？

（3）国际融资有哪些融资形式？

融资，即融通资金，是指为了调剂资金余缺，资金从盈余部门流向短缺部门的活动。如果发生在本国资金持有者之间的融资活动不能满足经济主体的资金需求，各经济主体可以到国际金融市场融通资金，在促进国内经济发展的同时，各经济主体也可以把闲置资金借给外国贷款人，以获取更高收益。

值得注意的是，与国内融资相比，国际融资的风险更大，但同时国际融资的方式更多、融资工具更丰富。筹资者可以根据各自的需求，选择不同的融资工具，从而较快地实现筹资目的。

国际融资具有以下特点：

1.国际融资主体和客体比较复杂

国际融资的主体包括筹资人和贷款人，大体可分为居民金融机构、居民非金融机构、非居民金融机构和非居民非金融机构四类。国际融资的借贷双方至少有一方属于非居民的金融机构或非居民的非金融机构。

国际融资的客体是指国际融资所使用的货币，必须是国际间可兑换货币。国际融资中经常使用的是一些国际通用货币，如美元、英镑、欧元、特别提款权（SDR）等。融资当事人使用何种货币是一个很复杂的问题，通常必须根据各种货币汇率的变化和发展趋势，结合融资条件等因素综合考虑，才能作出决策。

2.国际融资风险较大

国际融资与国内融资相比，贷款人和筹资人均面临较大风险。对国际融资中的贷款人来说，除了要面临债务人因经营管理不善到期无力偿还贷款或延期偿付的信用风险，还将面临债务人所在国家或地区不能或者不愿对外国贷款人履行其债务责任的风险，以及以外币计价的贷款因汇率变动而蒙受损失的外汇风险。对国际融资的筹资人而言，面临以外币计价的债务因外币对本币升值而使偿还的本币债务增加的风险。

3.国际融资易受管制

国际融资使得资本在不同国家的资金持有人之间流动，当事人所在的国家政府，从本国政治、经济利益出发，为调节本国国际收支，执行本国货币政策，以及审慎管理本国金融机构的需要，会对本国居民从事的国际融资行为加以干预或管制。

国际融资有多种形式，如国际贸易融资、国际银团贷款、国际项目融资、国际债券融资、国际租赁融资、政府间贷款、国际金融机构贷款等。本章主要介绍国际贸易融资、国际项目融资和国际债券融资。

任务一　　　　　　　国际贸易融资

随着各国经济开放程度不断加大、社会分工不断深化，各国之间的贸易往来越来越频繁，国际贸易对各国经济发展的作用越来越突出，而资金不足直接影响国际贸易的正常进行，进一步影响各国经济发展，各国应该善于利用一切可利用的资金资源，并尽可能降低融资成本，从而促进国际贸易的达成，推动经济发展。因此，我们有必要学习国际贸易融资的形式，并学会如何高效利用这些融资方式，这对利用外资、促进本国国际贸易发展具有实际意义。

国际贸易融资是国际融资中出现最早的形式，主要是指银行给从事国际贸易交易的进出口企业提供的资金融通便利。在国际贸易中，出口商在出口商品的过程中，或者进口商在进口商品的过程中，都希望获得低成本、小风险的资金支持，国际贸易融资应运而生。

国际贸易融资为国际贸易的达成提供支持，随着国际贸易和金融业的发展，其种类也不断发展。按照融资期限的长短，国际贸易融资，可分为短期国际贸易融资和中长期国际贸易融资；按照接受贸易融资的对象，可分为对出口方融资和对进口方融资。

一、短期国际贸易融资

短期国际贸易融资，是指进出口商在国际贸易过程中，利用各种手段和途径而获得的期限在1年以下（含1年）的短期资金融通行为。因为很多短期国际贸易融资经常和结算方式相关，所以也可将短期国际贸易融资称为国际贸易结算融资。

短期国际贸易融资的常见期限有1个月、2个月、3个月和6个月，后两种使用较多。

短期国际贸易融资的形式很多，这里主要介绍对出口方融资、对进口方融资和国际保理业务。

（一）短期出口贸易融资

在国际贸易过程中，出口商在出口产品的过程中要支付各种费用，需要大量资金支持，而各种费用支付容易引起出口商流动性资金不足，所以此时获得短期资金融通就成为出口顺利的保障。对出口方融资主要包括银行对出口方融资及进口方对出口方融资。

1.银行对出口方融资

银行对出口方融资包括短期信用贷款、商品抵押贷款、打包放款、出口押汇、远期票据贴现。

（1）短期信用贷款。

短期信用贷款是指银行为了支持出口，专门给出口商品的生产商提供的无抵押贷款。采用这种融资方式，要求出口商与银行有密切的业务关系，而且出口商要有良好的资信。

（2）商品抵押贷款。

如果出口商所出口的商品不是自行生产的，而是进行采购的，这时可以以国内货物作为抵押，从银行取得贷款。银行在提供此项贷款时，往往以货物市值的一定百分比贷出资金，而且随市价变动而调整。如果银行已贷出资金，且抵押品市价下跌，那么银行往往要求出口商归还部分贷款，或提供新的抵押品。

（3）打包放款。

打包放款通常是指在国际贸易中，出口商在发出货物前，收到进口商开证行开立的信用证之后，将正本信用证抵押给银行，向银行申请一定数额的贷款（一般不超过信用证金额的80%）用来备货。该项融资期限一般不会超过信用证的有效期。

银行在发放打包放款时，主要考虑下列两个因素：一是开证行资信好，信用证条款明确，出口商执行无困难；二是出口商资信好，履约能力强，能按信用证条款及时出口收汇。

（4）出口押汇。

出口押汇是指出口商发货后，将出口商品的货运单据抵押给出口方银行申请融资。根据不同的结算方式，出口押汇可分为信用证出口押汇和跟单托收出口押汇。

信用证出口押汇是指在信用证结算方式下，出口方自装运货物后至收到开证行支付的货款前，以信用证项下的出口单据作抵押，请求出口地议付行垫付信用证金额的一种融资方式。议付行审核出口商提交的信用证项下规定的单据后，若单证相符，则用信用证金额扣除利息及手续费后将剩余金额垫付给出口商。若信用证到期后，出口商无法从开证行获得货款，则议付行有权向出口商进行追索，要求出口商偿还本金和利息。

跟单托收出口押汇是指在跟单托收方式下，出口方装运货物后，将货运单据提交给出口地托收行，请求托收行预先支付部分或全部货款，待货款收到后偿还银行垫款的一种出口贸易融资方式。在这种融资方式下，托收行买入出口商交来的以进口商为付款人的跟单汇票和随附的商业单据后，扣除利息和有关费用将汇票余额付给出口商。若出口商无法从进口商处收回货款，则银行有权向出口商进行追索，要求出口商偿还本金和利息。

跟单托收出口押汇与信用证押汇的主要区别是，跟单托收出口押汇没有银行信用的保证，能否收回货款完全取决于进口商的资信，风险较大，因此押汇利率较高。

（5）远期票据贴现。

远期票据贴现是指银行或贴现公司有追索权买入未到期的已承兑的远期票据，为客户提供短期融资业务。在远期票据贴现中，最常见的是出口商以在远期信用证项下经开证行承兑的远期汇票向银行申请贴现，贴现金额等于票面金额扣除贴现利息。若到期开证行不能履行付款义务，则付款行有权要求出口商归还等于汇票金额的贷款。

2.进口方对出口方融资

进口商在收到货物单据前，会付出全部或部分货款，即进口商向出口商预付货款，这个融资方式手续简单、费用少，对出口方有利。

（二）对进口商提供的融资

1.银行对进口方融资

（1）为进口商开立信用证。

信用证是银行对出口商作出的付款承诺，一旦开证申请人（进口商）丧失偿债能力，银行就要承担款项收不回来的风险。因此，银行要求开证申请人缴纳一定的开证保证金或提供相应的抵押品或由第三方提供担保。银行为进口商开立信用证，相当于占用了银行的资金。

（2）进口押汇。

在信用证结算方式下，当出口商按照要求将所有单据交给银行要求进口商付款赎单时，如果进口商无足够的资金向开证行赎单，则可由开证行先行垫付货款，进口商从银行取得单据，在这种方式下相当于银行对进口商提供了融资。

（3）提货担保。

在信用证结算方式下，当货物先于提单到达目的地港时，进口商为了抓住市场有利机会及早提货，可要求银行出具提货担保书，并将提货担保书交给航运公司先行提货。待收到提单时，再将提单交给航运公司换回提货担保书。

（4）信托收据。

在跟单托收中采用远期付款交单结算方式时，进口商可向银行开立书面保证文件，即信托收据，以取出提货单据，以便把握市场有利机会尽快出售货物，待获得货款后支付给银行以换回信托收据。其具体过程为：

①代收行根据信托收据向进口商借出货运单据，使进口商在远期汇票未到期前先提货，提货后进行销售获得部分或全部货款；

②当汇票到期时，进口商将货款支付给代收行，同时收回信托收据；

③代收行收回货款后，将货款支付给托收行。

从信托收据的操作流程可以发现，进口商在整个过程中未使用自己的资金就完成了进口交易，在此过程中银行为其提供了融资。

（5）承兑交单。

在承兑交单结算方式下，出口商为保证安全收款，发货后要求银行承兑汇票。银行承兑后进口商可取得运输单据并提货，再将货物转售或用于生产，进口商必须在汇票到期日前将有关款项支付给银行，以便银行能在付款日准时兑付给出口商，这一过程中银行对进口商提供了融资。

2.出口方对进口方融资

为提高出口商品的竞争力，出口商可向进口商提供商业信用，为进口商提供延期付款的融资便利，即由进口商承兑出口商开立的远期汇票，便可获得单据提货，并于汇票到期日支付票面金额给出口商。

（三）国际保理业务

国际保理，也称承购应收账款，是指在出口商以商业信用出口货物时，货物发运后，出口商立即把应收账款的发票和装运单据无追索权地卖给保理商，取得部分或全部货款。如果将来出现进口商逾期付款或不付款，则由保理商承担责任。

国际保理业务是针对赊销而设计的，主要具有以下特点：

（1）应收账款必须是商业机构之间因货物销售产生的，该应收账款不属于个人或家庭消费或者类似使用性质。

（2）该商业机构必须将应收账款的权利转让给保理商。

（3）应收账款的转让通知必须送交债务人。

（4）保理商必须履行以下职能：以贷款或者预付款的形式向供货商融通资金；管理与应收账款有关的账户；收取应收账款；对债务人的拒付提供坏账担保。

二、中长期国际贸易融资

短期国际贸易融资只能解决临时性资金短缺问题，而在大型机械或成套设备的进出口贸易中主要存在中长期资金不足，因此需要进行中长期贸易融资。

中长期国际贸易融资是指在国际贸易过程中，进出口商通过不同方式或手段获得的期限在一年以上的资金融通。中长期国际贸易融资主要用于改善企业资本结构，解决中长期资金不足的问题。实际上，中长期国际贸易融资不仅是一种融资方式，也是企业争夺出口商品市场的竞争手段。

动画微课8-1

国际中长期
贸易融资

中长期国际贸易融资的方式主要包括出口信贷和福费廷等。

（一）出口信贷

随着各国之间大规模开展大型机器设备及技术的国际贸易，加之这类贸易涉及金额较大、资金占用时间较长，导致进出口商需要中长期融资的支持，所以出口信贷应运而生。

1.出口信贷的概念及特点

出口信贷是指为促进本国大型机械设备或技术的出口，增强出口商品的国际竞争力，一国银行金融机构或非银行金融机构对本国出口商或外国进口商（或银行）提供较低利率贷款的一种国际信贷方式。这种贷款由出口商提供，以推动出口为目的，因此称之为出口信贷。

出口信贷主要表现出以下特点：

（1）贷款发放对象为出口大型设备或技术的企业，为本国产品（主要是大型成套设备）及技术的出口提供服务。

（2）利率较低。出口信贷的利率明显低于国内市场利率，由国家给予利息补贴。出口信贷的利率一般会根据经济合作与发展组织的协议每半年进行一次调整。

（3）风险较大。由于出口信贷金额大、偿还期长，发放贷款的银行承担较大的风险。

（4）与保险、担保相结合。为了解决出口国贷款银行后顾之忧，保证其贷款资金的安全发放，出口国一般设有信贷保险机构，对银行发放的贷款提供担保，为提供保险服务的私人保险公司提供再保险服务。

2.出口信贷的形式

出口信贷主要有买方信贷和卖方信贷两种形式。

（1）买方信贷。

买方信贷是目前国际上出口信贷的主要类型，是指为了扩大本国大型机械设备或技术的出口，出口商所在地银行向外国进口商或进口商所在地银行提供的中长期贷款。由于买方信贷可以贷给进口商，也可以贷给进口商所在地的银行，因此买方信贷有两种形式，即出口方银行向进口商提供贷款、出口方银行向进口商所在地银行提供贷款。

①出口方银行向进口商提供贷款的流程，如图8-1所示。

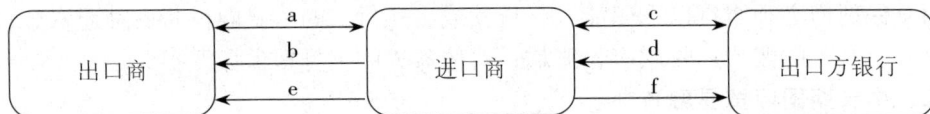

图8-1　出口方银行向进口商提供贷款

a.进出口商双方签订贸易合同；

b.进口商预付相当于货价15%的现汇定金；

c.进口商与出口方银行签订买方信贷协议；

d.进口商从出口方银行取得贷款；

e.进口商从出口方银行取得贷款后，以现汇方式向出口商支付货款；

f.进口商按贷款协议向出口方银行偿还贷款。

②出口方银行向进口商所在地银行提供贷款的流程，如图8-2所示。

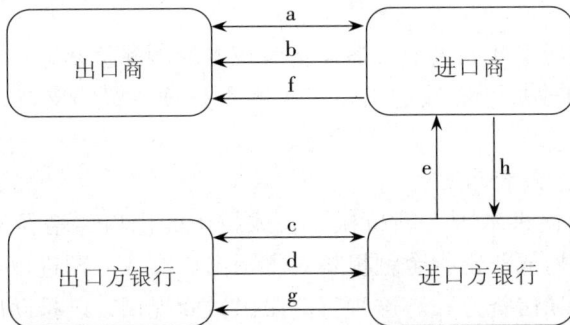

图8-2　出口方银行向进口商所在地银行提供贷款

a.进出口商双方签订贸易合同；

b.进口商预付相当于货价15%的现汇定金；

c.进口方银行与出口方银行签订买方信贷协议；

d.根据协议，进口方银行从出口方银行取得贷款；

e.进口方银行取得贷款后，将款项贷给进口商；

f.进口商从进口方银行取得贷款后，以现汇方式向出口商支付货款；

g.进口方银行按贷款协议向出口方银行偿还贷款；

h.进口商按协议向进口方银行偿还贷款。

③买方信贷下各方利弊分析。

a.对出口商来说，出口方银行对进口商或进口方银行提供贷款，不仅能收到现汇、承担风险小、资金周转快，还能够简化手续和改善财务状况。由于收到的是现汇，出口商在制定出口价时无须考虑附加的信贷手续费等费用。同时，由于各项费用由进口商负担，出口商只能报现汇价，获利较少。

b.对出口方银行来说，出口方银行贷款给进口方银行，风险较小；若出口方银行贷款给进口商，则须担保，由银行或其他金融机构担保，也无太大风险。

c.对进口商来说，若采用出口方银行贷款给进口方银行的买方信贷，则进口商可以集中精力谈判技术条件和商务条件。由于使用现汇成交，可不用考虑延期付款的利息问题。信贷条件由双方银行另行协商，手续费也由双方银行直接协商解决，减少了收费数额和中间环节，使进口商在贸易谈判中处于有利地位。但如果采用出口方银行贷款给进口商的买方信贷，则进口商须同出口方银行打交道，办理贷款手续。

d.对进口方银行来说，出口方银行对进口方银行提供贷款，可以拓宽与进口企业联系的渠道，扩大业务量，增加收益。

（2）卖方信贷。

卖方信贷，是指为促进大型机械或成套设备的出口，出口方银行或非银行金融机构对出口商提供贷款融资，使得出口商允许进口商以延期付款的方式进口大型机械或成套设备。延期付款的货价一般高于现汇支付的货价。

①卖方信贷业务流程，如图8-3所示。

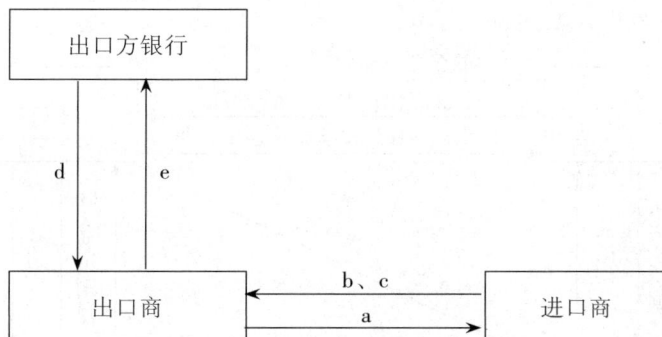

图8-3　卖方信贷业务流程

a.进出口双方签订贸易合同，进口商以延期付款方式向出口商购买大型设备；

b.进口商预先支付货款的10%～15%作为定金；

c.在分批交货验收及保证金期满时，进口商再支付10%～15%的货款，剩余货款则在出口商全部交货后的规定期限内支付（一般为每半年支付一次），并由进口商承担延期付款产生的利息；

d.出口商以贸易合同为基础，向所在地银行申请融资，并签订贷款协议，取得所需资金；

e.出口商以进口商分期支付的货款分期偿还银行贷款。

②卖方信贷下各方利弊分析。

a.对出口商来说，在卖方信贷下，出口商除了跟进商品外，还要与出口地银行打交道，办理贷款手续。虽然可以由进口商负担一切费用和风险，但是由于货款没有进口方银行的担保，有可能出现不能按期收回的风险。

b.对出口方银行来说，在卖方信贷下，出口方银行要经常关注出口商的经营状况和贷款清偿情况。

c.对进口商来说，在卖方信贷下，进口商与出口商洽谈、签订贸易协议时不需要自己向银行贷款，省时省力，而且采用延期付款的方式可以减少进口商的资金占用。但是，由于出口商须向银行贷款，要承担贷款利息、保险费等费用，因此货价较高，且进口商须向出口商支付延期付款产生的利息。

d.对进口方银行来说，在卖方信贷下，只有出口商、出口方银行、进口商三方当事人，与进口方银行不产生关系。

（二）福费廷

福费廷（forfaiting，原意为放弃，音译为福费廷），也称票据包买或票据买断，是指在采用延期付款方式的大型机械设备的中长期国际贸易中，出口商将经过担保方担保的、进口商承兑的、期限在3~12年的远期汇票或本票，无追索权地卖给出口商所在地银行或大金融公司，以提前取得现款的一种融资方式。

福费廷业务是一种无追索权的贴现业务，即如果进口商到期不付款，贴现银行不能向出口商行使追索权。实际上，它是一种较复杂的、变相的出口卖方信贷，是专门的代理融资技术，包括出口商、进口商、担保方和福费廷方四方当事人。

1.福费廷业务流程（如图8-4所示）

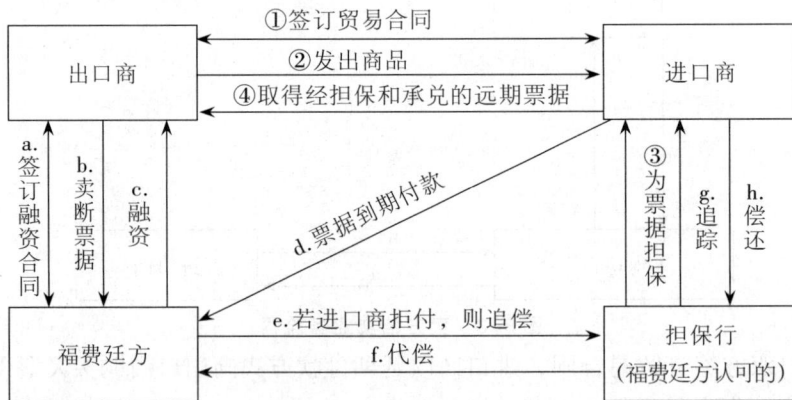

图8-4 福费廷业务流程

（1）出口商与进口商进行贸易洽谈。如果使用福费廷，则出口商提前与当地银行或金融公司约定，以便做好各项信贷准备。

（2）出口商根据福费廷方的报价，将融资费用全部或部分计入出口商品价格向进口商报价，一旦进口商同意，双方签订贸易合同。与此同时，出口商确认福费廷方的报价并与其签订融资合同。

（3）出口商按贸易合同发货后，取得经进口商承兑并经担保银行担保的远期汇票。对票据担保的形式是在汇票上签字盖章保证到期付款或者出具保函。担保银行需要经过福费廷方认可。如果福费廷方认为担保银行资信不高，则进口商需要更换担保银行。

（4）出口商取得承兑汇票后，按照与福费廷方的约定，将票据卖断给福费廷方，取得现款。

（5）票据到期结算。票据到期时，福费廷方与进口商清算货款，若进口商拒绝支付，则福费廷方可向担保行追偿，要求担保行付款。

2.福费廷业务对各方利弊分析

（1）对出口商的利弊。

使用福费廷对出口商有利，主要体现在：出口商办理福费廷手续简便，提交单据较少，可以向进口商转移部分融资费用，在交货后可立即获得无追索权的融资，减少和避免了出口收汇风险。由于福费廷方承担了较多风险，相应地提高了融资利率，使得出口商的融资成本较高。此外，出口商很难找到一个令福费廷方满意的担保方。

（2）对进口商的利弊。

进口商以延期付款的方式进口大型机械或成套设备，可以减少资金占用。对进口商不利的方面是：出口商可能将部分融资成本转移到货价中，使得货价较高；担保方对票据提供了担保，进口商要需支付担保费，同时银行担保将长期占用进口商的银行信用额度。

（3）对福费廷方的利弊。

福费廷方给出口商提供融资，可以获得较高的收益，并且福费廷业务中使用的汇票和本票可以在二级市场上流通转让。对福费廷方不利的方面是：福费廷方买进的票据对出口商无追索权，须承担较高的融资风险。此外，福费廷方必须调查担保人的资信情况，了解进口国有关商业票据和保函的法律规定。

（4）对担保行的利弊。

担保行不仅能获得担保费，还能扩大担保行在国际市场上的影响力。对担保行不利的方面是：如果票据到期，进口商拒付货款，则担保行对到期票据负有绝对的、无条件的付款责任。

知识链接8-1

区块链福费廷交易平台

2020年8月6日，中国人民银行清算总中心与中信银行、中国银行、中国民生银行正式签署区块链福费廷交易平台合作协议。这意味着由中信银行倡议建立的区块链福费廷交易平台正式成为行业平台。

根据协议，人民银行清算总中心将借鉴三家商业银行前期区块链福费廷交易平台建设实践经验，完善人民银行国内电子信用证系统资产交易功能。相关功能建设将充分利用和发挥区块链技术优势，将区块链的多边信任、防篡改、共识算法等技术与电子信用证资产交易业务结合，开发一个福费廷资产交易平台。新平台将统一业务标准，与人民银行大额支付系统对接，便利银行间福费廷资产买卖，提高福费廷领域的贸易融资效率，降低企业融资成本。

目前，中信银行、中国银行、中国民生银行三家商业银行在运行的区块链福费廷交易平台，是基于区块链技术和区块链思维，共同设计、共同开发的资产交易联盟链平台，用于国内福费廷资产的二级市场交易。平台集合了资产发布、资金发布、要约、债权转让等一系列环节，解决了福费廷业务缺乏公开报价市场、交易流程脱节等长期以来的痛点。目前，该平台联盟成员已增至43家，累计办理业务超过3 000亿元人民币。

经中国人民银行批准，人民银行清算总中心于2019年12月9日上线了电子信用证信息交换系统，该系统将吸收借鉴三家银行已有福费廷交易平台建设成果，基于区块链技术实现资产登记、交易功能，预计将成为国家公共金融基础设施的重要组成部分。

资料来源：佚名. 央行清算总中心与中信银行等三家银行签署区块链福费廷交易平台合作协议［EB/OL］.［2020-08-19］. https：//m.gmw.cn/baijia/2020-08/19/34100147.html.

任务二　　　　　　　　国际项目融资

一、国际项目融资概述

国际项目融资是一种特殊的融资方式，是指以境内建设项目的名义在境外筹措资金，并以项目自身的现金流收入、自身的资产与权益，承担偿还债务责任的融资方式，属于无追索权或有限追索权的一种融资方式。

项目融资被广泛应用于自然资源开发项目、豪华饭店的建设项目以及大型农业发展项目等。当今的项目融资主要集中应用于大规模的基础设施建设项目，如发电站、高速公路、铁路和机场等。在中国、东南亚以及新兴工业化国家中，这些项目经常采用BOT（build-operate-transfer，建设—运营—转让）融资方式。

国际项目融资由于融资金额大、期限长、风险大，往往采用银团贷款方式融资，具有以下特点：

（1）贷款人不以主办单位的资产和信誉作为发放贷款的依据，而以该工程项目预期的经济效益和承办单位资产状况作为发放贷款的依据。

（2）项目融资的还款来源是该项目未来的收益。项目的成败对贷款人能否收回贷款具有决定性的意义。

（3）国际项目融资风险大，需要与工程项目有利害关系的更多单位进行担保以回避风险。

（4）项目所需资金来源多样化，除从银团贷款取得资金外，还能够得到政府、国际组织的支持。

（5）项目融资以"有限追索权"筹资方式为主，利率较高。有限追索权项目融资除了以项目经营性收入作为还款来源和取得物权担保外，贷款人还要求项目以外的第三方（如项目主办人、项目产品购买人或项目设施使用人、项目工程承包人等）提供担保。当项目收益不佳或经营失败时，贷款人有权向第三方担保人追索，担保人承担债务的责任以他们各自提供的担保金额为限。

知识链接8-2

BOT项目融资的前世今生

近些年，BOT项目融资方式被一些发展中国家用来进行基础设施建设，并取得了一定的成功，引起了各国的青睐，被当成一种新型的投资方式进行宣传。然而，BOT项目融资方式远非一种新生事物，它自出现至今已有至少300年的历史。

17世纪英国的领港公会负责管理海上事务，包括建设和经营灯塔，并拥有建造灯塔和向船只收费的特权。但是，据专家调查，从1610年到1675年，领港公会连一个灯塔也未建成，而同期私人建成的灯塔至少有10座。这种私人建造灯塔的投资方式与现在的BOT项目融资方式如出一辙，即私人首先向政府提出准许建造和经营灯塔的申请，申请中必须包括许多船主的签名以证明将要建造的灯塔对他们有利，并且表示愿意支付过路费。在申请获得政府批准后，私人向政府租用建造灯塔必须占用的土地，在特许期内管理灯塔并向过往船只收取过路费；特许期满后由政府将灯塔收回并交给领港公会管理和继续收费。在1820年，全部的46座灯塔中，有34座是私人投资建造的。可见，BOT项目融资方式在投资效率上远高于行政部门。

二十世纪六七十年代以后，国际上大型工程开发项目日益增多。这类大型项目包括石油、煤炭、天然气等自然资源开发项目，也包括交通运输、电力、农林等基础建设工程项目。国际项目融资往往耗资巨大，开发周期长，动辄需要几亿、几十亿甚至上百亿美元的投资金额和几年、十几年甚至几十年的投资周期。项目的投资风险超出了项目投资者所能够和所愿意承担的限度，传统的融资方式已经不能满足此类大型项目融资的要求。针对这种情况，国际项目融资为适应开发大型项目的需要，利用项目本身的资产价值和现金流量安排项目贷款。这种新型融资方式就应运而生，并获得了很大发展。

资料来源：佚名. BOT项目融资模式案例分析［EB/OL］. ［2016-11-18］. https://www.xuexila.com/chuangye/rongzi/1888842.html.

二、项目融资的参与方

项目融资的参与方包括项目发起人、项目公司、借款人、银行、安排行、管理行、代理行、工程银行、担保受托人、财务顾问行、专家、律师、国际金融机构、项目所在国政府、保险公司、租赁公司、评级机构。

（一）项目发起人

项目发起人可以是一个公司或一个由像承包商、供应商、项目产品的购买方或使用方构成的多边联合体或财团，甚至可以是与项目无直接利益关系的成员。

（二）项目公司

项目公司是经营项目的实体，其身份、注册地址和法定形式取决于多种因素。

（三）借款人

借款人可以是或者不是项目公司。一个项目融资可能有多个借款人，他们分别筹资以满足各自参加项目的需要，如建筑公司、经营公司、原料供应商等。

（四）银行

许多大规模的项目需要银团贷款。尽量组成一个由许多国家银行参加的银团，从而避免所在国政府对项目的干涉，因为项目所在国政府可能不愿意因此破坏与这些国家的经济关系。商业银行可以作为担保行参加银团。

（五）安排行

银行贷款的安排行通常在贷款条件和担保谈判中起主导作用。

（六）管理行

参加项目融资的银团贷款可指定银团贷款的管理行。管理行通常不对借款人或贷款人承任何特殊责任。

（七）代理行

代理行对贷款人的贷款决定不负任何责任，其职责是协调用款、帮助各方交流融资文件内容、送达通知和传递信息。

（八）工程银行

工程银行的责任是监控技术进程和项目业绩，并负责项目工程师和独立专家之间的联络。工程银行很大可能是代理行或安排行的分支机构。

（九）担保受托人

在一个涉及银团贷款的项目融资中，经常有一个具有信托资格的代理行来保管担保资产。

（十）财务顾问行

财务顾问行准备项目情况备忘录的提纲，以及项目的特点和经济效益可行性分析，提出与项目成本、市场价格和需求、汇率等有关的假设，并报告各项目发起人的情况。

（十一）专家

被项目发起人或财务顾问选中的具有国际声望的技术专家负责准备或至少检查项目的可行性报告，通常情况下，专家会继续参加项目的监控。当项目发起人和贷款人对项目文件规定的竣工测试有争议时，专家还会充当仲裁人。

（十二）律师

大规模项目融资所涉及的项目文件十分复杂，加上来自不同国家的参与方，这使律师的作用变得非常重要。

（十三）国际金融机构

许多发展中国家的项目是由世界银行及活跃在私人企业界的国际金融公司或区域发展银行共同提供融资的。

（十四）项目所在国政府

在许多情况下，项目所在国政府不会作为借款人或项目公司的所有人直接参与项目融资，而是可能通过一个代理人获得项目的股权利益，成为项目的购买者或项目所提供服务的使用者。所在国政府在项目中起到非常关键的作用，如给予项目有关批准或运营特许，或给予项目优惠待遇或保证外汇来源。

（十五）保险公司

必要的保险是项目融资的一个重要方面。

（十六）租赁公司

租赁公司的作用是通过获得项目公司所需的部分或全部资产，并将这些资产租给项目公司来定期收取租金。

（十七）评级机构

一些项目在银行的支持下，可能通过发行债券来筹资。如果债券要被评级，则应在早期咨询有关评机机构。

三、项目融资的风险

项目融资的风险包括信用风险、建设和开发风险、市场和运营风险、金融风险、政治风险、法律风险和环境风险。

（一）信用风险

项目融资中，即使对借款人、项目发起人有一定的追索权，贷款人也应评估项目参与方的信用、业绩和管理技术。

（二）建设和开发风险

贷款人在评估建设和开发阶段的风险时，应仔细研究可行性报告中使用的方法和假设，必须考虑以下因素的影响：矿藏量不足，能力、产量和效率不足，成本过高，竣工延期，土地、建筑材料、燃料、原材料和运输的可获得性，劳动力、管理人员和可靠的承包商的可获得性，不可抗力等。

（三）市场和运营风险

在项目的运营阶段，可能存在下列风险：

（1）该项目产品是否存在国内和国外市场。

（2）可能存在的竞争情况，是否有相似的项目竣工。

（3）市场准入情况，潜在的顾客是否能自由购买产品，政府是否可控制市场。

（4）当项目到运营阶段时，项目产生的产品或提供的服务是否仍有市场，项目所用的技术是否可能被超越或被取代。

（四）金融风险

在项目筹资和还款阶段，可能面临汇率波动、利率上升的风险；在项目建设阶段，可能面临国际能源和原材料价格上涨的风险；在项目运营阶段，可能面临项目产品价格下跌的风险，或者面临通货膨胀的风险。

（五）政治风险

在项目融资中，借款人和贷款人都面临政治风险，如借款人所在国现有政治体制的崩溃，或颁布新税制、汇兑限制、国有化，或其他可能损害项目投资安全、偿债和变现的法律。

（六）法律风险

许多项目都是在第三世界国家进行的，其法律系统不健全，现有法律可能排除对不动产的所有权，对知识产权保护不够，可能缺乏有关公平贸易和竞争的法律，争议可能难以解决，当地律师和法院可能对项目中的争议不熟悉，当地法律系统可能运行迟缓、费用高。

（七）环境风险

公众越来越关注工业化进程对自然环境和人类健康的影响，许多国家颁布了法律来控制辐射、废弃物、有害物质的运输和低效使用能源、不可再生资源。因此，在项目融资过程中，借款人可能受到因污染而产生的罚款和惩罚，以及可能付出的其他环境成本。

四、项目融资的典型方式：BOT融资

BOT融资是项目融资的一种典型方式。BOT是英文 "biuld-operate-transfer"，即 "建设-运营-转让"，是指项目所在国政府将政府支配、拥有或控制的项目以招标形式选择国际商业资本或私人资本等发展商，政府通过与其签订协议，授权其为此项目筹资、设计、建设、运营、维护，并授予项目公司在项目建成后一定期限内的特许经营。在特许经营期限内，项目公司向用户收取费用，以此回收项目投资、经营和维护成本并获得合理回报。特许期满后，项目公司把基础设施无偿移交给政府。

BOT融资方式实质上是政府与承包商合作经营基础设施项目的一种特殊运作模式，在我国这种融资方式被称为 "特许权融资方式"。我国采用特许权融资方式建设的较有代表性的项目有北京京通高速公路、广西来宾电厂B厂、四川成都自来水厂六厂B厂、上海黄浦江延安东路隧道复线工程、海南东线高速公路等。

采用BOT融资方式，对东道国的有利之处在于：

（1）项目由外国投资者投资，无须本国政府投资，无须资金投入，只需授权，项目建成后且投资者特许经营期满，即可无偿得到基础设施项目，因此BOT融资方式很受各国政府青睐。

（2）国家无须对项目的债务提供担保，因此项目的债务不会构成国家债务。

（3）项目的绝大部分财政和回收投资风险由投资者承担。

东道国利用这种方式建成社会需要的基础设施，无疑对本国是有利的。

采用BOT融资方式，对东道国的不利之处在于：

项目建成后，投资者在经营项目期间，可能会对使用该项目产品或服务的公众收取较高的费用，引起公众的不满。

采用BOT融资方式，对投资者而言有利之处在于：

（1）可以直接进入东道国具有长期发展潜力的基础设施建设项目，并由此获得其他商业机会。

（2）在项目建设阶段，投资者可以推销设备，并带动本国劳务输出和贸易的出口。

（3）在项目运营阶段，可以从所拥有的项目公司获得红利收入。

（4）在项目运营期满阶段，可从高价出售的项目股份中获得可观的投资回报。

知识链接8-3

BOT融资在中国

我国第一个BOT基础设施项目是1984年以香港合和实业公司和中国发展投资公司等作为承包商在深圳建设的沙头角B电厂。之后，我国广东、福建、四川、上海、湖北、广西等地区也出现了一批BOT融资项目。如广深珠高速公路、重庆地铁、地沧高速公路、上海延安东路隧道复线、武汉地铁、北海油田开发等。比较典型的BOT融资

案例是深圳地铁4号线的建设。

深圳地铁4号线由港铁公司获得运营及沿线开发权。根据深圳市政府和港铁公司签署的协议，港铁公司在深圳成立项目公司以BOT融资方式投资建设全长约16千米、总投资约60亿元的4号线二期工程。同时，深圳市政府将已于2004年年底建成通车的全长4.5千米的4号线一期工程在二期工程通车前（2007年）租赁给港铁深圳公司，4号线二期通车之日始，4号线全线将由港铁公司成立的项目公司统一运营，该公司拥有30年的特许经营权。此外，港铁公司还获得4号线沿线290万平方米建筑面积的物业开发权。在整个建设和经营期内项目公司由港铁公司绝对控股，自主经营、自负盈亏，运营期满时全部资产无偿移交深圳市政府。

资料来源：佚名. 大全了，BOT/TOT/PPP/EPC等十余种项目承包模式全面解析［EB/OL］.［2017-07-16］. https：//www.sohu.com/a/157519797_221394.

任务三　　　　　　　　　国际债券融资

国际债券融资是指一国政府当局、金融机构、工商企业以及国际金融机构，通过在国外市场上发行以某种货币为面值的债券进行筹集资金的活动。

国际债券融资包括外国债券融资和欧洲债券融资。外国债券是指债券的发行者在境外发行的、以发行市场所在国货币为面值的债券。欧洲债券是指债券的发行者在境外发行的、不以发行市场所在国货币为面值的债券。此处的欧洲不是地理上的"欧洲"，指的是"境外"。

外国债券和欧洲债券的区别是：

（1）外国债券的发行市场与债券面值货币属于同一个国家，与发行者属于不同的国家或地区；而欧洲债券的发行者、发行市场、债券面值货币属于三个不同的国家或地区。

（2）发行方式不同。外国债券一般由发行市场所在国的证券公司、金融机构承销；而欧洲债券则由一家或者几家大银行牵头，组成十几家或者几十家国际性银行在一个国家或者几个国家同时承销。

（3）受发行市场所在国的法律限制不同。外国债券的发行受发行市场所在国有关法律、法规管制和约束；而欧洲债券不受发行地所在国有关法令管制和约束。

一、外国债券融资

发行外国债券时，可以面向发行地所在国广大投资者公募发行，也可面向发行地所在国少数投资者私募发行。外国债券的承销由发行所在国国内承销团承购，投资者主要是该国国内居民。外国债券的利率取决于发行国国内资本市场利率，以固定利率发行。外国债券的期限较长，约20～30年，期限较长的债券通常会向投资者提供回售保护，即投资者有权在债券到期前要求发行人以一定价格提前赎回该债券。

按照国际惯例，国外金融机构在一国发行外国债券时，一般以发行市场所在国最具该国特征的代表性物品命名，如在英国发行的外国债券称为"猛犬债券"，在美国发行的外国债券称为"扬基债券"，在日本发行的外国债券称为"武士债券"，在中国发行的外国债券称为"熊猫债券"。

当前主要的外国债券市场包括美国的扬基债券市场，日本的武士债券市场，瑞士外国债券市场、欧元债券市场等。

二、欧洲债券融资

欧洲债券融资具有的优点有：

（1）以不记名方式发行，转让极为便利。

（2）发行不受发行地所在国法令管制和约束，但每一笔销售都必须遵守销售国的法律和法规。债券发行前应注明发生纠纷时，应以哪一国家的法律为准。

（3）欧洲债券的利率受货币标价国国内资本市场利率影响，如欧洲美元债券收益率根据纽约债券市场的收益率而定，多数情况下，欧洲债券的收益率低于相应货币标价国国内资本市场利率。

在欧洲债券市场中，占比份额最大的是欧洲美元债券。除此之外，还有其他币种的债券，如欧洲英镑债券、欧洲日元债券、欧洲欧元债券等。

欧洲债券市场起源于20世纪60年代，发展极为迅速。欧洲债券融资总量目前已远远超过外国债券的融资总量，已成为跨国公司、外国政府和发展中国家政府筹集资金的重要渠道。

当前主要的欧洲债券市场包括欧洲美元市场、欧洲日元市场、欧洲英镑市场、欧洲特别提款权债券市场，其中欧洲美元债券市场的容量最大，而欧洲特别提款权债券市场的发行额与前三个市场相比较小。

思政小课堂

科技创新使贸易金融迎来崭新时代，人工智能和大数据的运用有效提升了决策的准确性，区块链技术的渗透大幅提升了业务处理效率，使得商业银行贸易融资未来发展呈现出六大趋势：以企业为中心的综合化贸易金融服务需求增加；国内贸易蕴含巨大业务机遇；大宗商品融资业务面临增长机遇；跨境电商的迅速崛起；"一带一路"沿线贸易金融和对外担保业务需求增长；金融科技变革贸易金融业务模式。

商业银行应当加快培育国际经济合作和竞争新优势，在贸易金融领域贯彻"利益共同体"和"命运共同体"的理念，为贸易金融发展注入新动力。

请思考：（1）金融科技未来将对银行贸易金融业务带来什么样的变化？

（2）商业银行如何在贸易金融领域贯彻"利益共同体"和"命运共同体"的理念？

项目思维导图

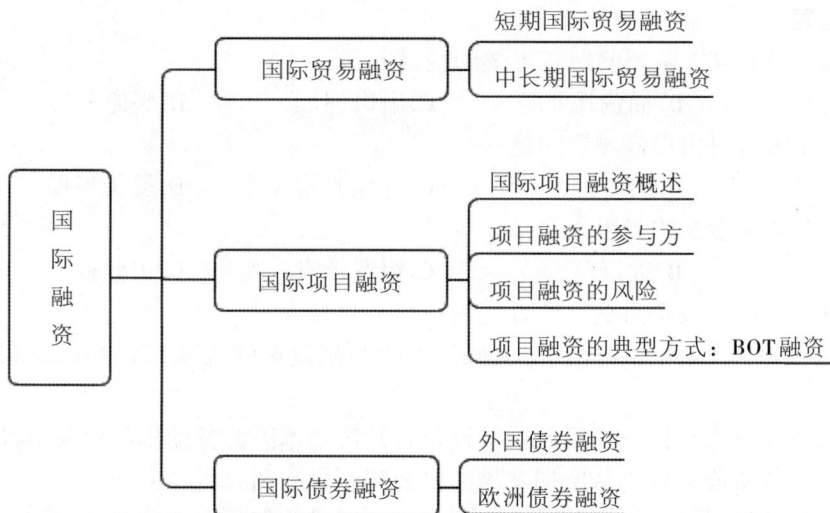

```
                                        短期国际贸易融资
                       国际贸易融资
                                        中长期国际贸易融资

                                        国际项目融资概述

                                        项目融资的参与方
           国际
           融资      国际项目融资
                                        项目融资的风险

                                        项目融资的典型方式：BOT融资

                                        外国债券融资
                       国际债券融资
                                        欧洲债券融资
```

项目训练

一、单选题

1.下列属于短期国际贸易融资方式的是（　　　）。

A.出口信贷　　　　　B.福费廷业务　　　　C.国际保理业务　　　D.买方信贷

2.下列不属于银行对进口商融资的是（　　　）。

A.卖方信贷　　　　　B.提货担保　　　　　C.买方信贷　　　　　D.信托收据

3.下列说法中，错误的是（　　　）。

A.外国筹资者在英国债券市场上发行的以英镑为面值的债券称为"猛犬债券"

B.外国筹资者在美国债券市场上发行的以美元为面值的债券称为"扬基债券"

C.外国筹资者在日本债券市场上发行的以美元为面值的债券称为"武士债券"

D.日本筹资者在瑞士债券市场上发行的以美元为面值的债券属于欧洲债券

4.下列说法中，错误的是（　　　）。

A.出口商办理福费廷手续简便，提交单据较少，可以向进口商转移部分融资费用

B.进口商以延期付款的方式进口大型机械或成套设备，可以减少资金占用

C.福费廷方给出口商提供融资，可以获得较高的收益，但是福费廷业务中使用的汇票和本票不可以在二级市场上流通转让

D.担保行不仅可以获得担保费，还可以扩大担保行在国际市场上的影响力

5.下列说法中，正确的是（　　　）。

A.BOT 的意思是"买断—转让"

B.出口信贷包括买方信贷和卖方信贷

C.在福费廷业务中，担保行的选择不需要福费廷方认可

D.国际保理业务属于中长期国际贸易融资

二、多选题

1.下列属于中长期国际贸易融资方式的是（   ）。

A.提货担保　　　　B.福费廷业务　　　　C.出口押汇　　　　D.买方信贷

2.下列属于银行对出口商融资的是（   ）。

A.卖方信贷　　　　B.出口押汇　　　　C.打包放款　　　　D.提货担保

3.福费廷业务中涉及的当事人有（   ）。

A.出口商　　　　B.进口商　　　　C.福费廷方　　　　D.担保行

4.在 BOT 融资中，投资者获得的好处包括（   ）。

A.可以直接进入东道国具有长期发展潜力的基础设施建设项目，并由此获得其他商业机会

B.在项目建设阶段，投资者可以推销设备，并带动本国劳务输出和贸易出口

C.在项目运营阶段，可以从所拥有的项目公司获得红利收入

D.在项目运营期满阶段，可从高价出售的项目股份中获得可观的投资回报

5.下列说法中，错误的是（   ）。

A.买方信贷是指出口地银行对进口商或进口商所在地银行提供的贷款形式

B.外国债券的发行人和债券面值货币属于同一个国家

C.福费廷方买断票据后，对出口商依然具有追索权

D.在 BOT 融资方式下，项目公司在特许经营期满时，将项目无偿移交给政府

三、判断题

1.打包放款是指在国际贸易中，出口商在发出货物之后，收到进口商开证行开立的信用证时，将正本信用证抵押给银行，向银行申请一定数额的贷款。（   ）

2.出口押汇是指出口商发货后，将出口商品的货运单据无追索权地卖给出口方银行申请融资。（   ）

3.出口信贷是指为促进本国大型机械设备或技术的出口，增强出口商品的国际竞争力，一国银行或非银行金融机构对本国出口商或进口商及进口商所在地银行提供较低利率贷款的一种国际信贷方式。（   ）

4.在 BOT 融资中，政府无须投入资金进行项目的建设。（   ）

5.欧洲债券融资是指外国筹资者在欧洲金融市场上发行债券筹集资金。（   ）

四、实践分析题

杭州某出口企业拟向国外出口大型成套设备，但国外进口企业短期内无法实现现汇付款，为保证贸易顺利进行，请为该企业设计一个出口方案。

项目九
外汇风险管理

学习目标

知识目标

掌握外汇风险的含义、要素及类型；了解外汇风险管理内容及外汇管制的具体方法和措施。

能力目标

能够辨识具体案例中的外汇风险情况。

操作目标

能够分析外汇风险管理案例并给出基本措施。

课程导入

外汇风险准备金率从20%下调为0，央行大动作有何深意？

2020年国庆节后首个交易日，在岸人民币对美元强势补涨近1 100点，离岸人民币对美元延续假期的强势。截至10月10日，在岸、离岸人民币双双破6.70关口，创下2019年4月以来新高。

人民币涨势迅猛

2020年第三季度，在岸人民币升幅达3.8%，实现了自2008年以来的最大季度涨幅，同期离岸人民币涨幅逾4%。人民币在三季度的表现，超过了包括瑞士法郎和日元等传统避险货币在内的G10货币。

统计数据显示，从2020年5月末以来，人民币掀起了一拨上涨行情，在岸人民币对美元汇率累计上涨4 000多点，离岸人民币对美元汇率累计上涨近5 000点。

以离岸人民币汇率简单计算，汇率从7.19到6.69，一个居民假如换汇10万美元，需要71.9万元人民币，到了今天最低只要66.9万元人民币，相差超5万元人民币。

央行出手：20%下调为0

中国人民银行10日发布消息：2020年以来，人民币汇率以市场供求为基础双向浮动，弹性增强，市场预期平稳，跨境资本流动有序，外汇市场运行保持稳定，市场供求平衡。

为此，中国人民银行决定自 2020 年 10 月 12 日起，将远期售汇业务的外汇风险准备金率从 20% 下调为 0。下一步，中国人民银行将继续保持人民币汇率弹性，稳定市场预期，保持人民币汇率在合理均衡水平上的基本稳定。

远期售汇业务是银行对企业提供的一种汇率避险衍生产品。企业通过远期购汇能在一定程度上规避未来汇率风险。

专家解读：此举有何深意？

中国民生银行首席研究员温彬表示，如果提高外汇风险准备金率，则企业从银行远期购买美元的成本就会上升，现在下调到 0，实际会降低企业购买远期美元的成本，从而增加远期购汇的需求。

2020 年以来，人民币对美元汇率波动加大，总体看呈现了由贬值转升值的走势。特别是随着中国经济基本面持续向好，近期人民币对美元升值显著。

这个时刻外汇风险准备金率下调为 0，一方面，有助于降低企业远期购汇成本，更好地利用人民币衍生品管理汇率风险；另一方面，远期美元购汇的需求增加，也可以抑制人民币即期汇率的过快升值，从而实现人民币对美元的汇率继续保持在合理均衡水平上的双向波动。

资料来源：顾志鹏. 外汇风险准备金率从 20% 下调为 0，央行大动作有何深意？[EB/OL]. [2020-10-12]. http://zj.zjol.com.cn/news/1540425.html.

思考讨论：

（1）什么是外汇风险？

（2）外汇风险准备金率的作用是什么？

任务一　　外汇风险概述

一、外汇风险的含义

外汇风险（foreign exchange exposure），又称汇率风险，是指由于国际外汇市场汇率变动，引起企业、银行等经济组织或国家、个人以外币计价的资产（债权、权益）和负债（债务、义务）的价值发生变化，从而给外汇交易主体带来的不确定性。

外汇风险有广义和狭义之分。广义的外汇风险是指既有损失的可能，又有盈利的可能；狭义的外汇风险仅指因汇率变动给经济主体带来损失的可能。一般我们所说的是狭义的外汇风险。

外汇风险通常由外汇敞口来体现。外汇敞口，又称受险部分，是指经营活动中受汇率变动影响的外币金额。外汇敞口包括两种情况：

（1）当以外币计价的资产或负债的金额不相等时，就会出现一部分外币资产或负债净额受汇率变动的影响，这一净额就是"外汇敞口头寸"。

（2）当以外币计价的资产或负债的期限不同时，就会出现期限缺口。

【例9-1】某跨国公司出口收入200万美元，进口支付100万美元，因此形成100万美元的外汇敞口，如果美元升值5%，则收益5万美元；相反，则损失5万美元。因此，暴露的100万美元外汇，就是受险部分。

二、外汇风险的构成要素

外汇风险有本币、外币和时间三个构成要素，这三个要素在外汇风险中同时存在，缺一不可。

（一）本币

本币是衡量企业经济效益的共同货币指标。在涉外经营活动中，如果企业发生外币应收账款、应付账款、外币资本的借入和借出等，均需用本币进行折算，以考核其经营绩效。在外币与本币的折算过程中，由于汇率不断变化可能引起按本币计算的现金流等发生变动，如果因此造成损失，则说明存在外汇风险。如果涉外经济活动中企业未使用外币而用本币计价，则不存在外汇风险。

【例9-2】美国某出口企业出口一批货物给德国进口商，3个月后收回货款，同时要求以美元进行结算。在这笔交易中，该出口企业是以本币计价，不涉及本币与外币的折算，因此不存在外汇风险。

（二）外币

在国际经济活动中，常常需要用外币进行结算，尤其是本国货币不能在国际市场上流通的经济实体，更需要使用外币进行结算。因此，这些经济主体在本币与外币的折算过程中，不可避免地会存在外汇风险。

【例9-3】我国某出口企业出口一批货物给德国进口商，6个月后支付货款，要求以美元结算。在这笔交易中，该出口企业以外币计价，收回美元货款后需要折算成人民币，就可能会受到汇率波动的影响，即6个月后美元货款兑换的人民币金额发生变化，因此存在外汇风险。

（三）时间

在国际经济活动中，从交易达成到账款实际收付、借贷本息偿付的完成都有一个期限，这个期限就是时间因素。在一定的时间内，外币与本币的折算比率有可能发生变化，从而产生外汇风险。

【例9-4】在【例9-3】中，该出口企业6个月后收回货款，这6个月内美元对人民币汇率时刻发生变化，从而产生外汇风险。

一般来说，时间越长，汇率波动的可能性和幅度越大，外汇风险就越大；反之，外汇风险就越小。

三、外汇风险的类型

根据外汇风险发生的时间，外汇风险可分为折算风险、交易风险和经济风险三种。

（一）折算风险

折算风险，又称会计风险或转换风险，是指经济主体进行会计处理时，在将功能货币（即经济活动中使用的货币，一般为外币）转换成记账货币（一般为经济主体的本国货币）时，由于汇率波动而呈现账面损失的可能。

折算风险不是交割时发生的实际损失，而是会计评价上的损失，是一种存量风险。跨国公司在编制合并会计报表时，要将国外分公司的财务报表按照相应会计准则转换为本国货币。一般企业以外币计价的资产、负债、收益和支出等，通常也都要转换成本国货币。很明显，如果汇率发生波动，即使企业以外币计价的资产、负债的数额没变，但是在会计账目中，本币数值却会发生相应变化，因此企业会计账目会出现一定的损益。这种损益会影响企业向股东和社会公开财务报表的结果。

【例9-5】我国某企业因业务需要在美国的银行存放了10万美元，当时美元与人民币的汇兑比率为USD1=CNY6.9146，在该企业的会计账目上，其存款折算成人民币为69.146万元。如果一段时间后，美元与人民币的汇兑比率为USD1=CNY6.8146，则在该企业的会计账目上，其存款折算成人民币为68.146万元。显然，相同数额的美元存款以不同的汇率进行折算，最终账面价值减少了1万元人民币，这就是折算风险，会对企业的盈利、财务报表等带来很大影响。

（二）交易风险

交易风险，又称交易结算风险，是指在以外币计价的交易中，由于本币与外币之间的汇率变化，造成资产或负债价值变化的风险。交易风险是一种流量风险，自交易合同生效时产生，到交易完成交割时终了。在国际经济活动中，只要涉及外币计价或收付的交易活动或国际投资等都会存在交易风险。根据涉外活动的情况，交易风险主要包括以下三种情况：

1.对外贸易结算风险

在进出口业务中，一般从签订贸易合同到货款的最终收付都需要经历一段时间，在这段时间内汇率可能发生变化，使得出口商收入减少或进口商支出增加，这就是对外贸易结算风险。

【例9-6】我国某出口商向美国进口商出口一批价值100万美元的货物，3个月后收款。在签订贸易合约时，美元与人民币的汇兑比率为USD1=CNY6.8201，按此汇率该出口商收款时可获得682.01万元人民币。但是，如果在3个月后人民币升值，汇率变为USD1=CNY6.7201，那么该出口商收款时只能获得672.01万元人民币，损失了10万元人民币，即该出口商收入比预期的减少了。同理，进口商从签订合约到结算为止也要承担外汇风险，原理与出口商相同，汇率变动与出口商刚好相反。

2.外汇买卖风险

在待交割的即期或远期外汇交易中，由于汇率变化，使得合同到期时交易一方可能要遭受少收或多付本币（或其他货币）的损失，这种情况构成了外汇买卖风险。

【例9-7】假定某银行与客户进行外汇买卖，当天汇率为EUR1=USD1.1300，买入100万欧元，卖出113万美元，次日交割。如果第二天欧元贬值，汇率变为EUR1=USD1.1200，则银行买入100万欧元，只需支付112万美元，客户损失1万美元，这就是外汇买卖风险。

3.国际投资风险

在以外币计价的国际投资和国际借贷活动中，在债权债务未清偿之前，由于汇率变动而引起债权人收入减少或债务人支出增加的风险，就构成国际投资风险。这种风险存在的前提是，开始买进或卖出外汇，将来必须反过来卖出或买进外汇。

【例9-8】某美国企业借入500万欧元国际借款，期限为2年，当时的汇率为EUR1=USD1.1217。如果2年后汇率变为EUR1=USD1.1317，则该企业需要565.85万美元（500×1.1317）才能偿还500万欧元借款，比借款时多支付5万美元（500×1.1217-565.85）。

（三）经济风险

经济风险，也称经营风险，是指由于意料之外的汇率变动，使企业在未来的收益发生变化的可能。具体来说，经济风险是一种潜在风险，汇率变动通过对产量、销量、生产成本和销售价格的影响，使企业最终收益发生变化；收益变化的幅度则取决于汇率变化对产品数量、价格和成本的影响程度。

对一个企业来说，经济风险涉及企业生产的各个阶段，需要从企业整体进行预测和分析。经济风险的分析主要取决于企业的预测分析能力，存在主观性和动态性，其影响是长期的；而折算风险和交易风险的影响则是一次性的，所以经济风险带来的损失比折算风险或交易风险严重。

【例9-9】当某国货币贬值时，出口商品的外币价格下降，会刺激出口增加，使出口商的出口额增加；如果出口商生产使用的生产要素主要是进口商品，本币贬值则会使其成本增加。综合考虑，该出口商最终收益可能增加，也可能减少。这种风险就是经济风险。

任务二　　　　　　　　外汇风险管理

一、外汇风险管理概述

在涉外经济活动中不可避免地存在外汇风险，给涉外经济主体带来很大影响。因此，各经济主体应该正视外汇风险客观存在的事实，努力分析其发生的原因，并采取相关措施加以防范。

（一）外汇风险管理的含义

外汇风险管理，是指外汇资产持有者对外汇市场可能出现的变化作出相关决策，以预防、规避、转移或消除外汇业务中的风险，从而避免或减少汇率变化可能造成的经济损失。

虽然外汇风险是客观存在的，但是通过采取相关措施是可以规避或消除的。外汇风险管理包括一般管理和综合管理，不管进行一般管理还是综合管理，都应该遵循相关原则。

（二）外汇风险管理的原则

各经济主体进行外汇风险管理，都应该遵循以下原则：

1. 结合宏观经济原则

各企业、部门等微观经济主体在处理自身利益与国家宏观利益的问题时，通常都是尽可能降低或避免外汇风险损失，而将风险转嫁给银行机构、保险公司等。但是，在实际业务中，各经济主体应尽可能将微观主体利益与宏观经济结合起来，共同防范风险。

2. 分类防范原则

针对不同种类的外汇风险产生的原因不同，各经济主体应该采取不同措施进行分类防范。例如，针对交易风险，各经济主体应该以选好结算货币作为主要的防范方法；对于证券投资的汇率风险，各经济主体应该采取各种保值为主的防范方法。

3. 避损得利原则

在实际业务中，应注意在采取措施转嫁或消除外汇风险的同时，将可能的收益转移出去。因此，各经济主体应该在转嫁或消除外汇风险的同时，尽可能做到"避损得利"。

案例探析9-1

2018年1月，中华集团公司与美国某公司签订出口订单1 000万美元，当时美元对人民币的汇率为USD1=CNY6.5063，6个月后交货时，人民币已经大大升值，美元对人民币的汇率为USD1=CNY6.3063，由于人民币汇率的变动，该公司损失了200万元人民币。

这一事件发生后，该公司为了加强外汇风险管理，切实提升公司外汇风险防范水平，于2018年7月召开了关于公司强化外汇风险管理的高层会议，总结本次损失发生的经验教训，制定公司外汇风险管理对策。有关人员的发言要点如下：

总经理张某：（1）加强外汇风险管理工作十分重要，对于这一问题必须引起高度重视。（2）外汇风险管理应当抓住重点，尤其是对于交易风险和折算风险的管理，必须制定切实的措施，防止汇率变化对公司利润的侵蚀。

总会计师宋某：加强外汇管理的确十分重要。我最近对外汇风险管理的相关问题进行了初步研究，发现进行外汇风险管理的金融工具还是比较多的，在采取任何一种金融工具进行避险的同时，也就失去了汇率向有利方面变动带来的收益，外汇的损失和收益主要取决于汇率变动的时间和幅度，因此强化外汇风险管理，首先必须重视对汇率变动趋势的研究，根据汇率的不同变动趋势，采取不同对策。

资料来源：佚名. 国际金融复习提纲 [EB/OL].［2011-02-17］. https://wenku.baidu.com/view/03130e0ff12d2af90242e6ea.html.

思考题：

（1）案例中体现的是哪一种风险？

（2）从外汇风险管理基本原理的角度，指出总经理张某和总会计师宋某在会议发言中的观点有何不当之处，并分别简要说明理由。

（三）外汇风险管理的战略

外汇风险管理的战略，是指涉外经济主体对外汇风险持有的态度，即应不应该防范风险、应该进行多大程度的防范。根据对风险的不同态度，涉外经济主体可以采取完全防范战略、完全不防范战略和部分防范风险战略。

1.完全防范战略

完全防范战略，是指采取严格措施防范外汇风险，完全消除不确定性因素的战略。虽然这种措施能有效防范外汇风险，但不是最有利的战略，因为在进行风险防范的同时，丧失了获利机会。

2.完全不防范战略

完全不防范战略，是指对外汇风险不采取任何防范措施的战略。如果汇率朝不利方向变化，则自愿承担损失；如果汇率朝有利方向变化，则能获得收益。一般来说，在固定汇率制度下，外汇业务量小或投机活动中采取完全不防范战略的较多；而在浮动汇率制度下，企业或银行几乎没有采取此战略的。

3.部分防范风险战略

部分防范风险战略，是指对外汇风险的一部分采取防范措施，其他部分则不予防范的战略。采取部分防范风险战略的关键在于：在全部的外汇暴露中，哪些部分需要采取防范措施，哪些部分不需要采取防范措施。采取此战略不仅要考虑防范风险的成本，还要考虑防范风险的难易程度、对汇率走势预测的准确度等因素。

二、涉外企业外汇风险管理

由于市场汇率水平的不断变化，涉外企业随时可能会遭受外汇风险。因此，如何防范外汇风险成为涉外企业经营管理的主要内容之一，涉外企业应该针对不同类型的外汇风险，遵循"成本最小、风险管理效果最佳"的原则，设计和选择防止和减少损失发生的管理方案。下面将对涉外企业的折算风险管理、交易风险管理和经济风险管理进行介绍。

（一）折算风险管理

根据折算风险的传递机制，折算风险管理的方法主要包括资产负债保值法、资产负债中性化法、风险对冲法和净额支付法。

1.资产负债保值法

资产负债保值法，是指企业对资产、负债进行相应调整，以防止或减少外汇风险的方法。

在企业的资产、负债中，有些容易调整，有些则难以调整或无法调整，因此企业进行资产、负债调整前应对资产负债进行定性分析，确定调整的重点对象。一般来说，企业的长期资产、长期负债都缺乏流动性，短期内无法迅速增加或减少，因而难以进行调整；在短期资产、负债中，有一些企业也不能按照自己意愿进行调整，如应交税额等。因此，企业对资产、负债调整的重点是短期资产中的应收账款、现金、存货、银行存款和短期投资等，以及短期负债中的应付账款和票据等。

【例9-10】某跨国企业预期某外币将升值，增加了以此外币计价的短期资产，减少了以此外币计价的短期负债；反之，当预期某种货币将贬值时，应减少以此货币计价的短期资产，增加以此货币计价的短期负债。

2.资产负债中性化法

资产负债中性化法，是指对资产和负债进行调整，使得以各种功能货币（日常经营活动中使用的货币）表示的资产和负债的数额相等，从而折算风险头寸（受险头寸，即受险资产与受险负债之间的差额）为零的防范折算风险的方法。

资产负债中性化法的具体操作流程为：

（1）计算资产负债表中各种外币资产和外币负债的数额，确定净折算风险头寸的大小。

（2）根据风险头寸的性质确定受险资产和受险负债的调整方向。

（3）对具体情况进行认真分析和权衡比较，决定调整的种类和数额，使调整的综合成本最小、效果最佳。

【例9-11】假定某跨国企业仅有美元资产300万美元、美元负债400万美元，即美元负债大于美元资产，这时需增加美元资产或减少美元负债，或同时进行，当美元资产和美元负债的数额相等时，折算风险头寸为零。

3.风险对冲法

风险对冲法，是指企业在金融市场进行相应操作，利用外汇合约的盈亏来冲抵折算盈亏。具体来说，企业先确定可能出现的预期折算损失，再进行相应远期外汇交易避免风险。

【例9-12】假定在美国的英国子公司预期其资产负债表中存在5万英镑的损失，在预期英镑将贬值的情况下，期初时可以在远期市场卖出英镑，到期末再买进等额的英镑，并进行远期合约的交割。显然，如果期初远期汇率大于期末即期汇率，则期初卖出英镑获得的美元肯定大于购回等额英镑所花的美元数额，交易有利可图。由此可见，风险对冲法是以折算结果为基础，并且与预期期末折算货币密切相关，只要预测准确就可以避免外汇风险。

风险对冲法存在一定的局限性：

（1）期初签订外汇合约时，折算风险头寸是未知的，远期或期货合约的避险金额可能不同于折算风险头寸。

（2）风险对冲法实际上是用实现的外汇合约盈亏来冲抵未发生的账面折算盈亏，外汇合约盈亏要计入应税所得，折算盈亏则不在应税所得范围内，这种差异使得风险对冲不能有效地减少企业的实际风险。

4.净额支付法

债务净额支付法，是指涉外企业在清偿内部交易产生的债权和债务，对各子公司、母公司与子公司之间的应收账款和应付账款进行划转与冲销时，仅定期对净额部分进行支付，从而减少支付数额和次数，降低折算风险。

【例9-13】某跨国公司各子公司之间发生内部交易，美国子公司欠英国子公司价值500万美元的英镑，英国子公司欠香港子公司价值300万美元的港元，香港子公司欠美国子公司300万美元，经过冲销后，美国子公司支付价值200万美元的预先商定的货币，减少了支付的次数和数额，大大降低了折算风险。

拓展阅读9-1

企业汇率风险管理不到位导致汇率浮动恐惧症

11月28日，"2020中国新经济企业500强"发布会在浙江杭州举办，中国企业评价协会发布了《2020 中国新经济企业 500 强发展报告》及"2020 中国新经济企业 500 强"榜单。发布会上，国家外汇管理局副局长王春英做了主题演讲。

"汇率问题是我们各界高度关注的一个问题，在一个汇率波动幅度加大的世界里，如何做好汇率风险管理，对企业尤其是国际业务占比较高企业的财务绩效十分重要。"

王春英表示，从外汇局的调查结果来看，目前我国企业避险保值意识亟待加强。为了解企业汇率风险管理现状，外汇局对 2 400 多家企业开展了问卷调查。调查显示，在人民币汇率市场化进程中，企业的汇率风险管理水平不断提升，但也存在一些值得关注的问题。

第一，风险管理意识相对薄弱。大多数企业汇率风险敞口对冲比例较低，甚至有企业不进行任何金融避险。一些大型外资企业超过 100 万美元以上的敞口就会制定汇率风险管理策略，而部分国内企业持有上亿美元的风险敞口，仍缺乏汇率风险管理意识。

第二，风险管理较为被动。调查显示，仅 20% 的企业能够严格遵照财务纪律，主动、及时规避汇率风险。相当一部分企业习惯在汇率波动加剧时才重视汇率风险管理，一些企业甚至利用外汇衍生品谋取收益或从事套利，偏离主业。

第三，汇率风险管理不到位导致"汇率浮动恐惧症"。市场供求变化决定了汇率双向波动的自然特征，但一些企业不习惯汇率波动。越缺少科学有效的汇率风险管理，越担心汇率波动。

对影响企业选择汇率避险的因素，王春英表示有四个方面：

一是以往汇率单边走向助长企业押注汇率。历史上人民币汇率长期处于单边走向，波动幅度很窄，人民币汇率趋势预测比较容易，客观上助长了部分企业押注人民币汇率的倾向。

二是企业不熟悉外汇衍生产品。相当数量的企业认为，现有外汇衍生品总体够用，增加新品种的需求并不十分迫切。对外汇衍生产品越熟悉的企业，办理外汇衍生品套保的比例越高。但仍有相当数量的企业不熟悉外汇衍生品。

三是部分企业仍存在"赌博投机"心态。很多企业对套期保值认识不到位，习惯将外汇衍生品价格和到期市场价格比较，并以此作为财务管理的业绩考核依据。这表明企业对套期保值认识不到位，风险中性意识仍有待提升。

四是部分企业认为套保成本较高。部分企业的资产负债管理存在过度顺周期问题。在人民币升值期间，通过增加外币债务（包括向境内银行借用外汇贷款）和加杠杆等方式，进行过度"资产本币化、负债外币化"资产配置，赚取人民币汇率升值收益；在人民币贬值期间，通过增加外币资产和加杠杆等方式，进行过度"资产外币化、负债本币化"资产配置，赚取人民币汇率贬值收益。

"盲目的顺周期财务运作极易引发风险，从微观层面来看，企业不结合主业、经营实际状况合理布局自身资产负债结构，而通过财务运作过度增加杠杆和负债，盲目增大外汇风险敞口，在人民币汇率波动时将面临风险。"

资料来源：王蒙. 外汇管理局王春英：企业汇率风险管理不到位导致汇率浮动恐惧症［EB/OL］.［2020-11-28］. https://finance.sina.com.cn/meeting/2020-11-28/doc-iiznezxs4136108.shtml.

（二）交易风险管理

交易风险是涉外企业面临的最主要的外汇风险，是企业进行风险管理的重点内容。下面介绍涉外企业交易风险管理的主要方法。

1.币种选择法

币种选择法，即选好和搭配好计价货币，是企业通过选择涉外经济交易中使用的计价货币的种类来防范外汇风险的方法。在涉外经济交易中，双方签订合同，合同中支付条款会说明结算货币。选择哪一种计价货币，直接关系到交易主体将来是否会承担外汇风险。

（1）选择本国货币计价。

在签订进出口贸易合同时，应该尽量选择本币作为计价货币。选择本国货币作为计价货币，就不涉及本币与外币的折算，对于进出口商中的一方就可以完全防范外汇风险。

对出口商来说，以本国货币作为计价货币，由于不需要进行本币与外币的兑换，因此出口商完全不会有外汇风险，但是对进口商来说存在外汇风险；对进口商来说，以本国货币作为计价货币，也不存在外汇风险，但是对出口商来说存在外汇风险。

【例9-14】英国某企业出口一批货物给我国进口商，以英镑作为计价货币，3个月后收回货款。在这笔交易中，英国出口商选择英镑（本币）作为计价货币，就不会涉及本币与外币的折算，不存在外汇风险；而对我国进口商来说，英镑对人民币汇率可能会发生变化，因此存在外汇风险。

【例9-15】美国进口商从中国购买一批电脑，以美元作为计价货币，3个月后支付货款。在这笔交易中，美国进口商选择美元（本币）作为计价货币，就不会涉及本币与外币的折算，不存在外汇风险；而对我国出口商来说，美元对人民币汇率可能会发生变化，因此存在外汇风险。

选用本国货币计价的优点是简便易行。由于这种方式会受到本国货币国际地位的限制，同时贸易双方也会因计价货币的选择而产生矛盾，因此需要综合考虑本币的国际地位和双方的交易习惯来选择计价货币。

（2）选择自由兑换货币计价。

选用可以自由兑换的货币作为计价货币，有利于外汇资金的运用，在汇率可能发生不利影响时，可以立即兑换成另一种有利货币。

【例9-16】假如日本一家出口企业，与加拿大进口商达成一笔交易，规定使用美元作为计价货币，6个月后支付货款。如果收到货款时，美元对日元汇率下跌，即美元贬值，而英镑对日元汇率上升，即英镑升值，那么日本出口商就可以立即将美元兑换成英镑。

（3）选择有利货币计价。

一般来说，出口选择硬货币计价，进口选择软货币计价，即"收硬付软"。

硬货币是指汇率稳定且有升值趋势的货币；软货币是指汇率不稳定且具有贬值趋势的货币。出口商以硬货币作为计价货币，由于硬货币将来升值，在出口商收到货款时，就可以将这部货款兑换成更多数额的本国货币；同样，进口商以软货币作为计价货币，由于软货币将来贬值，在进口商支付货款时，就可以用较少的本币兑换这笔货款。

【例9-17】假定当前美元对人民币汇率为USD1=CNY6.7000，美元汇率稳定且有升值趋势，当前英镑对人民币汇率为GBP1=CNY8.5900，英镑汇率不稳定且有贬值趋势。

分析：（1）如果某中国出口商出口一批货物给日本进口商，价值100万美元，3个月后收回货款，那么此时中国出口商应该选择美元作为计价货币。因为美元是硬货币，假定3个月后美元升值，美元对人民币汇率为USD1=CNY6.8800，那么中国出口商就可以多获得18万元人民币（100×（6.8800-6.7000））。

（2）如果某中国进口商从日本进口一批货物，价值100万英镑，3个月后支付货款，那么此时中国进口商应该选择英镑作为计价货币。因为英镑是软货币，假定3个月后英镑贬值，英镑对人民币汇率为GBP1=CNY8.5000，那么中国进口商就可以少支付9万元人民币（100×（8.5900-8.5000））。

实质上，选择有利货币计价是将汇率变动的好处留给自己，而将汇率变动带来的坏处推给对方。采用此方法一般会受到两个方面的影响：一是贸易双方的交易习惯；二是货币的"软""硬"是相对的，所以此方法不能保证进出口商完全消除外汇风险。

（4）选用"一篮子"货币计价。

"一篮子"货币是指按一定比例构成的一组（两种以上）货币。由于"一篮子"货币中既有硬货币又有软货币，硬货币升值带来的收益可以与软货币贬值带来的损失基本相抵，因此"一篮子"货币的币值相对稳定。对贸易双方来说，此方法可以有效减少或消除外汇风险。

2.货币保值法

贸易双方在签订进出口贸易合同和借贷合同时，在合同中加列保值条款，以防范外汇风险。常见的保值条款包括以下三种：

（1）黄金保值条款。

黄金保值，是指在签订合同时，按当时市场上的黄金价格将支付的货币折算为相应单位的黄金，到实际支付时，再按照同期黄金的市场价格折算成应支付的货币金额。

【例9-18】某笔货款为50万美元，签订合同时1美元折合黄金为1克纯金，则50万美元折合黄金为50万克纯金。到实际支付时，美元贬值，1美元的含金量为0.90克纯金，则50万克纯金折合成美元为55.56万美元，因此进口商应支付货款55.56万美元。由于美元贬值，结算时进口商支付的55.56万美元相当于签订合同时的50万美元。

黄金保值条款在固定汇率制度下经常被使用，如今很少使用了。

（2）外汇保值条款。

在计价货币已确定的情况下，为避免其币值变动给双方带来风险，可以选用币值稳定的货币为计价货币来保值。其具体操作是：

①贸易双方交易时，确定合同计价货币；

②选择计价货币以外的一种或"一篮子"货币作为保值货币，并在合同中规定计价货币与保值货币之间的固定比价；

③一旦结算时计价货币汇率发生不利变动，交易一方可以要求对方按计价货币与保值货币的比价调整其收汇或付汇数额。

（3）"一篮子"货币保值条款。

"一篮子"货币保值条款是交易双方在合同中规定计价货币与"一篮子"货币的价值挂钩的保值条款。其具体做法为：

①签订合同时，按照当时汇率和各保值货币的权重，将货款分别折算成各保值货币；

②到货款支付时，再按照当时汇率将保值货币折算成计价货币。

【例9-19】某笔货款为1 000万美元，合同中规定用美元、日元、英镑组成的"一篮子"货币对货款进行保值，其中各货币的权重分别为0.3、0.3、0.4。假设签订合同时的汇率为：1美元=105日元、1美元=0.7845英镑，则1 000万美元折合为保值货币为：1 000×0.3×1=300（万美元）；1 000×0.3×105=31 500（万日元）；1 000×0.4×0.7845=313.8（万英镑）。假设货款支付时的汇率为：1美元=110日元、1美元=0.7950英镑，则各保值货币分别折回美元为：300万美元；31 500÷110=286.36（万美元）；313.8÷0.7950=394.72（万美元），即货款结算时进口商向出口商支付981.08万美元（300+286.36+394.72）。

3.调价保值法

调价保值法是通过价格调整来防范外汇风险的方法。在进出口贸易中，"收硬付软"只是一种理想的选择，实际交易中会因各种因素的限制而无法实现。在实际交易中，当出口收软货币，进口付硬货币时，可以采用价格调整的方法来规避外汇风险。调价保值法主要分为加价保值法和压价保值法两类。

（1）加价保值法。

加价保值法用于出口交易中，当出口商接受软货币计价时，提高出口商品价格以规避外汇风险。加价的幅度等于软货币预期贬值的幅度，即将汇率变动可能带来的损失摊入出口商品价格中。根据国际惯例，其计算公式为：

加价后商品价格=原单价×（1+预期货币贬值率）

【例9-20】某公司出口商品以英镑计价，现在成交，1年后结汇。假设英镑为软货币，预期年贬值率为6%，每单位商品的原价为200英镑，则加价后的商品价格为：

200×（1+6%）=212（英镑）

（2）压价保值法。

压价保值法用于进口交易中，当进口商接受软货币计价时，压低进口商品价格以规避外汇风险。降价的幅度等于硬货币预期升值的幅度，即将汇率变动可能带来的损失从进口商品价格中剔除。根据国际惯例，其计算公式为：

压价后商品价格=原单价×（1-预期货币升值率）

值得注意的是，调价保值法只是将外汇风险转移出去了。运用这种方法时会受到商品的市场需求、商品质量等因素的限制。

4.易货贸易法

易货贸易，也称以物易物贸易法，是指贸易双方直接进行等值的货物交换。同时，双方将互换商品单价事先确定，交易时双方无须收付外汇，不存在外汇风险，但交易双方都存在自身商品涨价和对方商品跌价的风险。

5.期限调整法

期限调整法，是指通过调整收支时间来防范外汇风险的方法，包括提前收付或拖延收付。具体地说，就是进出口商根据对计价货币汇率变动趋势的预测，提前或延迟货款收付日期，进而规避外汇风险，获得汇率变动收益的方法。

一般来说，当预测计价货币有贬值趋势时，出口商或债权人应尽量提前收汇，以避免将来收到的外汇兑换成本币的数额减少；而进口商或债务人则应尽量延迟支付外汇，以有利于将来用较少的本币就可以兑换到同样数额的外汇。

当预测计价货币有升值趋势时，出口商或债权人应尽量延迟收汇，以获得将来收到的外汇兑换更多数额的本币；而进口商或债务人则应尽量提前支付外汇，以避免将来用更多的本币才能兑换到同样数额的外汇。

6.金融市场交易法

金融市场交易法，是指涉外企业利用金融市场，特别是外汇市场和货币市场的交易来防范外汇风险的方法。金融市场交易法主要包括以下方法：

（1）即期合同法。

即期合同法，是指拥有外汇应收或应付账款的企业与银行签订买卖外汇的即期合同，以消除外汇风险的方法。

即期外汇交易是在成交后的两个营业日内办理交割的，这两天的汇率波动就会带来外汇风险。因此，如果这两天内有外汇收入，企业则要与银行签订卖出相同币种、相同金额外汇的即期合同来消除外汇风险；如果这两天内有外汇支出，企业则要与银行签订买入相同币种、相同金额外汇的即期合同来消除外汇风险。

（2）远期合同法。

远期合同法，是指拥有外汇应收或应付账款的企业与银行签订买卖外汇的远期合同，以消除外汇风险的方法。其具体操作是：

①出口商在签订贸易合同后，按当时的远期汇率预先卖出与合同币种相同、金额相等的远期外汇，在收到货款时，再按约定的远期汇率进行交割；

②进口商在签订贸易合同后，按当时的远期汇率预先买入与合同币种相同、金额相等的远期外汇，在支付货款时，再按约定的远期汇率进行交割。

【例9-21】中国某出口企业3个月后会收到500万美元货款，为消除外汇风险，该企业与银行签订卖出500万美元的远期外汇合同，假设3个月期的远期汇率为USD1=CNY6.8805，则该企业3个月后可用收到的500万美元兑换3 440.25万元人民币。由此可知，远期外汇交易合同锁定了美元与人民币的兑换比率，消除了3个月内美元对人民币汇率可能波动的风险。

案例探析9-2

中国海尔集团在美国南卡来罗那州设立了一家生产电视机的工厂。海尔集团决定从日本引进一条彩色显像管生产线，总额为1 000 000日元，2个月后支付货款。海尔集团财务人员担心2个月后日元升值。一个解决办法是委托中国银行买入2个月期的远期外汇合约。2个月期的远期汇率为1日元=0.007042美元。但是，海尔集团又不想通过远期外汇合约锁定固定汇率，因为海尔集团希望在日元贬值时也能受益。也就是说，海尔集团希望在日元升值时能得到保护，而在日元贬值时又能受益。

花旗银行为海尔集团设计了一个套期保值方案：海尔集团买进一份协定价格为1日元=0.007143美元的日元看涨期权，合约金额为140 000 000日元，期权价格为50 000美元。同时，海尔集团卖出一份协定价格为1日元=0.006667美元的日元看跌期权合约，合约金额和期权价格都与看涨期权相同。由于两份期权合约的期权费相同，海尔集团开始时没有任何现金支出。到时不外乎有三种情况：

1.当日元汇率大于0.007143美元时：

（1）看涨期权有价，海尔集团行使该期权，按协定价格买进140 000 000日元，支付1 000 000美元。

（2）看跌期权无价，买方放弃期权。海尔集团无任何负担。

2.当日元汇率小于0.007143美元，但大于0.006667美元时：

（1）看涨期权无价，海尔集团不会行使期权，而是按当时的即期汇率买进所需的140 000 000日元，假设当时的即期汇率为0.006888美元，则海尔集团支付964 320美元。

（2）看跌期权无价，买方不会行使期权。海尔集团无任何负担。

3.当日元汇率小于0.006667美元时：

（1）看涨期权无价，海尔集团放弃期权。

（2）看跌期权有价，买方决定行使期权，按0.006667美元卖给海尔集团140 000 000日元。海尔集团别无选择，只能按此价格买进这笔日元，支付933 380美元。

资料来源：佚名. 海尔外汇风险管理案例［EB/OL］.［2020-05-26］. https：//wenku.baidu.com/view/12e6af4050d380eb6294dd88d0d233d4b14e3 f8e.html.

思考题：

（1）银行制定的这套期权组合策略为海尔集团提供了何种保护和受益机会？

（2）银行制定的这套期权组合策略同远期和单一的期权策略相比，有何优点和缺点？

（3）期货交易法。

期货交易法，是指拥有外汇应收或应付账款的企业通过签订外汇期货合同来防范外汇风险的方法，即涉外企业委托银行或经纪人购买或出售相应外汇期货，以消除外汇风险的方法。其具体操作是：

①拥有外汇应收账款的企业担心收汇时计价货币贬值，可以进入期货市场利用空头套期保值避免外汇风险；

②拥有外汇应付账款的企业担心付汇时计价货币升值，可以进入期货市场利用多头套期保值避免外汇风险。

【例9-22】2020年2月10日，美国某出口商预计3个月后将收到一笔100万欧元的货款。2月10日签订合同时，美元对欧元即期汇率为EUR1=USD1.1340，按此汇率水平，该出口商可收入113.4万美元。为了防止欧元贬值，该出口商在期货市场卖出8份5月份到期的欧元期货合约（每份合约为12.5万欧元），成交价格为EUR1=USD1.1396。3个月后，欧元贬值，汇率变为EUR1=USD1.1290，现汇市场上，该出口商出售100万欧元，只能兑换到112.9万美元，比2月10日少收0.5万美元。但是，3个月后期货市场上成交价为EUR1=USD1.1346，该出口商此时可以买进8份5月份到期的欧元期货合约，以冲抵原来卖出的欧元期货，因此在期货市场上可以获得0.5万美元（（1.1396-1.1346）×12.5×8），刚好弥补了现汇市场上出现的损失。

（4）期权交易法。

期权交易法，是指拥有外汇应收或应付账款的企业通过签订外汇期权合同来防范外汇风险的方法。根据期权的特征，出口商应买入看跌期权，进口商应买入看涨期权。

由于期权赋予期权买者相应权利，期权买者可以根据市场汇率变动选择执行或不执行期权，最多损失期权费。

（5）掉期交易法。

掉期交易法，是指具有远期外汇债权或债务的企业，在与银行签订买入或卖出即期或远期外汇的同时，卖出或买入相应的远期外汇，以防范外汇风险的方法。

掉期交易涉及两笔币种、金额相同，方向相反的交易，多被运用于短期投资、借贷业务。

【例9-23】某企业进行短期国际投资，在美国以500万美元投资6个月，在购买即期美元用于投资的同时，可以卖出500万美元6个月远期外汇，以规避6个月后美元汇率变动带来的风险。

（6）货币互换法。

货币互换法，是指交易双方互相交换期限相同、金额相当，但币种不同的两种货币，以降低筹资成本，进而防范外汇风险的方法。货币互换属于一种新型的衍生金融产品。

【例9-24】假定汇率为1英镑=1.5000美元，A想借入5年期的1 000万英镑，B想借入5年期的1 500万美元，A、B借入的本金换算成美元是等值的。由于A、B信誉不同，市场提供给他们的固定利率存在差异（见表9-1）。

表9-1   A、B面临的市场利率

	美元	英镑
A	8.0%	11.6%
B	10.0%	12.0%

A在美元市场上具有比较优势（2.0%大于0.4%），B在英镑市场上具有比较优势，二者可以进行互换。A以8%的利率借入5年期的1 500万美元，B以12.0%的利率借入5年期的1 000万英镑。不合作时总成本为10%+11.6%=21.6%，合作时总成本为8%+12%=20%，即总成本下降了1.6%。假定双方各分享一半，即0.8%。

（7）借款法。

借款法运用于拥有应收账款（外汇收入）的情形。出口商在签订合同后，可以向银行借入与未来应收外汇币种、金额和期限都相同的款项，并在即期外汇市场上兑换成本币，当借款到期时，以外汇收入偿还借款，以防范外汇风险。

【例9-25】某美国公司3个月后将收入500万英镑，为避免3个月后英镑汇率下跌的风险，该公司从银行借入500万英镑，期限为3个月，并将这笔英镑在即期外汇市场上兑换成美元。该公司3个月后收入500万英镑偿还银行借款，到时即使英镑汇率下跌，也不用承担汇率风险。

（8）投资法。

投资法运用于拥有应付账款（外汇支出）的情形。进口商在签订合同后，可在现汇市场买入与未来应付外汇币种、金额和期限都相同的外汇，并将其投资于短期资金市场（货币市场）；到货款支付日，以投资到期的外汇款项支付货款，以防范外汇风险。

【例9-26】某英国公司3个月后将支付货款100万美元，为避免3个月后美元汇率上升的风险，该公司在现汇市场上买入100万美元，并用这100万美元购买了3个月期的国库券，3个月后该公司再以投资到期的100万美元支付货款。

（9）BSI（borrow-spot-invest）法。

BSI法，又称借款—即期合同—投资法，是一种防范外汇风险的综合方法，是指具有应收账款或应付账款的企业综合运用借款、即期合同和投资来防范外汇风险的方法。

公司在拥有应收账款的情况下，BSI法的具体做法是：

①从银行借入与应收外汇的币种、金额、期限相同的外币，同时将借入的外币进行即期交易，卖给银行换回本币；

②将换回的本币存入银行或进行投资，以投资收益抵补相关费用（如借款利息等）；

③以外汇收入归还银行借款，这样就消除了外汇风险。

【例9-27】某德国企业出口一批货物，预计3个月后收回货款100万美元。为防止美元对马克汇率变动的风险，该企业运用BSI法进行操作。首先，该企业向银行借入100万美元，期限为3个月；同时该企业在即期外汇市场上，将这100万美元按1美元=0.5823马克的价格卖给银行，获得58.23万马克。然后，该企业将58.23万马克投放于德国货币市场，投资期限为3个月。3个月后，该企业以100万美元的应收账款归还银行，这样就消除了外汇风险。

公司在拥有应付账款的情况下，BSI法的具体做法是：

①向银行借入购买应付外汇所需的本币，同时在即期外汇市场用借入的本币购买未来支付所需的外币；

②用这笔外币进行短期投资，投资收益可以抵补相关费用（如借款利息等）；

③到货款支付日，收回投资支付货款。

（10）LSI（lead-spot-invest）法。

LSI法，又称提早收付—即期合同—投资法，是一种防范外汇风险的综合方法，是指具有应收账款或应付账款的企业在征得债务人或债权人的同意后，综合运用提前收付或延迟收付货款、即期合同和投资来消除外汇风险的方法。

公司在拥有应收账款的情况下，LSI法的具体做法是：

①由债权人（出口商）允诺给予进口商一定的折扣，并在获得对方同意后，让进口商提前支付货款，进而消除时间风险；

②出口商与银行签订即期合同，将收回的外币换成本币，从而消除价值风险；

③将兑换的本币进行投资，投资收益可以抵补因提前收汇造成的损失。

公司在拥有应付账款的情况下，LSI法的具体做法是：

①进口商先从银行借入购买应付外汇所需金额的本币，以消除时间风险；

②进口商与银行签订即期合同，将借入的本币兑换成外币，以消除价值风险；

③用兑换的外币提前支付给出口商，并得到一定数额的折扣，所获得的折扣可以全部或部分抵补借款利息。

（三）经济风险管理

汇率的变动对企业的收益、成本和竞争地位等都会产生一定的经济影响，因此企业需要从长期利益出发，采取相关措施来对经济风险进行管理。企业进行经济风险管理的一般原则是，尽量降低汇率变动对现金流量的影响。经济风险的管理主要包括以下两个方面：

1. 经济风险的市场营销管理

（1）市场选择与分割。

汇率波动时，出口企业需要考虑的问题之一就是市场选择。一般情况下，当一国货币升值时，其出口产品的外币价格将上升，那么该国出口产品的价格竞争力就会减弱。此时，国外企业就可以依靠其产品的价格优势扩大其在该国的市场份额。

另外，适当地将产品的出口市场进行分割也是必要的。例如，发达国家对进口商品价格变动的敏感度低于发展中国家。因此，当本国货币升值时，出口企业可以适当增加对发达国家的出口，减少对发展中国家的出口；反之，当本国货币贬值时，则增加对发展中国家的出口。

（2）定价策略。

企业进行定价策略调整时需要考虑市场占有率和利润率。

当本币升值时，本国出口商品的国际竞争力减弱，此时出口商有两种选择：维持价格、降低市场份额；降低价格、维持市场份额。

当本币贬值时，本国出口商品的国际竞争力增强，此时出口商也有两种选择：维持价格、扩大市场份额；提高价格、维持市场份额。

当然，企业在调整定价策略时，还需要考虑很多因素，如出口商品的需求价格弹性、产品的可替代性、汇率变动的时间性、潜在的竞争是否激烈等。

（3）促销策略。

任何企业，特别是涉外企业，在安排用于广告、推销和滞销的预算时，应该考虑因汇率变化可能带来的风险，合理安排促销预算。

当本国货币升值时，促销支出带来的回报，将因本国产品竞争力减弱而减少，此时企业需要进行产品策略调整；当本国货币贬值时，出口企业用于促销的支出所带来的回报将增加。

（4）产品策略。

产品策略，是指企业在新产品的研制、新生产线的建立及新产品投放市场的时机选择等方面进行调整，以防范外汇风险。

在新产品的研制方面，企业应注重在研究与开发方面投入足够的资金，以确保向市场不断投放新产品，增强竞争力，同时应根据市场汇率变化，针对不同的消费市场投放相应的新产品。

在建立新生产线方面，当本国货币贬值时，产品国际竞争力增强，企业可以在国内外建立新的生产线，扩大市场份额；当本国货币升值时，企业可以将新生产线建立在对价格变动不敏感的发达国家。

在产品投放市场的时机选择方面，当本国货币贬值时，企业可以利用贬值对出口带来的价格优势投放新产品。

2.经济风险的多样化管理

由于经济风险是由意料之外的汇率变化给企业带来的一种长期性、综合性外汇风险，而意料之外的汇率变化很难准确预测，因此防范经济风险的有效方法是企业实行多样化管理。多样化管理的基本思想是，企业进行风险分散，并使风险损失和风险收益相互冲抵，从而降低风险。企业实行多样化管理主要表现在以下两个方面：

（1）经营多样化。

经营多样化，是指企业将其业务活动分散于不同行业，或将生产原料的采购地、产品的生产地和销售地在全球范围内进行优化配置。如果企业实现了经营多样化，当汇率出现意外变化时，一方面，企业在某些市场获得风险收益，在另一些市场出现风险损失，但是风险收益基本可以抵补风险损失，使经济风险得以自动防范；另一方面，企业可以比较不同市场的销售价格、不同产地的要素等，而对经营策略进行迅速调整，改善经营条件，使汇率变动带来的风险降到最低。

（2）财务多样化。

财务多样化，即投资多样化和融资多样化，是指企业在不同国家金融市场上，以多种货币寻求资金来源和资金去向。这样，有的外币贬值，有的外币升值，企业的外汇风险就可以相互抵消；同时，企业可根据汇率变动，调整各种货币的资产与负债，更易于实现资金的配对组合，实现风险抵补。

在投资方面，企业可以选择多种货币进行投资，同一币种选择不同类型、不同期限的证券进行投资，并根据对市场的预测，不断调整投资对象，增加收益，实现降低风险的目的。

在融资方面，全面考虑汇率和利率的变化趋势，在货币由贬值趋势的市场借入该种货币，如果预测准确，就可以获得收益；还可以借入多种货币，以降低汇率变动的风险。

三、商业银行外汇风险管理

商业银行是外汇市场的主体之一，而外汇业务又是商业银行主要的一项业务。因此，银行的外汇风险管理是外汇风险管理的重要部分。商业银行通过买卖外汇，从中赚取买卖差价和手续费，如果买卖外汇过程中出现外汇风险，将直接影响银行的收益。因此，商业银行有必要进行外汇风险管理，主要包括外汇头寸管理和外汇资产负债管理。

（一）银行的外汇头寸管理

所谓外汇头寸，是指银行持有的外汇数额。银行每天都会买卖大量的外汇，并且会出现买入量和卖出量不相等，即买入额大于卖出额（即外汇多头），或卖出额大于买入额（即外汇空头）。

外汇多头或空头统称为敞口头寸或头寸暴露。敞口头寸会受汇率变动影响，使银行面临外汇风险。当银行处于某种外汇的多头时，就会面临该外汇贬值的风险；当银行处于某种外汇的空头时，就会面临该外汇升值的风险。因此，银行应重视外汇头寸的管理。

1.外汇头寸的额度管理

通常来说，商业银行对不同的外汇头寸（如现汇头寸或期汇头寸）会制定不同的持有限额，对不同层次的外汇交易人员所持有的外汇头寸也会有限制。

（1）规定头寸限额。

规定头寸限额是指银行通过规定外汇头寸的限额来防范外汇风险。

商业银行在制定外汇头寸限额时，应考虑以下因素：

一是本银行在外汇市场上的地位，即本银行是市场领头者、市场活跃者，还是一般参与者。在外汇市场上，那些资本规模大、交易金额高、职员素质好的大银行、大券商都有能力影响市场汇率水平，成为造市者。如果银行想要成为造市者，其交易金额一定要大；如果银行只是成为一般参与者，其交易额肯定不能太高。

二是银行最高领导层对外汇业务的期望收益、对外汇风险的态度。汇率变动既可能带来收益，也可能带来损失。一般来说，风险控制比实现盈利目标更容易。所以，最高领导层对外汇业务的期望收益越高，对外汇风险的容忍程度越高，交易金额就可以越大。

三是本银行外汇交易人员的整体素质。外汇交易人员的整体素质越高，规定的交易限额就可以越大。

四是交易货币的种类。一般情况下，交易货币种类越多，交易笔数和交易规模越大，制定的交易限额就会越大。

在实际外汇交易中，外汇头寸限额一般都是由外汇交易员掌握的。

（2）制定止损点限额。

制定止损点限额是指银行通过对外汇交易制定止损点限额以防范外汇风险。

所谓止损点限额，是银行能忍受的由于外汇风险所造成的最大损失。当市场汇率变动不利时，一旦亏损到达止损点限额，交易人员应该立刻斩仓，以防止发生更大的损失。

所谓斩仓，是一种止损措施，是在建立头寸后，当所持货币汇率下跌时，为防止亏损过大而采取的一种手段。

2.外汇头寸调整

为了防范外汇风险，除了对外汇头寸额度进行管理外，银行还可以调整外汇敞口头寸，或尽量缩小外汇敞口头寸，使外汇敞口头寸的状况与汇率走势一致。

商业银行进行头寸调整的具体做法为：想办法缩小受险部分，即尽量减少外汇多头与外汇空头之间的差额，如银行可以通过拓展业务来实现买卖头寸的平衡，还可以通过相反交易来平衡买卖头寸。所谓相反交易，是指为了平衡多头头寸或空头头寸而在银行间市场进行的即期交易或利用远期交易进行的套期保值或掉期交易。

（1）单一货币头寸的调整。

当银行只存在某一种货币的敞口头寸时，为防范外汇风险，就只需要对这一种货币的头寸进行调整，即单一货币头寸调整。对单一货币头寸的调整主要包括以下方面的内容：

①即期头寸的调整。

例如，某银行某营业日的外汇买卖情况为：买进500万美元，卖出300万美元，结果该银行出现多头200万美元。为了防范外汇风险，该银行就要想办法抛出这200万美元，使美元头寸平衡。

②即期头寸和远期头寸的综合调整。

银行在进行实际外汇交易时，一般不会只涉及即期交易，还会涉及远期外汇交易。所以，银行不仅会在即期交易中出现敞口头寸，也会在远期交易中出现敞口头寸，此时银行就需要对即期头寸和远期头寸进行综合调整。

【例9-28】某银行某营业日的外汇买卖情况为：即期交易买进800万美元，卖出500万美元，持有多头300万美元；远期交易买进500万美元，卖出900万美元，持有空头400万美元，该银行的综合头寸为空头100万美元。对上述头寸的调整有两种方法：

第一，使即期头寸和远期头寸都为零，即卖出300万美元的即期，买入400万美元的远期。此时，在远期交易上，如果买进的400万美元的远期期限与原来买进的500万美元和卖出的900万美元的期限相同，就可以完全消除外汇风险。当然，在实际交易中，很难做到将不同外汇的不同期限的远期头寸完全吻合，所以商业银行通常是对综合头寸进行调整。

第二，抛补综合头寸，使综合头寸为零。针对上例，银行有两种选择：一是买进100万美元的即期，使即期交易的多头增加至400万美元，此时综合头寸为零；二是买进100万美元的远期，使远期交易的空头减少至300万美元，与即期交易的多头300万美元匹配，此时综合头寸为零。

③不同交割日的远期头寸的综合调整。

【例9-29】某银行2月1日的交易情况为：第一笔远期交易买入200万美元，5月31日交割，第二笔远期交易卖出200万美元，6月30日交割。显然，该银行的远期综合头寸为零，但是由于两笔交易的交割日不同，银行依然面临外汇风险，即5月31日交割的美元存在贬值风险，而6月30日交割的美元存在升值风险。

对此，银行可以利用掉期交易来防止外汇风险产生，即2月1日，银行卖出200万美元，交割日为5月31日；同时买入200万美元，交割日为6月30日。值得注意的是，该例中买入和卖出美元的金额相等，只是交割日不同，而有可能会出现交割日和买卖金额都不同的情况，对此银行可以运用掉期交易防范部分风险，后期再通过外汇交易来平移。

（2）多种货币头寸的调整。

当银行同时存在多种货币的敞口头寸时，为防范外汇风险，就需要将这些头寸结合起来进行调整，即多种货币头寸的调整。对多种货币头寸的调整主要包括以下两个方面的内容：

①分别调整各种货币的头寸。

银行主要通过具有敞口头寸的货币与美元之间的交易来转换。例如，某银行同时存在欧元多头和英镑空头，在调整头寸时，银行先将欧元多头转换为美元，同时以美元补进英镑的空头，将欧元和英镑的敞口头寸转换为美元的敞口头寸，再通过美元与本币之间的交易消除美元的敞口头寸。

②调整综合头寸，即允许各种货币的敞口头寸同时存在，只对综合头寸进行调整，使来自各种货币的风险相互抵消。

例如，当某银行持有瑞士法郎空头时，可以买进金额相当的英镑，当汇率发生变动时，用英镑多头的收益或损失抵补瑞士法郎的损失或收益。

（二）银行的外汇资产负债管理

银行的自营外汇交易和代客外汇交易带来的外汇风险，可以通过外汇头寸管理进行防范；而银行的外汇存贷业务和投资业务所带来的外汇风险，则需要通过对外汇资产和负债的管理进行防范。外汇资产负债管理主要包括以下内容：

1.调整资产负债的币种

银行应该尽量做到分散筹资和投资，即筹到哪种货币，就贷出哪种货币；贷款到期收回哪种货币，筹款到期就支付哪种货币，尽可能保证借贷和收付货币时不需要通过外汇交易来转换货币。

2.调整资产负债的期限

在同一货币的资产负债中，尽量做到未来任一时间到期的资产，都能抵付到期的负债，尽量使存款和贷款的期限相同或接近。

3.调整存贷款的金额

同一种货币，利率和期限均匹配的外汇存款和贷款，应使之金额相等；市场利率上浮时，应使浮动利率的贷款额大于浮动利率的存款额，或者固定利率的贷款额小于固定利率的存款额；市场利率下跌时，应争取浮动利率的贷款额小于浮动利率的存款额，或者固定利率的贷款额大于固定利率的存款额。

4.调整存贷款利率

以外币收付的存贷款利息也是受险部分，而利息高低取决于利率的高低，因此存贷款利率的高低直接影响银行面临的外汇风险的程度。一般做法是：压低以硬货币吸收的外汇存款利率，提高以软货币发放的外汇贷款利率。

任务三 　　　　　　　　　　外汇管制

一、外汇管制概述

（一）外汇管制的含义

外汇管制，也称外汇管理，是指一国政府为平衡国际收支、维持汇率水平稳定、集中外汇资金并根据政策需要加以分配，而利用各种法律、法规等方式对外汇市场、外汇资金来源与运用、汇率和外汇买卖进行的干预。

外汇管制是一国政府对外汇收支、结算和使用等采取的限制性措施，主要通过法令、条文对外汇活动进行管理和干预，其目标是维持本国国际收支平衡，限制资本流入与流出，保持汇率稳定，保证外汇的有效运用，保障金融市场的有序运行。

（二）外汇管制的原因

外汇管制是资本主义发展到一定阶段的产物，它与资本主义经济危机和经济发展的不同阶段紧密相关。

第一次世界大战爆发之前，资本主义各国普遍实行金本位制度，黄金可以自由输出、输入，各国未采取任何外汇管制措施。第一次世界大战爆发后，国际金本位制度处于崩溃边缘，各参战国为了保护本国经济，开始实行外汇管制。第一世界大战结束后，各国开始恢复经济生产，为促进经济发展、扩大对外贸易，各国又逐步解除了外汇管制。1929—1933年，资本主义国家爆发了严重的经济危机，各国国际收支不断恶化，国际金本位制度崩溃，为了应对激烈的市场竞争，西方各国纷纷采取贸易保护政策，并重新实行外汇管制。

第二次世界大战期间，各主要参战国为应对巨额战争支出，都进一步加强了外汇管制。第二次世界大战结束后，西方各国为恢复经济，继续实行严格的外汇管制。

20世纪50年代，西欧各国经济慢慢恢复，对外贸易不断扩大，国际收支状况得到改善，各国才开始逐渐放松外汇管制。20世纪70年代以来，西欧各国国际收支状况良好，使得他们进一步放松外汇管制，有的国家甚至取消了外汇管制。20世纪80年代以来，西方国家加快放缓外汇管制的速度，而发达国家普遍放松了外汇管制。同时，随着发展中国家经济的快速发展，外汇管制也出现放松趋势。

从外汇管制的演变历程可以发现，外汇管制与资本主义经济危机紧密相关，而外汇管制的宽松程度又与一国的国际收支状况和经济发展水平相关。

案例探析9-3

西班牙华人涉嫌非法携带40万欧元现金被没收

据西班牙《欧华报》报道，西班牙阿利坎特警方在El Altet机场，逮捕了一名涉嫌非法携带大量现金而不进行申报的华人男子。警方从他所托运的行李中搜查到了几十万欧元的现金，这些现金最后全部遭到没收。

这名男子当时正打算从阿利坎特机场乘坐飞机前往奥地利首都维也纳，他当时携带了一件手提行李，还托运了一件体积更大的行李。机场安检在他托运的行李中，发现了两包用金属纸包裹起来的纸张，打开一看里面全部都是崭新的欧元钞票。

经过清点，这些被藏在托运行李内的现金总额达到了39.3万欧元，之后警方又在其随身携带的行李中同样发现了大量的现金，其金额为4 000欧元。这些纸币加在一起，总额接近40万欧元。

虽然这名男子前往的目的地是奥地利，同样属于欧盟国家，但是法律规定欧盟居民即便在成员方之间旅行，不经申报可以直接携带的现金总额不得超过10万欧元。最后，这名男子所携带的现金被全部没收，他必须去西班牙银行解释其来源之后，才有可能重新拿回这些现金。

资料来源：佚名. 西班牙华人涉嫌非法携带 40 万欧元现金被没收［EB/OL］.［2013-03-28］.
http：//news.sina.com.cn/w/2013-03-28/111726668177.shtml.

思考题：案例中的男子为什么被没收现金？他违反了什么规定？

二、外汇管制的主体和客体

（一）外汇管制的主体

外汇管制的主体，即执行外汇管制的机构。目前，世界各国实行外汇管制都是由政府授权中央银行或设立专门机构作为执行外汇管制的机构。例如，在英国，外汇管制的职能由英格兰银行行使；我国设立了专门的外汇管制机构——外汇管理局，由其行使全国外汇管理职能。

（二）外汇管制的客体

外汇管制的客体就是外汇管制的对象。通常来说，外汇管制可分为对人、对物、对地区、对行业和对国别五个层次。

（1）对人的管制，包括对法人和自然人的管制。根据法人与自然人居民地或营业地的不同，又可分为居民与非居民。一般来说，因为居民的外汇收支情况对本国国际收支影响较大，所以管制较严，而对非居民管制相对宽松。

（2）对物的管制，是指对不同形式的外汇进行管制，包括外国货币、外币支付凭证、外币有价证券和贵金属等。另外，对本国货币输出、输入的管制也属于对物的管制。

（3）对地区的管制，是指对本国不同地区实施不同的外汇管制政策。一般来说，各国对出口加工区、保税区、经济特区等的管制比较宽松，而对其他地区的管制较严格。

（4）对行业的管制，是指国家根据产业政策，对不同的进出口企业实行不同的外汇管制政策。这是拉美地区一些新兴工业化国家采取的一种管制方法，对传统出口行业实行严格管制，而对高技术和重工业出口实行相对优惠政策；对生活必需品进口采取较优惠政策，而对生活奢侈品进口则采取相对严格的政策。我国曾经实行的外汇留成制度，就属于典型的行业差别政策。

（5）对国别的管制，是指对不同国家、不同地区的情况采取不同的管制政策。

三、外汇管制的方法和措施

外汇管制主要包括数量管制和价格管制。数量管制是指对外汇交易的数量进行限制，通常采用的方法有进出口结汇、外汇配给、进口许可证等；价格管制主要是指采用复汇率制度和本币高估的方式。

进行外汇管制的国家，通常对贸易和非贸易的外汇收支、资本的输出和输入、汇率等采用一定的措施。

（一）贸易外汇管制的方法和措施

对外贸易外汇收支占一国国际收支比重最大，因此对贸易外汇收支的管制是整个外汇管制的重要部分。贸易外汇管制主要包括进口外汇管制和出口外汇管制两个方面的内容。

一般来说，进行外汇管制的国家首先会对进口实行管制，进口企业需要的外汇必须向外汇管理部门申请，经批准后才能购汇。对出口实行外汇管制的国家，通常规定出口企业收入的外汇必须出售给指定的银行。为了扩大出口，很多国家对出口实施税收、信贷和汇率等一系列优惠政策，同时对国内某些供不应求的商品实行出口数量限制；还有一些国家与相关国家达成协议，对某些产品实行出口数量限制。

（二）非贸易外汇管制的方法和措施

除了贸易、资本输出、输入以外的外汇收支都属于非贸易收支，其目的主要是集中非贸易外汇收入，限制非贸易外汇支出。

非贸易外汇收支的范围较广，主要包括运输费、保险费、佣金、股利、利息、专利费、许可证费、特许权使用费、技术劳务费、版权费、稿费、奖学金、留学生费用、驻外机构费用、旅游费等。其中，与贸易有关的费用，一般都按贸易外汇管制的方式处理，其他非贸易外汇收支都需要向指定银行报告或取得批准。

（三）资本输出、输入管制的方法和措施

一般来说，各国都会对资本输出、输入实行不同程度的管制。资本输出管制，是指对购买外汇作为资本输出，本国货币、投资利润和股息的汇出，有价证券和基金的输出等方面的管理。资本输入管制，是指对外国资本流入、非居民购买本国有价证券等方面的管理。相对来说，发展中国家很重视资本输出、输入的管理，只是存在管制程度的不同，而发达国家较少实施外汇管制。

（四）汇率的管理

很多国家直接对汇率进行管理，可以改善国际收支和稳定汇率水平。对汇率的管理主要可以采取以下两种方式：

1.法定汇率制度

法定汇率制度，是指依据本国宏观经济政策、国际收支状况等，外汇管理机构以法定形式规定、调整对外汇率，同时规定本国外汇收付的价格。

2.复汇率制度

复汇率制度，是指一国同时实行两个或两个以上的汇率制度。复汇率制度是经济水平较落后国家调节国际收支逆差的主要手段，一般发挥"奖出限入"的作用。值得注意的是，作为外汇管制政策的复汇率，是指外汇管制机构人为地、主动地制定和实行多种汇率，以达到预期的目的，这与经济中实际存在的复汇率现象存在一定的差别。复汇率制度常见形式有双重汇率制和多重汇率制。

（1）双重汇率制。

双重汇率制，是指官方汇率与市场汇率并存，以便于鼓励或限制某些经济活动。例如，对鼓励出口的多数商品，允许收汇后按市场汇率高价卖出，以提高出口商收入；对限制进口的多数商品，则规定进口商从自由市场高价购买全部或部分所需外汇，以增加进口商成本；对鼓励进口的国内紧缺物品，允许进口商按官定汇率购买外汇，以降低进口成本支出；对限制出口的少数商品，则规定出口商必须将收入外汇按官定汇率卖给指定银行，以减少其出口收入。

（2）多重汇率制。

多重汇率制，即多种汇率同时混合使用，是针对不同形式交易制度下不同的优惠性或限制性汇率。例如，对出口商来说，对国际竞争力强的商品；对国际竞争力较弱的商品按高汇率结汇。

拓展阅读9-2

外汇管制与人民币国际化如何兼得？

"在全球大变局下，未来人民币前景是值得大家关注的。"

10月21日，在"2020金融街论坛年会"上，博鳌亚洲论坛副理事长、中国金融学会会长、清华大学五道口金融学院名誉院长周小川就人民币国际化的机遇和所需要做的准备详述看法。

在谈到近期人民币持续走强时，周小川指出，不必过度关注人民币币值、指数的近期走势，这其中有疫情管理、经济增长差异带来的影响，也有大家对美元存疑的连锁反应。由于我国实行浮动汇率制度，随着人民币对美元汇率波动，购买人民币资产情况就会有相应变化，但这都不是人民币国际化最关键的因素。

周小川认为，真正对人民币国际化有利的是：

第一，中国在世界范围内保护主义明显的背景下坚持走实体经济对外开放的道路，加大对外开放措施，包括加码自贸区、自由港、临港新片区等建设。

第二，国内金融市场逐步突破各类障碍和保护主义，如开设沪港通、深港通、债券通等。

第三，近年来，大家突破了一些心理障碍，市场对于汇率"破7"、外汇储备"破3万亿美元"等象征性关口的担忧正在逐渐减轻。

"货币的开放应该为实体经济的开放服务，那么实现高水平开放型经济，货币也必然是配合趋势。"周小川强调。

周小川谈到，对于既想做好外汇管制又想实现人民币国际化的想法，需要进一步理清思路。"我们总希望把不同东西的好处都抓到手里，最后发现有些东西是结合不了的。"

他提到，今后一段时间，要下更大决心大幅度提高人民币可自由使用程度，最大限度减少资本项下管控，这其中涉及到研究、思维方式、政策体系变革及应急准备。

在上述背景下，周小川提出几个要点想法：

第一，推进人民币国际化和资本项目可兑换过程中一个主要的权衡要点是进行利弊分析，明确哪些需要结合，哪些只能做取舍。不必过度依赖"控制"导向，不能产生对市场价格存在不信任甚至恐惧的心理，分析研究应进一步深入。

第二，关于资本流动。外界通常认为在当前国际经济秩序下资本流动对发展中国家会造成冲击，因此决定保留哪些管控措施时总会有讨论甚至争论。但实际上，涉及资本流动，除了经济、币值因素外，更重要的是信心，后者可以减少很多不正常的流动。

第三，在走向开放经济的过程中，外汇管制效果究竟如何，是需要评估的。

此外，周小川还指出，进一步推进资本项目可兑换并不意味着百分之百实现自由化。全球都有反洗钱、反恐融资等要求，很多金融交易、汇款都会受到限制。另外，国际货币基金组织（IMF）在2008年全球金融危机过后，对于跨境资本流动的观点也有校正，对应急状况下的资本流动管理也有新的政策导向。

"随着人民币可自由使用程度大幅提高，对于短期投资性产品、个别衍生产品交易等，还需要研究哪些要管理、哪些不需要管理，以迎接更高水平开放型经济。"周小川说。

除了全球共性的题目，周小川同时还提到中国特色的内容。他表示，中国是拥有14亿人口的大国、世界第二大经济体、第一大贸易国，做决策主要依靠分步推进，通过试点逐步取得经验，进而复制推广。

另外，过去一些政策在大幅推广的过程中，曾出现双轨问题，这就要求合并过程中应处理好体制、机制、价格、利益等因素。而人民币国际化过程中也可能存在双轨问题，如在股票市场，有A股、B股、H股，还有红筹股，不同壳里的实际资产内容一样，价格却不同。

在他看来，同股不同权的产品价格有较大差异可以理解，但是同股同权产品出现明显价差，可能主要是因为货币不可兑换等原因造成，未来需要把这些问题解决。

资料来源：曹家宁. 外汇管制与人民币国际化如何得兼？周小川提出三个要点 [EB/OL]. [2020-10-23]. https：//www.thepaper.cn/newsDetail_forward_9694853.

四、外汇管制的影响

外汇管制的有利影响在于：外汇管制当局通过一定的管制政策来实现平衡国际收支、稳定汇率、奖出限入和稳定国内物价等目标。但在外汇管制发挥作用时，也会出现一些不利影响，主要表现在以下方面：

（一）影响国际贸易健康发展和对外开放进程

外汇管制阻碍自由多边结算体系的形成，也阻碍了国际贸易和国际资本流动的正常运行。对发展中国家来说，高估本币汇率和限制外汇供求都会打击出口商的创汇积极性，同时外汇短缺又会影响该国进口贸易；而限制资本输出、限制投资收益回流等措施，则会打击外国投资者对该国投资的积极性。很多国家的经验证明，要改善国际收支逆差、外汇储备不足、外汇管制、对外开放程度低、经济发展缓慢之间的恶性循环，需要在逐步取消外汇管制上找出路。

（二）汇率扭曲，资源配置效率低

外汇管制中，政府规定官方汇率或采取限制外汇买卖的措施，会使汇率偏离市场的均衡汇率，即汇率扭曲。对发展中国家来说，汇率扭曲常常表现为本币汇率过高，原因可能是政府规定的本币的官方牌价较高，也可能是政府限制外汇供求的结果。而这种扭曲的汇率会影响资源合理配置。首先，它会冲击发展中国家的农业。由于发达国家普遍对农产品出口提供高额补贴，使得全球农产品价格偏低；而高估本币汇率又会进一步降低进口农产品的本币价格，发展中国家的农产品价格随之下降，从而严重影响发展中国家的农业发展。其次，本币汇率高估会给本国出口和进口的替代产业带来冲击，主要原因在于高估本币汇率会抬高本国出口商品的本币价格、压低进口商品的本币价格。最后，从全球范围来看，汇率是引导国际资本流动的价格信号之一，汇率扭曲就会使人们难以正确判断投资方向。

（三）出现外汇黑市交易

由于政府规定的外汇牌价过低，催生了外汇黑市交易。当外汇黑市交易规模较大时，政府就有必要开放外汇调剂市场，使该国出现合法的双轨制汇率。同时，为了以较低的官价购汇，某些个人或企业可能会向拥有外汇配给权的官员行贿，助长不良风气。

对于世界经济的长远发展来说，各国逐步取消外汇管制是一种趋势，但是其过程是十分漫长的。世界各国特别是发展中国家应结合本国实际，考虑如何尽可能利用外汇管制的积极作用，而避免或减少其带来的消极影响。

思政小课堂

阅读下列一则新闻，请选择其中一个案例网上查阅资料进行详细了解，并分析其违反了什么规定？为什么？

据外汇局网站消息，2018年以来，国家外汇管理局深入贯彻落实十九大精神和党中央、国务院工作部署，紧紧围绕服务实体经济、防控金融风险、深化金融改革三项任务，加强外汇市场监管，依法查处各类外汇违法违规行为，严厉打击虚假、欺骗性交易。根据《中华人民共和国政府信息公开条例》（国务院令第492号）等的相关规定，现将部分违规典型案件通报如下（节选）：

案例1：交通银行厦门前埔支行违规办理转口贸易案

2016年1月至8月，交通银行厦门前埔支行未按规定尽职审核转口贸易真实性，在企业提交虚假提单的情况下，违规办理转口贸易付汇业务。

该行上述行为违反《中华人民共和国外汇管理条例》第十二条。根据《外汇管理条例》第四十七条的规定，处以罚款600万元人民币，暂停对公售汇业务三个月，并责令追究负有直接责任的高级管理人员和其他直接责任人员的责任。

案例2：中国银行莆田分行违规办理个人外汇业务案

2016年1月至2017年4月，中国银行莆田分行为个人分拆办理售付汇和外币现钞提取业务。

该行上述行为违反《个人外汇管理办法》第七条和第三十四条。根据《中华人民共和国外汇管理条例》第四十七条和第四十八条的规定，处以罚款70万元人民币。

案例3：智付电子支付有限公司逃汇案

2016年1月至2017年10月，智付电子支付有限公司凭借虚假物流信息办理跨境外汇支付业务，金额合计1 558.8万美元。

该行为违反《中华人民共和国外汇管理条例》第十二条，构成逃汇行为，严重扰乱了外汇市场秩序，性质恶劣。根据《中华人民共和国外汇管理条例》第三十九条的规定，处以罚款1 530.8万元人民币。

案例4：支付宝（中国）网络技术有限公司违反外汇管理规定案

2014年1月至2016年5月，支付宝（中国）网络技术有限公司超出核准范围办理跨境外汇支付业务，且国际收支申报错误。

上述行为违反《支付机构跨境外汇支付业务试点指导意见》第六条、《国际收支统计申报办法》第七条的规定。根据《中华人民共和国外汇管理条例》第四十八条的规定，处以罚款60万元人民币。

案例5：河北籍赵某分拆逃汇案

2016年1月至2017年12月，赵某为实现非法向境外转移资产的目的，利用本人及他人（共计55人）的个人年度购汇额度，将个人资产分拆购汇后汇往境外账户，非法转移资金合计245.31万美元。

该行为违反《个人外汇管理办法》第七条，构成逃汇行为。根据《中华人民共和国外汇管理条例》第三十九条的规定，处以罚款116万元人民币。

资料来源：王擎宇. 外汇管理局通报外汇违规案例　华夏民生等多银行上榜［EB/OL］.［2018-07-24］. http://finance.china.com.cn/news/20180724/4709011.shtml.

项目思维导图

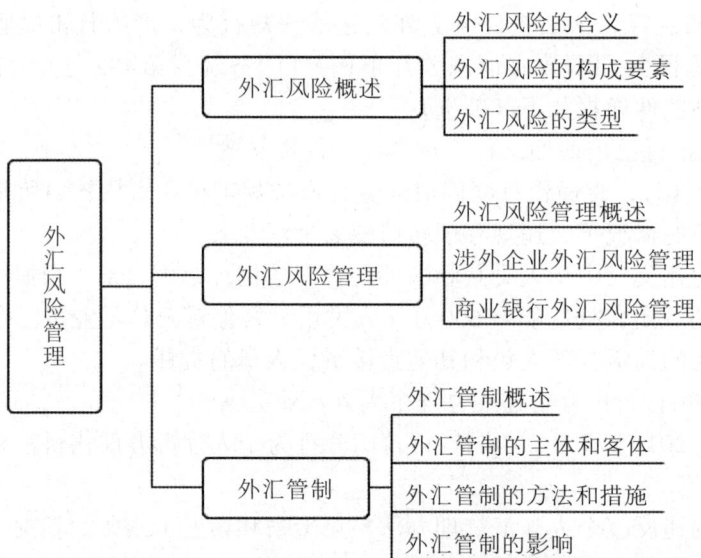

外汇风险管理
- 外汇风险概述
  - 外汇风险的含义
  - 外汇风险的构成要素
  - 外汇风险的类型
- 外汇风险管理
  - 外汇风险管理概述
  - 涉外企业外汇风险管理
  - 商业银行外汇风险管理
- 外汇管制
  - 外汇管制概述
  - 外汇管制的主体和客体
  - 外汇管制的方法和措施
  - 外汇管制的影响

项目训练

一、单选题

1.外汇风险的不确定性是指（　　　）。

A.外汇风险可能发生，也可能不发生

B.外汇风险给持汇者或用汇者带来的可能是损失也可能是盈利

C.给一方带来的是损失，给另一方带来的必然是盈利

D.外汇汇率可能上升，也可能下降

2.一笔应收或应付外币账款的时间结构对外汇风险的大小具有直接影响。时间越长，外汇风险（　　　）。

A.越大　　　　　　B.越小　　　　　　C.没有影响　　　　D.无法判断

3.进口商与银行订立远期外汇合同，是为了（　　　）。

A.防止因外汇汇率上涨而造成的损失

B.防止因外汇汇率下跌而造成的损失

C.获得因外汇汇率上涨而带来的收益

D.获得因外汇汇率下跌而带来的收益

4.某家外贸公司于9月1日签订了价值10万美元的出口合同，收汇日期定在11月20日，此期间该公司面临的外汇风险属于（　　　）。

A.时间风险　　　B.经济风险　　　　C.交易风险　　　　D.折算风险

5.在同一时期内，创造一个与存在风险相同货币、相同金额、相同期限的反方向资金流动为（　　　）。

A.提前收付　　　B.套期保值　　　　C.平衡法　　　　　D.组对法

二、多选题

1.外汇风险的构成要素包括（　　　）。

A.本币　　　　　　B.外币　　　　　　C.时间　　　　　　D.汇率

2.在以下例子中，无外汇风险的是（　　　）。

A.以本币收款

B.流入与流出外币币种相同、金额相同、时间相同

C.以本币付款

D.不同时间的相同外币、相同金额的流出

3.软、硬货币此降彼升，具有负相关性质。对软、硬货币进行合理搭配，能够减少汇率风险，其主要方式有（　　　）。

A.软、硬货币对半　　　　　　　　B.软货币多些或硬货币多些

C.介于软、硬货币之间　　　　　　D.随意配比

4.企业防范外汇风险的方法有（　　　）。

A.选择合同货币　　　B.使用"一篮子"货币　　C.掉期交易

D.远期交易　　　　　E.期权交易

5.按照行使期权的时间是否具有灵活性，外汇期权分为（　　　）。

A.看涨期权　　　　　B.看跌期权　　　　　　C.欧式期权

D.美式期权　　　　　E.买方期权

6.外汇管制的目标是（　　　）。

A.维持本国国际收支平衡　　　　　B.限制资本流入与流出

C.保持汇率稳定　　　　　　　　　D.保证外汇的有效运用

E.保障金融市场的有序运行

三、判断题

1.外汇风险不仅意味着风险损失，也可能是风险盈利。　　　　　　　（　　）

2.采用合理的外汇风险管理方法，企业可以完全消除汇率风险。　　　（　　）

3.外汇管制仅仅发生在发展中国家，发达国家没有外汇管制。　　　　（　　）

4.当以本币计价时，任何时候都没有外汇风险，但可能会面临通货膨胀的风险。　　　　　　　　　　　　　　　　　　　　　　　　　　　　　（　　）

5.进出口企业可以通过"收软币付硬币"的方法来降低汇率损失。　　（　　）

四、实践分析题

某美国公司准备7月1日从法国进口一批货物，价值为100万欧元，该年12月31日付款，假定7月1日欧元期货价格为1欧元=1.1380美元。请问该公司可以如何利用欧元期货来防范外汇风险？

项目十
国际货币体系

课程导入

Libra出现将会改变国际货币体系，调整世界金融格局

　　Libra概念的横空出世正在给全球带来前所未有的震撼。近日，美国众议院连续举行两场听证会，针对Facebook的Libra项目的问题进行询问。虽然Facebook自称希望Libra是支付工具，不会和主权货币竞争，但是从Libra的属性来看，其不仅仅只是一种支付工具，而是具备了数字货币的功能。可以预见，Libra项目一旦推进，将会深刻改变当前的国际货币体系，这一变革将会是颠覆性的。

　　Libra的出现将会深刻改变国际货币体系，调整世界金融格局：

　　一是加剧货币竞争。一旦Libra广泛使用，那么将会成为国际储备货币，Libra实际上对现有的货币制度形成了挑战，尤其是对美元的世界货币地位形成了挑战。因此，Libra的货币之路不会一帆风顺，必然会面临美元既得利益集团的围剿，真正意义上拉开了主权货币与数字货币战争的序幕。从美国社会各界的反应也可以印证这一点，美国总统发表了对Libra的不信任评价，国会也迅速地开展听证，

Facebook 保证在未取得监管部门支持之前，暂时取消 Libra 计划，这与对比特币放之任之的态度有根本的区别。

二是将全面改变社会信用体系。货币制度建立在信用基础之上，而数字化货币的诞生恰恰是因为国家货币滥发引发通胀导致公众的不信任。一旦 Libra 成功，很有可能会引起连锁反应，导致信用体系的改变，金融体系与资本市场的运行模式将会根本改变。

三是面临货币调控的考验。如果 Libra 能成为货币，即使在全额准备金的制度下，Libra 供给数量的变化也将导致全球货币市场的波动，存在不同货币之间的协调问题。Facebook 作为货币的发行机构，将成为与美联储、欧洲央行等同等重要的机构，Libra 的借贷利率将成为利率体系的重要基准，一旦放开全额准备金制度，Facebook 将可能成为全球的"网联储"，对各国货币调控形成考验。

Libra 带来的冲击是巨大而未知的，国内的金融界也已经意识到这一点，周小川、朱民等专家纷纷指出 Libra 的颠覆性和可行性。中国在移动支付上的全球领先地位，面临 Libra 的颠覆，人民币在国际货币中不断扩大的影响，也可能因为 Libra 戛然而止。央行应当积极参与到数字化货币的变革中，加快研究推出中国数字化货币，在全球数字化货币中取得一席之地。

资料来源：骆振心. Libra或带来巨大冲击 中国应积极参与数字化货币变革［EB/OL］.［2019-07-20］. http:/finance.eastmoney.com/a/201907201183776595.html.

思考讨论：

(1) 通过网络搜索，了解Libra是什么，如何诞生的。

(2) 什么是国际货币体系？它包括哪些内容？

任务一　　国际货币体系概述

一、国际货币体系的含义

国际货币体系就是各国政府为适应国际贸易与国际支付的需要，对货币在国际范围内发挥世界货币职能所确定的原则、采取的措施和建立的组织形式的总称。国际货币体系是国际金融领域中的中心课题。这里说的"体系"是从英文翻译过来的，也称国际货币制度。由于各国货币是由各个主权国家发行，而国际经济交易是跨国进行的，这就需要一种国际性货币体系来协调、规范各国的经济交易，从而保证和促进国际贸易和国际支付的顺利进行。

国际货币体系的核心是国际汇率制度。各国为了本国经济的发展，维护共同的利益，往往就货币汇率的安排达成共识，按照较为合理的原则在世界范围内规范汇率的变动，从而形成一种各国共同遵守的汇率体系。

二、国际货币体系的主要内容

一个健全的国际货币体系能够促进国际贸易和国际资本的顺利进行，从而促进整个国际经济的发展。国际货币体系一般包括以下主要内容：

（一）关键货币与汇率制度的确定

关键货币是在国际货币体系中充当基础性价值换算工具的货币。各国使用的货币不同，只有确定了关键货币，才能确定各国货币之间的兑换比率、汇率调整及国际储备构成等。在国际货币体系发展的不同历史阶段，黄金、英镑都曾充当过关键货币的角色。目前，美元在当今世界上使用最广泛、在外汇储备中占比最大，是最重要的国际货币，各国一般把美元作为关键货币。但非洲一些国家由于历史原因把英镑作为关键货币。

一国货币与其他货币之间的汇率应按何种规则确定与维持，并保持汇率稳定，有效防止各国货币间汇率的竞争性贬值。由于汇率变动可直接影响到各国之间经济利益的再分配，因此形成一种较为稳定的为各国共同遵守的国际间汇率安排成为国际货币体系所要解决的核心问题。同时，各国政府还规定一国货币与其他货币之间的汇率如何决定与维持、货币比价确定的依据、货币比价波动的界限、货币比价的调整、维持货币比价所采取的措施、对同一货币是否采取多元化比价、一国货币能否成为自由兑换货币、采取何种汇率制度等。

（二）国际储备资产的确定

一国政府应用什么货币来保有自己的贸易盈余和债权，以在保证国际支付和满足国际清偿力的同时维持人们对储备货币的信心。

为平衡国际收支的需要，一国需要有一定数量的国际储备，保存一定数量的、为世界各国普遍接受的国际储备资产以及它们的构成是国际货币体系的一项重要内容。另外，采用何种货币作为国际间的支付货币；在一个特定时期中心储备货币如何确定，以维护整个储备体系的运行；世界各国的储备资产如何选择，以满足各种经济交易的要求等都是国际货币体系的重要内容。

（三）国际收支及其调节机制的确定

确定一种有效的国际收支调节机制，通过该机制的运作能够使各国公平、合理地承担国际收支失衡的调节责任，并使调节所付出的代价最小。确定国际收支调节机制能够帮助国际收支不平衡的国家进行调节，促进各国经济平衡发展和世界经济稳定。

国际货币体系的主要内容之一是有效地帮助与促进国际收支出现严重失衡的国家通过各种措施进行调节，使其在国际范围内能公平地承担国际收支调节的责任和义务。由于各国实行的金融货币政策会对相互来往的国家乃至整个世界经济产生影响，因此如何协调各国与国际金融活动有关的金融货币政策，通过国际金融机构制定若干为各成员所认同与遵守的规则、惯例和制度，建立国际货币合作的结构和形式也构成了国际货币体系的重要内容。

此外，有不少因素影响着国际货币体系。

在结算国家间的债权债务时，采取什么样的结算方式、是否施加限制（即外汇管制）等也都是国际货币体系的内容。一国对外的债权债务，或者立即进行结算，并在国际结算中实行自由的多边结算；或者定期进行结算，并实行有限制的双边结算。

为进行国际支付，各国政府都要确定本国货币能否自由兑换成其他任何国家的货币，在对外支付方面是否加以全部或部分限制，或者完全不加限制，包括对经常项目、资本金融项目管制与否的规定和国际结算原则的规定，黄金、外汇的流动与转移是否加以限制而不能自由流动，或者只能在一定地区范围内自由流动，或者完全自由流动，都须由国家明确规定。

三、国际货币体系的类型与作用

（一）国际货币体系的类型

判定一种货币体系的类型，可以依据国际储备资产形式和货币合作程度两种标准划分。

1.按照国际储备资产形式的标准划分

据此，国际货币体系可分为金本位制和信用本位制两类。

（1）金本位制。

根据黄金充当国际储备资产与国际货币的作用程度，金本位制可以细分为金币本位制、金块本位制、金汇兑本位制。从19世纪到第一次世界大战爆发，国际通行的货币体系是金币本位制；第一次世界大战后至20世纪30年代经济危机爆发，国际通行的货币体系是金块本位制；其后至第二次世界大战结束以及1944—1973年通行的布雷顿森林体系是金汇兑本位制。

（2）信用本位制。

信用本位制是20世纪30年代经济危机爆发，金本位制崩溃之后，世界各国转而采用的货币制度。1976年至今通行的国际货币体系就是信用本位制。

2.按照货币合作程度的标准划分

据此，国际货币体系可分为单一货币体系和多元货币体系两类。

国际金本位制（也称英镑本位制时代）、布雷顿森林体系（也称美元本位制时代）实施的都是以某一国家的货币充当国际货币的单一货币体系。自信用本位制实施以来，特别是欧元的诞生标志着国际货币体系进入了多元货币体系时代。

（二）国际货币体系的作用

不同历史时期的国际货币体系都有其产生的背景，同时也发挥着重要作用。

（1）确定了国际收支调节机制与各国可遵守的调节政策，为各国纠正国际收支失衡状况提供了基础。

（2）建立了相对稳定的汇率机制，很大程度上防止了不公平的货币竞争。

（3）创造了多元化的储备资产，为国际经济的发展提供了足够的清偿力，同时借此抵御区域性或全球性金融危机。

（4）促进各国经济政策的协调。在统一的国际货币体系框架内，各国都要遵守一定的共同准则，任何损人利己的行为都会遭到国际指责，因而各国经济政策在一定程度上可得到协调与相互谅解。

任何一个国际金融体系都有它的缺陷，因此国际金融体系仍然需要改革，并在此基础上寻求发展。

任务二　　　　　　　国际货币体系的演变

　　国际货币体系是随着历史的发展不断演变的。不同的国际货币体系，意味着各国在实现内外平衡时，对国际货币的基本问题要遵循的准则不同。国际货币体系的发展，体现了为适应不同的历史条件而对这些准则所进行的变革。

　　从时间先后来看，国际货币体系大体可分为三个阶段，即国际金本位制阶段，布雷顿森林体系阶段和现行的牙买加货币体系阶段。国际货币体系演变简表见表10-1。

表10-1　　　　　　　　　　　　　　国际货币体系演变简表

国际货币制度	年份
国际金本位制	1880—1914年
	1918—1939年（恢复时期）
布雷顿森林体系	1944—1973年
向浮动汇率制过渡时期	1973—1976年
牙买加货币体系	1976年至今

资料来源：根据相关资料整理所得。

一、国际金本位制

（一）国际金本位制的形成

动画微课10-1

　　世界上首次出现的国际货币体系是国际金本位制，它大约形成于1880年年末，到1914年第一次世界大战爆发时结束。金本位制是以黄金为本位货币的一种制度。在金本位制下，流通中的货币除金币外，还存在可兑换为黄金的银行券及少量其他金属辅币，但只有金币才能完全执行货币的全部职能，即价值尺度、流通手段、贮藏手段、支付手段和世界货币。国际金本位制以各国普遍采用金本位制为基础。

国际货币体系及其演变

（二）国际金本位制的特点

　　金本位制是一种比较稳定的、健全的货币制度，它具有以下三个特点：

1.固定汇率制度

　　在金本位制下，各国货币都规定了含金量，各国本位货币所含纯金之比称为铸币平价，铸币平价是各国货币汇率的物质基础。由于外汇供求关系，外汇市场的实际汇率围绕铸币平价上下波动，但汇率的波动有一个限度，这个限度就是黄金输送点。铸币平价加运送费是黄金输出点，这是汇价上涨的最高限度；铸币平价减去运送费是黄金输入点，这是汇价下跌的最低限度，由于黄金输送点限制了汇价的变动幅度，因此汇率波动的幅度较小，基本上是稳定的。

　　在金本位制下，币值比较稳定，生产成本易于计算，促进了商品的流通和信用的扩大，生产规模和固定投资的规模不会因币值的变动而波动，从而促进了商品经济的发展。

2.自动调节国际收支

在金本位制下，资本主义各国的国际收支是自发进行调节的，因为国际收支的不平衡会引起黄金的流动，黄金的流动使黄金输入国的银行准备金增加，并减少黄金输出国的银行准备金，而银行准备金的变动则会引起货币数量的变化，造成贸易国双方国内物价和收入的变动，从而纠正国际收支的不平衡，制止黄金的流动。任何国家都不会发生因黄金储备枯竭而不能维持金本位制的情况。具体来讲，当一国发生国际收支逆差时，外汇的供给小于需求，外汇汇率上升，当汇率上升超过黄金输送点时，就会引起黄金外流，减少了作为银行准备的黄金数量，从而减少了货币发行量。于是，金融市场银根吃紧，短期资金利率上升，当国内利率高于国外利率时，就会产生套利活动，促使短期资金内流；短期资金利率上升，也会促使长期资金利率上升，引起长期资金内流。如果一国发生国际收支顺差，则会发生相反的情形，这种资金流动可以在短期改善国际收支，稳定国际金融市场。

教学视频10-1

3.各国经济政策协调机制

金本位制的国家把对外平衡（即国际收支平衡和汇率稳定）作为经济政策的首要目标，而把国内平衡物价、就业和国民收入的稳定增长放在次要地位，服从对外平衡的需要，因此国际金本位制也使主要资本主义国家有可能协调其经济政策。

认识国际金
本位制度

（三）国际金本位制的优缺点

1.优点

在国际金本位制盛行时，正值资本主义自由竞争的全盛时期，国内和国际政治都比较稳定，经济发展迅速。当时世界的工业制成品主要来自英国，其他国家的贸易赤字可以得到英国贷款资金的弥补，国际收支可以大体上保持平衡，在这样有利的条件下实行国际金本位制，它所带来的固定汇率对发展国家间的贸易和投资非常有利。

2.缺点

国际金本位制本身也存在一些缺陷，国际金本位制的自动调节机制并不像理论上所说的那么完善，其作用的发挥要受到许多因素的限制。这些缺陷表现在以下方面：

（1）在实行国际金本位制的30多年时间中，黄金在各国之间的流动并不频繁，一国发生贸易赤字，不一定要输出黄金，它可以利用国外的贷款（主要是英国贷款）来弥补赤字；同样，发生盈余的国家也可以利用资本输出来减少盈余，也不一定要输出黄金，因此贸易的不平衡就难以通过双方货币供应量和价格的相反变动来纠正。

（2）金本位制的自动调节机制的作用必须通过各国间的物价变动，才能使进出口贸易发生变化，进而引起黄金的流动，以维护国际收支平衡，汇率稳定。事实上，在金本位制时期，主要资本主义国家的物价变动趋势相当一致，并没有发生因物价变动而引起黄金流动的现象。

（3）国际金本位制的正常运行是建立在各国政府都遵守金本位制的基本要求，以及对经济不加干预的基础之上。然而，在金本位制的末期，各国的中央银行或货币管理当局已经不是听凭金本位制发挥自动调节作用，而是经常设法抵消黄金流动对国内货币供应量的影响。当黄金流入国内时，货币管理当局会采取措施抑制货币供应量的增加，以稳定物价；反之亦然。于是，金本位制的自动调节机制难以实现。事实上，在资本主义制度下，各国之间的矛盾使国际金本位制不可能自动调节达到国际收支平衡。

（四）国际金本位制的演化

随着资本主义矛盾的深化，破坏国际货币体系稳定性的因素也日益增长起来。到1913年年末，英国、美国、法国、德国、俄罗斯五国拥有世界黄金存量的2/3，绝大部分黄金被少数国家占有这就削弱了其他国家货币制度的基础，一些国家为了准备战争，政府支出急剧增长，大量发行银行券。于是，银行券兑换黄金越来越困难，这就破坏了自由兑换的原则。在经济危机时期，商品输出减少，资金外逃严重，引起黄金大量外流，各国纷纷限制黄金流动，黄金不能在国际间自由转移。由于维持金本位制的一些必要条件逐渐遭到破坏，国际货币体系的稳定性也就失去了保证。

1.金币本位制

传统的、最典型的金本位制指的是金币本位制。不少学者认为金本位制时期是世界经济发展的"黄金期"，有人甚至认为应该重建金本位制。

在金币本位制下，黄金作为重要的支付工具，具有以下特点：

（1）黄金规定货币所代表的价值——每一货币单位都有法定的含金量，各国货币的比价由其含金量决定。

（2）金币可以自由铸造。任何人可以自由地将黄金交给国家铸币局铸造成金币，由于金币可以自由铸造，金币的面值与其所含黄金的价值就可保持一致，金币数量就能自发地满足流通中的需要。

（3）金币是无限法偿的货币，具有无限制的支付手段的权利。

（4）各国的货币储备是黄金，国际间的结算也使用黄金，黄金可以自由输入、输出，由于金币可以自由兑换，各种价值符号（如金属辅币和银行券）就能稳定地代表一定数量的黄金进行流通，从而保持币值的稳定，不致发生通货膨胀现象。

由于黄金可以在各国间自由流通，这就保证了外汇市场的相对稳定与国际金融市场的统一。

2.金块本位制

第一次世界大战爆发后，各国停止银行券兑现并禁止黄金输出。战争期间，各国实行自由浮动的汇率制度，汇价波动剧烈，国际货币体系的稳定性已不复存在。第一次世界大战结束后，各国已无力恢复金币本位制。1925年，英国首先实行金块本位制。不久，法国，意大利等国家也相继推行金块本位制。金块本位制是以黄金为准备金，以有法定含金量的价值符号作为流通手段的一种货币制度。在金块本位制下，货币仍然规定含金量，但黄金只作为货币发行的准备金集中于中央银行，不再铸造金币和实行金币流通，流通中的货币黄金由银行券等价值符号代替，银行券在一定数量上可按含金量兑换黄金，黄金的输入、输出由中央银行负责，禁止私人输出黄金。

虽然金块本位制仍对货币规定含金量，并以黄金作为准备金，但是金币的自由铸造和流通以及黄金的自由输入、输出已被禁止，价值符号与黄金的兑换也受到限制。此时，黄金已难以发挥自动调节货币供求和稳定汇率的作用，因此金块本位制实际上是一种残缺不全的金本位制。

3.金汇兑本位制

金汇兑本位制，又称虚金本位制，是以存放在金块本位制或金币本位制国家的外汇资产为准备金，以有法定含金量的纸币作为流通手段的一种货币制度。在第一次世界大战前，许多殖民地国家曾经实行过这种货币制度；在第一次世界大战后，一些无力恢复金币本位制但又未采用金块本位制的资本主义国家，便推行了金汇兑本位制。

第一次世界大战后各国勉强恢复的国际金汇兑本位制，终于在1929年爆发的世界性经济危机和1931年的国际金融危机中全部瓦解。由于经济危机的影响，英国的国际收支已陷入困境，在1931年的国际金融危机中，各国纷纷向英国兑换黄金，使英国难以应付，终于被迫在1931年9月终止实行金本位制。同英镑有联系的一些国家，也相继放弃了金汇兑本位制。1933年3月，在大量银行倒闭和黄金外流的情况下，美国也不得不停止兑换黄金，禁止黄金输出，从而放弃了金本位制。20世纪30年代，国际金汇兑本位制的崩溃是资本主义货币制度的第一次危机。

国际金本位制彻底崩溃后，20世纪30年代的国际货币体系一片混乱，正常的国际货币秩序遭到破坏，当时主要的三种国际货币，即英镑、美元和法郎，各自组成相互对立的货币集团——英镑集团、美元集团、法郎集团，各国货币之间的汇率再次变为浮动汇率，各货币集团之间普遍存在严格的外汇管制，货币不能自由兑换。在国际收支调节方面各国也采取了各种各样的手段，为了解决国内严重的失业，各国大打汇率战，竞相实行货币贬值以达到扩大出口、抑制进口的目的，而且各种贸易保护主义措施和外汇管制手段也非常盛行，结果使国际贸易严重受阻，国际资本流动几乎陷于停顿。

1936年9月，英国、美国、法国三国为恢复和稳定国际货币秩序，达成了"三国货币协定"。该协定保证尽力维持协定成立时的汇价，减少汇率的波动，共同合作以保持货币关系的稳定。1936年10月，英国、美国、法国三国又签订了三国相互间自由兑换黄金的"三国黄金协定"。然而，由于不同货币集团的对立，国际货币体系关系仍然充满矛盾和冲突。后来，由于帝国主义国家忙于准备战争、购置军火，导致黄金外流，"三国货币协定"遂被冲垮。不过，该协定在制止外汇倾销方面取得了一些成效，并为以后的国际货币体系的建立创造了一定条件。

二、布雷顿森林体系

（一）布雷顿森林体系的形成

在第二次世界大战后期，美国、英国政府出于本国利益的考虑，构思和设计战后国际货币体系，分别提出了"怀特计划"和"凯恩斯计划"。

"怀特计划"是以美国财政部官员名字命名的，于1943年4月提出的，全称为联合国外汇稳定方案。该方案的主要内容是建立一个国际货币稳定基金机构，各国必须缴纳基金来建立外汇稳定基金；各国的发言权和投票权取决于其向基金组织缴纳的份额；基金组织拟定一种国际货币单位"尤尼他"，其含金量相当于10美元；采用固定汇率，各国货币汇率非经基金组织机构同意，不能任意变动；基金组织的主要任务是稳定汇率，提供短期信贷，平衡国际收支；基金办事处设在拥有份额最多的国家。"怀特计划"反映了美国试图操纵和控制基金，获得国际金融领域的统治地位。

"凯恩斯计划"由英国经济学家凯恩斯提出，实际上，它是一个国际清算联盟方案，主要内容是建立世界性的中央银行、国际清算联盟，各国在其中所占的份额以第二次世界大战前三年进出口贸易的平均额计算。这一计划的内容明显对英国有利。

经过长达3个月的讨论，美国、英国终于达成协议。在此基础上，1944年7月，在美国的新罕布什尔州的布雷顿森林召开了由美国等四国参加的联合国国际货币金融会议，会议通过了以"怀特计划"为基础制定的《国际货币基金协定》和《国际复兴开发银行协定》，宣布了第二次世界大战后国际货币体系——布雷顿森林体系的建立。

（二）布雷顿森林体系的特点

1.各国货币比价的挂钩

（1）双挂钩体制。

美元与黄金挂钩，其他国家货币与美元挂钩，布雷顿森林体系以黄金为基础，以美元作为最主要的国际储备货币，美元直接与黄金挂钩，各货币则与美元挂钩，并可按35美元一盎司的官价向美国兑换黄金。

（2）实行可调整的固定汇率。

《国际货币基金协定》规定，各国货币对美元的汇率只能在法定汇率上下各1%的幅度内波动。若市场汇率超过法定汇率1%的波动幅度，则各国政府有义务在外汇市场上进行干预，以维持汇率的稳定；若成员的法定汇率变动超过1%，则必须得到国际货币基金组织的批准。布雷顿森林体系的这种汇率制度被称为"可调整的钉住汇率制"。

2.各国货币的兑换性与国际支付结算的原则

各国货币自由兑换的原则是：任何成员对其他成员在经常项目往来中积存的本国货币，若对方为支付经常项目货币，则换回本国货币。考虑到各国的实际情况，《国际货币基金协定》又作了"过渡期"的规定，还规定了国际支付结算的原则；成员未经基金组织同意，不得对国际收支经常项目的支付或清算加以限制。

3.确定国际储备资产

《国际货币基金协定》中关于货币平价的规定，使美元处于"等同"黄金的地位，成为各国外汇储备中最主要的国际储备货币。

4.国际收支的调节

国际货币基金组织成员份额的25%以黄金或可兑换成黄金的货币缴纳，其余则以本国货币缴纳。成员发生国际收支逆差时，可用本国货币向基金组织按规定程序购买（即借贷）一定数额的外汇，并在规定时间内以购回本国货币的方式偿还借款。成员所认缴的份额越大，得到的贷款越多。贷款只限于成员用于弥补国际收支赤字，即用于经常项目的支付。

5.成立国际货币基金组织

建立永久性国际金融机构——国际货币基金组织，是布雷顿森林体系的一大特色。《国际货币基金协定》确定了国际货币基金组织的宗旨：建立国际货币基金组织机构，促进国际货币合作；促进国际贸易和投资的均衡发展，提高成员的就业和实际收入水平，扩大生产能力，促进汇率

教学视频10-2

认识布雷顿森林体系

稳定，维护正常汇兑关系，避免竞争性货币贬值；建立多边支付体系，设法消除外汇管制；为会员提供资金融通，纠正国际收支失衡；缩小或阻止国际收支赤字或盈余的扩大。

（三）布雷顿森林体系的优缺点

1.优点

布雷顿森林体系的双挂钩，使美元等同于黄金，各国货币只有通过美元才能与黄金发生联系，从而确立了美元在国际货币体系中的中心地位。因此，第二次世界大战后的国际货币体系实际上是一种美元本位制，布雷顿森林体系的建立和运转对战后国际贸易和世界经济的发展起了一定的积极作用。

（1）固定汇率稳定了国际金融秩序。

布雷顿森林体系确立了美元与黄金、各国货币与美元的"双挂钩"原则，实行可调整的钉住汇率制，汇率的波动受到严格的约束，货币汇率保持相对稳定。布雷顿森林体系的建立结束了国际货币金融领域的动荡混乱状态，使得国际金融关系进入了相对稳定时期，对国际商品流通和国际资本流动非常有利，为世界经济的稳定发展创造了良好的外部条件。

（2）美元发挥了世界货币的职能。

美元成为最主要的国际计价单位、支付手段和国际储备货币，弥补了国际清算能力的不足，这在一定程度上解决了由于黄金供应不足所带来的国际储备短缺的问题，提高了全球的购买力，促进了国际贸易和跨国投资。

（3）两种方法调节国际收支的失衡。

在布雷顿森林体系下，国际收支的失衡有两种调节方法：短期失衡通过国际货币基金组织提供的信贷资金来解决；长期失衡通过汇率平价来解决。

（4）国际性的货币机构发挥重大作用。

国际货币基金组织和世界银行等国际金融机构为一些工业国家，尤其是一些发展中国家提供各种类型的短期贷款和中长期贷款，监督各国汇率变动，在一定程度上缓和了各成员的国际收支困难，使它们的对外贸易和经济发展得以正常进行，从而有利于世界经济的稳定增长。

2.缺点

布雷顿森林体系是战后国际货币合作的一个比较成功的事例，它为稳定国际金融和扩大国际贸易提供了有利条件，但该体系存在以下缺陷：

（1）美元的特权地位。

美元享有的特殊地位使美国货币政策对各国经济产生重要影响。由于美元是主要的储备资产，享有"纸黄金"之称，美国可以利用美元直接对外投资，购买外国企业，或利用美元弥补国际收支逆差（这种现象被称为"铸币税"，即货币发行国通过货币转移可获得净收益），各国货币汇率盯住美元，形成了各国货币对美元的依附关系，美国货币金融当局的一举一动都将波及整个金融领域，从而导致世界金融体系的不稳定。

（2）特里芬难题。

1960年，美国经济学家罗伯特·特里芬在《黄金与美元危机——自由兑换的未来》一书中提出，布雷顿森林体系这一国际货币制度存在其自身无法克服的设计结构的矛盾——由于美元与黄金挂钩，而其他国家的货币与美元挂钩，美元虽然因此而取得了国际核心货币的地位，但是各国为了发展国际贸易，必须用美元作为结算与储备货币，这样就会导致流出美国的货币在海外不断沉淀，对美国来说就会发生长期贸易逆差；而美元作为国际货币核心的前提是必须保持美元币值稳定与坚挺，这又要求美国必须是一个长期贸易顺差国。这两个要求互相矛盾，因此是一个悖论。

动画微课10-2
特里芬难题

我们将这一国际储备增长与对储备货币信心之间的矛盾称为"特里芬难题"。如果美国保持国际收支平衡，稳定美元，将阻断国际储备来源，导致国际清偿能力不足，这又是一个不可调和的矛盾。

（3）汇率机制缺乏弹性，国际收支调节机制失灵。

布雷顿森林体系过分强调汇率的稳定，各国不能利用汇率的变动来达到调节国际收支平衡的目的，只能消极地实行外汇管制，或放弃稳定国内经济的政策目标，前者必然阻碍国际贸易的发展，后者则违反了稳定和发展本国经济的原则，这二者都是不可取的。可见，缺乏弹性的汇率机制不利于各国经济的稳定发展。

自20世纪50年代开始，上述种种缺陷不断地动摇着布雷顿森林体系的基础，在20世纪70年代布雷顿森林体系陷入崩溃的境地。

（四）布雷顿森林体系的演化

第二次世界大战后，美国的经济实力空前增强，1949年美国拥有世界黄金储备的71.2%，当时饱受战争创伤的西欧、日本为发展经济需要大量美元，但由于无法通过商品和劳务输出来满足，形成了普遍的美元荒，20世纪50年代初期，美国发动侵朝战争，国际收支由顺差转为逆差，黄金储备开始流失，1960年爆发了第一次美元危机，1968年发生了第二次美元危机，1971年爆发了新的美元危机，1971年8月15日美国政府宣布实行"新经济政策"，其内容之一就是对外停止履行美元兑换黄金的义务，切断了美元与黄金的直接联系，从根本上动摇了布雷顿森林体系。

美元停兑黄金以后，引起了国际金融市场的极度混乱。"十国集团"于1971年2月通过了《史密森协议》。其主要内容是，美元贬值7.89%，黄金官价升至每盎司38美元，西方各国主要货币的汇率也作了相应的调整，并规定汇率的波动幅度不超过货币平价的±2.25%。此后，美国的国际收支状况并未好转，1973年1月下旬，国际金融市场又爆发了新的美元危机。美元被迫再次贬值，幅度为10%，黄金官价升至42.22美元。

美元第二次贬值后，为维持本国的经济利益，西方各国纷纷放弃固定汇率，实行浮动汇率。各国货币的全面浮动，使美元完全丧失了中心货币地位，这标志着以美元为中心的国际货币体系的彻底瓦解。

案例探析10-1

"布雷顿森林：75年后"会议在巴黎召开与会代表反对贸易保护主义

2019年是布雷顿森林会议75周年。当地时间7月16日，一场名为"布雷顿森林：

75年后"的高级别会议在法国巴黎召开。在此次会议上，多国代表及专家针对国际合作、多边主义及未来全球经济治理发表了自己的意见，与会者反对贸易保护主义，呼吁多边合作，改变美元霸权地位。

此次会议由法国央行主办，美国、英国、法国等国家政府代表、部分央行行长及专家学者参加，法国央行行长在欢迎辞中再次强调了世界贸易组织和多边主义在处理国际贸易问题中的重要作用。

法国央行行长弗朗索瓦·维勒鲁瓦表示：新的多边主义必须将在三个方面起到重要的作用。首先就是贸易。"二十国集团"一致同意加强世界贸易组织功能的必要性，世界贸易组织应该继续加强贸易自由，特别是在服务领域的贸易自由，在这一方面已经落后……

资料来源：节选自央视网（2019-07-17）。

思考题：

（1）1944年的布雷顿森林会议发生了什么？

（2）美元霸权与贸易保护主义是如何联系的？

三、牙买加货币体系

（一）牙买加货币体系的形成

20世纪60年代初期，联邦德国因为贸易持续较大顺差而对马克币值进行重估，甚至被国际货币基金组织公开批评。1976年，国际货币基金组织（以下简称基金组织）的国际货币体系临时委员会在牙买加首都金斯敦召开会议并达成了《牙买加协议》，与《国际货币基金组织章程（第二修订案）》一道终结了布雷顿森林体系，正式形成了国际货币关系的新格局。

1.增加会员的基金份额

根据该协议的规定，成员的基金份额从原来的292亿特别提款权增至390亿特别提款权，即增长了3.6%；各成员的基金份额比例也有所调整，其中石油输出国比重提高，其他发展中国家基本不变，美国的份额比例有所下降。

2.汇率浮动合法化

《牙买加协议》正式确认了浮动汇率制的合法化。成员可以自行选择汇率制度（事实上，承认固定汇率制与浮动汇率制并存），但成员的汇率政策应同基金组织协商，并接受监督。基金组织协调成员的经济政策，促进了金融稳定，缩小了汇率波动范围。浮动汇率制应逐步恢复固定汇率制，在条件具备时，国际货币基金组织可以实行稳定但可调整的固定汇率制。

3.降低了黄金在国际货币体系中的作用

《牙买加协议》作出了逐步使黄金退出国际货币的决定：废除了原协定中所有的黄金条款，并规定黄金不再作为各国货币定值的标准；废除黄金官价，成员间可以在市场上买卖黄金；成员间及其与基金组织间取消以黄金清算债权债务的义务；基金组织持有的黄金部分出售，部分按官价退还给成员，剩下的酌情处理。

4.规定特别提款权作为主要的国际储备资产

增强特别提款权的作用，主要是提高特别提款权的国际储备地位，扩大其在国际货币基金组织业务中的使用范围，并适时修订特别提款权的有关条款。《牙买加协议》规定，特别提款权可以作为各国货币定值的标准，也可以供有关国家用来清偿对基金组织的债务，还可以用作借贷。

5.扩大对发展中国家的资金融通

用按市价出售的黄金超过官价的收益部分设立一笔信托基金，以优惠条件向最不发达的发展中国家提供援助，帮助其解决国际收支问题；扩大基金组织信用贷款的额度；增加基金组织"出口波动补偿贷款"的数量。

教学视频10-3

认识牙买加
货币体系

（二）牙买加货币体系的特点

牙买加货币体系继承并强化了布雷顿森林体系下的国际货币基金组织，放弃了"双挂钩"制度，主要有以下特点：

1.储备货币多元化

与布雷顿森林体系下国际储备结构单一、美元地位十分突出的情形相比，在牙买加货币体系下，国际储备呈现多元化局面，虽然美元仍是主导的国际货币，但美元地位明显削弱了，美元垄断外汇储备的情形不复存在。目前，国际储备货币已日趋多元化，欧元在国际储备中比重增加。黄金仍然是最稳定的价值手段和最终国际清偿手段。除黄金和主要国家货币外，还有特别提款权。

2.汇率安排多样化

在牙买加货币体系下，浮动汇率制与固定汇率制并存，以浮动汇率为主的多种汇率安排体系能够较为灵活地适应世界经济形势多变的状况和主要储备货币国家经济政策的需要。一般而言，发达工业国家多数采取单独浮动汇率或联合浮动汇率，但有的也采取钉住自选的货币篮子。

对发展中国家而言，多数是钉住某种国际货币或货币篮子，采取单独浮动汇率的很少，不同汇率制度各有优劣，浮动汇率制可以为国内经济政策提供更大的活动空间与独立性，而固定汇率制则减少了本国企业可能面临的汇率风险，方便生产与核算，各国可根据自身的经济实力、开放程度、经济结构等因素去权衡得失利弊。

3.多种渠道调节国际收支

（1）国内经济政策。

国际收支作为一国宏观经济的有机组成部分，必然受到其他因素的影响，一国通常运用国内经济政策改变国内的需求与供给，从而消除国际收支不平衡。比如，在资本项目逆差的情况下，可提高利率，减少货币发行，以此吸引外资流入，弥补缺口。需要注意的是，在运用财政或货币政策调节外部均衡时，往往会受到"米德冲突"的限制，在实现国际收支平衡的同时，牺牲了其他政策目标，如经济增长，财政平衡等，因此内部政策应与汇率政策相协调，才不至于顾此失彼。

（2）汇率政策。

在浮动汇率制或可调整的钉住汇率制下，汇率是调节国际收支的一个重要工具。其原理是：在经常项目赤字时，本币趋于下跌，外贸竞争力增加，出口增加、进口减少，经常项目赤字减少或消失；在经常项目顺差时，本币币值上升，有利于国内进口贸易，不利于对外出口，经常项目顺差得以降低。但是，在实际经济运行中，汇率的调节作用受到"马歇尔—勒纳条件"和"J曲线效应"的制约，其功能往往令人失望。

（3）国际融资。

在布雷顿森林体系下，国际融资功能主要由国际货币基金组织完成，在牙买加货币体系下以国际货币基金组织为中心，通过各国政府和商业银行，给逆差国提供贷款。值得注意的是，随着石油危机的爆发和欧洲货币市场的迅猛发展，各国逐渐转向欧洲货币市场，利用该市场比较优惠的贷款条件融通资金，调节国际收支中的顺逆差。

（4）国际协调。

国际协调功能主要体现在：以国际货币基金组织为桥梁，各国政府通过磋商谈判商，就国际金融问题达成共识与谅解，共同维护国际金融形势的稳定与繁荣。新兴的七国首脑会议上西方七国达成共识，多次合力干预国际金融市场，主观上是为了各自的利益，但客观上也促进了国际金融与经济的稳定与发展。

（三）牙买加货币体系的优缺点

1.优点

（1）多元化的储备结构摆脱了布雷顿森林体系下各国货币间的僵硬关系，为国际经济提供了多种清偿货币，在较大程度上解决了储备货币供不应求的矛盾。

（2）多样化的汇率安排可适应不同发展水平的各国经济，为维持各国经济的稳定与发展提供了灵活性与独立性，有助于保持各国国内经济政策的连续性与稳定性。

（3）多种渠道并行，使国际收支调节更为有效与及时。

2.缺点

（1）在多元化国际储备下，储备货币发行国仍享有"铸币税"等多种好处。同时，在多元化国际储备下，缺乏统一的、稳定的货币标准，这本身就可能造成国际金融的不稳定。

（2）汇率大起大落，变动不定。汇率体系的不稳定，增大了外汇风险，从而在一定程度上抑制了国际贸易与国际投资活动。对发展中国家而言，这种负面影响尤为突出。

（3）国际收支调节机制并不健全。各种现有的汇率渠道都有各自的局限性，牙买加货币体系并没有消除全球性的国际收支失衡问题。

（四）牙买加货币体系的演化

如果说在布雷顿森林体系下，国际金融危机是偶然的、局部的，那么在牙买加货币体系下，国际金融危机则是经常的、全面的和影响深远的，1573年浮动汇率普遍实行后，西方外汇市场货币汇价的波动、金价的起伏经常发生，小危机不断，大危机时有发生。

1978年10月，美元对其他主要西方货币汇价跌至历史最低点，引起整个西方货币金融市场的动荡。这就是著名的1977—1978年西方货币危机。由于金本位制与金汇兑本位制的瓦解，信用货币无论在种类上还是金额上都大大增加，信用货币（如各种形式的支票、支付凭证，信用卡等）占西方各通货流通量的90%以上，现金在某些国家的通货中只占百分之几，货币供应量和存放款的增长大大高于工业生产的增长速度，而且国民经济的发展对信用的依赖越来越深。总之，现有的国际货币体系被人们普遍认为是一种过渡性的、不健全的体系，需要进行彻底的改革。

任务三　国际货币体系的改革

　　经济全球化是生产力发展和科技进步的必然趋势，是生产社会化向国际化的延伸。在开放经济条件下，国际货币体系发挥着越来越重要的作用。国际货币体系是维持全球金融稳定、促进世界经济发展的一系列制度安排，是影响全球经济金融系统安全与稳定的一个重要因素。合理有效的国际货币体系可以促进全球金融稳定和世界经济增长，是全球经济持续、稳定、健康运行的重要条件。

一、国际货币体系改革概况

（一）国际货币体系改革势在必行

　　自20世纪90年代东南亚金融危机、墨西哥金融危机以来，国际社会就对改革国际货币体系提出了各种方案，面对金融危机有人提出重塑布雷顿森林体系，对国际货币基金组织重新定位。2007年由美国次贷危机引起的世界范围的金融危机，引发了各国对当前货币体系的思考。

　　第一，美元霸权地位助长了此次金融危机的发展。此次金融危机发生后，人们普遍认为布雷顿森林体系确立的美元在国际货币体系中的主导地位助长了美国的过度负债和过度消费，而后者又助长了本次金融危机的发展。

　　第二，欧盟期待通过改革提升欧元在国际货币体系中的地位。基于这一战略，2008年11月，法国总统萨科齐反复强调有必要改革美元独霸的现行国际货币体系。

　　第三，在现有美元储备货币体制下，中国等外汇储备大国面临美元贬值的风险，因此这些国家希望建立、健全国际储备货币体系。

　　以美元为主导的国际货币体系在战后世界经济恢复和发展中发挥过积极的作用，但是随着中国等新兴经济体的崛起和全球经济多元化发展，现行国际货币体系已经不能适应世界经济格局的深刻变化。同时，美国转向"逆全球化"和美元霸权的滥用，对国际金融危机后全球经济恢复和发展起着消极作用，因此改革国际货币体系势在必行。

　　首先，世界经济的全球化并没有带来国际货币体系的全球化。现行的国际货币体系仍延续发达国家和发展中国家的"中心—外围"格局，未能反映世界经济格局的新变化。2017年，美元占全球储备货币的比例为63%，远远高于美国在全球国民生产总值中所占的比例（24%）。国际金融风险和责任集中于少数发行国际货币的国家，形成了大国利用储备货币发行权绑架全球经济的局面。当储备货币发行国面临国内政策需求与国际责任要求不一致时，储备货币发行国往往会基于本国利益，优先选择满足国内政策需求，忽视或轻视国际责任。储备货币发行国的政策效应可能在全球范围内产生负面的溢出效应，给其他国家增加了不确定性和风险。

　　其次，国际金融危机的形成和爆发都有国际货币和国际货币体系方面的因素。在金融危机发生的过程中，基本上都存在汇率大幅贬值、国际收支调节机制失衡等现象。随着金融衍生品市场的高度发展，国际货币之间的联系越来越紧密，不稳定的国际货币体系造成的危害也越来越大。国际金融危机的爆发进一步暴露了现行国际货币体系的缺陷。国际货币体系改革需要更加全面地考虑发达国家、发展中国家、新兴市场国家之间平衡的、互利共赢的关系。

最后，国际货币体系改革的重要性已经成为国际社会的共识。国际货币体系的不平衡、不稳定发展是全球经济失衡的重要因素。为了有效维护全球经济、贸易和金融结构，改革国际货币体系已成为推动全球经济和金融稳定发展的重要基础，也是完善全球经济治理体系的重要内容。现行的全球经济治理体系是由发达国家主导的，具有不合理、不公正、不平等的一面，对发展中国家的利益诉求关注不足。

因此，改革国际货币体系、提升新兴市场国家和发展中国家的代表性和发言权，是完善全球经济治理的重要方向和内容。中国作为最大的发展中国家，要推动各国加强宏观经济政策协调，改革国际货币金融体系，积极参与全球治理体系变革，并在其中发挥建设性作用，推动国际秩序朝着更加公正、合理的方向发展，特别要在建设稳定、抗风险的国际货币体系中发挥应有的作用。

（二）国际货币体系改革目标

从国际货币制度的总体发展趋势来看，它的长远目标是创立一种既不依赖黄金，又不依附于单一国家的统一的世界货币，这是国际货币制度发展的必然趋势。然而，距实现这一目标还相当遥远，需要若干个发展阶段，并且有赖于全球经济的高度一体化及国际范围内强大、统一的政治经济联合体的形成。虽然这一目标十分遥远，但是变革的进程已经开始。20世纪70年代国际货币基金组织创立的"特别提款权"及"欧洲货币单位"的出现，打破了美元一统天下的格局。前者无疑是既脱离黄金本位又不依附于单一国家经济实力的、统一的世界货币的雏形，后者则是统一的世界货币形成过程中必然要经历的国际区域货币的发展阶段。

ECU（欧洲货币单位）经过30年的发展已演变为一种崭新的国际区域货币。欧元的出现标志着国际货币制度演变到了一个新的历史阶段——国际区域货币创立及几种国际区域货币并存的发展阶段。

作为国际区域货币的欧元，未来的发展道路也许坎坷不平，然而它的诞生，无疑是国际货币制度发展史上的一个里程碑。

创立一种既不依赖黄金，又不依附于单一国家的统一的世界货币还为时过早，条件尚不具备。因为统一的世界货币需要以高度一体化的世界经济、统一的世界政府、全球性的中央银行为基础，很显然这是一个相当遥远的目标。经济全球化的发展规律和各国国民经济相对独立化的运行规律，将会在相当长的历史时期内相互影响、相互作用。

（三）国际货币体系的发展趋势

现行国际货币体系在汇率制度、资本账户开放、国际储备货币等关键问题上均面临两难的选择，任何选择都并非完美无缺，未来必将是一个多种选择并存的、竞争性的国际货币体系安排。

1.多变性

汇率制度和资本流动管理没有放之四海而皆准的选择。浮动汇率制度、资本可自由流动都曾经被各国改革推动者奉为准则，但随着经济金融形势的演变以及经济金融危机的反复洗礼，很多经济体尤其是发展中经济体开始感受到这一选择的弊端，并且已经在实践中不断修正原有的改革路径，寻找适合自己的发展道路。实际上，各国经济结构、市场发育程度的差异一直存在，不同时期又会出现不同的经济目标和问题，一成不变的制度安排和管理思路难以时刻发挥正向的作用。从发达经济体的角度来看，经济金融相关政策的制定并没有考虑其较大的外溢性，如量化宽松货币政策的推出就大幅增加了资本可自由流动的风险，也加大了浮动汇率制下的汇率波动性。发展中经济体和新兴经济体则需充分考虑国际环境的变化、国内经济的运行状况、金融市场的深度、市场管理者和参与者的能力与水平，总结历史经验教训，积极应对现实挑战，防范外部冲击风险。例如，亚洲金融危机后，相关经济体普遍增加储备积累，相当于摒弃了自由浮动汇率制度的不干预原则；国际金融危机后很多新兴经济体，甚至部分发达经济体都不得不加强跨境资本流动管理，也体现了应对国际金融市场变化的需要。

2.多元化

布雷顿森林体系是基于规则的国际货币体系安排，牙买加货币体系是没有体系的体系，即没有规则约束，是一个开放、包容的体系。一方面，关于各国汇率制度的选择和跨境资本流动的管理，早已不大可能出现和试图寻求统一的标准与规定。事实证明，适合自身经济金融发展状况和发展阶段的制度才是最优的制度，有利于国内经济金融稳定的管理措施才是有效的措施。另一方面，当前各国实力对比意味着以美元为主的国际货币体系在短期内无法发生颠覆性改变，国际货币体系改革不可能走得太快。20世纪60年代，黄金总库与特别提款权的建立和引进，均是对美元本位下国际清偿能力不足的补充。20世纪70年代初期，美元与黄金脱钩以后，国际储备货币体系就已经进入了多元化的时代。

3.弹性化

至于选择什么货币作为计价、结算和投资的货币，包括是否将本币推向国际市场，是否选择超主权货币或者虚拟货币作为国际货币，各国均有自主权，只是任何选择都要与现存的国际货币竞争，由市场优胜劣汰。尽管新兴市场国家在现有国际货币体系中的话语权和代表性依然不足，但国际货币体系改革已被提上全球治理框架改革日程。例如，国际货币基金组织的经济政策监督已经从汇率政策扩展至整个宏观经济政策，从对发展中国家的监督扩大至对所有国家尤其是全球系统性重要国家的监督；金融稳定论坛、巴塞尔委员会、国际证监会组织等机构从各自领域提出了诸多改进和加强金融监管的建议；全球范围内建立了各种层次的货币合作；2010年，世界银行通过了向发展中国家转移3.13个百分点投票权的改革方案，同时国际货币基金组织也在努力推动份额改革。

二、欧洲货币一体化

（一）欧盟与欧元的诞生

20世纪以前，欧洲统一的思想业已出现。历史上的欧洲也曾在某些时期以帝国或国家联盟形式成为命运共同体。1948年，荷兰、比利时、卢森堡三国组成关税联盟，以免除关税，开放原料、商品自由贸易。

第二次世界大战后，1946年9月，英国首相温斯顿·丘吉尔提议建立"欧洲合众国"。

1949年，欧洲委员会成立，成为第一个泛欧组织。

1950年5月，鉴于煤、钢产品是军事武器的必要原料，法国外交部长罗伯特·舒曼提出欧洲煤钢共同体计划（即舒曼计划），旨在约束德国。

1951年4月18日，法国、意大利、比利时、荷兰、卢森堡与德国六国联合签署为期50年的《关于建立欧洲煤钢共同体的条约》（又称《巴黎条约》），于1952年成立欧洲煤钢共同体，在接管鲁尔区管理权并取消部分德国工业生产限制的同时，合作推动煤与钢铁的生产销售。1955年6月1日，欧洲煤钢共同体六国外长在意大利的墨西拿举行会议，提议将煤钢共同体的原则推广到其他经济领域并建立共同市场。

1957年3月25日，欧洲煤钢共同体六国首脑及外长在罗马签署《欧洲经济共同体条约》和《欧洲原子能共同体条约》，这两份条约统称为《罗马条约》。

1958年1月1日，《罗马条约》正式生效，欧洲经济共同体正式成立，旨在创造共同市场，取消成员之间的关税，促进成员之间劳动力、商品、资金、服务等的自由流通。同一天，欧洲投资银行（The European Investment Bank）成立，于1959年正式开业，总行设在卢森堡。

1965年4月8日，德国、法国、意大利、荷兰、比利时、卢森堡六国签署《布鲁塞尔条约》，决定将欧洲煤钢共同体、欧洲原子能共同体、欧洲经济共同体统一起来，统称为"欧洲共同体"，此为欧盟的前身。

1987年7月1日，欧洲单一法案生效。

1991年12月11日，欧共体马斯特里赫特首脑会议通过并草签了《欧洲经济与货币联盟条约》和《政治联盟条约》，统称为《欧洲联盟条约》，即《马斯特里赫特条约》。

1992年2月7日，欧共体12国外长和财政部长在荷兰小镇马斯特里赫特正式签署《马斯特里赫特条约》，设立理事会、委员会、议会，逐步由区域性经济共同开发转型为区域政经整合的发展。

1993年11月1日，《马斯特里赫特条约》正式生效，欧洲联盟正式成立，欧洲三大共同体纳入欧洲联盟。

1994年3月30日，奥地利、瑞典、芬兰和挪威的入盟协商完成。各国举行公民投票，除了挪威以外，其他各国均通过加入欧盟的提案。1994年1月1日，挪威与冰岛、列支敦士登等欧洲自由贸易联盟成员加入欧洲经济区。

1994年1月1日，欧洲经济与货币联盟（Economic and Monetary Union of the European Union）成立欧洲货币管理局。

1998年1月，欧洲中央银行成立。

1999年1月1日，欧盟正式启动欧元（Euro）；欧元自此在奥地利、比利时、法国、德国、芬兰、荷兰、卢森堡、爱尔兰、意大利、葡萄牙和西班牙11个国家正式使用，11国实行统一的货币政策，由欧洲中央银行负责。

2002年1月1日零时，欧元正式流通。

2002年7月，欧元成为欧元区唯一合法货币。截至2018年年末，欧元为欧盟19个国家所使用；此外，欧元也是非欧盟中6个国家或地区的货币，分别是摩纳哥、圣马力诺、梵蒂冈、安道尔、黑山和科索沃地区。

欧洲中央银行

欧洲中央银行（European Central Bank，ECB）于1998年6月1日成立，总部设在德国金融中心法兰克福，是根据1992年《马斯特里赫特条约》规定而设立的欧元区中央银行，是共同货币政策的制定者、实施者、监督者。欧洲中央银行是欧洲经济一体化的产物，是世界上第一个管理超国家货币的中央银行，也是为了适应欧元发行和流动而设立的金融机构。欧洲中央银行的职责和结构以德国联邦银行为模式，独立于欧盟机构和各国政府之外。欧洲中央银行的主要任务是维持欧元购买力，保持欧元区物价稳定。欧洲中央银行管理主导利率、货币储备与发行，以及制定欧洲货币政策。虽然欧元区货币政策的权力集中了，但是具体执行仍由欧元区成员方央行负责。欧元区各国央行仍保留自己的外汇储备，欧洲中央银行的储备由各成员方央行根据本国在欧元区内的人口比例和国内生产总值的比例来提供。

欧洲中央银行管理委员会是最高决策机构，负责制定利率和执行货币政策，由6名执行董事会成员和欧元区成员方央行行长组成，每月定期召开会议。

随着欧洲银行联盟的建立，欧洲中央银行被赋予了监管欧盟内主要银行的职能，将从2014年11月起，和成员方主管机构共同履行该职能。

资料来源：根据网络资料整理所得。

（二）欧洲货币体系

欧洲货币体系主要有三个组成部分：欧洲货币单位（European Currency Unit，ECU）、欧洲货币合作基金（European Monetary Cooperation Fund，EMCF）、稳定汇率机制（Exchange Rate Mechanism，ERM）。

1.欧洲货币单位

欧洲货币单位，类似于特别提款权，其价值是欧共体成员货币的加权平均值，每种货币的权数根据该国在欧共体内部贸易中所占的比重和该国国民生产总值规模进行确定。以这种方式计算出来的欧洲货币单位具有价值比较稳定的特点。欧洲货币单位的创设是欧洲货币体系与联合浮动的最大区别所在，其发行有着特定的程序。

欧洲货币单位的作用主要有：作为欧洲稳定汇率机制的标准；作为决定成员货币汇率偏离中心汇率的参考指标；作为成员官方之间的清算手段、信贷手段和外汇市场的干预手段。

2.欧洲货币合作基金

为保证欧洲货币体系的正常运转，欧共体在1973年4月设立了欧洲货币合作基金，集中了成员20%的黄金储备和美元储备，作为发行欧洲货币单位的准备。

欧洲货币合作基金的主要作用是向各成员提供相应的贷款，以帮助它们进行国际收支调节和外汇市场干预，保证欧洲汇率机制的稳定。欧洲货币合作基金给各成员提供的贷款种类因期限不同而有所不同。期限最短的45天以下（含45天）贷款只向稳定汇率机制的参与国提供；9个月以下的短期贷款用于帮助成员克服短期国际收支失衡问题；中期贷款的期限为2～5年，用于帮助成员解决结构性国际收支问题。欧共体通常在向各成员提供贷款时附加一定的条件。

3.稳定汇率机制

欧洲货币体系内部的汇率制并非完全固定的，各成员之间货币汇率有一个可波动的范围。每一成员的货币都与欧洲货币单位定出一个中心汇率，这个汇率在市场上的波动幅度为±2.25%，对英镑来说是6%。

（三）欧元对现行国际货币体系的挑战

欧元的诞生助推了欧盟经济实力与政治地位的提升，为其他经济组织的金融合作提供了可效仿的成功案例。

汇率制度安排多样化、黄金非货币化以及国际政策协调艰难，是目前牙买加货币体系被称为"非体系"的重要原因。欧元将以其汇率稳定、跨国界的协调及统一的中央银行对这一"非体系"直接提出挑战。

欧元是人类历史上第一次可用于非官方结算的跨国界信用本位货币的一种创造，它的诞生及其发展，将为未来统一世界货币的创造提供宝贵经验，也将为其他区域性经济合作组织货币一体化起到示范作用。

许多学者预言，世界货币最终的统一将建立在几大区域性国际货币基础之上，并在广泛的国际协调与制度框架内执行其世界货币的职能。未来，国际货币基金组织的货币改革进程将和区域内国际货币一体化发展进程相交织，并最终创造出一种完善的世界货币。尽管这个过程很漫长，但是这或许就是未来国际货币体系演化的趋势。

三、人民币国际化

经济学家托马斯·弗里德曼曾说："地球是圆的，但世界是平的。"深度全球化的现代社会是一个互相影响的整体。脱胎于世界经济大国的人民币注定要承载一定的历史使命，在世界经济的舞台上发挥着越来越重要的作用。

（一）人民币国际化的含义

一般认为，一国货币成为国际化货币至少要具备三项基本职能，即结算职能、投资职能和储备职能。其中，结算职能是货币国际化的必要条件，而不是充分条件。

人民币国际化是指人民币获得国际市场的广泛认可和接受，并发挥计价单位、交换媒介和价值储藏的功能，成为国际结算货币、投资货币和储备货币。

人民币国际化的本质含义应包括以下三个方面：

第一，人民币现金在境外享有一定的流通度，国际贸易中以人民币结算的交易要达到一定的比重。

第二，以人民币计价的金融产品成为国际各主要金融机构包括中央银行的投资工具，以人民币计价的金融市场规模不断扩大。

第三，世界多数国家接受人民币作为本国的储备货币。这是衡量货币包括人民币国际化的通用标准。

（二）人民币国际化进程

人民币诞生于1948年12月1日。20世纪70年代末改革开放前，在高度集中的外汇管理体制下，人民币仅作为国内货币这一单一角色，原则上既不允许携带出境，也不允许用于对外贸易、投融资等活动的计价结算。

随着改革开放的不断深入，我国对外人员交往日趋频繁，其中包括出入境旅游、探亲的个人，还包括大量往返港澳台与内地间的外商。另外，海外分布数千万的华侨华裔，改革开放密切了境内外居民之间的联系。为满足市场使用现钞量上升的需要，政府适应性地调整了人民币跨境政策，放宽了个人携带人民币出入境的限制。1993年2月，中国公民和外国人出入境，每人每次携带人民币限额为6 000元；在开放边民互市和小额贸易的地区，允许当地根据实际情况确定限额，并在报批后实施。2005年1月，出入境携带人民币现钞标准进一步提高到2万元。

1973年浮动汇率普遍实行后，西方外汇市场货币汇价的波动、金价的起伏经常发生，中国在对外贸易中有较大的顺差，大量资本流入，意味着国家要大量持有外汇储备，如果外汇不稳定，中国的经济安全就很难保住。

当人民币成为国际储备货币，国际贸易可以用人民币支付时，就不需要持有大量的外汇储备，其他国家汇率变动对中国经济所能造成的影响就会减少。

2003年3月，国家外汇管理局发文，明确规定境内机构在签订进出口合同时，可以采用人民币作为计价货币，但实际对外交割的货币，仍然是按当日银行牌价折成等值外汇进行收付和结算。2003年9月，外汇局再次发文，允许边境贸易中用人民币计价结算和办理进出口核销，允许境外贸易机构在我国边境地区银行开立人民币边境贸易结算专用账户，办理边贸结算项下的资金收付，同时鼓励边境地区银行与毗邻国家边境地区商业银行建立代理行关系，开通银行直接结算渠道，并可加挂人民币兑毗邻国家货币的汇价。

2007年6月，人民币债券登陆中国香港。

2008年12月，中俄磋商在贸易中改用本国货币结算；中韩签署1 800亿元货币互换协议。

2009年7月，跨境贸易人民币结算试点正式启动。

2011年9月，尼日利亚计划将10%的外汇储备投资人民币。智利、泰国、巴西和委内瑞拉拟将人民币纳入央行储备。

2011年12月，人民币合格境外机构投资者试点计划相关规则发布。

2012年10月，开启日元/人民币直接报价。

2013年6月，中英签署200亿英镑双边本币互换协议。

2013年10月，中欧签署3 500亿元货币互换协议。

2015年6月，中国人民银行首次发布《2015年人民币国际化报告》。

2015年11月30日，国际货币基金组织决定将人民币纳入特别提款权（SDR）货币篮子，SDR货币篮子相应扩大至美元、欧元、人民币、日元、英镑5种货币，人民币在SDR货币篮子中的权重为10.92%，美元、欧元、日元和英镑的权重分别为41.73%、30.93%、8.33%和8.09%。这无疑是人民币和中国金融市场迈向国际舞台的新起点。

环球银行金融电信协会（SWIFT）统计显示，2016年12月，人民币成为全球第6大支付货币，市场占有率为1.68%。2016年10月1日，国际货币基金组织宣布纳入人民币的特别提款权（SDR）新货币篮子正式生效，这是人民币国际化的重要里程碑。

（三）人民币国际化的利弊

1.人民币国际化之利

（1）国际铸币税收入增加。

在现代货币制度下，铸币税并不是税收体系下的一个税种，而是指发行者凭借其发行货币的特权所获得的货币面值大于发行成本之间的差额，即货币发行带来的收入。一国货币成为国际货币可以获得丰厚的铸币税收入。同样，国际铸币税收入是实现人民币国际化之后的最大收益。发行国际货币便可以从其他国家征收铸币税，而且这种收益是无成本的。因此，如果人民币成为国际计价和支付货币，甚至成为储备货币后，我国将获得高额的铸币税税收。人民币国际化带来的国际铸币税收入将会成为我国财政收入的一个重要来源。

（2）节省外汇储备，规避汇率风险。

目前，我国的外汇储备高度集中于美元资产，无论是美国国债价值下跌还是美元汇率大幅贬值，都会导致我国外汇储备大幅缩水。实现人民币国际化，可以使人民币成为国际结算的主要货币之一，其自身既是一种计价货币，又是一种储备货币，减少外汇储备可以在一定程度上缓解因外汇储备过多而导致的流动性过剩问题，有助于内外均衡。与此同时，对外贸易的快速发展使外贸企业持有大量外币债权和债务，这些都会因外币汇价动荡而产生巨大的风险，汇价波动会对企业的生产经营带来不利影响。实现人民币国际化后，可以减少因使用外币引起的财富流失，可以用本国货币进行对外贸易和投资，企业能够有效地规避汇率风险，降低贸易成本，推动和扩大对外贸易。

（3）优化世界货币结构。

第二次世界大战之后，美元成为全球货币的霸主，在全球外汇储备中占了很大比例。其中，在全球外汇储备中占了60%以上，在发达国家外汇储备中占比更是超过70%。人民币国际化能够在币种上分散各国储备的风险，为发展中国家争取更多权利。各国国际储备中多了人民币这一选择，将大大有利于本国所持有财富的稳定，减少以往面对美元大幅贬值造成的财富缩水却束手无策的无奈。

（4）助推金融创新发展。

当前，我国金融市场存在诸多问题，金融创新滞后于实体经济，创新不足问题突出。反观欧美发达国家，其金融市场不断推陈出新，各种金融衍生品工具和结构性产品层出不穷，且其金融体制相对健全和完善。这些都与美元、欧元在国际上的巨大话语权密不可分。人民币国际化能够推动我国金融不断完善，金融衍生品不断更新，有利于分散并降低风险，增强市场流动性，丰富市场投资品种，增加投资。

（5）增强政治经济话语权。

人民币国际化既非可做可不做，也非贪大求洋。这是中国经济发展到现阶段，不论从经济发展还是从国家战略与地缘政治考虑，均有必要迈出的战略步伐。

2.人民币国际化之弊

（1）宏观调控难度加大。

目前，央行通过收放银根就可以相对有效地调控市场流动性以及与流动性关联的一系列资产和投资问题。而一旦人民币国际化以后，央行在制定货币政策时，由于来自国际的需求导致面临的货币需求更复杂，货币操作思路就将由中国境内从上到下的线性系统转变为遍布全球和央行联动的网状系统。由于市场机制本身的缺陷以及各种市场信号检测的滞后性，将使确定货币供应量成为一个技术难题。人民币国际化之后，国际金融市场上将流通一定量的人民币，并随着人民币国际化程度的提高而增加，这将削弱中央银行对国内人民币的控制能力，影响国内宏观调控政策的实施效果。

（2）货币政策自主性削弱。

国际金融交易的猛增使各国中央银行更难以应付，导致相关国家不得不放弃金融全球化的利益，通过实施资本项目的管制来控制资本流动。实行浮动汇率制和资本自由流动的国家在利用世界储蓄资源时处于不利地位。一国实施浮动汇率制，虽能控制短期利率，但货币国际化使得汇率对利率的影响更为明显，利率的变化更为敏感地受到来自汇率变化的影响。货币国际化后，如果本币的实际汇率与名义汇率出现偏离，或者即期汇率、利率与预期汇率、利率出现偏离，都将给国际投资者套利的机会，刺激短期投机性资本的流动。

（3）国际投机资本对中国金融市场的冲击加重。

人民币国际化之后，中国经济与世界经济的联系必然更为密切，国际金融市场的任何风吹草动都有可能对中国金融市场产生影响。无论是亚洲金融危机还是国际金融危机，中国相对稳定的经济和金融正是得益于其相对封闭的经济和金融市场，以及对外汇的严格管制。一旦开放金融市场，外部"热钱"必然会大量流入。因此，人民币实现国际化之后，很可能成为一种金融危机的传导工具，降低中国经济和金融市场抵御风险的能力。

（4）更大的货币需求与汇率波动。

人民币成为国际货币后，将会被许多国家储存和使用。一旦国外货币需求的偏好发生变化，将会导致国内货币供需发生波动，从而导致汇率的波动。

（5）出口企业面临冲击。

目前，我国已经成为世界第一大出口国。改革开放多年来，经济飞速的发展得益于高额的出口。同时，人民币国际化将进一步增大人民币的升值压力。人民币升值以后，为维持同样的人民币价格，当前用美元表示的我国出口产品价格将有所提高，这就削弱了其价格上的竞争力，而要使出口产品的美元价格不变，势必挤压出口企业的利润空间，这就不可避免地对出口企业造成冲击。

思政小课堂

《货币》是中央电视台制作的一部10集大型纪录片，这部纪录片由货币的起源开始，到货币的发展、货币的崛起、货币的灾难和货币的未来，对货币和政治、经济、文化以及社会运行秩序之间的关系进行一次较为全面深入的梳理，以一种开放、通俗、生动的方式来解读货币。

请观看纪录片《货币》第九集《跨越国界》，完成下列任务：

（1）说一说世界几大国际货币出现的时间及发展脉络。

（2）试着总结国家货币演变为国际货币的条件有哪些。

（3）思考在全球化视野下人民币如何才能实现真正的国际化？

项目思维导图

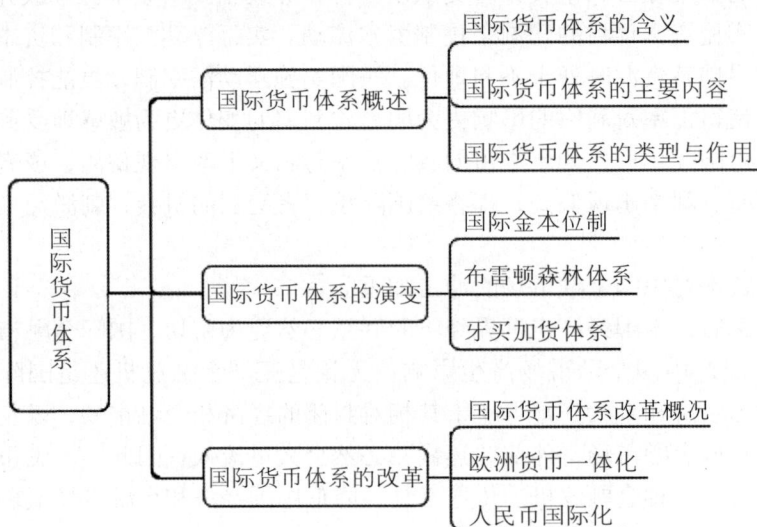

项目训练

一、单选题

1.国际货币体系进入到浮动汇率时代开始于（　　）。

A.国际金本位制度　　　　　　　　B.布雷顿森林体系

C.牙买加货币体系　　　　　　　　D.欧元诞生之后

2.维持布雷顿森林体系运转的基本条件不包括（　　）。

A.美国国际收支保持顺差，美元对外价值稳定

B.世界各国有充足平衡的黄金储备，以维持对黄金的充分兑换

C.美国有充足的黄金储备，以保持美元对黄金的有限兑换性

D.黄金价格维持在官价水平上

3.特里芬难题中提及的一个基本矛盾是（　　）。

A.维持美元汇价与美国国际收支平衡的矛盾

B.维持美元与黄金比价和维持美元与各国货币汇率之间的矛盾

C.美元与黄金挂钩和各国货币与美元挂钩之间的矛盾

D.浮动汇率与管制汇率之间的矛盾

4.历史上第一个国际货币体系是（　　　）。

A.国际金本位制　　　　　　　　　B.国际金汇兑本位制

C.布雷顿森林体系　　　　　　　　D.后布雷顿森林体系

5.欧元启动的时间是（　　　）。

A.2002年1月　　　　　　　　　　B.1999年1月

C.2000年10月　　　　　　　　　　D.2002年3月

二、多选题

1.国际货币体系的内容包括（　　　）。

A.关键货币与汇率制度的确定

B.国际储备资产的确定

C.国际收支及其调节机制的确定

D.在结算国家间债权债务时采取什么样的结算方式

E.是否施加限制（即外汇管制）

2.以下关于国际货币基金组织的说法，正确的是（　　　）。

A.是联合国系统的一个专业机构，其总部设在华盛顿

B.作为该组织创始国之一，中国一直保有该组织的合法席位

C.是以成员入股的方式组成的企业性金融机构，成员的基金份额构成其主要的资金来源

D.普通提款权的期限不超过5年，贷款最高额度为成员所缴份额的100%

3.人民币国际化的好处有（　　　）。

A.国际铸币税收入增加

B.节省外汇储备，规避汇率风险

C.优化世界货币结构

D.助推金融创新发展

E.增强政治经济话语权

4.在布雷顿森林体系下，下列说法正确的是（　　　）。

A.黄金与美元挂钩

B.各国货币与美元挂钩

C.各国货币直接与黄金挂钩

D.各国货币间接与黄金挂钩

5.当前国际货币体系的特点是（　　　）。

A.多种汇率制度并存

B.基本上以美元为中心国际货币

C.多种中心国际货币并存

D.普遍采用盯住一种国际中心货币

三、判断题

1.按照国际储备资产形式的标准划分，国际货币体系可分为金本位制和信用本位制两大类。   （   ）

2.关键货币是在国际货币体系中充当基础性价值换算工具的货币。   （   ）

3.世界上首次出现的国际货币体系是国际银本位制度。   （   ）

4.国际货币基金组织是在牙买加货币体系时期成立的。   （   ）

5.欧元诞生于1999年。   （   ）

四、实践训练

通过网络、书籍等资料收集信息，了解人民币国际化的最新进展，并分析人民币国际化的有利因素和不利因素有哪些。

主要参考文献

[1] 陈雨露. 国际金融（精编版）[M]. 6版. 北京：中国人民大学出版社，2019.

[2] 王晓光. 国际金融 [M]. 5版. 北京：清华大学出版社，2019.

[3] 姜波克. 国际金融新编 [M]. 6版. 上海：复旦大学出版社，2018.

[4] 刘淑娥，赵秀艳. 国际金融与实务 [M]. 2版. 北京：清华大学出版社，2018.

[5] 孙连铮. 国际金融 [M]. 4版. 北京：高等教育出版社，2019.

[6] 李敏. 国际金融实务 [M]. 3版. 北京：中国金融出版社，2019.

[7] 张宗英，纪建新. 国际金融实务 [M]. 2版，北京：对外经济贸易大学出版社，2017.

[8] 李军燕，楼昳江. 国际金融实务 [M]. 3版. 大连：东北财经大学出版社，2021.

[9] 刘玉操，曹华. 国际金融实务 [M]. 6版. 大连：东北财经大学出版社，2021.

[10] 何泽荣. 国际金融原理 [M]. 3版. 成都：西南财经大学出版社，2015.

[11] 王宗湖. 国际金融实务 [M]. 2版. 北京：对外经济贸易大学出版社，2015.

[12] 傅海龙. 国际贸易理论与实务 [M]. 5版. 北京：对外经济贸易大学出版社，2018.

[13] 程祖伟，等. 国际贸易结算与融资 [M]. 4版. 北京：中国人民大学出版社，2016.

[14] 姚君. 国际结算实务 [M]. 北京：中国人民大学出版社，2018.

[15] 许南. 国际结算 [M]. 北京：中国人民大学出版社，2014.

[16] 刘金波. 外汇交易原理与实务 [M]. 2版. 北京：人民邮电出版社，2016.

[17] 张元萍. 金融衍生工具 [M]. 5版. 北京：首都经济贸易大学出版社，2018.

[18] 任金秀. 新编国际贸易理论与实务 [M]. 2版. 北京：北京大学出版社，2016.

[19] 国际货币基金组织. 国际收支和国际投资头寸手册 [M]. 6版. 北京：中国金融出版社，2012.

[20] 国家外汇管理局国际收支司. 诠释国际收支统计新标准 [M]. 北京：中国经济出版社，2015.

［21］国际货币基金组织网站，https：//www.imf.org/zh/home

［22］国家外汇管理局网站，https：//www.safe.gov.cn/

［23］中国外汇交易中心网站，http：//www.chinamoney.com.cn/chinese/index.html

［24］世界黄金协会网站，https：//www.gold.org/

［25］中国金融新闻网，https：//www.financialnews.com.cn/

英 文 篇

Project One
Balance of Payments

Learning Objectives

Knowledge Objectives:

Understand the concept and meaning of the balance of payments; learn the principles of the compilation of the balance of payments statement, and to master the content and structure of the balance of payments statement.

Competence Objectives:

Master the analysis methods of the balance of payments statement; understand the causes and effects of imbalances in the balance of payments, and to master the means and measures of the balance of payments adjustment.

Operational Objectives:

To be able to apply the knowledge and to make a preliminary analysis of China's balance of payments.

Course Introduction

The State Administration of Foreign Exchange released data on China's international trade in goods and services for May 2020

In May 2020, China's international trade in goods and services, as measured by the balance of payments, generated revenues of RMB 1 589.4 billion and expenditures of RMB 1 165.4 billion, resulting in a surplus of RMB 424 billion. Of these, the revenue from trade in goods was RMB 1 459.2 billion while the expenditure was RMB 965 billion, resulting in a surplus of RMB 494.2 billion; the revenue from trade in services was RMB 130.2 billion and the expenditure was RMB 200.4 billion, resulting in a deficit of RMB 70.2 billion.

In US dollar terms, China's international trade in goods and services in May 2020, as measured by the balance of payments, generated US$ 223.9 billion in revenue and US$ 164.2 billion in expenditure, resulting in a surplus of US$ 59.7 billion. Of this amount, trade in goods generated US$ 205.5 billion and the expenditure was US$ 135.9 billion, resulting in a surplus of US$ 69.6 billion. While the trade in services revenue was US$ 18.3 billion and the expenditure was US$ 28.2 billion, resulting in a deficit of US$ 9.9 billion.

Source: The State Administration of Foreign Exchange (SAFE). The State Administration of Foreign Exchange released data on China's international trade in goods and services for May 2020 [EB/OL]. [2020-06-29]. http: //www.safe.gov. cn/safe/2020/0629/16534.html.

Discussion: How to understand the terms such as balance of payments, surplus, deficit, trade in goods, trade in services? After learning this project, students will be able to make a preliminary analysis of China's balance of payments based on the understanding of basic concepts.

The history of world economic development tells us that the origin of international economic transactions is international trade, and the initial form of international trade is cross-border trade in goods, which is inevitably accompanied by the transfer of resources, the movement of wealth and the cross-border payment of money. Global advances in science and technology have driven the development of social productivity while international economic relations have become increasingly closer. Thus, international trade today is not limited to the initial trade in goods but extends to trade in services, capital flows and direct investment between countries, transfer payments between governments (aid, donations, etc.) and other areas of political and economic activities.

Task 1   Balance of Payments Overview

I. The concept and meaning of balance of payments

Once the different types of international economic transactions have taken place, various debt relationships and the monetary payments take place subsequently. For example, a resident of a country who exports a shipment of goods receives an external credit while an imported shipment of goods creates an external debt. In international finance, the relationship between credits and debts is referred to as international borrowing and lending which indicates the combination of a country's external debts and credits at a certain date (point in time).

The debt relationship represented by international borrowing and lending needs to be liquidated and settled within a certain period of time in the currency of the creditor's income and the debtor's payment. This liquidation, settlement or payment results in a balance of payments. To some extent, the balance of payments reflects a country's external income and payments over a period of time.

The International Monetary Fund (IMF) defines the balance of payments as a systematic record of all economic transactions that take place between residents and non-residents of an economic entity during a given period.

Teaching Video 1-1

Understanding the International
Monetary Fund

II. Understanding the concept of balance of payments

To understand the concept of balance of payments, following aspects are needed to be considered:

1. The balance of payments is a flow concept, not a stock concept.

The balance of payments records the number of changes in a country's external income and expenditure that occur in a given period (quarterly, half-yearly or annually). Flows are the values of quantities that change over a certain period, such as the number of changes in deposits, the number of births.

2. The balance of payments records all economic transactions of a country.

Economic transactions include not only tangible trade, such as trade in goods but also intangible trade, such as services and technology transfer.

3. The balance of payments records transactions between residents and non-residents.

A resident is an economic unit with a centre of economic interest that has been living in the economic territory of a country for one year or more. A person who does not meet the above conditions is a non-resident. A resident may be a natural person, a government institution or a legal person. The difference in residence is the basis for the classification of residents and non-residents, that is, the location where residents engage in economic activities and transactions such as production and consumption.

(Knowledge Link 1-1)

The Scope of Chinese Residents

The State Administration of Foreign Exchange (SAFE) stipulates in the "Operational Guidelines on Balance of Payments Statistics Reporting through Banks (2019 Edition)" that institutions determine their resident and non-resident status according to the country or region of registration. International organizations in China, China's office of international organizations and foreign consulates in China are not considered Chinese residents.

Individuals are identified as residents or non-residents according to their valid personal identity documents.

Individuals holding a valid document such as a permanent residence permit outside of

China, a foreign passport, a Mainland Travel Permit for Hong Kong and Macao Residents or a Mainland Travel Permit for Taiwan Residents are determined to be non-residents of China.

Individuals who hold a Chinese resident identity card, a foreigner's permanent residence identity card or other valid Chinese documents are deemed to be Chinese residents.

Individuals who hold both an identity document of the nationality (region) to which they belong and a permanent residence document are given priority for resident status on the basis of the permanent residence document, given that the centre of economic interest principle of residency is used for balance of payments statistics.

Individuals holding a Chinese passport must be identified in conjunction with other valid documents, that is, individuals who hold both a Chinese passport and a permanent residence permit abroad are identified as non-Chinese residents, while individuals who do not hold a permanent residence permit abroad are identified as Chinese residents.

Source: The State Administration of Foreign Exchange (SAFE). Notice of the State Administration of Foreign Exchange on the Issuance of the "Operational Guidelines on Balance of Payments Statistics Reporting through Banks (2019 Edition)" [EB/OL]. [2019-09-18]. http: //www.gov.cn/xinwen/2019-09/18/content_5430887.htm.

Task 2   Balance of Payments Statement

I. Concept of the Balance of Payments Statement

Animation Micro-lesson 1-1

Balance of Payments and Balance of Payments Statement

A country's balance of payments can only be effectively represented by specific statistics, so the balance of payments statement is indispensable. A balance of payments statement is a statistical statement reflecting all the external economic transactions of an economic entity expressed in monetary units over a certain period of time (annually, semi-annually or quarterly). Therefore, the balance of payments statement is the external expression of the balance of payments.

II. Principles of Balance of Payments Statement Presentation

The balance of payments statement is prepared on a double-entry bookkeeping basis, i.e., "where there is a debit, there is a credit, and debits and credits are equal". According to this principle, all income items, increases in liabilities or decreases in assets are shown as credits, indicated by a " + " sign, while all expenditure items, increases in assets or decreases in liabilities are shown as debits, indicated by a " − " sign. Each transaction must be recorded with the corresponding debit and credit in equal amounts at the same time. In practice, any transaction that results in a payment to foreigners or a demand for foreign currency, i.e., an increase in assets and a decrease in liabilities, is recorded as a debit; any transaction that results in an income from foreigners or a supply of foreign currency, i.e., a decrease in assets and an increase in liabilities, is recorded as a credit.

In principle, therefore, the total debits and credits of all balance of payments statement items are always equal with a net difference of zero. In practice, however, the debits and credits (i.e., income and expenditure) for each specific item of the balance of payments statement are often unbalanced and there is always a difference between income and expenditure. When the income is greater than the expenditure, i.e., the amount credited is greater than the amount debited, the difference is positive (+) and is referred to as a surplus; conversely, when the expenditure is greater than the income, i.e., the amount credited is less than the amount debited, the difference is negative (−) and is referred to as a deficit. The total balance of payments is the sum of the differences between items.

III. Composition of the Balance of Payments Statement

(i) Structure of the Balance of Payments Statement

As the content and scope of international economic transactions vary from country to country and the needs of economic analysis are not identical, balance of payments statements are prepared differently. To guide members in preparing their balance sheets and to make them comparable across countries (regions), the Balance of Payments and International Investment Position Manual (sixth edition) prepared by the IMF divides the overall balance of payments into two main accounts. They are the current account, which reflects real resource flows such as imports and exports of goods and services and net factor payments, and the capital and financial account, which reflects asset ownership flows. In addition, artificially balanced accounts are set up with the errors and omissions account. The details of China's Balance of Payments Account are shown in Table 1−1.

Table 1−1 　　　　　　　China's Balance of Payments　　　　　Unit: US$ billion

Projects	Difference	Credit (+)	Debit (−)
I. Current account			
A. Goods and services			
a. Goods			
1. General merchandise			
2. Goods for processing			
3. Repair of goods			
4. Goods purchased at the port by various means of transport			
5. Non−monetary gold			
b. Services			
1. Processing services			
2. Maintenance and repair services			
3. Transport			

续表

Projects	Difference	Credit（＋）	Debit（－）
4. Travel			
5. Construction			
6. Insurance and pension services			
7. Financial services			
8. Intellectual property royalties			
9. Telecommunications， computer and information services			
10. Other business services			
11. Personal， cultural and recreational services			
12. Government services not mentioned elsewhere			
B. Initial income			
a. Compensation of employees			
b. Investment income			
C. Secondary income			
a. Individual transfers			
b. Other secondary income			
II. Capital and financial accounts			
A. Capital accounts			
B. Financial accounts			
a.Financial accounts of a non−reserve nature			
1. Direct investment			
2. Portfolio investment			
3. Financial derivatives			
4. Other investments			
b.Reserve assets			
1. Monetary gold			
2. Special Drawing Rights			
3. Reserve position with the International Monetary Fund			
4. Foreign exchange reserves			
5. Other reserve assets			
III. Net errors and omissions			

Source: 1. International Monetary Fund. Balance of Payments and International Investment Position Manual ［M］. 6th ed. Beijing: China Finance Press, 2012.

2. Balance of Payments Analysis Group, State Administration of Foreign Exchange. China's Balance of Payments Report 2018 ［R］. Beijing: State Administration of Foreign Exchange, 2019.

（ii）**Elements of the Balance of Payments Statement**

1.Current account（items）

The current account is the flow of real resources, including imports and exports of goods, imports and exports of services, external receivables and payables. It also includes current transfers of economic value provided or received with other countries or regions that occur without equivalent returns. The current account is the most basic and important item in a country's balance of payments statement. Taking the items in China's balance of payments statement as an example, the current account includes four sub - items: goods, services, primary income and secondary income.

（1）Goods. This account records a country's imports and exports of commodity goods. The goods item is most basic in a country's current account and is the largest item in terms of revenue and expenditure. Imports are debited, exports are credited, and the difference between the two is known as the balance of trade. Goods include items such as general merchandise, goods used for processing, repairs to goods, goods purchased by various means of transport at ports, and non-monetary gold.

（2）Services. Services are the second largest item in the current account and mainly record changes in receipts and payments arising from intangible trade inputs and outputs. The output of services is credited and the input of services is debited. Services include processing services, maintenance and repair services, transport, tourism, communications, construction, insurance and pension services, financial services, intellectual property royalties, telecommunications, computer and information services, other business services, personal, cultural and recreational services, and government services not mentioned elsewhere.

（3）Primary income. Primary income comprises two main types of transactions between residents and non−residents. The first type is employee compensation, which is primarily the remuneration of wages paid to non−resident workers（e.g., seasonal short-term workers）. The second type is investment income, which includes income and expenses from direct investments, portfolio investments and other investments. The most common types of investment income are income from equity（dividends）and income from debt（interest）.

（4）Secondary income. Secondary income is a transfer of goods, services or financial assets between residents and non - residents that is not compensated and rewarded, and is therefore referred to as an uncompensated or unilateral transfer. It includes all transfers that are not capital items, including unremunerated transfers between governments（such as war reparations, government aid, regular government contributions to international organizations and regular transfers from international organizations to governments as a matter of policy）and private unremunerated transfers（such as remittances, donations, inheritances, subsidised remittances, pensions, etc.）. Non-reimbursable transfers from home to foreign countries are debited while non−reimbursable transfers from foreign to home countries are credited.

2.Capital and financial account（items）

The capital and financial account, which is the account that records the movement of ownership of assets between countries, consists of two main parts: the capital account and the financial account.

（1）The capital account, which reflects the transfer of assets between residents and non-residents. The transfer of assets from residents to non-residents increases residents' external claims and reduces residents' external liabilities. The opposite is true for the transfer of assets from non-residents to residents. Therefore, this account shows how the country's assets and liabilities have increased or decreased over a period of time.

Unlike the current account, which is recorded on a gross debit and gross credit basis, the capital account is debited and credited on a net basis （the difference between debits and credits）. Net decreases in claims or assets and net increases in debts or liabilities are recorded as credit items; net increases in claims or assets and net decreases in debts or liabilities are recorded as debit items.

（2）The financial account reflects the changes in investments and borrowing between residents and non-residents. Like the capital account, the financial account is recorded on a net basis. Net increases in investments and credit provided by residents to non-residents are debited; net increases in investments and credit provided by non-residents to residents are credited.

Financial projects can be classified according to the type or function of the investment:

① Financial accounts of a non-reserve nature, including direct investments, portfolio investments, financial derivatives and other investments.

② Reserve asset accounts, including monetary gold, special drawing rights, reserve positions with the International Monetary Fund, foreign exchange reserves and other reserve assets.

Reserve assets exist primarily to reconcile the imbalance in the overall balance caused by the current account balance and the capital and financial account balance. If the overall balance is in surplus, official reserves increase; if the overall balance is in deficit, official reserves decrease. The increase or decrease in reserve assets is the result of a change in the volume of the balance of payments.

3.Net errors and omissions

The net errors and omissions account is an artificially created offsetting account used to offset the net debit or credit balances that arise at the time of the balance sheet. In principle, a balance of payments statement uses double-entry accounting and the total debits and credits should be equal, with the difference being zero. In practice, however, it is inevitable that a country's balance of payments statement will have a net debit balance or a net credit balance and it is difficult to balance. This balance is the result of errors or omissions in statistical information. For this reason, a separate "errors and omissions" item needs to be artificially created in the balance sheet to bring the difference to zero. If there is a balance on the credit side of the current account, capital and financial accounts (including the reserve assets account), a figure equal to the balance is shown on the debit side under net errors and omissions; if there is a balance on the debit side of these accounts, a figure equal to the balance is shown on the credit side under net errors and omissions.

Task 3　　Balance of Payments Imbalances and Reconciliation

I. Balance of Payments Balances and Imbalances

1.Balance of payments balances

The balance of payments statement is always balanced to some extent, in terms of the principles of its preparation, and its balance is expressed in two ways:

(1) Because of the double-entry bookkeeping principle, the total debits and credits to the balance of payments are always equal.

(2) Because of the creation of balancing items, the combined difference between the current account and the capital account can always end up being balanced by increases or decreases in official reserves and by net errors and omissions items, so that the final book balance i.e., the overall balance is necessarily zero. This balance thus becomes an account balance rather than a balance in the true sense of the word.

2.Balance of payments imbalances

On the other hand, the balance of payments is often unbalanced, and the imbalance manifests itself in two ways:

(1) The various items in the balance of payments statement are generally unbalanced, always with certain differences. It is known as partial differences which are likely to give rise to an overall balance of payments balance.

(2) By the nature of the international economy, a country's balance of payments activity is caused by a wide range of external economic transactions making it impossible to achieve a complete balance of payments. Therefore, a country's true balance of payments activity is often either in surplus or in deficit, but the size of the difference varies.

II. Criteria for Judging Balance of Payments Imbalances

There are two types of balance of payments imbalances: surpluses and deficits in external trade. A surplus is usually characterised by more income than expenditure from external economic transactions, while a deficit is characterised by more expenditure than income. The total external economic transactions recorded by a country's balance of payments can be divided into autonomous and regulated transactions. The balance of payments resulting from autonomous transactions is an active balance, while the balance of payments resulting from reconciliation transactions is a passive balance.

1.Autonomous trading

Autonomous trading are transactions carried out by economic agents or resident individuals, such as financial institutions, importers and exporters, international investors, etc., for certain autonomous purposes, such as the pursuit of profit, risk reduction, asset preservation, tax evasion and avoidance, regulatory evasion or speculation. From the point of view of motivation, these transactions are completely unrelated to whether a country's balance of payments will be imbalanced as a result, so they are called autonomous transactions. Autonomous transactions reflect the individual will of economic agents or residents and do not represent the will of any one country or government, and are characterised by the ex ante, spontaneous and decentralised nature.

2.Regulated trading

Regulated trading also known as compensatory transactions, refer to various transactions carried out by the central bank or monetary authority to adjust the balance of payments, maintaining the balance of payments and maintaining the stability of the currency exchange rate, including international capital financing, capital absorption and introduction, international reserve changes, etc. Regulated transactions are transactions carried out by the government in order to make up or adjust the difference in autonomous transactions, reflecting the will of the government, and are characterised by their ex post facto, centralised and passive nature.

How do you determine whether the balance of payments is in balance? It depends primarily on whether a country's autonomous transactions are in balance. Active balance, achieved by autonomous transactions, is the goal of balance of payments. The balance of autonomous transactions is the criterion for judging whether a country's balance of payments is truly balanced or not.

III. Causes of the Balance of Payments Imbalance

Balance of payments equilibrium is temporary, while the balance of payments imbalance is long-term. There are many reasons for the imbalance of payments, and the main reasons can be analysed in the following four aspects.

1.Economic cycles

A balance of payments imbalance caused by fluctuations in a country's economic cycle is known as a cyclical imbalance. In a market economy, a country's economy goes through four stages - boom, bust, recession and recovery - as an economic cycle. Different stages of the economic cycle have different effects on the balance of payments. In a boom period, due to strong domestic demand, imports increase accordingly and exports decrease instead, and the balance of payments may run a deficit. While in a recession, due to insufficient demand, imports fall and exports rise instead will result in a surplus.

2.National income

A balance of payments imbalance arising from changes in national income is known as an income imbalance. As a country's economic growth rate varies, its national income increases or decreases accordingly. The increase in purchasing power caused by an increase in national income will lead to an increase in imports and, as a result, an increase in external expenditure on services, donations, tourism and investment, resulting in a balance of payments deficit. Conversely, a decrease in national income will lead to a balance of payments surplus.

3.Monetary value

Monetary imbalances are balance of payments imbalances caused by relative changes in the money supply. Excessive growth in a country's money supply can lead to higher inflation in that country. With lagging exchange rate movements, higher domestic currency costs, relatively higher prices for exports and lower prices for imports may result in a balance of payments deficit. Monetary imbalances can be short or medium or long-term in nature.

4.Economic structure

Structural imbalances are balance of payments imbalances that occur when a country's industrial structure does not adapt to changes in world markets. Structural imbalances have two meanings:

(1) A balance of payments imbalance caused by lagging and difficult changes in a country's national economy and industrial structure. When the international market changes, new styles and high-quality products are constantly eliminating old styles and low-quality products. When new alternatives are emerging, if the country's production structure does not adjust to the situation in time, its original trade balance will be disrupted and a trade deficit will emerge. Conversely, if the adjustment is timely, a trade surplus may emerge.

(2) Balance of payments imbalances caused by a country's homogeneous industrial structure and the high price elasticity of its products. A typical example is the huge balance of payments surpluses and deficits of the Middle East oil-exporting countries that have resulted from the sharp rise and fall in oil prices since 1970s. Structural imbalances are long-term in nature and can be quite difficult to reverse.

In addition to the above factors causing balance of payments imbalances, changes in international political relations, natural conditions, psychological expectations and other factors, as well as government policies, can affect the stability of a country's balance of payments and thus lead to imbalances.

(Case Analysis 1-1)

Pegged exchange rate regimes, balance of payments imbalances and the Mexican financial crisis

The Mexican financial crisis erupted in December 1994 and soon spread to Brazil, Argentina and Chile, creating a Latin American economic crisis that shocked the world. The peso's exchange rate system pegged to the US dollar was the root cause of the crisis and the imbalance in the balance of payments was the trigger for this crisis.

Before 1982, Mexico had a predominantly state-owned economy which means all prices, including commodity prices, interest rates and exchange rates, were strictly regulated by the government. Like many Latin American countries, Mexico opted for an import-substitution industrialisation development strategy, hoping that this would lead to a rapid modernisation of its economy and bridge the gap with the major developed countries. Over time, Mexico encountered a problem that is difficult to avoid in all countries pursuing an import-substitution development strategy — a balance of payments imbalance. Initially, it seemed that this problem could be solved by borrowing on the international financial markets, but when the economy slowed down, the government was unable to pay its international debts as they fell due; when the domestic political situation became unstable, foreign creditors stopped providing new loans and a debt crisis erupted.

In August 1982, the debt crisis in the third world countries began with the announcement that the Mexican government was unable to pay its foreign debts as they fell due. The debt crisis announced the failure of government-led economic growth and import-substitution development strategies. After the crisis, the Mexican government resolved to push ahead with its economic reform programme. The main measures included the promotion of privatisation, the introduction of market mechanisms and the creation of market competition; the opening up of the domestic market by reducing tariffs, eliminating import licenses and subsidies; accelerating the convertibility of the peso and joining the Common Market (NAFTA) comprised by the United States, Canada and Mexico.

At the same time that economic reforms were being fast-tracked, the Mexican government remained committed to the peso's exchange rate peg to the US dollar. As the rate of inflation in Mexico at the time was much higher than that in the US, the pegged exchange rate system caused an overvaluation of the peso, which had the effect of encouraging imports and discouraging exports, creating a large trade deficit and a huge current account deficit. In order to maintain the balance of payments, the Mexican government accelerated the opening of capital markets to attract foreign capital inflows. However, a large amount of capital did not enter the real economy but the capital market. When the political and economic situation at home and abroad changed, the international capital flow reversed, which eventually led to the Mexican financial crisis.

Source: Researcher, Research Bureau, The People's Bank of China. The pegged exchange rate system, balance of payments imbalance and the Mexican financial crisis [N/OL]. First Financial Daily, 2015-01-26 [2021-06-08]. https://www.yicai.com/news/4067360.html.

Discussion: The internal logic between the balance of payments imbalance and the Mexican crisis.

IV. Impact of Balance of Payments Imbalances on the Economy

A large and persistent surplus or deficit in a country's balance of payments can be detrimental to the economy. A persistent deficit can lead to a steady loss of official reserves, which puts domestic economic activity under austerity pressure and inhibits economic growth. Conversely, a persistent large surplus can lead to an increase in the exchange rate of the national currency, which weakens export competitiveness, or to an excessive accumulation of official reserves, which means giving up access to real resources and triggering inflation. It may sometimes generate and deepen contradictions and conflicts with other countries, resulting in trade disputes.

1. The negative impact of a persistent balance of payments deficit

Firstly, in the external economy, the persistent balance of payments deficit creates pressure for the currency to depreciate, which affects the stability of the exchange rate of the currency, reduces the credibility of the currency and causes a deterioration in the terms of trade. To maintain the stability of the exchange rate of the local currency, the government must use its foreign exchange reserves to intervene in the foreign exchange market when the country has a large balance of payments deficit, thus causing a reduction in the country's official reserves.

Secondly, accompanied by a large balance of payments deficit, the export multiplier effect shrinks, bringing about a domestic economic slump and high unemployment. Under market conditions, the reduction in reserves may also lead to a lower domestic money supply and higher interest rate levels, exacerbating deflation and affecting the growth rate of the national economy.

Finally, a persistent balance of payments deficit can reduce a country's external creditworthiness, causing large capital outflows and exacerbating domestic economic deterioration.

2. The negative impact of a persistent balance of payments surplus

Excessive balance of payments surpluses can also hurt a country's external economic relations and domestic economy.

Firstly, in terms of external economic relations, a large balance of payments surplus will cause a rapid increase in a country's reserve assets, bringing pressure on the local currency to appreciate externally, which in turn will cause the relative price of domestic exports to rise and that of imports to fall, thus discouraging exports and favouring imports and turning the balance of payments into a deficit.

Secondly, a large balance of payments surplus can also lead to dissatisfaction among trading partners, causing trade frictions and international disputes as well as affecting the normal development of foreign economic and political relations.

Finally, the increase in the balance of payments surplus and reserve assets is accompanied by an increase in the domestic money supply and inflationary pressures. As a result, internal imbalances may arise alongside external imbalances in a country's economy, making it more difficult to regulate its macroeconomy.

V. Reconciliation of Balance of Payments Imbalances

If a country has a temporary imbalance in its balance of payments i.e., an imbalance that is short‑term and caused by uncertain or fortuitous factors, then the imbalance is generally mild, short-lived and reversible. Therefore, it is unnecessary to apply policy adjustment, just waiting for self-correction. However, if a country's balance of payments imbalance is persistent due to some deep-rooted causes, and is characterised by a large surplus or deficit, then it is a fundamental imbalance that is not reversible, so it must be corrected by appropriate policy responses.

(i) Automatic balance of payments adjustment

Short−term, sudden imbalances in the balance of payments are spontaneously adjusted by the "invisible hand" within the market mechanism to bring them back into balance. The more market−oriented a country's economy is, the more pronounced the spontaneous adjustment of the balance of payments will be. Under different monetary regimes, the spontaneous balance of payments adjustment takes different forms.

Under the international gold standard, a deficit in a country's international trade balance forces the exchange rate of the country's currency to fall to the point of gold export, resulting in an outflow of gold. The outflow of gold leads to lower bank reserves and a reduction in currency issuance, causing prices to fall, which in turn increases the competitiveness of the country's goods internationally, and leads to an increase in exports. At the same time, the relative rise in the price level abroad also discourages imports. Eventually, external revenue increases and external expenditure decreases, gradually eliminating the deficit and restoring balance of payments. The price−cash flow mechanism is illustrated in Figure 1−1.

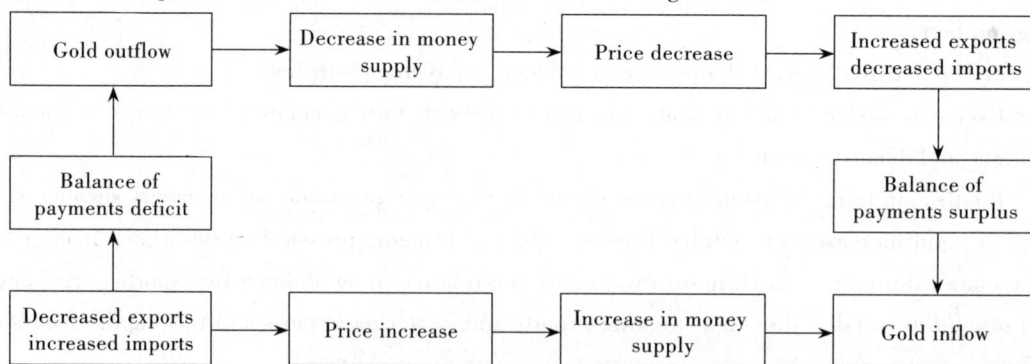

Figure 1−1 Price−cash flow mechanism

Under paper money circulation, although the role of gold flows in the balance of payments no longer exists, the automatic balance of payments adjustment mechanism can still work through prices, exchange rates, interest rates, income and other economic variables to bring the balance of payments into balance. For example, a deficit in the balance of payments can

lead to an oversupply of foreign exchange, a fall in the national exchange rate, an increase in
the price of imports and a relative fall in the price of exports, leading to an increase in exports
and a reduction in imports, and an improvement in the balance of payments. The automatic
balance of payments adjustment mechanism under a floating exchange rate is illustrated in
Figure 1-2.

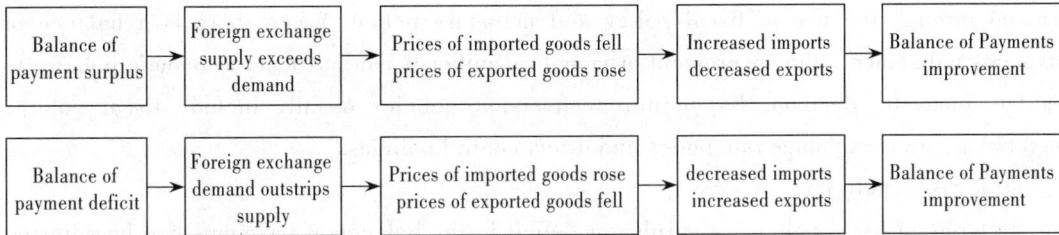

| Balance of payment surplus | → | Foreign exchange supply exceeds demand | → | Prices of imported goods fell prices of exported goods rose | → | Increased imports decreased exports | → | Balance of Payments improvement |

| Balance of payment deficit | → | Foreign exchange demand outstrips supply | → | Prices of imported goods rose prices of exported goods fell | → | decreased imports increased exports | → | Balance of Payments improvement |

Figure 1-2 Automatic balance of payments adjustment mechanism under a
floating exchange rate

(ii) Balance of payments policy reconciliation

Balance of payments policy adjustment is the process by which a government, in
particular the monetary authority, takes certain policy measures to arrest or even reverse the
original trend in the balance of payments and thereby restore balance.

Under the modern system of dishonoured paper money standard, the financial system has
become increasingly complex while the government has intervened more and more in the foreign
exchange market, resulting in a significant weakening of the automatic balance of payments
adjustment effect. Therefore, when there is an imbalance in the balance of payments, the
authority of a country cannot rely solely on the automatic adjustment mechanism of the
economic system but need to adopt appropriate policies to regulate it.

1. Foreign exchange buffer policy

Foreign exchange buffer policy refers to the government's intervention in the foreign
exchange market to regulate the balance of payments imbalances through changes in foreign
exchange reserves or short-term external borrowing. The central bank regulates the balance of
payments by buying and selling foreign exchange in the foreign exchange market, changing the
supply and demand of foreign exchange, or by financing from foreign governments,
international financial institutions or international financial markets to make up for the balance
of payments deficit. The main role is to offset the negative impact of the imbalance in the
balance of payments but it is only used to address temporary imbalances in the balance of
payments.

A foreign exchange buffer policy can keep the negative impact of a balance of payments
imbalance to international reserves but not to the domestic economy and finance. However, the
implementation of a foreign exchange buffer policy can only address the short-term balance of
payments deficits, but not those with a large, long-term balance of payments deficits. Because
a country's official reserves are limited, the central bank's long-term buying and selling of

large amounts of foreign exchange in the foreign exchange market will lead to an excess or depletion of foreign exchange reserves, which in turn lead to new conflicts and problems.

2. Expenditure conversion policy

Expenditure conversion policies, also known as demand management policies, are policies that regulate the balance of payments imbalances by changing aggregate domestic demand through the use of fiscal policy and monetary policy. When there is a balance of payments imbalance, the government or monetary authority can use macroeconomic policies to regulate domestic demand. Expenditure conversion policies usually include fiscal policy, monetary policy, exchange rate policy and direct control policies.

(1) Fiscal policy.

In terms of fiscal policy, a surplus or deficit in the balance of payments can be adjusted by increasing or decreasing fiscal expenditure and adjusting tax rates to influence total social demand. When a country has a balance of payments deficit, the government can implement a tight fiscal policy, i.e., cutting fiscal expenditure or raising tax rates to keep the domestic economy in a state of contraction, so as to reduce total domestic demand and lower prices, thereby stimulating exports, discouraging imports, and bringing the balance of payments back into balance; Conversely, when a country has a balance of payments surplus, it can adopt an expansionary fiscal policy, expanding government expenditure and lowering tax rates to expand domestic aggregate demand and raise prices, thereby increasing imports and reducing exports and restoring the balance of payments.

(2) Monetary policy.

Monetary policy refers to the regulation of the balance of payments through the adjustment of interest rates. When the balance of payments is in deficit, the government can adopt a tight monetary policy, i.e., the central bank can reduce the domestic money supply by increasing the rediscount rate, raising the legal reserve ratio or selling government bonds in the open market, raising interest rates and suppressing domestic aggregate demand, thereby increasing exports and reducing imports, in order to eliminate the deficit and restore the balance of payments.

(3) Exchange rate policy.

Exchange rate policy refers to the monetary authority regulating the balance of payments by changing the level of the exchange rate. There are two main types of policies: devaluation of the local currency and appreciation of the local currency. For example, if the balance of payments is in deficit, a policy of devaluation of the local currency is used to increase exports and reduce imports, thus improving the balance of payments. Conversely, if the balance of payments is in surplus, a policy of appreciation of the local currency is used. The advantage of the exchange rate policy is that it can avoid deflation. The disadvantage is that frequent fluctuations in the exchange rate can increase economic instability and easily cause inflation. Therefore, exchange rate policy is implemented in conjunction with a tight fiscal or monetary policy and is mainly used to regulate monetary imbalances in the balance of payments.

(4) Direct control policy.

Direct control is the practice of government regulation of imports, exports and foreign exchange purchases and sales through compulsory administrative means such as rules and regulations. The starting point of direct control is to restrict transactions involving external payments, such as imports and purchases of foreign exchange, and to encourage transactions involving external income, such as exports and sales of foreign exchange, with the aim of improving the balance of payments. Direct controls on imports and exports are usually referred to as trade controls, while direct controls on the purchase, sale, receipt and deposit of foreign exchange are referred to as foreign exchange controls. The advantages of direct controls are that they are more flexible and can be used to restructure products, increase tariffs or reduce quotas, and encourage exports to be subsidized or preferential, with quick results. The disadvantage is that they are likely to cause "trade wars" between countries. Direct controls are mainly used to regulate the short-term, structural balance of payments imbalances.

3. International economic cooperation policy

In the context of global economic integration, in addressing the balance of payments imbalance, countries should focus on strengthening international economic and financial cooperation.

(1) Coordinating economic policies. To avoid trade frictions, trading partner countries should enhance consultation and dialogue to coordinate their economic policies, which will help to regulate their balance of payments imbalances.

(2) Strengthening credit cooperation between countries. When a country is vulnerable to financial crises due to a balance of payments imbalance, especially a serious deficit, emergency credit between countries is needed to regulate the balance of payments imbalance.

(3) To give full play to the role of international financial institutions such as the IMF in balancing a country's balance of payments.

Task 4 Analysis of the Balance of Payments Statement

The balance of payments statement gives some simple figures, but each specific figure represents a specific external economic transaction. Thus, a historical and scientific approach must be taken in analysing the balance of payments statement.

Through scientific analysis of the balance of payments statement, it is possible to gain a comprehensive and timely understanding of the country's economic interactions and to find out the reasons for the formation of the balance of payments surpluses and deficits so that corresponding adjustment measures can be taken. It also enable the monetary and financial authorities to grasp the sources and use of the country's foreign exchange funds promptly as well as the increase or decrease in international reserves. Moreover, the country's economic status and strength should be fully grasped to formulate corresponding policies of trade, financial and foreign exchange etc.

I. Methods of analysis of the balance of payments statement

1.Static analysis

Static analysis is a detailed item-by-item analysis of a country's balance of payments statement for a given period. Generally, static analysis involves calculating and analysing the individual items of the balance of payments statement and their differences, and analysing the reasons for the formation of the differences in each item and their impact on the total balance of payments.

2.Dynamic analysis

Dynamic analysis, also known as vertical analysis, is the analysis of a country's balance of payments statement over successive periods. Due to the continuity of a country's external economic policy and the time-sensitive nature of economic restructuring, the balance of payments of one period is generally closely linked to the balance of payments of the previous and next periods. Therefore, the analysis of the balance of payments statement should also link the balance of payments of different periods in order to capture trends over time.

3.Cross-sectional comparative analysis

Cross-sectional comparative analysis is the analysis and comparison of the balance of payments statements of different countries over the same period to understand a country's economic status and strength, to understand the external economic development of each country, and to better grasp the development trend of the world economy.

The analysis of a country's balance of payments statement must include a comprehensive examination and analysis of the macroeconomic and political background at home and abroad, and an understanding of the possible impact of various factors on the balance of payments. Only in this way can the conclusions drawn from the analysis be more comprehensive, objective and scientific.

II. Overall analysis of China's balance of payments statement

1.The current state of preparation of China's balance of payments statement

State Administration of Foreign Exchange (SAFE) prepares and publishes quarterly balance of payments. The balance of payments is classified under the criteria set out in the Balance of Payments and International Investment Position Manual (Sixth Edition) from 2015. In principle, the balance of payments covers all transactions between Chinese residents and non-Chinese residents; transactions are valued at market prices where they are available, mostly at nominal value for debt instruments and FOB price for exports of goods; import data from customs are CIF price data, with an adjustment factor of 5% to obtain FOB price data. Exports and imports are recorded when the goods pass through the customs border and other balance of payments transactions are recorded on an accrual basis.

2.Analysis of China's balance of payments for the year 2018

In 2018, China's balance of payments continued to be in basic balance. The current account remained in a reasonable surplus range, with a surplus of US$49.1 billion for the year, or 0.4% of GDP. Of this, the combined surplus of trade in goods and services was US $102.9 billion, or 0.8% of GDP, making the trade balance more balanced.

Animation Micro-lesson 1-2

China's Balance of Payments

The financial account of a non-reserve nature maintained a surplus of US$130.6 billion for the year. Of these, the surplus on direct investment was US$107 billion, still a relatively stable source of surplus; the surplus on portfolio investment was US$106.7 billion, a record high, mainly reflecting the effect of further liberalisation of the capital market; the deficit on other investment was US$77 billion, remaining stable in a two-way fluctuation.

Overall, capital inflows for medium and long-term investment and asset allocation still remain dominant and China's outward investment is rational. In 2018, the foreign exchange reserve assets formed by transactions grew slightly and remained stable, indicating that China's balance of payments continued to show an autonomous balance pattern.

At the end of 2018, China's external financial assets and liabilities increased by 2.5% and 2.9% respectively compared to the end of 2017, while net external assets were US$2.13 trillion with an increase of 1.4%. China's Balance of Payments Statement in 2018 (overview table) can be seen in Table 1-2.

Table 1-2   2018 China's Balance of Payments Statement (Overview Table)

Projects	Row	RMB billion	US$ billion	Billion SDR
1. Current account	1	352.7	49.1	36.2
Credit	2	19 305.3	2 913.6	2 060.1
Borrower	3	−18 952.6	−2 864.5	−2 023.9
1.A Goods and services	4	705.4	102.9	74.1
Credit	5	17569.4	2651.0	1874.7
Borrower	6	−16 864.0	−2 548.1	−1 800.6
1.A.a Goods	7	2636.6	395.2	280.4
Credit	8	16 023.7	2 417.4	1 709.6
Borrower	9	−13 387.1	−2 022.3	−1 429.2
1.A.b Services	10	−1931.2	−292.2	−206.4
Credit	11	1545.7	233.6	165.0
Borrower	12	−3 476.9	−525.8	−371.4

Projects	Row	RMB billion	US$ billion	Billion SDR
1.B Initial income	13	−339.4	−51.4	−36.4
Credit	14	1 552.6	234.8	165.9
Borrower	15	−1 892.0	−286.2	−202.2
1.C Secondary income	16	−13.3	−2.4	−1.6
Credit	17	183.3	27.8	19.6
Borrower	18	−196.6	−30.2	−21.2
2. Capital and financial accounts	19	723.1	111.1	77.7
2.1 Capital accounts	20	−3.8	−0.6	−0.4
Credit	21	2.0	0.3	0.2
Borrower	22	−5.8	−0.9	−0.6
2.2 Financial accounts	23	726.9	111.7	78.1
Assets	24	−2 443.6	−372.1	−262.1
Liabilities	25	3 170.5	483.8	340.2
2.2.1 Financial accounts of a non-reserve nature	26	830.6	130.6	90.4
2.2.1.1 Direct investment	27	696.4	107.0	75.0
Assets	28	−639.3	−96.5	−68.2
Liabilities	29	1 335.7	203.5	143.2
2.2.1.2 Portfolio investment	30	695.4	106.7	75.1
Assets	31	−348.1	−53.5	−37.4
Liabilities	32	1 043.5	160.2	112.5
2.2.1.3 Financial derivatives	33	−41.5	−6.2	−4.4
Assets	34	−32.6	−4.8	−3.4
Liabilities	35	−8.9	−1.3	−0.9
2.2.1.4 Other investments	36	−519.8	−77.0	−55.2
Assets	37	−1 319.9	−198.4	−140.7
Liabilities	38	800.2	121.4	85.4
2.2.2 Reserve assets	39	−103.7	−18.9	−12.3
3.Net errors and omissions	40	−1 075.8	−160.2	−113.8

Note: Data from the website of the State Administration of Foreign Exchange.

Mini Case

A report released by the State Administration of Foreign Exchange (SAFE) shows that China's balance of payments was generally in balance in 2019, showing a strong degree of robustness and adaptability. Please download the Balance of Payments Statement of China for 2019 and analyse it. Thinking how our economy is robust and adaptable and what are the reasons for our country's great economic success.

Mind Map

```
                              ┌─ Concept of balance of payments
              ┌ Balance of ───┤
              │ Payments Overview└ Understanding the meaning of balance of payments
              │
              │                  ┌ Concept of Balance of Payments statement
              │ Balance of Payments┤ Principles of Balance of Payments statement Preparation
              │ statement        └ Composition of the balance of payments statement
Balance of ──┤
Payments      │                  ┌ Balance of Payments Balances and Imbalances
              │                  ├ Criteria for Judging Balance of Payments Imbalances
              │ Balance of Payments├ Causes of the Balance of Payments Imbalance
              │ Imbalances and   ├ Impact of Balance of Payments Imbalances on the Economy
              │ Reconciliation   └ Reconciliation of Balance of Payments Imbalances
              │
              │ Analysis of the  ┌ Methods of analysis of the balance of payments statement
              └ Balance of Payments┤
                statement        └ Overall analysis of China's balance of payments statement
```

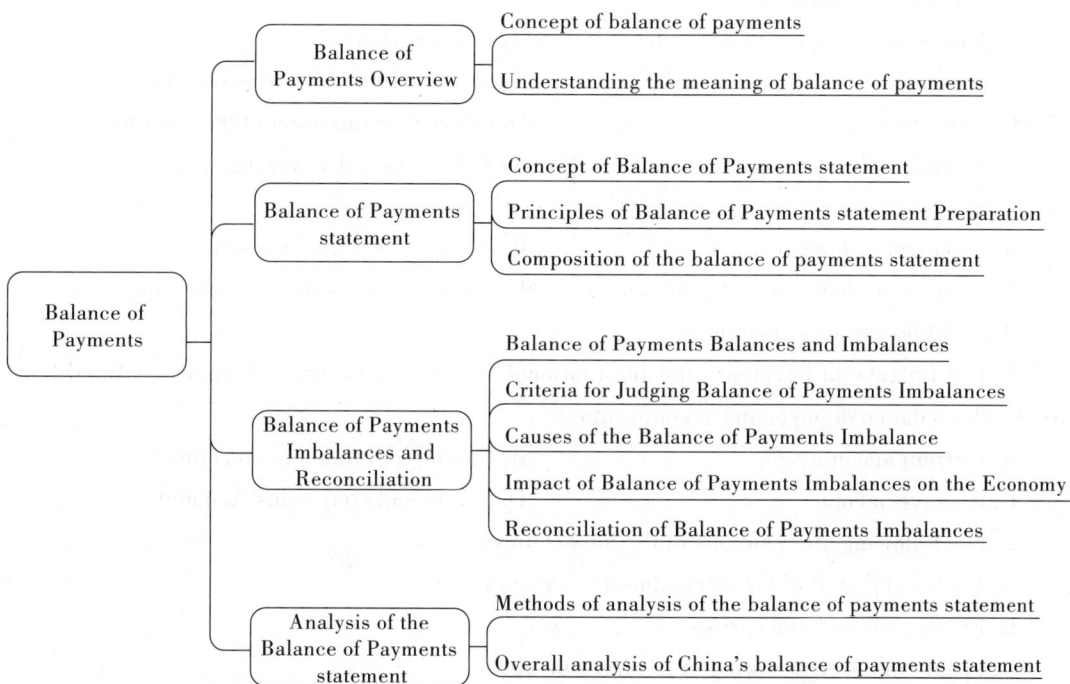

Project Training

I. Single-choice questions

1. The following (　　) are not classifiable as residents of the State.

A. A business that has just been registered

B. Natural persons who have resided in the country for two years

C. International Monetary Fund representatives in the country

D. Local employees employed by foreign consulates in their home countries

2. If the reserve assets item in the balance of payments statement is US$100 billion, this means that the country (　　) .

A. increased reserves by US$ 100 billion

B. decreased reserves by US$100 billion

C. artificial book balance, not indicative

D. impossible to judge

3. The following (　　) provide a better measure of the pressure on international reserves from the balance of payments.

A. balance of trade balance

B. balance of current account

C. capital and financial account balances

D. consolidated account balances

4. A persistent surplus in a country may lead to or exacerbate (　　) .

A. inflation   B. domestic financial constraints

C. economic crisis   D. external devaluation of the currency

5. Balance of payments statements are recorded statistically according to the (　　) principle.

A.single-entry bookkeeping   B. double-entry bookkeeping

C. increase or decrease in bookkeeping   D. receipt and payment bookkeeping

II. Multiple choice questions

1. The Balance of Payments and International Investment Position Manual (sixth edition) divides the balance of payments account into (　　) .

A. Current account   B. Capital and financial account

C. Reserve account   D. Errors and Omissions Account

2. The following are residents of the host country (　　) .

A. Diplomatic staff of foreign embassies and consulates

B. Foreign-owned enterprises

C. Local employees working in foreign consulates

D. National Disabled Persons' Federation

3. The current account of the Balance of Payments includes (　　) .

A. Goods and services   B. Direct investment

C. Primary income   D. Secondary income

4. In the balance of payments statement, (　　) is obtained directly from the statistics.

A. Current account   B. Capital and financial account

C. Net errors and omissions account   D. Reserves and related items

5. The effects of the emergence of a balance of payments surplus are (　　) .

A. appreciation of the exchange rate of the local currency

B. growth in the supply of the local currency

C. depreciation of the exchange rate of the local currency

D. deflation

III. Judgment questions

1. The balance of payments is a flow, ex-post concept...   (   )

2. The consolidated account balance provides a more comprehensive picture of the autonomous balance of payments and is of great significance for the overall measurement and analysis of the balance of payments situation.   (   )

3. Since a country's balance of payments cannot be exactly equal to its balance of payments, the final balance of payments is never zero.   (   )

4. Theoretically, a balance of payments imbalance is an imbalance in autonomous transactions, but it is statistically difficult to achieve.   (   )

5. The capital and financial account can finance the current account without restriction.

(   )

IV. Practical training

Go to the website of the State Administration of Foreign Exchange to access our balance of payments statement data for the period 2015-2020 and compare and analyse the changes and reasons for them.

The teacher can give guided explanations, divide the class into groups as appropriate, and let students look up the information, discuss and analyse it on their own, and finally produce a brief analysis report and a PPT presentation, which the teacher will review.

Project Two
International Reserve

Learning Objectives

Knowledge Objectives:

Understand the definition and features of the international reserve, master composition and source of the international reserve.

Competence Objectives:

Understand the moderation principles and management methods of international reserve management, grasp the current situation of international reserve diversification.

Operational Objectives:

In light of the country's current international reserve situation, analyze the rationality of the level and composition of China's foreign exchange reserves.

Course Introduction

RMB assets in global foreign exchange reserves

Foreign exchange reserves are foreign assets held in reserve by individual countries that can be converted into foreign currency, which can be said to be foreign currency. However, not all foreign currencies can be used as foreign exchange reserves. The currencies that can be used as foreign exchange reserves must have at least a certain degree of international recognition. And the higher the percentage of assets or currencies held as foreign exchange reserves, the higher the international recognition of that currency. What percentage of the global foreign exchange reserves are RMB assets?

With $3.1 trillion in foreign exchange reserves, China has the largest amount of foreign exchange reserves in the world, but the proportion of our

RMB in global foreign exchange reserves is not high. According to IMF data, At the end of 2019, the global foreign exchange reserves are 11.08 trillion US dollars. Among these foreign exchange reserves, RMB assets are only US \$217.7 billion, accounting for about 1.97%, ranking behind US dollars, Euros, Japanese yen and Sterling. At present, the proportion of the RMB as a global foreign exchange reserve asset is not high, but it has been growing, and the growth rate is not slow. Compared to 2018, 2019 grew by roughly \$14.6 billion, the growth rate reached 7.2%, and at this rate of growth could exceed \$500 billion by 2031.

Source: Anonymous. Why are more than 60% of global foreign exchange reserves US dollar assets? [EB / OL]. [2021-06-26]. https: //view. inews. qq. com / w2 / 20200403A0O7VB00.

Discussion: What are foreign exchange reserves? What are international reserves? What are the forms of a country's international reserves? And what are their specific contents? This project will introduce the relevant contents.

The international reserve is the final result of a country's foreign economic exchanges. It is also an important symbol of a country's international financial strength and its status in international economic competition. The moderate scale, reasonable structure and scientific management of a country's international reserves are the prerequisites for it to make up for its balance of payments deficit, maintain its external payment capacity and intervene foreign exchange market, and maintain exchange rate stability, as well as the credit guarantee for its external debt and foreign debt repayment.

Task1	**Overview of International Reserve**

I. Concept and Characteristics of International Reserve

Animation Micro-lesson 2-1

The international reserve is an internationally accepted liquid asset held by a country's monetary authority to cover the balance of payments gap and stabilize the exchange rate.

International Reserve

The assets that can be used as international reserves (short for reserve assets) generally have the following typical characteristics:

1. Official holdings

International reserve assets must be assets held by the monetary authorities of a country (usually the central bank or the Ministry of Finance). Gold and foreign exchange assets held by unofficial financial institutions, enterprises and individuals cannot be counted as international reserves. Therefore, international reserves are also called official reserves.

2. Universal acceptance

As assets of international reserves, they must be generally recognized and accepted in the foreign exchange market and intergovernmental settlement of balance of payments. This widely accepted characteristic of reserve assets is universal acceptance. Financial assets that cannot be transferred and exchanged internationally cannot be used as reserve assets.

3. Sufficient liquidity

International reserves should have sufficient ability to become cash and be ready to be used when a country runs a balance of payments deficit or intervenes in the foreign exchange market. Therefore, reserve assets are mainly in the form of demand deposits in foreign exchange in banks and easily liquidated securities（especially foreign government bonds）.

4. Free convertibility

International reserve assets must be freely convertible with other assets that can be paid. If they lack convertibility, their ability to pay will be limited, so they cannot play their role in making up for the balance of payments deficit and intervening in the foreign exchange market.

5.Non-local currency

Foreign exchange reserves cannot be assets that are denominated in local currency, because the currencies of some countries are widely accepted internationally, such as the US dollar and Euro. Sometimes, these countries directly use their own currencies for external payments. If they count their own currencies as foreign exchange reserves, it is impossible to make quantitative statistics on international reserves.

II. International reserve and international solvency

From the perspective of ultimate ownership, the international reserves actually held by a country can be divided into two sections: self-owned reserves and borrowed reserves. Self-owned reserves include monetary gold, foreign exchange reserves, reserve positions in the IMF and special drawing rights; The borrowed reserve consists of standby credit, reciprocal credit agreement, general loan arrangement and foreign short-term convertible monetary assets of a country's commercial banks.

Another concept closely related to international reserves is international solvency. International solvency refers to the ability of a country to finance to make up for the balance of payments deficit. It includes not only various international reserves held by monetary authorities but also the country's ability to borrow funds from foreign governments or central banks, international financial organizations and commercial banks. International solvency is the sum of the actual and possible external solvency of a country. Therefore, generally speaking, international reserves we say are the one in a narrow sense, that is, self-owned reserves. According to the definition of the IMF, international reserves in a broad sense refers to international solvency, that is, the sum of a country's self-owned reserves and borrowed reserves.

The relationship between international solvency and international reserves is shown in

Figure 2-1.

```
                        ┌─────────────────┐
                        │  International  │
                        │    solvency     │
                        └─────────────────┘
                   ┌──────────────┴──────────────┐
          ┌─────────────┐              ┌─────────────┐
          │  Self-owned │              │  Borrowed   │
          │   reserves  │              │  reserves   │
          └─────────────┘              └─────────────┘
      ┌──────────────┐                        ┌──────────────┐
      │Gold reserves │                        │Standby credit│
      └──────────────┘                        └──────────────┘
      ┌──────────────┐                        ┌──────────────┐
      │   Foreign    │                        │  Reciprocal  │
      │   exchange   │                        │    credit    │
      │   reserves   │                        │   agreement  │
      └──────────────┘                        └──────────────┘
      ┌──────────────┐                        ┌──────────────┐
      │   Reserve    │                        │ General loan │
      │position in IMF│                       │ arrangement  │
      └──────────────┘                        └──────────────┘
      ┌──────────────┐                        ┌──────────────────┐
      │     SDR      │                        │ Commercial banks'│
      └──────────────┘                        │ short-term foreign│
                                              │ exchange courses │
                                              └──────────────────┘
```

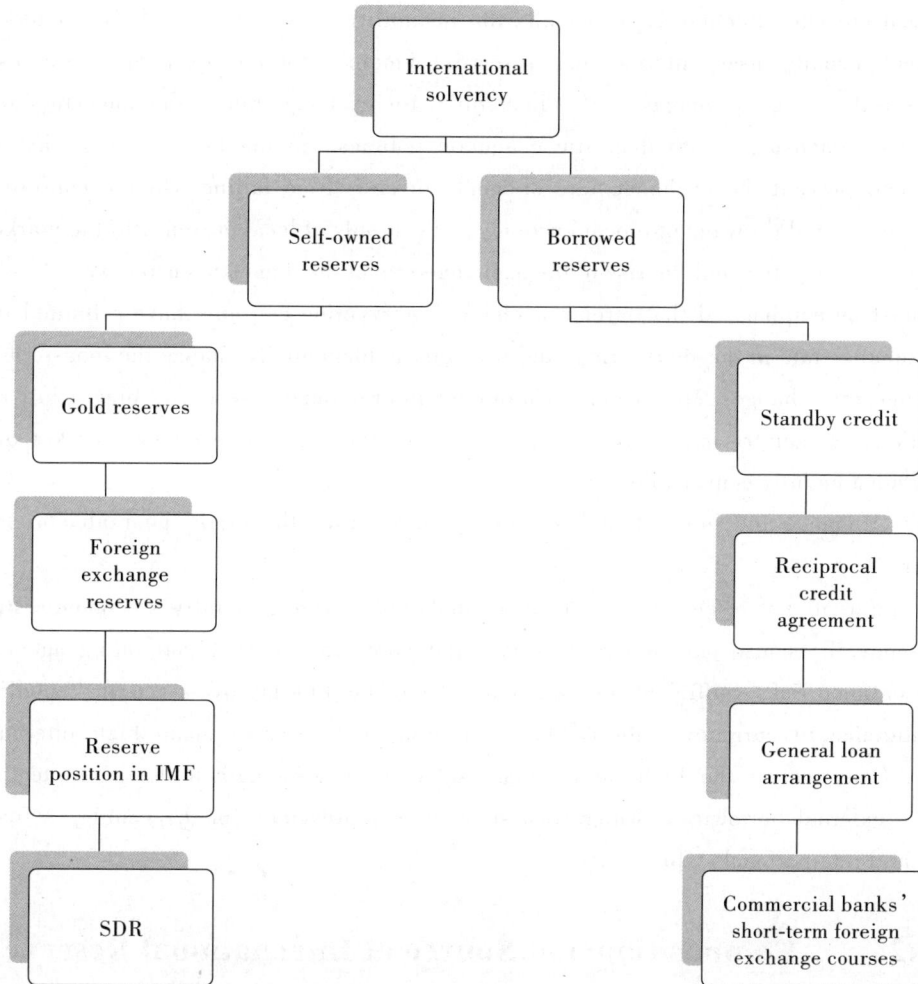

Figure 2-1 Relationship between international solvency and international reserve

III. The role of the international reserve

(i) Adjusting the balance of payments imbalances

When a country has a temporary balance of payments deficit due to various reasons, it can make up for the balance by using international reserves to prevent the adverse effects such as economic recession and rising unemployment rate caused by the adoption of fiscal or monetary policies affecting the macro economy. Even if a country has a structural imbalance in its balance of payments and has to take adjustment measures, the use of international reserves can form a certain buffer for the implementation of policy adjustment, so as to avoid the fluctuation of the domestic economy caused by policy adjustment.

(ii) Intervene in the foreign exchange market and stabilize the exchange rate of domestic currency

The amount of a country's international reserves reflects the strength of the government's ability to intervene in the foreign exchange market to a certain extent. When the exchange rate of the local currency fluctuates, especially the instability caused by speculative factors, the government usually uses international reserves (mainly foreign exchange reserves) to intervene in the foreign exchange market to stabilize the exchange rate of the domestic currency at a level commensurate with domestic economic policies. Buying local currency by selling reserves can prevent the exchange rate of local currency from falling. On the contrary, by buying reserves and throwing out local currency, the supply of local currency in the market can be increased, so as to avoid the rise of the exchange rate of the domestic currency.

It must be emphasized that foreign exchange intervention can only have a limited impact on the exchange rate in the short term, and it cannot fundamentally change the long-term trend of exchange rate changes. Moreover, in order for international reserves to play a full role of intervention, a country must have a relatively developed foreign exchange market and its currency must be fully convertible.

(iii) Enhance the international solvency and improve the credit guarantee of foreign borrowings

The international reserve is one of the symbols to measure a country's economic strength and solvency. It is also one of the important indicators for international rating agencies to evaluate national risks. Sufficient international reserves help to improve a country's confidence and confidence in currency stability. Large international reserves mean high international solvency. Conversely, the high international solvency will strengthen the guarantee of the country's external borrowing, which also shows the improvement of the country's financial strength and international status.

Task2　　Composition and Source of International Reserve

I. Evolution of the composition of international reserves

The composition of international reserves refers to the types of assets that act as international reserve assets. In different historical periods, the types of assets serving as international reserve assets are different.

Animation micro-lesson 2-2

Composition of China's
International Reserves

The composition of international reserve assets changes with the development of history. Under the international gold standard system, gold is a natural international currency, and all countries in the world accept its status as a means of payment and a representation of wealth. During the Bretton Woods System, international reserves were mainly composed of gold and US dollars. After the collapse of the Bretton Woods System, reserve currencies began to diversify. Today, there are mainly four forms: gold reserves, foreign exchange reserves, reserve positions in the IMF and special drawing rights (SDRs) in the IMF. As of January 31, 2019, the data of China's official reserve assets and other foreign currency assets are shown in Table 2-1.

Table 2-1　China's official reserve assets and other foreign currency assets

(approximate market value) in January 2019

Item	100 million USD	100 million SDR
A. Official reserve assets	31 863.52	22 748.33
(1) Foreign exchange reserves (in convertible foreign currencies)	30 879.24	22 045.61
(a) Securities	30 737.14	21 944.16
(b) Total currency and deposits with:	142.10	101.45
(i) Other national central banks, BISand IMF	10.68	7.63
(ii) Banks headquartered in the reporting country	45.91	32.77
Of which: located abroad	45.91	32.77
(iii) Banks headquartered outside the reporting country	85.51	61.05
(2) IMF reserve position	84.85	60.58
(3) SDRs	107.86	77.01
(4) Gold (including gold deposits and, if appropriate, gold swapped)	793.19	566.29
volume in millions of fine troy ounces	59.94	59.94
(5) Other reserve assets (specify)	−1.63	−1.16
Financial derivatives	−1.63	−1.16
B. Other foreign currency assets (specify)	1 839.35	1 313.17

Note: since April 2016, in addition to the template of international reserves and foreign currency liquidity data published in US dollars, relevant data published in IMF Special Drawing Rights (SDRs) have been added. The conversion exchange rate is from the website of the International Monetary Fund, of which USD/SDR =0.71393 in January 2019.

Source: State Administration of Foreign Exchange.

II. Composition of international reserves

(i) Gold reserve

The gold reserve is the monetarized gold held by the monetary authority of a country, excluding gold as a commodity reserve to meet the needs of industrial gold and private gold.

Gold is the oldest reserve asset. During the period of The International Gold Standard and Bretton Woods System, gold has always occupied an important position. After the disintegration of the Bretton Woods System, with the non-monetization of gold, gold can no longer be used as a means of direct external payment, but as a special commodity. It can be sold in the international gold market and exchanged for freely convertible foreign exchange.

1. Ways to increase gold reserves

Two ways to increase gold reserves:

(1) Monetary authorities purchase gold in the domestic market, that is, the so-called monetization of gold.

(2) Buy gold in the international gold market. However, for non-reserve currency issuers, buying gold in the international market needs to use their own foreign exchange. Therefore, it will not change the total amount of their international reserves, but the structural transformation between gold reserves and foreign exchange reserves.

2. Characteristics of gold reserve

The reason why gold has become an important part of international reserves is that it has the characteristics that any other form of reserve assets does not have. First, gold itself is a special commodity and a reliable means of preserving its value; second, gold reserves belong to the national wealth owned by one country's sovereignty and are not dominated and interfered with the rights of other countries.

However, compared with foreign exchange reserves, gold reserves have poor liquidity and no interest, so the amount of gold reserves depends on a country's gold policy.

However, in the turbulent international situation, especially in the danger of war or in the war, the gold reserve is the most solid part of a country's international reserves. Keynes, a western economist, vividly summed up the role of gold in the monetary system, saying: "the important role of gold in our system, as the last guard and reserve in times of emergency, there is nothing better to replace it." According to the statistics of the World Gold Council, the ranking of gold reserves of various countries in the world in 2018 is shown in Table 2-2.

Table 2-2   Ranking of gold reserves in the world in 2018 (part)

Ranking	Country (region, organization)	Tons	% of international reserves
1	US	8 133.5	73.4%
2	Germany	3 369.7	68.8%
3	IMF	2 814.0	n/a
4	Italy	2 451.8	65.1%
5	France	2 436.0	59.1%
6	Russia	2 036.2	16.9%
7	China	1 842.6	2.2%
8	Switzerland	1 040.0	5.0%
9	Japan	765.2	2.3%
10	Netherland	612.5	65.5%

续表

Ranking	Country (region, organization)	Tons	% of international reserves
11	India	579.9	5.5%
12	European Central Bank	504.8	25.1%
13	Chinese Taiwan	423.6	3.4%
14	Portugal	382.5	63.1%
15	Kazakhstan	335.1	42.5%
16	Saudi Arabia	323.1	2.4%
17	UK	310.3	7.7%
18	Lebanon	286.8	19.5%
19	Spain	281.6	15.8%
20	Austria	280.0	46.9%

Source: According to data released by the World Gold Council.

(Knowledge Link 2-1)

The history of gold's function as a currency

After the outbreak of World War II, gold lost its status as a currency in advanced economies. At the end of World War II, the Bretton Woods System of fixed exchange rates was established. In 1971, the United States unilaterally terminated its gold standard and the Bretton Woods System collapsed. The U.S. gold standard stipulates that an ounce of gold can be exchanged for $35.

The gold standard generally refers to two key periods in history: the period of the classical gold standard and the period following the Bretton Woods gold-pegged exchange rate system.

The Classical Gold Standard Period

The gold standard is a system under which all countries tie the value of their currency to a certain amount of gold, or to the currency of another country that is already pegged to a certain amount of gold. Domestic currency can be freely exchanged for gold at a fixed price, and the import and export of gold are not restricted. Gold coins circulate as domestic currency along with other metal coins and banknotes and the composition of gold coins varies from country to country. Since the value of each currency is determined by a certain amount of gold, the exchange rate between the various currencies participating in this system is also determined.

Bretton Woods System period

After the Second World War, the world needed a new international system to replace the gold standard, which was more obvious during the Second World War. The Bretton Woods conference held in the United States in 1944 drafted the blueprint of the system. The political and economic status of the United States naturally puts the dollar at the core of the system. After the chaos between the two world wars, countries yearned for stability, because a fixed exchange rate was seen as important for trade, and they also yearned for greater flexibility than the traditional gold standard. The system established at the meeting pegged the US dollar to gold at the gold parity of US $35 an ounce at that time. At the same time, the currencies of other countries were pegged to the US dollar, but the exchange rate could be adjusted. Unlike the classical gold standard, the system allows countries to carry out capital controls to stimulate their economies without being punished by financial markets.

Source: Anonymous. History of gold [EB/OL]. [2021-06-20] .https: //www.gold.org/cn/page/9372.

(ii) Foreign exchange reserves

The foreign exchange reserve is an external liquid asset, expressed in reserve currency held by a country's monetary and financial management authority. Its main forms are cash, foreign bank deposits and foreign government bonds, money market instruments, foreign exchange derivatives contracts, etc.

The IMF defines foreign exchange reserve as the creditor's rights that can be used in the event of balance of payments deficit held by the monetary and financial management authorities in the form of bank deposits, treasury bills of the ministry of finance, long-term and short-term government bonds, etc.

Foreign exchange reserve is the main component of international reserve assets at present. Reserve currency refers to the currency widely used as foreign exchange reserves by various countries, including the US dollar, Euro, British pound, Japanese yen, etc. Since the RMB joined the SDR at the end of 2016, the RMB has also occupied a place in the foreign reserve currencies of central banks. According to the 2018 IMF report, China's foreign exchange reserves reached the US $316.15 billion, ranking first in the world. See Table 2-3 for specific data.

Table 2-3   Countries (regions) of world foreign exchange reserves in 2018 (top 10)

Ranking	Country/Region	Foreign exchange reserve (billion)
1	China	3 161.50
2	Japan	1 204.70
3	Switzerland	785.7
4	Saudi Arabia	486.6
5	Hong Kong China	437.5
6	India	397.2
7	Republic of Korea	385.3
8	Brazil	358.3
9	Russia	356.5
10	Singapore	279.8

Source: Collation, according to IMF data.

（ⅲ）Reserve position

The third form of the international reserve is the reserve position of members in IMF, short for to the reserve position, also known as general drawing rights, which is the assets that the IMF members can withdraw and use freely in the general account of IMF at any time. The reserve position includes:

（1）25% share subscribed in gold, foreign exchange or SDR.

（2）The domestic currency used by the IMF to meet the borrowing needs of its members shall account for 75% of the subscribed share and may be paid in its currency.

（3）The net amount of IMF borrowing from a member is also referred to as the member's claim on the International Monetary Fund.

The general drawing rights belongs to the creditor's rights of the members in the IMF, so the members of the IMF can withdraw unconditionally to make up for the balance of payments deficit. If a country wants to use its reserve position in the IMF, it only needs to make a request to the IMF, and the IMF will satisfy it by providing the currency of another country. General drawing rights account for a small proportion of the total international reserve assets of IMF members.

（ⅳ）Special Drawing Rights

Compared with general drawing rights, SDR is an intangible currency created by the IMF. It is allocated to members as a means of supplementing existing reserve assets. It is the book assets of members in the IMF. Because it is a special right to use funds other than ordinary drawing rights, that is, reserve positions, it is called "Special Drawing Rights", also known as "Paper Gold".

1. Functions of Special Drawing Rights

SDR is an important part of a country's international reserves. It can be used for the settlement between the governments of IMF members, can be used as international reserves together with gold and foreign exchange, and can be used to exchange convertible currencies with other members, pay the balance of payments and repay IMF loans, but it cannot be directly used for trade and non-trade payments.

2. Characteristics of Special Drawing Rights

SDR has the following characteristics:

（1）It is an asset issued by credit and has no intrinsic value. It is a purely book-based asset artificially created by the International Monetary Fund.

（2）SDRs are freely allocated to members by the IMF in proportion to their quota, and the recipients do not pay any price.

（3）SDR is a state-owned asset, which can only be held by the member monetary authorities and plays a role between the International Monetary Fund and governments. Unofficial financial institutions are not allowed to hold and use.

III. Source of international reserves

1. Balance of payments surplus

Most of the international reserve assets are accumulated by the balance of payments surplus. A country's balance of payments is in surplus, and its international reserve amount increases. The current account surplus in the balance of payments is the main source of international reserves. The surplus of capital and financial accounts in the balance of payments is an important supplement to international reserves.

2. International lending

International lending refers to the direct borrowing from foreign countries by a government or bank, such as obtaining loans from international financial institutions or other governments and reciprocal credit between central banks.

3. Purchasing foreign exchange in the foreign exchange market

This refers to the increased international reserve stock of a country's monetary management authority to ensure the external stability of its currency value and intervene in the foreign exchange market to buy foreign exchange. Typically, central banks typically intervene in the foreign exchange market through open market operations, selling local currency and buying foreign exchange, so as to increase their international reserves.

4. SDRs allocated by the IMF

The special drawing rights allocated by the International Monetary Fund to its members are also a source of countries' international reserves. Due to the small amount of distribution and uneven distribution for developing countries, special drawing rights cannot become the main source of their international reserves.

Task3   Management of International Reserve

I. Management principles of international reserves

International reserve assets management refers to the process in which a country's government and monetary authorities adjust and control the scale and structure of international reserves and the use of reserve assets according to the requirements of its balance of payments and the law of economic development in a certain period of time, so as to realize the moderation of the scale and optimization of the structure of reserve assets. The following principles should be followed in the management of international reserve assets:

1.Security

Security refers to the stable value and reliable storage of reserve assets. First of all, foreign exchange reserves should choose those currencies with a stable exchange rate. Currencies with large exchange rate fluctuations and vulnerable to foreign exchange market fluctuations should reduce reserves. Secondly, reserve assets should be deposited in countries with developed economies and loose market supervision. Many countries choose to deposit their gold reserves in the United States, on the one hand, because the American market is stable and safe, on the other hand, the United States has the largest gold market, which is stored in the United States to facilitate trading and reduce transportation costs.

2.Liquidity

Liquidity refers to the availability and use of reserve assets at any time. In reserve assets, different assets' liquidity are different. For example, cash, demand deposits, bills of exchange and other assets have high liquidity and can be used as the primary reserves. Gold, foreign medium-term treasury bonds and other assets have weak liquidity and can only be used as the secondary reserves. When managing international reserves, various reserve assets with different liquidity should be used for investment of different periods, which can not only maintain and increase the value but also maintain the liquidity without affecting the use.

3.Profitability

Profitability refers to the higher returns of reserve assets on the basis of hedging. When managing reserve assets, a country should generally improve the profitability of reserve assets as much as possible on the premise of meeting the security and liquidity, so as to reduce the opportunity cost of holding reserve assets.

The international reserve is essentially a kind of reserve for external payment at any time, which is used to make up the deficit when a country's balance of payments is unbalanced. This characteristic of international reserve determines its three properties: liquidity, security and profitability. Among these three properties, liquidity is the most important, and security is second only to liquidity. Only when the liquidity and security are fully guaranteed can the profitability of the investment be considered. At the same time, these three properties are not completely independent. They are the embodiment of the essence of international reserves and are indispensable.

II. Management methods of international reserves

The management of international reserves can be divided into two aspects: one is the management of the scale of international reserves; the other is the management of the structure of international reserves. Through reasonable and scientific management, the purpose of maintaining a country's balance of payments and improving the efficiency of the use of international reserves can be achieved.

(i) International reserve scale management

The so-called international reserve scale management refers to the determination and adjustment of the international reserve scale to keep a country's international reserve at an appropriate level. The scale of a country's international reserves should not only meet the needs of national economic growth and external payments but also avoid asset waste due to excessive reserves.

Determining an appropriate reserve scale is the most important task of the international reserve management. Internationally, the more popular method is the ratio analysis method, which is proposed by American economist Robert Triffin. It measures the demand of a country's international reserves by measuring the ratio of a country's international reserves to imports (expressed in R/M). The R/M ratio of a country should be 40% as the highest limit and 20% as the lowest limit. According to the proportion of annual reserves to imports, it is about 25%~30%. In other words, a country's international reserves should ensure the payment of imports for 3~4 months, or the proportion of reserves to imports (annual figure) should not be less than 25%.

However, due to the different levels of economic development of countries all over the world, it is unreasonable to use one standard. In practice, developed countries tend to choose a lower level of international reserves and developing countries tend to choose a higher level of international reserves. This is mainly due to the strong borrowing capacity of developed countries. Despite their international reserves cannot pay for imports for 3 months, their international solvency is not lower than that of developing countries and often higher than that of developing countries.

(Knowledge Link 2-2)

Why does not the US need foreign exchange reserves?

Many people say that the United States has no foreign exchange reserves. As an economic power in the world, how can the United States ensure sustained and stable economic development and resist economic risks without foreign exchange reserves?

Strictly speaking, the United States also has foreign exchange reserves, but the scale is very small, accounting for about 0.59 month of its imports. Germany, France, Britain, Canada and other developed countries have foreign exchange reserves accounting for about 1.1 ~ 1.9 months of their imports. In contrast, Japan's economic development is third only to the United States, China. It is also a large country of financial assets and capital exports. It has an extreme surplus of capital and has 13 months of foreign exchange reserves. China's foreign exchange reserves are higher than Japan's.

The main reason why the United States does not have foreign exchange reserves is that the US dollar is the dominant currency, while the Euro, Sterling, RMB and Yen are reserve currencies. The dollar is directly linked to gold and the currencies of various countries are linked to the dollar, making the US dollar the center of the international currency, which also leads to the lack of foreign exchange reserves in the United States.

Another important reason why the United States does not need foreign exchange reserves is that as an international reserve currency, it can be directly used for international payments in foreign trade. There is no need to use foreign exchange reserves to regulate the balance of payments, foreign exchange market and international payments.

Source: according to the relevant data collation.

（ⅱ）Structural management of international reserves

The management of international reserve structure refers to how to achieve the best combination of various reserve assets and how to maintain an appropriate proportion of various reserve currencies in foreign exchange reserves.

The four components of international reserves are very different in terms of liquidity, security and profitability. Their different proportions directly determine the liquidity, security and profitability of the entire international reserve. Monetary authorities should constantly optimize the reserve structure in line with the principle of developing strengths and avoiding weaknesses, so as to maximize its efficiency. As the reserve position and the number of special drawing rights are determined by the IMF distribution, it is difficult for a country to change, so the structural management of international reserves is mainly concentrated on gold and foreign exchange reserve assets.

1. Gold reserve management

Due to the relatively stable value of gold, the quantity and scale of gold reserves in various countries remain basically unchanged or change very little. However, due to the global economic downturn in recent years, the dominance of the US dollar in the global reserve currency has been shaken and governments have changed their gold reserve strategies.

According to the official data of the World Gold Council, since 2018, the number of gold reserves purchased by countries around the world has maintained a rapid growth trend. As of the first half of 2018, the total number of the gold purchased by countries was 193.3 tons, an increase of 8% compared with the total purchase in the first half of 2017. Russia, China, India, the Philippines, Thailand and other countries are also actively increasing their gold reserves in 2018.

2.Structural management of foreign exchange reserves

Foreign exchange reserves account for a high proportion of international reserves, so the structural management of foreign exchange reserves is the core of the structural management of international reserves. The determination of foreign exchange reserve management includes two meanings: one is the determination of the proportion of foreign exchange reserve to gold reserve and other reserve assets. The second is the determination of the proportion of various currencies in foreign exchange reserves, that is, the determination of the optimal structure. Because the proportion of gold reserves is basically unchanged, the discussion is of little significance. The main content of foreign exchange reserve structure management includes the choice of currency structure and asset form.

（1）Currency management of foreign exchange reserve

When choosing the currency of foreign exchange reserves, countries should consider the actual situation of their foreign trade and follow the principles:

① Try to choose the currency required for domestic international trade and international payment, which is consistent with the currency required to make up the deficit and intervene in the market. This can avoid exchange rate risk and reduce transaction costs to a certain extent；

② Choose "hard" currency reserves and reduce "soft" currency reserves，so as to ensure the stability of the value of the reserve currency；

③Increase the reserves of currencies with small exchange rate fluctuations and reduce the reserves of currencies with large exchange rate fluctuations；

④Maintain the diversification of monetary reserves and diversify risks.

Figure 2-2 reflects the proportion of major reserve currencies in the foreign exchange reserves of central banks around the world in 2018.

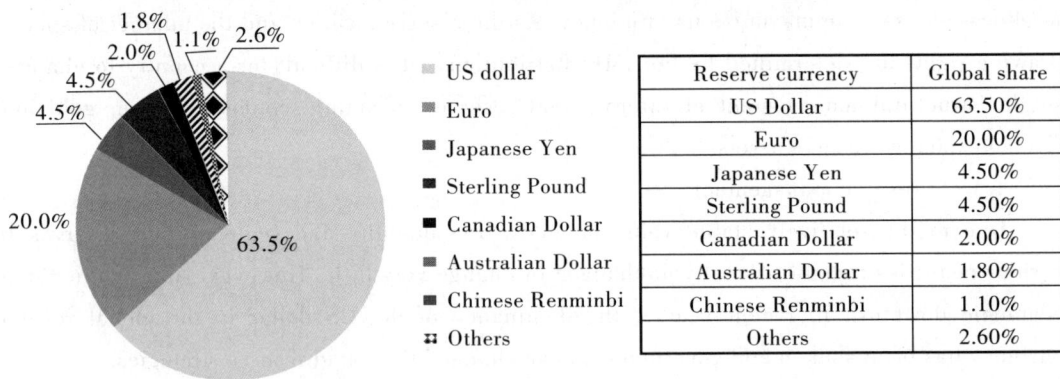

Reserve currency	Global share
US Dollar	63.50%
Euro	20.00%
Japanese Yen	4.50%
Sterling Pound	4.50%
Canadian Dollar	2.00%
Australian Dollar	1.80%
Chinese Renminbi	1.10%
Others	2.60%

Figure 2-2 The proportion of major reserve currencies in the foreign exchange

Source：IMF data.

（2）Asset structure management of foreign exchange reserves

Since the main role of international reserves is to make up for the balance of payments deficit，the monetary authorities of various countries pay more attention to the liquidity of reserve assets. According to the level of liquidity，foreign exchange reserves can be divided into the following three categories：

①Tier 1 reserves：the most liquid，but the least profitable，including demand deposits in foreign banks，foreign currency commercial bills and foreign short-term government bonds. The profitability of these highly liquid assets is very low.

② Tier 2 reserves：the profitability is higher than Tier 1 reserves，but the liquidity is lower than Tier 1 reserves. Various certificates of deposit，2-year and 5-year medium-term foreign government bonds，etc belong to Tier 2 reserves. These reserves are mainly used in case of temporary and unexpected events in a country.

③ Tier 3 reserves：the profitability is higher than Tier 2 reserves，but the liquidity is lower than Tier 2 reserves. Tier 3 reserves are mainly used to make up for the low return of the primary reserve. It is a long-term investment，so its rate of return is the highest. Tier 3 reserves include long-term foreign government bonds，AAA European bonds，etc. After maturity，it can be converted into Tier 1 reserves，but if it converts into cash in advance before maturity，it will suffer huge losses in return.

Different countries in the world have different economic development conditions，so the asset forms of foreign exchange reserves are also different. However, in general, countries with a deficit in the balance of payments prefer to retain a relatively large proportion of Tier 1 reserves to maintain their liquidity. Countries with surpluses do not need too many Tier 1 reserves and can focus on retaining more profitable Tier 3 reserves, because the surplus country itself has a relatively strong ability to borrow reserves and does not need to 1 a large amount of Tier 1 reserves.

Case Analysis 2-1

China's foreign exchange reserves account for 30% of the world, and many countries increase their holdings of gold and sell off US bonds

Foreign exchange reserves refer to the foreign exchange assets centrally controlled by the central banks and other government agencies of various countries to meet the needs of international payment. The 10-year average yield of China's foreign exchange reserves from 2005 to 2014 was 3.68%, while by the end of 2018, China's gold reserves had reached 1 852 tons, ranking sixth in the world. IMF statistics show that China's foreign exchange reserves account for nearly 30% of the global foreign exchange reserves.

Although China's gold reserves only rank sixth in the world, a large country accounting for nearly 30% of the world's foreign exchange reserves, China's foreign exchange changes will naturally attract much attention. In addition to China's increased holdings of gold, emerging market countries are hoarding gold at an unprecedented rate in 50 years. According to the latest data of the World Gold Council, as of the end of June 2019, the net purchase of gold by the global central bank was 247.3 tons, a year-on-year increase of 73%, and Russia, China, Turkey and Kazakhstan became the four largest buyers of gold.

Due to the increasingly strong desire for "de-dollarization", many countries are increasing their holdings of gold and selling US bonds sharply. According to the latest report of the Federal Reserve, the debt of the U.S. financial system has reached $72 trillion, and the total debt of U.S. Treasury bonds has exceeded $22.5 trillion. When the sharp sell-off of U.S. debt is combined with the increase of gold holdings, as long as the debt deficit risk of the U.S. economy breaks out, the countries with gold are likely to become the leaders after the global financial market is reset.

Source: Financial fresh news. China's foreign exchange reserves account for 30% of the world's, and many countries increase their holdings of gold and sell off US bonds [EB/OL]. [2019-07-30]. https://baijiahao.baidu.com/s? id=1640447399684891842&w fr=spider&for=pc, modified.

Combined with the above materials, please think:

1. Why is China's foreign exchange reserve so huge?

2. What are the reasons for the increase of gold reserves in various countries in recent years?

3. How can we reasonably manage a country's international reserves?

Mini Case

In November 1996, China's foreign exchange reserves exceeded the US $100 billion for the first time. In 2001, this figure doubled to $200 billion. Since then, the growth rate of China's foreign exchange reserves has accelerated. At the end of February 2006, China surpassed Japan for the first time and ranked first in the world. In October of the same year, China's foreign exchange reserves exceeded the $1 trillion mark for the first time. In June 2009, foreign exchange reserves exceeded the US $2 trillion. Since then, foreign exchange reserves have increased to the US $3 trillion in less than a year, an increase of 50% in less than a year. Since then, China's foreign exchange reserves have been at a high level of more than $3 trillion.

More than one-third of China's huge foreign exchange reserves of up to US $3 trillion are invested in US Treasury bonds. The gold reserves are less than 2 000 tons, accounting for only 2.2% of China's foreign exchange reserves. The gold reserves held by some developed countries basically constitute the majority of their foreign exchange reserves.

Please thinking: How did China's huge foreign exchange reserves come into being? What are the characteristics? How does China manage international reserves?

Mind Map

```
                                        ┌─ Concept and characteristics of international reserve
                      ┌─ Overview of   ─┼─ International reserve and International solvency
                      │  International  └─ The role of international reserve
                      │  Reserve
                      │
                      │                 ┌─ Evolution of the composition of international reserves
  International ──────┼─ Composition   ─┼─ Composition of international reserves
  reserve             │  and source of  └─ Source of international reserves
                      │  international
                      │  reserves
                      │
                      │  Management of  ┌─ Management principles of international reserves
                      └─ International  ─┴─ Management methods of international reserves
                         reserve
```

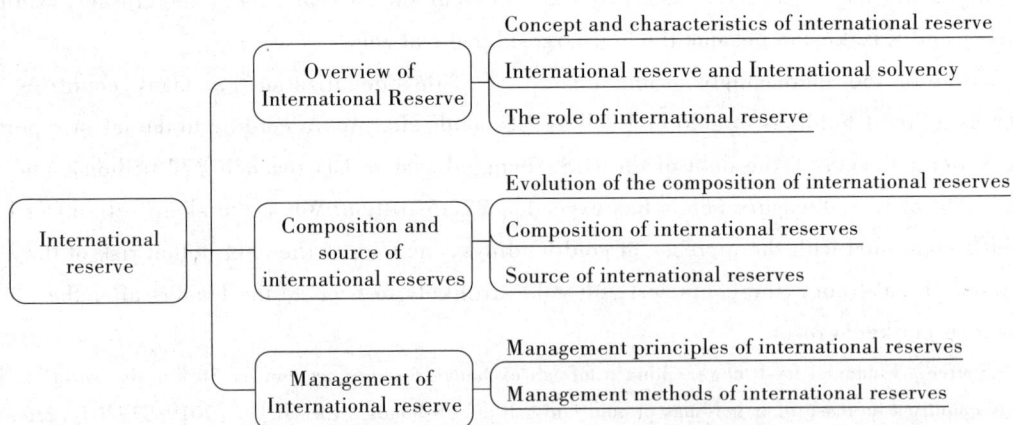

Project Training

I. Single-choice questions

1. International reserves do not include （   ）.

A. commercial bank reserves　　　　　B. foreign exchange reserve

C. reserve position in IMF　　　　　　D. SDR

2. There are three basic principles for the operation and management of international reserves: (　　) .

A. security, liquidity and profitability　　B. security, fixity and hedging

C. security, fixity and profitability　　　D. liquidity, hedging and appreciation

3. Tier 3 international reserve assets include (　　) .

A. special drawing rights

B.general drawing rights

C.long-term bonds

D.yields are lower than Tier 1 international reserve assets

4. The most basic role of international reserves is (　　) .

A. intervene in the foreign exchange market

B. act as means of payment

C. cover the balance of payments deficit

D. as a guarantee of foreign debt repayment

5. SDR is (　　) .

A. the currency created by the European Economic and Monetary Union

B. the central currency of the European monetary system

C. IMF-created reserve assets and units of bookkeeping account

D. World Bank-created special access to funds

6. The focus of China's international reserve management is (　　) .

A. foreign exchange reserves　　　　　B. special drawing rights

C. gold　　　　　　　　　　　　　　D. ordinary drawing rights

7. (　　) amount of import is widely used all over the world as the standard for determining the appropriate amount of international reserves.

A. 6 months　　　B. 3 months　　　C. 9 months　　　D. 1 year

8. SDR is a (　　) .

A. actual assets　　　　　　　　　　B. book assets

C. current assets　　　　　　　　　　D. fixed assets

9. The maximum limit for ordinary loans is (　　) of the member's share.

A. 100%　　　B. 25%　　　C. 75%　　　D. 125%

10. In international reserves, (　　) had historically occupied an extremely important position, but since the beginning of the 1950s, its share in total international reserves has tended to decline.

A. gold　　　　　　　　　　　　　　B. ordinary drawing rights

C. foreign exchange reserves　　　　　D. special drawing rights

II. Multiple-choice questions

1. International reserves have the following characteristics: (   ).

A. official holding   B. convertibility

C. full liquidity   D. general acceptability

2. International reserves mainly include (   ).

A. gold reserve   B. foreign exchange reserves

C. land fund   D. ordinary drawing rights

E. special drawing rights

3. Which of the following statements is true about SDR? (   )

A. SDR is a currency actually issued.

B. SDR can be used as a means of circulation

C. SDR is a book asset.

D. SDR has a strictly limited purpose

E. SDR has no intrinsic value

4. The following financial assets can be used as international reserves: (   ).

A. SDR

B. individuals invest abroad

C. residents holding foreign currencies

D. gold

5 International reserve management should follow (   ) principle.

A. moderation   B. security   C. liquidity   D. profitability

III. True or false questions

1. SDRs are mainly used to make up for members' balance of payments deficits or to repay IMF loans, and cannot be held and used by any individuals or enterprises, nor can they be used for trade or non-trade payments.   (   )

2. The acquisition of gold by a country's central bank in the international gold market has not only changed the structure of international reserves but also increased the total amount of international reserves significantly.   (   )

3. The current international reserve currency structure has been diversified, and the US dollar is no longer the main reserve currency.   (   )

4. International reserves held by a country can adjust the balance of payments deficit and stabilize the exchange rate of the local currency, so the more international reserves the better.
                                                                          (   )

5. Generally speaking, the size of international reserves is inversely proportional to the size of a country's economic activities.   (   )

IV. Practical training

1. Log on to the website of the State Administration of Foreign Exchange and check the basic data about China's balance of payments, import and export amounts, foreign debt size

and foreign exchange reserves in recent years, and choose one of the years' data for analysis.

　　2. Understand the operation of China's international reserve assets and try to write the "Analysis Report on the Size and Moderation of China's Foreign Exchange Reserves in 2020".

　　The teacher can give a guided explanation, then divide the class into groups according to the situation, let the students check the information themselves, discuss and analyze, and finally form a brief analysis report, and make a PPT to explain, finally the teacher will comment.

Project Three
International Financial Markets and Financial Institutions

Learning Objectives

Knowledge Objectives:

Understand the meaning and classification of international financial markets and grasp the concept and composition of international monetary markets, international capital markets and Eurocurrency markets.

Competence Objectives:

Master the operations and functions of the international monetary market, the international capital market and the Eurocurrency market.

Operational Objectives:

Master the range of major international financial institutions and identify financing opportunities for businesses or organizations.

Course Introduction

China's first issue of Euro sovereign bond with a negative interest rate

On 18 November 2020, the Chinese Ministry of Finance successfully issued €4 billion of sovereign bonds. Of these, the issue yielded −0.152% for a 5-year term of €750 million, 0.318% for a 10-year term of €2 billion and 0.664% for a 15-year term of €1.25 billion.

The issuance was the second consecutive year after the relaunch of Euro sovereign bond issuance in 2019 and achieved the lowest yield level for China's offshore sovereign bond issuance to date. The 5-year issue was issued at a premium with a zero coupon, achieving a negative interest rate for the first time. The issue was listed on the London Stock Exchange, the Luxembourg Stock Exchange and the Hong Kong Stock Exchange in a "triple listing, double custody" model. At the same time, to support the development of Hong Kong as an international financial center, the 5-year Euro sovereign bond was cleared for the first time in the Hong Kong Central Moneymarkets Unit (CMU), contributing to the development of Hong Kong's financial infrastructure. In addition, international rating companies have assigned credit ratings.

From the book-entry situation, international investors were well subscribed, with the order size reaching 4.5 times the issue size and a wide range of investor groups covering central banks, sovereign funds, super-sovereign and pension funds, capital management and banks. The final investment ratio of European investors was as high as 72%, reflecting the confidence of international capital market investors in China's stable and improving economy. The successful issuance of Euro sovereign bonds further reflects China's determination and confidence in opening up to the outside world at a higher level, in line with the trend of economic and financial globalization, and will further deepen China's accomodation with international capital markets and cooperation with international investors.

Sovereign bonds are bonds issued by a government in foreign currency in the international market. This type of bond called a sovereign bond because it is a government-issued bond and it is backed by government credit. The reasons for the emergence of negative interest rate issues are related to the current global economic environment. In recent years, many countries have adopted accommodative monetary policies in response to downward economic pressures, and negative interest rates are an unconventional monetary policy tool that has emerged in recent years. At present, the benchmark deposit rate in the Eurozone is already negative. The yields on long-term government bonds of many European countries are also in the period of negative interest rates. The 5-year Euro sovereign bonds are issued by China's Ministry of Finance this time, although the issue yield is −0.152%, it is still higher compared to the yields on other Eurozone sovereign bonds. Furthermore, the market expects the benchmark Eurozone interest rate to continue to fall, and the price of the bond will then rise. For investors, this means that even if they do not hold to maturity, they can make profits by selling through the secondary market.

The credit of sovereign bonds relies on the credit of the state. International capital is keen on China's sovereign bonds, which is in essence a vote of confidence in China's economic development. For China, the issuance of euro sovereign bonds is conducive to furthering the internationalization of the RMB and is also of great significance to the integration of China's financial markets into the world economy. With the internationalization of the RMB, China's government bonds will also go global in the future, and will certainly be issued more often, including sovereign bonds in USD, EUR, and even JPY and GBP, which is a concrete manifestation of the optimization of our government bond structure. In fact, this is also a concrete move in the context of the internationalization of the RMB. In addition to attracting a lot of foreign exchange to the country, the RMB also needs to "go out".

Source: Ministry of Finance of the People's Republic of China. Ministry of Finance successfully issues €4 billion sovereign bonds [EB/OL]. [2020-11-19]. http://www.mof.gov.cn/zhengwuxinxi/caizhengxinwen/202011/t20201119_3626191.htm.

Discussion:

(1) What is a sovereign bond?

(2) Why are European investors keen to invest in negative-rate euro sovereign bonds issued by China?

Task 1   Overview of International Financial Markets

I. The meaning of international financial markets

There are narrow and broad definitions of international financial markets. International financial markets in the narrow sense are places where international funds are borrowed or financed. The international financial market in the broad sense refers to the place and transaction network for engaging in various international financial transactions, including international financial business such as funds borrowing and lending, issuance and trading of marketable securities internationally, which can be subdivided into the international monetary market, international capital market, international gold market, international foreign exchange market and financial derivatives market. Due to the widespread use of computer technology in banking, various cross-border financial transactions are generally conducted through telephones, telegrams, telexes and other telecommunication tools. Therefore, the international financial market is not limited to a geographical location but is more embodied as an invisible network of transactions. The international financial markets described in this project refer to international financial markets in a broad sense.

II. Classification of international financial markets

（ⅰ）To classify according to the region of the trading entity and the extent of control over financial transactions by the country where the market is located

International financial markets can be divided into onshore and offshore financial markets according to the region of the trading entity and the degree to which the financial transaction is of control over financial trasactions by the country where the market is located.

（ⅱ）To classify according to the presence or absence of a fixed trading venue

International financial markets can be divided into tangible and intangible markets according to the presence or absence of a fixed trading venue.

Tangible markets refer to international financial markets with fixed trading venues, such as international stock markets. Intangible markets refer to the absence of fixed physical trading places, international financial transactions between the supply and demand sides through the telephone, telex, computer and other communication equipment and trading networks for transactions, such as the international foreign exchange market. Most of the international financial markets are intangible markets.

（ⅲ）To classify by the type of business conducted

The international financial markets can be divided into the international lending market, the international securities market, the international foreign exchange market, the international gold market and the financial derivatives market according to the type of business operated.

（ⅳ）To classify by duration of the transaction

The international financial markets can be divided into international monetary market and international capital market according to the duration of the transactions.

The international monetary market is the market for cross - border trading of financial instruments with a maturity of one year or less, also known as the short-term funding market.

The international capital market is the international financial market for international medium and long - term funds borrowing and lending and securities buying and selling operations with maturities of one year or more.

（ⅴ）To classify by mode of delivery of financial assets

The international financial markets can be divided into spot market, futures market and options market according to how financial assets are delivered.

III. The formation and development of international financial markets

Animation Micro-lesson 3-1

The Evolution of International Financial Markets

International financial markets have been formed and developed gradually with the internationalization of international trade, capital export and production.

Before World War I, Britain's industrial revolution and overseas expansion saw its economic power leap to the top of the world, and the pound became the world's leading international reserve and settlement currency. London also took the lead as the world's first international financial market.

Between the outbreak of World War I and the end of World War II, the British economy was severely damaged, the role of London's international financial markets was weakened and the pound declined in stature. The New York financial market in the USA took advantage of the situation and the US dollars became the main reserve and settlement currency for all countries. As a neutral country, Switzerland was not damaged by the war, its economy was stable and the Swiss franc was freely convertible, making the Zurich financial market a leap forward. During this period, New York, London and Zurich became the world's three largest international financial markets.

The international financial markets of this period were essentially domestic financial markets with international operations, i.e., "traditional international financial markets". The international business carried out was mainly international credit and bond business between residents and non-residents of the countries where the market was located, and was regulated by the financial laws and regulations of the host governments. It is essentially a form of capital export.

In the late 1950s, the Eurocurrency market emerged and its credit transactions became more international, allowing foreign lenders to trade with foreign borrowers in almost all western currencies. From then on, the international financial markets were no longer confined to a few traditional financial centers but rapidly expanded to include Paris, Frankfurt, Brussels, Amsterdam, Stockholm, Tokyo, Luxembourg, Singapore, China's Hong Kong, China and the Cayman Islands. International financial transactions during this period were extended to non-residents of the countries in which the markets were located, and were not subject to any domestic financial laws or regulations.

After the 1970s, with the rapid development of global economic integration, international capital and industrial technology were exported to many developing countries. Countries have taken the initiative to align themselves with international practices and establish a financial environment that is in line with them. For example, the financial markets of developing countries such as Malaysia, the Philippines and Thailand in Asia, oil-exporting countries in the Middle East, as well as countries in Latin America and Africa, have gradually emerged.

IV. The role of international financial markets

The formation and development of international financial markets play an extremely important role for both developed and developing countries, and the world economy as a whole.

(i) Positive effects

International financial markets have accelerated the flow of capital and contributed to global economic development in the following ways.

(1) Promoting the development of the world economy. International financial markets

facilitate the financing of international trade, providing foreign capital for countries with capital shortages, expanding production and thus contributing to the development of the world economy.

(2) Regulating the balance of payments. International financial markets are increasingly becoming an important source of foreign exchange funds for all countries. On the one hand, the countries with a balance of payments surplus put their foreign exchange surplus funds on the international financial markets; on the other hand, the countries with a balance of payments deficit borrow from the international financial markets to make up for the balance of payments deficit.

(3) Optimizing the international division of labor and promoting the integration of the world economy. The international financial markets have made it possible to reduce the cost of transferring funds between countries, which has facilitated the development of international trade and accelerated the movement of international capital, making it possible for funds to flow in the direction of optimizing the distribution of resources in the world economy and promoting the establishment of an international division of labor system.

(ii) Negative effects

International financial markets also have their adverse effects, which are reflected in the following areas.

(1) A disproportionate share of speculation and a small share of real economy transactions and investments in international financial transactions have led to increasing financial risks in international markets.

(2) International financial markets bring financial risk to the world. With international capital flows, transitory investments, economic bubbles and international debt are also carried around the world. In addition, financial institutions and financial markets are so closely linked to each other that a problem in any one place can spread the risk to the entire international financial system.

(3) The international financial markets have become a venue for international smuggling, drug trafficking and other financial crimes to launder money, which has to some extent weakened the enforcement efforts of the countries concerned in this regard.

(Knowledge Link 3-1)

International Financial Centre

An international finance centre (IFC) is a city or region where a large number of financial institutions and related service industries are located, with a comprehensive concentration of international capital lending, bond issuance, foreign exchange transactions, insurance and other financial services. It is a city that provides the most convenient international financing services, the most efficient international payment and clearing system and the most active international financial trading venue. The basic characteristics of the international financial center are a complete financial market, a high density of services and a radiating influence on the surrounding area or even the world.

The status of an international financial center is based on the combined advantages of multiple resource conditions, and is formed and consolidated by a series of supply and demand factors. Based on historical experience and relevant research findings, these conditions can be summarized as follows: (1) a strong and prosperous economic base; (2) a stable and peaceful political environment; (3) an efficient and sound financial system; (4) a concentrated financial institution; (5) a supportive policy orientation; (6) low and reasonable taxation costs; and (7) a complete and comprehensive infrastructure.

On 25 September 2020, the 28th edition of the Global Financial Centre Index (GFCI 28), jointly compiled by the China (Shenzhen) Institute of Comprehensive Development, a high-end national think tank, and Z/Yen Group, a UK-based think tank, was released simultaneously in Shenzhen, China and Seoul, Korea. The report evaluates and ranks the world's leading financial centers in terms of the business environment, human resources, infrastructure, financial sector development and reputation. A total of 111 financial centers were listed, with the top 10 financial centers in the world being New York, London, Shanghai, Tokyo, Hong Kong, Singapore, Beijing, San Francisco, Shenzhen and Zurich. Shanghai overtook Tokyo and entered the top three for the first time.

Source: Anonymous. The 28th edition of the Global Financial Centre Index: Shanghai in top three, Shenzhen in top ten [EB/OL]. [2020-09-25]. https://www.thepaper.cn/newsDetail_forward_9345476, with deletions and modifications.

Task 2   International Monetary Markets

I. The meaning of international monetary market

The international monetary market is a market for cross-border transactions in financial instruments with maturities of one year or less, also known as the short-term funding market. The participants in the international monetary market are mainly commercial banks, central banks, the financial departments of national governments, monetary institutions, multinational companies, bill acceptors, discounters, securities companies, multinational banks and so on. Multinational banks are in a key position in the market and are the main suppliers and demanders of funds in the international monetary market.

Instruments and securities issued and circulated in the money market, such as treasury bills, commercial paper, banker's acceptances and large negotiable time deposits, are short-term in nature. These instruments and securities are characterised by their short maturity, low risk and high liquidity, all of which have an active secondary market and can be sold for realization at any time.

II. Characteristics of the international monetary market

International monetary markets are generally characterised by several aspects.

(1) Short maturity, with the shortest financing period being only one day and the longest being one year.

Teaching Video 3-1

The Composition and Role of the International Monetary Market

(2) The purpose of the transaction is to address the need for short-term liquidity. The sources of funds on the international monetary market are mainly the temporarily idle funds of the owners of the funds, and the demanders are only there to cover the short-term liquidity shortage.

(3) Financial instruments have a high degree of liquidity. Financial instruments traded on international monetary markets are generally short term, highly liquid and highly liquid in realization.

(4) High creditworthiness of the traders, large scale of financing, low borrowing costs, fast turnover of funds and large flows.

Because the international monetary market has the above characteristics, it requires that the market has a good regulatory control mechanism and provides a fairly matured social and economic development environment. In other words, international monetary markets can only be formed and developed under conditions of a highly developed economy, a highly developed central banking system, fairly well-developed credit instruments, very favorable market conditions and a very well-developed legal system.

III. Composition of the international monetary market

The international monetary market can be divided by type of business into the short-term credit market, the short-term securities market and the discount market.

(i) Short-term credit market

The short-term credit market refers primarily to the interbank market. This market offers short-term loans of one year or less and is designed to address temporary funding needs and position shifting. Loans are available for periods as short as one day and as long as one year, but also for periods of three days, one week, one month, three months, six months, etc. Interest rates are usually based on LIBOR; transactions are usually conducted on a wholesale basis, ranging from a few hundred thousand pounds to several million or tens of millions of pounds; transactions are simple, require no security or collateral and are conducted by telephone and telex completely on the basis of reputation.

(ii) Short-term securities market

The short-term securities market is an international venue for trading in short-term securities with a maturity of up to one year. Short-term treasury bills, large negotiable time deposits, bankers' acceptances and commercial acceptances are traded. Treasury bills are short-term bonds issued by Western finance ministries to raise seasonal funds or for short-term economic and financial regulation, usually with a maturity of three months or six months, depending on the circumstances, and usually marketed at a discount on the face value and by auction.

A banker's certificate of deposit is a certificate of time deposit in a bank which can be transferred and circulated. Banker's acceptances and commercial acceptances are both credit payment instruments, with the former being accepted by banks and the latter being accepted by enterprises, which can be endorsed and transferred after acceptance and can be held at maturity to demand payment from the payer. Due to the higher creditworthiness of banks, bankers' acceptances are more liquid than commercial acceptances.

(ⅲ) Discount market

Discounting is a financial transaction in which the holder pledges the outstanding instrument to a bank or discounting company, which hands over the remaining funds to the holder at the face value of the instrument, less discounted interest. A discount market is a place where outstanding bills are financed on a discounted basis. The discounting transaction allows the holder to obtain the amount of the instrument at maturity (the balance of the face amount less the discounted interest) in advance, while the discounting firm provides credit to the holder who requests it and obtains the discounted interest. Discounting is an important way of financing the money market. The main instruments discounted are treasury bills, bank bonds, corporate bonds, bankers' acceptances and commercial acceptances, and the discount rate is generally higher than the bank rate. The discounter can apply to other commercial banks for rediscounting of the discounted bills, or to the central bank for rediscounting. The central bank uses this rediscounting business to regulate credit, interest rates and macro-finance.

Task 3   International Capital Markets

I. The meaning of international capital markets

The international capital market is an international financial market for the lending, buying and selling of international medium, long-term funds and securities with a maturity of one year or more. The main suppliers of funds to the international capital markets include the following types:

(1) Various institutional investors, such as commercial banks, investment banks, insurance companies, fund companies and multinational companies.

(2) National monetary authorities as well as international financial institutions.

(3) Private investors.

The main demanders of funds in the international capital markets include governments, international financial institutions, commercial banks and multinational corporations.

The transactions mainly include borrowing and lending of medium and long-term funds, buying and selling of medium and long-term securities and international leasing.

II. Characteristics of international capital markets

Due to the relatively long maturity of the objects traded, international capital markets have the following characteristics:

(1) Longer terms of financing, usually over a year or even up to several decades.

(2) The size of the transaction is substantial and the purpose of the transaction is generally to add capital or cover a financial deficit.

(3) The financial instruments traded have longer maturities, less liquidity and greater risk.

III. Composition of international capital markets

The international capital markets mainly consist of the medium and long-term credit markets, the medium and long-term securities markets and the international leasing markets. The most significant businesses in the international capital markets at present remain the medium and long-term credit business and the securities business.

Teaching Video 3-2

The Composition and Role of
International Capital Markets

(i) Medium and long-term credit market

The medium and long-term credit market is primarily a market in which governments, international financial organizations and multinational banks provide medium and long-term funding to their customers.

Government loans have relatively long terms and low-interest rates but have certain conditions attached to them. Government loans can have terms of up to 30 years and interest rates can be as low as zero, while conditions are generally attached to restrict the use of the loan, such as stipulating the use of the loan or requiring the borrowing country to make certain commitments or adjustments in its economic or foreign policy. Therefore, government loans are binding loans.

Multinational bank loans are generally unrestricted as to the purpose of the loan and the interest rate is based on market conditions and the reputation of the borrower. For larger loans, united or syndicated loans are generally used to spread the risk.

United loan or syndicated loan is a joint loan from several or even a dozen banks to a particular customer, with one bank as the lead bank, several banks as the managing banks and the remaining banks as the participating banks.

(ii) Medium and long-term securities market

The international medium and long-term securities market generally consists of the international stock market and the international medium and long-term bond market.

1.International Stock Market

International stocks refer to generally stocks issued by a country's business enterprises outside its territory and denominated in the currency of the country in which the market is located. The issuer and the investor of international shares, or the issuer and the currency in which the shares are denominated, belong to different countries or regions. Examples include China's S-shares issued in Singapore and N-shares issued in New York, such as Chinese enterprise NetEase, Youdao, which issued shares denominated in US dollars on the New York Stock Exchange on 25 October 2019.

An international stock market is a venue or trading network where shares are issued and traded on an international scale. Some of the better-known international stock markets are the New York Stock Exchange in the US, the London Stock Exchange, the Singapore Stock Exchange and the Hong Kong Stock Exchange.

2.International Medium and Long-Term Bond Market

International bonds are bonds denominated in the foreign currency issued by a country's government, enterprises, financial institutions, etc., to raise funds outside the country, or bonds issued by international financial institutions in the financial markets of various countries to raise funds. Most international bond issues are underwritten by banks or securities companies. International medium and long-term bonds have a maturity of more than one year.

International bonds are divided into two categories: foreign bonds and Eurobonds.

Foreign bonds refer to bonds denominated in the currency of the country where the market is located issued by a government, enterprise or financial institution in the overseas bond market, or bonds denominated in the currency of that country issued by an international financial institution in the bond market of a country, such as bonds denominated in US dollars issued by a UK company in the US bond market, or bonds denominated in RMB issued by an international financial company in the bond market of China Bonds. The issuance of foreign bonds by fundraisers is subject to regulation by the securities regulator and financial laws of the country in which the market is located.

The larger foreign bonds include the US Yankee Bonds (US dollar-denominated bonds issued by foreign funders in the US bond market), the UK Mighty Dog Bonds (sterling-denominated bonds issued by foreign funders in the UK bond market), the Japanese Samurai Bonds (yen-denominated bonds issued by foreign funders in the Japanese bond market) and the Chinese Panda Bonds (RMB-denominated bonds issued by foreign funders in the mainland Chinese bond market).

Eurobonds are bonds denominated in the currency of a third country issued by a government, enterprise or financial institution in a foreign bond market, or by an international financial institution in the bond market of a third country. The term "Europe" here is not geographically European but refers to "offshore". For example, a bond issued by a US company in the Tokyo bond market is denominated in sterling. The issuance of Eurobonds by fundraisers is generally less subject to the financial regulations of the country in which the market is located.

The comparison of the foreign bonds and Eurobonds is shown in Table 3-1.

Table 3-1   Comparison of foreign bonds and Eurobonds concepts

classification	concept
Foreign bonds	The bond issuer and the place of issue belong to different countries or regions, but the place of issue and the currency in which the bond is denominated belong to the same country or region
Eurobonds	The bond issuer, the place of issue and the currency in which the bond is denominated belong to different countries or regions

(iii) International leasing market

A lease is an arrangement whereby the lessee pays the lessor a certain amount of money at regular intervals for the right to use an asset. It allows the lessee to obtain the right to use the required equipment without having to purchase equipment that is needed for a short period of time or seasonally, by paying the lessor a certain amount on a regular basis, which is tantamount to the lessor providing credit to the lessee in disguise. In economic life, many manufacturing industries not only sell equipment but also engage in equipment leasing. In addition, banks are also heavily involved in leasing, which is in effect a form of capital financing. When leasing crosses national borders, it becomes a form of capital financing between countries.

Task 4   Eurocurrency Markets

I. The meaning of the Eurocurrency market

The Eurocurrency market is a market for lending and borrowing of a currency between non-residents, with banks acting as intermediaries, outside the borders of the country of issue, also known as the offshore financial market. The currency that is traded outside the country of issue is known as "Eurocurrency", and the bank that deals in Eurocurrency is known as "Eurobank".

The "Eurobank" uses its global network of branches and clients, its modern communication tools to connect Eurocurrency suppliers and demanders around the world, forming a global, invisible market based on a number of offshore financial centers.

There are several points to note regarding the meaning of the Eurocurrency market.

(1) Eurocurrency, also known as offshore currency, is a general term for all types of currency that are stored and borrowed outside the country of issue, not the currency of a European country. The term "Europe" is not a geographical concept and is not limited to the European region, but means "offshore". For example, US dollars deposited and lent outside the United States are referred to as "Eurodollars"; sterlings deposited and lent

outside the UK is referred to as "Europounds". Currently, the Eurocurrency often used in the offshore financial markets include the US dollar, Swiss franc, Japanese yen, pound sterling and euro, with the US dollar still dominating.

Animation Micro-lesson 3-2

RMB Offshore Market

(2) The Eurocurrency Market is the market in which Eurocurrencies are traded. Similarly, the term "Europe" is not a geographical concept but refers to the "offshore" of the currency-issuing country. For example, the "offshore RMB market" is a market for the deposit and lending of RMB outside of China, currently mainly in Singapore and Hong Kong, China. A Eurocurrency market (or offshore financial market) can also be established in China.

Knowledge Link 3-2

Offshore Finance Scope of Business

Offshore finance is a product of financial globalization and openness, which can effectively promote the optimal allocation of financial resources in the world, facilitate international capital financing and international debt settlement, and promote the rapid development of international trade. Offshore financial services mainly include financial services such as banking, insurance and securities, as well as non-financial services such as ship registration.

Some of the more prominent offshore financial centers are the British Virgin Islands, the Cayman Islands, the Bahamas, Bermuda and the Solomon Islands. Offshore banking has also grown rapidly in offshore financial centers. Bank of Asia, for example, is incorporated in the British Virgin Islands and uses the latest financial technology to provide comprehensive cross-border financial services to its global clients. The scope of offshore banking often includes providing payments and settlements to offshore business partners (e.g., companies engaged in import / export trade, consulting - type businesses); receiving proceeds from offshore investments in offshore accounts; accepting funds from investors and investing them in portfolio projects; and being able to set up time deposits for temporarily unused funds.

The global offshore financial markets are also making progress in terms of regulation and information transparency, creating a favorable atmosphere and environment for the further development of offshore business.

Source: Anonymous. What is the scope of offshore banking services in the offshore financial market? [EB/OL] . [2020-12-16] .http: //cn.dailyeconomic.com/roll/2020/12/16/139530. html.

II. The creation and development of the Eurocurrency market

(i) The creation of the Eurocurrency market

The Eurocurrency market arose in the 1950s and its predecessor was the Eurodollar market. After the end of the Second World War, the United States adopted a policy of hostility and containment towards the Soviet Union and other socialist countries. The Soviet Union and the Eastern European countries feared that their dollar funds held in the United States would be frozen, so they transferred some of these dollar funds to British banks. The British government needed large sums of money to restore the status of the pound and to support its domestic economy, so the major commercial banks in London were allowed to deposit and lend abroad in US dollars. This led to the creation of the Eurodollar market.

(ii) Development of Eurocurrency markets

The development of the Eurodollar market has been the result of a variety of factors.

After 1958, the US balance of payments deficit began to grow in size. Large outflows of US dollars out of the US provided the Eurodollar market with large amounts of capital. In order to prevent further deterioration of the balance of payments, the US adopted a policy of restricting capital outflows, forcing residents outside the US to shift their dollar borrowing and lending operations to the Eurodollar market, and US banks opened many branches in Europe accordingly, all of which stimulated the development of the Eurodollar market.

From the 1960s onwards, in addition to the US dollar, currencies such as the Deutsche Mark and the Swiss franc were also traded on the Eurodollar market. In addition, the Asian financial markets of Singapore and Hong Kong, China, began to operate lending operations in US dollars and marks. At this point, the Eurodollar market evolved into the European currency market. The term "Europe" no longer refers to a geographical location, but rather to "offshore". The term "European currency" refers to currencies circulating outside the country of issue.

The two sharp increases happened in world oil prices after the 1970s. On the one hand, petroleum exporting countries accumulated a large amount of petrodollars, most of which were invested in the Eurodollar market. On the other hand, the balance of payments deficits of the non-oil-exporting developing countries led them to borrow funds in the Eurodollar market to cover their deficits, thus increasing the demand for funds in this market.

The significance of Eurocurrency markets changed again after the 1980s. In 1981 the Federal Reserve (US Federal Reserve Bank) approved the establishment of an international banking facility in New York, which allowed US depository institutions and foreign banks to operate US dollar deposits and other foreign currency deposits from foreign customers at their branches or managers, and this portion of US dollar deposits and foreign currency deposits were not subject to US domestic deposit reserves and interest rates, and also allows these institutions to extend credit to foreign customers with funds taken from non-residents in US dollars and foreign currency deposits. It follows that international banking facilities may operate the non-resident business that are not subject to the financial policies of the currency-issuing country and belong to the broad Eurocurrency market.

Animation Micro-lesson 3-3

Eurocurrency Market and Eurocurrency

III. Operating characteristics of the Eurocurrency market

The Eurocurrency market is a fully internationalized financial market, the mainstay of international financial markets, with the following operating characteristics.

(1) The market is extensive and not limited by geography. Transactions are mainly made through modern communication networks.

(2) The market is huge with a wide variety of transactions and currencies and is extremely dynamic in terms of financial innovation. The vast majority of individual transactions on the Eurocurrency market exceed US$1 million, such as the US dollar, the Japanese yen, the Deutsche Mark, the Swiss franc, the pound sterling and the Canadian dollar, as well as in currencies of many developing countries and even in SDRs and Eurocurrencies. These transactions bring the Eurocurrency market and the foreign exchange market closer together.

(3) A unique interest rate structure. The Eurocurrency market interest rate system is based on the London Interbank Offered Rate (LIBOR) and the market has a small spread between deposits and loans. On the one hand, as the Eurocurrency market is not subject to statutory reserve and deposit rate ceilings, banks offer higher interest rates on deposits; on the other hand, as the Eurocurrency market is an interbank market and the lending customers are usually large banks, large companies or government agencies with high creditworthiness, the scale of transactions is huge, the risk of lending is low and the cost of lending is low, making the interest rates on lending lower.

(4) With less regulation, market risks are increasingly intensified. As the Eurocurrency market involves lending and borrowing in foreign currencies, the participants are mainly non-residents and generally not regulated by the domestic laws of any country, which makes the risks in this market increasingly intensified.

IV. Types of Eurocurrency markets

(i) Integrated type

An integrated currency market means that there are no strict boundaries between onshore operations participated by domestic residents and offshore operations carried out by non-residents, and in which domestic funds and offshore funds can be readily interchanged. The London financial market and the Hong Kong financial market are examples of such markets.

(ii) Separated type

A separated currency market refers to the separation between onshore operations pariticipated by domestic residents and offshore operations carried out by non-residents. Separated currency market helps to isolate the impact of international capital flows on domestic currency stocks and the macro economy. The international banking facilities set up in the US offshore financial markets, the offshore special accounts set up in the Tokyo offshore financial market in Japan, and the Asian currency accounts set up in the Singapore offshore financial market all fall into this category.

(ⅲ) Book-entry or bookkeeping type

These markets have little or no actual offshore financial transactions, but act as bookkeeping and transfers for other financial market transactions to avoid taxation and regulation. Offshore financial markets such as Canada, Cayman and Bermuda fall into this category.

V. Composition of the Eurocurrency market

The Eurocurrency market can be divided into the Eurocurrency credit market and the Eurobond market according to the type of borrowing and lending, the maturity of the borrowing and the nature of the business.

(ⅰ) Eurocurrency and credit markets

The Eurocurrency credit market comprises the Eurocurrency short - term credit market (borrowing periods of one year or less) and the Eurocurrency long - term credit market (borrowing periods of more than one year).

1. Eurocurrency short-term credit market

This market is primarily an interbank lending market, operating mainly in short - term funds lending of up to one year, with the shortest maturities being daily. The market relies on the creditworthiness of the participants, no collateral is required and transactions are generally concluded by telephone or telex, with turnover in the millions or tens of millions of US dollars or more. The majority of deposits in this market are the short - term idle funds of companies, banks, institutions and individuals. These funds are in turn made available through banks to companies, banks, private and official institutions in other countries for short - term working capital.

The characteristics of the European currency short - term credit market include the following:

(1) The short maturity of the traded species, generally less than 3 months.

(2) The transaction is wholesale in nature with relatively large individual transaction amounts.

(3) The transaction is flexible and convenient transactions with a wide choice of borrowing periods, borrowing currencies and borrowing locations.

(4) Based on LIBOR, the interest rates shall be negotiated between the parties.

2. Eurocurrency medium and long-term credit market

The Eurocurrency medium and long-term credit markets lend and borrow funds for periods of one year or more. The main financiers are state-owned or private companies, governments and international financial organizations around the world. Due to the long maturity of the loans, they are less liquid and therefore riskier. Lending rates are generally adjusted based on the London Interbank Offered Rate (LIBOR) and are mostly floating. The main features of transactions in this market include as follows.

(1) Longer loan terms, usually 2 to 10 years, some even up to 20 years.

（2）Loans are large, typically between \$20 million and \$50 million, but also in the billions of dollars.

（3）International syndicated loans or syndicated loans are generally used to diversify the risk.

（4）Variable interest rate, adjusted every three months or six months according to market changes.

（5）Loans must be subject to agreements and in some cases even require guarantees from governments.

（ii）European currency bond market

The European currency bond market, or Eurobond market, is a market formed by non-residents issuing bonds in the bond market of one country in the currency of a third country in order to raise funds. This market is an important part of the Eurocurrency market. The types of bonds in the Eurobond market mainly include ordinary fixed-rate bonds, floating-rate bonds, convertible bonds, warrant bonds, synthetic bonds, etc.

VI. The role of the Eurocurrency market

（i）The positive role of the Eurocurrency market

The positive effects of the Eurocurrency market on the world economy include the following:

1. Promoting financial globalization

The Eurocurrency market has broken down the national boundaries of the international financial markets, strengthening financial ties between countries and creating a global financial market through the 24-hour operation of numerous money markets.

2. Promoting international trade

The Eurocurrency market has facilitated the financing of international trade, solved the problem of foreign exchange scarcity for some countries in international payments and promoted the development of international trade.

3. Promoting the economic development of some countries

The huge amounts of money available on the Eurocurrency markets enabled the economies of Western European countries and Japan to recover and develop rapidly after the Second World War. A number of developing countries, particularly non-oil producing countries, also raised some of the funds needed for their development from the Eurocurrency markets, thus contributing to the development of their economies.

（ii）Negative impact on European currency markets

1. Increased operational risk for banks operating in the Eurocurrency deposit and loan business

The lending business in the Eurocurrency market is basically short-term deposits and long-term loans, i.e., most of the Eurocurrency deposits taken by banks are short term, while most of the Eurocurrency loans granted are long term, with a maturity mismatch, which undoubtedly increases the operational risk of the banks operating these businesses. On the other hand, Eurocurrency loans are mainly syndicated loans, and these banks will suffer losses if their customers are unable to repay them when they fall due.

2.Exacerbated volatility in the foreign exchange market

The European currency market is not subject to the financial regulations of the market location and is prone to massive international capital flows, making the foreign exchange markets of both capital inflowing and capital outflowing countries volatile and unstable.

3.Weakening the effectiveness of the implementation of national financial policies

When a country implements a tight monetary policy and raises interest rates to curb inflation, domestic companies and banks have easy access to funds from the Eurocurrency market at lower interest rates; when a country implements an expansionary monetary policy and lowers interest rates to stimulate the domestic economy, domestic banks may move funds abroad in search of higher interest income. This makes it difficult for domestic financial policy to achieve the desired effect.

Task 5 International Financial Institutions

I. International Monetary Fund

Animation Micro-lesson 3-4

International Financial Institutions, World Bank and International Monetary Fund

The International Monetary Fund, or IMF for short, was formally established by its members on 27 December 1945 in accordance with the Agreement on the International Monetary Fund signed at the Bretton Woods Conference in July 1944, with its headquarters in Washington, D.C., USA. Together with the World Bank Group and the World Trade Organization, it constitutes one of the three pillars of the international order after the Second World War.

(ⅰ) The purposes for which the International Monetary Fund was established

The International Monetary Fund was established for the following purposes:

(1) To promote international monetary cooperation and provide a means for consultation and collaboration on international monetary issues.

(2) To promote the expansion and balanced development of international trade in order to increase and maintain high levels of employment and internship income, as well as to develop the productive resources of the member parties.

(3) To stabilize international exchange rates, manipulating orderly exchange rate arrangements between members and avoiding competitive exchange rate depreciation.

(4) To assist in the establishment of a multilateral payment system for current transactions between members and the elimination of exchange controls that impede world trade.

(5) To provide temporary bonuses to members to help them correct balance of payments imbalances.

（ii）Organizational structure of the International Monetary Fund

The Board of Governors is the highest decision-making body of the IMF and is composed of a Governor and Deputy Governors appointed by each member for a five-year term. The Director is usually the Minister of Finance or the Governor of the Central Bank of the member and has stock voting rights. The deputy director has stock voting rights only in the absence of the Director. The main function of the Board is to approve new members.

（iii）Functions of the International Monetary Fund

The functions of the International Monetary Fund include are as follows：

（1）To establish and monitor exchange rate policy and rules on current account payments and currency convertibility between members.

（2）To provide emergency financial facilities, where necessary, to members experiencing balance of payments difficulties to avoid other countries （or regions） being affected by them.

（3）To provide meeting space for members on international monetary cooperation and consultation, etc.

（4）To promote cooperation between countries in the financial and monetary fields.

（5）To maintain the exchange rate order between countries.

（6）To assist in the establishment of a recurring multilateral payment system between members, etc.

（iv）Funding of the International Monetary Fund

The IMF is mainly financed by the fund shares paid by members, borrowings and trust funds from the sale of gold. Of these, the Fund's shares paid by members are the main source of funding for the IMF.

1.Fund shares paid by members

The IMF is financed primarily by contributions from its members, which are used to finance its members. A share is a certain amount of money that a member has to contribute to participate in the IMF. Each member is allocated a share, which is broadly based on the relative size of the member in the world economy. The amount of the member's share is determined by taking into account economic indicators such as the member's national income, gold and foreign exchange reserves, average imports, the rate of change in exports, and the ratio of exports to national income, and is determined through consultations among the IMF members.

2.Borrowing

Borrowing is another important source of funding for the IMF. External borrowing by the IMF, through its members or otherwise, makes up for the shortfall in quota as a source of funding. It plays an important role in providing temporary replenishment to the Fund in emergencies.

3.Gold for sale

The IMF holds approximately 90.5 million ounces of gold, making one of the largest official holders of gold globally. The IMF Articles of Agreement severely restrict the use of gold and the sale of gold is a temporary source of funding.

The IMF may sell gold or accept payments in gold from members if an 85% majority of the total voting rights of the members agrees, but the IMF cannot purchase gold or engage in other gold transactions.

(ⅴ) Main operational activities of the International Monetary Fund

1. Provision of various loans to member parties

The main day-to-day operational activity of the IMF is the provision of different types of loans to members experiencing balance of payments difficulties. The types of IMF loans have evolved. In the early days the IMF only granted ordinary loans, but later on medium-term loans, compensatory loans, buffer stock loans and some temporary loans were added.

(1) Ordinary loan.

It is the most basic IMF loan, with a maturity of up to five years, and is mainly used to cover a member's balance of payments deficit. The maximum amount of the loan is 125% of the member's share. The loan is divided into two components: a reserve component and a credit component. The former is 125% of the member's contribution and is unconditional and interest-free, but is guaranteed by the member's share of foreign currency or SDRs; the latter is 100% of the member's contribution and is divided into four tranches of 25% of each.

The first tranche is relatively easy for members to obtain and generally requires only a loan to be approved, while the second to fourth tranches are high grade credit loans with more stringent conditions that require members to provide comprehensive financial stabilization plans and to be monitored by the IMF at the time of use.

(2) Medium-term loan.

The medium-term loan, also known as the extension loan, was established in 1974 as a special loan for the long-term adjustment of members due to structural problems in production, trade, etc. The loan amount is higher than the normal loan. Its maximum loan amount is 140% of the borrowing member's share, with a standby period of 3 years and repayment starting in the fourth year after drawdown to be repaid within 10 years. The IMF disburses the loan by instalments according to the member's actual performance in achieving the objectives of the plan and implementing the policy.

(3) Export Fluctuation Compensation Loan.

The IMF established the Export Volatility Compensation Facility in February 1963. In May 1981, the IMF added that a member could also apply for a compensatory loan when the price of food imports exceeded the average price of the previous five years, causing balance of payments difficulties. In August 1988, the IMF adopted a revised proposal to combine the Contingency Facility with the original Compensatory Loan and to change the name of the loan to Compensatory and Contingency Loan.

Members may apply for this loan in the event of sudden, temporary economic factors that cause the current account balance to deviate from the desired adjustment target in the implementation of an IMF-supported economic adjustment program.

2. Exchange rate monitoring and policy coordination

In addition to providing financial loans, the International Monetary Fund carries out the following activities:

(1) Regulating the supply and allocation of international reserve assets through the issuance of SDRs.

(2) Promoting exchange rate stability through exchange rate monitoring.

(3) Coordinating balance of payments reconciliation activities of members.

(4) Promoting international monetary system reform.

3. Providing training, advice and other services to members

(1) Providing training, advice and other services to members.

(2) Collection and exchange of financial information and statistics.

II. The World Bank Group

The World Bank Group is an evolving international financial institution comprising five relatively independent institutions: the International Bank for Reconstruction and Development, the International Development Association, the International Finance Corporation, the Multilateral Investment Guarantee Agency and the International Centre for Settlement of Investment Disputes.

(i) The World Bank

The World Bank was established in December 1945 by the International Bank for Reconstruction and Development (IBRD) Agreement adopted at the Bretton Woods Conference in July 1944, with its headquarters in Washington, D.C. It opened its doors in June 1946 and became a specialized agency of the United Nations in November 1947. It is closely linked to the IMF and only IMF members are eligible to apply for membership of the World Bank. In 1980, China was reinstated as a member of the Bank and received its first loan from the Bank the following year. At present, the World Bank has 189 members.

1.The purpose of the World Bank

Although the World Bank is a for-profit organization, it does not operate to maximize profits. In accordance with the Articles of Agreement of the International Bank for Reconstruction and Development, the purposes of the World Bank are showed as follows:

(1) To assist the economic recovery and construction of member countries through investment in production undertakings and to encourage the exploitation of resources in underdeveloped countries.

(2) To promote private outward investment by way of guarantees or participation in private loans and other private investments. The use of the Bank's capital or funds raised to supplement private investment when private capital is not available to a member on reasonable terms.

(3) To encourage international investment, assisting members to increase their

productive capacity, and promoting balanced development of their international trade and improved balance of payments position.

(4) To coordinate with other international loans in providing loan guarantees.

When the World Bank was first established, it was primarily to finance the recovery of the war-torn economies of some European countries, but after 1948 when European countries began to rely mainly on the Marshall Plan of the United States for their post-war economic recovery, the World Bank shifted to providing medium and long-term loans and investments to developing countries to promote their economic and social development.

The World Bank is working to close this gap, turning the resources of rich countries into an engine of economic growth for poor countries. As one of the world's largest providers of development assistance, the World Bank supports governments in developing countries in their efforts to build schools and hospitals, supply water and electricity, prevent and treat disease and protect the environment.

2.Organization

(1) The Board Govenrs.

The Board of Governors is the supreme authority of the World Bank and consists of one Governor and one Deputy Governor from each member. Governors and Deputy Governors are appointed for a five-year term and may be re-elected, with the Deputy Governors having the right to vote in the absence of the Governors. The members of the Council are generally the Ministers of Finance or the Governors of the Central Banks of each member. The Council meets once a year, usually in conjunction with the IMF's Board of Governors.

(2) Executive Board.

The Executive Board is the body responsible for organizing and conducting the day-to-day business, exercising the powers delegated to it by the Board of Governors. The Executive Board consists of 25 Executive Directors. The President of the World Bank is a U.S. citizen who serves a five-year term and is eligible for re-election. The President is the Chairman of the Executive Board and is responsible for the overall management of the Bank. In general, the President does not have the right to vote and may only cast a casting vote in the event of a tie between the votes of the Executive Board. The Executive Director cannot exercise any authority alone, nor can he make commitments or represent the Bank alone, without the express authority of the Executive Board.

(3) Administrative bodies.

The Bank's executive management consists of the President, a number of Vice-Presidents, Directors and other staff. The President is the head of the Administration and is responsible for the day-to-day management of the Bank and the appointment and dismissal of the Bank's officers and staff.

3.Sources of funding

(1) World Bank shares paid by each member party.

Like the IMF, the World Bank was established on a shareholding basis, with each member subscribing to the Bank's shares. Countries' contributions are based on their national income, their total trade and their share of the IMF.

The World Bank was established with an authorized capital of US$10 billion, of which 20% was paid-in, of which 2% was paid in gold or US dollars and 18% in national currencies; 80% of the capital to be paid-in was kept by the members and paid in gold, US dollars or the required currency when needed. After several capital increases by the World Bank, the paid-up capital is only 6% of the contributed share capital.

(2) External borrowing.

The World Bank disburses an average of over US$20 billion in loans each year, and relying on paid-up equity from its members is far from sufficient to meet its funding needs. The Bank relies primarily on borrowing from international financial markets as its main source of credit funding.

Of these, funds borrowed from the issuance of international bonds, which cover 70% of the funds required for loan disbursement, are the main source of World Bank credit facilities.

The World Bank issues bonds in two ways: one is to sell medium and short-term bonds directly to member governments and central banks; the other is to sell bonds to the private investment market through underwriters such as investment banks and commercial banks. At present, the World Bank has become the world's largest non-resident borrower.

(3) Assignment of claims.

In order to speed up and expand the liquidity of the credit facilities, the World Bank assigns the claims on the loaned funds to private investors such as commercial banks, thereby recovering a portion of the credit facilities, which has also become a source of funding for the Bank.

4. The World Bank operations

(1) Loans to Members. The World Bank provides long-term loans to members and private enterprises guaranteed by member governments. The terms of the loans can be up to 30 years (with a grace period of 5 years) and the loans have a variable interest rates, but the rates of the loans are generally below market rates.

Loans must be used for specific projects, such as agriculture, transport, energy and sanitation, and the borrowers must be able to repay. The loan processes are rigorous and the approval time is long, usually taking one and a half to two years.

The World Bank's loans are denominated in US dollars and only provide the foreign exchange component required for the project, which is approximately 30% to 40% of the total project amount.

(2) Provide extensive technical assistance to members; dispatch experts, provide advisory services and help train middle and senior officials of members in economic management, especially project management.

(ⅱ) The International Development Association

The International Development Association (IDA), a subsidiary of the World Bank, was founded in September 1960 and opened for business in November 1960. It is based in Washington, D.C. and it has 169 members.

In 1980, China resumed its legal seat in the World Bank Group and became a member party of the International Development Association (IDA) at the same time. China's voting power in the IDA is 344 829 votes, accounting for 1.88% of the total voting power. As of July 1999, the IDA had provided a total of US$10.2 billion in soft loans to China, implementing 69 projects. As of July 1999, IDA stopped lending to China. In December 2007, China contributed US$30 million to IDA.

1. The aim of the IDA

The aim of the IDA is to help members in less developed parts of the world to promote economic development and improve productivity and living standards.

2. Organizational structure

The directors, executive directors and managers of the International Development Association are all staffed by their World Bank counterparts. It can be said that there are "two heads and one set of staff", but they are legally and financially independent of each other.

3.Sources of funding

(1) Capital contributed by member parties. Member parties are divided into two groups according to their level of economic development.

Group I: Developed countries (regions) or countries with higher incomes (regions), where contributions must be paid in gold or foreign currency.

Group II: Developing countries (territories), where 10% of the contributed shares are payable in foreign currency and the remaining 90% are payable in local currency.

(2) Supplementary funding from Members, mainly from Group I countries, has reached US$10 billion.

4. IDA's operations

The IDA specializes in providing lenient, long-term, interest-free loan financing to member governments in less developed regions, i. e., countries that cannot afford to borrow from the International Bank for Reconstruction and Development, to address the development needs of these countries (regions). For this reason, the IDA is known as the Bank's "soft-loan window".

(1) Loan recipients: Low-income developing countries (GNP per capita below US$925).

(2) Loan term: Long-term concessional loan of up to 50 years (including a 10-year grace period). The first 10 years are a grace period, the second 10 years are repayable at 1% per annum and the next 30 years at 3% per annum.

(3) Interest on loan: Interest-free loan with only 0.75% handling fee.

(4) Loans are denominated in SDRs and may be repaid in part or in full in national currency.

(ⅲ) International Finance Corporation

Founded on 24 July 1956, the IFC became a specialized agency of the United Nations in February 1957 and now has 175 members. The IFC was the first intergovernmental organization to have the promotion of private enterprise as its main objective.

1. Purpose of the IFC

To encourage international private capital flows to developing countries (regions) by providing loans or investments without government guarantees to priority private enterprises of members, particularly in developing countries (regions), in conjunction with World Bank operations to promote the growth of private enterprise in these countries (regions) and to foster their economic development.

2. Organizational structure

The directors, executive directors and managers of the IFC are also held by their World Bank counterparts, "two brands, one set of people", but the IFC has its own operational staff.

3. Sources of funding

The IFC was established with an authorized capital of US$100 million. The remainder was financed mainly by borrowings from the World Bank and the financial markets, in addition to net proceeds from operations in investments and lending.

4. IFC's business activities

The IFC provides loans to private enterprises of developing country (regional) members, generally tending to manufacturing, processing and mining industries. There are two types of loans, A and B. A is provided directly by the IFC; B is a loan provided by commercial banks organized by the IFC. The specific loan conditions are as follows.

(1) Productive private enterprises cannot obtain capital from other sources on reasonable terms.

(2) The maturity period is normally 7 to 15 years and repayments must be made in the original borrowed currency.

(3) It is a profitable project that does not require a government guarantee.

(4) Below market rates and slightly above World Bank lending rates.

In addition, the IFC can also take a direct equity stake, generally not exceeding 25%, but with a return of 10% or more, and with a strict selection of projects.

Mini Case

In 2013, during a visit to Southeast Asia, President Xi Jinping proposed the establishment of the Asian Infrastructure Investment Bank (referred to as "AIIB"), which received positive responses from many Asian countries. In June 2015, representatives of 50 intending founding members signed the Agreement on the Asian Infrastructure Investment Bank

(AIIB), followed by seven other countries. In December 2015, the AIIB Agreement met the legal requirements for entry into force and the AIIB was formally established. In January 2016, the AIIB officially opened for business. As of 29 July 2020, the number of members of the AIIB has increased from 57 at the time of its opening to 103, covering six continents, including Asia, Europe, Africa, North America, South America and Oceania. The majority of members are developing countries, but developed countries, including the UK, France, Germany and Canada, have also been included.

The AIIB is an intergovernmental Asian regional multilateral development institution established to promote regional infrastructure connectivity and economic integration in Asia, and to strengthen cooperation between China and other Asian countries (regions).

In the context of what you have learnt in this project, please consider what the establishment of the Asian Infrastructure Investment Bank means for our country and what impact it will have on global economic development.

Mind Map

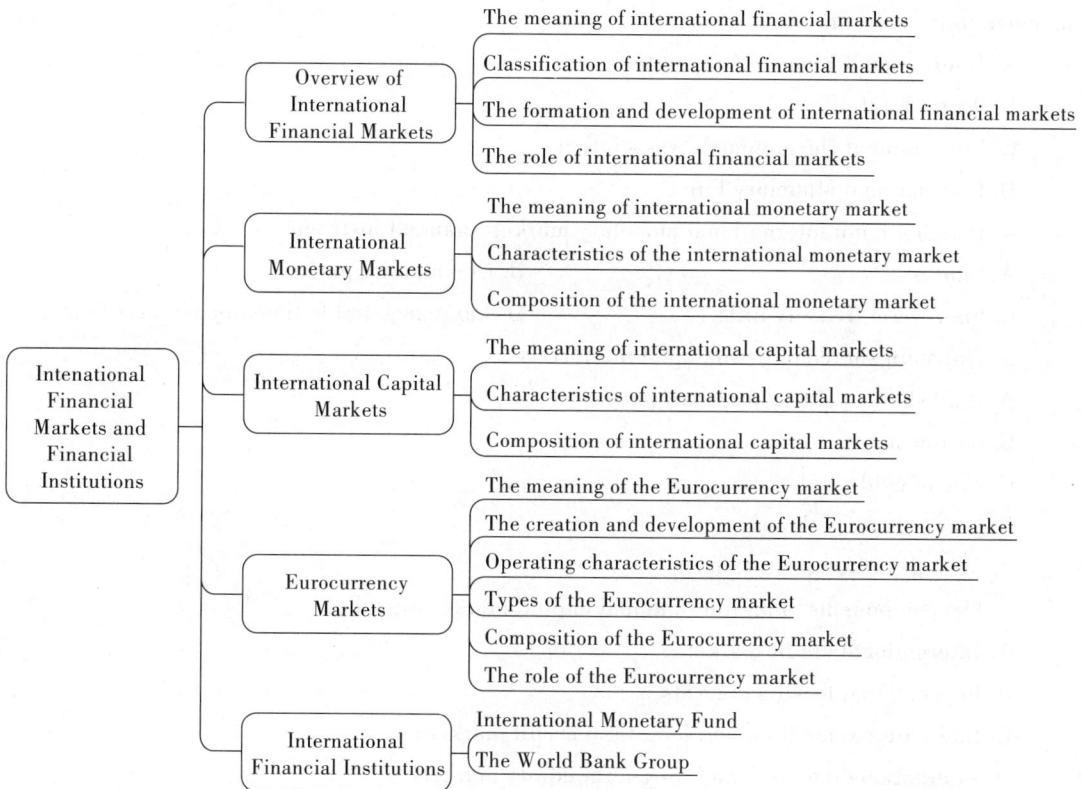

Project Training

I. Single-choice questions

1. Which are not characteristics of international monetary markets: (   ) .

A. Short terms, with the shortest financing term being only one day and the longest being no more than one year

B. The purpose of the transaction is to address the need for long-term underfunding

C. Financial instruments are highly liquid and those traded on international monetary markets are generally short term, highly liquid and highly liquid in realization

D. High creditworthiness of the dealers, large scale of financing, low borrowing costs, fast turnover of funds and high liquidity

2. Bonds issued by non-residents in the US financial market in US dollars are called (   ) .

A. Mighty Dog Bonds   B. Samurai Bonds

C. Yankee Bonds   D. Panda Bonds

3. The international financial institution that lends to productive private enterprises in member countries is the (   ) .

A. International Finance Corporation

B. World Bank

C. International Development Association

D. International Monetary Fund

4. Which are not international monetary market financial instruments: (   ) .

A. Shares   B. Commercial papers

C. Short-term treasury bills   D. Large negotiable time deposit certificates

5. The main source of financing of the IMF is (   ) .

A. fund shares paid by member parties

B. borrowing

C. sale of gold

D. proceeds from claims

II. Multiple choice questions

1. The components of an international capital market include (   ) .

A. International credit markets

B. International leasing markets

C. International medium and long-term credit markets

D. International medium and long-term equity markets

2. Which of the following statements about the characteristics of international capital markets are correct: (   ) .

A. Longer financing terms, typically over one year or even decades

B. The size of the transaction is huge and the purpose of the transaction is generally to add capital or cover the fiscal deficit

C. The financial instruments traded have long maturities, are less liquid and are more risky

D. None of the above options are correct

3. According to the classification of financing term, the international financial market can be divided into (   ).

A. international foreign exchange market

B. international currency market

C. international capital markets

D. offshore financial markets

4. Which of the following are the operating characteristics of the Eurocurrency market: (   ).

A. The market is extensive, not limited by geography; and transactions are mainly made through modern communication networks

B. The market has a huge trading scale, a wide variety of transactions and currencies, and is extremely active in financial innovation

C. Less regulated and increasingly risky markets

D. Higher spreads on deposits and loans in the Eurocurrency market

5. Which of the following are the components of the Eurocurrency market: (   ).

A. Eurocurrency short-term credit market

B. Eurocurrency medium and long-term credit market

C. Eurocurrency bond market, i.e., Eurobond market

D. All of the above

III. Judgement Questions

1. International financial markets can be classified into international monetary markets and international capital markets according to the content of the business they operate. (   )

2. The issuer, the market for the issue and the nominal value of the Eurobond belong to different countries. .   (   )

3. European currency refers to the currency issued by European countries.   (   )

4. The Eurocurrency market was formerly known as the Eurodollar market.   (   )

5. IFC loans are made to the governments of the respective member parties.   (   )

IV. Practical analysis questions

Since November 2003, the People's Bank of China has been providing RMB clearing services in Hong Kong. 2004 saw the beginning of the development of the offshore RMB market when Hong Kong banks began to offer personal RMB business, including deposits, remittances, exchange and credit card business, on a trial basis outside Mainland China.

In 2010, the offshore RMB market took initial shape when the People's Bank of China and the Hong Kong Monetary Authority signed the Hong Kong RMB Business Clearing

Agreement and issued a joint announcement that RMB could be settled in Hong Kong from 19 July 2010. With this, the offshore RMB market was officially launched and Hong Kong has since taken its first step towards building an offshore RMB financial market, which has taken shape after more than a decade of development.

On 18 April 2012, London became the world's second largest offshore RMB trading center after Hong Kong with the launch of the City's RMB Business Centre. With the growing international recognition and acceptance of the RMB, the development of the offshore RMB market has entered the fast lane. After Hong Kong and London, more and more international financial centers are looking to become offshore RMB financial markets.

In February 2013, the People's Bank of China authorized the Industrial and Commercial Bank of China Singapore Branch to act as the clearing bank for RMB business in Singapore, which means that RMB supply can be obtained directly through the USD RMB market.

Based on the above materials, please work in groups to collect further information and research why China should vigorously develop an offshore RMB market, then create a PPT presentation.

Project Four
Foreign Exchange and Exchange Rates

Learning Objectives

Knowledge Objectives:

Understand the concepts and types of foreign exchange and exchange rates; be able to correctly identify different types of exchange rates; understand the stages, characteristics, similarities and differences, advantages and disadvantages of fixed and floating exchange rate systems; understand the history of RMB exchange rate regime; understand the factors affecting exchange rate fluctuations and the impact of exchange rate fluctuations.

Competency Objectives:

·Be able to distinguish the characteristics, advantages and disadvantages of fixed and floating exchange rates correctly; be able to analyze how various factors affect the movement of exchange rates and how changes in exchange rates affect each factor.

Operational Objectives:

Correctly identify the method of marking up in exchange rate quotations; be able to perform exchange rate hedging.

Course Introduction

A day as a foreign exchange trader

Michael Bamber is a foreign exchange trader, let's take a look at his day:

1. Get up at 6:00 am and turn on his computer at 6:10 am to check orders, rain or shine!

2. After checking his orders and the latest market situation, Bamber does not rush to start trading, but to meditate. (Note: meditation is a highly prized practice among many traders abroad).

3. After this, Bamber begins to analyze the target trade. He is a technical trader, specializing in trend analysis and K-chart analysis.

4. Lunch is simpler than instant noodles. The food provides enough energy and keep him in shape.

5. At 3:00 pm, the market is at its peak and Bamber is busy. From time to time, he also communicates with the broker account manager on trading issues.

6. Trading GBP / CHF is profitable. Overall, the day is good and Bamber is satisfied.

7. At 7:00 pm, Bamber drives to the gym on time to do some exercise as his best way to refresh his mind.

8. At 9:00 pm, when he gets home, Bamber reviews his trading strategy for the day and looks for opportunities to continue trading.

9. At almost 00:00 am, Bamber is not eager to rest, but writes his trading diary before going to bed, making it a habit to record his daily trading highlights.

10. At 00:45, Bamber goes to bed.

We can see from Bamber's trading routine that he is definitely serious about his work. As a full-time trader, Bamber has never slacked off. His strong self-discipline is also the reason why he is able to help his clients make money.

Source: Compiled by the author from relevant sources.

Discussion: Seeing the day of a forex trader, think about if you were him, would you be willing and able to do this job?

Task 1   Overview of Foreign Exchange and Exchange Rates

I.The concept of foreign exchange

Most countries in the world have their own currencies, China uses the RMB, the USA uses the US dollar and the UK uses the pound sterling. However, any foreign economic interaction is inseparable from foreign exchange.Trade between countries gives rise to the exchange of different currencies. For example, when a Chinese investor purchases goods, services or financial assets from a foreign country, he or she must convert the RMB into foreign currencies. In China, with the growing reform and opening up, foreign trade and economic transactions are becoming more and more frequent, and more and more business involving foreign exchange is being conducted. Therefore, it is essential to learn the basics of foreign exchange as part of the international finance curriculum.

(i) The concept of dynamic and static foreign exchange

1. The concept of dynamic foreign exchange

Dynamic foreign exchange is an activity whereby the currency of one country is exchanged for the currency of another country in the settlement of international claims and debt relationship of specialised business activity. This activity is not expressed as direct delivery of cash, but it takes the form of entrusted payments or transfers of claims.

For example, a Japanese exporter exporting cars to the United States settles an account with the US importer by sending a cheque in US dollars payable to Bank A in New York. The bank in New York as the payer pays the Japanese exporter a cheque in US dollars, which in turn is deposited in foreign currency with Bank A. In this way, the US importer transfers its claim in Bank A to the Japanese exporter's account in Bank A. The Japanese exporter then has a foreign exchange claim in Bank A in the United States. As can be seen, dynamic foreign exchange refers to international settlement activities and behaviours.

2. The concept of static foreign exchange

Static foreign exchange can be further divided into two categories: broad and narrow.

Broadly, foreign exchange refers to the international debt settlement process of the formation of the financial assets. Specifically, it can be divided into the payment documents in foreign currency, letters of credit and foreign currency cash, such as bills in foreign currency and the foreign debt.

Foreign exchange in a narrow sense simply refers to the international settlement of debts in the process of payment documents in foreign currency, such as the foreign currency cash.

The Regulations of the People's Republic of China on Foreign Exchange Administration (amended in August 2008) clearly state that foreign exchange in China refers to various means of payment and assets expressed in foreign currencies that can be used to settle debts internationally.

The scope of foreign exchange is: ① foreign currency cash, including banknotes, minted coins; ② foreign currency payment documents or payment instruments, including bills, bank deposit certificates including bills, bank deposit certificates, bank cards, etc.; ③ foreign currency securities, including bonds, stocks, etc.; ④ special drawing rights; ⑤ other foreign exchange assets.

Animation Micro-lesson 4-1

Foreign Exchange and Major Foreign Currencies

Regarding the definition of foreign exchange, the following two points need to be clarified:

(1) Foreign exchange must be assets expressed in a foreign currency. Take the example of an import/export trade, suppose a British business imports a batch of goods from the US and both parties agree to settle in US dollars. Accordingly, the UK importer should pay the US exporter in US dollars. The US dollar is a foreign currency to the company in the UK, so this company does pay for assets expressed in foreign currency, i.e., foreign exchange. However, the US

dollar received by the US exporter is only the national currency but not foreign currency, so the US exporters receiving US dollars cannot be called foreign exchange. If they had agreed upon to use the euro for settlement, then both the American and the British companies use a foreign currency.

（2）Foreign exchange must be internationally redeemable, accepted and transferable by countries, freely convertible into other forms of assets, or means of payment currency and foreign currency certificates that are convertible into other forms of assets or means of payment. On the contrary, all foreign currency certificates, bad checks or dishonored bills of exchange that cannot be reimbursed internationally shall not be regarded as foreign exchange.

（ii）Names and symbols of the major world currencies

Today, in the process of currency exchange, it is popular to use codes to indicate the names of currencies in the world. The table below gives a brief overview of the major currencies in the world today, including the countries and regions in which they are used, their standard Chinese/English names, currency symbols and the system of currency conversion. The table below provides a brief overview of the world's major currencies today, including the countries and regions in which they are used, their standard Chinese/English names, currency symbols and the system of currency conversion. According to the International Organization for Standardization（ISO）4217 standard, each currency is defined by a three-letter code. Each currency is represented by a three-letter code（as shown in Table 4-1）.

Table 4-1　　　　　　　　Currency names and symbols

Country	Curency name		Curency symbol	Subsidiary curency carry system
	Chinese	English	Standard symbol	
China	人民币元	Renminbi Yuan	CNY	1 CNY=10 jiao=100cents
USA	美元	U.S. Dollar	USD	1 USD=100 cents
EUR	欧元	Euro	EUR	1 EUR=100 euro cents
Japanese	日元	Japanese Yen	JPY	（none）
Hong Kong China	港元	Houn Kong Dollar	HKD	1 HKD=100 cents
UK	英镑	Pound	GBP	1 GBP=100 new pences
Australia	澳大利亚元	Australian Dollar	AUD	1 AUD=100 cents
New Zealand	新西兰元	New Zealand Dollar	NZD	1NZD=100 cents
Singapore	新加坡元	Singapore Dollar	SGD	1SGD=100 cents
Swiss	瑞士法郎	Swiss Franc	CHF	1 CHF=100 centimes
Canada	加元	Canadian Dollar	CAD	1 CAD=100 cents
Malaysia	马来西亚林吉特	Malaysian Ringgit	MYR	1MYR=100 cents
Thailand	泰铢	Thai Baht	THB	1THB=100 satang

Source: Collated based on relevant information.

II. Exchange rate and pricing method

An American wants to visit Italy, but he holds US dollars, while the currency in Italy is the euro. If he wants to fulfil his wish, he must exchange his dollars for euros. There must be an exchange rate between dollars and euros. This rate is the "Foreign Exchange Rate", that is, a certain unit of a country's currency and a certain number of another country's currency in exchange for the proportional relationship. For example, on 30 June 2019, the exchange rate of the euro against the US dollar is US$1.15. The exchange rate is the ratio of the euro to the dollar, or the price of one euro expressed as US$1.15.

The exchange rate is an exchange ratio that reflects the value of different national currencies in relation to each other. The exchange rate plays an important role in international economic trade.

(ⅰ) Changes in exchange rates

Changes in exchange rates are usually expressed in terms of appreciation and depreciation. For example, a commodity is worth 100 RMB and if the exchange rate of the dollar to the RMB is 6.85, the price of this item on the international market is US$14.60. If the USD/CNY exchange rate rises to 7, i.e., the USD appreciates (the RMB depreciates) , then the item can be bought for less USD. The price of this commodity on the international market would then be US$14.29, so the price of the commodity on the international market will be lower, which is beneficial to the buyer. Conversely, if the exchange rate of the US dollar against the RMB falls to 6.5, i.e., the dollar depreciates (the RMB appreciates) , the price of the good on the international market would be US$15.38. The price of the commodity on the international market is US$15.38, which is favorable to the buyer. This is the effect of changes in the exchange rate on international trade.

Knowledge Link 4-1

Comparison and contrast of exchange rates and interest rates

The exchange rate is the ratio of the exchange of two currencies while the interest rate is the cost of using the currency. The two are the different manifestations of the external and internal value of a country's currency, but they are closely related.

Generally speaking, if the interest rate of a country is relatively higher than that of other countries, it will stimulate the inflow of foreign funds into the country and the outflow of domestic funds will decrease. This will lead to a capital account surplus and a higher exchange rate for the domestic currency. Conversely, this will lead to a decline in the exchange rate of a country's domestic currency.

(ⅱ) Methods of exchange quotation

Since the exchange rate is the rate of exchange between two currencies, when making a mark-up, it is necessary to determine whether it is expressed in the domestic currency or in a foreign currency. The method of expressing the exchange rate varies depending on the standard chosen. Currently, there are two main methods of expressing exchange rates in the world, namely the direct and indirect methods.

Animation Micro-lesson 4-2

Exchange Rate and its Pricing Methods

Direct Quotation is a method of quotation in which a certain number of units (usually multiples of 1 or 100) of foreign currency are used as a standard and converted into a certain amount of domestic currency. In other words, the price of a foreign currency is expressed in the national currency. Since this method uses a certain unit of foreign currency as a basis for the amount of domestic currency payable, i.e., the amount of domestic currency payable to obtain a certain unit of foreign currency. Therefore, we also call it the "giving quotation". For example, the foreign exchange trading centre in China publishes the 100USD = 687.85CNY, where 100USD is a unit of foreign currency and 687.85CNY is the price payable in RMB for 100USD.

Indirect Quotation refers to a quotation method in which a certain integer unit (usually a multiple of 1 or 100) of the domestic currency is converted into several foreign currencies. In contrast to the direct quotation method, the indirect quotation method calculates the amount of foreign currency receivable based on a certain unit of domestic currency, that is, how much foreign currency requires payment of a certain unit of domestic currency, so it is also called the "receivable quotation method". For example, the listed price of Thai Baht published by China's Foreign Exchange Trade Center is 1CNY= 4.5005 THB, where 1 CNY is a certain unit of local currency, and 4.5005 Baht is the price of Thai Baht obtained by spending 1 CNY.

(iii) The difference and connection between the two pricing methods

1. Different criteria for the two mark-up methods

In general, we refer to the currency that remains constant in quantity as the "base currency" and the currency that changes in quantity over time as the "quoted currency".

In the direct method, the foreign currency is the base currency and the local currency is the quoted currency.

In the indirect method, the local currency is used as the base currency and the foreign currency is used as the quoted currency.

2. The difference between two pricing methods in their ability to indicate a rising or falling foreign exchange market

An increase in the foreign exchange rate means a rise in the value of the foreign currency and a fall in the value of the domestic currency. A fall in the foreign exchange rate means a fall in the value of the foreign currency and a rise in the value of the national currency. Due to the existence of these two valuation methods, the expression of the ups and downs of foreign exchange rates is different.

Under the direct method of valuation: the amount of foreign currency is fixed, if the value of the foreign currency rises, it is necessary to pay more than the original amount of the national currency in order to exchange the same amount of foreign currency; conversely, if the value of the foreign currency falls, in order to exchange it for the same amount of foreign currency, you will only have to pay less than the original amount in the national currency.

Under the indirect method of valuation: the amount of domestic currency remains unchanged and the amount of foreign currency receivable increases or decreases with the value of the domestic currency. If the foreign exchange rate rises, the amount of foreign currency received is less than before; If the exchange rate falls, the amount of foreign currency received is more than before.

3. Direct quotation and indirect quotation are reciprocal

$$\frac{1}{\text{Direct bidding method}} = \text{Indirect quotation method}$$

$$\frac{1}{\text{Indirect bidding method}} = \text{Direct quotation method}$$

For example, 1USD is worth 6.8785 CNY, which is the direct pricing method. Conversely, it is the indirect pricing method, i.e.,1 CNY is worth about 0.1454 USD （1/6.8785）.

III. Types of exchange rates

According to different classification criteria, we can divide the exchange rate into the following categories:

（i）Division according to the bank trading of foreign exchange perspective

Teaching Video 4-1

Types of Exchange Rates

The exchange rate can be divided into the buying rate, the selling rate and the intermediate rate from the perspective of the bank buying and selling foreign exchange.

1. Buying Rate Price

Buying Rate/Bid Price, also known as the buying price, is the price banks use when buying foreign currency. It also includes the buying rate of foreign cash and the buying rate of foreign currency. The cash buying price refers to the price that banks use to buy foreign exchange cash in their home currency, while the spot buying price refers to the price that banks use to buy foreign exchange cash in their home currency. Normally, the cash buying price is lower than the spot buying price. This is because when buying foreign currency notes, banks are usually required to accumulate to a certain amount after which the pile of notes will be deposited. The bank is not earning interest during the interval of time.

In addition, in the process of transporting foreign currency notes to foreign banks, freight and insurance costs have to be paid, and banks have to pass these costs on to the sellers of foreign currency notes. The bank must transfer these costs to the customer who sells the foreign currency notes, so the bank usually buys the foreign currency notes at a price lower than the spots price.

2. Selling Rate Price

Selling Rate/Offer Price, also known as the selling price, is the price banks use when selling foreign currency. It also includes the Selling Price of Cash and the Selling Price of Foreign Exchange. As there is no process of interest generation and transportation when banks sell foreign currency, the selling price of banknotes is usually the same as the selling price of foreign currency. There are also some banks that simply indicate the "selling price" without specifying whether the currency is in cash or foreign currency.

3.Intermediate exchange rates

The arithmetic average of the buying rate and the selling rate, namely: （Buying rate + selling rate） /2. It's called the central rate, also known as the central price.

Interbank foreign exchange transactions are converted at the mid-rate; the exchange rate announced by the media such as TV and the Internet is also often for the intermediate exchange rate. Economists' analysis of economic phenomena and foreign exchange market experts' analysis of the market usually quote intermediate exchange rate. However, the intermediate exchange rate is generally not used for customer trading.

4. Notes on bank quotes

It is important to emphasize that both the buying rate and the selling rate are introduced from the perspective of the quoting bank. The purpose of selling foreign exchange is to make a profit, i.e., to make a difference by buying low and selling high. The difference between the buying and selling price of foreign exchange is the amount that the bank gains from buying and selling foreign exchange, generally 1‰~5‰ of the differerce between the buying and selling price of foreign exchange. In the foreign exchange market, the difference between the purchase and sale price is usually expressed as "basis points", and each basis point stands for one over ten thousand （that is 0.0001）.

The foreign exchange market usually uses two-way quotes to offer, that is, to quote the bid price and the ask price at the same time. The exchange rates quoted are small in the first case and large in the second. However, the meaning of the exchange rate is different under different pricing methods.

（1） Under the direct pricing method, the first local currency digit of a given amount of foreign currency represents the "bid price", i.e., the amount of local currency that the bank will pay to the customer when it sells the foreign currency. The latter figure represents the "selling price", i.e., the amount of local currency that the bank receives from the customer when selling a foreign currency.

（2） Under the indirect method, the first foreign currency figure after a certain amount of local currency represents the "selling price", i.e., the amount of foreign currency paid to the customer when the bank receives a certain amount of local currency and sells the foreign currency; The next foreign currency number after a certain amount of local currency represents the "bid price", i.e., a certain amount of local currency the bank pays to buy foreign currency is the amount of foreign currency charged to the customer.

For example, on 28 July 2019, in the Bank of China's foreign exchange quotation （using the direct mark-up method）, the exchange rate of USD to RMB is 1USD=6.8661/6.8952CNY. The former figure, CNY6.8661/USD, is the bid price of the US dollar, i.e., the bank buys 1 USD and pays the customer 6.8661 CNY. The latter figure CNY6.8952/USD is the selling price of the US dollar, i.e., the bank sells 1 USD and receives 6.8952 RMB from the customer. The difference of 0.0291RMB （6.8952 - 6.8661） is the bank's profit on this transaction.

Furthermore, on 28 July 2019, in the Bank of China's foreign exchange quotation （using the indirect quotation method）, the exchange rate between RMB and Thai Baht is 1CNY= 4.4841/4.4909THB. The former figure THB4.4841/CNY is the selling price of Thai Baht, i.e., the bank charges the customer 1RMB for selling 4.4841 THB; the latter figure THB4.4909/CNY is the buying price of the Thai Baht., i.e., the bank buys 4.4909 Baht and pays the customer 1RMB. The difference is 0.0068RMB （4.4909 - 4.4841）.

It is important to note that in both the direct and indirect mark-up methods, banks buy foreign currency at a low price and sell it at a high price.

Knowledge Link 4-2

Cash and spot exchange

Cash and spot exchange are caused by China's foreign exchange management system, and are two different forms of foreign exchange assets held by China's residents. Cash points to the foreign currency in paper money held by domestic reidents,and it is specific,real foreign notes and coins,such as US dollar, Japnese yen,euro,Australian dollar and Canadian dollar. Spot exchange refers to the foreign exchange deposits remitted to China from foreign banks, as well as foreign currency bills, promissory notes, traveler's checks and other international settlement documents that banks can directly enter into their accounts through electronic transactions. Spot exchange can also be understood as the foreign currency on the book,which is the foreign currency held in the customer's bank account and cannot be taken out, as it becomes cash if it is withdrawn.

In essence, both foreign exchange cash and spot exchange are the amount of foreign exchange owned by customers, and there is no essential difference in value. However, in terms of the use and management, there is still a big difference: while transferring abroad, spot exchange can be imported and exported directly, under the limit of China's foreign exchange management policy,freely transfer out or from outside the entry,and there is no transfer of phisical form,can be directly remitted or direct import,just the transfer on bookkeeping. Accordingly, foreign spot exchange transfer and remittance are more convenient. And cash is different, theoretically, the cash on the account cannot be remitted directly abroad, the cash in the hand of client can only be carried out of the country along with client. Certainly, our country has certain limitation and requirement to the foreign currency cash that carries by persons, and any amount that exceeds this scale should be declared.

The difference between cash and spot exchange is that cash can be deposited or withdrawn, while spot exchange can only be withdrawn after it has been converted into cash; cash cannot be remitted directly to foreign countries and can only be remitted after it has been converted into spot exchange and the spot exchange can be made directly.

Source: Compiled by the author from relevant sources.

Animation Micro-lesson 4-3

Bank of China foreign exchange rates are shown in Table 4-2.

Foreign Exchange Price

Table 4-2 Bank of China Foreign Exchange Rates

No.	Name	Buying Rate	Cash Buying Rate	Selling Rate	Cash Selling Rate
1	ZAR	48.0500	44.3600	48.3700	52.0600
2	USD	686.6100	681.0200	689.5200	689.5200
3	TWD	–	21.3400	–	23.0100
4	THB	22.1900	21.5100	22.3700	23.0500
5	SGD	500.2800	484.8500	503.8000	505.3000
6	SEK	72.1100	69.8800	72.6900	72.8900
7	RUB	10.8000	10.1400	10.8800	11.3000
8	NZD	454.5500	440.5300	457.7500	463.3600
9	NOK	78.5300	76.1100	79.1700	79.3900
10	MYR	167.3100	—	168.8200	—
11	MOP	85.5100	82.6400	85.8500	88.3600
12	KRW	0.5789	0.5585	0.5835	0.6047
13	JPY	6.3065	6.1106	6.3529	6.3564
14	HKD	87.8100	87.1600	88.1600	88.1600
15	GBP	848.6900	822.3200	854.9400	857.0100
16	EUR	762.2300	738.5500	767.8500	769.5600
17	DKK	101.9900	98.8400	102.8100	103.1000
18	CHF	689.7000	668.4100	694.5400	696.8300
19	CAD	519.9800	503.5600	523.8100	525.0800
20	AUD	473.5000	458.7900	476.9800	478.1500

Source: The author collates the information based on the relevant information.

(ii) Different calculation methods

According to the different calculation methods, it can be divided into base exchange rates and arbitrage exchange rates.

1. Base exchange rate

Base exchange rate is a rate based on the exchange rate between a country's currency and a key currency in the international arena. All countries generally choose a key currency that is most commonly used in their foreign economic transactions. The exchange rate is the base rate.

Many countries choose the US dollar as their key currency. The exchange rate between the national currency and the US dollar is used as the base rate. When banks quote exchange rates between countries, they usually only quote the base rate. The exchange rate between other foreign currencies and the national currency is converted according to the base rate of each country.

2. Arbitrage exchange rates

The exchange rate between the two currencies is calculated indirectly by using the exchange rate of each currency in the key currency. The exchange rates of currency A to currency B and currency A to currency C are known, and you want to know the currency of country B to country C or the currency of country C to country B, where currency A is the key currency.

Under the two-way quotation method, the calculation process of the arbitrage exchange rate is as follows:

Example 1 :The known USD/HKD and EUR/USD exchange rates are:

USD/HKD=7.7586/7.7665,　EUR/USD=1.3885/1.3975

Multiplication of the same side: To know the exchange rate of EUR/HKD, you can calculate it as follows:

EUR/HKD = （EUR/USD）× （USD/HKD）

　　　　 = （7.7586×1.3885）/ （7.7665×1.3975）

　　　　 =10.773/10.854

1EUR = 10.773/10.854 HKD

1USD=7.7586 / 7.7665 HKD

（multiply by the same side）

1EUR=1.3885 / 1.3975 USD

Example 2: The known exchange rates for EUR/USD and GBP/USD are:

EUR/USD=1.3885/1.3975, GBP/USD=1.5695/1.5760

Cross Division: To know the exchange rate of EUR/GBP, you can apply it as follows:

EUR/GBP = （EUR/USD）÷ （GBP/USD）

　　　　 = （1.3885÷1.5760）/ （1.3975÷1.5695）

　　　　 =0.8810/0.8904

1EUR = 0.8810/0.8904 GBP

1EUR=1.3885 /1.3975 USD

（cross division）

1GBP=1.5695 /1.5760 USD

According to this, the rules and steps for arbitrage exchange rates can be summarized as follows:

（1）Step 1: Determine whether to "multiply" or "divide".

（2）Step 2: Judge "who multiplies whom" or "who divides whom".

If multiplied, then: （decimal × decimal）/ （large × large）

If divided, then: （decimal ÷ large）/ （large ÷ decimal）

(iii) Division according to the delivery period of foreign exchange transactions

According to the delivery period of foreign exchange transactions, the exchange rate can be divided into spot exchange rate and forward exchange rate.

1. Spot Rate

It refers to the exchange rate on which delivery is made in principle within two business days (T+2) after the transaction of foreign exchange. Spot rate is the basis for quotations in the foreign exchange market.

2. Forward Rate

It refers to the exchange rate of which delivery will be made in a future period of time after the foreign exchange transaction is completed (the transaction and delivery will not be carried out at the same time), and it is to be agreed upon the time of the transaction. The delivery period for forwarding foreign exchange, is usually 1 month to 1 year. Unlike spot rates, at the same point in time, there will be multiple forward rates for different delivery periods in existence. For example, 30 days, 90 days, 180 days, 360 days, etc. Forward rates are based on spot rates and reflect changes in spot rates. They are based on spot rates and reflect trends in spot rates. In general, spot rates and forward rates move in the same direction.

(iv) Division from the instruments used in foreign exchange trading

Divided by the instruments used in foreign exchange trading, the exchange rate can be divided into telegraphic transfer rate, mail transfer rate and demand draft transfer rate.

1. Telegraphic Transfer Rate (T/T Rate).

The telegraphic transfer rate is the rate used by a bank to notify its foreign branches or correspondent banks of payments by quicker means of telecommunication. The time taken to receive payment for a transaction by wire transfer is quick and the bank can hardly tie up the customer's funds. Therefore, the telegraphic transfer rate is the highest. In market economy countries, the buying and selling prices used in inter-bank foreign exchange transactions are the rate of telegraphic transfer. The daily newspaper reports on foreign exchange quotes in the spot exchange rate are also the telegraphic exchange rate. The telegraphic exchange rate is the basis for calculating other exchange rates in the current market.

2. Mail Transfer Rate (M/T Rate).

Mail transfer rate is the rate used when a bank notifies its foreign branches or correspondent banks of payment by letter communication. The mail transfer rate is lower than the telegraphic transfer rate as it takes longer for the letter to travel than the telegraphic notification.

3. Demand Draft Transfer Rate

The demand draft transfer rate is the exchange rate used by banks when buying and selling foreign exchange bills, cheques and other instruments. In the form of a bill of exchange, the bank sells the instrument and often pays the money between a period of time. During this time, the bank can tie up the customer's funds and therefore the D/T rate is lower than the telegraphic transfer rate.

(v) Division according to the degree of tightness of foreign exchange control

In terms of the degree of tightness of exchange controls, they can be divided into official and market exchange rates.

1. Official rate

The official exchange rate is the rate set and published by the national foreign exchange authority (e.g., the central bank, the Ministry of Finance or the designated foreign exchange management bank). In countries with strict exchange controls, free trading of foreign exchange is prohibited. If there is no market exchange rate, all foreign exchange transactions will be conducted at this rate.

2. Market rate

The market exchange rate is the actual exchange rate for buying and selling foreign exchange in the free foreign exchange market. The market exchange rate is determined by the supply and demand in the foreign exchange market. It changes with the change of foreign exchange supply and demand.

(vi) Division from the perspective of the business hours of foreign exchange banks

From the perspective of the opening and closing rates of foreign exchange banks, they can be divided into opening exchange rates and closing exchange rates.

1. Opening rate

The opening exchange rate is the foreign exchange bank in each working day when the business began to deal with the first foreign exchange trading. It is also called the opening price.

2. Closing rate

The closing rate refers to the rate used by foreign exchange banks for the last foreign exchange transaction before the close of business on each working day. It is also known as the closing price.

(Extended Reading 4-1)

Must-heard stories for the novice in the foreign exchange

An experienced forex trader often tells novices the following story which is very similar to investor behavior.

San Mao's father gave him a penny to get some soy sauce. The owner of the grocery shop filled the bowl San Mao took with soy sauce and said with difficulty, "San Mao, there's still a little bit of soy sauce left, what should I do?" San Mao took a look and giggled, "Boss, isn't that easy? I have an idea!" He turned the bowl full of soy sauce over and said, "Can't the bottom of this bowl hold it?"

When San Mao returned home, his father looked dumbfounded and scolded him, "San Mao, you are so stupid, you bought such a little soy sauce for a penny? You've been cheated!" San Mao said proudly, "Father, do you think your son is that stupid? There's more here!" He said he turned the bowl over again and poured the only bit of soy sauce at the bottom of the bowl as well.

Many investors are very smart in their daily life and work, but once they enter the currency market, IQ is dumbfounded. Some investors tend to sell foreign exchange at the lowest point and buy at the highest point. The following are some examples of investors who have failed in their investments and we hope that they will not be in this situation again:

1. Any short-term fluctuations can affect sentiment, with the worst sentiment at the lows and the best at the highs.

This situation is most typical of the three concepts （no real-world experience, no real-world information, no real-world mentality） of investors. The key to grasping the key, simple things in the actual battle, using the two key points of the price difference they can grasp to make money, not through most of the time impossible to guess the right short term fluctuations, in the foreign exchange market to make money, one must endure the torment of time and reverse volatility.

2. A single eye blinded by a single leaf can't see the mountain

Portfolio investment activity is very much a test of an investor's ability to analyze issues holistically, both in terms of trends and individual foreign exchange, but also to analyze risks and operational instruments, while comparing them with emerging opportunities. Many investors, however, focus on only one point in their investment activity that they wish to see, while fail in other relevant factors. In particular, some investors have only analysis and no operational tools, as soon as the exchange rate does not move as they have analyzed. If the exchange rate does not fluctuate in accordance with their own analysis, they immediately become suspicious. When an investment activity is not yet ripe, they rush into it and end up in a hurry. The result is self-evidently very unsatisfactory.

3. Letting misguided investments get out of control

Due to human nature, certain mistakes will inevitably occur in investment activities and when they do you must do the following things: the first thing is to analyse the risk following a mistake, because only operations with a large risk are bound to be short, things with small risks can be reversed by time or other efforts, and in addition to opportunity analysis there is also risk analysis. The second thing is to analyse whether the key points for profit still exist, and if they do, and they are far greater than the risks, then you can use the operation to take advantage of them. If they exist and are far greater than the risk, then you can use operational tools to correct them and not end the programme so easily. The third thing is that if you find that the opportunity has disappeared and the risk is high, then you should end the project decisively, otherwise you could make a big mistake.

Source: The author collates the information based on the relevant information.

Discussion:

1. What did the story of "San Mao" inspire you?

2. What do you think are the requirements for a beginner to invest in financial products

such as foreign exchange and stocks?

Task 2　　Exchange Rate System

An exchange rate system is a set of arrangements or regulations made by a country's monetary authority regarding the determination of the level of its exchange rate, and the way of exchange rate fluctuation. Traditionally, exchange rate systems have been divided into two main categories: fixed exchange rate systems and floating exchange rate systems.

I.Fixed rate system

A fixed exchange rate system is one in which the exchange rate between the two currencies is essentially fixed, or in which fluctuations in the exchange rate between the two currencies are limited to a small range of fluctuations within a small floating range. Historically, the international gold standard and the Bretton Woods exchange rate system were both fixed exchange rate systems. Under this system, a country's monetary authority is obliged to maintain the exchange rate of its currency within a specified range. It cannot exceed the upper limit or fall below the lower limit.

（i）A fixed exchange rate system under a typical international gold standard

The typical international gold standard is the gold standard system, which is characterized by the fact that each monetary unit （mint） has a legal. The gold content of the currency then becomes the basis for the exchange rate of each country's currency. The ratio between the currencies of two countries is the ratio of the gold content of two gold coins. This ratio is known as 'mint parity'. Mint parity was the basis for exchange rate determination under the international gold standard system.

For example, the gold content of a British pound gold coin is 113.0016 grams, and the gold content of a US dollar coin is 23.22 grams. The ratio between the British pound and the US dollar is 113.0016/23.22 = 4.8665. That is, 1 British pound = 4.8665 US dollars. If there is a disproportionate change in the gold content of a gold coin between the pound and the dollar, then the minting parity will also change.

1. Gold delivery point

However, under a typical international gold standard system, the real exchange rate in the foreign exchange market is not always consistent with the mint parity, but fluctuate with the supply and demand relationship in the foreign exchange market, i.e., the exchange rate is based on the mint parity and around the mint parity up and down. No matter how strong the supply and demand forces of foreign exchange, the exchange rate fluctuations are always limited. This boundary is the gold input point and gold output point. They are called "gold transmission point".

2. Changes in gold delivery points and exchange rates

So, how is the exchange rate affected by the gold delivery point?

The mechanism by which the exchange rate works is this: when the foreign exchange rate in a particular country's foreign exchange market has an upward trend and exceeds the gold output point, gold starts to flow out of the country. When the exchange rate has a downward trend and falls below the gold input, the gold begin to flow in. The direction of gold flow is exactly opposite to the direction of supply and demand changes in the foreign exchange market. Thus, it has the role of offsetting the foreign exchange market supply and demand forces, so that exchange rate changes do not exceed the boundary of gold transport point.

See Figure 4-1 and Figure 4-2.

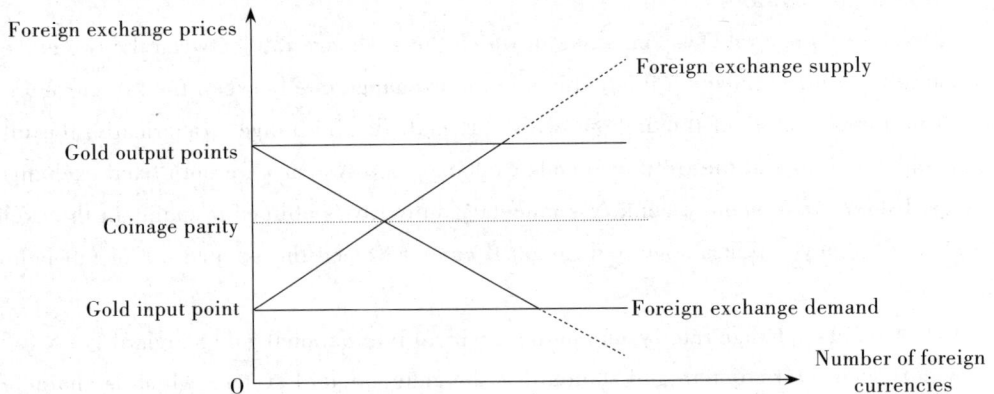

Figure 4-1 Gold delivery points for exchange rate movements

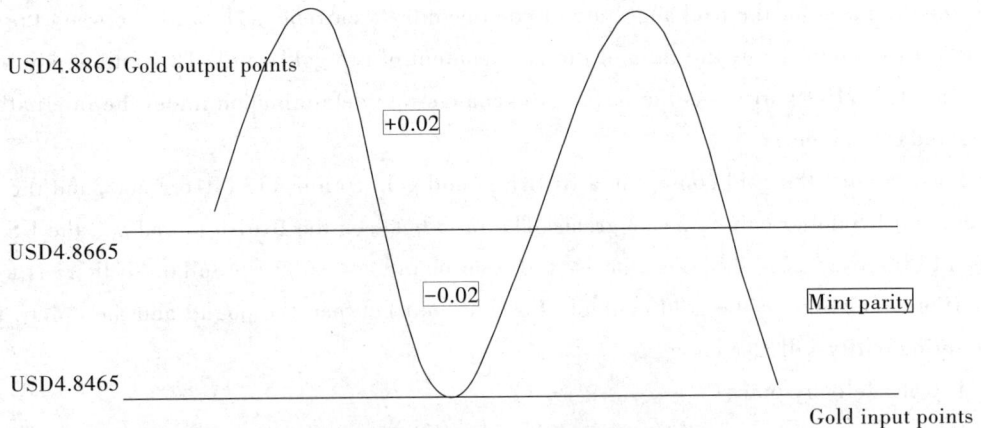

Figure 4-2 Gold delivery point = seigniorage parity± freight

For example, in the New York foreign exchange market, the mint parity between the pound and the US dollar is 1GBP = 4.8665USD. The cost of transporting gold from New York to London is US$0.02. In New York, the output point for gold is mint parity + gold transportation cost = 4.8665USD + 0.02 USD. Gold transportation cost = 4.8665 + 0.02 = USD 4.8865. Assume that the demand for the British pound in the New York foreign exchange market exceeds the demand for the British pound. The demand for pounds exceeds the supply of pounds, forcing the exchange rate of pounds to rise from mint parity 1GBP = 4.8665 USD to gold output 1GBP = 4.8865USD. At this point, the pound exchange rate will not rise any further because if it rises above USD 4.8865, US importers will not buy pounds. They will instead buy gold from the US monetary authorities in US dollars at US$4.8665−US$4.8865 and ship the gold to London and sell it to the British monetary authorities in exchange for pounds sterling, which can then be used to settle debts between them. As a result, the US importers receive pounds sterling at mint parity plus transportation costs, with only a US $0.02 increase in transportation costs. The result is that the American importer receives pounds sterling at mint parity plus transportation costs, adding only US $0.02 to his transport costs. Otherwise, it would have had to buy the pound at a higher price than the gold export point. Therefore, the US importer was exporting gold to settle their debts when the pound rate rose to the gold export point rather than having to reduce the demand for the pound and naturally the pound exchange rate cannot continue to rise.

Similarly, if the supply of pounds in the New York market exceeds the demand, it forces the pound exchange rate down to the gold input point （4.8665−0.02）. London importers will not sell pounds at a low price below 1GBP= 4.8465USD, preferring to use pounds to buy gold from the British monetary authorities and channel it to the United States, where it will be sold to the US monetary authorities in exchange for dollars and liquidation of the debt. At this point the London importers' dollars were obtained at mint parity less the cost of transportation of US $0.02. If it did not do this, the importer in London would have to buy dollars at a price lower than the point at which gold was imported, and he would then have to spend more pounds in order to exchange them for the original required amount of US dollars. In New York, because the continuous inflow of gold will reduce the supply of pounds, the supply and demand of pounds tend to balance, and the pound exchange rate will naturally not fall further, but will rise back above the gold input point.

This is the automatic mechanism for regulating the exchange rate under a typical gold standard system. The gold delivery point depends mainly on the cost of gold delivery, which in turn depends mainly on the distance between the two countries, which in turn depends primarily on the distance between the two countries, as geographical distance determines the cost of freight, insurance and interest payments during transit. Therefore, the point of delivery of gold varies from country to country.

（ii）Fixed exchange rate system under the Bretton Woods System （dollar-gold standard）

Due to specific historical circumstances, the international monetary system after the Second World War and until 1973 was a fixed exchange rate system centred on the US dollar, at which time the US government set the gold content of a US dollar note at 0.888671 grams. For example, in 1946, the United Kingdom set the gold content of the British pound note at 0.888671 grams, and other countries also set the gold content of their currency units. For example, in 1946, the United Kingdom stipulated that the gold content

Teaching Video 4-2

Exchange Rate Formation Mechanism

of one British pound note was 3.58134 grams. Thus, the ratio of the gold content of the two countries' banknotes becomes the decision of the exchange rate. This ratio is called the "gold parity". For example, the exchange rate between the pound and the US dollar is 3.58134 / 0.888671 = 4.03, i.e., 1 GBP = 4.03 USD.

As with the typical international gold standard, the actual exchange rate in the foreign exchange market is not likely to be exactly equal to the gold parity due to supply and demand. However, at the time, the International Monetary Fund (IMF) stipulated that exchange rates could fluctuate by ±1% (e.g. the upper limit of the fluctuation of the pound against the US dollar is 4.03 + 4.03 × 1% = 4.0703 US dollars, and the lower limit is 4.03−4.03×1%=3.9897 US dollars) .

With more than this range, the relevant national government should intervene in the foreign exchange market, so that the exchange rate back to the range of this fixed. In order to intervene in the foreign exchange market, all countries should establish, including the local currency, foreign exchange, gold, including the "foreign exchange parity fund". When the foreign exchange rate changes below parity of 1%, the government will use the fund in local currency or gold to buy foreign exchange, so that the supply of foreign exchange is less than the demand and the foreign exchange rate can back up.

Then later the International Monetary Fund adjusted this movement to ±2.25%, but governments still have to intervene in the foreign exchange market to stabilize foreign exchange rates. Not only that, but at the time the IMF also stipulated that Countries should not easily change their parity. Only when there is a basic imbalance in the balance of payments, i.e. when the measures taken to regulate the imbalance conflict with the balanced development of the domestic economy, can the parity be changed more substantially; and that such changes are subject to the arrangements and supervision of the International Monetary Fund.

It follows that the fixed exchange rate system under the Bretton Woods regime was an adjustable pegging system. This adjustable peg equates the US dollar with gold, with national currencies maintaining a fixed legal ratio to the US dollar. The US dollar is at the centre of the international monetary system, acting as the international standard currency for international reserves, settlement and intervention. Other national currencies are dependent on the US dollar.

(iii) Comparison of two fixed exchange rate regimes

Animation Micro-lesson 4-4

Big Mac Index

The fixed exchange rate system under a typical gold standard system and the fixed exchange rate system under the Bretton Woods System have something in common. Both exchange rate systems are based on the gold content of national currencies. However, there are clear differences between them.

1. The connection with gold is different

The fixed exchange rate system under the typical gold standard system is based on the coinage parity of two countries' currencies. The Bretton Woods fixed exchange rate system was based on gold parity and centered on the US dollar equal to gold.

2. The adjustment mechanism of exchange rates is different

Under the typical gold standard system, the exchange rate fluctuates around the coinage parity of the currencies of the two countries, but the fluctuation range does not exceed the gold delivery point. When it exceeds the gold delivery point, the exchange rate is stabilized within the gold delivery point through the automatic adjustment of the free output and input of gold. For the fixed exchange rate system under the Bretton Woods System, its floating range is artificially stipulated and artificially maintained, that is, if the Specified range is exceeded, the exchange rate can be stabilized within the specified range through the direct intervention of the governments of various countries or the central bank.

3. The scope of impact of exchange rate changes is different

Under a typical gold standard, when exchange rates change, only the currencies and trade balances of the two countries are concerned. Under the Bretton Woods System, if the key currency of the US dollar is unstable due to the deterioration of the balance of payments of the United States, the adjustment of the value of the US dollar will affect all currencies pegged to it, thus affecting the stability of the trade balance and exchange rate of other countries besides the issuing country of the key currency. Therefore, the United States, the issuer of the key currency, had sufficient gold reserves and a good balance of payments position, which was the basis for the Bretton Woods system to be maintained.

4. The gold content varies

Under a typical gold standard, the amount of money generally does not change, and does so without the consent of other countries. Under the Bretton Woods System, any adjustment in the amount of gold in a country's currency must be made in the event of a balance of payments imbalance and should be agreed by the International Monetary Fund.

(iv) The advantages and disadvantages of the fixed exchange rate system

1. Advantages

The greatest advantage of a fixed exchange rate system is the low risk of exchange rate fluctuations. The exchange rate is relatively stable because the currency ratio between the two countries is essentially fixed. Thus, the economic agents of international trade, international credit and investment are able to make the cost, benefit and profit accounting relatively clear and unambiguous. This effectively facilitates the development of the international economy.

2. Disadvantages

(1) The fixed exchange rate basically cannot play the economic adjustment role of the international balance of payments. Exchange rate fluctuations have a deep impact on the balance of payments, so the exchange rate is also known as the economic lever to adjust the balance of payments. Under the fixed exchange rate system, the currency exchange rate is basically fixed, so it is difficult to adjust the balance of payments.

(2) The fixed exchange rate system cannot satisfy the internal and external simultaneous equilibrium of a country. Under the fixed exchange rate system, the exchange rate basically can-

not play the economic leverage of borrowing the international balance of payments. When a country has a balance of payments deficit, it needs to adopt tight monetary and fiscal policies to adjust, which will restrain domestic economic growth and expand unemployment, thus sacrificing internal balance. On the contrary, if the expansionary monetary and fiscal policies are adopted for adjustment, they will aggravate domestic inflation and price rise, thus sacrificing internal equilibrium.

II. Floating Exchange Rate System

Floating exchange rate system is to show each country monetary authority announces the gold content of home currency, no longer stipulate local currency to the fluctuation range of foreign currency exchange rate change, also no longer bear to maintain exchange rate fluctuation to a certain extent within the scope of the obligation , the exchange rate fluctuates freely in accordance with the supply and demand of foreign exchange in the foreign exchange market.

Under the floating exchange rate system, coinage parity, gold parity and the upper and lower limits of exchange rate fluctuations no longer exist. Since there is no central axis for the fluctuation of the exchange rate, we can only explain the fluctuation of the exchange rate of the currency by comparing it with the previous period. If demand for foreign exchange exceeds supply, the exchange rate rises. A currency that tends to rise in value is called a Hard Currency. On the other hand, if the supply of foreign exchange exceeds the demand, the exchange rate will fall. The currency is called Soft Currency.

(i) The type of floating exchange rate

1. Divided by the different degrees of government intervention in the foreign exchange market.

The floating exchange rate can be divided into free floating and managed floating according to the different levels of government intervention in the foreign exchange market.

(1) Free floating, also known as clean floating, means that a country's monetary authorities on the exchange rate fluctuations generally do not take intervention measures. The exchange rate fluctuates freely and adjusts spontaneously depending on the changes of supply and demand in the foreign exchange market. The government does not undertake to maintain the rate fluctuation rate of obligation. Only when the exchange rate changes abnormally and unfavorable to the national economy, the monetary authorities will directly or indirectly intervene in the foreign exchange market , so that it is conducive to the development of the national economy. Currencies such as the United States dollar, the British pound and the Japanese yen belong to the free floating currency.

(2) Managed floating, also known as unclean floating, refers to the various measures taken by a country's monetary authorities to intervene in the foreign exchange market from time to time, so that the exchange rate is in the direction of the country's economic development. For example, China's RMB belongs to the floating currency.

2. Divided according to the different ways of exchange rate fluctuations

According to the different ways of exchange rate fluctuation, the floating exchange rate can be divided into Independent Floating, Joint Floating and Pegged Floating.

（1） Independent Floating is a system in which a country's currency does not form a bloc with the currencies of other countries, but floats on its own, with its exchange rate adjusting to changes in supply and demand in the foreign exchange market. The exchange rate is adjusted according to changes in demand and supply in the foreign exchange market, without the influence of any national currency. Currencies like the US dollar, the British pound, the Japanese yen and the Swiss franc belong to the independent floating currency.

（2） Joint Floating refers to a group of countries that form a currency bloc, within which currency is a fixed exchange rate system with exchange rate fluctuations within a certain range, while externally the exchange rate is unified to rise and fall. For example, the European Monetary System （EMS） was established by the former European Community countries in March 1979. After the establishment of the EMS, member currencies were set against the European monetary units within the EMS, and it was reaffirmed that a fixed exchange rate was maintained between members with a joint float for non-members. The UK joined the joint float in October 1990, but withdrew from the joint float in favor of a separate float until today due to the significant devaluation of the pound prior to the European unification of the Great Market in 1992. It has been floated independently until today.

（3） Pegged Floating is when a country's currency is pegged to a reserve currency or to a basket of currencies and maintains a fixed exchange rate with the pegged currency, while floating freely against other currencies. For example, many developing countries have pegged their currencies to a single currency such as the US dollar and the British pound. Currencies such as Saudi Arabia and the United Arab are pegged to SDRs. The exchange rate is relatively stable compared to separate and joint floats, but exchange rate adjustments are easily controlled by the currency to which they are pegged and lack autonomy.

（ii） Advantages and disadvantages of floating exchange rates

1. Advantages

（1） Prevent the loss of large foreign exchange reserves. Under a floating exchange rate system, monetary authorities are not obliged to maintain a fixed exchange rate. When the currency falls, foreign exchange reserves do not have to be used to buy the currency being sold, thus avoiding a massive drain of foreign exchange reserves.

（2） Automatic balance of payments adjustment. Under the floating exchange rate system, the balance of payments of a country can be adjusted through the fluctuation of the exchange rate, which plays the role of economic leverage. For example, when the demand for domestic goods and services declines, the balance of payments deficit occurs. The floating exchange rate devalues the domestic currency, which lowers the price of domestic goods and services and promotes the growth of exports, partially offsetting the adverse impact brought by the decline in demand.

（3） Monetary policy is more autonomous. If central banks were no longer forced to intervene in currency markets for fixed exchange rates, governments would have the flexibility to use monetary policy to achieve domestic and external balances.

2. Disadvantages

(1) Increased risk in international economic transactions. The large changes in the exchange rate may bring great uncertainty to international trade. Accounting for costs and profits are difficult to grasp, which is not good for multinational companies to make the right business decisions.

(2) Promote international speculative activities. The unlimited fluctuations in exchange rates give international speculators opportunities for arbitrage and exchange arbitrage, and even local, worldwide financial crisis, such as the global financial crisis in 2008 and the European debt crisis in 2009.

III. RMB exchange rate system

RMB is the unique, unified and stable currency of the People's Republic of China. Due to historical reasons, the Chinese government has not stipulated the gold parity of RMB, which determines that the determination of the RMB exchange rate with other currencies has its own particularity. The RMB exchange rate arrangement has always adhered to the principle of independence, equality and mutual benefit, fairness and rationality, which is conducive to the development of China's foreign economic relations and promote the economic and trade progress of other countries. The evolution of the RMB exchange rate against the currencies of western countries can be divided into the following stages:

(i) The RMB exchange rate system before the reform and opening up

1. Management of the floating system phase (1949–1952) .

In the early days of the birth of RMB, before the planned economic system was established, the government announced that RMB would not be based on gold, and in practice, the floating management system was implemented. The RMB/USD exchange rate is determined based on the weighted average of the RMB/USD export price, import price and daily living cost of overseas Chinese. During this period, the RMB exchange rate was determined based on prices and its function was actually to adjust foreign trade and take care of overseas remittance income.

2. Fixed exchange rate system (1953–1972) .

Since 1953, China has entered a period of socialist industrialization construction and socialist transformation. The national economy was planned, and prices set by the state were basically stable. During this period, the RMB exchange rate was mainly used for the settlement of non-trade foreign exchange. The exchange rate based on the comparison of domestic and foreign consumer prices has taken proper account of overseas Chinese remittances and other non-trade foreign exchange income, and there was no need to adjust it. Since the currencies of capitalist countries adopted a fixed exchange rate system during this stage, the exchange rate did not often change, so the RMB exchange rate remained stable, essentially a fixed exchange rate system.

3. The RMB implemented a basket of currencies to nail the exchange rate system （1973–1980）.

In March 1973, western currencies adopted a floating exchange rate system and the exchange rate fluctuated frequently. In order to maintain a relatively reasonable foreign exchange rate, the RMB must be adjusted upwards or downwards according to the fluctuation of the international market exchange rate. The RMB exchange rate is determined on the basis of the exchange rate level established. The exchange rate is set against the currencies of western countries based on a "basket of currencies" principle.

（ii）The RMB exchange rate system after the reform and opening up

1. Internal settlement price of trade （1981–1984）.

In order to encourage exports and restrict imports, strengthen the economic accounting of foreign trade and adapt to the reform of China's foreign trade system, China has implemented two types of exchange rates to encourage exports and restrict imports since 1981. One is the foreign exchange rate applicable to non-trade foreign exchange receipts and payments. The other is the internal settlement price of foreign exchange applicable to foreign exchange payment. During this period, China had three exchange rates. The first was external which applied to the non-trade balance of payments of the official quotation; the second was the intra-trade settlement price applied to the trade balance ; the third was the foreign exchange adjustment price in the foreign exchange adjustment market .

2. Limited flexible exchange rate system based on the United States dollar （1985–1993）.

On 1 January 1985, the use of intra-trade settlement prices was discontinued while trade and non-trade receipts and payments were settled at official rates. Both trade and non-trade receipts and expenditures were settled according to official quotations. Although the intra-trade settlement price and the official price were in line, the transfer foreign exchange market still existed . In fact, in addition to the official price, there was still a foreign exchange transfer price.

3. Supply–demand–based, single and managed floating exchange rate system （1994–2005）.

On 1 January 1994, China made a major reform of the RMB exchange rate system by implementing a single and managed floating exchange rate system based on market supply and demand. The RMB exchange rate was brought into line in one step to 8.7 RMB per US dollar. The national foreign exchange reserves rose significantly. A new foreign exchange management system was introduced. Under this new system, the RMB exchange rate had the following characteristics:

（1）The RMB exchange rate was no longer directly designated by the official monetary authority.

（2）The designated foreign exchange banks could set their own foreign exchange rates based on the market supply and demand.

（3）The exchange rate formed based on the market supply and demand was uniform.

4. Managed floating exchange rate system adjusted by reference to a basket of currencies (2005-present)

Since 21 July 2005, China has adopted a managed floating exchange rate system based on market demand and supply and adjusted by reference to a basket of currencies. The RMB exchange rate is no longer pegged to a single US dollar.

As for the way of the exchange rate adjustment, China implements a managed floating exchange rate regime based on market supply and demand and adjusted with reference to a basket of currencies.

Determination of central parity and daily floating range: The People's Bank of China announces the closing price of several major currencies in the inter-bank foreign exchange market against RMB after the market closes each working day, which serves as the intermediate price of the currencies against RMB in the next working day.

At 19: 00 on 21 July 2019, the trading price of US dollar against RMB was adjusted to 7.1158 RMB per US dollar, which was the midpoint for transactions between designated foreign exchange banks in the inter-bank foreign exchange market the next day. Designated foreign exchange banks can adjust the quoted exchange rate to customers from this time. The adjustment mainly depends on the degree of China's trade surplus and the needs of structural adjustment, and also considers the adaptability of domestic enterprises to adjust.

Task 3　　Factors Affecting Exchange Rate Movements

In today's floating exchange rate system, there are many factors affecting exchange rate movements, and various economic, political, man-made, social and natural factors can make foreign exchange rates fluctuate frequently and even produce large waves leading to financial crises. Specifically, the following factors are:

I. In the long run, inflation is the fundamental factor influencing exchange rate movements.

If a country issues too much currency and the amount of money in circulation exceeds the actual demand for goods in circulation, it will cause inflation.

Inflation directly leads to a decrease in the purchasing power of a country's currency domestically, causing it to depreciate internally, which, all else being equal, will inevitably lead to a depreciation of the currency externally. Because the exchange rate is a comparison between the currencies of two countries, a country that issues too much currency will have a smaller value per unit of currency and therefore pay more of that country's currency than would otherwise be the case when that country's currency is converted into an equivalent amount of foreign currency.

As a result, the prices of domestic goods and services are correspondingly higher when converted into foreign currency, which weakens the competitiveness of domestic goods and services in the international market and discourages exports. At the same time, it makes domestic residents turn to buy relatively cheaper foreign goods and services, thus promoting imports.

At the same time, inflation can cause real interest rates to fall. When the nominal interest rate remains unchanged, capital will flow to countries with high interest rates, which will eventually lead to capital outflow of the country, affecting the domestic currency demand and leading to the decline of the local currency exchange rate.

In short, a country with inflation higher than most other countries, will lead to the decline of its currency exchange rate, so as to realize the transmission of internal devaluation to external devaluation. The effect of inflation on the exchange rate is shown in Figure 4-3.

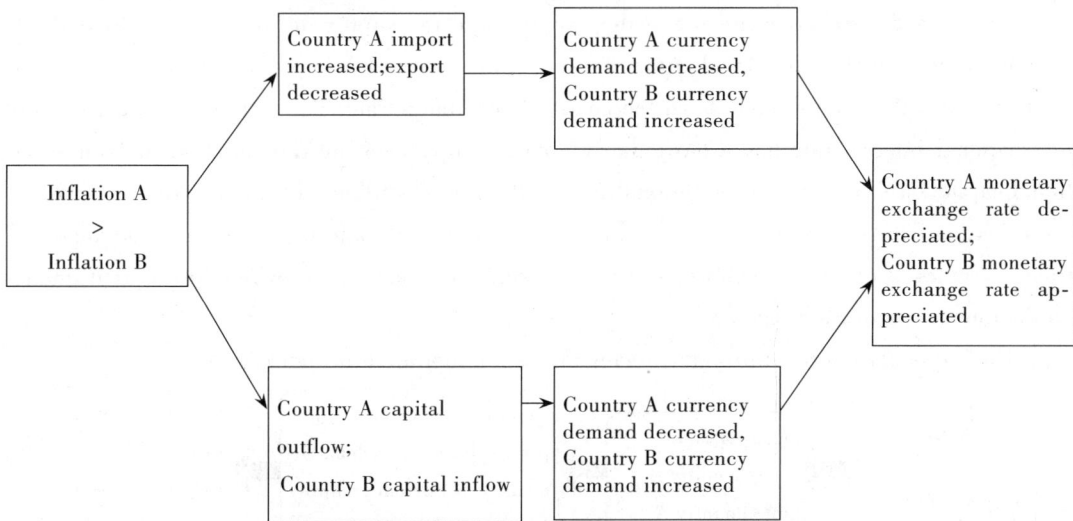

Figure   4-3 Effect of inflation on the exchange rates

II.In the short term, the balance of payments is a direct factor affecting changes in the exchange rate.

The balance of payments and exchange rates are closely linked, and sometimes even cause and affect each other. The surplus or deficit of international balance of payments will directly affect the change of exchange rate, and the change of exchange rate will in turn affect the change of surplus or deficit. If a country's balance of payments has a large surplus, its foreign exchange income must be greater than its foreign exchange expenditure, indicating that the supply of foreign exchange in the domestic market is greater than the demand, while the domestic currency is in short supply. Therefore, the local currency will appreciate against the foreign currency. On the contrary, the local currency will depreciate against the foreign currency.The impact of the balance of payments on the exchange rate is illustrated in Figure 4-4.

Balance of payments surplus	→	Foreign exchange income is greater than Foreign exchange expenditures	→	Foreign exchange is oversupplied Local currency is in short supply	→	The local currency appreciated Foreign currency depreciated

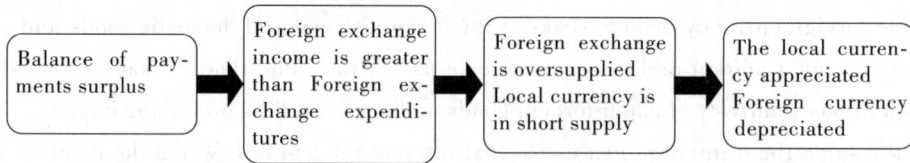

Figure 4-4   Impact of balance of payments on exchange rates

III.Interest rates are an important factor influencing exchange rate movements.

Interest rate difference is a very important factor affecting exchange rate fluctuation. As the price of borrowing funds, the interest rate directly affects the input and output of a country's capital. If the interest rate of a country is generally higher than that of other countries, foreign capital holders will invest their funds in the country to pursue higher interest income. This will increase the foreign exchange income of the country, and the supply of foreign currency exceeds demand, thus promoting the devaluation of foreign currency and the appreciation of local currency. Otherwise, that would push down the country's exchange rate. The difference in the level of international interest rate has a particularly obvious impact on the flow of short-term international capital, while today's international financial market is filled with huge amounts of short-term floating capital. These international hot capital flows into and out of foreign exchange and financial markets of various countries on a large scale for speculation, which has a great impact on the fluctuation of exchange rate.

The impact of interest rates on exchange rates is illustrated in Figure 4-5.

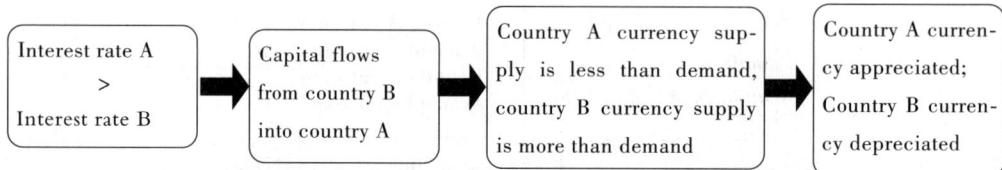

Interest rate A > Interest rate B	→	Capital flows from country B into country A	→	Country A currency supply is less than demand, country B currency supply is more than demand	→	Country A currency appreciated; Country B currency depreciated

Figure 4-5 The impact of interest rates on exchange rates

IV. The psychology of market expectations is a factor that cannot be ignored in influencing exchange rate movements.

Market psychological expectation is the main factor affecting exchange rate fluctuation in the short term, which is changeable and unpredictable. If participants in the foreign exchange market expect a country to have high inflation, a large balance of payments deficit, low real interest rates, or other adverse factors for the country's economy, the currency will be expected to depreciate. In reality, the country's currency will be sold in the foreign exchange market, so that the country's currency exchange rate becomes a real devalued currency. Otherwise,the currency would appreciate.

V. National macroeconomic policies are another important factor influencing exchange rate movements.

The macroeconomic policies implemented by each country will have a certain impact on its economic growth （especially foreign trade growth）, price level and international balance of payments, which is bound to have a certain impact on exchange rate fluctuations. For example, monetary policy affects the exchange rate through changes in the money supply and interest rates. If a government implements an expansionary monetary policy, increasing money supply and lowering interest rates, the exchange rate of the country's currency will decline. Otherwise, if the government adopts a tight monetary policy, reducing money supply and raising interest rates, the currency exchange rate will rise. The effect of monetary policy on the exchange rate is illustrated in Figure 4-6.

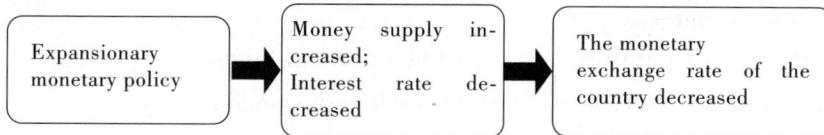

Expansionary monetary policy	→	Money supply increased; Interest rate decreased	→	The monetary exchange rate of the country decreased

Figure 4-6   The impact of monetary policy on the exchange rate

VI. Direct central bank intervention is a factor that should not be overlooked in influencing exchange rate movements.

As mentioned above, whether in a fixed exchange rate system or a floating exchange rate system, the central bank intervenes in the foreign exchange market passively or actively to stabilize the local currency exchange rate and to avoid the adverse impact of exchange rate fluctuations on the economy. Central banks intervene mainly by buying and selling foreign exchange directly in the foreign exchange market, thus affecting supply and demand in the foreign exchange market. Specifically, if the foreign exchange rate falls, the central bank will buy a large amount of foreign exchange to increase the demand for foreign exchange, and the foreign exchange will appreciate when the foreign exchange supply remains unchanged. On the other hand, if the foreign exchange rate rises, the central bank sells the foreign exchange in large quantities, causing the exchange rate to fall.

The impact of direct central bank intervention on the exchange rate is illustrated in Figure 4-7.

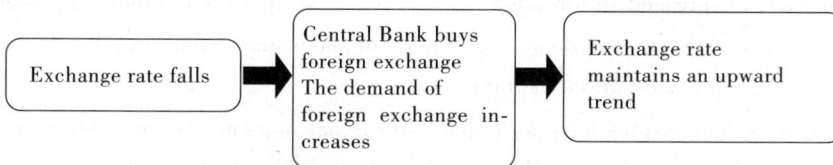

Exchange rate falls	→	Central Bank buys foreign exchange The demand of foreign exchange increases	→	Exchange rate maintains an upward trend

Figure 4-7   Effects of direct central bank intervention on the exchange rate

In addition to the six factors listed above, there are many other factors affecting exchange rate fluctuations, such as major international political events, vicious speculation, natural disasters (Japanese tsunami in 2013) , and wars. Because the factors affecting exchange rate movements are varied and complex, their effects sometimes cancel each other out and sometimes reinforce each other. Therefore, when analyzing exchange rate fluctuations, we should make a comprehensive investigation and analysis in light of different situations to reach a more correct judgment.

Task 4   Impact of Exchange Rate Fluctuations

The exchange rate is the special price in the foreign exchange market and the link center of all currencies. Under the conditions of open economy, exchange rate is closely linked with various economic factors, making exchange rate become an important variable in the macro-economy of various countries.

I. The impact of exchange rate changes on the balance of payments

(i) The impact on the balance of tangible trade and intangible trade

The tangible trade means the import and export of a country's goods, while intangible trade refers to the import and export of a country's services exports. The impact of exchange rate changes on both is the same, mainly through changes in the relative prices of goods and services caused by exchange rate movements.

When the exchange rate of a country's currency falls, the price of domestic goods and services expressed in foreign currency goes down. This stimulates demand for domestic goods and services from foreign customers, resulting in increased exports of goods and services. For example, a Chinese import of the Huawei P30 Pro is priced at €1,024 in Germany （the exchange rate of the RMB to the euro was 1EUR=8CNY on 15 June 2019）. When the RMB exchange rate fell by 30 July, the exchange rate of RMB against euro was 1EUR=8.2CNY. For the same Huawei mobile phone sold for 1 024 euros, the Chinese exporter would have received RMB 8 192 at the exchange rate before the devaluation of the RMB, and RMB 8 396.8 at the exchange rate after the devaluation. Compared to the pre-devaluation rate, the exporter would have received an additional RMB 204.8. This has greatly stimulated the exporter's motivation.

Conversely, when the exchange rate of a country's currency rises, the price of domestic goods and services, expressed in foreign currency, will rise, thereby dampening foreign demand for domestic goods and services and causing exports of goods and services to decrease.

(ii) the impact on international capital flows

Changes in exchange rates have an impact on the earnings of capital holders and therefore on the domestic and external flows. When a country's currency exchange rate is on a downward trend but has not yet started to fall, this can give rise to expectations of a depreciation of the local currency exchange rate. The capital holders of the local currency will then move their capital abroad, resulting in capital outflows. Such capital outflows will continue until the end of the exchange rate decline. When it is expected that the decline in the local currency exchange rate has come to an end and is about to rebound （i.e., the local currency exchange rate rises）, capital outflows will continue until the end of the decline （i.e., a rise in the local currency exchange rate）, the transferred capital will return to the country and may cause further capital flows into the country. The impact of exchange rate fluctuations on short-term primary flows is particularly pronounced.

II. The impact of exchange rate changes on foreign exchange reserves

(ⅰ) The impact on the amount of foreign exchange reserves

The amount of capital transfers directly affect the increase or decrease of country's foreign reserves through the volume of export and import trade. Generally speaking, a stable exchange rate of a country's currency is conducive to the country's attraction of foreign investment, thus promoting the country's foreign exchange reserves. Conversely, it will cause capital outflows and reduce foreign exchange reserves.

(ⅱ) The impact on the value of foreign exchange reserves

If the exchange rate of the reserve currency held by a country declines, the real value of the foreign exchange reserves of the country holding this reserve currency will decrease, while the reserve currency country will reduce the debt burden and benefit from it. Conversely, this would increase the real value of the reserves of the reserve currency holders, while the reserve currency holders would increase their debt burdens. For example, the US dollar against the RMB has been in a declining trend in recent years, which reduces the value of China's dollar-dominated foreign exchange reserves and the US debt.

At the same time, the depreciation of the reserve currency as a result of exchange rate movements will cause the country's central bank to consider whether to adjust the currency structure of its foreign exchange reserves by reducing the proportion of the US dollar held and increasing the proportion of other reserve currencies held. For example, in the State Administration of Foreign Exchange Annual Report 2018 published by the State Administration of Foreign Exchange of China, it is noted that in the 20 years from 1995 to 2014, the proportion of US dollars in China's foreign exchange reserves, alone, fell from 79% to 58%.

III. The impact of exchange rate changes on the domestic economy

(ⅰ) The impact on national income and employment

Economists often compare exports, demand and investment to the triumvirate that drives economic growth. As the local exchange rate depreciation favours the export of goods and services, the depreciation of the local currency activates idle factors of production, expands the scale of production and raises employment and national income. Conversely, as the appreciation of the local currency is detrimental to the export of goods and services, it may have a dampening effect on economic growth, national income and employment. The appreciation of the currency may have a dampening effect on economic growth, national income growth and employment.

(ⅱ) The impact on domestic prices

Other things being the same, the change of domestic currency exchange rate will lead to the change of domestic prices in the opposite direction to the change of exchange rate. That is to say, when the exchange rate of a country's currency declines, the devaluation promotes the export of goods and services and increases the foreign exchange income, thus leading to the increase in the demand for domestic currency and thus promoting the rise of domestic price level.

On the contrary, the rise of the local currency will lead to a decline in the domestic price level.

IV. The impact of exchange rate changes on international trade

The world market can be likened to a big cake, which will be unevenly distributed. In order to occupy more shares, some countries may take advantage of exchange rate depreciation to expand exports, thus affecting the interests of other countries. To safeguard their interests, other countries take the same way to devalue their currencies （called "competitive currency devaluation"）, or adopt trade protectionism, so as to cause trade wars between countries, which will harm the development of international trade, thus affecting international relations. For example, the "China–US trade dispute" has been a hot topic in recent years.

(Knowledge Link 4-3)

Commodity dumping and foreign exchange dumping

Commodity dumping is the sale of goods abroad by exporters in concentrated or sustained quantities at export prices below normal prices. According to the specific purpose of dumping, commodity dumping can be divided into occasional dumping, intermittent or predatory dumping and long-term dumpling. The three forms of dumping are shown as follows.

1. Incidental dumping usually refers to the sale of backlogged stock on foreign markets at lower prices because the peak season in the home market has passed or the company has switched to other products that are difficult to sell in the domestic market. The backlog of stock that is difficult to sell on the domestic market is sold on the foreign market at a lower price.

2. Intermittent or predatory dumping refers to selling in foreign markets at prices lower than domestic prices or below cost, in order to beat competitors and form a monopoly. After defeating all or most of its competitors, it then uses its monopoly power to raise prices and obtain high monopoly profits.

3. Long-term dumping means selling goods in foreign markets at a lower price than in the domestic market for an indefinite period of time continuously. The ultimate aim of dumping is to open markets, beat competitors, expand sales and create monopolies.

Exchange dumping is the use by a government to devalue its currency to achieve increase the price competitiveness of export commodities and expand exports. Exchange dumping cannot be carried out without restriction and conditions. Only when the following conditions are in place, can foreign exchange dumping play a role in expanding exports.

1. The degree of currency depreciation is greater than the degree of domestic price inflation. A devaluation of a country's currency abroad inevitably leads to an internal devaluation of the currency. It will lead to an increase in domestic prices. When domestic price rises to catch up with or exceed the degree of currency devaluation, the export price of goods will rise to or exceed the original price, i.e., the price before the currency devaluation. Thus, foreign exchange dumping cannot be implemented.

2. Other countries do not simultaneously implement the same degree of currency devalua-

tion. When a country's currency is devalued, if other countries also implement the same degree of currency devaluation, this will keep the exchange rate between the two currencies unchanged, thus making the export price of goods also remain unchanged, so that foreign exchange dumping cannot be achieved.

3. Other countries do not simultaneously take another retaliatory measures. If a foreign country takes retaliatory measures such as raising tariffs, that will also raise the price of export goods in foreign markets, thus offsetting the effect of foreign exchange dumping.

Source: The author collates the information based on the relevant information.

V. Exchange rate movements drive innovation in international financial instruments

The instability of exchange rate will aggravate the exchange rate risk of international trade and investment. In order to prevent and reduce the occurrence of such risks, financial instruments used in the financial market continue to innovate, such as currency futures, currency options, currency swaps and other financial derivatives with currency （mainly foreign exchange） as the underlying assets continue to emerge, which mitigate the risks brought by exchange rate fluctuations to a certain extent. The innovation of financial products is the inevitable outcome of the further development of national financial market.

Mini Case

In November 2020, the "Proposal of the CPC Central Committee on Formulating the 14th Five-Year Plan for National Economic and Social Development and the 2035 Vision" proposed to "promote the internationalization of the RMB prudently, adhere to market-driven and independent choices of enterprises, and create a new type of mutually beneficial partnership based on the free use of the RMB". It is clear that the future internationalization of the RMB will be market-oriented to cultivating real demand.

On 15 November 2020, the Regional Comprehensive Economic Partnership （RCEP） was officially signed by ten ASEAN countries, China, Japan, Korea, Australia and New Zealand. The RCEP covers a population of more than 3.5 billion and a total economic volume of US$29 trillion, accounting for 30% of the global total. The signing of the Agreement provides a broad market base for the internationalization of the RMB.

Please consult the information and think about:

1. What achievements have been made in the internationalization of the RMB?

2. What are the opportunities and challenges for the internationalization of the RMB?

Mini Map

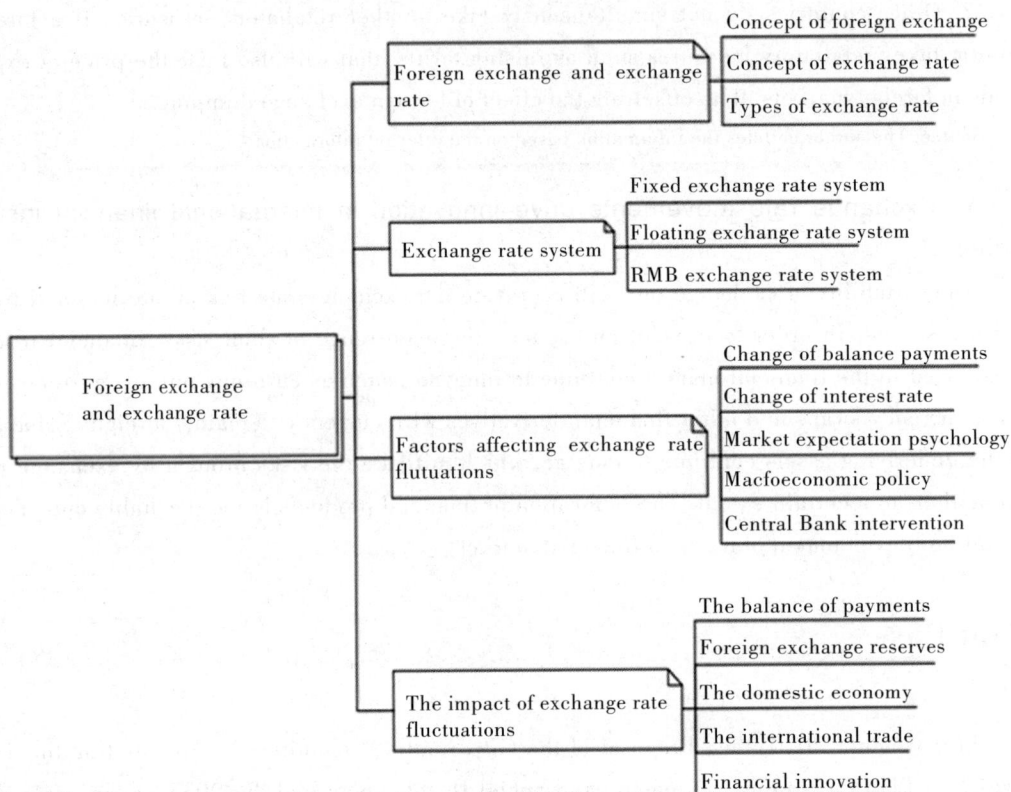

Foreign exchange and exchange rate

- Foreign exchange and exchange rate
  - Concept of foreign exchange
  - Concept of exchange rate
  - Types of exchange rate
- Exchange rate system
  - Fixed exchange rate system
  - Floating exchange rate system
  - RMB exchange rate system
- Factors affecting exchange rate flutuations
  - Change of balance payments
  - Change of interest rate
  - Market expectation psychology
  - Macfoeconomic policy
  - Central Bank intervention
- The impact of exchange rate fluctuations
  - The balance of payments
  - Foreign exchange reserves
  - The domestic economy
  - The international trade
  - Financial innovation

Project Training

I. (1) Single-choice questions

1. In a narrow sense, static foreign exchange is a means of payment that can be used for international settlement denoted by (   ).

A. National currency

B. Foreign currency

C. Foreign Securities

D. Special Drawing Rights

2. On a given day, the exchange rate in the Tokyo foreign exchange market is 1 USD = 115.20 JPY, if the exchange rate on the previous trading day was 1 USD = 112.80 JPY. Then which of the following descriptions is correct (   ).

A. Compared with the previous trading day, it indicates the depreciation of the US dollar and the appreciation of the Japanese yen; the pricing method is the direct pricing method

B. Compared with the previous trading day, it indicates the appreciation of the US dollar and the depreciation of the Japanese yen; the pricing method is the direct pricing method

C. Compared with the previous trading day, it indicates the appreciation of the US dollar and the depreciation of the Japanese yen; the pricing method is the indirect pricing method

D. Compared with the previous trading day, it indicates the depreciation of the US dollar and the appreciation of the Japanese yen; the price method is the indirect price method

3. Under the direct pricing method, the number of national currencies is reduced, which means (   ) .

A. the local currency exchange rate decreased

B. the local currency exchange rate increased

C. foreign currency exchange rate increased

D. foreign currency exchange rates declined

4. The exchange rate system is divided into individual floats and joint floats are classified according to (   ) .

A. whether the government intervenes

B. how the exchange rate fluctuates

C. nature of the exchange rate

D. the degree of tightness of floating management

5. When the exchange rate of a foreign currency is too high, a country's government can (   ) in order to curb further increases in the foreign exchange rate measures to regulate.

A. limit foreign exchange spending

B. buy a lot of foreign exchange

C. do massive selling of Forex

D. take restrictions on the circulation of local currency

II. Multiple-choice questions

1. Foreign exchange in a broad sense is a general term for financial assets formed in the process of international debt settlement, including specifically (   ) .

A. Foreign Currency Payment Voucher

B. Credit certificate

C. Foreign Government Bonds

D .Foreign currency deposits

2. Which of the following assets belongs to the category of foreign exchange (   ) .

A.Foreign Currency Securities

B. Foreign exchange payment voucher

C.Foreign currency

D. Foreign currency deposit certificate

3. According to the different calculation methods, the exchange rate can be divided into ( ).

A. Arbitrage exchange rate

B. Basic exchange rate

C. Official Exchange Rate

D. Market exchange rates

4. The main factors affecting the exchange rate change are ( ).

A. Inflation

B. Balance of payments

C. People's psychological expectations

D. International political events

5. Among the following factors, the factors that may cause the devaluation of a country's currency are ( ).

A. Balance of Payments Deficit

B. Inflation is higher than in other countries

C. Domestic interest rates rise

D. Tight monetary policy

III. Judgement questions

1. The direct quotation method of the exchange rate is based on the national currency as the base currency and the foreign currency as the quotation currency.   ( )

2. The base exchange rate is the ratio of the exchange rate between a country's currency and a key international currency.   ( )

3. Under a fixed exchange rate system, the exchange rate of the two currencies will not change once it is determined.   ( )

4. Generally speaking, if the inflation rate of a country increases, it will increase the local currency exchange rate and the foreign currency exchange rate will decrease.   ( )

5. A decline in the exchange rate of a country's currency is conducive to the improvement of the country's tourism and other services revenue and expenditure.   ( )

IV. Practical application questions

1. A Chinese company wants to invest in the United States and is quoted a bank price of 1USD = 6.8355/6.8366 RMB. How much RMB would it cost for the company to invest US$10 million?

2. Exchange rate arbitrage

(1) The exchange rate quoted on the foreign exchange market on a given day is known to be:

1USD=1.2179/1.2183CHF,1USD=1.0491/1.0496CAD

Try to calculate the arbitrated exchange rate between the Swiss franc and the Canadian dollar and explain its meaning.

（2）The exchange rate quoted on the foreign exchange market on a certain date is known to be:

1USD=1.2179/1.2183CHF,1GBP=2.0110/2.0115USD

Try to calculate the hedged exchange rate between the British pound and the Swiss franc and explain its meaning.

Project Five

Foreign Exchange Market and Traditional Foreign Exchange Transactions

Learning Objectives

Knowledge Objectives:

Master the meanings, characteristics, participants and classifications of the foreign exchange market. Understand and master the meanings, functions, quotation rules and transaction processes of spot foreign exchange transactions and forward foreign exchange transactions.

Competence Objectives:

Master the principles of the spot, forward, swap, arbitrage and other foreign exchange transactions, and be flexible.

Operational Objectives:

Design foreign exchange trading schemes with different trading tools for hedging operations.

Course Introduction

China foreign exchange market

China foreign exchange market is an important part of China financial market. It has played an irreplaceable role in improving the exchange rate formation mechanism, promoting RMB convertibility, serving financial institution, promoting the change of macro - control mode and improving the financial market system. Since 1994, China foreign exchange market has begun to transition from the foreign exchange adjustment market to the inter bank foreign exchange market with China foreign exchange trading center as the core, which is undoubtedly a significant progress in China foreign exchange market.

In recent years, the total transaction volume of China foreign exchange market has shown a steady growth trend. In 2018, the total transaction volume of China foreign exchange market was 192,974.8 billion yuan, up 18.92%

year-on-year, and it reached 200,561.9 billion yuan in 2019, a year-on-year increase of 3.93%. There into, the bank-to-customer market turnover increased to 28, 379.1 billion yuan, and the interbank foreign exchange market volume was 172, 182.8 billion yuan. Short-term transaction volume grew to 78,317.3 billion yuan, accounting for 39.05%. Long-term transaction volume was 2,625.7 billion yuan, accounting for 1.31%. The foreign exchange and currency swap transaction amounted to 113, 760.9 billion yuan, accounting for 56.72%, and the volume of options were 5,858 billion yuan, accounting for 2.92%.

Table 5-1 shows the transaction volume of varieties in China foreign exchange market from 2015 to 2019.

Table 5-1   Transactions in China foreign exchange market from 2015 to 2019

Unit: 100 million yuan

Year	Short-term	Long-term	Foreign exchange & currency swap	Option
2015	515,521	30,712	537,838	25,219
2016	588,349	25,253	674,412	63,967
2017	640,077	28,631	913,426	40,607
2018	734,966	35,488	1,102,877	56,415
2019	783,173	26,257	1,137,609	58,580

Source: Data collected from the State Administration of Foreign Exchange.

Discussion:

(1) What is the development trend of foreign exchange transactions in China?

(2) Looking for information and thinking about the future changes in China foreign exchange market.

Generally speaking, international trade is the main reason for the establishment of foreign exchange market. Because the monetary system of each country is different, so the currency of each country is different. When paying off international creditor's rights and debts, the exchange of currencies between different countries should be solved first. In trade, we need to exchange a certain amount of one currency for another, and the solution of this problem needs to rely on foreign exchange market transactions. At first, the foreign exchange market was mainly created to meet the needs of international trade settlement. Later, with the modernization of trading means and the continuous expansion of global international trade scale, the foreign exchange market has gone far beyond the basic functions of the initial trade settlement. The derivative transactions brought by financial innovations such as spot transaction, forward transaction, foreign exchange swap, foreign exchange future and options have further enriched the products in the foreign exchange market.

Task 1   Overview of Foreign Exchange Market

I. The Meaning of Foreign Exchange Market

The market in which international currency trades take place is called the foreign exchange market. The foreign exchange market is a trading place where banks, various financial institutions, foreign exchange demanders and suppliers, trading intermediaries and individuals engage in foreign exchange trading and adjust foreign exchange supply and demand.

The foreign exchange market is an important part of the international financial market. International trade, international financing and other international economic activities involve the exchange of different currencies. All of them should be realized through foreign exchange trading, so these activities are inseparable from the foreign exchange market. To be brief, the foreign exchange market refers to the place where foreign exchange is traded, that is, the place where different currencies are exchanged with each other. What is traded in this market is a special commodity-foreign currency.

Animation micro-lesson 5-1

Foreign exchange market and characteristics

The foreign exchange market is the exchange between different currencies, which could be the exchange between domestic currency and foreign currency, or the exchange between two different foreign currencies. For example, in China foreign exchange market, traders can use RMB to buy foreign currencies such as US dollars, euros and Japanese yen. In the international foreign exchange market, traders can buy euros, Australian dollars, Japanese yen and other foreign exchange in US dollars. Traders can buy or sell foreign exchange according to their own trading intentions.

II. Characteristics of the Foreign Exchange Market

1. The foreign exchange market is a global market that can be traded 24 hours a day

At the stage when communication and network technology were not developed enough, foreign exchange transactions were mainly limited to local areas, with a small radiation range. With the progress of technology, it is possible to connect the scattered foreign exchange markets around the world, and the regional transactions are gradually transformed into global transactions. Because of the time zone, foreign exchange transactions can take place anywhere and at any time in the world. The major foreign exchange markets in the world are in different time zones. It is theoretically possible to close one market and open another market. Therefore, global foreign exchange transactions are continuous and can be carried out 24 hours a day.

(Knowledge Link 5-1)

Is foreign exchange trading 24 hours a day?

Digital currencies can be traded 365*24 hours without interruption, while foreign exchange is not traded 7*24 hours at any time. Unlike stocks and digital currencies, foreign exchange trading has no centralized exchange. It must be traded and settled through dealers (usually commercial banks). Essentially, the foreign exchange market is decentralized: trading regions, dealers and trading varieties are scattered.

One of the most unique features of the forex market is that it is comprised of a global network of financial centers that transact 24 hours a day, closing only on the weekends. As one major forex hub closes, another hub in a different part of the world remains open for business. This increases the liquidity available in currency markets, which adds to its appeal as the largest asset class available to investors. That means it takes place from one market to another which is from different time zones in different countries around the world: from Oceania to Asia, to Europe, to the Americas. As shown below (in Beijing time):

1. Australia opened a new week of deals at 5 a.m. Monday morning.

2. At 7 a.m., trading in Tokyo, Japan, marked the start of trading in the Asia-Pacific region, with Singapore and Hong Kong, China, starting an hour later.

3. Bank Frankfurt, Germany, received the stick before Australian and Japanese staff left work and European trading hours opened.

4. Then London, the world's biggest foreign exchange trader, appeared at 3 p.m.

5. At 8 p.m., New York joined London as they combined to perform the world's most active hours of the day in foreign exchange, ending early in the morning.

6. The New York trading session continued until the next day and coincided seamlessly with Australia.

Source: Anonymity. One of foreign exchange fundamentals: is foreign exchange trading 24 hours a day? [EB/OL]. [2019-07-21] .https://zhuanlan.zhihu.com/p/74506940.

2. The market with diversified trading methods and the largest trading scale

The original purpose of the birth of foreign exchange market is to carry out trade settlement. With the expansion of the scale of global international trade, the increasing volume and scope of foreign exchange market, the risk of foreign exchange market is also increasing. In order to reduce foreign exchange risks and based on the traditional foreign exchange transactions, a large number of new foreign exchange trading methods and products (financial derivatives) have been produced in the market by financial innovation. The financial market presents a diversified trading pattern, and foreign exchange trading activities are becoming more and more complicated, and the transaction scale is expanding rapidly.

3. Violent price fluctuation and widespread speculation

Under Jamaica monetary system, the floating exchange rate system is widely implemented in many countries around the world, and the exchange rate is directly affected by the market supply and demand, so it fluctuates relatively frequently and violently. Speculative foreign exchange transactions, in particular, have aggravated the instability of exchange rate and further aggravated market risks.

4. Increasing proportion of intangible market

Foreign exchange market is the place where foreign exchange transactions take place. This place can be tangible or intangible. At present, most foreign exchange transactions in the world are carried out through modern electronic communication equipment, which is free from the limitation of site and time, with high transaction speed and high market efficiency. Therefore, in the global foreign exchange transactions, the intangible market has become the main form of the contemporary foreign exchange market, which also further promotes the expansion of foreign exchange transactions scale.

5. Central banks constantly intervene in foreign exchange market

The central bank is an important participant in the foreign exchange market. The purpose of its participation in foreign exchange transactions is not to avoid foreign exchange risk and speculation, but to intervene in the foreign exchange market, to maintain the stability of the exchange rate of domestic currency and to make the exchange rate develop in a direction beneficial to domestic interests through foreign exchange intervention. For example, intervention in the foreign exchange market can promote the balance of domestic international payments and achieve the goal of influencing or stabilizing domestic economic development. Governments in both developed and developing countries have never stopped intervening in foreign exchange markets.

III . Classification of the Foreign Exchange Market

The foreign exchange market can be divided into different types according to different classification standards. Here are three main categories:

(i) Classified by organizational form

The foreign exchange market can be divided into tangible foreign exchange market and intangible foreign exchange market according to organizational forms.

1.Tangible foreign exchange market

The initial foreign exchange trading activities were carried out in a specific fixed trading place. The parties of the transaction trade in the exchange houses with fixed trading places and facilities （usually located in stock exchanges） within the specified business hours, which are called the tangible foreign exchange markets. The well-known tangible foreign exchange markets are mainly concentrated in continental European countries, such as Zurich in Switzerland, Paris in France, Frankfurt in Germany and Amsterdam in the Netherlands.

2.Intangible foreign exchange market

Today's foreign exchange market is more often invisible. This is a huge foreign exchange trading system that connects buyers and sellers by means of telephone, telex, fax, internet and other communication tools. Any party to the transaction can enter this market for trading by telecommunication, so the current foreign exchange market is more of a trading network, an abstract and intangible market.

Since the intangible foreign exchange market makes foreign exchange transactions more convenient and more efficient, it develops rapidly. Even in continental European countries, most foreign exchange transactions are conducted in the intangible market. Intangible foreign exchange market is the dominant form of foreign exchange market today.

（ii）Classified by transaction entities

The foreign exchange market can be divided into foreign exchange retail market and foreign exchange wholesale market according to transaction main bodies.

1. Foreign exchange retail market

The retail market of foreign exchange is a market for buying and selling foreign exchange between banks and customers. Customers may buy and sell foreign exchange because they need to import and export, or to invest in a certain foreign exchange asset. In either case, banks play an intermediary role between the ultimate foreign exchange supplier and the ultimate foreign exchange demander, that is, on the one hand, they buy foreign exchange from customers, on the other hand, they sell foreign exchange to customers who need it, so as to earn the bid-ask price difference from the deal. Compared with the foreign exchange wholesale market, this level of foreign exchange market is called the foreign exchange retail market because the amount of each transaction is relatively small.

2. Foreign exchange wholesale market

Corresponding to the foreign exchange retail market is the foreign exchange wholesale market. It is a market for foreign exchange transactions among banks. Because of the large number of transactions and high starting point, it is called the foreign exchange wholesale market. The foreign exchange wholesale market brings together huge supply and demand flows, so it determines the immediate exchange rate in the foreign exchange market. The exchange rate in the foreign exchange retail market is formed on the basis of the exchange rate in the foreign exchange wholesale market, so the exchange rate of the retail market is higher than that in the foreign exchange wholesale market.

（Ⅲ）Classified by trading instruments

The foreign exchange market can be divided into traditional foreign exchange market and new foreign exchange market according to trading instruments.

Animation micro-lesson 5-2

Traditional foreign exchange markets include spot market, forward market and swap market.

Classification of foreign exchange transactions

The new foreign exchange market is the result of foreign exchange market innovation, also known as foreign exchange financial derivative market which specifically includes forward exchange market, foreign exchange options market and swap market. It will be introduced in detail in the following projects, and only briefly explained here.

Ⅳ. Participants in the Foreign Exchange Market

The trading objects in the foreign exchange market are currencies of various countries, while the traders in the foreign exchange market include commercial banks, foreign exchange brokers, enterprises and individuals engaged in business or investment activities, speculators and arbitrators, central banks, etc. They are collectively referred to as participants in the foreign exchange market. They participate in the foreign exchange market for different purposes and in different ways.

1. Commercial banks

Commercial banks in developed countries usually engage in foreign exchange trading, foreign exchange deposit, exchange and discount. In some countries that implement foreign exchange control, foreign exchange business is handled by banks that are authorized by the central bank of each country to handle foreign exchange operations. Commercial banks are the main bodies of the foreign exchange market and the center of foreign exchange business. 90% of the trading volume in the foreign exchange market comes from foreign exchange transactions among banks.

In the foreign exchange retail market, commercial banks can accept the entrustment of importers and exporters to handle the international settlements, act as the intermediary of foreign exchange trading to earn fees, and can also obtain the trading price difference by buying and selling foreign exchange by themselves. In the foreign exchange wholesale market, if a bank sells more foreign exchange than it buys, it can use its foreign exchange account to sell the additional part to make up the difference, or trade with other banks to maintain the original foreign exchange balance. Commercial banks sometimes speculate in the foreign exchange market, and gain profits through speculation. For example, the banks predict that the US dollar will appreciate in the next three months, so they buy the dollar at the moment and then sell it for speculative gain after three months. However, the premise of speculative trading is to have a more accurate judgment on the exchange rate, so as to ensure the accuracy of the decision-making, otherwise it will lose money.

2. Foreign exchange brokers

A foreign exchange broker is an intermediary agency that specializes in introducing transactions or buying and selling foreign exchange on behalf of customers, and collects fees from it. The foreign exchange broker itself being not a transaction entity, does not hold foreign exchange, and only provides services for commissions. Generally, foreign exchange brokers don't contact with the final suppliers and demanders of foreign exchange. Their main clients are major commercial banks engaged in foreign exchange business, providing commercial banks with appropriate transaction prices and suitable counterparties to facilitate transactions. Typically, foreign exchange transactions facilitated by foreign exchange brokers are usually huge. The reason why foreign exchange brokers can be favored by commercial banks is that they can collect global foreign exchange market information and master foreign exchange market, save information collection costs for customers and hide their trading identities for banks to obtain favorable trading conditions. The existence of foreign exchange brokers is conducive to the rapid closing of foreign exchange transactions, and improve the efficiency of the foreign exchange market.

3. Suppliers and demanders of foreign exchange

Commercial enterprises, multinational investors and individuals engaged in import and export trade are the ultimate demanders and suppliers of the foreign exchange market, and their foreign exchange transactions have different purposes. For example, importers need to buy foreign exchange to pay for foreign goods. In order to avoid the risk of exchange rate fluctuation, exporters can use foreign exchange forward contracts to minimize the losses from foreign currency depreciation.

4. Foreign exchange speculators and arbitrators

The trading purpose of speculators and arbitrators is to obtain profits from the bid-ask spread. Their transactions have no trading background and do not generate any value, and their profits are the losses of counterparties. Therefore, foreign exchange transactions are called the "zero-sum game" in a sense.

5. Central banks

Central banks are indirect participants in the foreign exchange market, and generally do not directly participate in foreign exchange market transactions, usually conducting transactions through foreign exchange brokers. The motive of trading is not profit, but stability of the exchange rate. In the foreign exchange market, the central bank can stabilize the exchange rate of domestic currency by increasing foreign exchange reserves or selling excess foreign exchange assets through foreign exchange brokers or commercial banks, so as to realize its monetary policy and adjust the development of the macro economy.

(Knowledge Link 5-2)

Global foreign exchange market

The foreign exchange market has no borders, and foreign exchange transactions are also globally integrated transactions that span the concepts of time, region, and country. While there are many kinds of foreign exchange markets, which are distributed on all continents of the world. The five most important foreign exchange markets are: London in the UK, New York in the US, Sydney in Australia, Tokyo in Japan and Hong Kong in China.

London foreign exchange market in the UK

London is the world's oldest financial center and the first place to start foreign exchange trading. The long history of London foreign exchange market makes it habitual for banks in various countries to start large foreign exchange transactions after its opening. Therefore, the fluctuation of the global foreign exchange market begins to intensify with the opening of London foreign exchange market. The trading hours are from 15: 30 to 23: 30 Beijing time.

New York foreign exchange market in the US

New York foreign exchange market is one of the important international foreign exchange markets, and its daily trading volume is second only to London. The high activity creates profit opportunities for a large number of investors. Currently, more than 90% of US dollar transactions in the world are finally settled through the interbank clearing system in New York, so the New York market has become the international settlement center of the US dollar. In addition to the US dollar, the major trading currencies are the euro, British pound, Swiss franc, Canadian dollar, Japanese yen, etc. The trading hours are from 20: 00 Beijing time to 4: 00 the next day.

Sydney foreign exchange market in Australia

According to Beijing time, Sydney foreign exchange market is one of the earliest foreign exchange markets to open every day in the world. The trading currencies are mainly AUD, NZD and USD. The trading time is about 6: 00−15: 00 Beijing time.

Tokyo foreign exchange market in Japan

Tokyo foreign exchange market is the largest exchange market in Asia. During Tokyo's foreign exchange trading hours, the yen may be more likely to fluctuate. As a major exporter, Japan's import and export trade is relatively concentrated, so it is vulnerable to interference. Trading currencies in the Tokyo market are mainly the Japanese yen, the US dollar and the euro. The trading hours are 8: 00− 15: 30 Beijing time.

Hong Kong foreign exchange market in China

Hong Kong foreign exchange trading market is significantly different from the other four trading markets mentioned above, because Hong Kong is a fixed trading place for the US dollar, foreign exchange traders can conduct foreign exchange transactions through the Internet or other communication facilities. Therefore, Hong Kong foreign exchange market is an intangible market, but invisibility does not mean inactivity. As an international financial center, Hong Kong has a large influx of international capital, and Hong Kong foreign exchange market has always been one of the most active markets in the world. The trading currencies are mainly Hong Kong dollar and US dollar. The trading hours are 9: 00−16: 00 Beijing time.

Source: Anonymity. Detailed explanation of the world's five major foreign exchange trading centers ［EB/OL］. ［2018−03−01］. https://www.sohu.com/a/224621165_249239.

V. China Foreign Exchange Market

China foreign exchange market is an important part of China financial market, which plays an irreplaceable role in perfecting the exchange rate formation mechanism, promoting the convertibility of RMB, serving financial institutions, promoting the change of macro-control mode and improving the financial market system. Although China foreign exchange market started late, it is developing rapidly, mainly using an advanced electronic trading platform for foreign exchange transactions at home and abroad.

From the perspective of market structure, China foreign exchange market is divided into three levels:

1. The retail market

It is the market between customers and designated foreign exchange banks.

In China, the foreign exchange retail market, also known as the customer market, refers specifically to the foreign exchange trading activities and places between banks and individual and corporate customers. Banks play an intermediary role in foreign exchange transactions with customers. On the one hand, they buy foreign exchange from customers. On the other hand, they sell foreign exchange to customers to earn the difference between foreign exchange buying and selling, which is the foreign exchange service provided by banks to customers and the basis for the existence of foreign exchange market.

In the retail market, trading customers mainly include enterprises, importers and exporters, individuals and so on. Banks take part in foreign exchange trading for the needs of international trade, investment and other aspects. The retail business of foreign exchange consists of foreign exchange transactions between banks and individuals or corporate customers, such as currency exchange, import and export settlement and foreign exchange trading. Individuals and enterprises usually trade directly with banks. The retail foreign exchange market is dominated by sporadic transactions, with no minimum transaction amount limit. The transactions are scattered, the transaction volumes are small, the cost is relatively high, and the bid-ask spread is large.

2. The wholesale market (inter bank foreign exchange market)

All financial institutions operating in China should conduct foreign exchange transactions through the inter bank foreign exchange market, which is also called the wholesale market. Authorized by the People's Bank of China and the State Administration of Foreign Exchange, domestic financial institutions (including Chinese banks, foreign banks and non bank financial institutions) are allowed to conduct foreign exchange transactions through the China Foreign Exchange Trade System (CFETS), and the market in which the transactions between RMB and foreign currencies conduct is called the Inter bank Foreign Exchange Market.

Designated foreign exchange banks may be overbought or oversold in the process of settlement and sale of foreign exchange. They can conduct foreign exchange transactions through the interbank foreign exchange market to balance their foreign exchange positions. In addition, the floating exchange rate is implemented in the Jamaica monetary system, the fluctuating exchange rate brings many profit opportunities for speculative foreign exchange trading. Banks will engage in foreign exchange transactions such as arbitrage, hedging and swap for speculative purposes.

The wholesale market is characterized by large-scale transactions, mainly adopting integer wholesale transactions, and there are limits on the minimum transaction amount (for example, in the European foreign exchange market, the minimum transaction volume of US dollars is 1 million). Due to the huge trading volume, the transaction cost is lower and the bid-ask spread is smaller. The wholesale market is the mainstream of the foreign exchange market, and its transactions account for more than 90% of the total foreign exchange transactions. The foreign exchange market we generally mentioned in news reports usually refers to the interbank foreign exchange market.

3. Market between the central bank and designated foreign exchange bank

For the purpose of macro-control, the central bank buys or sells foreign exchanges through open business operations in the wholesale market. It can timely enter the market as an ordinary member, intervene in the market, adjust the supply and demand of foreign exchange and maintain the stability of the exchange rate, which is an effective way for the People's Bank of China to regulate and manage the foreign exchange market.

In addition, the interbank RMB market consists of the transaction of spot ,forward , swap and option, etc. These transactions will be introduced in detail in the following projects.

Knowledge Link 5-3

The China Foreign Exchange Trade System

Founded on April 18, 1994, the China Foreign Exchange Trade System （CFETS）, also known as the National Interbank Funding Center, is a sub-institution directly affiliated to the People's Bank of China （PBC）. Its headquarter is in Shanghai and its sub-center is in Beijing. CFETS aims to provide a trading system and organize transactions for interbank foreign exchange market, money market, bond market and derivatives market, and at the same time perform the market monitoring function to ensure the stable, healthy and efficient operation of the market. China Foreign Exchange Trading Center's main business and services include:

1.The interbank FX market

The interbank FX market consists of the interbank RMB/FX market, the foreign currency pairs market, the foreign currency lending market, and the related derivatives market. With the membership system and a market-making mechanism, it supports FX trading among market participants.

CFETS provides the interbank FX market with a unified and efficient e-trading system that supports anonymous trading, bilateral trading and matched trading, and offers system services such as trade analysis, market-making interface, and real-time communication tool.

In addition, CFETS supports bilateral trading of gold spot, forward and swap transactions with the cooperation of Shanghai Gold Exchange.

2.The interbank RMB market

The interbank RMB market consists of money market, bond market, and the related derivative market, serving as an important platform for financial institutions to manage their liquidity, asset-liability, investment and trade, interest rate and credit risk, as well as being a major platform for transmitting the monetary policies of PBC.

CFETS provides various institutional investors of the interbank RMB market with an efficient and convenient trading system that covers a range of interest rates and credit products and supports various trading methods such as bilateral trading, market-making quotations, requesting for quotations, and bilateral matching. The system also allows market participants to issue interbank negotiable certificates of deposit and offers them standing lending facility.

Source: According to the information on the website of China Foreign Exchange Trade System. http://www. chinamoney.com.cn/.

Task 2   The Spot Foreign Exchange Transaction

There are many types of foreign exchange transactions. The spot foreign exchange transaction , forward foreign exchange transaction and foreign exchange swap are known as the basic transactions in the foreign exchange market, which are called traditional forms of foreign exchange transactions. With technology continually improving, the continuous development of the international financial industry and the endless innovation of financial instruments, many innovative forms of foreign exchange transactions have appeared in the foreign exchange market, such as foreign exchange futures, foreign exchange options, foreign exchange swaps, etc. They are called foreign exchange derivatives. This section introduces the basic principles and applications of spot transactions, forward transactions, swap transactions and arbitrage.

I. The Spot Transaction

The spot transaction refers to the foreign exchange transaction in which the buyer and seller have to settle on the day of the transaction or within two business days after the foreign exchange transaction. The spot transaction is also called the spot trade ,and it is the most common and popular transactions in the foreign exchange market.

The following contents must be clarified for better understanding spot foreign exchange transactions.

（i）Dealing and delivery

In foreign exchange transactions, dealing refers to the confirmation of a foreign exchange trading agreement, which stipulates the buyer and seller, the currency, quantity and price of the foreign exchange transaction and the delivery standard. Dealing refers to determine the buying and selling relationship, and no actual payment behavior occurs.

Delivery refers to the payment of currency by the buyer and seller after the transaction, and the two parties respectively remit the sold currency to the bank account designated by the other party according to the requirements of the other party. The day when delivery takes place is called the "delivery date".

（ii）Delivery method

The delivery date, also known as the settlement date and the value date, refers to the date when the buyer and seller exchange monetary funds with each other, which is also the date when the monetary funds of both parties are transferred to the designated account bank and interest begins to accrue. According to different market rules, the delivery date of spot foreign exchange transactions is different, and there are mainly the following three types:

1. The value spot （T+2）

The value spot （T+2） generally adopt the delivery method of T+2, which is synchronized with the settlement of European accounts, that is, the parties will exchange the currencies on the second business day after the deal is applied in the spot transaction. At present, some major foreign exchange markets basically adopt the T+2 mode of delivery. For instance, an American buyer imports printing presses from Germany, pays after the goods are verified on May 10th, and completes the delivery on May 13th, according to the current bank foreign exchange quotation of that day.

2. The value tomorrow （T+1）

The value tomorrow （T+1） also known as cash delivery, applys the deliverys method of T+1, which means the delivery occurs at the first business day after the deal. Some countries or regions apply T+1 due to time difference. For example, in Hong Kong foreign exchange market, spot transactions of HKD/JPY, HKD/SPD, HKD/AUD apply the value tomorrow. The spot transaction of USD/CAD and USD/MXN in New York market also deliver at the next day after the deal. Because these countries or regions basically belong to the same time zone.

3. The value today （T+0）

The value today （T+0） is used in the spot transaction . In this manner, the exchange of the currencies is executed on the trading day, which is called the value today （T+0）. The transactions between banks and local customers can generally close the deal on the same day.

The value spot （T+2） is usually used in the international foreign exchange market. If the day of delivery falls on a bank holiday, it will be postponed. The spot transaction adopts spot exchange rate, which is usually the quoted price on the day of the bank that handles foreign exchange business, or refers to the price comparison between major currencies in the local foreign exchange market plus a certain service charge.

II . The Role of Spot Transaction

The spot trading can be applied to the remittance of foreign exchange, and serve individual customers, customers of import and export enterprises and foreign exchange speculators. The functions of spot transaction are as follows:

1. Meeting the temporary payment needs

Temporary foreign exchange demand of enterprises or individuals in daily business or life can be met by spot foreign exchange transactions. Customers can exchange their local currency or foreign currency into another currency through spot foreign exchange transaction for external payment. For example, when individuals need to exchange foreign currency for overseas travel, they can exchange their local currency into foreign currency at the exchange rate of the day at the bank counter.

2. Avoiding foreign exchange risks

As import and export enterprise hold different foreign currencies, fluctuations in exchange rates will lead to foreign exchange risks. Enterprises can adjust their foreign exchange positions at any time to avoid the risk of exchange rate fluctuations by taking spot foreign exchange trans-actions.

3. Foreign exchange speculations

Speculators conduct foreign exchange speculative transactions by buying and selling spot exchange. They can obtain profits through the operation of "buy low and sell high". However, foreign exchange speculation is a risky activity. All the gains achieved are based on the ability to seek the bid-ask spreads and accurate forecast about the trend of the future exchange rate. Otherwise, there will be the opposite result-loss.

Ⅲ. Quotation Rules and Procedures for Spot Foreign Exchange Transactions

（ⅰ）Quotation rules for spot transactions

The quotation is the basis of the spot transaction. The institution that provides the transac-tion price (exchange rate)is generally referred to as the offeror, the foreign exchange bank usual-ly plays this role; in contrast, the one who inquire the price is called the bidder. The bidder could be foreign exchange banks, foreign exchange brokers, individuals, central banks, etc. They make inquires to the offeror and make deals with them at the spot exchange rate provided by the offeror. Foreign exchange banks should follow certain practices and rules when quoting in spot transactions.

1.Two-way quotation

Foreign exchange banks generally adopt two-way quotation, that is, banks quote both the bid rate and the offer rate at the same time. The difference between them is called Bid-Ask Spread. For instance, the spot foreign exchange quotation of EUR/CNY on August 10, 2018 was EUR/CNY = 7.8561/7.9141. In this quotation, the euro is the base currency and the RMB is the quoted currency; 7.8561 is the bank's buying price, and 7.9141 is the bank's selling price. That is, the bank needs to pay 7.8561 RMB for every euro it buys; Banks can charge 7.9141 RMB for every euro sold.

2. Only the last two digits of the exchange rate are quoted

In spot transactions, the exchange rate quoted by banks is generally expressed by five sig-nificant figures, which consists of two parts: the large number and the decimal number. Large numbers are an essential part of the exchange rate and are usually not quoted by traders, unless the parties need to confirm the transaction or when the market changes rapidly. Suppose USD/CNY=6.8271/85, where 6.82 is a large number, 71 and 85 are decimals, and the difference of 14 between 71 and 85 is called the spread. In general, the decimal change of exchange rate is relatively active, and the large number is relatively stable. The exchange rate will change every second during foreign exchange trading, so the quotation should be concise and fast. Quotations between foreign exchange banks are usually quoted in the last two digits, that is, the decimal part.

3. Concept of basis point

The smallest unit and the last digit after the decimal point in the quotation is called a basis point or one point. In the transaction, 1 basis point =0.0001. Changes in currency exchange rates are usually indicated by changes in points. For example, the exchange rate of the US dollar against RMB rose from 6.8271 to 6.8285, which can be said that the exchange rate of the US dollar rose by 14 basis points.

(ⅱ) Procedures for spot foreign exchange transactions

Most foreign exchange transactions are interbank transactions. There is a standard set of procedures for spot transactions. Its trading procedures generally go through the inquiry, quotation, transaction, confirmation, record delivery and so on. Here's how two forex traders traded EUR /USD swaps:

A: HIHI FRD ANY INT TO SWAP EUR 2 MIO AG USD

B: FOR TOM/1W?

　　3.38 3.48

A:DONE I S/B EUR

B: CFM I B/S EUR 2 MIO AG USD AT+3.48

　　REATS ARE 1.2310 N 1.231348

　　MY EUR TO DEUTDEFF

　　MY USD TO BKTRUS33

A: ALL AGREE

　　MY EUR TO DRESDEFF

　　MY USD TO CITIUS33

A: Hello, friend. Quotes for EUR /USD FX swaps? The amount is 2 million euros. （Inquiry）

B: The spot will be delivered tomorrow, and the forward will be delivered one week later? Spot buy euro forward sell dollar at 3.38, spot sell euro forward buy US dollar at 3.48. （Quote）

A: OK, that's a deal. I'm selling EUR forward and buying USD at the spot. （Make a deal）

B: To confirm, I will buy and sell 2 million euros against the US dollar at the spot, with the swap rate is 3.48, the spot exchange rate is 1.2310, and the forward exchange rate is 1.231348. My EUR is transferred to the account DEUTDEFF, and the US dollar is transferred to the account BKTRUS33. （Confirm and record delivery）

A: Confirm the deal. My euro to the account DRESDEFF and USD to the account CITIUS33. （Confirm and record delivery）

It can be seen from the above conversations between foreign exchange traders that foreign exchange traders are very professional positions, and spot transactions between banks usually have special standard terms. As a professional trader, you must have super comprehensive quality, strong pressure-bearing ability, good at observation and learning, the ability to capture details, risk awareness and stop-loss awareness, etc., which are indispensable skills and qualities for foreign exchange traders.

Ⅳ. Arbitrage Trading

The arbitrage transaction is typically spot transactions. Arbitrage refers to the process of buying a currency in one market at a lower rate and immediately selling it in another market at a higher rate. The difference between these two rates is the profit to the participant. According to the distribution of arbitrage locations, arbitrage transactions can be divided into direct arbitrage and indirect arbitrage.

1. Direct arbitrage （locational arbitrage）

Direct arbitrage, which is also known as locational arbitrage, refers to the behavior that the arbitrage trader buys a certain foreign exchange in the market with low exchange rate and sell it in the market with a high exchange rate, so as to profit from it.

［Example 5-1］ On a certain day, GBP/USD = 1.6260/70 in London foreign exchange market and 1.6280/90 in New York foreign exchange market. How to carry out direct arbitrage?

The analysis of the arbitrage operation process is as follows:

In this case, the GBP/USD rate is 1.6260/70 in London market, and at the same time, the rate is 1.6280/90 in New York market. There is an arbitrage opportunity if a trader buys one GBP from London for \$1.6270 and then sells the same in New York market for \$1.6280. In the transaction, the trader would make \$0.01 per GBP. （Excluding arbitrage cost）.

As a result, the exchange rate of the British pound rose and the US dollar fell in the London foreign exchange market. In New York foreign exchange market, the exchange rate of the British pound fell and the exchange rate of the US dollar rose. Finally, the exchange rates in the two markets tend to be the same, and arbitrage automatically terminates. Due to the development of electronic communication systems, arbitrage opportunities between the two markets can be quickly captured, which greatly reduces the difference of foreign exchange quotation between the two markets and the opportunities of the direct arbitrage.

2. Indirect arbitrage （triangular arbitrage）

Indirect arbitrage, also known as triangle arbitrage, is a process where two related goods set a third price. In the triangular arbitrage, a trader tries to benefit from the discrepancy in the exchange rate between three foreign currencies with one basis currency and two supporting currencies, such as EUR/USD, EUR/GBP, and USD/GBP. In this, USD is the basis currency.

The first step in triangular arbitrage is to identify the opportunity of indirect arbitrage. The method is to unify the quotation form to direct quotation or indirect quotation, and then multiply them. If the product is 1, there is no chance; On the contrary, there is an opportunity, and the larger the deviation between the product and 1, the higher the arbitrage income.

［Example 5-2］ On a certain day, USD/ CHF =0.9807 in New York foreign exchange market, GBP /USD= 1.6782 in London foreign exchange market and GBP /CHF=1.6052 in Zurich foreign exchange market. How to carry out indirect arbitrage?

The analysis of arbitrage operation process is as follows:

Step 1: unifying the quotation form.

Both New York and London market adopt the indirect quotation, while Zurich market adopts direct quotation. Therefore, the quotation in Zurich foreign exchange market is converted into indirect pricing, that is, CHF/GBP =0.6630. Then, multiply the right of the equal sign of the three exchange rates by $0.9807×1.6782×1/1.6052 = 1.0253 \neq 1$, which shows that there is an opportunity for arbitrage among these three markets.

Step 2: Carry out the market operation.

The GBP is the most expensive in London foreign exchange market among the three markets and collected in New York and Zurich foreign exchange market is cheaper. Therefore, the arbitrage trader buy GBP in New York and Zurich, and sell it in London foreign exchange market, thus gaining profits （that is, buy CHF sell USD in New York foreign exchange market, then buy GBP sell CHF in Zurich foreign exchange market, finally sell GBP in London foreign exchange market and get US dollars）. If the principal is USD 1, the profit can be USD 0.0253 （$1×0.9807×1/1.6052×1.6782-1$）, and the profit rate is 2.53%. （Excluding transaction costs）

If the two-way quotation is adopted, the issue of transaction price should be considered when calculating the profits of triangular arbitrage. Triangular arbitrage can only be carried out by professional exchange traders, and it is difficult for public participants to make such arbitrage transactions.

Task 3　　Forward Exchange Transactions

I. Overview of Forward Transactions

The forward exchange transaction refers to a transaction in which two parties (at least one of which is a bank) sign a foreign exchange transaction contract, and do not deliver immediately, but execute the deal on an agreed date in the future (after the third business day after the contract signed).

The forward exchange rate is not the future spot exchange rate. It is stipulated by the buyer and seller in the contract in advance and cannot be changed. The future spot exchange rate is the true market price at a certain time, which might rise or fall in the future. The spread of the two rates is the profit of the transaction.

Animation micro-lesson 5-3

Forward foreign exchange transactions

Forward transactions are completed through forwarding contracts. Generally, there are at least five kinds of information in the contract, such as currency type, exchange rate, quantity, delivery date and the type of foreign exchange trading.

1. Delivery period of forward foreign exchange transactions

Foreign exchange deals sometimes specify a future transaction date—may be 30 days, 90 days, 180 days, or even several years away. In practice, 90 days forward transactions are the most common, while transactions over 1 year are rare. The reason is that the longer the delivery period, the greater the uncertainty of the transaction, so the greater the risks that traders will take.

The way to calculate the forward delivery date is to add the spot delivery date to the corresponding forward months. For example, for 90 days forward transaction signed on June 7th, the delivery date is September 9th, which is the spot delivery date of June 9th plus 90 days. The delivery date should be postponed later if this day happens to be bank holidays. The exchange rate used for forward transactions is the forward exchange rate.

(Knowledge Link 5-4)

How to calculate the value date?

The value date is the date when a trade is expected to be settled. Customers who buy foreign exchange should deliver their own currency, while sellers should deliver the foreign currency they sell. The qualified delivery date must be the business day of the currency issuer. Even if both parties to the transaction are holidays, as long as the country of currency issuer is business day, it is still a qualified delivery date.

The value date can be divided into two categories: value date for the spot transaction and value date for forward foreign exchange transaction.

For spot transactions, or those involving the sale or purchase of currency for another, the value date is usually two business days after the date upon which the transaction and exchange rates were agreed to. The value date is the date that the two currencies are traded and not the date of the agreement. Of course, the two business days do not include Saturdays, Sundays, or public (bank) holidays in either of the two countries of the currencies involved.

For FX forward transactions, value date refers to the date agreed upon by both parties for the delivery of funds, but unlike spot transactions, this date can be settled on any business day that is beyond the spot value date.

For example, the transaction will be agreed on Monday, November 25th, 2019, and the delivery date of spot exchange will be Wednesday, November 27th. The delivery date of 30 days, 60 days ,90 days forward transactions are December 27th (Friday), January 27th, 2020 (Monday), February 27th, 2020 (Thursday)respectively.

---

2. Generation of forward foreign exchange transactions

Forward transactions are created to avoid foreign exchange risks. Compared with domestic trade, international trade activities are more complicated, and there will be a period of time between signing the contract and settling the payment. It usually takes several months for importers and exporters to sign an export contract, to receive and to pay for the goods. During this period, one of the traders will take a loss if the value of the currency used for payment changes. Those countries that adopt the floating exchange rate system will suffer the risk from the fluctuation of the exchange rate. And this will further aggravate the exchange rate risk of traders. Similarly, the benefits and costs of financial traders who invest and finance internationally will also be affected by the exchange rate changes. Forward foreign exchange transactions can reduce or avoid the losses caused by exchange rate fluctuations.

II. Quotation of Forward Transactions

(i) Direct quotation

Banks will quote the buying price and selling price of forward foreign exchange at the same time. Direct quotation is used in the forward transaction between the bank and individuals.

For instance, on a certain day, the 30 days forward exchange rate of the US dollar against the Japanese yen is USD/JPY=119.77/119.83, which indicates that the bank's buying price of 30 days forward US dollar is 119.77 Japanese yen and the selling price is 119.83 yen per US dollar.

On December 1st, 2018, the Bank of China reported that the exchange rate of 30 days forward the US dollar was USD/CNY=6.8660/6.8770, which indicated that the bank bought 30 days forward US dollar at 6.8660 yuan per US dollar, and sold it at 6.8770 yuan per US dollar.

(ii) Quotation of swap rate

Animation micro-lesson 5-4

At premium and at discount

The quotation of swap rate only marks the difference between the forward exchange rate and spot exchange rate, not the buying price and selling price of forward exchange rate directly. It is usually adopted in the international foreign exchange market. The difference between the forward exchange rate and spot exchange rate is called the forward spread or forward point. The forward price difference is expressed in terms of premium, discount and parity in the foreign exchange market.

1. Premium and discount

In the foreign exchange market, there are two columns of figures expressing the forward exchange rate, representing the purchase price and the selling price respectively. For example, at premium means that forward foreign exchange is more expensive than spot foreign exchange, while the forward foreign exchange is cheaper than spot foreign exchange, it is called a discount. Parity (at par) means that the forward foreign exchange rate and spot foreign exchange rate are equal.

The scope of the forward margin is determined by the difference in the interest rate of the two currencies. Generally speaking, the currency with a higher interest rate shows a discount in the forward market, while the currency with a lower interest rate shows a premium in the forward market.

In the practical application of forward foreign exchange transactions, banks only quote the spot exchange rate and the swap points of forward exchange, they do not report whether it is premium or discount. The forward exchange rate can be calculated by adding or subtracting the swap points. It is necessary to judge whether the forward exchange rate is premium or discount before adding or subtracting the premium and discount.

2. Calculation of forward exchange rate

The formulas for calculating forward exchange rates are different due to the different quotation methods used.

Under the direct quotations, forward exchange rate = spot rate +/− premium / discount points.

In this case , the method to judge the premium/discount of the base currency is: the first digital is small and the last is large, it is at premium, addition is used to calculate the forward exchange rate, while the first digital is large and the last is small ,it is at discount, subtract will be adopted.

Under the indirect quotation, forward exchange rate= spot rate −/+ premium /discount points.

〔Example 5-3〕 One certain day, the Bank of New York quoted the spot exchange rate GBP/USD = 1.6783/93, and the swap point of 90 days forward GBP/USD was 80/70.

Analysis: the direct quotation was adopted for GBP/ USD=1.6783/93, and the 90 days forward GBP/USD swap point was 80/70. According to the above judgment method, "Large in front and small in back means at discount, subtract will be adopted", the forward exchange rate of GBP is calculated as follows:

forward GBP bid = 1.6783−0.0080 = 1.6703
forward GBP ask = 1.6793−0.0070 = 1.6723
90−day forward GBP/USD=1.6703/1.6723

〔Example 5-4〕 On a certain day, in New York foreign exchange market, the spot exchange rate was GBP /USD= 1.5575/81. Suppose the swap point of 30 days forward GBP was10/20, calculate the 30 days forward exchange rate of GBP.

Analysis: Under the direct quotations, the spot exchange rate GBP/USD =1.5575/81, 30 days forward pound was at premium, so the forward exchange rate = spot exchange rate+premium points, namely:

30 days forward GBP buy = 1.5575 + 0.0010 = 1.5585
30 days forward GBP sell = 1.5581 + 0.0020 = 1.5601
30 days forward GBP/USD=1.5585/1.5601

As long as the order of swap point is from small to large （20/30）, use addition; while the swap point order is from large to small （60/40）, subtraction is used. At the same time, the order of swap point"small in the front and large in the back" means the premium of base currency and the discount of quote currency. The order of the swap points "large in the front and small in the back" means that the basis currency is discount, and the quote currency is premium.

Ⅲ. Application of Forward Transactions

The type of currency, amount, value date, exchange rate in the forward contract can be determined by both parties through negotiation, therefor the forward contract can be called a tailor−made contract for customers, which is welcomed by importers and exporters. However, because of its "personality", or nonstandardized characteristics, its liquidity is poor, the contract cannot be suspended and must be executed when it expires, so it is difficult to change hands in the market. The nonstandardized characteristics make forward foreign exchange transactions generally adopt over-the-counter transactions.

Teaching video 5-1

Forward foreign exchange transactions

In practice, importers and exporters will sign forward transaction contracts with banks to avoid exchange risk. The buyer transfers the future exchange rate risk to the bank. Of course, the bank will adjust its own position in time, and transfer the risk to other investors through the currency market and foreign exchange market.

(i) Importers and exporters manage exchange rate risk by forward transactions

[Example 5-5] In mid-February, 2020, the spot exchange rate in New York foreign exchange market was GBP/USD = 1.6700, with a 90 days forward discount of 16 bps. An American exporter signed a contract to export goods worth 625,000 pounds to the UK. It was expected that he would not receive the pounds until three months later, then the British pound would need to be converted into US dollars for accounting. Suppose the American exporter expected that the spot exchange rate will depreciate to GBP/USD=1.6600 in 3 months. What strategy could the exporters take to manage exchange rate risk? Try to analyze his profit and loss in forward transactions (suppose no transaction cost).

The specific analysis is as follows:

(1) Strategy for the American exporter.

The American exporter expected to take the loss due to the discount of the forward exchange rate. Once the selling contract was signed, the American exporter should sign a forward contract with the bank to sell 3-month forward pounds to avoid the risk. The contract agreed to sell 625,000 pounds to the bank after 3 months, and the exchange rate was the result negotiated by both parties. No matter how the spot exchange rate changes after 3 months, the specified exchange rate would be implemented according to the contract.

(2) Profit and loss of the exporter in forward transactions.

Based on given conditions, the spot exchange rate was GBP/USD = 1.6700, and the 3-month forward discount was 16 bps. The exchange rate of 3-month forward GBP could be calculated as follows:

GBP/USD=1.6700-0.0016=1.6684

In the case of a forward transaction, the US exporters receive 625,000 pounds after 3 months, which can be converted for US dollars as:

625,000*1.6684=1,042,750 USD

Without forward transactions, the exporter would receive 625,000 pounds after 3 months, that will be :

625,000*1.6600=1,037,500 USD

As compared to the spot transaction, the forward transaction can earn an extra $5,250 (1,042,750-1,037,500). In the above case, the American exporter can sell forward GBP to lock in future earnings in order to avoid the depreciation of the foreign currency. In fact, importers can also determine the balance of local currency to be paid in the future by buying forward foreign exchange in advance. Similarly, international borrowers can also hedge the risk through forward transactions.

〔Example 5-6〕 On March 20th, 2018, a Chinese buyer imported a batch of goods from the United States, and would pay USD 1 million three months later. The spot exchange rate was USD/CNY = 6.3141/6.3409, and the 3-month forward exchange rate was USD/CNY = 6.4620/6.4822. To avoid higher costs due to exchange rate movements, the Chinese importer signed a forward contract with the local bank to buy $1 million. Suppose the spot exchange rate on the date of payment after 3 months was 6.4648/6.4922. What was the impact of the Chinae importer not doing forward transactions (suppose no transaction cost)?

Analysis: the Chinese importer bought USD1,000,000,000 for three months and was expected to pay in CNY:

1,000,000*6.4822=6,482,200

Suppose the Chinese importer did not carry out the foreign exchange forward transaction, the amount to be paid after 3 months for USD at spot exchange rate was:

1,000,000*6.4922=6,492,200

So if the Chinese importer didn't make the forward foreign exchange transaction, he would pay 10,000 RMB （6,492,200-6,482,200） more.

(**Knowledge Link 5-5**)

What is forex hedge?

A forex hedge is a transaction implemented to protect an existing or anticipated position from an unwanted move in exchange rates. Forex hedges are used by a broad range of market participants, including investors, traders and businesses. By using a forex hedge properly ,the traders can sell or buy the foreign exchange which would be settled at the future date in the foreign exchange market to protect against upside or downside risk.

By hedging, the original foreign currency will suffer losses at maturity due to exchange rate change, while trading in the foreign exchange market generates profits, the loss can be offset. Similarly, if the transactions in the foreign exchange market suffer losses, the original foreign currency will gain profits instead, which can also offset the losses. It can be seen that as long as the transaction in the foreign exchange market is contrary to the original foreign currency position due to the exchange rate change, the profit and loss can be offset.

For example, when a Chinese company exports goods to Germany, the contract stipulates that the Chinese company will receive 5 million euros in three months. If the euro exchange rate fall in three months, the Chinese company will suffer losses. Therefore, it would sell 5 million 90 days euro in advance. Three months later, the forward contract would be executed at stipulated price. Of course the Chinese company will not be able to make profits if the euro exchange rate rises in three months.

Obviously, a forex hedge is meant to protect from losses, not to make a profit. Holders of forward foreign exchange bonds or debts, such as importers, exporters and international fund borrowers, can make profits or fix foreign exchange costs in advance by signing forward contracts, so as to remove a portion of the exposure risk.

Source: Compiled by the editor according to the network.

(ii) Balance banks' positions by means of forward foreign exchange transactions to avoid foreign exchange risks

Banks are the counterparties of importers and exporters in the forward transaction market. Contract buyers pass on foreign exchange risks to banks, it is inevitable that banks will have an imbalance of forward positions in a certain currency. To avoid the risk, banks also try to balance their forward exchange positions by selling long positions and buying short positions in the foreign exchange market.

(Ⅲ) Speculators make profits from forward transactions

Forward foreign exchange transactions can also meet the needs of speculators. The purpose of foreign exchange speculators is to take advantage of fluctuations in the exchange rate and obtain the spread in the exchange rate. There are two types of forex speculative trading: short selling and buy long.

Short selling is the behavior of "selling before buying" in the foreign exchange market by speculators who expect the foreign exchange rate to fall. The specific operation mode of short selling is: the foreign exchange rate is expected to fall in the future, traders make an appointment to sell first when the current exchange rate is relatively high, and then buy back the same amount of foreign exchange to make a profit. Buy long is the behavior of "buying first and then selling" when the foreign exchange rate is expected to rise, that is, buying foreign exchange at the current low price and selling it after the exchange rate rises in the future. Whether it is short selling or buy long, speculators receive the price difference of exchange rate fluctuation on the maturity date, and do not have sufficient delivery funds. Moreover, foreign exchange speculators' foreign exchange trading is not based on real trade. If the forecast direction is opposite, they will face losses.

Ⅳ. Classification of Forward Transactions

1. Fixed forward transaction

Fixed Forward transaction refers to an agreement between the two parties to carry out foreign exchange delivery on a fixed date in the future. Importers and exporters or creditors and debtors who sign such forward contracts generally have already signed a trading contract, and the contract stipulates the date of paying/receiving the foreign exchange. The fixed forward transaction is commonly used in real trading. If the foreign exchange market suddenly changes, fixed forward transactions cannot be temporarily changed.

2. Optional forward transaction

Optional forward transaction of foreign exchange refers to the foreign exchange forward deal that enables customers to settle with a prescribed foreign exchange rate on any working day within a certain contracted period in the future. Customers can choose the settlement date by themselves. When the settlement date is uncertain, optional forward transaction would be a good choice.

For customers, optional forward transaction is more flexible and convenient, while the bank will take more risks in this transaction. This is the reason why the bank will choose the exchange rate favorable to itself.

Task 4   Foreign Exchange Swap Transactions

A swap transaction is an agreement between two parties to exchange two currencies at a certain exchange rate at a certain time in the future. There are two types of swap transactions. One is a currency swap and the other is an interest swap. The swap trading, like futures and options trading, is one of the rapidly developing financial derivatives in recent years, and has played an important role for international financial institutions to avoid exchange rate risk and interest rate risk.

I. Foreign Exchange Swap Transaction

A foreign exchange swap is a simultaneous purchase and sale of identical amounts of one currency for another with two different value dates. In other words, traders sell or buy the same currency with different maturities as buying or selling a certain currency. For example, to sell currency A (spot transaction) and buy currency B (forward transaction); or buy currency A (spot transaction) and sell currency B (forward transaction).

To summarize, the characteristics of the above two cases:one purchase, one sale, for two different value dates, one of which is spot or forward, the other is forward.

Teaching video 5-2

Foreign exchange swap transactions

II. Classification of Foreign Exchange Swap Transactions

According to the delivery time of the transaction, swaps can be classified into spot – forward swaps, spot – spot swaps and forward–forward swaps.

1. spot – forward swaps

Spot–forward swap transactions refer to buying or selling a spot foreign exchange and simultaneously selling or buying a futures exchange. For example, a Japanese bank bought USD 10 million for business needs and deposited it in New York for three months. The US dollar deposited in New York can't be exchanged for the original number of Japanese yen if the USD exchange rate fall in 3 months. The bank would adopt swap transactions to avoid its risk, buying 10 million US dollars in spot exchange and selling 10 million US dollars at the same time, so as to transfer the risk arisen by the US dollar's depreciation in the next three months.

2. spot-spot swaps

The spot-spot swap transaction refers to buying or selling one spot foreign exchange while selling or buying another spot foreign exchange of the same currency, but the delivery dates of the two spot transactions are inconsistent. Spot-spot swaps are mostly used in the overnight market.

3. forward-forward swaps

Forward-forward swap transactions mean that the trader buys or sells a forward exchange, concurrently sells or buys the same currency with different delivery times. In the forward to forward swap transaction, if the settlement dates of two forward transactions are relative close , it would be the short-term to forward swap transaction. For example, ABC Company of the United States is going to invest 10 million euros in French bond market after three months and recover it after six months. ABC Company could purchase a 90 days forward contract for 10 million euros and sell a 180-days forward contract to avoid exchange rate risk.

(Knowledge Link 5-6)

Famous swaps transactions in history

In 1981, IBM and the World Bank conducted a currency swap transaction between Swiss francs and Deutsche marks and US dollars. At that time, the World Bank was able to raise US dollars in Eurodollar market with more favorable conditions, but what was actually needed was Swiss francs and Deutsche marks. Meanwhile, IBM, which held the Swiss francs and Deutsch marks, wanted to change its currencies into US dollars to avoid interest rate risk.

As an intermediary, the Salomon Brothers started a swap transaction. The World Bank provided the US dollars raised at low interest rates to IBM, and IBM sold the Swiss francs and Deutsche marks to the World Bank. The World Bank raised the required Swiss francs and Deutsche marks in a more favorable condition, while IBM avoided the exchange rate risk and raised the US dollars at a low cost.

This is the first currency swap in the world officially announced so far. Through this swap transaction, the World Bank and IBM raised their own funds at a low cost without changing the legal relationship with the original creditors.

In 1982, Deutsche Bank conducted an interest rate swap transaction ,which based on a loan with a long-term floating interest rate to an enterprise. It expected that the interest rate would rise, so it might be more advantageous to raise long-term funds in the form of fixed interest rate. Deutsche Bank's solution was to issue long-term fixed-rate bonds, then use interest rate swap to convert fixed interest rate into floating interest rate. This transaction was considered to be the first formal interest rate swap transaction in the word.

Source: Anonymity: What is a foreign exchange swap? [EB/OL] . [2006-10-20] . https://www.233. com/zq/jichu/Instructs/20061020/102020497.html.

Ⅲ. Application of foreign exchange swaps

The swap is an important tool for hedging with forward foreign exchange transactions. We will further discuss how to use swaps for hedging.

〔Example 5-7〕 Suppose that ABC Company needs 10 million euros to invest in the French security market (assuming that the investment products are fixed-income securities), and plans to recover it after three months. It is known that the spot euro to US dollar exchange rate is 1.3372/1.3374, and the swap rate is 20/24. How to manage the exchange rate risk by swap transaction?

The specific analysis is as follows:

（1）Calculate the forward exchange rate.

EUR/USD=1.3392/1.3398

（2）Calculate the US dollars needed for euros.

10,000,000*1.3374=13,374,000（The first transaction）

（3）Calculate the US dollars obtained by selling forward euros.

10,000,000*1.3392 = 13,392,000（The second transaction）

Finally, no matter how the spot exchange rate changes after 3 months, ABC company can fix its investment cost and benefit exactly in advance.

Task 5   Arbitrage

Arbitrage, also known as interest arbitrage, refers to the transaction that funds transfer from low interest rates countries to high interest rates countries for the interest difference when two countries' short-term interest rates are different.

For example, the short-term interest rate in the US financial market is 7% per annum, while that in the UK is 9.5%, so short-term investors can borrow US dollar at 7% per annum in the US then buy British pound and remit it to the UK. If the handling fee and other factors are not taken into account, the profit of using sterling funds in Britain is 2.5%, which is higher than that in the United States, that is, the price difference is 2.5% in the short- term. Since the funds transferred to the UK, whether owned or borrowed, must bear the risk of exchange rate fluctuations in the pounds to avoid losses caused by fluctuations in the exchange rate of the pounds, this is called the covered arbitrage. If arbitrageurs move funds to countries with high interest rates without making forward foreign exchange transactions, then the arbitrage is the non-covered arbitrage.

The arbitrage is the important trading activity in the foreign exchange market. Because the foreign exchange markets are closely linked, large banks or companies will quickly invest when-ever there is an arbitrage opportunity. This transaction eventually makes the spreads and the swap rates almost the same, thus making arbitrage unprofitable. The arbitrage trading connects interest rates and exchange rates together, which influence and restrict each other and promote the integration of international financial markets.

Mini Case

China is the first country to produce paper money. The first paper currency, named Jiaozi was born in the Northern Song Dynasty. At that time, the core of the world economy was in East Asia, and the Northern Song Dynasty was undoubtedly the richest and most developed region in the world. Today, the center of gravity of the world economy shifts to the east again as the internationalization of RMB sweeping across the world. The Belt and Road Initiative and Asian Infrastructure Investment Bank （AIIB） bring us to a new era.

Think and discuss: with the full opening of China financial market and the development of RMB internationalization, what opportunities and challenges will China foreign exchange market face?

Mind Map

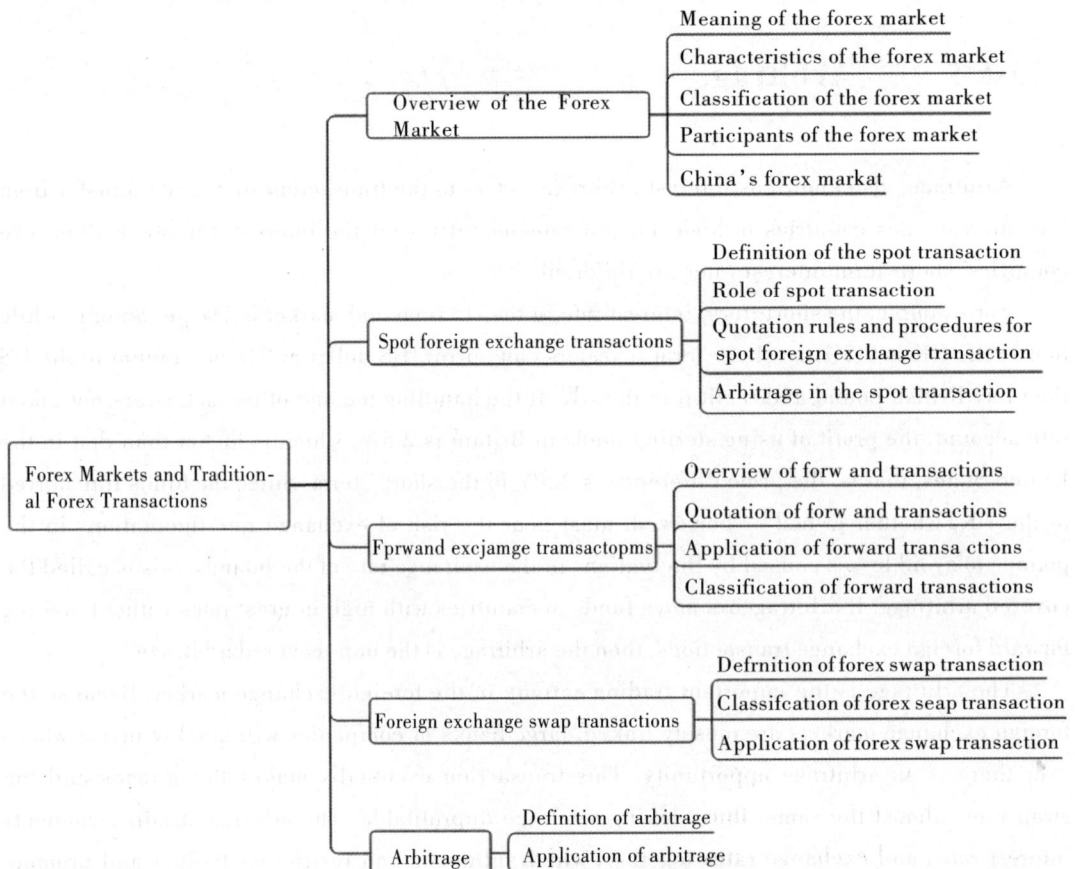

Project Training

I. Single-choice questions

1. The foreign exchange transactions between banks and customers in the foreign exchange market are also called (　　) .

A. Retail market   B. Wholesale market

C. Intangible market   D. Tangible market

2. The spot foreign exchange market usually adopts (　　) quotation.

A. Two-way   B. Buying price

C. Selling price   D. Middle price

3. The interbank market refers to (　　) .

A. The market between banks and companies

B. The bank to bank market

C. The market between central banks and commercial banks

D. The commercial market

4. The most important participants in the foreign exchange market are (　　) .

A. Commercial banks   B. Foreign exchange brokers

C. Clients   D. Central Banks

5. If there is a big exchange rate difference between two foreign exchange markets, people will do (　　) .

A. Indirect arbitrage   B. Direct arbitrage

C. Hedging arbitrage   D. Non-hedging arbitrage

6. The spot foreign exchange transaction refers to the trading which is settled at (　　) after the buyer and the seller have concluded the transaction.

A. in two business days   B. on the same day

C. in one month   D. after two business days

7. The ultimate supplier and demander of foreign exchange markets are (　　) .

A. Foreign exchange banks   B. Foreign exchange brokers

C. Central Banks   D. Customers

8. Assuming that the spot exchange rate quoted by a foreign exchange bank is EUR/USD =1.3219/49, and the swap rate is 20/40, the forward exchange rate of euro to USD for one month is (　　) .

A.1.1219/0.9249   B.1.3199/1.3209

C.1.3239/1.3289   D.1.5219/1.7249

9. The spread of two currencies determines the forward exchange rate. The currency with a higher interest rate will have a forward exchange rate (　　) .

A. Premium   B. Discount

C. Parity   D. Unchanged

10. In the import trading, if the foreign exchange rate is higher than the exchange rate agreed in the contract, the local currency paid by the importer will be （　　） .

A. Less   B. More

C. Constant   D. Uncertain

Ⅱ .Multiple-choice questions

1. What are the following functions of the foreign exchange market （　　） ?

A. Adjust the supply and demand of foreign exchange

B. Form a foreign exchange price system

C. Facilitating the international transfer of funds

D. Providing foreign exchange financing

E. Preventing foreign exchange risks

2. Participants in the foreign exchange market are （　　） .

A. Foreign exchange banks   B. Importers and exporters

C. Foreign exchange brokers   D. Central Banks

E. International students

3.The foreign exchange retail market includes （　　） .

A. A Chinese clothing company purchased US dollars from the Bank of China to import suit fabrics

B. Xiao Li went to study in an American university and bought 20,000 US dollars from the Bank of China

C. A company invested a color TV production line in the United States and purchased 50 million US dollars from Citibank

D. The Bank of China Shanghai Branch had too much USD, and sold USD 100 million to Citibank Shanghai Branch

4. When the foreign exchange bank quotes, it is generally reports at the same time （　　） .

A. The delivery price   B. The middle price

C. The buying price   D. The Selling price

E. The market price

5. Swap transactions consist of （　　） .

A. Two forward transactions

B. Two spot transactions

C. A spot transaction, a forward transaction

D. None of the above

Ⅲ . Practical application

1. A foreign exchange trader conducts foreign exchange transactions and predicts that the pound will appreciate, so he buys 5 million pounds when the quotation is GBP/USD=1.5740/60.

An hour later, the bank quotation becomes 1.5775/95, and the trader immediately sells 5 million pounds. What is the trader's profit?

2. On a certain day, the spot exchange rate in London foreign exchange market is GBP/USD =1.6955/1.6965, the 3-month swap rate is 50/60. What is the 3-month forward exchange rate?

3. Assume that the spot exchange rate in the foreign exchange market on a certain day is GBP/USD=1.5520/1.5530, and the 2-month swap rate is 20/10. An American seller exports 2 million British pounds machinery to British importers, and the contract stipulates that the payment will be made in pounds two months later.

（1）How much can the American exporter receive if the British importer pay now （the payment at sight）?

（2）If the market exchange rate at maturity is GBP/USD = 1.5115/1.5145, how many dollars can the American exporter recover? How about profit and loss?

（3）If the exporter wants to manage risks, what strategy should the seller take? How many dollars can be recovered at maturity? How about profit and loss?

IV. Practical training

1. Scene: in the bank lobby, the bank manager is dealing with the foreign exchange business for a customer. One student plays the customer and an other plays the bank manager in class to display the bank routine duties.

2. Log in to the websites of five banks, collect the information of their foreign exchange wealth management products, and choose one product to share in the class.

Project Six
Forex Derivatives Trading

Learning Objectives

Knowledge Objectives:

Understand the definition, classification and characteristics of foreign exchange futures, foreign exchange options and currency swaps; know the process of foreign exchange futures trading; master the application strategies of foreign exchange futures, foreign exchange options and currency swaps.

Competence Objectives:

Master various application strategies of foreign exchange futures, foreign exchange options and currency swaps.

Operational Objectives:

To be able to apply the application strategies of foreign exchange futures, foreign exchange options and currency swaps in the simulation system for simulated operation.

Course Introduction

The story of derivatives

Scenario 1: Song wants to buy 10 catties of pork, and goes to the pork shop to find the owner, Rui offers 50 yuan per catty of pork, and Song pays 500 yuan and brings 10 catties of pork home. This is a spot transaction, which is the underlying asset.

Scenario 2: Song plans to buy 10 catties of pork in a month, fearing that the price of pork will rise, he goes to the pork shop to find the owner, and tells his request. Rui agrees, but the price is no longer 50 yuan per catty, but 51 yuan per catty. Why? Rui says that he is also afraid of the price of pork, and he is not sure about the price in a month. He will buy 80 catties of pork and freezes it in the cold storage and sells to Song a month later. Because Rui has to pay the money in advance to purchase the goods and occupy the cold storage, he has to charge some costs. In addition, Rui is also worried that Song will forget about it a month later, so he requires to receive a guarantee deposit of 50 yuan at first. This is the futures trading.

Scenario 3: Song also plans to buy 10 catties of pork in a month, and goes to the pork shop to find the owner Rui, who recommends the transaction of Scenario 2 to him. But Song keeps a careful thought: maybe the price of pork will drop in a month, so I still buy it at 51 yuan per catty. Isn't it expensive? So, Song says to Rui, Can I discuss it with you, and sell me 10 catties of pork a month later? the price is 51 yuan, which is called the strike price. However, if I don't want it anymore, I can give up. " Rui shakes his head and refuses, saying that "you can't take all the good things". At this time, Song hands a pack of cigarettes worth 20 yuan, and Rui happily agrees.

Source: Anonymity. Introduction and transaction of forex derivatives [EB/OL]. [2019-12-29]. https://zhuanlan.zhihu.com/p/100041382.

Thinking and discussion: if you were Song in the story, which trading model would you choose and why?

Task 1   Forex Futures Trading

I. Overview of Foreign Exchange Futures Trading

The forex futures trading means that both parties to a foreign exchange transaction buy or sell a specific foreign exchange through brokers in the futures exchange by open bidding, but the date is pre-agreed, the exchange rate is also pre-agreed, which is a standardized foreign exchange transaction mode for futures contracts.

Due to the risk of price fluctuations in the spot market, many traders enter the futures market to the avoid price risk in the spot market. However, there are still many traders who enter the futures market simply to earn the price difference and few are willing to make physical delivery, but to hedge before the contract expires, so-called hedging, meaning that a person who buys (or sells) a futures contract and then sells (or buys) a futures contract before the contract expires. In the futures exchange, these buy-before-sell or sell-before-buy behaviors are allowed, but the scale is limited.

（i）Characteristics of foreign exchange futures trading

The foreign exchange futures trading provides traders with hedging and speculation opportunities through futures contracts, but the foreign exchange futures trading has its characteristics:

1.Contract standardization

Contract standardization is the standardization of foreign exchange futures contracts. A foreign exchange futures contract is a legal contract formulated by the exchange, which stipulates that both parties to the transaction pay a certain margin and commission, and buy or sell a certain amount of foreign exchange according to the transaction currency, transaction quantity, delivery month and location. Foreign exchange futures contracts have strict requirements on contract units, which are embodied in the following aspects:

(1) The trading unit per contract is standard.

Each foreign exchange has special regulations on the denomination of foreign exchange futures contracts, and the denominations of contracts in different currencies are also different. For example, in the Chicago International Currency Market, the standard denomination of each foreign exchange futures contract is 100,000 Canadian dollars, 12.5 million Japanese yen, 125,000 Swiss francs, and 25,000 sterling pounds. The number of transactions in each currency must be an integer multiple of the contract denomination.

(2) The delivery month and delivery date are standard for each contract.

The delivery months for all foreign exchange futures contracts are March, June, September and December of each year. The Wednesday of the third week of the delivery month is the delivery day of the month. If this day is not a business day, it will be postponed to the next business day. If the trading deadline is the second business day before the delivery day, and the exchange rate of the last trading day is the transaction settlement price.

[Example 6-1] A person sold a three-month euro futures contract on June 6, 2021, if he did not hedge before September 6 (that is, he did not buy an identical euro futures contract before September 6), then he must sell euros at the spot rate at the contract price on September 19 (the third Wednesday of this month).

2.Quoted in US dollars

In foreign exchange futures trading, the trading currency is quoted in terms of how many US dollars a unit currency is converted into. As the underlying currency of a foreign exchange futures contract (a foreign exchange), like the underlying commodity futures, its value should be expressed in the settlement currency (usually US dollars). For example, the quotation of a foreign exchange futures transaction is: 1 CAD = 0.7511 USD, 1 SGD = 0.7393 USD, 1 CHF = 0.9978 USD.

3.Minimum price movement and price ceiling

In the international financial market, the prices of various currencies are changing almost every minute and every second, and the price fluctuations of some currencies are relatively large, while the price fluctuations of some currencies are relatively small. Based on the difference in the fluctuation range of currency prices, in order to facilitate bidding, the foreign exchange futures exchange provides uniform regulations on the minimum price fluctuation of each currency involved in the foreign exchange futures contract, that is, the "minimum price fluctuation". For example, a GBP futures contract specifies a minimum price movement of $ 6.25, indicating a minimum price movement of $ 6.25 per GBP contract.

The price ceiling, also known as the maximum daily price fluctuation, refers to the maximum range of the daily price fluctuation of the contracted currency in foreign exchange futures trading. If the price of a foreign exchange futures contract fluctuates beyond this limit, the transaction will automatically stop. For example, a GBP futures contract specifies a price ceiling of $ 125, which means that each GBP contract has a daily ceiling price of $125.

4.Implement a margin system

Foreign exchange futures trading relies on standardized futures contracts, and futures contracts are formulated by foreign exchange futures exchanges, so the exchange acts as a third-party guarantees in foreign exchange futures trading. In order to protect the interests of both parties, the exchange requires both parties to open margin accounts and pay a certain amount of "Initial Margin", generally 5%~10% of the contract value. A concept related to "Initial Margin" is "Maintenance Margin". In the process of foreign exchange futures trading, the open positions should be liquidated according to the closing price of the day, and the specific profit and loss will be reflected by the settlement price, and the amount of the margin account will be adjusted at the same time. If there is a surplus, the margin account balance will increase. If there is a loss, the margin account balance will decrease. If the balance of the margin account decreases below the minimum margin limit (that is maintenance margin)stipulated by the exchange, the exchange will issue a margin call notice to the customer. If the customer does not make a margin call within the specified period, the exchange will forcibly close the position.

5.Daily mark-to-market settlement system

The so-called "mark-to-market" means that in the process of foreign exchange futures trading, at the end of each day's trading, the clearing house (for-profit institutions under the exchange) shall settle each transaction according to the closing price. The settlement price, which is the floating profit and loss, is reflected on the margin account. In this way, both parties to the transaction can clearly grasp the profit and loss situation. Table 6-1 shows the simulated trading contracts of EUR/USD futures on China Financial Futures Exchange.

Table 6-1　EUR/USD futures simulated trading contracts on China Financial Futures Exchange

Contract subject	EUR/USD spot exchange rate(EUR/USD)
Contract face value	10,000 euros
Minimum price change	USD 0.01 / EUR 100
Contract month	The last three consecutive months and the following three quarterly months, quarterly months refer to March, June, September and December
Transaction hour	9:00 to 11:30; 13:00 to 15:15
Last trading day trading hours	9:00 to 11:30; 13:00 to 15:00

Maximum daily price fluctuation limit	±3% of the settlement price of the previous trading day
Minimum trading margin	3% of contract value
Last trading day	On the third Wednesday of the contract expiry month, it will be postponed in case of a national statutory holiday
Delivery date	Same as last trading day
Delivery mode	Cash delivery
Transaction code	EF
Listed exchange	China Financial Futures Exchange

Source: China Financial Futures Exchange.

(ⅱ) The operational process of foreign exchange futures trading

Foreign exchange futures are traded on exchanges, and its participants mainly include foreign exchange futures exchanges, foreign exchange futures traders, brokers (acting as intermediaries) and clearing companies. Foreign exchange futures trading is completed through these four types of participants, and the specific steps include:

1.Select a broker and open a margin account

The foreign exchange futures exchange implements a membership system, and only members of the exchange can enter the exchange for trading. In addition, the number of members is generally fixed, and new members can only obtain trading seats through a replacement for trading. At the same time, in order to obtain membership, it is necessary to apply for and is approved by the relevant departments, and members must pay huge membership fees every year. Therefore, if an individual or enterprise wants to trade foreign exchange futures as soon as possible, it must go through a foreign exchange futures broker.

Brokers' conditions of service vary more or less and traders can choose brokers according to their own wishes. After the broker is selected, foreign exchange futures traders need to open a margin account with the broker as required and pay the "initial margin" according to the transaction size.

2.Placing trading orders, entrusting buying and selling

Placing a trading order means that a foreign exchange futures trader places an order to a broker and entrusts the broker with an order for corresponding foreign exchange futures trading. The entrusted order should mainly include the following contents: transaction location, transaction direction (buy or sell), transaction currency, delivery month, price type and validity period.

(1) The broker executes the order.

After receives the trading order, the broker immediately communicates the specific order content to the company's (pure) floor broker (also known as "marketing representative" or "waiting person") on the exchange through communication means such as telex or telephone; the floor broker fills in the order after receiving the order, and stamps it with a timestamp; then the order is handed over to the "runner" to the traders in the trading circle. After receiving the order, the floor trader will conduct bidding transactions according to the principle of "price priority and time priority". After the transaction is completed, the transaction price and transaction quantity will be recorded on the order, and then the order will be handed over to the "runner" and the transaction price will be reported to "yellow vest". If there is a new transaction price, the "yellow vest" needs to enter the latest price into the exchange's market quotation system, and display it on the exchange's large screen to report the latest transaction price on the market at any time.

Knowledge Link 6-1
Why do they wear shirts of different colors in the futures exchange?

The exchange stipulates that the personnel on the floor must wear specific shirts and ties. At the same time, in order to meet the actual needs of the exchange, shirts that are light, loose and easy for traders to move freely have appeared.

There are many traders from different brokerage companies in the exchange. In order to find people with the same company in the crowd, all the staff of the same brokerage company wear the same color shirts, sometimes with the company's name or logo embroidered on the shirts. At the same time, the different colors of the tops of different companies help to identify counterparties in fast transactions.

(2) Transaction registration, daily clearing.

After the floor trader handed the order to the "runner", the "runner" immediately handed the order to the floor broker (waiting person). After the "waiting person" receives the transaction order, on the one hand, notifies the broker to order the transaction, and the broker registers and clears the client's margin account on a daily basis. Each transaction of the day is registered and cleared after the market closes.

II . Application of Foreign Exchange Futures Trading

The application of foreign exchange futures trading mainly includes two aspects: hedging and speculation.

(i) Foreign exchange futures trading is used for hedging

The use of futures contracts to reduce the risk of exchange rate fluctuations in the spot foreign exchange market, so the foreign exchange futures transactions conducted by traders are for the purpose of hedging.

The specific operation of hedging using foreign exchange futures trading is: according to the characteristics that the foreign exchange futures price and the spot exchange price change in the same direction, the foreign exchange futures market is traded in the opposite direction to the spot exchange market, so as to hold foreign exchange claims or debt hedging. Hedging of foreign exchange futures is divided into long hedging and short hedging.

1. Long hedging

Long hedging means that when a certain foreign exchange is expected to be purchased in the spot foreign exchange market at a certain time in the future, in order to avoid the increased cost due to the rise of the foreign exchange rate, the corresponding foreign exchange futures are first purchased in the foreign exchange futures market and are in a long position. When buying spot foreign exchange in the spot foreign exchange market at a specified time, the traders simultaneously sell the foreign exchange futures previously bought in the foreign exchange futures market (that is to close the position).

[Example 6-2] Suppose a company in the US imported a batch of goods from the UK in the beginning of March, worth 500,000 pounds, and will pay the payment three months later. In order to avoid the increase in cost due to the rise of the sterling exchange rate after 3 months, the American company enters the foreign exchange futures market and buys sterling futures (the face value of each sterling futures contract is 62,500 pounds) for hedging. The specific operation is shown in Table 6-2.

Table 6-2 　　　　The specific operation of long hedging

Spot market	Futures market
Early March	Early March
Prepaid £ 500,000	Buy 8 sterling futures expiring in June
Exchange rate: £ 1 = $1.5950	Price: £ 1 = $1.5955
Converted to USD: 500,000*1.5950=797,500（USD）	Value: 62,500 * 8 * 1.5955 = 797,750（USD）
Early June	Early June
Buy £ 500,000	Sell 8 sterling futures expiring in June
Exchange rate: £ 1 = $1.6040	Price: £ 1 = $1.6090
Converted to USD: 500,000 * 1.6040 = 802,000 (USD)	Value: 62,500 * 8 * 1.6090 = 804,500 (USD)
797,500 -802,000 = −4,500 (USD)(Loss)	804,500 − 797,750=6,750 (USD)(Profit)

From Table 6-2, although the rise in the exchange rate of sterling causes the company to pay an extra USD 4,500 in the spot foreign exchange market three months later, it makes long hedging in the foreign exchange futures market and a profit of USD 6,750, thus making up for the losses in the spot exchange market. Of course, if the exchange rate in the spot foreign exchange market falls after 3 months, the company will suffer losses in the foreign exchange futures market, but at this time, the spot foreign exchange market can obtain risk benefits, thereby making up for the losses in the foreign exchange futures market.

2. Short hedging

Short hedging means that when it is expected that a certain foreign exchange will be sold in the spot foreign exchange market at a certain time in the future, in order to avoid the decline in the foreign exchange rate leading to a decrease in profit, the corresponding foreign exchange futures transactions are first sold in the foreign exchange futures market and are in a short position. When selling foreign exchange in the spot foreign exchange market at a specified time, at the same time, the traders will close the foreign exchange futures transaction that has been sold at the beginning in the foreign exchange futures market (that is, the corresponding foreign exchange futures contract will be bought).

[Example 6-3] Suppose a company in the US exports a batch of goods to the UK on March 10, worth 500,000 Swiss francs, and receives the payment two months later. In order to avoid the losses due to the fall of the Swiss franc exchange rate two months later, the British company enters the foreign exchange futures market and sells Swiss franc futures (the face value of each Swiss futures contract is 125,000 Swiss francs) for hedging. The specific operations are shown in Table 6-3.

Table 6-3   The specific operation of short hedging

Spot market	Futures market
March 10	March 10
Receive 500,000 CHF in advance	Sell 4 CHF futures expiring in May
Exchange rate: 1 USD = 1.0105 CHF	Price: 1 CHF = 0.9850 USD
Converted to USD: 500,000/1.0105=494,805 (USD)	Value: 125,000*4*0.9850=492,500 (USD)
May 10	May 10
Sell 500,000 CHF	Buy 4 CHF futures expiring in May
Exchange rate: 1 USD = 1.0315 CHF	Price: 1 CHF = 0.9645 USD
Converted to USD: 500,000/1.0315=484,731 (USD)	Value: 12,5000*4*0.9645=482,250(USD)
484,731-494,805 = -10,074 (USD)(Loss)	492,500-482,250=10,250 (USD)(Profit)

From Table 6-3, although the exchange rate of Swiss franc falls two months later, the company losses USD 10,074 in the spot foreign exchange market, but makes short hedging in the foreign exchange futures market and a profit of USD 10,250, thus making up for the losses in the spot exchange market. Of course, if the exchange rate in the spot foreign exchange market rises two months later, the company will suffer losses in the foreign exchange futures market, but at this time, the spot foreign exchange market can obtain risk benefits, thereby making up for the losses in the foreign exchange futures market.

(ii) Foreign exchange futures trading is used for speculation

Through the analysis of foreign exchange futures hedging, everyone should know that the premise of foreign exchange futures hedging is that traders have foreign currency claims or assume foreign currency debts. Speculators using foreign exchange futures to speculate do not require actual foreign currency claims or foreign currency debts. They only need to earn the difference by buying low and selling high in the foreign exchange futures market. According to their expectations of exchange rate changes. Foreign exchange futures trading for speculation mainly includes short selling and short buying.

1. Short selling

Short selling means that when speculators expect that the exchange rate of a certain currency will fall in the future, they first sell the futures contracts of this currency in the foreign exchange futures market, and then buy the futures contracts of this currency.

[Example 6-4] Suppose a speculator in early March expects that the exchange rate of GBP against the US dollar will decline in 3 months, so the speculator enters the foreign exchange futures market and sells 10 sterling futures maturing in 6 months at a price of 1 GBP = 1.3040 USD (each sterling futures contract has a denomination of £62,500). If the exchange rate of GBP against the US dollar does fall after 3 months, the speculator buys 10 sterling futures contracts expiring in 6 months at the price of 1 GBP = 1.2950 US dollars and can obtain a profit of 5,625 US dollars (62,500 * 10 * (1.3040−1.2950)).

2. Short buying

Short buying means that when speculators expect that the exchange rate of a certain currency will rise in the future, they first buy the futures contracts of this currency in the foreign exchange futures market, and then sell the futures contracts of this currency.

[Example 6-5] Suppose a speculator in early June expects that the exchange rate of Japanese yen against the US dollar will rise in 3 months, so the speculator enters the foreign exchange futures market to buy 10 9-month yen futures contracts at 1 JPY = 0.008940 USD (each yen futures contract has a denomination of 12,500,000 yen). If the JPY/USD exchange rate does rise in 3 months, the speculator sells 10 yen futures contracts with a 9-month maturity at 1 JPY = 0.009055 USD and can earn a profit of USD 14,375 ((12,500,000)*10*(0.009055 − 0.008940)).

Ⅲ. The Differences Between Foreign Exchange Futures and Foreign Exchange Forward Transactions

Foreign exchange futures transactions and foreign exchange forward transactions are the transactions that agree to buy and sell a certain amount of foreign exchange at an agreed price at a certain time in the future. However, the two use different forms. Foreign exchange futures transactions rely on futures contracts, which are standardized contracts. Foreign exchange forward transactions rely on forwarding contracts, which are non-standardized. Therefore, foreign exchange futures transactions and foreign exchange forward transactions belong to two different transaction forms. There are many differences between them (see Table 6-4).

Table 6-4　The differences between foreign exchange futures trading and foreign exchange forward trading

Difference	Forex Futures Trading	Forex Forward Trading
Different transaction objects	Futures contract	Forward contract

The relationship between the two parties is different	Can be completely ignorant of each other	It is necessary to fully understand the reputation and strength of the other party
Different trading venues	There is a fixed place, and transactions are carried out in the exchange, and over-the-counter transactions are generally not allowed	There is no fixed venue and transactions are usually carried out on an invisible market
Different transaction results	Most are settled by liquidation	The vast majority will be delivered on the delivery date
Default risk and management ways are different	The margin system and daily settlement system are adopted, and the clearing company is involved, and the risk of default is almost zero	Guaranteed only by the creditworthiness of both parties, the risk of default is high
Settlement methods are different	Daily settlement, reflecting floating profit and loss through a margin account	The settlement will be carried out only after the expiration date, and no settlement will be carried out during the period

Task 2　　**Forex Options Trading**

I. Overview of Foreign Exchange Options Trading

The option refers to giving the option buyer the right to buy or sell a certain amount of a commodity or financial asset at an agreed price at a certain time in the future. Commodity trading was the first to introduce options trading and was later introduced into financial asset trading.

The so-called foreign exchange options transaction refers to a trading activity in which the option buyer obtains the right to decide whether to buy or sell a certain amount of currency at the agreed price within the agreed time after paying a certain fee. In short, in foreign exchange options trading, both sides of the transaction are actually trading "options". After buying the "options", the buyer has the right to decide whether to buy or sell some foreign exchange option at the price specified in the option contract.

The basic idea of the option buyer is: when the spot foreign exchange market is unfavorable for the buyer's transaction (such as increased costs), the buyer can execute the option contract, that is, buy or sell a certain foreign exchange from the option seller at the price specified in the contract. When the situation in the spot foreign exchange market is favorable to the buyer for the relevant transaction (such as cost reduction), the buyer will give up the execution of the option contract, that is, instead of buying or selling a certain foreign exchange from the option seller at the price specified in the option contract, it will go to the spot foreign exchange market at the current price (for the price is favorable to self-interest)buy or sell a certain foreign exchange.

（ⅰ）Classification of foreign exchange options transactions

According to different criteria, foreign exchange options trading can be divided into many different categories.

1. Divided according to the term of validity of the option executed by the option buyer

According to the term of validity of the option for buyers to execute the option, foreign exchange options can be divided into European-style options and American-style options.

（1）European-style option is that the option buyer can only execute the option on the expiration date. This option is more popular in European countries, so it is called the European option.

（2）American-style options are options that can be exercised by the option buyer on any business day before the option expires. Compared with European-style options, American-style options are more flexible and the buyer can choose a favorable time to execute the option within the validity period. However, for the seller, it is very disadvantageous, that is, the seller has a greater risk, so the option premium of American-style options is higher than that of European-style options.

2. Divided by option buyer's rights

According to the rights of option buyers, foreign exchange terms can be divided into call options and put options.

（1）The call option, refers to an option that an option buyer has the right to buy a certain amount of foreign exchange at an agreed price within a specified period of time after paying a certain amount of premium.

（2）The put option, refers to the option buyer having the right to sell a specified amount of a certain foreign exchange option at an agreed price within a specified period of time after paying a certain amount of option premium.

3.Divided by transaction content

According to different transaction content, foreign exchange options can be divided into spot options, forex futures options and futures-style options.

（1）The spot option refers to an option in which an option buyer has the right to buy or sell an agreed amount of certain foreign exchange in the spot market at an agreed price within a specified period of time after paying a certain amount of option premium.

（2）The forex futures option refers to an option in which an option buyer has the right to buy or sell a certain amount of foreign exchange, futures contracts at an agreed price within a specified period after paying a certain amount of premium.

（3）Futures-style options refer to the way that both parties to an options trade, buy or sell the option according to the rise and fall of the futures price by means of futures trading.

（ⅱ）Characteristics of foreign exchange options trading

Compared with foreign exchange, futures trading, foreign exchange options trading has the following characteristics.

1. Rights and obligations are not equal

Forex options transactions are completed with the help of options contracts, and in option contracts, the buyer only has rights but not obligations, while the seller only has obligations but not rights. Simply put, when the exchange rate agreed in the contract is favorable to the buyer of the foreign exchange option compared with the spot exchange rate in the future market, the buyer has the right to execute the contract, which is unfavorable to the seller at this time, but the seller must execute the contract according to the regulations. On the contrary, the buyer can choose to give up the option, and the seller must also accept the buyer's decision.

2. Low transaction risk and high flexibility

For the option buyer, no matter how the market exchange rate changes, the biggest loss is the option premium paid, that is, the amount of loss is limited and the transaction risk is small. In addition, options trading does not require daily liquidation, and there will be no cash flow before expiration. When the market situation is favorable for the buyer, the option can be exercised, and when the market situation is unfavorable for the buyer, the option can be abandoned, which has great flexibility.

3. Option premiums are not recoverable

Option premiums, also known as insurance premiums, are what the buyer of an option pays the seller to acquire the right, that is, the option premium is the price of the option. When the option contract is concluded between the two parties, the buyer pays the option premium in full, and the option premium cannot be recovered regardless of whether the buyer exercises the option during the validity period of the option. In addition, the option premiums of different options contracts are different and the level of option premiums is mainly related to the length of the option contract's validity period and the fluctuation of exchange rate.

Ⅱ. Application of foreign exchange options trading

According to the characteristics of foreign exchange options trading, based on the purpose of foreign exchange options traders, foreign exchange options trading includes buying call options and buying put options.

(ⅰ) Buying call options

For borrowers or importers with foreign exchange debts, if the foreign exchange rate rises, it will lead to an increase in liabilities (such as an increase in import payments, etc.)by buying foreign exchange call options, the exchange rate level can be locked in, avoiding the risk of exchange rate rises to achieve the purpose of value preservation. During the validity period of the call option, when the spot exchange rate in the spot exchange market is greater than or equal to the agreed price in the option contract, the buyer can execute the option; when the spot exchange rate in the spot exchange market is less than the agreed price in the option contract, the buyer should give up the option.

[Example 6-6] Assume that in early April 2021, a US company expected to pay 500,000

Swiss francs in 2 months, at this time, the market spot exchange rate is 1 USD = 1.1135 CHF. In order to prevent the increase in costs caused by the rise in the exchange rate of the Swiss franc, the company bought four Swiss franc European - style call options expiring in June (each Swiss franc option contract denominated 125,000 CHF), the agreed price was 1 USD = 1.1173 CHF, the option premium was 1 CHF = 0.02 USD. It was assumed that the following two situations may occur in the spot foreign exchange rate after 2 months: (1)1 USD = 1.0005 CHF;(2)1 USD = 1.1350 CHF. Please calculate the import cost of the company in the two cases separately.

Analysis:

（1） When the market spot foreign exchange rate was 1 USD = 1.0005 CHF, the option strike price was 1 USD = 1.1173 CHF, which was lower than the spot price, so the company could execute the option, buying 500,000 CHF at the strike price.

Paid USD = 500,000÷1.1173 = 447,507 (USD)

Paid option premium = 500,000 × 0.02 = 10,000 (USD)

Total payment in USD = 447,507 + 10,000 = 457,507 (USD)

（2） If the company did not buy the Swiss franc call option, it needed to buy 500,000 Swiss francs (1 USD = 1.0005 CHF)at the spot rate, it needed to pay 500, 000/1. 0005=499,750 (USD) and the total payment in USD = 499,750 + 10,000 = 509,750 (USD).

So, buying the Swiss franc call option could save the company $ 52,243 (509,750−457, 507), when the market spot foreign exchange rate rises.

（3） When the spot rate in the market was 1 USD = 1.1350 CHF, the option agreed price (1 USD = 1.1173 CHF)was higher than the market spot rate. At this time, the company gived up the option and directly bought 500,000 Swiss francs from the spot market.

Paid USD = 500 000 ÷ 1.1350 = 440,529 (USD)

Paid option premium = 500,000 × 0.02 = 10,000 (USD)

Total payment in USD = 440,529 + 10,000 = 450,529 (USD)

According to the actual payment situations about the company in the two cases, the two parties involved in the foreign exchange call option transaction are: during the term of validity of the option, when the market spot rate is higher than the call option agreed price, it is beneficial to the option buyer. The option should be executed to obtain profit (reduce cost payment). The profit is the difference between the spot rate and the option agreed price, and the higher the market spot rate, the greater the profit of the option buyer, which may be unlimited. However, for the option seller, its profit - and - loss situation is just opposite to that of the buyer, so in this case, the seller's loss may be unlimited. When the spot rate in the market is lower than the call option agreed price, it is unfavorable to the option buyer and the option should be abandoned. The buyer's loss is only the option premium (the option premium is limited), which is limited loss. For option sellers, limited returns can be obtained in this case, which is the option premium.

Without considering transaction fees, the distribution of buyer's profit and loss for foreign exchange call options is shown in Figure 6-1(a), X is the option agreed price, C is the option premium, E is the spot rate in the foreign exchange market. Since options contracts are zero-sum games, the profit and loss of the buyer are just opposite to the profit and loss of the seller. Therefore, the profit and loss distribution of the seller of the foreign exchange call option can be drawn as shown in Figure 6-1 (b).

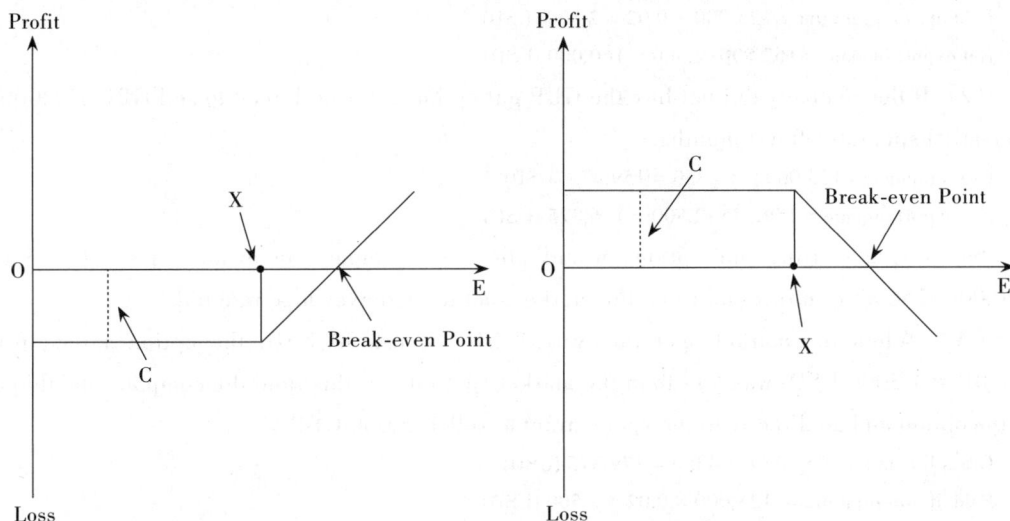

(a) Forex call option length (buyer)   (b) Forex call option short (seller)

Figure6-1 Distribution of profit and loss of foreign exchange call options

(ii) Buying put options

For investors or exporters with foreign currency claims, if the foreign exchange rate falls, the asset will depreciate (such as the decrease in export income, etc.), by buying foreign exchange put options, the exchange rate level can be locked in, the risk of exchange rate falling can be avoided, and the purpose of value preservation can be achieved. During the validity period of the put option, when the spot exchange rate in the spot exchange market is less than or equal to the agreed price in the option contract, the buyer can execute the option; when the spot exchange rate in the spot exchange market is greater than the agreed price in the option contract, the buyer should give up the option.

[Example 6-7] Assuming that a company in the US exported a batch of goods to the UK in early March 2018, it was expected that it would receive payment of 125,000 GBP after 3 months. At this time the market spot rate is 1 GBP = 1.2990 USD. In order to prevent the decline in the exchange rate of sterling from reducing export revenue, the company bought 2 European put options on sterling expiring in June (each sterling option contract had a face value of 62,500 GBP), with an agreed price of 1 GBP = 1.3000 USD, the option premium was 1 GBP = 0.02 USD. It was assumed that there were two situations in the market spot rate after 3 months: (1) 1 GBP = 1.2750 USD; (2) 1 GBP = 1.4350 USD. Please calculate the export revenue of the company in the two cases separately.

Analysis:

(1) When the market spot rate was 1 GBP = 1.2750 USD, the option agreed price (1 GBP = 1.3000 USD) was greater than the market spot rate, so the company could execute the option and sell at the agreed price of GBP 125,000 (2 × 62,500).

Gross income: USD = 125,000 × 1.3000 = 162,500 (USD)

Paid option premium = 125,000 × 0.02 = 2,500 (USD)

Net export income = 162,500−2,500 = 160,000 (USD)

(2) If the company did not buy the GBP put options, it would need to sell GBP 125,000 at the market spot rate after 3 months.

Gross income = 125,000 × 1.2750 = 159,375 (USD)

Net export income = 159,375−2,500 = 156,875 (USD)

So, buying sterling put options would allow the company to avoid a loss of $ 3,125 (160,000−156,875) in revenue when the market spot foreign exchange rate fell.

(3) When the market spot rate was 1 GBP = 1.4350 USD, the option agreed price (1 GBP = 1.3000 USD) was less than the market spot rate, at this time the company should give up the option and go directly to the spot market to sell 125,000 GBP.

Gross Income = 125,000 × 1.4350 = 179,375 (USD)

Paid option premium = 125,000 × 0.02 = 2,500 (USD)

Net export income = 179,350-2,500 = 176,875 (USD)

According to the actual payment situations about the company in the two cases, the two parties involved in the foreign exchange put option transaction are: during the term of validity of the option, when the market spot rate is lower than the put option agreed price, it is beneficial to the option buyer. The option should be executed to obtain profit (avoid income reduction), which is the difference between the options agreed price and the market spot rate. The lower the market spot rate, the greater the profit of the option buyer, and it may be unlimited. However, for the option seller, the profit-eand-eloss situation is just opposite to that of the buyer, so in this case, the seller's loss may be unlimited. When the spot rate in the market is higher than the put option agreed price, it is unfavorable to the option buyer and should give up the execution of the option. The buyer's loss is only the option premium (the option premium is limited), which means it has the limited loss. For option sellers, in this case, they can obtain limited income (that is option premium).

Assume that transaction fees are not considered, the distribution of buyer's profit and loss of foreign exchange put option is shown in Figure 6−2(a), X is the option agreed price, C is the option premium, E is the spot rate in the foreign exchange market. Since options contracts are zero-sum games, the profit and loss of the buyer are just opposite to that of the seller. Therefore, the profit and loss distribution of the foreign exchange put option seller can be drawn, as shown in Figure 6−2(b).

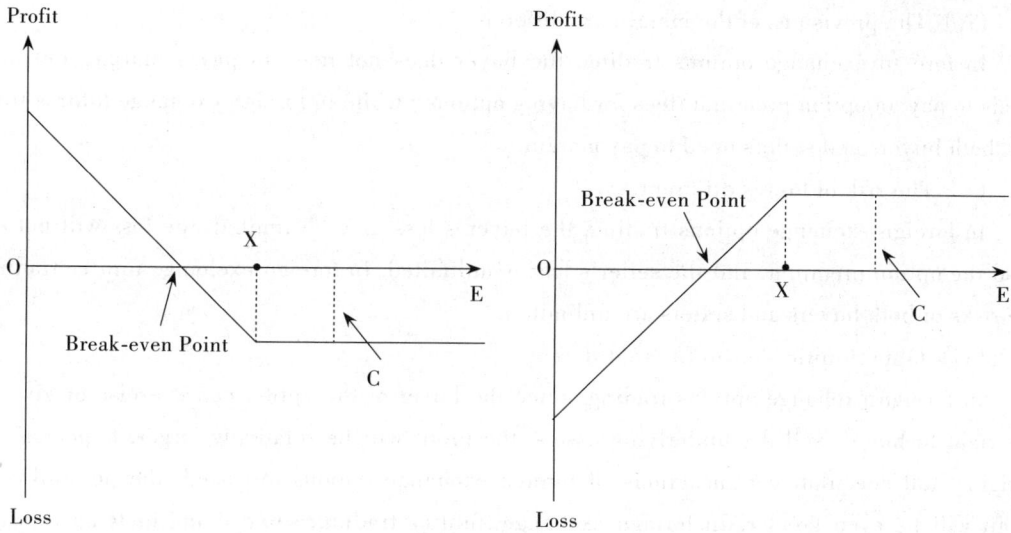

(a) Long FX put option   (b) Short FX put option

Figure6-2 Forex put option profit and loss distribution chart

III. The Difference Between Foreign Exchange Options and Foreign Exchange Futures

(i) The rights and obligations of the buyer and the seller are different

The risk-reward for the buyer and seller of foreign exchange options trading is asymmetric. The buyer of the option can choose to execute or not execute the right during the validity period of the contract. If the price change is beneficial to him, he can execute the right. Otherwise, he cannot execute the right. However, the seller of the option cannot refuse to execute the right when the buyer proposes to execute the right, so the rights and obligations of the buyer and the seller are asymmetrical, while the risk-reward for buyers and sellers of foreign exchange futures trading is symmetric. With the content stipulated in the contract, both the buyer and seller must execute the contract when the contract expires (unless hedging before the expiration).

Animation Micro-lesson 6-1

Forex derivatives trading

(ii) The content of the transaction is different

The foreign exchange option transaction is a kind of "right", that is, the right to buy or sell foreign exchange at a predetermined price at a certain time in the future; while the foreign exchange, futures transaction is a certain amount of foreign exchange objects, which will be stated in the contract.

(III) The Price of the Transaction is Different

The trading price of foreign exchange options is determined according to the regulations of the exchange when the option contract is launched, and it is written in the contract; the trading price of foreign exchange, futures is formed by market competition, and this price is the price expectation of all participants in the market of the expiration date of the contract.

(ⅳ) The provisions of the margin are different

In foreign exchange options trading, the buyer does not need to pay a margin, but only needs to pay an option premium (fees for buying options); while in foreign exchange futures trading, both buyers and sellers need to pay margin.

(ⅴ) The risk of loss is different

In foreign exchange options trading, the buyer's loss may be limited, the loss will not exceed the option premium, and the seller's loss is unlimited. In foreign exchange futures trading, the risks of both buyers and sellers are unlimited.

(ⅵ) Opportunities for profit are different

In foreign exchange options trading, since the buyer of the option can exercise or give up the right to buy or sell the underlying assets, the profit will be relatively larger. Especially in hedging and speculative transactions, if foreign exchange options are used, the possibility of profit will be even greater. In foreign exchange, futures trading, when doing hedging transactions. There will always be losses in either the spot market or the futures market, which undoubtedly dilutes the profit. When making speculative trades, one can be rewarded handsomely or lose everything.

Case Analysis 6-1

CITIC Pacific hit the legal red line; Australian dollar foreign exchange derivatives investment suffered huge losses

CITIC Pacific is a Hong Kong-funded enterprise that invests in and operates iron ore projects in Australia. It needs Australian dollars to invest and some equipment imported from Europe. In order to hedge against the risk of the appreciation of the Australian dollar and the euro, the cost of US dollar expenditures is locked in. From August 2007 to August 2008, CITIC Pacific signed 24 "Forex forward contracts" with 13 banks, including HSBC and Citibank respectively, long Australian dollars and euros. The contract stipulated that within the next 2 years, CITIC Pacific would pay counterparties in USD to receive AUD (average exchange rate would be 1 AUD =0.87 USD). At that time, the market generally believed that the Australian dollar's market price was higher than 0.87 USD after the signing.

However, the subprime mortgage crisis in the US had increased the risk of global economic recession, and the Australian central bank had to cut interest rates to stimulate the economy. The Australian dollar fell almost straight against the US dollar. From mid-July to mid-August 2008, the Australian dollar fell as much as 10.8% against the US dollar, nearly erasing its gains since 2008. At the same time, the exchange rate of the euro against the US dollar continued to decline. The risks of foreign exchange contracts signed by CITIC Pacific were also fully exposed, which eventually resulted in huge losses.

The foreign exchange forward contract that brought disaster to CITIC Pacific is called the "cumulative target redeemable forward contract". It restricts CITIC Pacific to continue to buy a specific amount of Australian dollars and euros at the price agreed in the contract in a specific period of time in the future. The average exercise price of the Australian dollar contract is 1 AUD = 0.87 USD, that is, CITIC Pacific has the right and is obliged to buy a certain amount of Australian dollars from the other party at the price of 1AUD = 0.87 USD every month, regardless of the exchange rate of the Australian dollar against US dollar in the market until the cumulative amount specified in the contract is reached. If the market exchange rate of the Australian dollar is higher than US$ 0.87, CITIC Pacific will gain by buying the Australian dollar at a cheaper price. If the market exchange rate of the Australian dollar is lower than US$ 0.87, CITIC Pacific will suffer losses by buying the Australian dollar at this exercise price.

Generally speaking, the rights and obligations of the long and short parties under the forward contract are equal, and the risks are the same. However, the "cumulative target redeemable forward contract" is different from this, and its "redeemable" feature limits the maximum profit that the long party may obtain. This is achieved through a " knock-out" clause in the contract, that is, the contract will be terminated when pre-agreed conditions are met. For example, in the Australian dollar contracts signed by CITIC Pacific, each contract stipulated a profit cap ranging from $ 1.5 million to $ 7 million. When CITIC Pacific makes a profit due to a favorable change in the Australian dollar exchange rate, the contract is terminated if the profit level reaches the top line. Due to the existence of the "knock-out clause", CITIC Pacific can make a profit of up to US$ 51.5 million, about HK$ 400 million, under this series of Australian dollar foreign exchange forward contracts. But on the other hand, if CITIC Pacific loses money under the contract, that is, if the market exchange rate of the Australian dollar falls below US$ 0.87, there is no termination clause in the contract. That is to say, as long as the Australian dollar continues to depreciate against the US dollar, CITIC Pacific must continue to receive goods at high levels and increase the number of goods received until the total amount reaches the cumulative target. For this reason, CITIC Pacific has obtained limited benefits but has suffered an infinite risk of loss.

On March 25, 2009, CITIC Pacific released its 2008 annual report, announcing a loss of HK $ 12.7 billion, of which the realized loss caused by the foreign exchange contract was HK$ 14.6 billion, becoming the first loss in the 19 -year history of the famous blue-chip company. If the losses on foreign exchange contracts were excluded, CITIC Pacific could have handed over a beautiful annual report with an after-tax profit of HK$ 1.9 billion in 2008. However, the huge loss of CITIC Pacific's foreign exchange derivatives trading shocked the world and was called "the largest loss suffered by a global non-financial institution since the subprime mortgage crisis in the US". So, who should be responsible for this?

CITIC Pacific admitted after the incident that the loss of foreign exchange transactions stemmed from the unauthorized operation of the relevant functional departments of the company and the failure to correctly estimate the potential maximum risk in the contract. In other words, CITIC Pacific is "the ignorant without fear" . Among them, in terms of ultra vires, the main reason is that "Zhang Lixian, the financial director in charge of the group's hedging strategy, conducted foreign exchange transactions without obtaining the permission of the chairman in advance according to the established procedures, which exceeded the scope of authority, while the financial director Zhou Zhixian failed to fulfill his supervisory responsibilities. There was also no alert to the chairman of an unusual hedging transaction".

In view of the huge scale of CITIC Pacific's foreign exchange contracts, some investors exposed to the media: CITIC Pacific's above explanation concealed the true process of foreign exchange derivative transaction decision-making, which raised doubts about the conspiracy of CITIC Pacific's management to defraud. Eventually, it led to the intervention of the Hong Kong police. Regardless of the final findings on CITIC Pacific's internal decision—making process, one thing certain is that CITIC Pacific's corporate governance is indeed deeply flawed. First, the management lacks sufficient knowledge of complex derivatives transactions; second, the company's decision—making procedures and risk control procedures are almost completely ineffective when concluding such a large-scale and risky transaction. It is foreseeable that the shareholders of the company will hold relevant executives and directors responsible for their dereliction of duty.

CITIC Pacific discovered losses on foreign exchange contracts on September 7, 2008. At this time, the exchange rate of the Australian dollar against the US dollar had fallen below US\$ 0.84, and the fair value loss of the CITIC Pacific Australian dollar contract had exceeded HK\$ 2 billion, which constituted a significant loss, at this time, the information should be disclosed immediately. However, CITIC Pacific delayed the disclosure until October 20, at which time the loss had reached HK\$ 15.5 billion. The delay in disclosure not only prevented the shareholders of CITIC Pacific from selling their stocks in time to reduce losses, but more importantly, it was the eve of the Wall Street storm in September 2008. A few days later, Lehman Brothers filed for bankruptcy protection and overthrew its first "dominoes" of the Wall Street storm. It was conceivable that if CITIC Pacific disclosed significant losses in foreign exchange contracts in a timely manner, shareholders might even get away with the Wall Street storm. Therefore, CITIC Pacific's failure to disclose promptly not only violated company laws and securities regulations but also caused very serious damage.

Not only that, on September 12, CITIC Pacific issued a shareholder circular at the shareholders' meeting of its subsidiary DCH. It responded to market rumors about significant losses from the company's foreign exchange contracts, stating that "... as far as the directors know, there has not been any material adverse change in the Group's financial or trading position since December 31, 2007". The range of information covered by this announcement is available until September 9 at the latest. This means that CITIC Pacific may still announce to the outside world that the company has no "material adverse changes" two days after the discovery of the contract losses. If this situation is finally confirmed, the content of CITIC Pacific's announcement on September 12 is untrue and misleading and constitutes a standard false statement.

Source: Wei Ke. Decryption of the incident: does CITIC Pacific hit every legal redline? [EB/OL]. [2009-04-16]. https://business.sohu.com/20090416/n263432186_1.shtml.

Questions to think:

1. What problems did CITIC Pacific face when making trading decisions? Do these issues violate relevant laws and regulations or professional ethics?

2. What should enterprises pay attention to in the process of financial derivatives venture capital investment?

Task 3　　Forex Swaps Transactions

I. Meaning of Foreign Exchange, Swap Transactions

A swap is a contract in which both parties agree to exchange a series of cash flows within a certain period of time according to agreed conditions. Swap is the most typical application of the theory of comparative advantage in the financial field. According to the theory of comparative advantage, as long as the following two conditions are met, the exchange can be carried out:

(1) Both parties have demands on the other's assets or liabilities.

(2) Both parties have comparative advantages in both assets or liabilities.

The types of swaps mainly include currency swaps and interest rate swaps. The following mainly introduces currency swaps.

The currency swap, that is foreign exchange swap, refers to the exchange of the principal of one currency to the equivalent principal of another currency within a specified period. Due to the exchange rate risk in the foreign exchange market, currency swaps, which convert assets or debts denominated in one foreign exchange into assets or debts denominated in another foreign exchange, can avoid exchange rate risks, reduce costs, and achieve the purpose of preserving value.

II. Application of Foreign Exchange, Swap Transactions

The application of forex swap is mainly hedging, which generally includes three steps: principal swap at the beginning of the period, interest exchange during the period, and principal re-exchange at the end of the period. The following examples illustrate the application and specific operations of foreign exchange swaps.

[Example 6-8]　A company has a loan in RMB with an amount of RMB 1,000,000,000.

The interest rate is a fixed rate of 4.35% for 5 years, with interest payment dates on June 10 and December 10 each year. Withdrawal on December 10, 2015, due to be returned on December 10, 2020. After the company withdraws the money, it converts RMB into US dollars to purchase raw materials for production; the export income of the products is in US dollars, and there is no income in RMB. In this case, the company's RMB loans are subject to exchange rate risk. The reason is: the company borrows RMB, uses US dollars, and earns US dollars as well. On December 10, 2020, the company needs to convert the US dollar income into RMB for repayment. If the RMB appreciates against the US dollar at that time, the company needs to use more US dollars to purchase the same amount of RMB for repayment. In this way, due to the inconsistency of currency in borrowing, using and repaying the company's RMB loans, there is exchange rate risk.

In view of the above situation, the company can make a foreign exchange swap transaction with Bank A to control the exchange rate risk. Both parties stipulate that the transaction will take effect on December 10, 2015, and expire on December 10, 2020, using the exchange rate of 1 USD = 6.7030 RMB.

The specific operation process of this foreign exchange swap is as follows:

(1) On the date of withdrawal (December 10, 2015), the company exchanged principal swap with the Bank. The company withdraws the loan principal from the lending bank and pays it to Bank A at the same time, and Bank A pays the corresponding amount to the company at the agreed exchange rate of US dollars.

(2) On the interests payment date (June 10 and December 10 of each year from 2015 to 2020), the company and the bank exchange interest. Bank A pays the company RMB interest at the RMB interest level, and the company pays RMB interest to the lending bank, at the same time, the company pays US dollar interest to Bank A at the agreed US dollar interest rate level.

(3) On the expiry date (December 10, 2020), the company and Bank A exchange the principal again: Bank A pays the principal in RMB to the company, and the company returns the principal in RMB to the lending bank, at the same time, the company pays the corresponding amount in US dollar to Bank A at the agreed exchange rate of US dollar.

According to the foreign exchange, swap process, at the beginning and end of the swap period, the company and Bank A exchange principal at the same exchange rate (1 USD = 6.7030 RMB) as agreed in advance, and during the loan period, the company only pays US dollar interest, the RMB interest is just used to repay the RMB loan interest, so that the company completely avoids the risk of future exchange rate changes.

(Extended Reading 6-1)

The Development of China's RMB Foreign Exchange Derivatives Market

The modern foreign exchange market in China began in the early 1990s. In recent years, in order to more effectively support the implementation of a series of major reform measures such as RMB current account convertibility, RMB exchange rate marketization, cross-border trade, RMB settlement, and cross-border direct investment RMB settlement, the China Foreign Exchange Trade System has successively launched in August 2005, April 2006, August 2007 and April 2011 officially launched RMB foreign exchange forwards, RMB foreign exchange swaps, currency swaps, foreign exchange options and other products in the interbank foreign exchange market, forming the structure of derivatives in China's foreign exchange market system.

The development of the domestic foreign exchange market has enhanced the international status and market share of RMB, and effectively accelerated the pace of reform in the internationalization of RMB. However, from a global perspective, comparing the domestic and international markets, China's domestic, foreign exchange market still has certain deficiencies, mainly in the following aspects:

1. The size of the market is not commensurate with the global status of our economy. At present, China's gross national product accounts for nearly 15% of the global gross national product, while the average daily transaction volume of the domestic foreign exchange market is only about 1% of the global foreign exchange market, which has a huge difference.

2. The rapid development of the RMB market has put pressure on the onshore market. The RMB internationalization report released by the People's Bank of China shows that the average daily trading volume of RMB and foreign exchange in major offshore markets such as Hong Kong, Singapore, and London is more than four times that of the domestic market.

3. At present, the structure of participants in the foreign exchange market is too single, resulting in low market activity. From July 2005 ,since China started the reform of the RMB exchange rate formation mechanism, the interbank RMB foreign exchange market has developed rapidly, but the restrictions on the participants are still relatively strict. The main players in the market are financial institutions, which objectively restricts the development of the market. In 2015, interbank transactions accounted for 67.7% of the entire foreign exchange market, and the proportion of transactions between banks and non-financial customers was 30.5%, while in the international foreign exchange market, the proportion of banks in the total foreign exchange market transaction value has decreased from 70% in the 1990s to around 30% nowadays.

The reasons for the contrast between the domestic and international foreign exchange markets are that, in addition to macro factors such as the incomplete reform of the RMB exchange rate formation mechanism and the insufficient opening of the domestic foreign exchange market to the outside world, there are also insufficient varieties of RMB derivatives transactions in the onshore market. The transactions of foreign exchange options and foreign exchange forwards were not active enough, and the exchange rate risk management tools were not balanced enough.

Source: Jun Kong. Promoting the development of China's RMB foreign exchange derivatives market 〔EB/OL〕. 〔2017-02-16〕. https://www.financialnews.com.cn/sc/wh/201702/t20170216_112731.html.

Thinking and discussion:

1. Please talk about the problems facing the development of China foreign exchange market based on the materials.

2. Please continue to check the documents, discuss what opportunities are there for the further improvement of China foreign exchange market?

Mini Case

In April 2020, Zhuhai Gree Electric Appliances Co., Ltd., issued a business report "About the Development of Foreign Exchange Derivatives Trading in 2020". The report pointed out: the board agreed that the company will use no more than 10 billion US dollars to carry out foreign exchange derivatives transaction business. In 2019, the company's foreign exchange receivables from exports were about 2.5 billion US dollars, and the import foreign exchange payments amounted to about 500 million US dollars. In order to avoid the exchange rate risks of the above two businesses, it is necessary for the company to carry out foreign exchange derivatives trading business. The company conducts foreign exchange derivatives trading business for foreign exchange hedging, management of exchange rate risks of import and export business and adjustment of surplus and shortage of funds, and there is no speculative operation.

Please further inquire about more materials, combined with the analysis of the content learned in this project:

(1) Why did the company trade foreign exchange derivatives?

(2) What types of transactions are included in the company's foreign exchange derivatives transactions?

(3) Combined with the new goals of China's 14th Five-year Plan, let's talk about the prospects for the development of China's foreign exchange market.

Source: Anonymoity. Gree Electric Appliances: special report on foreign exchange derivatives trading in 2020 [EB/OL]. [2020-04-30]. https://stock.zdcj.net/f10new/php?newid=ggmx000651_6226555.html.

Mind Map

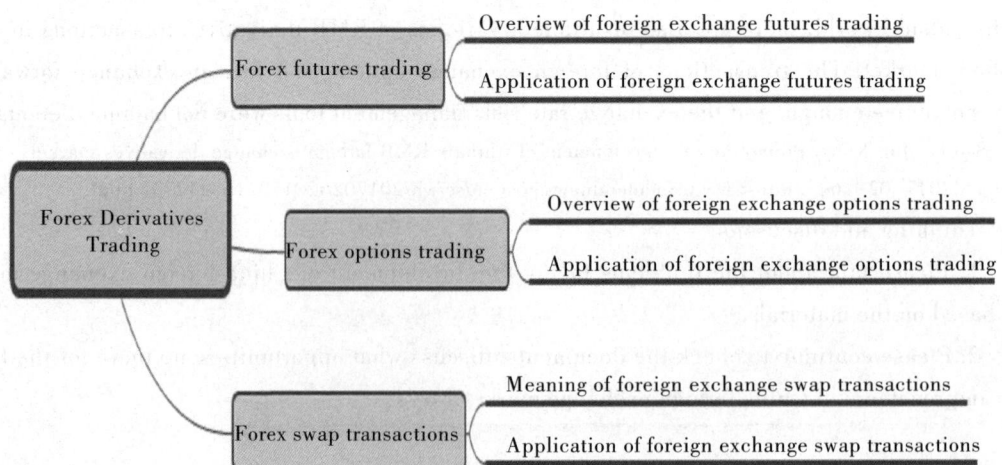

Project Training

I. Single-choice questions

1. Use (   ) to avoid exchange rate risks caused by exchange rate fluctuations.

A. Interest rate futures   B. Forex futures

C. Commodity futures   D. Metal futures

2. (   ) has the right to buy or sell a certain amount of foreign exchange assets at a certain exchange rate at a given time in the future after paying a certain fee to the seller.

A. Forex futures   B. Forex swaps

C. Forex swaps   D. Forex options

3. Investors trade in the opposite direction of the spot foreign exchange market in the foreign exchange futures market, thereby preserving the value of their foreign exchange claims or debts. This process is called (   ) .

A. Hedging   B. Arbitrage

C. Swap   D. Speculation

4. The following characteristics of interest rate swaps are (   ) .

A. Exchange the interest difference, but not the principal

B. Exchange both the interest difference and the principal

C. Neither the interest balance nor the principal is exchanged

D. None of the above

5. An investor sells two GBP futures contracts on the US International Money Market (IMM) at £ 1 = $1.5000, holding to expiry. The settlement price on the delivery day is £ 1= $1.4500. If the position is closed at this time. Then the investor's profit and loss are (   ) . (The face value of each GBP futures contract is 62,500 GBP)

A. Profit of $6,250   B. Profit of $3,125

C. Loss of $6,250   D. Loss of $3,125

II . Multiple-choices questions

1.Which of the following statements about financial futures are correct (   ) .

A. The content of financial futures contracts is at the discretion of the buyer and the seller

B. Financial futures trading requires a margin

C. Most financial futures are settled in US dollars

D. When a financial futures contract expires, physical delivery is generally required

2.An importer of US institutional equipment needs to pay 3 billion Japanese yen for import payment is required after 3 months, the importer (   ) .

A. May bear the risk of yen appreciation   B. Can buy JPY/USD futures for hedging

C. May bear the risk of yen depreciation   D. Can sell JPY/USD futures for hedging

3. A complete financial options contract should contain at least the following elements （   ）.

A. The nature of the option, that is, whether it is a call or a put

B. The price of the option, the option premium

C. The agreed price of the underlying asset

D. The contract amount of the option

4. Assuming that a European exporter will receive a payment in USD after 3 months, the strategies that the exporter can take to guard against the risk of devaluation of USD are （   ）.

A. Buy 3-month EUR on the futures market

B. Sell 3-month EUR on the futures market

C. Buy 3-month USD put options

D. Sell 3-month USD call options

5. To carry out a currency swap, two cash flows with （   ） must be required.

A. The same amount

B. The same term

C. The method of calculating the interest rate is the same

D. Different currencies

Ⅲ. True or false questions

1. There are a lot of speculative transactions in the financial derivatives market and the existence of speculative transactions disrupts the market order.   （   ）

2. Forex futures trading can only avoid risks for participants, and cannot be used by speculators to gain profits.   （   ）

3. Forex options products are bought and sold as the right, so the buyer can either execute this right or waive this right.   （   ）

4. The rights and obligations of buyers and sellers of forex futures are equal, while the rights and obligations of buyers and sellers of forex options are not equal.   （   ）

5. The precondition for a currency swap is that both parties have demands for each other's currency.   （   ）

Ⅳ. Practical application questions

1. Suppose an investor predicts that the exchange rate of sterling against US dollar will fall in 3 months in early September, so the investor sells 1 sterling futures expiring in December at 1 GBP = 1.3050 USD. Question: if the spot exchange rate of GBP/USD in December is 1 GBP = 1.2950 USD, can the investor make a profit? If he could get a profit, please calculate the specific value.

2. Assuming that a British company expects to pay 25 million Japanese yen for import goods in 2 months in early April 2020, the market spot rate at this time is 1 GBP = 147.050 JPY. In order to avoid exchange rate risk, the company buys 2 Japanese yen option contracts expiring in June (the face value of each Japanese yen option contract is 12,500,000 yen), the

agreed price is 1 JPY = 0.0075 GBP, and the option premium is 1 JPY = 0.0002 GBP. It is assumed that there are two situations in the market spot rate after 2 months: 1 GBP = 146.850 JPY; 1 GBP = 147.350 JPY. Please calculate the import cost of the company in the two cases separately.

Project Seven

International Settlement

Learning Objectives

Knowledge Objectives:

Understand the concept and meaning of international settlement; know the evolution of international settlement modes; master the characteristics of international settlement tools.

Competence Objectives:

Master traditional international settlement tools such as remittance, collection and letter of credit; master international settlement tools such as standby letter of credit and bank guarantee.

Operational Objectives:

Operate exchange rate, collection, letter of credit and other business with the help of the simulation system.

Course Introduction

The membership of the RMB settlement system continues to increase

With the rapid growth of Chinese economy, 984 financial institutions from 97 countries and regions have joined China's Cross-border Interbank Payment System by the end of July 2020. It is estimated that the number will exceed 1 000 by the end of this year.

Today's international settlements are mainly in US dollars. Banks exchange remittance information through the system of the Society for Worldwide Interbank Financial Telecommunication (SWIFT) headquartered in Belgium. The average daily settlement amount is 5~6 trillion US dollars, of which USD accounts for about 40% and RMB accounts for less than 2%.

The RMB international settlement system, also known as the Cross-border Interbank Payment System (CIPS), is an independent settlement system developed by the People's Bank of China. It aims to further integrate the existing RMB cross-border payment and settlement channels and resources, improve the efficiency of cross-border settlement and meet the development needs of RMB business in all major time zones. The system was constructed on April 12th, 2012 and officially started on October 8th, 2015.

There are 865 banks from 89 countries and regions have joined CIPS since October 2015. CIPS serves its customers in English, every transaction is settled instantly, and the scope of RMB settlement and clearing is expanded. CIPS consists of "direct participating banks" that open accounts in the system and "indirect participating banks". Funds can be easily transferred to the accounts of Chinese enterprises as long as the transaction is completed. According to the official announcement of the CIPS, RMB settlement is gradually increasing since its launch. The number of transactions was 1.44 million in 2018, increased by 15% over the previous year.

As of April 2019, 865 banks all over the world, including Chinese banks, have joined the system, such as Japan's Mitsubishi UFJ and Mizuho, 21 local banks, and Tokyo branches of 7 foreign banks, a total of 30 banks to participate in. The two super-large banks—Mitsubishi UFJ and Mizuho have become direct participating banks. It is interesting to note that 23 banks in Russia have participated in the system, and the rate of Russian enterprises using RMB to pay for imports from China has increased from 9% in 2014 to 15% in 2017. As of September 2018, the Central Bank of Russia has increased the ratio of RMB in foreign exchange reserves to 14%, a significant increase compared with 1% in September 2017, while the ratio of US dollar has been lowered from 46% to 23%.

Another obvious feature of the Cross-border Interbank Payment System is that 31 banks from African countries such as South Africa and Kenya have participated in, which is more than that of North America. The countries joined the Cross-border Interbank Payment System mostly come from the partners of China's "The Belt and Road Initiative", their demands for RMB settlement is rising. However, there is still a long way to go for RMB to become an international currency. As of March 2019, the rate of RMB in SWIFT's fund settlement was only 1.89%, which was lower than USD, Euro, GBP and JPY, ranking fifth. Compared with SWIFT, which sends and receives more than 30 million messages every day, the scale of the Cross-border Interbank Payment System is still very small.

Source: The "friend circle" of the RMB settlement system continues of expand [EB/OL]. [2020-08-27]. https: //www. guancha. cn / internation / 2019_05_22_502562.shtml.

Think and discuss:

(1) Why should China launch Cross - border Interbank Payment System?

(2) What is the connection between Cross-border Interbank Payment System and "The Belt and Road Initiative"?

International trade activities ultimately depend on the recovery and expenditure of transaction funds, which requires certain tools and means to realize the repayment of creditor's rights and debts and complete the transfer of funds. The international settlement business of banks provides a channel for completing this process. However, with the receipt and payment of funds for trade activities, the import and export companies may have an imbalance between the surplus and shortage of funds, and the buyer, seller or both parties may need financing, which brings trade financing with international settlement to banks. This project mainly introduces international settlement and trade financing activities based on settlement.

Task 1   Overview of International Settlement

I. Definition of international settlement

International settlement refers to financial activities in which payments are made to settle accounts, debts and claims, etc, occurring among different countries. It means money transfer across national borders. Parties in two different countries or regions use certain financial instruments to transfer funds through banks or other financial institutions for business such as commodity trading, service provision, fund allocation and international lending.

Because most of the international payments are due to international trade, emphasis is generally laid on how to deal with the international payments and settlements for the import and export activities, especially for the international trade in tangible goods.

Therefore, international settlement can be classified into trade settlement with tangible goods and non - trade settlement with service trade. Non - trade settlement is mainly based on remittance, which is relatively simple to operate and low in risk. Trade settlement is complicated and risky. This book mainly introduces trade settlement.

From the micro level, international settlement is the intermediary business of banks, which is more complicated than domestic settlement. It is based on international trade and closely related to international finance. From the macro level, international settlement uses the most scientific and effective method to settle the international creditor's rights and debts expressed in currency or transfer funds across countries. The research objects of the international settlement are mainly means of payment, settlement modes and bank-centered transfer methods. On the one hand, international trade is inseparable from international settlement and financing and trade financing doesn't work without international settlement. On the other hand, international trade financing can also promote the development of international settlement business, help banks to absorb deposits, strengthen their capital strength and improve their capital quality.

Knowledge Link 7-1

Evolution of international settlement

The international settlement before the 19th century is called traditional international settlement. The traditional international settlement evolves along with the development of international trade and the emergence of modern commercial banks. It develops from cash settlement to non-cash settlement, from goods payment to cash against documents, from direct sales settlement to bank settlement, and then to the combination of international settlement and trade financing.

The international settlement come to a modern stage after the 19th century. The characteristics of the international settlement are based on bills, conditioned by documents, centered by banks, combined with financing and increasingly standardized. With the continuous development, international settlement appeared the following characteristics in the international field: document standardization, processing by express mail, the electronic settlement , increase of non-L/C settlement and extended financing period. Documents become the basic carrier of international trade and an important basis for international settlement.

Source: According to the network information.

II. International settlement instruments

(i) Settlement instruments

Bill is one of the payment instruments used in international settlement. It is a written payment certificate issued by the drawer that unconditionally agrees with himself or requires others to pay a certain amount, and it can be transferred after endorsement. Bills generally include bill of exchange, promissory note and check.

1.Bill of exchange

Bill of exchange is the main payment instrument for international settlement, and it is a written payment order issued by the drawer to the drawee requiring the counterparty to unconditionally pay a certain amount to a person or holder at sight or at a certain time in the future. A bill of exchange is essentially a certificate of creditor's rights issued when a creditor provides credit. Its circulation and use must go through legal procedures such as drawing, endorsement, presentation, acceptance, payment, etc. If payment is refused, the right of recourse can be exercised according to law.

Bill of exchange includes for types are as follow:

Teaching video 7-1

Classification of bill of exchange

(1) According to the drawer, there are bank draft and commercial draft. The drawer and payer of bank bills are both banks, and the issuer of commercial draft is enterprises or individuals.

(2) According to the different payment times, there are sight draft and usance draft. The draft at sight will be paid at presentation or sight. A usance draft is a bill of exchange payable at a specified time or date, it also be called a time draft or a term draft.

(3) It can be divided into clean bill and documentary bill according to whether there are attached documents or not. A clean bill is not accompanied by a document, while a documentary bill is accompanied by a shipping document.

(4) According to different acceptors, there are bank acceptance bills and commercial acceptance bills. Bank acceptance bills are usance bills accepted by banks, and commercial acceptance bills are usance bills accepted by enterprises or individuals.

Figure 7-1 is a completed bill of exchange:

```
No.            SS-02-158

For            US$168,000.00                                    SHANGHAI,CHINA     18TH-JUN-2002
      (amount in figure)                                        (place and date of issue)

At             XXX                    sight of this    FIRST    Bill of exchange(SECOND being unpaid)

pay to         BANK OF CHINA, SHANGHAI BRANCH                            or order the sum of

SAY TOTAL U.S. DOLLARS ONE HUNDRED AND SIXTY EIGHT THOUSAND ONLY
                                       (amount in words)

Value received for       23,600PCS       of    100% SILK SCARVES
                        ( quantity )           ( name of commodity )

Drawn under              BANK OF TOKYO, THE TOKYO

L/C No.    S-188CN                            dated       MAY 3RD, 2002

To:        BANK OF TOKYO, THE TOKYO            For and on behalf of
           15-1, 1-CHOME,CHUO-KU, TOKYO, JAPAN  SHANGHAI SHENGSHI IMP./EXP. CO, LTD

                                                        XXX
                                                      (Signature)

ENDORSEMENT:    SHANGHAI SHENGSHI IMP./EXP. CO., LTD
                           XXX
                        (Signature)
```

Figure 7-1　bill of exchange

2. Promissory note

Promissory note is a written certificate issued by the drawer promising to pay a certain amount unconditionally to the payee or holder at sight or at a certain time. Promissory notes include the following form: commercial promissory note, bank promissory note, international money order, traveler's check, negotiable certificate of deposit, central banker's note, etc. Figure 7-2 is a completed promissory note:

<u>USD 8 000.00</u>   <u>New York, 6 Jun, 2020</u>

At 60 days after date we promise to pay Nanjing Import and Export Corp. or order the sum of US dollars eight thousand only.

For CITIC BANK New York

(Signature)

Figure 7-2   promissory note

3. Check

Check is a written, dated, and signed instrument that directs a bank to pay a specific sum of money to the bearer.

Check must contain the following main contents, such as:

(1) Stating the word "check";

(2) Unconditional payment order;

(3) Name of the paying bank;

(4) Signature of drawer;

(5) Date and place of issuance;

(6) Place of payment;

(7) Certain amount;

(8) Payee or his/her instructions.

Figure 7-3 is a completed check:

Cheque for <u>USD 10 000.00</u>   <u>London, 26th Sept, 2020</u>

Pay to the order of <u>ABC CO., LTD</u>

the sum of <u>TEN THOUSAND POUNDS ONLY</u> .

To <u>Midland Bank Ltd.</u>

For D CO., LTD London

(Signature)

Figure 7-3   check

(ii) Documents in international settlement

Documents in international settlement aredivided into basic documents and subsidiary documents.

Basic documents refer to the documents provided by the exporter to the importer, including commercial documents, transport

Teaching video 7-2

Differences among bill of exchange, promissory note and check

documents and insurance documents. These documents are introduced in international trade practice, so this book will not repeat them.

Subsidiary documents refer to the special documents provided by the exporter to comply with the government regulations of the importer, which are also called official documents or government documents. Besides import and export licenses, there are customs invoice, consular invoice, certificate of origin, etc.

Task 2   Traditional International Settlement Methods

Animation micro-lesson 7-1

International settlement business

The international settlement, also known as international payment, or payment terms in import and export contracts. Traditional international settlement methods include remittance, collection and letter of credit. While standby letter of credit, letter of guarantee, factoring and forfaiting are new comprehensive settlement methods integrating functions of financing, guarantee and settlement, and these are the direction of the future international settlement. International settlement is mainly conducted through financial institutions such as banks.

I. Remittance

(i) Definition of remittance

Remittance is a payment of money that is transferred to another party. More specifically, it refers to a settlement method in which the payer applies to the bank to remit a certain amount of money to the designated payee through the bank or its agent bank and foreign correspondent bank.

Remittance can be divided into direct remittance and reverse remittance according to the direction of fund flow and settlement instruments. Remittance refers to the transfer of funds from one party to another among different countries. That is, a bank (the remitting bank), at the request of its customer (the remitter), transfers a certain sum of money to its overseas branch or correspondent bank (the paying bank), instructing them to pay to a named person or corporation (the payee or beneficiary) domiciled in that country. The reverse remittance is that creditors issue bills and entrust banks to collect money from foreign debtors, and the funds flow in a contrary direction to the payment instructions transmitted there from.

(ii) The parties to the remittance

1. Remitter

The remitter is a person who requests the bank to remit funds to a beneficiary in a foreign country. Usually it refers to the importer or buyer in import and export business.

2. Remitting bank

Remitting bank is a bank transferring funds at the request of a remitter to its correspondent or its branch in another country and instructing the latter to pay a certain amount of money to a beneficiary. In effect, it is usually the importer's bank.

3. Paying bank

Paying bank is a bank entrusted by the remitting bank to pay a certain amount of money to a beneficiary named in the remittance advice. It is usually the bank where the exporter is located, and paying bank is usually the overseas branch or agent bank of the remitting bank.

Teaching video 7-3

Comparison of draft, wire transfer and mail

4. Payee

Payee refers to the person who receives remittance, that is, the beneficiary of remittance, exporter.

(iii) Types of remittance

1. Telegraphic transfer

Telegraphic transfer (T/T) is a remittance method in which the remitting bank instructs the paying bank (branch or agent bank of remitting bank) to pay to the designated payee in the form of tested cable, telex or SWIFT at the request of the remitter.

T/T is generally handled on the same day in banking business, so it is fast, safe, reliable and efficient. While these advantages make the remitter bear a higher price. Nowadays the cost of T/T has been greatly reduced due to the rapid development of telecommunication technology. Today T/T is wildly used in international remittance, especially for urgent payment and large remittance.

The procedure of T/T is shown in Figure 7-4.

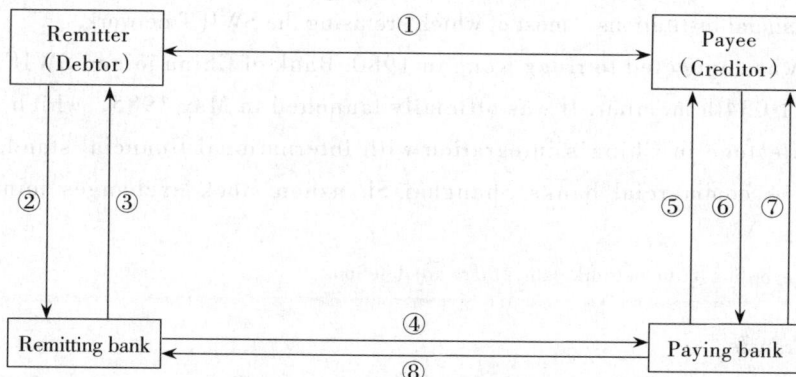

Figure 7-4   the procedure of T/T

Steps of T/T:

①The remitter and the payee establish trade relations and agree to settle by T/T;

② The remitter fills in the application and delivers the remittance funds and handling charges;

③ The remitting bank issues a receipt to the remitter, and establishes the entrustment relationship between the remitting bank and the remitter;

④ The remitting bank sends the indication to the paying bank by means of telegraph, telex, SWIFT, etc;

⑤ After receiving the instruction, the remitting bank shall check the secret key and make a telegraphic transfer notice to the payee;

⑥ The payee withdraws money from the inward bank with the telegraphic transfer notice and identity certificate;

⑦ The paying bank checks the documents and pays the remittance;

⑧ The paying bank issues a payment notice to the remitting bank.

Knowledge Link 7-2

SWIFT

Society for World-wide Interbank Financial Telecommunications (SWIFT), an international cooperation organization among international banks, was established in 1973, and banks in most countries around the world have entered the SWIFT system. SWIFT provides safe, reliable, fast, standardized and automated communication services for interbank settlement, improving the settlement speed of banks.

Headquartered in Brussels, Belgium, SWIFT has set up switching center in Amsterdam, Netherlands and New York, USA, and set up national concentration centers for participating countries to provide fast, accurate and excellent services. SWIFT operates a world - class financial message network, through which banks and other financial institutions exchange messages to complete financial transactions. In addition, SWIFT also sells software and services to financial institutions, most of which are using the SWIFT network.

SWIFT was connected to Hong Kong in 1980. Bank of China joined SWIFT in 1983, which is the 1 034th member. It was officially launched in May 1985, which became an important milestone in China's integration with international financial standards. After that, China's commercial banks Shanghai Shenzhen stock exchanges joined SWIFT successively.

Source: According to the network data, there are deletions.

2.Mail Transfer

Mail transfer (M/T) is to transfer funds by means of the payment order or mail advice issued by a remitting bank, at the request of the remitter.

Remittance by mail is low in cost, but its speed is slower than that of telegraphic transfer. At present, it is rarely used among banks in developed countries. The process of mail transfer is similar to that of telegraphic transfer.

3. Demand draft

Demand draft（D/D）refers to a remittance method in which the remitting bank at the request of the client draws a banker's draft on its overseas branch or correspondent abroad ordering the latter to pay on demand the stated amount to the holder of the draft. The payment instruction used in D/D is a bank's demand draft, in which the remitting bank is the drawer, the paying bank is the payer, and the remittance payee is the payee of the draft. D/D is characterized by relatively poor security and less bank participation, so it is also the cheapest.

The financial risks of remittance are under took by on the payer, it is mostly used to pay the advance payment or the final payment in China, and it is seldom used in the international settlement. The remittance is still one of the main settlement methods used in developed countries because a large amount of trade is internal transactions of multinational companies, and foreign trade companies also have reliable trading partners abroad.

Teaching video 7-4

Comparison of basic elements of collection

In practice, to choose the remittance method, buyers and sellers should be considered enterprise transaction situations, market sales, counterparty credit status, etc, and the remittance method shall be determined by both parties through negotiation.

II. Collection

（ⅰ）Definition of collection

Collection is an arrangement whereby the seller draws a draft on the buyer, and /or shipping documents are forwarded to his bank, authorizing it to collect the money from the buyer through its correspondent bank.

Collection is still based on commercial credit instead of bank credit and the bank act only as a collector of funds and provide a channel to transfer funds between the buyer and the seller. It only acts as an agent for collection and does not assume the responsibility of payment. In the collection business, the exporter/seller takes greater risks.

（ⅱ）Parties to collection

1.Principal

Principal is the party entrusting the handling of a collection to a bank, is generally the exporter（seller）, creditor and beneficiary. Because principals issue bills of exchange to entrust banks to collect money from foreign payers, they are often called the drawer.

2. Collection bank

Collection bank is the bank to which the principal has entrusted the handling of a collection. On the one hand, the remitting bank accepts the entrustment of the principal. On the other hand, it entrusts its foreign correspondent bank or agency bank to collect money from the debtor. The collection bank is generally the client's opening bank. It is responsible for receiving documents and making collection instructions and should comply with international practice.

3. Collecting bank

The "collecting bank" which is any bank, other than the remitting bank, involved in processing the collection. It is the bank that receives the entrustment to collect money from the debtor (buyer), usually the overseas branch or agent bank of the collection bank. Because it is the agent bank of the collection bank, all its activities need to follow the instructions of the collection bank. In general, the collecting bank is allowed to release the documents to the drawee only against the acceptance of a draft, and will not be responsible for any consequences caused by the delay of delivery.

4. Payer

Payer refers to debtor or importer. And it is also called drawee in celletion. Drawee will pay to collect the documents as receiving the notice of collection from the collecting bank.

The collection also involves the role of presenting bank and agent when needed. The presenting bank is the collecting bank making a presentation to the drawee. Generally, the collecting bank is the presenting bank. The agent on demand refers to the person who handles the follow-up matters in place of the principal at the place of payment when the payer refuses to pay the goods.

(iii) Types of collection

Collection can be divided into clean collection and documentary collection according to whether the shipping documents are attached to the collection.

1. Clean collection

Clean collection refers to the collection of financial instruments without being accompanied by commercial documents, that is, the seller submits the bill of exchange and entrusts the bank to collect the money on its behalf. Bills of exchange collected by the clean bill could be sight and forward. In practice, bills of exchange payable at sight are more common used because the collection amount is small.

2. Documentary collection

Documentary collection means that the seller issues a draft together with a set of shipping documents to the domestic collecting bank, and then entrusts the foreign collecting bank to make the collection. Documents are very important in the documentary collection. Documentary collection can be divided into D/P and D/A in terms of the release of documents.

(1) D/P is an arrangement in which a seller directs the presenting bank to release shipping and title documents to the buyer only if the importer completely pays the accompanying bill of exchange or draft. D/P can be divided into two types: D/P at sight and D/P at forward in terms of the different conditions of bills of exchange. Figure 7-5 is the process of D/P payment:

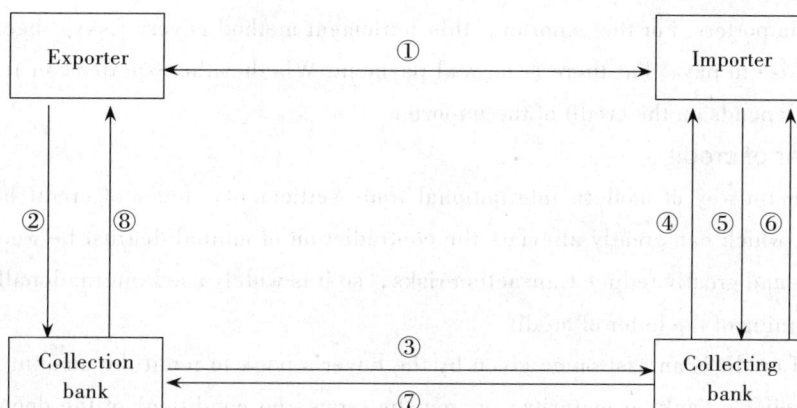

Figure 7-5   process of D/P

Procedures of D/P:

① The buyer and the seller establish a trade relationship and agree to adopt D / P settlement;

② The exporter prepares the goods and shipment receipts, fills in the collection application, and draws the draft (at sight or at forward) together with the commercial documents and deliver it to the collection bank;

③The collection bank checks the documents, fills in the collection order, and submits the draft and commercial documents to the presenting bank or the collecting bank;

④The collecting bank presents the payer for payment (under D/P at sight) or acceptance (under D/P at forward);

⑤Drawee pays (under D/P at sight), or drawee accepts (under D/P at forward);

⑥The collecting bank presents the documents (under D/P at sight), when the usance bill is due, the collecting bank prompts the drawee to pay, the drawee pays and the collecting bank delivers documents (under D/P at forward);

⑦The collecting bank will transfer the payment to the collection bank;

⑧The collecting bank will hand over the payment to the exporter.

The process of D/A only has one more acceptance process than D/P, and other steps are the same.

(2) D/A is an arrangement in which an exporter instructs a bank to discharge shipping and title documents to an importer only if the importer accepts the accompanying bill of exchange (or draft) by signing it. In this case, the documents required to take possession of the goods are released by the clearing bank only after the buyer accepts a time draft drawn upon him. D/A is only applicable to the collection of time drafts.

The process of D/A is similar to D/P after sight, the latter means that the buyer can only withdraw the documents from the collecting bank after payment; while D/A means that the collecting bank can release the bill after the importer accepts the bill. When the importer has signed the bill in acceptance, he can take the documents and clear his goods, thus D/A is beneficial to importers. For the exporter, this settlement method is very risky, because D/A is only the promise to pay, but there is no real payment. Whether the exporter can really receive the payment depends on the credit of the importer.

III. Letter of credit

As the main way of modern international trade settlement, letter of credit based on the bank credit, which can greatly alleviate the contradiction of mutual distrust between importers and exporters and greatly reduce transaction risks, so it is widely used internationally.

(ⅰ) Meaning of the letter of credit

Letter of credit is an assurance given by the buyer's bank to remit the amount to the seller through the seller's bank on maturity, as per the terms and conditions of the document based

Teaching video 7-5   on the contractual agreement between buyer and seller.

In short, the letter of credit is a conditional bank payment commitment. L/C can be divided into two categories: clean L/C and documentary L/C. Documentary L/C is mainly used in international trade.

Basic contents of letter of credit

(ⅱ) Characteristics of the letter of credit

(1) L/C is a kind of bank credit, and the issuing bank fulfills the payment responsibility. For exporters, foreign exchange collection guarantees are higher and therefore safer.

(2) The letter of credit is an independent document, and its execution is not bound by the sales contract between the two parties.

(3) The letter of credit is a kind of document trading. The bank pays against the document without checking the goods. Therefore, the L/C settlement business is prone to fraud.

(4) The letter of credit is cumbersome and costly. The process is complicated and the fees that importers have to pay to banks far exceed the settlement methods such as remittance and collection.

The process of the letter of credit is shown in Figure 7-6:

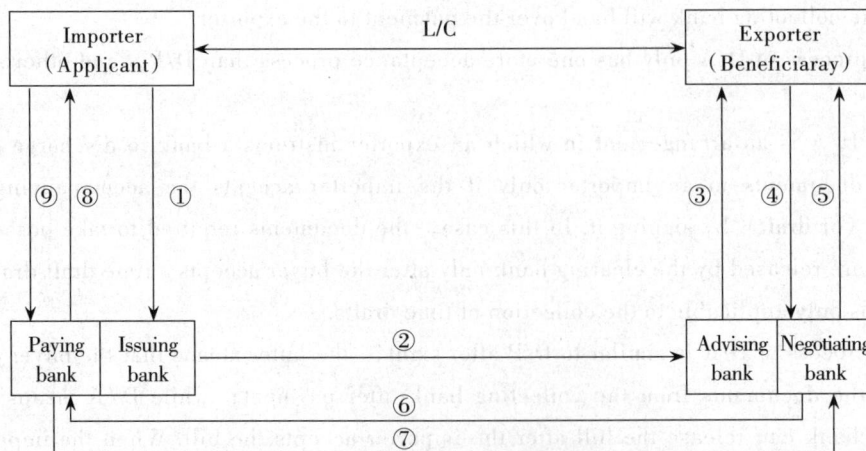

Figure 7-6   process of letter of credit

Procedures of letter of credit:

① The importer fills in the application for L/C, pays the deposit or provides other guarantees, and applys to the issuing bank for opening the L/C;

② The issuing bank accepts the application, issues the L/C according to the contents of the application after collecting the deposit, and sends it to the advising bank where the exporter is located;

③ L/C is presented to the beneficiary (exporter) after the advising bank has verified the apparent authenticity of the L/C;

④ The exporter shall ship the goods according to the provisions of the L/C, prepare all shipping documents and draw a draft, then send these documents to the negotiating bank within the delivery period stipulated in the L/C;

⑤ The negotiating bank pays the balance to the exporter by deducting the discount tax and handling charge according to the amount of the bill of exchange after reviewing the documents in accordance with the terms of the L/C;

⑥ The negotiating bank sends the draft and shipping documents to the issuing bank or the paying bank for compensation;

⑦ Payment shall be made by the issuing bank or the paying bank to the negotiating bank after checking the documents;

⑧ The issuing bank or paying bank notifies the importer of the payment order;

⑨ The importer makes the payment for the bill of lading.

The letter of credit is based on bank credit instead of commercial credit, which once dominated international settlement for a hundred years. However, the international settlement has changed since the 1990s, with the commercial credit settlement increasing year by year and the letter of credit settlement gradually decreasing.

(1) Higher costs and expenses. Importers are required to pay L/C deposit, application fee and telegraph fee, etc, which are occupied in a fixed period of time and this increases enterprise costs. The exporters have to pay notification fees and negotiation fees as well.

(2) L/C settlement procedures are numerous and complicated. L/C is considered to be the most complicated settlement method, which involves the issuing, reviewing and modifying of L/C, as well as various document preparation procedures, collection and transmission of bank documents and shipping documents.

(3) The quality of the goods in the transaction is difficult to guarantee. The letter of credit is the trade of document, the bank is only responsible for transferring document and not checking the goods. As long as the document on the surface show that document is consistent, the bank will receive the document and fulfill the payment obligation.

In view of the above reasons, both sides of the trade should know each other better and not rely too much on banks. Parties should investigate the credit status of each other to ensure the smooth progress of the transaction.

Knowledge Link 7-3

Development trend of international settlement

Although L/C settlement is widely used in the world, it is not the case in all countries and regions. At present, more than 60% of settlements are the open account (O/A) in some developed countries because of the high efficiency. Therefore, the trend of international settlement is the use of simple payment methods such as O/A, D/P and D/A. However, these methods are based on commercial credit, which is a great risk to the seller. They must be supplemented by other methods, such as requiring the buyer to provide a bank guarantee to protect the seller's benefits. The new trend of international settlement is a growing use of standby letter of credit, letter of guarantee, factoring, forfaiting, and so on.

Sources: According to the network data, there are deletions.

Task 3   New International Settlement Methods

I. Bank guarantee

(i) Definition of bank guarantee

Teaching video 7-6

The types of bank guarantee

A Letter of Guarantee refers to a written commitment granted by a bank on the request of a client who has engaged in a sale agreement to purchase goods from a supplier, providing assurance that the customer will fulfill the obligations of the contract entered into with the supplier.

Apart from the purchase of goods, a letter of guarantee may also be issued in technology trade, contracting and construction, financing from a financial institution, large equipment leases, and goods import-export declaration. There is no certain format in the form of bank guarantee, and no certain convention on the provisions and handling procedures of the rights and obligations of relevant parties.

(ii) Parties

The main parties of the letter of guarantee are the principal, the beneficiary and the guarantor. In addition, the advising bank, confirming bank and counter guarantor are the participators.

1. Principal

The principal, also known as the applicant, is the person who applies to the guarantee bank for issuing a letter of guarantee. In a specific trade, the principal may be a bidder, a seller, a buyer, a lessee, etc.

2. Beneficiary

Beneficiary refers to the party who receives the letter of guarantee and claims against the bank, and is usually the principal of the letter of guarantee.

3. Guarantor

Guarantor, also known as guarantee bank, refers to a bank or financial institution that accepts the entrustment to issue a letter of guarantee to the beneficiary and assumes the payment responsibility when the client defaults.

4. Advising bank

Advising bank refers to the bank that receives the entrustment of the guarantee bank to deliver the letter of guarantee to the beneficiary, which is generally the overseas subsidiary or business cooperation bank of the entrusting bank.

The creditor/debtor relationship between the principal and the beneficiary is based on the contract signed by each other, while there is a guarantee relationship between the principal and the bank, the letter of guarantee signed by two parties is the evidence for the bank to recover from the principal after charging the handling fee and performing the guarantee responsibility. Therefore, the bank should carefully evaluate and review the client's credit, debt, guarantee content and operation risk to minimize its own risk after receiving the client's application for guarantee.

(iii) Classification of bank guarantee

With the continuous development and innovation of international trade forms, bank guarantee can be widely used in the fields of goods and services trade, cross-border project contracting / construction and foreign labor cooperation. The common letters of guarantee include:

1. Loan guarantee

Loan guarantee is a pledge by one party to become liable for a debt obligation if a borrower defaults. The guaranteeing party is called the guarantor. In specifically, it is a payment guarantee commitment made by the bank to the loan bank to ensure that the borrower can repay the principal and interest of the loan to the lender on schedule according to the provisions of the loan contract.

2. Financing lease guarantee

Financing lease guarantee is a payment guarantee commitment that the lessee requests the bank to issue a guarantee to the lessor in accordance with the provisions of the lease agreement to ensure that the lessee pays rent to the lessor on time.

3. Bid guarantee

Bid guarantee is a written guarantee issued by banks to tender, as requested by the bidder (applicant for the guarantee). The bank guarantees that the bidder will abide by its promise and will sign the contract with the tenderee within a certain time.

4.Performance security

Performance security is a written guarantee issued by banks to the beneficiary, as requested by the applicant. Banks undertakes to pay to the beneficiary the amount specified in the guarantee in the event of the applicant being unable to fulfill the obligation of the contract signed with the beneficiary.

5. Advance payment guarantee

Advance payment guarantee refers to a written commitment issued by bank to importer or owner, as requested by exporter or contractor. Once the client is unable to fulfill the principal contract, the guarantee bank returns or pays in advance the equivalent amount upon receipt of the claim from the importer or owner, or equivalent to the advance payment on the part of the contract not yet performed.

6. Payment guarantee

Payment guarantee is a written guarantee issued to the exporter by banks. The bank undertakes to pay the amount specified in the guarantee to the exporter in the event that the importers are unable to perform the payment obligation of the contract signed with the exporter.

(iv) Functions of the bank guarantee

1. Enhance the principal's credit

Bank guarantee provides bank credit to the enterprise and helps it to get a reasonable price accordingly.

2. Expand trade opportunities

The counterparties often require enterprises to submit bank guarantees to ensure the smooth development of trade, especially in the commodity trade, service trade and technology trade.

3. Reduce capital pressure

For enterprises that use credit lines to open letters of guarantee, it can reduce the occupation of their own funds and ease the financial pressure of enterprises.

II. Standby letter of credit

Traders' demands for financial services are becoming more and more comprehensive because of the considerations such as paying off debts, obtaining financing facilities, reducing transaction costs and avoiding risks. As a multi-functional financial product integrating guarantee, financing, payment and related services, standby letter of credit (SBLC) is widely used in international trade.

(i) Concepts of the standby letter of credit

Teaching video 7-7

SBLC and commercial L/C

Standby letter of credit is an independent undertaking by the bank to pay the beneficiary a certain sum of money within a specified period if the applicant fails to fulfill his contractual or other obligations of an underlying transaction. It is usually used to secure either a financial or performance obligation of the principal. SBLC is a popular way for modern banks to replace bank guarantee.

The standby letter of credit originated in the United States. In 1879, U.S. federal law prohibited commercial banks from handling guarantee for customers. Some commercial banks used the derivative form of commercial letter of credit, that is the standby letter of credit to provide guarantee services. Since then, the scope of application of standby letter of credit has gradually expanded and it has rapidly evolved into an international financial instrument.

(ii) Classification of standby letters of credit

1. According to the practice, international standby practice (ISP98) advises that SBLC be applied to different fields such as performance, bidding, advance payment, direct payment, financing, insurance, etc.

(1) The performance SBLC supports an obligation to perform other than to pay money, including for the purpose of covering losses arising from a default of the applicant in completion of the underlying transactions.

(2) The tender bond SBLC supports an obligation of the applicant to execute a contract if the applicant is awarded a bid.

(3) The advance payment SBLC supports an obligation to account for an advance payment made by the beneficiary to the applicant.

(4) The direct payment SBLC is a special form of standby letter of credit. The issuing bank directly pays to the beneficiary. It does not include any clause of performance or non-performance from the seller.

2. According to whether the standby letter of credit can be revoked, it can be divided into revocable SBLC and irrevocable SBLC.

(1) Revocable SBLC refers to a letter of credit with clauses that can be revoked or modified when the applicant's financial status changes. This letter of credit is designed to protect the interests of the issuing bank, which opens the credit according to the applicant's request and instructions. Without the instruction of the applicant, the issuing bank will not cancel the letter of credit at will.

(2) Irrevocable SBLC refers to a letter of credit that the issuing bank cannot unilaterally revoke or amend. For the beneficiary, the irrevocable payment promise of the issuing bank gives him a more reliable payment guarantee.

(iii) Functions of standby letter of credit

1.International settlement function

Internationally, the application rate of letters of credit in developed countries has dropped to less than 20%, while the open account (O/A), document against acceptance (D/A), and factoring are widely used in today's international settlement. In practice, SBLC is not directly used for payment of trade goods and related expenses, but forms a payment combination with O/A, D/A, and other commercial payment methods, i.e., O/A+SBLC, D/A+SBLC, etc. This mode of operation can take into account the interests of both parties; simplify the payment procedure, improve the efficiency of trade. It can effectively reduce the transaction cost, increase the trader's means of risk control, and is conducive to reducing the risk in the process of trade.

2.International guarantee function

As a dual financial instrument, the standby letter of credit is widely used in international project contracting, BOT project, compensation trade, processing trade, international credit, financial leasing, insurance and reinsurance. As long as the creditor considers that the commercial contract is not sufficiently secure to bind the debtor, the debtor can be required to apply to a bank to issue a standby letter of credit in which it (the creditor) is the beneficiary, in order to avoid risks and ensure the realization of the creditor's rights.

The advantage of the standby letter of credit lies in the guarantee obligation and the flexibility of its application. First of all, after the standby letter of credit is issued, the bank's payment responsibility is always positive and clear, which helps to reduce misunderstandings and disputes, and improve the quality and efficiency of guarantee services. Secondly, most of the beneficiaries take standby L/C as supplementary to avoid risks. In practice, a standby letter of credit is usually "standby" if the underlying transaction contract is successfully performed.

3.International financing function

The standby letter of credit is also an international financing instrument. It is good for enterprises to expand international financing channels.

The financing standby letter of credit mainly supports the performance of payment obligations including repayment of loans. Overseas investment enterprises can obtain funds from the host country through the financing standby letter of credit. The direct payment SBLC supports the fulfillment of the basic payment obligations related to the financing standby letter of credit. In practice, commercial paper financing support is widely used.

As the comprehensive financial instruments, international factoring and forfaiting will be introduced in detail in the international financing part.

Mini Case

In 2020, the "China Trade and Finance Industry Development Report (2019—2020)" released by China Banking Association showed that the international settlement business volume of Chinese commercial banks in 2019 was 6.89 trillion US dollars, slightly lower than that in 2018. The report showed that state-owned commercial banks are the main force in the international settlement business occupying a major position in the whole industry. In terms of international trade financing, the international trade financing business showed a slight downward trend in 2019, while the domestic letter of credit settlement grew rapidly in 2019.

Please use what you have learned in this project, think and discuss:

Under the background of the global economic slowdown, sharp reduction of investment and financial turbulence, what are the reasons for the contrarian growth of China's domestic letter of credit?

Mind Map

- International Settlement
  - Overview of international settlement
    - Meaning of international settlement
    - International settlement instruments
  - Traditional international settlement methods
    - Remittance
    - Collection
    - Letter of credit
  - New international settlement methods
    - Bank guarantee
    - Standby letter of credit

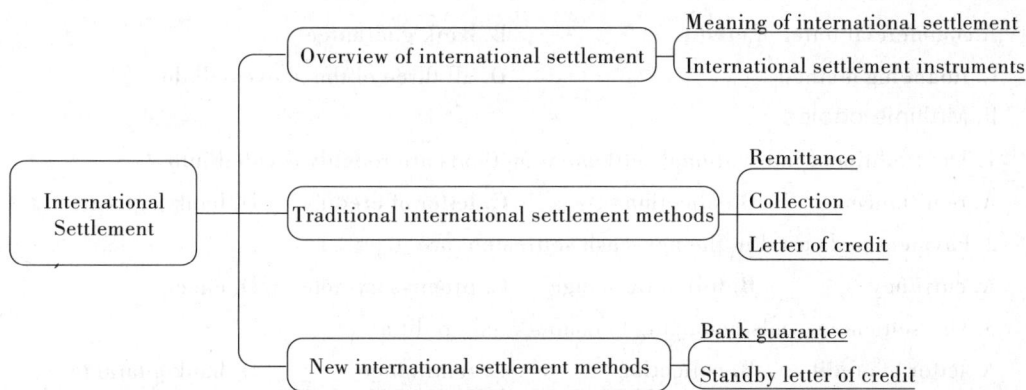

Project Training

I. Single-choice

1. Telegraphic transfer (T/T) is generally (　　).

A. small payment   B. large payment with urgent payment time

C. trade subsidiary expenses   D. non-urgent money

2. The settlement basis of the collection business is commercial credit, because (　　).

A. no bank involved in

B. the draft is a commercial draft

C. banks are not obligated to guarantee payment

D. importers can borrow bills with trust receipts

3. The function of L/C for exporters is (　　).

A. instead of occupying funds, exporters can get incomes from the opening fee

B. get a considerable settlement fee

C. with the trust receipt, the issuing bank can be required to deliver the documents first and then deliver the payment after the goods are sold

D. as long as the shipping documents that meet the terms of the letter of credit are handed over to the bank, the payment for goods can be fully obtained and the capital turnover can be accelerated

4. The basic principle of auditing documents is （　　　）.

A. the documents are consistent with the trade contract

B. only the documents are consistent and the documents and L/C are consistent

C. the letter of credit is consistent with the trade contract

D. the documents are consistent with the application for issuing the letter of credit

5. Standby L/C originated in the United States and has the function of guarantee, which actually is a kind of （　　　）.

A commercial letter of credit   B. bank guarantee

C. financing method   D. all three of the above will do

II. Multiple-choice

1. The traditional international settlement methods are roughly divided into （　　　）.

A. remittance   B.collection   C. letter of credit   D. bank guarantee

2. Payment tools used in the non-cash settlement are （　　　）.

A. currency   B. bill of exchange   C. promissory note   D. check

3. The settlement tools belonging to commercial credit are （　　　）.

A. letter of credit   B. collection   C. remittance   D. bank guarantee

4. SWIFT is a （　　　）.

A. US dollar international payment system

B. telecommunication system for transferring interbank financial transactions

C. sterling bill clearing system

D. large-scale clearing system of central banks of Eurozone

5. There are two main types of credit in traditional international trade and settlement: （　　　）.

A. system credit and bank credit   B. system credit and judicial credit

C. commercial credit and judicial credit   D. commercial credit and bank credit

III. Judgment questions

1. Collection is an international settlement method that relies on bank credit.   （　　　）

2. The development of international trade settlement is closely related to the reform of payment methods.   （　　　）

3. International settlement has gone through the development process from cash settlement to non-cash settlement, from commodity sales to document sales, from direct sales settlement to bank settlement, from using simple terms of trade to relatively complete terms of trade combining delivery and payment.   （　　　）

4. Remittance from expatriates, travel expenses, service reimbursement are tangible trade settlement.   （　　　）

5. The importer's payment by telegraphic transfer can accelerate the exporter's capital turnover, thus reducing the exporter's exchange rate risk.   （　　　）

IV. Practical training

The Chinese exporter A shipped a batch of goods, issued a 60 days usance draft and handed in a complete set of attached documents, and entrusted bank H to collect payment from abroad by D/P. After the documents are sent to the collecting bank M, when the payer goes through the acceptance procedures, the goods have arrived in the port and the market is promising, but the payment period has not yet arrived. The payer immediately issues a trust receipt to the bank to guarantee the payment due, so as to borrow the documents from the bank. After the goods were sold, the payer went bankrupt due to his debt and was unable to pay. In this case, should the foreign collecting bank allocate the payment to the exporter on the due date of the draft?

Project Eight
International Financing

Learning Objectives

Knowledge Objectives:

Understand the types of international trade financing, and master the contents of short-term trade financing and medium and long-term trade financing; master the concept and typical methods of international project financing; understand the concept and types of international bond financing.

Competence Objectives:

Use the knowledge of international financing that has been learned to propose financing solutions for import and export enterprises, and analyze the financing scheme of BOT project.

Operational Objectives:

Be able to design appropriate financing scheme according to the actual situation of the enterprise or project.

Course Introduction

Bonds named after "Panda" have been issued for more than 400 billion RMB

On June 11, 2020, the Asian Infrastructure Investment Bank issued 3 billion RMB of Panda Bonds in the China Interbank Bond Market. This is the first time that the Asian Infrastructure Investment Bank has issued Panda Bonds. The bonds issued this time are the COVID-19 epidemic prevention and control bonds registered by the National Association of Financial Market Institutional Investors.

According to Wind data statistics, as of June 11, 2020, the cumulative issuance of Panda Bonds in the interbank market and exchange market has exceeded 400 billion RMB. In the first half of 2020, the issuance of Panda Bonds has exceeded 30 billion RMB.

The development of the Panda Bonds market has gradually accelerated, along with the deepening of financial reforms, the opening of China's capital market to the outside world and the process of RMB internationalization.

As the first overseas entities to enter the domestic RMB bond market for financing, overseas high-quality sovereign institutions, local governments, and international development institutions play the key role in the development of Panda Bonds. Zhao Qingming, an international financial expert, believes that the issuance of Panda Bonds by these institutions not only enriches China's bond market, but also shows confidence in the development of China's economy and China's financial market.

Experts believe that, this will further improve the efficiency of the Panda Bonds issuance, reduce the cost of communication, enhance the attraction of the market to international issuers and investors, improve the demonstration effect of using Panda Bonds financing, and further promote the healthy development of Panda Bonds market.

The market expects that, along with the acceleration promotion of the reform process of Panda Bonds market, including the foreign countries central governments along with "The Belt and Road" may be significantly accelerate the process of the issuance of Panda Bonds. In the context of the deep integration of China's economy and finance into globalization, it is of great significance to improve the issuance rules of Panda Bonds, so as to enrich the group of overseas issuers and investors in China's bond market and form a more open and market-oriented financial system.

Source: LIU K X. Bonds named after "Panda" have been issued for more than 400 billion RMB [EB/OL]. [2020-06-16]. http://www.xinhuanet.com/fortune/2020-06/16/c_1126121417.html.

Thinking and Discussion:

(1) What is the kind of international bonds that the Panda Bonds belongs to?

(2) What is the difference between Foreign bonds and Europe bonds?

(3) What are the forms of international financing?

Financing, that is, financing funds, refers to the activities of funds flowing from surplus departments to shortage departments in order to adjust the surplus and shortage of funds. If the financing activities between domestic capital holders cannot meet the capital needs of economic entities, economic entities can borrow funds in the international financial market, while promoting domestic economic development, economic entities can also lend idle funds to foreign lenders to obtain higher returns.

It is worth noting that compared with domestic financing, international financing has greater risks, more financing methods, and more financing tools. Fundraisers can choose different financing tools according to their needs to quickly achieve the purpose of financing.

International financing has the following characteristics:

1. The subject and object of international financing are relatively complex

The subjects of international financing include fundraisers and lenders, which can be roughly divided into four categories: resident financial institutions, resident non‑financial institutions, non‑resident financial institutions and non‑resident non‑financial institutions. At least one of the borrowers and lenders of international financing belongs to non‑resident financial institution or non‑resident non‑financial institution.

The object of international financing refers to the currency used in international financing, which must be an internationally convertible currency. Some international common currencies are often used in international financing, such as the US dollar, pound, euro, and special drawing right (SDR). For financing parties, which currency to use for financing is a complex issue. The financing parties must generally consider the changes and development trends of various currency exchange rates in combination with financing conditions and other factors before making decisions.

2. International financing risk is relatively high

Compared with domestic financing, both lenders and fundraisers face greater risks in international financing. For lenders in international financing, they will not only face the credit risk that the debtor is unable to repay the loan or has deferred payment due to poor management, but also face the national risk that the debtor's country or region is unable or unwilling to perform its debt obligations to foreign lenders, as well as the foreign exchange risk that loans denominated in foreign currencies suffer losses due to changes in exchange rates. For fundraisers of international financing, they face the risk that foreign currency denominated debt will increase in local currency debt due to the appreciation of foreign currency against the local currency.

3. International financing is regulated

International financing allows capital to flow between fund holders in different countries. Based on its political and economic interests, the government of the country where the parties are located will intervene or regulate the international financing activities of its residents to adjust its balance of payments, implement its monetary policy and prudently manage its financial institutions.

There are many forms of international financing, such as international trade financing, international syndicated loans, international project financing, international bond financing, international lease financing, intergovernmental loans, and loans from international financial institutions, etc. This project mainly introduces three forms of international trade financing, international project financing and international bond financing.

Task 1　International Trade Financing

With the accelerating process of economic opening and the deepening of the social division of labor in various countries, trade contact between countries are becoming more and more frequent, so the role of international trade in the economic development of various countries is becoming more and more prominent. The lack of funds directly affects the normal conduct of international trade, and further affects the economic development of various countries. Countries should make good use of all available financial resources and reduce financing costs as much as possible, so as to facilitate the achievement of international trade and promote economic development. Therefore, it is necessary for us to learn the forms of international trade financing and how to make efficient use of these financing methods, which are of practical significance for using foreign capital to promote the development of domestic international trade.

International trade financing is the earliest form of international financing, which mainly refers to the financing facilities provided by banks to import and export enterprises engaged in international trade transactions. In international trade, exporters in the process of exporting goods, or importers in the process of importing goods, all hope to obtain low-cost and low-risk financial support. This gave rise to international trade financing.

According to the length of the financing period, international trade financing can be divided into short-term international trade financing and medium and long-term international trade financing. According to the object receiving trade financing, it can be divided into financing for exporters and financing for importers.

I. Short-term international trade financing

Short-term international trade financing refers to the short-term financing behavior with a term of less than one year (including one year) obtained by importers and exporters through various means and channels in the process of international trade. Because much short-term international trade financing is often related to settlement methods, short-term international trade financing can also be called international trade settlement financing.

The common terms of short-term international trade financing are 1 month, 2 months, 3 months and 6 months, and the latter two are more used.

There are many forms of short-term international trade financing. Here we mainly introduce the financing for exporters, financing for importers and international factoring business.

(ⅰ) Short-term export trade financing

In the process of international trade, the seller had to pay all kinds of fees in the process of export, which required a large amount of financial support. Moreover, the payment of all kinds of fees would easily cause insufficient liquid capital for the export business. Therefore, short-term funding is the guarantee of export success at this time. The financing for the export side mainly includes bank financing to exporters and importers financing to exporters.

1. Bank financing to exporters

Bank financing to exporters includes short-term credit loans, commodity mortgage loans, package loans, export documentary bills and forward bill discounts.

(1) Short-term credit loans.

Short-term credit loans refer to unsecured loans provided by banks to producers of export commodities in order to promote exports. This financing method requires a closely business relationship with the bank and good credit of the exporter.

(2) Commodity mortgage loans.

If the goods exported by the exporter are not produced by themselves but purchased, then the exporter can obtain loans from the bank by using the domestic goods as collateral. When a bank has offered this loan, it would usually lend out a certain percentage of the market value of the goods, and adjust it with the market price. If the bank has lent out money and the market price of the collateral falls, the bank will often require the exporter to repay a portion of the loan or provide new collateral.

(3) Package loans.

Packing loans usually refer to that the exporter mortgages the original L/C to the bank and applies for a certain amount of loan (generally not more than 80% of the L/C value) from the bank to prepare the goods after receiving the L/C issued by the importer's issuing bank and before sending the goods in international trade. Generally, the term of this financing would not exceed the validity of the L/C.

When issuing package loans, banks mainly consider the following two factors: first, the issuing bank has good credit, the terms of the letter of credit are clear, and the exporter has no difficulty in implementing it; second, the exporter has good credit, strong ability to perform the contract, and can collect foreign exchange in time according to the terms of the letter of credit.

(4) Export documentary bills.

Export documentary bills refer to that the exporter mortgages the shipping documents of exported commodities to the exporter's bank to apply for financing after delivery.

According to different settlement methods, export documentary bills can be divided into L/C export documentary bills and documentary collection export bills.

a. L/C export documentary bills.

L/C export documentary bills refer to a financing method in which the exporter uses the export documents under the L/C as collateral and requests the negotiating bank at the place of export to advance the amount of the L/C during the period between shipment and receipt of payment from the issuing bank.

After reviewing the documents specified in the L/C submitted by the exporter, if the documents are consistent, the negotiating bank will advance the remaining amount to the exporter after deducting interest and handling charges from the amount of the L/C. If the exporter cannot obtain the payment from the issuing bank after the expiry of the L/C, the negotiating bank has the right to recover from the exporter and require the exporter to repay the principal and interest.

b. Documentary collection export bills.

Documentary collection export bills refer to an export trade financing method in which the exporter, after shipping the goods, submits the shipping documents to the collecting bank at the place of export, requests the collecting bank to pay part or all of the payment in advance, and repays the bank advance after receiving the payment.

Under this financing method, the collecting bank will pay the balance of the bill to the exporter after buying the documentary bills and the attached commercial documents paid by the importer from the exporter, deducting interests and relevant expenses. If the exporter cannot recover the payment from the importer, the bank has the right to recourse to the exporter and require the exporter to repay the principal and interest.

The main difference between documentary collection export bills and L/C export documentary bills is that the former does not use the guarantee of bank credit. Whether the payment can be recovered depends entirely on the credit of the importer, so the risk is relatively high. That's why the interest rate of the documentary bills is always relatively high.

(5) Forward bill discounts.

Forward bill discounts refer to the fact that banks or discount companies have the right of recourse to buy the accepted forward bills that are not due and provide short-term financing business for customers.

In the process of forward bill discounts, the most common is that the exporter applies to the bank for a discount with the forward bill accepted by the issuing bank under the forward L/C. The discount amount is equal to the face amount minus the discount interest. If the issuing bank fails to fulfill its payment obligation at maturity, the paying bank has the right to require the exporter to repay the loan equal to the amount of the draft.

2. Importers financing to exporters

The importer pays all or part of the payment before receiving the goods documents, that is, the importer prepays the exporter for the goods. This financing method has simple procedures and low costs, which is beneficial to the exporter.

(ii) Financing for importers

1. Bank financing to importers

(1) Open a letter of credit for the importer.

Letter of credit (L/C) is a payment commitment made by the bank to the exporter. Once the applicant (importer) for issuing the L/C loses its solvency, the bank will bear the risk that the payment will not be recovered. Therefore, the bank requires the applicant to pay a certain percentage of the security deposit or provide corresponding collateral or guarantee from a third party. The bank opens a letter of credit for the importer, which is equivalent to occupying the bank's funds.

(2) Import documentary bill.

Under the L/C settlement method, when the exporter submits all documents to the bank as required and requires the importer to pay for the redemption documents, and if the importer does not have enough funds to redeem the documents from the issuing bank, the issuing bank can offer the payment in advance, and the importer obtains the documents from the bank. In this way, it is equivalent to the bank financing the importer.

(3) Delivery guarantee.

Under the L/C settlement method, when the goods arrive at the destination port before the bill of lading, in order to seize the favorable market opportunity to pick up the goods as soon as possible, the importer can request the bank to issue a delivery guarantee letter, and give the delivery guarantee letter to the shipping company to pick up the goods firstly. When the bill of lading is received, the bill of lading will be handed over to the shipping company in exchange for the delivery guarantee.

(4) Trust receipt.

When adopting the D/P settlement method in the documentary collection, the importer can issue a written guarantee document, i.e., trust receipt to the bank to take out the bill of lading. The importer can grasp the favorable opportunity of the market to sell the goods as soon as possible, and pay to the bank in exchange for the trust receipt after obtaining the payment. The specific process is as follows:

①The collecting bank lends the shipping documents to the importer according to the trust receipt, so that the importer can pick up the goods before the expiry of the forward draft, and then sell the goods to obtain part or all of the payment;

②When the draft is due, the importer pays the payment to the collecting bank and takes back the trust receipt;

③After the collecting bank collects the payment, it will pay the payment to the remitting bank.

It can be seen from the operation process that the importer completes the import trade without using its funds throughout the process, and the bank provides financing for it in the process.

(5) Documents against acceptance (D/A).

Under the settlement method of D/A, the exporter requires the bank to accept the bill after delivery in order to ensure safe collection. After acceptance by the bank, the importer can obtain the transport documents and take delivery of the goods, and then resell the goods or use them for production. The importer must pay the relevant money to the bank before the arrival date of the bill, so that the bank can cash it to the exporter on time on the payment date. In this process, the bank provides financing to the importer.

2. Exporters financing to importers

In order to improve the competitiveness of export commodities, the exporter can provide commercial credit to the importer and provide the importer with financing facilities for deferred payment, that is, the importer can obtain the document for delivery after accepting the usance bill issued by the exporter, and pay the face value on the due date of the bill to the exporter.

(ⅲ) International factoring business

International factoring business, also known as off-taking accounts receivable, means that when the exporter exports goods with commercial credit after the goods are shipped, the exporter immediately sells the invoices and shipping documents of accounts receivable to the factoring agent without recourse to obtain part or all of the payment. If the importer delays or fails to pay in the future, the factoring agent shall be liable.

The international factoring business is mainly designed for credit sales and has the following characteristics:

(1) Accounts receivable must be generated from the sale of goods between commercial institutions. The accounts receivable do not belong to personal or household consumption or other similar uses.

(2) The business organization must transfer the rights of accounts receivable to the factoring agent.

(3) Notification of assignment of accounts receivable must be sent to the debtor.

(4) The factoring agent must perform the following functions: financing the supplier in the form of a loan or advance payment, managing the accounts related to accounts receivable, collecting accounts receivable, and providing a bad debt guarantee for the refusal of the debtor.

II. Medium and long-term international trade financing

Short-term international trade financing can only solve the problem of temporary capital shortage. In the import and export trade of large machinery or complete sets of equipment, there is a problem of medium and long-term capital shortage, so it is necessary to carry out medium and long-term trade financing.

Animation micro-lesson 8-1

International medium and long-term trade financing

Medium and long-term international trade financing refers to the financing with a term of more than one year obtained by importers and exporters through different ways or means in the process of international trade. Medium and long-term international trade financing is mainly used to improve the capital structure of enterprises and solve the problem of insufficient medium and long-term funds. In fact, medium and long-term international trade financing is not only a financing method but also a competitive means for enterprises to compete for the export commodity market.

Medium and long-term international trade financing mainly includes export credit and forfaiting.

(i) Export credit

Along with the implementation of international trade of the large-scale machinery and equipment or technology between countries, and due to the large amount of money involved in such trade and the long-time of capital occupation, importers and exporters need the support of medium and long-term financing, so export credit comes into being.

1. The concept and characteristics of export credit

Export credit refers to an international credit method in which a bank or non-bank financial institution of a country provides loans with lower interest rates to domestic exporters or foreign importers (or banks) in order to promote the export of domestic large-scale machinery and equipment (or technology) and enhance the international competitiveness of export commodities. This kind of loan is provided by exporters for the purpose of promoting exports, so it is called export credit.

Export credit mainly shows the following characteristics:

(1) Loans are granted to enterprises that export large-scale equipment or technology and provide services for the export of domestic products (mainly large-scale complete sets of equipment) and technology.

(2) Lower interest rates. The interest rate of export credit is significantly lower than the domestic market interest rate, and the state provides interest subsidies. Interest rates for export credit are generally adjusted semi-annually in accordance with OECD agreements.

(3) Greater risks. Due to a large amount of export credit and long repayment period, the banks that issued loans undertake greater risks.

(4) Combined with insurance and guarantee. In order to solve the worries of lending banks in exporting countries and ensure the safe issuance of their loan funds, exporting countries generally have credit insurance institutions to guarantee the loans issued by banks and provide reinsurance services for private insurance companies providing insurance services.

2. The forms of export credit

There are mainly two forms of export credit: buyer's credit and seller's credit.

(1) Buyer's credit.

Buyer's credit is currently the main type of export credit in the world. It refers to the medium and long-term loans provided by the bank where the exporter is located to the foreign importer or the bank where the importer is located in order to expand the export of domestic large-scale machinery and equipment or technology. The buyer's credit can be lent to the importer or to the bank where the importer is located. Therefore, buyer's credit includes two forms: one is that the exporter's bank provides loans to the importer, and another is that the exporter's bank provides loans to the bank where the importer is located.

①The process of the exporter's bank providing loans to the importer is shown in Figure 8-1.

Figure 8-1　The exporter's bank provides loans to the importer

a. Both importers and exporters sign trade contracts;

b. The importer shall pay a cash deposit equivalent to 15% of the goods price in advance;

c. The importer signs a buyer's credit agreement with the exporter's bank;

d. The importer obtains a loan from the exporter's bank;

e. After the importer obtains a loan from the exporter's bank, the importer shall pay the payment to the exporter in cash exchange;

f. The importer repays the loan to the exporter's bank according to the loan agreement.

②The process of the exporter's bank providing loans to the importer's bank is shown in Figure 8-2.

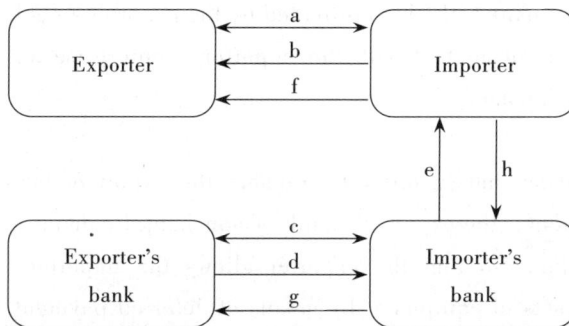

Figure 8-2　The exporter's bank provides loans to the importer's bank

a. Both importers and exporters sign trade contracts;

b. The importer shall pay a cash deposit equivalent to 15% of the goods price in advance;

c. The importer's bank signs the buyer's credit agreement with the exporter's bank;

d. According to the agreement, the importer's bank obtains loans from the exporter's bank;

e. After the importer's bank obtains the loan, it will lend the money to the importer;

f. After the importer obtains the loan from the importer's bank, the importer shall pay the payment to the exporter in cash exchange;

g. The bank of the importer shall repay the loan to the bank of the exporter in accordance with the loan agreement;

h. The importer reimburses the importer's bank according to the agreement.

③Analysis of the advantages and disadvantages of all parties under buyer's credit.

a. For the exporter, the exporter's bank provides loans to the importer or importer's bank. On the one hand, it can receive cash exchange with less risk and fast capital turnover, and also simplify the procedures and improve the financial situations. Due to the cash exchange received, there is no need to consider additional credit charges and other expenses when formulating the export price. On the other hand, since various expenses are borne by the importer, the exporter can only report the current exchange rate and make less profit.

b. For the exporter's bank, the exporter's bank loans to the importer's bank is less risky. If the loan is given to the importer, it must be guaranteed by a bank or other financial institution, and there is no great risk.

c. For the importer, if the buyer's credit loaned by the exporter's bank to the importer's bank is adopted, the importer can concentrate on negotiating technical and commercial terms. Due to the use of spot exchange for transactions, there is no need to consider the interest issue of deferred payment. The credit items shall be negotiated separately by the banks of both parties, and the handling fee shall also be negotiated directly by the banks of both parties. This reduces the number of charges and intermediate links, so that the importer is in a favorable position in the trade negotiation. However, if the buyer's credit is loaned to the importer by the exporter's bank, the importer must deal with the exporter's bank and go through the loan procedures.

d. For the importer's bank, the loan provided by the exporter's bank to the importer's bank can broaden the channels of contact with the importer's enterprise and expand the business volume and increase the income.

(2) Seller's credit.

Seller's credit means that in order to promote the export of large-scale machinery or complete sets of equipment, the exporter's bank or non-bank financial institution provides loan financing to the exporter, so that the exporter allows the importer to import large-scale machinery or complete sets of equipment by means of deferred payment. The price of deferred payment is generally higher than that of spot exchange payment.

① Specific process of seller's credit.

The specific process of seller's credit is shown in Figure 8-3.

a. The import and export parties sign the trade contract, and the importer purchases large-scale equipment from the exporter with deferred payment;

b. The importer shall pay 10% ~15% of the payment in advance as a deposit;

c. When the batch delivery is accepted and the deposit expires, the importer will pay another 10%~15% of the payment, and the remaining payment will be paid within the specified period after the exporter has delivered all the goods (usually once every half a year), and the importer will undertake the interest arising from the deferred payment;

d. Based on the trade contract, the exporter applies to the local bank for financing and signs a loan agreement to obtain the required funds;

e. The exporter repays the bank loan in installments with the instalment payment by the importer.

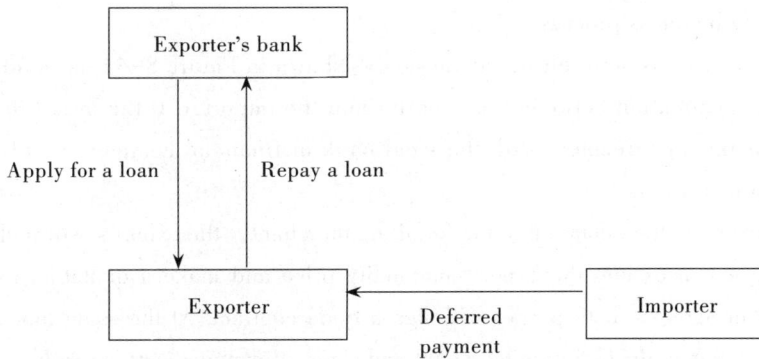

Figure 8-3　Seller's credit business process

②Analysis of the advantages and disadvantages of all parties under seller's credit.

a. For the exporter, under the seller's credit, the exporter should not only follow up with the suppliers but also deal with the banks in the export place and go through the loan procedures. Although the importer can bear all costs and risks and add them to the price to increase the profit of the exporter, there may be a risk that the payment for goods cannot be recovered on time because it is not guaranteed by the importer's bank.

b. For the exporter's bank, under the seller's credit, the exporter's bank should often pay attention to the operation of the exporter and the loan repayment of the exporter.

c. For the importer, under the seller's credit, the importer does not need to obtain bank loans when negotiating and signing trade agreements with the exporter, which saving time and effort, and the use of deferred payment can reduce the occupation of funds by the importer. However, since the exporter has to take a loan from the bank and bear the loan interest, insurance premium and other expenses, the price of the goods is relatively high, and the importer has to pay the interest generated by the deferred payment to the exporter.

d. For the importer's bank, under the seller's credit, there are only three parties: the exporter, the exporter's bank, and the importer.

(ii) Forfaiting

Forfaiting (or forfeiting, the original meaning is to give up, and transliterated as "fufeiting" in Chinese), also known as bill package purchase or bill buyout, refers to a time bill or promissory note with a term of 3~12 years guaranteed by the guarantor and accepted by the importer in the medium and long-term international trade of large machinery and equipment with deferred payment, the financing method of selling to the bank or large financial company where the exporter is located without recourse to obtain cash in advance.

Forfaiting business is a non-recourse discount business, that is, if the importer fails to pay when the deadline, the discount bank cannot exercise the right of recourse against the exporter. In fact, it is a more complex and disguised export seller's credit. It is a special agency financing technology, including exporters, importers, guarantor banks and forfaiting merchants.

1. Forfaiting business process

The specific process of forfaiting business（as shown in Figure 8-4）is as follows:

（1）Trade negotiation between the exporter and the importer. If the forfaiting is used, the exporter shall make an agreement with the local bank or financial company in advance to make various credit preparations.

（2）According to the quotation of the forfaiting merchant, the exporter will include all or part of the financing expenses into the export commodity price and make a quotation to the importer. Once the importer agrees, both parties will sign a trade contract. At the same time, the exporter confirms the quotation of the forfaiting merchant and signs a financing contract with it.

（3）After the exporter delivers the goods according to the trade contract, it obtains the usance bill accepted by the importer and guaranteed by the guarantee bank. The form of guarantee for bill is to sign and seal on the bill to ensure due payment or issue a letter of guarantee. The guarantee bank needs to be approved by the forfaiting merchant. If the credit of the guarantee bank is not high, the importer needs to change the guarantee bank.

（4）After obtaining the acceptance bill, according to the agreement with the forfaiting merchant, the exporter shall sell the bill to the forfaiting merchant and obtain cash.

（5）Bill maturity settlement. When the bill is due, the forfaiting merchant will settle the payment with the importer. If the importer refuses to pay, the forfaiting merchant will first claim reimbursement from the guarantee bank.

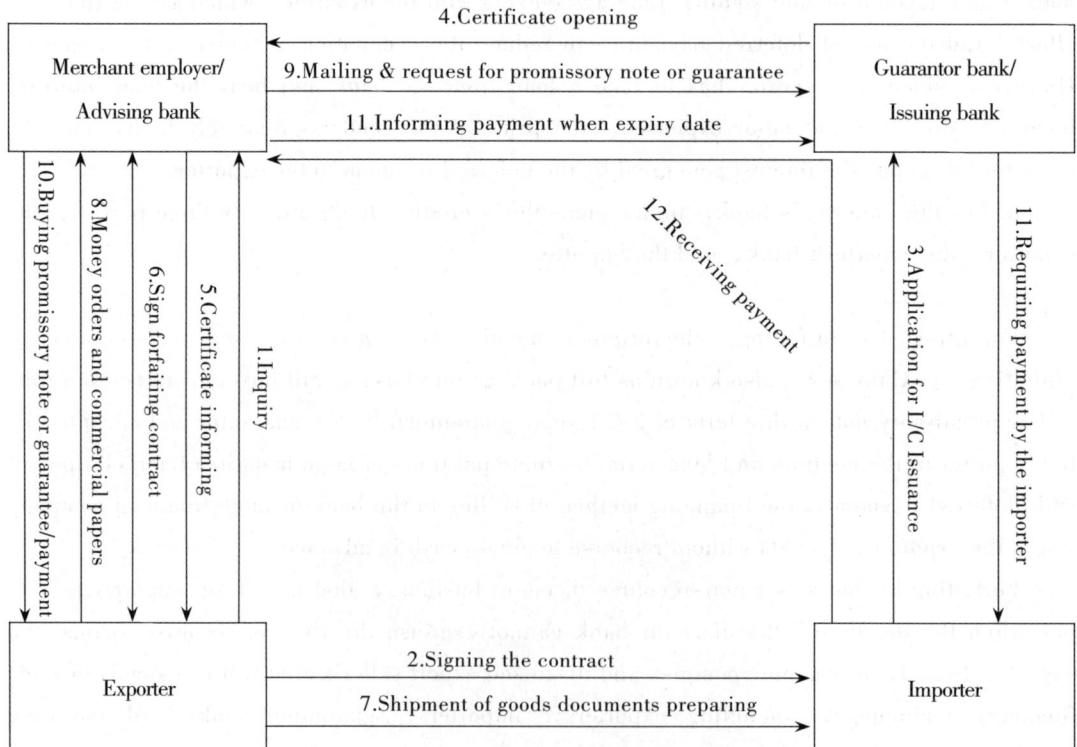

Figure 8-4　Forfaiting business process

2. Analysis of the advantages and disadvantages of all parties in forfaiting business

(1) Advantage and disadvantage for exporters.

The use of forfaiting is beneficial to exporters, which is mainly reflected in simple procedures and fewer documents to be submitted. Also, the exporter can transfer part of the financing expenses to the importer and obtain non - recourse financing immediately after delivery, which reduces and avoids the risk of export collection. As the forfaiting merchant has taken more risks, the interest rate of financing has also been increased accordingly, which makes the financing cost of exporters higher. In addition, it is difficult for exporters to find a guarantor that satisfies the forfaiting merchant.

(2) Advantage and disadvantage for importers.

Importers can import large machinery or complete sets of equipment by deferred payment, which can reduce capital occupation. The disadvantage for importers is that exporters may transfer part of the financing cost into the price of goods, making the price of goods higher. The guarantor provides a guarantee for the bill, the importer needs to pay the guarantee fee, and the bank guarantee will occupy the importer's bank credit line for a long time.

(3) Advantage and disadvantage for forfaiting merchants.

The forfaiting merchant provides financing to exporters, which can obtain higher income. Moreover, the bills of exchange and promissory notes used in forfaiting business can be circulated and transferred in the secondary market. The disadvantage for the forfaiting merchant is that the bills purchased by the forfaiting merchant have no recourse to the exporter and must bear higher financing risks. In addition, the forfaiting merchant must investigate the credit status of the guarantor and understand the legal provisions of the importing country on commercial paper and letter of guarantee.

(4) Advantage and disadvantage for guarantor banks.

The guarantor bank can not only obtain the guarantee fee income but also expand the influence of the guarantor bank in the international market. The disadvantage for the guarantor bank is that if the bill is due and the importer refuses to pay the payment, the guarantor bank has absolute and unconditional payment responsibility for the due bill.

(Knowledge Link 8-1)

Blockchain forfaiting trading platform

On August 6, 2020, the General Clearing Center of the People's Bank of China officially signed a cooperation agreement on the blockchain forfaiting trading platform with China CITIC Bank, Bank of China and China Minsheng Bank. This means that the blockchain forfaiting trading platform proposed by China CITIC Bank has officially become an industry platform.

According to the agreement, the General Clearing Center of the People's Bank of China will learn from the practical experience of three commercial banks in the construction of the early blockchain forfaiting trading platform to improve the asset trading function of the People's

Bank of China domestic electronic letter of credit system. Relevant function construction will make full use of and give full play to the technical advantages of blockchain, and combine the multilateral trust, tamper-proof, consensus algorithm and other technologies of blockchain with electronic L/C asset trading business to develop a forfaiting asset trading platform. The new platform will unify business standards, connect with the large-value payment system of the People's Bank of China, facilitate the trading of forfaiting assets between banks, improve the efficiency of trade financing in the field of forfaiting and reduce the financing cost of enterprises.

This platform currently in operation by China CITIC Bank, Bank of China and China Minsheng Bank is an asset trading alliance chain platform jointly designed and developed based on blockchain technology and blockchain thinking, which is used for the secondary market trading of domestic forfaiting assets. The platform integrates a series of links such as asset release, fund release, offer and creditor's right transfer, and solves the long-standing pain points such as the lack of open quotation market for forfaiting business and the disconnection of the transaction process. Until now, the number of members of the platform alliance has increased to 43, and the accumulated business has exceeded 300 billion RMB.

With the approval of the People's Bank of China, the General Clearing Center launched the electronic letter of credit information exchange system on December 9, 2019. The system will absorb and learn from the construction achievements of the existing forfaiting trading platforms of three commercial banks, realize the functions of asset registration and transaction based on blockchain technology, and is expected to become an important part of the national public financial infrastructure.

Source: Anonymity. General Clearing Center of the People's Bank of China officially signed a cooperation agreement on the blockchain forfaiting trading platform with three banks [EB/OL]. [2020-08-19]. https: // baijiahao.baidu.com/s?id=1674241307662421106&wfr=spider&for=pc.

Task 2   International Project Financing

I. Overview of international project financing

International project financing is a special financing method, which refers to the financing method of raising funds abroad in the name of domestic construction projects and bearing the responsibility of debt repayment with the project cash flow income, assets and interests. It belongs to a financing method with no or limited recourse.

Project financing is widely used in the development of natural resources such as oil and gas, the construction of luxury hotels and large-scale agricultural development projects. Nowadays, project financing is mainly used in large-scale infrastructure construction projects, such as power stations, highways, railways and airports. In China, Southeast Asia countries and other newly industrialized countries, BOT (build-operate-transfer) financing is often used for these projects.

Due to the large amount, long term and high risk of financing, international project financing mainly adopts syndicated loans for financing. It has the following characteristics:

(1) The lender does not take the assets and reputation of the sponsor as the basis for issuing loans, but the expected economic benefits of the project and the asset status of the undertaker as the basis for issuing loans.

(2) The repayment source of project financing is the future income of the project. The success or failure of the project is of decisive significance to whether the lender can recover the loan.

(3) International project financing risks are high, and more units with interests in the project need to be guaranteed to avoid risks.

(4) The sources of funds required for the project are diversified. In addition to obtaining funds from syndicated loans, it can also obtain support from the government and international organizations.

(5) Project financing is mainly based on the "limited recourse" financing method, and the interest rate is relatively high. In addition to taking the operating income of the project as the source of repayment and obtaining the real right guarantee, the lender also requires a third party other than the project (such as the project sponsor, the buyer of project products or the user of project facilities, the project contractor, etc.) to provide a guarantee. When the project income is poor or the operation fails, the lender has the right to recourse to the third party guarantor. The liability of guarantors for debts shall be limited to the amount of guarantee provided by each of them.

Knowledge Link 8-2

The past and present of BOT project financing

In recent years, BOT project financing has been used by some developing countries to carry out their infrastructure construction and has achieved certain success. It has attracted wide favor all over the world and is publicized as a new investment method. However, BOT project financing is far from a new thing. It has a history of at least 300 years since its emergence.

In the 17th century, the British pilotage association was responsible for managing maritime affairs, including the construction and operation of lighthouses, and had the privilege of building lighthouses and charging ships. However, according to the expert investigation, in the 66 years from 1610 to 1675, the pilotage association did not even build a lighthouse, while at least 10 private lighthouses were built in the same period. This investment method of private lighthouse construction is the same as the current BOT project financing method, that is, the private party first applies to the government for permission to build and operate lighthouses. The application must include the signatures of many ship owners to prove that the lighthouse to be built is beneficial to them and show their willingness to pay tolls. After the application is approved by the government, the private party rents the land that must be occupied for the construction of the lighthouse from the government, manages the lighthouse during the concession period and collects tolls from passing ships. After the expiration of the concession, the government will take back the lighthouse and hand it over to the pilotage association for management and continued charging. By 1820, of all 46 lighthouses, 34 were built with private investment. It can be seen that the investment efficiency of BOT project financing is much higher than that of administrative departments.

Since the 1960s and 1970s, large-scale international engineering development projects had increased day by day. Such large-scale projects include natural resources development projects such as oil, coal and natural gas, as well as infrastructure projects such as transportation, electric power, agriculture and forestry. International project financing often costs a lot and has a long development cycle. It often requires an investment amount of hundreds of millions, billions or even tens of billions of dollars and an investment cycle of several years, ten years or even decades. The investment risk of the project exceeds the limit that the project investors can and are willing to bear. The traditional corporate financing method cannot meet the financing requirements of such large-scale projects. In this situation, in order to meet the needs of developing large-scale projects, international project financing arranges project loans by using the asset value and cash flow of the project itself. This new type of financing comes into being and achieves great development.

Source: Anonymity. Case analysis of BOT project financing mode [EB/OL]. [2016-11-18]. https://www.xuexila.com/chuangye/rongzi/1888842.html.

II. Participants in project financing

The participants of project financing include the project sponsor, the project company, the borrower, the bank, the arranging bank, the management bank, the agent bank, the engineering bank, the security trustee, the financial consultant, the expert, the lawyer, the international financial institution, the host government, the insurance company, the leasing company and the rating agency.

1. Project sponsor

The project sponsor can be a company or a multilateral consortium or consortium composed of contractors, suppliers, purchasers or users of project products, or even members who have no direct interest in the project.

2. Project company

The project company is the entity operating the project, its identity, registered address and legal form depend on many factors.

3. Borrower

The borrower may or may not be the project company. A project financing may have several borrowers, who raise funds separately to meet the needs of their participation in the project, such as construction companies, operating companies, raw material suppliers, etc.

4. Bank

Based on the fact that the government of the country where the project is located may be reluctant to damage the economic relations with some countries, forming a syndicate with the participation of many national banks can avoid the interference of the government of the country where the project is located. Commercial banks can participate in syndicate as guarantee banks.

5. Arranging bank

The arranging bank is responsible for arranging financing and syndicated loans usually takes the lead in negotiating loan terms and security documents.

6. Management bank

The syndicated loan participating in the project financing can designate the management bank of the syndicated loan. The management bank generally does not assume any special liability to the borrower or the lender.

7. Agent bank

The agent bank is not responsible for the loan decision of the lender. The responsibility of the agent bank is to coordinate payment, facilitate the exchange of financing documents, serve notices and transmit information.

8. Engineering bank

The responsibility of the engineering bank is to monitor the technical progress and project performance, and to be responsible for the liaison between the project engineer and the independent expert. The engineering bank is likely to be a branch of the agent bank or the arranging bank.

9. Security trustee

In a project financing involving syndicated loans, there is an agent with trust qualification to keep the encumbered assets.

10. Financial consultant

The financial consultant will prepare the outline of the project memorandum, as well as the feasibility analysis of the characteristics and economic benefits of the project, put forward assumptions related to the project cost, market price and demand, exchange rate, etc., and report the situation of each project sponsor.

11. Expert

Technical experts with international reputations selected by the project sponsor or financial consultant will be responsible for preparing or at least inspecting the feasibility report of the project. Experts usually continue to participate in the monitoring of the project and act as arbitrators when the project sponsor and the lender have disputes over the completion tests specified in the project documents.

12. Lawyer

The role of lawyer is very important because of the complexity of project documents involved in large - scale project financing and the participation of parties from different countries.

13. International financial institution

Many developing country projects are jointly financed by the World Bank and the international finance corporations or regional development banks.

14. Host government

In many cases, the host government will not directly participate in project financing as the borrower or owner of the project company, but may obtain equity interests in the project through an agent and become the purchaser of the project or the user of the services provided by the project. The host government plays a key role in the project, such as giving relevant approval or operation license to the project, giving preferential treatment to the project or ensuring the source of foreign exchange.

15. Insurance company

Insurance is an important aspect of project financing.

16. Leasing company

The role of the leasing company is to collect rent regularly by acquiring some or all of the assets required by the project company and leasing these assets to the project company.

17. Rating agency

Some projects may be financed by issuing bonds with the support of banks. If bonds are to be rated, relevant rating agencies should be consulted at an early stage.

III. Risks of project financing

The risks of project financing include credit risk, construction and development risk, market and operational risk, financial risk, political risk, legal risk and environmental risk.

1. Credit risk

In project financing, the lender will evaluate the credit, performance and management skills of the project participants, even if they have certain recourse to the borrower and project sponsor.

2. Construction and development risk

The lender will carefully study the methods and assumptions used in the feasibility report when assessing the risks in the construction and development stage. The possibility and impact of the following factors must be considered: insufficient mineral reserve, insufficient capacity, output and efficiency, high cost, delay in completion, availability of land, construction materials, fuel, raw materials and transportation, availability of labor, management personnel and reliable contractors, force majeure, etc.

3. Market and operational risk

During the operational phase of the project, the following risks may exist:

（1） Whether the products of the project have domestic and foreign markets;

（2） Whether there might be competition and whether similar projects have been completed;

（3） Market access, whether potential customers can buy products freely, and whether the government controls the market;

（4） When the project reaches the operation stage, whether there is still a market for the products or services produced by the project, and whether the technology used in the project may be surpassed or replaced.

4. Financial risk

In the stage of project financing and repayment, it may face the risk of exchange rate fluctuation and interest rate rise. During the project construction stage, it may face the risk of rising price of international energy and raw materials. In the operation stage of the project, it may face the risk of falling price of products or the inflation.

5. Political risk

In project financing, both the borrower and the lender face political risks, such as the collapse of the existing political system in the borrower's country or the promulgation of a new tax system, exchange restrictions, nationalization or other laws that may damage the success of the project, the safety of project investment, debt repayment and project realization.

6. Legal risk

Many projects are carried out in the third world countries, and their legal system is not perfect. For example, the existing laws may exclude the ownership of the real estate; the protection of intellectual property rights is insufficient; there may be a lack of laws on fair trade and competition; disputes may be difficult to resolve; local lawyers and courts may not be familiar with disputes in the project; and the operation of local legal system can be slow and costly.

7. Environmental risk

There is growing public concern about the impact of industrialization on the natural environment and human health. Many countries have enacted increasingly stringent laws to control radiation, waste, the transport of hazardous materials, and the inefficient use of energy and non-renewable resources. As a result, borrowers may be subject to fines and penalties for pollution, as well as other environmental costs that may be incurred during the project financing process.

IV. Typical mode of project financing: BOT project financing

BOT refers to "build-operate-transfer", which means that the government of the country where the project is located selects international commercial capital or private capital developers in the form of bidding for the projects governed, owned or controlled by the government. By signing an agreement with them, the government authorizes them to raise funds, design, build, operate and maintain the project, and authorizes the project company to franchise within a certain period after the completion of the project.

During the franchise period, the project company collects fees from users to recover the project investment, operation and maintenance costs and obtain reasonable returns. After the expiration of the concession period, the project company will hand over the infrastructure to the government free of charge.

BOT financing is essentially a special operation mode of infrastructure projects operated by the government and contractors. In China, this financing mode is called "concession financing model".

The representative projects constructed by the way of concession financing in China include Beijing Jingtong Expressway, Guangxi Laibin Power Plant (Plant B), Sichuan Chengdu Water Supply Plant No. 6 (Plant B), Shanghai Huangpu River Yan'an East Road Tunnel Double Line Project and Hainan East Line Expressway, etc.

The advantages of BOT project financing for the host country are as follows:

(1) The project is invested by foreign investors without the investment of the local government. It only requires authorization without capital investment. After the project is completed, the investor can get the infrastructure project free of charge when the franchise expires. Therefore, the BOT financing method is highly valued by the local government.

(2) The country does not need to provide a guarantee for the debt of the project, so the debt of the project will not constitute national debt.

(3) The vast majority of the financial and investment recovery risks of the project are borne by the investors themselves.

It is undoubtedly beneficial for the host country to use this way to build the infrastructure needed by society.

The disadvantages of BOT project financing for the host country is that:

After the completion of the project, investors may charge higher fees for the public using the products or services provided by the project during the operation of the project, thus causing public dissatisfaction.

The advantages of BOT project financing for investors are as follows:

(1) It can directly enter the infrastructure construction projects with long - term development potential in the host country and obtain other business opportunities.

(2) In the project construction stage, investors can sell the equipment and drive the export of domestic labor service and trade.

(3) In the project operation stage, investors can obtain dividend income from the owned project company.

(4) At the expiration of the project operation period, the project company may obtain considerable investment return from selling the shares of the project at a high price.

BOT financing in China

The first BOT infrastructure project in China was the Shatoujiao Power Plant B built in Shenzhen by China Hong Kong Hehe Industrial Company and China Development Investment Corporation as contractors in 1984.

After that, several BOT financing projects also appeared in Guangdong, Fujian, Sichuan, Shanghai, Hubei and Guangxi. Such as the development of Guangzhou-Shenzhen-Zhuhai Expressway, Chongqing Metro, Diqia Expressway, Shanghai Yan'an East Road Tunnel Double Track, Wuhan Metro, Beihai Oilfield, etc. A typical BOT financing case is the construction of Shenzhen Metro Line 4.

Shenzhen Metro Line 4 is operated and developed by MTR Corporation. According to the agreement signed between Shenzhen Municipal Government and MTR Corporation, MTR Corporation established a project company in Shenzhen to invest in the construction of the Phase II project of Line 4 with a total length of about 16km and a total investment of about 6 billion RMB by means of BOT financing. At the same time, the Shenzhen Municipal Government would lease the 4.5km of Phase I project of Line 4, which had been completed and opened to traffic at the end of 2004 to MTR Corporation Shenzhen Company before the opening of the Phase II project (2007). From the date of opening of the Phase II project of Line 4, the whole line of Line 4 would be operated uniformly by the project company established by MTR, which had a 30-year franchise. In addition, MTR also obtained the property development right of 2.9 million square meters of construction area along Line 4. During the whole construction and operation period, the project company was absolutely controlled by MTR Corporation, operated independently and was responsible for its profits and losses. Upon the expiration of the operation period, all assets would be transferred to Shenzhen Municipal Government free of charge.

Source: Anonymity. Comprehensive analysis of project contracting modes such as BOT financing [EB/OL]. [2017-07-16]. https://www.sohu.com/a/157519797_221394.

Task 3　　　　　International Bond Financing

International bond financing refers to the activities of the government authorities, financial institutions, industrial and commercial enterprises and international financial institutions to raise funds by issuing bonds with the face value of a certain currency in the foreign market.

International bond financing includes foreign bond financing and European bond financing. Foreign bonds refer to bonds issued overseas by the issuer of bonds with the face value of the currency of the country where the issuing market is located. European bonds refer to bonds issued overseas by bond issuers and not denominated in the currency of the country where the issuing market is located. European here is not "Europe" geographically, but "overseas".

The difference between foreign bonds and European bonds is:

(1) The issuing market of foreign bonds belongs to the same country as the currency of the bond face value and belongs to different countries or regions from the issuer. The issuer, issuing market and face value currency of European bonds belong to three different countries or regions.

(2) Different distribution methods. Foreign bonds are generally underwritten by securities companies and financial institutions in the country where the issuing market is located. European bonds are led by one or several large banks to form more than a dozen or dozens of international banks to underwrite in one or several countries at the same time.

(3) It is subject to different legal restrictions in the country where the issuing market is located. The issuance of foreign bonds is regulated and bound by the relevant laws and regulations of the country where the issuing market is located. While European bonds are not subject to the relevant laws and regulations of the country where they are issued.

I. Foreign bond financing

When issuing foreign bonds, they can be publicly offered to the majority of investors in the country where they are issued, or privately offered to a minority of investors in the country where they are issued. The underwriting of foreign bonds is undertaken by the domestic underwriting syndicate of the issuing country and the investors are mainly domestic residents of the country. The interest rate of foreign bonds depends on the interest rate of the domestic capital market of the issuing country and is issued at a fixed interest rate. The term of foreign bonds is about 20~30 years. Bonds with a longer term usually provide resale protection to investors, that is, investors have the right to require the issuer to redeem the bonds in advance at a certain price before the maturity of the bonds.

According to international practice, when foreign financial institutions issue foreign bonds in a country, they are generally named after the most representative items with the characteristics of the country where the issuing market is located. For example, foreign bonds issued in the UK are called "bulldog bonds", foreign bonds issued in the United States are called "yankee bonds", foreign bonds issued in Japan are called "samurai bonds", and foreign bonds issued in China are called "panda bonds".

At present, the main foreign bond markets include the yankee bond market in the United States, the samurai bond market in Japan, the Swiss foreign bond market and the Euro bond market, etc.

II. European bond financing

The advantages of European bond financing are:

(1) European bond is issued in bearer form, which is very convenient for transfer.

(2) The issuance is not subject to the laws and regulations of the country where the issuance is located, but each sale must comply with the laws and rules of the country of sale. Before the issuance of the bond, it should be indicated that the country law shall prevail in the event of a dispute.

(3) The interest rate of European bonds is affected by the domestic capital market interest rate of the country with the currency price. For example, the yield of Eurodollar bonds is determined according to the yield of the New York bond market. In most cases, the yield of European bonds is lower than the domestic capital market interest rate of the country with the corresponding currency price.

In the European bond market, Eurodollar bonds account for the largest share. In addition, there are bonds in other currencies, such as European pound bonds, European yen bonds, European euro bonds, etc.

The European bond market was originated in the 1960s and developed very rapidly. At present, the total amount of European bond financing has far exceeded that of foreign bond financing. It has become an important channel for multinational corporations, foreign governments and developing country governments to raise funds.

At present, the main European bond markets include the European dollar market, the European yen market, the European pound market and the European special drawing right bond market. Among them, the capacity of the European dollar market is the largest, while the issuance volume of the European special drawing right bond market is relatively small compared with the first three markets.

Mini Case

Scientific and technological innovation has brought trade finance into a new era. The application of artificial intelligence and big data has effectively improved the accuracy of decision-making. The penetration of blockchain technology has greatly improved the efficiency of business processing, making the future development of commercial bank trade financing show six major trends: the increased demand for enterprise-centric comprehensive trade financial services; the huge business opportunities of the domestic trade; the growth opportunities of the commodity financing business; the rapid rise of cross-border e-commerce; the growth in demand for trade finance and external guarantee services along "The Belt and Road" and the financial technology transformation of trade finance business models.

Commercial banks should accelerate the cultivation of new advantages in international economic cooperation and competition, implement the concept of "community of common interests" and "community of common destiny" in the field of trade finance and inject new impetus into the development of trade finance.

Thinking questions:

(1) What the changes will financial technology bring to the bank trade finance business in the future?

(2) How can commercial banks implement the concept of "community of common interests" and "community of common destiny" in the field of trade finance?

Mind Map

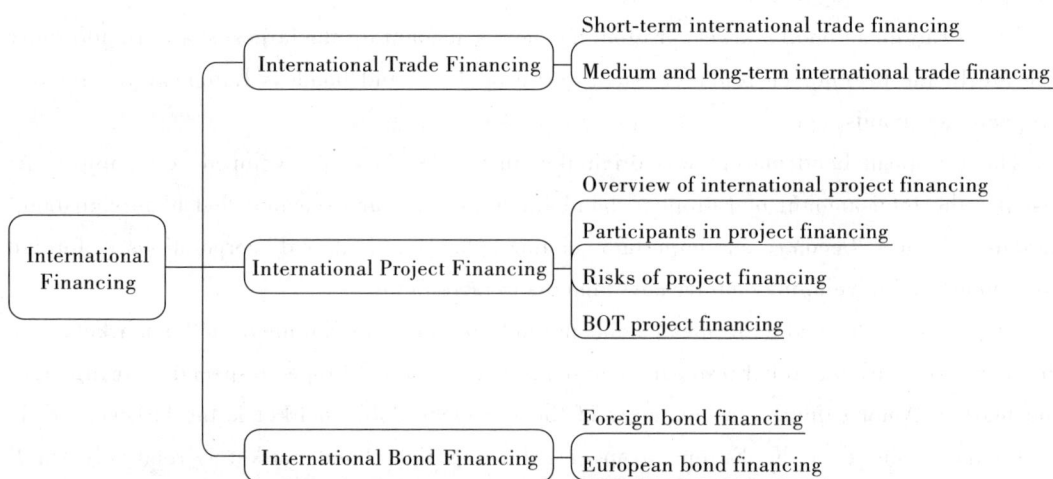

Project Training

I. Single-choice questions

1. Which of the following is a short-term international trade financing method (   ).

A. Export credit   B. Forfaiting business

C. International factoring   D. Buyer's credit

2. Which of the following does not belong to bank financing to importers (   ).

A. Seller's credit   B. Delivery guarantee

C. Buyer's credit   D. Trust receipt

3. In the following statements, the wrong statement is (   ).

A. Bonds denominated in sterling issued by foreign fundraisers in the UK bond market are called "bulldog bonds"

B. US dollar denominated bonds issued by foreign fundraisers in the US bond market are called "yankee bonds"

C. US dollar denominated bonds issued by foreign fundraisers in the Japanese bond market are called "samurai bonds"

D. US dollar denominated bonds issued by Japanese fundraisers in the Swiss bond market are European bonds

4. In the following statements, the wrong statement is （　　）.

A. The exporter's forfaiting procedures are simple and the documents submitted are less, and part of the financing costs can be transferred to the importer

B. Importers can import large machinery or complete sets of equipment by means of deferred payment, which can reduce the occupation of funds

C. The forfaiting merchant can obtain higher income by providing financing to exporters, but the bills of exchange and promissory notes used in forfaiting business cannot be circulated and transferred in the secondary market

D. The guarantee bank can obtain the guarantee fee income and expand its influence in the international market

5. Which of the following statements is correct （　　）.

A. BOT means "Buyout-Transfer"

B. Export credit includes buyer's credit and seller's credit

C. In the forfaiting business, the selection of the guarantee bank does not require the approval of the forfaiting merchant

D. International factoring business belongs to medium and long-term international trade financing

II. Multiple-choice questions

1. Which of the following are medium and long-term international trade financing methods （　　）.

A. Delivery guarantee   B. Forfaiting business

C. Export documentary bill   D. Buyer's credit

2. Which of the following are belong to bank financing to exporters （　　）.

A. Seller's credit   B. Export documentary bill

C. Package loan   D. Delivery guarantee

3. The parties involved in the forfaiting business include （　　）.

A. Exporter   B. Importer

C. Forfaiting merchant   D. Guarantor bank （guarantee bank）

4. In BOT project financing, the benefits for investors include （　　）.

A. It can directly enter the infrastructure construction projects with long-term development potential in the host country and obtain other business opportunities

B. In the project construction stage, investors can sell the equipment and drive the export of domestic labor service and trade

C. In the project operation stage, investors can obtain dividend income from the owned project company

D. At the expiration of the project operation period, the project company may obtain considerable investment return from selling the shares of the project at a high price

5. In the following statements, the wrong statements are （   ）.

A. Buyer's credit refers to the form of loan provided by the bank at the export place to the importer or the bank at the importer's location

B. The issuer of foreign bonds and the currency in which the bonds are issued belong to the same country

C. After the forfaiting merchant has bought out the bill, it still has the right of recourse against the exporter

D. Under the BOT project financing mode, the project company will hand over the project to the government free of charge when the franchise expires

III. Judgment questions

1. Package loan refers to that in international trade when receiving the letter of credit issued by the importer's issuing bank after delivering the goods, the exporter mortgages the original letter of credit to the bank and applies for a certain amount of loan from the bank.
（   ）

2. Export documentary bill is that the exporter sells the shipping documents of export commodities to the exporter's bank for financing without recourse after delivery.   （   ）

3. Export credit refers to an international credit type in which a bank or non-bank financial institution of a country provides loans at a lower interest rate to its exporters or importers or banks where importers are located in order to promote the export of large-scale machinery and equipment or technology and enhance the international competitiveness of export commodities.
（   ）

4. In BOT project financing, the government does not need to invest funds for the construction of the project.   （   ）

5. European bond financing refers to the issuance of bonds by foreign fundraisers in the European financial market to raise funds.   （   ）

IV. Practical questions

An export enterprise in Hangzhou plans to export large complete sets of equipment abroad, but the foreign import enterprise cannot realize cash exchange payment in the short term. In order to ensure the successful progress of trade, please design an export scheme for the enterprise.

Project Nine
Foreign Exchange Risk Management

Learning Objectives

Knowledge Objectives:

To master the meaning, elements and types of foreign exchange risk; to understand the contents of foreign exchange risk management and specific methods and measures of foreign exchange control.

Competence Objectives:

To be able to identify foreign exchange risks in specific cases.

Operational Objectives:

To be able to analyze foreign exchange risk management cases and give basic solutions.

Course Introduction

What is the significance of the central bank's drastic action to cut the foreign exchange risk reserve ratio from 20% to zero?

The onshore RMB strengthened nearly 1 100 points against the US dollar on the first trading day after the 2020 National Day holiday, while the offshore RMB extended its holiday strength against the US dollar. As of October 10, the onshore and offshore RMB both breached 6.70, its highest level since April last year.

The RMB is surging

The onshore RMB rose 3.8 percent in the third quarter of 2020, its biggest quarterly gain since 2008. The offshore RMB has risen more than 4 percent over the same period. In the third quarter, the RMB outperformed the G10, which includes traditional safe-haven currencies such as the Swiss franc and the Japanese yen.

Statistics show that since the end of May 2020, the RMB has set off a wave of upward trend, with the onshore RMB exchange rate rising by more than 4 000 points against the US dollar and the offshore RMB exchange rate rising by nearly 5 000 points against the US dollar.

Based on the simple calculation of the offshore RMB exchange rate, if the exchange rate ranges from 7.19 to 6.69, one resident needs RMB 719,000 to exchange USD 100,000, but today the lowest exchange rate is only RMB 669,000, a difference of more than RMB 50,000.

Central bank action: 20% down to 0

The People's Bank of China (PBOC) published the news: the RMB exchange rate has been floating on the basis of market supply and demand since 2020. The exchange rate has become more flexible, market expectations are stable, cross-border capital flows are orderly, the foreign exchange market has maintained stable operation and market supply and demand are in balance.

To this end, the People's Bank of China decided to lower the foreign exchange risk reserve ratio for forward foreign exchange sales from 20% to 0 on October 12, 2020. Next, the People's Bank of China would continue to maintain the flexibility of the RMB exchange rate, stabilize market expectations and keep the RMB exchange rate basically stable at a reasonable and balanced level.

Forward sale of foreign exchange is a kind of exchange rate hedging derivatives provided by banks to enterprises. Enterprises can avoid future exchange rate risk to a certain extent through the forward purchase of foreign exchange. So, what is the significance of the central bank's reduction of foreign exchange risk reserve ratio?

Expert interpretation: what is the meaning of this action

Wen Bin, the chief researcher at China Minsheng Bank, said: "If the foreign exchange risk reserve ratio is raised, the cost for enterprises to buy dollars from banks in the future will rise. Now it is lowered to zero, which will actually reduce the cost for enterprises to buy dollars in the future, thus increasing the demand for foreign exchange purchases in the future."

Since 2020, the exchange rate of RMB against the US dollar has become more volatile, and generally presents a trend from depreciation to appreciation. In particular, as the fundamentals of China's economy continue to improve, the RMB has appreciated significantly against the US dollar recently.

At this moment, the foreign exchange risk reserve ratio is lowered to 0. On the one hand, it helps reduce the cost of forward purchase of foreign exchange by enterprises and makes better use of RMB derivatives to manage exchange rate risks. On the other hand, the increased demand for forward purchase of US dollar can also restrain the rapid appreciation of the RMB spot exchange rate, so as to realize the two-way fluctuation of RMB against US dollar at a reasonable and balanced level.

Source: GU Z P. What is the significance of the central bank's drastic action to cut the foreign exchange risk reserve ratio from 20% to zero [EB/OL]. [2020-10-12]. http://www.cs.com.cn/yh/04/202010/t20201013_6100777.html.

Thinking and discussion:

1. What is the foreign exchange risk?

2. What is the role of foreign exchange risk reserve ratio?

Task 1   Overview of Foreign Exchange Risk

I. Meaning of foreign exchange risk

Foreign exchange risk, also known as exchange rate risk, refers to changes in the value of assets (claims and equity) and liabilities (debts and obligations) denominated in foreign currencies of enterprises, banks and other economic organizations, countries and individuals due to changes in exchange rates in the international foreign exchange market. Thus, it will bring uncertainty to foreign exchange trading subjects.

Foreign exchange risk has the broad and narrow definitions. Foreign exchange risk in a broad sense refers to the possibility of both loss and profit; and in a narrow sense, foreign exchange risk only refers to the possibility of loss to economic subjects due to exchange rate fluctuations. Generally, we refer to foreign exchange risk in a narrow sense.

Foreign exchange risk is usually represented by foreign exchange exposure. Foreign exchange exposure, also known as the at-risk portion, refers to the amount of foreign currency in business activities affected by exchange rate fluctuations. Foreign exchange exposure includes two scenarios:

(1) When the amount of assets or liabilities denominated in foreign currency is not equal, there will be a part of foreign currency net assets or liabilities affected by exchange rate changes, which is the "foreign exchange exposure position".

(2) Maturity gaps occur when assets or liabilities denominated in foreign currencies have different maturities.

【Example 9-1】 A multinational company earns 2 million dollars in export income and pays 1 million dollars in import income, so it has a foreign exchange exposure of 1 million dollars. If the dollar appreciates by 5%, the company will earn 50,000 dollars. Otherwise, it will lose 50,000 dollars. Therefore, the exposed 1 million dollars in foreign exchange is the portion at risk.

II. Components of foreign exchange risk

Foreign exchange risk consists of three elements: local currency, foreign currency and time. These three elements exist simultaneously in foreign exchange risk.

(ⅰ) Local currency

The local currency is a common currency indicator to measure the economic performance of enterprises. In foreign-related business activities, if an enterprise has foreign currency of accounts receivable, accounts payable, borrowing and lending of foreign currency capital, etc., it shall convert them into the local currency to assess its business performance. In the conversion process of foreign currency and local currency, the constant change of exchange rate may cause changes in cash flow calculated in local currency. If losses are caused, it indicates the existence of foreign exchange risk. If foreign economic activities in the enterprise do not use foreign currency and currency valuation, there is no foreign exchange risk.

【Example 9-2】 An American export enterprise exports a batch of goods to a German importer. The payment is due in 3 months. At the same time, the exporter requires the US dollar for settlement. In this transaction, the export enterprise is priced in local currency and does not involve the conversion of local currency and foreign currency, so there is no foreign exchange risk.

(ⅱ) Foreign currency

In international economic activities, it is often necessary to use foreign currency for settlement, especially for economic entities whose domestic currency cannot be circulated in the international market. Therefore, these economic entities will inevitably have foreign exchange risk in the conversion process of local and foreign currencies.

【Example 9-3】 A Chinese export enterprise exports a batch of goods to a German importer, and the payment will be made in six months. The exporter also requires settlement in the US dollar. Therefore, in this transaction, the export enterprise is denominated in foreign currency and needs to convert into RMB after receiving the payment for goods in USD, which may be affected by exchange rate fluctuations, that is, change of the RMB amount of the payment for goods in USD six months later, so there is foreign exchange risk.

(ⅲ) Time

In the process of international economic activities, there is a period from the transaction completed to the actual receipt of account payment and the completion of the loan principal and interest payment, and this period is the time factor. Over a certain period of time, the conversion ratio of foreign currency to local currency may change, resulting in foreign exchange risk.

【Example 9-4】 In the 【Example 9-3】, the export enterprise will recover the payment after six months, during which the exchange rate of USD against RMB changes constantly, resulting in foreign exchange risk.

Generally speaking, the longer the time, the greater the possibility and range of exchange rate fluctuations, and the greater the foreign exchange risk; otherwise, the smaller the foreign exchange risk.

III. Types of foreign exchange risk

According to the time of occurrence of foreign translation risk, foreign exchange risk can be divided into conversion risk, transaction risk and economic risk.

(i) Conversion risk

Conversion risk, also called the accounting risk or translation risk. It means that during economic subject accounting treatment, there is the possibility of book losses due to exchange rate fluctuations when the functional currency (the currency used in economic activity, usually the foreign currency) is converted into the bookkeeping currency (generally for the economic subject of local currency).

The conversion risk is not the actual loss that occurred at delivery, but the loss of accounting evaluation, which is a kind of stock risk. When preparing consolidated financial statements, a multinational company shall convert the financial statements of its foreign branches into its currency in accordance with relevant accounting standards. Generally enterprises in foreign currency denominated assets, liabilities, income and expenditure, usually also need to convert into the national currency. Obviously, if the exchange rate fluctuates, even if the amount of assets and liabilities denominated in foreign currency does not change, the local currency value in the accounting accounts will change accordingly, so the accounting accounts of enterprises will have certain gains and losses. This kind of profit and loss will affect the results of the financial statements that the company discloses to shareholders and the public.

【Example 9-5】 An enterprise in China deposits USD 100,000 in a bank in the United States because of business reasons. At that time, the exchange rate between USD and RMB is USD1=CNY6.9146, so in the enterprise accounting accounts, the deposit value is converted into RMB 691,460. If the exchange rate between USD and RMB is USD1=CNY6.8146 after a period of time, the deposit value of the enterprise will be converted into RMB 681,460 in the accounting accounts. Obviously, the same amount of dollar deposits is converted at different exchange rates, and the final book value is reduced by RMB 10,000. This is the conversion risk, which will have a great impact on the profits and financial statements of enterprises.

(ii) Transaction risk

Transaction risk, also known as transaction settlement risk, refers to the risk that the value of assets or liabilities changes due to the exchange rate changes between local and foreign currencies in transactions denominated in foreign currencies. Transaction risk is a kind of flow risk, which arises when the transaction contract becomes effective and ends when the transaction is completed. In the process of international activities, there will be transaction risks as long as the transaction activities involve foreign currency valuation or receipt and payment or international investment. According to the situation of foreign-related activities, transaction risks mainly include the following three situations:

1. Foreign trade settlement risk

In the import and export business, it generally takes a period of time from the signing of trade contracts to the final receipt and payment of goods. During this period, the exchange rate may change, which reduces the income of exporters or increases the expenditure of importers. This is the risk of foreign trade settlement.

【Example 9-6】 A Chinese exporter exports a batch of goods worth USD 1 million to an American importer and receives the payment 3 months later. At the time of signing the trade contract, the exchange rate between USD and RMB is USD1=CNY6.8201, according to which the exporter can get RMB 6.8201 million when receiving the payment. However, if RMB appreciates 3 months later and the exchange rate changes to USD1=CNY6.7201, then the exporter can only get RMB 6.7201 million when receiving payment at this exchange rate, losing RMB 100,000, that is, the exporter's income is reduced than expected. Similarly, the importer has to bear foreign exchange risk from the signing of contract to settlement. The principle is the same as that of the exporter, but the exchange rate changes are just opposite to that of the exporter.

2. Foreign exchange trading risk

In the spot or forward foreign exchange transactions to be delivered, due to the change of exchange rate, one party may suffer the loss of underpayment or overpayment of local currency (or other currency) when the contract expires, which constitutes the risk of foreign exchange trading.

【Example 9-7】 Assume that a bank buys and sells foreign exchange with a customer. On the same day, it buys 1 million euros at EUR1=USD1.1300 and sells 1.13 million dollars. If the euro depreciates the next day and the exchange rate changes to EUR1=USD1.1200, the bank will only have to pay 1.12 million dollars to buy 1 million euros and the customer will lose USD 10,000. This is the risk of foreign exchange trading.

3. International investment risk

In the international investment and loan activities denominated in foreign currency, the risk of the creditor's income decreasing or the debtor's expenditure increasing due to exchange rate fluctuation before the credit or debt is not repaid, which constitutes the international investment risk. This risk exists only if enterprises start buying or selling foreign exchange and then have to sell or buy it in reverse.

【Example 9-8】 An American company borrows 5 million euros for two years when the exchange rate of euro to the dollar is EUR1=USD1.1217. If the exchange rate changes to EUR1= USD1.1317 two years later, the enterprise will need 5.6585 million dollars (5×1.1317) to repay the loan of 5 million euros due to the change of exchange rate, and it will pay more USD 50,000 (5×1.1217-5.6585, in million) when borrowing.

(iii) Economic risk

Economic risk, also known as operational risk, refers to the possibility that the future earnings of an enterprise may change due to unexpected exchange rate fluctuations. Specifically, economic risk is a potential risk. Exchange rate fluctuations change the final earnings of enterprises by affecting output, sales volume, production cost and sales price. The size of the income change depends on the impact of exchange rate changes on product quantity, price and cost.

For an enterprise, economic risk involves every stage of enterprise production and needs to be predicted and analyzed from the whole enterprise. The analysis of economic risk mainly depends on the forecasting and analysis ability of enterprises, which is subjective and dynamic with long-term influence. However, the impact of conversion risk and transaction risk is one-time, so the loss caused by economic risk is more serious than that of conversion risk or transaction risk.

【Example 9-9】 When the currency of a country depreciates, on the one hand, the foreign currency price of exported goods decreases, which will stimulate the increase of exports, and then the export volume of the exporter increases. On the other hand, a weaker currency can raise costs for the exporter whose main factors of production are imported goods. Taken together, the exporter's final earnings may increase or decrease. That is the economic risk.

Task 2　　　　Foreign Exchange Risk Management

I. Overview of foreign exchange risk management

Foreign exchange risk inevitably exists in the process of foreign economic activities, which brings great influence to foreign economic subjects. Therefore, each economic entity should face up to the fact that foreign exchange risk exists objectively, try to analyze its causes, and take relevant measures to prevent it.

(i) Meaning of foreign exchange risk management

Foreign exchange risk management means that holders of foreign exchange assets make relevant decisions on possible changes in the foreign exchange market to prevent, avoid, transfer or eliminate risks in the foreign exchange business, so as to avoid or reduce possible economic losses caused by exchange rate changes.

Animation micro-lesson 9-1

Foreign exchange risk
management

Although foreign exchange risk exists objectively, it can be avoided or eliminated by taking relevant measures. Foreign exchange risk management includes general management and comprehensive management. Relevant principles should be followed regardless of general management or comprehensive management.

(ii) Principles of foreign exchange risk management

All economic entities should obey the following principles in the foreign exchange risk management:

1. Combining macro-economic principle

When dealing with the problems of their interests and national macro-economic interests, enterprises, departments and other micro-economic subjects usually try to reduce or avoid foreign exchange risk losses as much as possible, and transfer the risks to banks, insurance companies and so on. However, in the actual business, each economic subject should combine the interests of the micro-economic subject with the macro-economy as far as possible to prevent risks together.

2. Prevention-by-type principle

For different kinds of foreign exchange risks, different measures should be taken for classified prevention because of different causes. For example, to deal with the transaction risk, we should choose the settlement currency as the main prevention method; for the exchange rate risk of securities investment, we should take all kinds of preventive measures.

3. Avoiding loss and gaining profit principle

In practice, attention should be paid to transferring potential gains while taking measures to transfer or eliminate foreign exchange risks. Therefore, we should try our best to avoid losses and gain profits while transferring or eliminating foreign exchange risks.

Case Analysis 9-1

In January 2018, China Group Corporation signed an export order of USD 10 million with an American company. At that time, the exchange rate of the USD against RMB was USD1=CNY6.5063. When the goods were delivered six months later, RMB had appreciated greatly, and the exchange rate of the USD against RMB was USD1=CNY6.3063. The company lost RMB 2 million due to changes in the exchange rate.

After this incident, in order to strengthen foreign exchange risk management and effectively improve the company's foreign exchange risk prevention level, the company held a high-level meeting on strengthening foreign exchange risk management in July 2018. Managers summarized the experience and lessons of the loss and formulated foreign exchange risk management countermeasures. Highlights of the remarks made by the managers are as follows:

General manager Zhang: (1) it is very important to strengthen the management of foreign exchange risk, and great attention must be paid to this problem. (2) Foreign exchange risk management should focus on the emphasis, especially the management of transaction risk and conversion risk. Practical measures must be formulated to prevent the erosion of corporate profits by exchange rate changes.

Chief accountant Song: strengthening foreign exchange risk management is really very important. I recently conducted a study on issues related to the foreign exchange risk management and found that there are many financial instruments for foreign exchange risk management. When we take any kind of financial instruments to hedge, at the same time, we will lose the benefit from the exchange rate changes to the beneficial aspects. Foreign exchange losses and gains mainly depend on the timing and magnitude of exchange rate fluctuations. Therefore, to strengthen the foreign exchange risk management, we must firstly attach importance to the study of exchange rate trends and adopt different countermeasures according to the different trends of exchange rates.

Source: Anonymity. International finance review outline [EB/OL]. [2011-02-17]. https://wenku. baidu.com/view/03130e0ff12d2af90242e6ea.html.

Thinking and discussion:

(1) What kind of risk is reflected in the case?

(2) From the perspective of the basic principles of foreign exchange risk management, it points out that there is something wrong with the viewpoints of general manager Zhang and chief accountant Song in the speech of the meeting, and briefly explains the reasons respectively.

(iii) Strategies for foreign exchange risk management

The strategy of foreign exchange risk management refers to the attitude of foreign economic entities towards foreign exchange risks, that is, whether risks should be prevented and to what extent they should be prevented. According to their different attitudes toward risks, foreign economic entities can adopt a completely precautionary strategy, a completely non - precautionary strategy and a partially precautionary strategy.

1. Completely precautionary strategy

Completely precautionary strategy refers to the strategy of taking strict measures to prevent foreign exchange risks and completely eliminating uncertain factors. While this is an effective way to protect against foreign exchange risk, it is not the most profitable strategy because risk prevention is accompanied by a loss of profit opportunities.

2. Completely non-precautionary strategy

Completely non-precautionary strategy refers to a strategy that does not take any preventive measures against foreign exchange risks. Undertaking losses voluntarily if the exchange rate moves in an adverse direction while gains can be made if the exchange rate moves in a favorable direction. Generally speaking, under the fixed exchange rate system, there are more enterprises or banks adopt this strategy in the small foreign exchange business volume or speculative activities. But under the floating exchange rate system, almost no enterprises or banks adopt this strategy.

3. Partially precautionary strategy

Partially precautionary strategy refers to the strategy of taking preventive measures against part of foreign exchange risks while leaving other parts untouched. The key to adopting this strategy is to determine which parts of the total foreign exchange exposure need to be guarded against and which do not. This strategy should not only consider the cost of risk prevention, but also the difficulty of risk prevention and the accuracy of exchange rate prediction.

II. Foreign exchange risk management of foreign-related enterprises

As the level of market exchange rate changes from moment to moment, foreign enterprises may be exposed to foreign exchange risks at any time. Therefore, how to prevent foreign exchange risks has become one of the main contents of foreign-related enterprises operation and management. Foreign-related enterprises should design and select management schemes to prevent and reduce losses according to different types of foreign exchange risks and follow the principle of "minimum cost and best risk management effect". The following is an introduction to the scheme of conversion risk, transaction risk and economic risk faced by foreign-related enterprises.

(i) Conversion risk management

According to the transmission mechanism of conversion risk, the methods of conversion risk management mainly include asset-liability maintenance, asset-liability neutralization, risk hedging and net payment.

1. Asset-liability maintenance method

The asset-liability maintenance method refers to the method by which an enterprise adjusts its assets and liabilities accordingly to prevent or reduce foreign exchange risks.

Among the assets and liabilities of enterprises, some are easy to adjust, while others are difficult or impossible to adjust. Therefore, enterprises should conduct the qualitative analysis of assets and liabilities before adjusting assets and liabilities to determine the key objects of adjustment. Generally speaking, the long-term assets and liabilities of enterprises lack liquidity and cannot be rapidly increased or decreased in the short-term, so it is difficult to adjust. In the short-term assets and liabilities, some enterprises cannot be adjusted according to their wishes, such as tax payable. Therefore, enterprises focus on the adjustment of assets and liabilities, such as accounts receivable, cash, inventory, bank deposits and short-term investments in short-term assets, as well as accounts payable and bills in short-term liabilities.

【Example 9–10】 A transnational enterprise expects a foreign currency to appreciate, so it increases the short-term assets denominated in this foreign currency and reduces the short-term liabilities denominated in this foreign currency. Conversely, if a currency is expected to depreciate, the short-term assets denominated in that currency are reduced and the short-term liabilities denominated in that currency are increased.

2. Asset-liability neutralization method

Asset-liability neutralization method refers to the adjustment of the assets and liabilities, method of preventing conversion risk by equating the amounts of assets and liabilities expressed in various functional currencies (currencies used in daily business activities) so as to translate the risky position (the difference between the risky asset and the risky liability) to zero.

The specific operation process of the asset-liability neutralization method is as follows:

(1) Firstly, calculating the amount of various foreign currency assets and foreign currency liabilities in the balance sheet and determining the size of the net conversion risk position.

(2) Secondly, according to the nature of the risk position to determine the direction of the adjustment of the risk assets and liabilities.

(3) Finally, the specific situation is carefully analyzed and compared to determine the type and amount of adjustment, so that the overall cost of adjustment is minimum and the effect is the best.

【Example 9-11】 Assuming that a multinational enterprise has only 3 million dollars in assets and 4 million dollars in liabilities, that is, the dollar liabilities are greater than the dollar assets. Thus, it is necessary to increase the dollar assets or reduce the dollar liabilities, or at the same time, so that the dollar assets and the dollar liabilities are equal with the zero conversion risk position.

3. Risk hedging method

The risk hedging method refers to the corresponding operation of enterprises in the financial market, using the profit and loss of foreign exchange contracts to offset the profit and loss of conversion. To be specific, the enterprise first determines the possible expected conversion loss and then carries out the corresponding forward foreign exchange transaction to avoid risk.

【Example 9-12】 Suppose a British subsidiary in the United States expects a loss of 50,000 pounds on its balance sheet. In anticipation of a depreciation of the pound, it can sell pounds in the forward market at the beginning of the period and buy an equivalent amount of pounds at the end of the period and take delivery of the forward contract. Obviously, if the forward market exchange rate at the beginning of the period is higher than the final spot rate, the dollars gained from selling pounds at the beginning of the period must be greater than the dollars spent to buy back the equivalent amount of pounds, making the trade profitable. It can be seen that risk hedging is based on conversion results and is closely related to the expected currency at the end of the period. As long as the prediction is accurate, foreign exchange risk can be avoided.

However, risk hedging method has certain limitations:

(1) The conversion risk position is unknown at the beginning of the signing of the contract and the hedging amount of the forward or futures contract may be different from the conversion

risk position.

（2）In fact, the risk hedging method uses the realized gains and losses of foreign exchange contracts to offset the unrealized gains and losses of book conversion. The gains and losses of foreign exchange contracts should be included in the taxable income, while the converted gains and losses are not within the scope of taxable income. This difference makes the risk hedging unable to effectively reduce the actual risks of enterprises.

4. Net payment method

The method of net debt payment refers to that when a foreign-related enterprise pays off the creditor's rights and debts arising from internal transactions and transfers and writes off the receivables and payables between its subsidiaries, parent companies and subsidiaries, only the net part is paid regularly to reduce the amount and frequency of payment and reduce the conversion risk.

【Example 9-13】 A multinational company's internal transactions take place between various subsidiaries. The US subsidiary owed the UK subsidiary pounds worth of 5 million dollars, the UK subsidiary owed the China Hong Kong subsidiary HKD worth of 3 million dollars, and the Hong Kong subsidiary owed the US subsidiary 3 million dollars. After sterilization, the US subsidiary paid the preset monetary worth of 2 million dollars, so the number and amount of payments are reduced and the conversion risks are significantly reduced.

(Extended Reading 9-1)

Enterprise exchange rate risk management is not in place, resulting in exchange rate floating phobia

China Enterprise Evaluation Association released the 2020 China's Top 500 New Economy Enterprises Development Report and the 2020 China's Top 500 New Economy Enterprises list in Hangzhou, Zhejiang Province on November 28, 2020. Wang Chunying, deputy director of the State Administration of Foreign Exchange, delivered a keynote speech at the conference.

"The exchange rate issue is a matter of great concern to all of us. In a world where exchange rate fluctuations are increasing, how to manage exchange rate risk well is very important to the financial performance of enterprises, especially those with a high proportion of international business."

Wang Chunying said, from the SAFE survey results, the current Chinese enterprises' hedging awareness needed to be strengthen. In order to understand the current situation of enterprise exchange rate risk management, the SAFE conducted a questionnaire survey on more than 2,400 enterprises. The survey shows that in the process of RMB exchange rate marketization, enterprise exchange rate risk management level is constantly improving, but there are also some problems worth paying attention to.

First, the awareness of risk management is relatively weak. Most enterprises have a low hedging ratio of exchange rate risk exposure, and some enterprises even do not carry out any financial hedging. Some large foreign enterprises will formulate exchange rate risk management strategies when their exposure exceeds 1 million dollars, while some domestic enterprises with exposure of hundreds of millions of dollars still lack awareness of exchange rate risk management.

Second, risk management is more passive. According to the survey, only 20 percent of companies adhere to strict financial discipline and actively and promptly avoid currency risks. Quite a number of enterprises are used to attaching importance to exchange rate risk management only when exchange rate fluctuations are aggravated. Some enterprises even use foreign exchange derivatives to seek profits or engage in arbitrage, deviating from their main business.

Third, the exchange rate risk management is not in place, resulting in "exchange rate floating phobia". Changes in market supply and demand determine the natural characteristics of two-way exchange rate fluctuations, but some enterprises are not used to exchange rate fluctuations. The less scientific and effective exchange rate risk management, the more worried about exchange rate fluctuations.

Wang Chunying said four factors influence enterprises' choice of the exchange rate as a hedge:

First, the past unilateral exchange rate trend encouraged enterprises to bet on the exchange rate. Historically, the RMB exchange rate has been in a unilateral trend for a long time with a narrow fluctuation range. It is easy to predict the trend of the RMB exchange rate, which objectively encourages some enterprises to bet on the RMB exchange rate.

Second, enterprises are not familiar with foreign exchange derivatives. A significant number of companies believe that existing derivatives are sufficient overall and the need to add new ones is not very urgent. The more familiar enterprises are with foreign exchange derivatives, the higher the proportion of foreign exchange derivatives hedging. But there are still a significant number of companies unfamiliar with foreign exchange derivatives.

Third, some enterprises still exist a "gambling speculation" mentality. Many enterprises do not have a good understanding of hedging and are used to comparing the price of foreign exchange derivatives with the maturity market price as the basis for performance assessment of financial management. This shows that enterprises do not have a good understanding of hedging and their risk-neutral awareness still needs to be improved.

Fourth, some enterprises think hedging costs are higher. The assets and liabilities management of some enterprises is excessively pro-cyclical. During the period of RMB appreciation, the excessive asset allocation of "assets in local currency and liabilities in foreign currency" is carried out by increasing foreign currency debts (including borrowing foreign currency loans from domestic banks) and increasing leverage, so as to earn RMB exchange rate appreciation gains. During the period of RMB depreciation, the excessive asset allocation of "foreign currency of assets and domestic currency of liabilities" is carried out by increasing foreign currency assets and increasing leverage, so as to earn RMB exchange rate depreciation benefits.

"Blind pro-cyclical financial operation is easy to cause risks. From the micro-level, enterprises do not rationally arrange their asset and liability structure based on their main business and actual operating conditions, but excessively increase leverage and debt through financial operation, blindly increase foreign exchange risk exposure, and will face risks when the RMB exchange rate fluctuations."

Source: WANG M. Enterprise exchange rate risk management is not in place, resulting in exchange rate floating phobia [EB/OL]. [2020-11-28]. https://baijiahao.baidu.com/s?id=1684577162858082590&wfr=spider&for=pc.

(ii) Transaction risk management

Transaction risk is the most important foreign exchange risk faced by foreign-related enterprises and the key content of risk management. The following introduces the main methods of transaction risk management for foreign enterprises.

1. Currency selection method

Currency selection method, namely good selection and collocation of the currency. It is the method that the enterprise keeps on guard foreign exchange risk through the kind of valuation currency used in choosing foreign affairs economy to trade. In foreign economic transactions, both parties are usually required to sign a contract in which the payment terms specify the currency of settlement. The choice of pricing currency is directly related to whether the trading subject will bear foreign exchange risks in the future.

(1) Choose the local currency for pricing.

When signing import and export trade contracts, the local currency should be chosen as the valuation currency as far as possible. Choosing the local currency as the valuation currency does not involve the conversion of local currency and foreign currency, so one of the importers and exporters can completely prevent foreign exchange risks.

For exporters, taking domestic currency as the pricing currency, there is no need to exchange local currency with foreign currency, so they will have no foreign exchange risks at all, but there are still foreign exchange risks for importers. Otherwise, there is no foreign exchange risk for importers to use their domestic currency as the denomination currency, but there is still foreign exchange risk for exporters.

【Example 9-14】 A British company exports a batch of goods to a Chinese importer in pounds and gets the payment back three months later. In this transaction, the British exporter chooses pounds (local currency) as the pricing currency, which does not involve the conversion of local currency and foreign currency, so there is no foreign exchange risk. For the

Chinese importer, the exchange rate between pounds and RMB may change, so there is still foreign exchange risk.

【Example 9-15】 An American importer buys a shipment of computers from China, uses dollars as the currency, and pays for them three months later. In this transaction, the American importer chooses dollars (local currency) as the pricing currency, so there will be no conversion between the local currency and foreign currency and there will be no foreign exchange risk. For the Chinese exporter, the exchange rate between dollars and RMB may change, so there is still foreign exchange risk.

The advantage of using the local currency is simplicity and convenience. This method will be limited by the international status of the domestic currency, and both sides of the trade will also have conflicts due to the choice of the currency, so it is necessary to comprehensively consider the international status of the local currency and the transaction habits of both sides to choose the currency.

(2) Choose a freely convertible currency for pricing.

The use of a freely convertible currency as the denomination currency is conducive to the use of foreign exchange funds, which can be immediately converted into another favorable currency in the event of adverse exchange rate effects.

【Example 9-16】 Suppose that a Japanese exporter makes a deal with a Canadian importer that uses the US dollar as the currency for payment in six months. If the value of the dollar falls against the yen at the time the payment is received, the value of the dollar falls; while if the value of the pound rises against the yen, the value of the pound rises, and then the Japanese exporter can immediately convert the dollar into the pound.

(3) Choose a favorable currency for pricing.

Generally speaking, exports are denominated in hard currency and imports are denominated in soft currency, that is, "collecting hard and paying soft".

Hard currency refers to the currency with a stable exchange rate and appreciation trend. Soft currency refers to a currency with an unstable exchange rate and a tendency to depreciate. Exporters are denominated in hard currency, which will appreciate in the future, allowing them to convert their payments into larger amounts of local currency when they receive them. Similarly, importers use soft currency as the currency of account, and since the soft currency will depreciate in the future when importers make a payment, it will be able to exchange the payment for a smaller amount of local currency.

【Example 9-17】 Assume that the current USD/RMB exchange rate is USD1=CNY6.7000, and the US dollar exchange rate is stable and has an appreciation trend. The current GBP/RMB exchange rate is GBP1=CNY8.5900, and the pound exchange rate is unstable and has a depreciation trend.

Analysis: (1) if a Chinese exporter exports a batch of goods worth USD 1 million to a Japanese importer, and the payment is paid back three months later, then the Chinese exporter should choose the US dollar as the currency of valuation. Because the US dollar is a hard currency, assuming that the US dollar appreciates three months later and the exchange rate of the USD against RMB is USD1=CNY6.8800, then the Chinese exporter will get more RMB 180,000 (1× (6.8800-6.7000), in million) . (2) If a Chinese importer imports a batch of goods from Japan worth GBP 1 million and pays for them three months later, then the Chinese importer should choose the pound as the currency of valuation. Because the pound is a soft currency, assuming that the pound depreciates three months later and the exchange rate of GBP against RMB is GBP1=CNY8.5000, then the Chinese importer can pay less RMB 90,000 (1× (8.5900-8.5000), in million) .

In fact, choosing favorable currency valuation essentially means keeping the benefits of exchange rate fluctuations for oneself and pushing the disadvantages brought by exchange rate fluctuations to the other party. This method is generally affected by two aspects: firstly, the trading habits of both sides of the trade; secondly, the "soft" and "hard" currencies are relative, so this method cannot ensure that importers and exporters completely eliminate foreign exchange risks.

(4) Use a "basket" of currencies for pricing.

A "basket" of currencies is a group of two or more currencies in a given proportion. Since the "basket" consists of both hard and soft currencies, the gains from the appreciation of hard currencies can be roughly offset by the losses from the devaluation of soft currencies, so the value of the "basket" is relatively stable. This method can effectively reduce or eliminate foreign exchange risks for both sides of the trade.

2. Currency hedging method

When the two parties sign import and export trade contracts and loan contracts, they include hedging clauses in the contracts to prevent foreign exchange risks. Common hedging clauses include the following three:

(1) Gold hedging clause.

Gold hedging means converting the currency to be paid into corresponding gold units according to the gold price in the market at the time of signing the contract, and converting it into the currency amount to be paid according to the gold market price at the same time when the contract is actually paid.

【Example 9-18】 A certain amount of payment is USD 500,000. When signing the contract, USD 1 is equivalent to 1 gram of pure gold, so USD 500,000 is equivalent to 500,000 grams of pure gold. When the actual payment is made, the dollar depreciates, and the gold content of USD 1 is 0.90 gram of pure gold, then 500,000 grams of pure gold equals USD 555,556, so the importer should pay USD 55,556. Due to the depreciation of the dollar, the USD 555,556 paid by the importer at settlement is equivalent to USD 500,000 at the time of signing the contract.

Gold hedging clause, often used under the fixed exchange rate system, is however rarely used today.

(2) Foreign exchange hedging clause.

In the case that the valuation currency has been determined, the currency with a stable value can be selected as the valuation currency to maintain the value in order to avoid risks brought to both sides by the fluctuation of its value. Its specific operation is:

①When the two sides in transaction, the first is to determine the contract currency;

② Then choose a currency other than the currency of valuation or a "basket" of currencies as the value of hedging, and specify a fixed price ratio between the currency of valuation and the value of hedging in the contract;

③ Once the exchange rate of the valuation currency changes unfavorably at the time of settlement, one party to the transaction may require the other party to adjust the amount of foreign exchange it receives or pays according to the ratio between the valuation currency and the hedging currency.

(3) A "basket" of currencies hedging clause.

A "basket" of currencies hedging clause is a hedging clause stipulated in the contract between the trading parties that the valuation currency is linked to the value of a "basket" of currencies. The specific method is as follows:

① When signing the contract, the payment for goods shall be converted into each currency of hedging according to the current exchange rate and the weight of each currency of hedging.

② When the payment is made, the currency of hedging shall be converted into the currency of valuation according to the current exchange rate.

【Example 9-19】 The contract stipulates that a "basket" of currencies consisting of the US dollar, Japanese yen and British pound will be used to hedge the value of USD 10 million payment, with the weights of each currency being 0.3, 0.3 and 0.4 respectively. Assuming that the exchange rate at the time of signing the contract is: USD 1=JYP 105, USD 1=GPB 0.7845, then USD 10 million will be converted into a value hedging currency: $10 \times 0.3 \times 1 =$ USD 3 million; $10 \times 0.3 \times 105 =$ JYP 315 million; $10 \times 0.4 \times 0.7845 =$ GPB 3.138 million. Assuming that the exchange rate at the time of payment is: USD 1=JPY 110, USD 1=GPB 0.7950, then each insured currency is converted back to USD 3 million; $315 \div 110 =$ USD 2.8636 million; $3.138 \div 0.7950 =$ USD 3.9472 million, that is, the importer pays USD 9.8108 $(3 + 2.8636 + 3.9472)$ million to the exporter at the time of payment settlement.

3. Price adjustment hedging method

Hedging by price adjustment is a method to prevent foreign exchange risks through price adjustment. In import and export trade, "collecting hard and paying soft" is only an ideal choice, but it cannot be realized in actual trade due to various factors. In actual transactions, when soft currency is charged for exports and hard currency is paid for imports, price adjustment can be adopted to avoid foreign exchange risks. Price adjustment hedging method can be divided into two categories: value-increase hedging method and value-decrease hedging method.

(1) Value-increase hedging method.

The value-increase hedging method is used in export transactions to raise the price of exports to avoid foreign exchange risks when exporters accept soft currency pricing. The mark-up is equal to the expected depreciation of the soft currency, spreading the potential loss of the exchange rate into the price of exports. According to international practice, the calculation formula is:

Commodity price after value-increase = original unit price × (1 + expected currency depreciation rate)

【Example 9-20】 A company exports goods denominated in pounds. The transaction is made now and the exchange will be settled one year later. Assuming that the GPB is a soft currency, the expected annual depreciation rate is 6%, and the original price of each unit of a commodity is 200 pounds, the price of the product after value-increase is:

200 × (1+6%) = GPB 212

(2) Value-decrease hedging method.

The value-decrease hedging method is used in import transactions to lower the price of imported goods to avoid foreign exchange risks when importers accept soft currency pricing. The price cut is equal to the expected appreciation of the hard currency, taking the potential loss from exchange rate movements out of the price of imported goods. According to international practice, the calculation formula is:

Commodity price after value-decrease = original unit price × (1 − expected currency appreciation rate)

It is worth noting that price adjustment hedging method only transfers foreign exchange risk out. At the same time, the use of this method will be limited by the market demand of commodities, commodity qualities and other factors.

4. Barter trade method

The barter trade method refers to the direct exchange of goods of equivalent value between two trading parties. At the same time, the price of the commodities exchanged by both parties will be determined in advance. During the transaction, both parties do not need to receive and pay foreign exchange, so there is no foreign exchange risk. However, both parties are exposed to the risk of price rise of their own commodities and price decline of the other party's commodities.

5. Term adjustment method

The term adjustment method refers to the method of preventing foreign exchange risks by adjusting the time of receipt and payment, including the method of advance payment or delay payment. To be specific, it is a method for importers and exporters to advance or delay the payment date according to the prediction of the changing trend of the exchange rate of the valuation currency, so as to avoid foreign exchange risks and gain exchange rate changes.

Generally speaking, when the valuation currency is expected to depreciate, exporters or creditors should try their best to collect foreign exchange in advance to avoid the reduction in the amount of foreign exchange converted into local currency in the future. Importers or debtors, on the other hand, should defer payment of foreign exchange to the extent possible in order to facilitate the exchange of the same amount of foreign exchange for a smaller local currency in the future.

On the contrary, if the currency is expected to appreciate, the exporter or creditor should delay the receipt of foreign exchange as much as possible in order to receive a larger amount of currency in the future. The importer or debtor should try to pay in advance so as not to have to use more local currency to get the same amount of foreign currency in the future.

6. Financial market transaction method

The financial market transaction method refers to the method that foreign - related enterprises use financial market, especially foreign exchange market and currency market transactions to guard against foreign exchange risks. This method mainly includes the following:

(1) Spot contract method.

The spot contract method refers to a method whereby an enterprise with foreign exchange accounts receivable or accounts payable signs a sight contract with a bank to buy and sell foreign exchange to eliminate foreign exchange risks.

Spot foreign exchange transactions are settled within two business days after the transaction, the fluctuation of the exchange rate within these two days will bring foreign exchange risks. Therefore, if the foreign exchange income is received within two days, it is necessary to sign a spot contract with the bank to sell the same amount of foreign exchange in the same currency to eliminate foreign exchange risks. If a foreign exchange payment is made within two days, it is necessary to sign a spot contract with a bank to buy the same amount of foreign exchange in the same currency to eliminate foreign exchange risks.

(2) Forward contract method.

The forward contract method refers to the way that an enterprise with foreign exchange accounts receivable or accounts payable signs the forward contract with a bank to buy and sell foreign exchange in order to eliminate foreign exchange risks. Its specific operation is:

① After signing a trade contract, the exporter sells forward foreign exchange of the same currency and equivalent amount in advance at the forward exchange rate at the time, and makes delivery at the agreed forward exchange rate when receiving the payment for goods.

② After signing a trade contract, the importer will buy forward foreign exchange of the same currency and the same amount in advance according to the forward exchange rate at the time, and then make delivery according to the agreed forward exchange rate when the payment is made.

【Example 9-21】 A Chinese export enterprise will receive a USD 5 million payment in three months. In order to eliminate foreign exchange risk, the enterprise signs a forward foreign exchange contract with the bank to sell USD 5 million. Assume that the forward exchange rate is USD1=CNY6.8805. The company can then convert the USD 5 million received three months later into RMB 34.4025 million. Thus, the forward contract locks in the USD/RMB exchange rate, thus eliminating the risk that the USD/RMB exchange rate may fluctuate within three months.

Case Analysis 9-2

China Haier Group has set up a TV factory in South Carolina. Haier Group has decided to introduce a color picture tube production line from Japan, the total amount is 1,000,000 yen, the payment will be made two months later. Haier Group finance staff are worried about the yen appreciation two months later. One solution is to entrust the Bank of China to buy two-month forward contract. The two-month forward rate is: JYP 1=USD 0.007042. But Haier Group is reluctant to lock in fixed exchange rate through forward contract because it wants to benefit from a weaker yen. In other words, Haier Group wants to be protected from the rise of yen and to benefit from its fall.

Citibank designs a hedging scheme for Haier Group: Haier Group buys a yen call option with an agreed price of JYP 1=USD 0.007143, with the contract amount of 140,000,000 yen and the option price of 50,000 dollars.

1. When the yen exchange rate is above USD 0.007143

(1) The call option has a price and Haier Group exercises the option to buy 140,000,000 yen and pay 1,000,000 dollars at the agreed price of USD 0.007143.

(2) The put option is priceless and the buyer gives it up. Haier Group has no burden.

2. When the yen exchange rate is less than USD 0.007143, but greater than USD 0.006667

(1) The call option is priceless and Haier Group does not exercise the option, but buys the required 140,000,000 yen at the prevailing spot rate. Assuming the prevailing spot rate is USD 0.006888, Haier Group pays 964,320 dollars.

(2) The put option is priceless and the buyer will not exercise it. Haier Group has no burden.

3. When the yen exchange rate is less than USD 0.006667

(1) The call option is priceless, Haier Group gives up the option.

(2) The put option has a price and the buyer decides to exercise it, selling it to Haier Group for 140,000,000 yen at USD 0.006667. Haier Group has no choice but to buy the yen at that price, paying 933,380 dollars.

Source: Anonymity. Haier Group foreign exchange risk management case [EB/OL]. [2020-05-26]. https://wenku.baidu.com/view/12e6af4050d380eb6294dd88d0d233d4b14e3f8e.html.

Thinking and disscussion:

1. What protection and benefit opportunities do this option combination strategy developed

by the bank providing for Haier Group?

2. What are the advantages and disadvantages of this option combination strategy developed by the bank compared with forward and single option strategies?

(3) Futures trading method.

Futures trading method refers to the method that enterprises with foreign exchange accounts receivable or payable sign foreign exchange futures contracts to prevent foreign exchange risks, that is, foreign-related enterprises entrust banks or brokers to buy or sell corresponding foreign exchange futures to eliminate foreign exchange risks. Its specific operation is:

① Enterprises with foreign exchange accounts receivable can enter the futures market to use short hedging to avoid foreign exchange risks if they are worried about the depreciation of the valuation currency when receiving foreign exchange.

② Enterprises with foreign exchange accounts payable can enter the futures market to avoid foreign exchange risks by taking advantage of long hedging if they are worried about the appreciation of the valuation currency when they pay foreign exchange.

【Example 9-22】 On February 10, 2020, an American exporter expected to receive a payment of 1 million euros in three months. When the contract was signed on February 10, the USD/EUR spot exchange rate was EUR1=USD1.1340, which would have earned the exporter 1.134 million dollars. In an attempt to protect the euro from depreciation, the exporter sold eight euro futures contracts maturing in May at EUR1=USD1.1396 on the futures market (each contract is 125,000 euros). Three months later, the euro depreciated and the exchange rate became EUR1=USD1.1290. On the spot market, the exporter could only get 1.129 million dollars for selling 1 million euros, which was less than 5,000 dollars on February 10. However, if the trading price was EUR1=USD1.1346 on the futures market three months later, the exporter could now buy eight euro futures contracts due in May to offset the originally sold euro futures, so the exporter could get 5,000 ((1.1396−1.1346) ×125,000×8) dollars on the futures market, that just to cover the loss on the spot market.

(4) Option trading method.

Option trading method refers to the method that enterprises with foreign exchange accounts receivable or payable sign foreign exchange option contracts to prevent foreign exchange risks. According to the characteristics of options, exporters should buy put options and importers should buy call options.

Because the option entrusts the option buyer with the corresponding rights, the option buyer can choose to exercise or not exercise the option according to the market exchange rate fluctuation, and the maximum loss of the option fee.

(5) Swap trading method.

The swap trading method refers to the way in which enterprises with long-term foreign exchange claims or debts sign with banks to buy or sell spot or forward foreign exchange while selling or buying corresponding forward foreign exchange to prevent foreign exchange risks.

Swap transactions involve the same amount of money being traded in opposite directions in two currencies, and are mostly used for short-term investment and borrowing.

【Example 9-23】 An enterprise makes short-term international investments and invests 5 million dollars for 6 months in the United States. While buying spot dollars for investment, it can sell 5 million dollars for 6 months forward to avoid the risk caused by the change of the dollar exchange rate after 6 months.

(6) Currency swap method.

The currency swap method refers to the two sides of the transaction to exchange the same period of time, the same amount of money, but different currencies, in order to reduce the cost of financing, and then prevent foreign exchange risks. Currency swap is a new type of derivative financial product.

【Example 9-24】 Suppose that the exchange rate between the pound and the dollar is GPB 1=USD 1.5000. A wants to borrow 10 million pounds for 5 years, B wants to borrow 15 million dollars for 5 years, and they want to borrow the same amount of money. As A and B have different reputations, the fixed interest rates offered by the market are different (see Table 9-1).

Table 9-1   Market interest rates faced by A and B

Item	Dollar	Pound
A	8.0%	11.6%
B	10.0%	12.0%

A has a comparative advantage in the dollar market (2% is greater than 0.4%), and B has a comparative advantage in the pound market, the two are interchangeable. A borrows 15 million dollars for 5 years at 8% and B borrows 10 million pounds for 5 years at 12%.

When not cooperating, the total cost is: $10\% + 11.6\% = 21.6\%$; when cooperating, the total cost is: $8\% + 12\% = 20\%$, that is, the total cost decreases by 1.6%. Assuming that both parties share half and half, that is, 0.8%.

(7) Borrowing method.

The borrowing method is used in the case of accounts receivable (foreign exchange revenues). After signing the contract, the exporter can borrow from the bank in the same currency, amount and term as the future foreign exchange receivable, and convert it into local currency on the spot foreign exchange market. When the loan is due, the exporter can repay the loan with the foreign exchange income to prevent foreign exchange risks.

【Example 9-25】 An American company will earn 5 million pounds in three months. To avoid the risk that the pound will fall in three months, the company borrows 5 million pounds from the bank for three months and converts the pound into the dollar on the spot foreign exchange market. After three months, the company repays the bank loan with 5 million pounds, at which point it does not have currency risk even if the pound falls.

(8) Investment method.

The investment method applies to the situation of having accounts payable (foreign exchange expenses). After signing the contract, the importer may buy foreign exchange in the spot market in the same currency, amount and maturity as the foreign exchange payable in the future, and invest it in the short-term fund market (monetary market). On the payment date, the payment shall be made with the foreign exchange amount due to the investment to prevent foreign exchange risks.

【Example 9-26】 A British company will pay 1 million dollars in three months. To avoid the risk that the dollar will rise in three months, the company buys 1 million dollars in the spot market and uses the 1 million dollars to buy three-month treasury bills. After three months, the company pays 1 million dollars as the investment matures for the payment.

(9) BSI (Borrow-spot-invest) method.

BSI method, also known as the borrow - spot - invest, is a comprehensive method to prevent foreign exchange risks. It means that enterprises with accounts receivable or accounts payable use borrowings, spot contracts and investments to prevent foreign exchange risks.

In the case that a company has accounts receivable, the specific approach of the BSI method is as follows:

① Firstly, borrow the foreign currency in the same currency, amount and term as the foreign exchange receivable from the bank, and sell the borrowed foreign currency to the bank for spot transaction to exchange it back into local currency.

② Then, the local currency will be deposited in banks or invested, and the investment income will cover the related expenses (such as borrowing interest).

③ Finally, the foreign exchange income is used to repay the bank loan, thus eliminating the foreign exchange risk.

【Example 9-27】 A German company exports a batch of goods which is expected to recover 1 million dollars in three months. In order to prevent the risk of dollar to euro exchange rate fluctuations, the enterprise uses the BSI method to operate. Firstly, it borrows 1 million dollars from the bank for three months. At the same time, the company sells the 1 million dollars to a bank on the spot foreign exchange market at EUR 0.5823 for 582,300 euros. It then invests 582,300 euros in the German monetary market for three months. Three months later, the business returns the accounts receivable to the bank for 1 million dollars, thus eliminating the foreign exchange risks.

In the case that a company has accounts payable, the specific approach of the BSI method is as follows:

①Firstly, borrow from the bank to buy the local currency needed to meet the foreign exchange, and at the same time enter the spot foreign exchange market to buy the foreign currency needed for future payment with the borrowed local currency.

②Then, the foreign currency is used for a short-term investment, and the investment income can cover the related expenses (such as borrowing interest).

③Finally, on the payment date, the investment payment shall be recovered.

(10) LSI (Lead-spot-invest) method.

LSI method, also known as the lead-spot-invest method, is a comprehensive method to prevent foreign exchange risks. It means that enterprises with accounts receivable or accounts payable, with the consent of debtors or creditors, use a combination of early or delayed payments, spot contracts and investments to eliminate foreign exchange risks.

When a company has accounts receivable, the LSI method is as follows:

①After the creditor (exporter) promises to give the importer a certain discount and obtains the consent of the other party, the importer can make the payment in advance, thus eliminating the time risk;

②The exporter signs a spot contract with the bank to convert the collected foreign currency into local currency, thus eliminating the value risk;

③If the exporter invests in the converted local currency, the investment income can offset the loss caused by the early receipt of foreign exchange.

When a company has accounts payable, the LSI method is as follows:

①The importer first borrows from the bank to buy the amount of local currency needed to pay the foreign exchange, so as to eliminate the time risk;

②The importer signs the spot contract with the bank to convert the borrowed local currency into foreign currency to eliminate the value risk;

③The exporter is paid in advance with the foreign currency exchanged and receives a certain amount of discount, which can fully or partially offset the interest on the loan.

(iii) Economic risk management

The change of exchange rate will have a certain economic impact on the company's income, cost and competitive position, so the company needs to take relevant measures to manage economic risks from the perspective of long-term interests. The general principle of economic risk management for enterprises is to minimize the impact of exchange rate fluctuations on cash flow. The principle of economic risk management mainly includes the following two aspects:

1. Marketing management of economic risk

(1) Market selection and segmentation.

When the exchange rate fluctuates, one of the issues that export enterprises need to consider is market selection. In general, when the domestic currency of a country appreciates, the foreign currency price of its exports will rise, and the price competitiveness of its exports will be weakened. At this point, foreign enterprises can rely on the price advantage of their products to expand their market share in the country.

In addition, it is necessary to segment the export market of the product properly. For example, developed countries are less sensitive to changes in the price of imported goods than developing countries. Therefore, when the domestic currency appreciates, export enterprises can appropriately increase exports to developed countries, reduce exports to developing countries; conversely, when the domestic currency depreciates, exports to developing countries will increase.

(2) Pricing strategy.

Enterprises need to consider market share and profit margin when adjusting pricing strategy.

When the domestic currency appreciates, the international competitiveness of domestic exports weakens, and exporters have two choices: to maintain prices and reduce market share; or to lower prices and maintain market share.

When the domestic currency depreciates, the international competitiveness of domestic exports increases, and exporters have two choices: to maintain prices and expand market share; or to raise prices and maintain market share.

Of course, enterprises need to consider many factors when adjusting their pricing strategy, such as price elasticity of demand for export commodities, substitutability of products, the timing of exchange rate changes, potential competitions and so on.

(3) Promotion strategy.

Any enterprise, especially foreign-related enterprise, should consider the risks that may be brought by exchange rate changes and reasonably arrange the promotion budget when arranging the budget for advertising, marketing and poor sales.

When the domestic currency appreciates, the return brought by promotion expenditure will be reduced due to the weakening competitiveness of domestic products. At this time, enterprises need to adjust their product strategy. When the domestic currency falls, the return on the promotional spending of exporters will increase.

(4) Product strategy.

Product strategy refers to the adjustment of enterprises in the research and development of new products, the establishment of new production lines and the timing of new products to market, so as to prevent foreign exchange risks.

In the research and development of new products, enterprises should pay attention to investing enough money in research and development to ensure the continuous introduction of new products into the market and enhance competitiveness. Meanwhile, enterprises should launch corresponding new products in different consumer markets according to the changes in market exchange rates.

In terms of the establishment of new production lines, when the domestic currency devalues, the international competitiveness of products is enhanced, enterprises can establish new production lines at home and abroad, and expand market share. When the domestic currency appreciates, enterprises can construct the new production line in developed countries that are less sensitive to price changes.

In terms of the timing of new products to market, when the domestic currency devalues, enterprises can launch new products by taking advantage of the price brought by the devaluation on exports.

2. Diversified management of economic risk

Since economic risk is a long-term and comprehensive foreign exchange risk brought to enterprises by unexpected exchange rate changes, and unexpected exchange rate changes are difficult to predict accurately, the effective way to prevent economic risk is to implement diversified management. The basic idea of diversified management is to carry out risk diversification and make risk loss and risk gain offset each other, so as to reduce risk. Diversified management is mainly reflected in the following two aspects:

(1) Business diversification.

Business diversification refers to the enterprise diversification of its business activities into different industries, or the optimization of the procurement of raw materials, production and sales of products on a global scale. If the enterprise has achieved diversification and when the exchange rate changes unexpectedly, on the one hand, the enterprise achieves risk gains in some markets and suffers risk losses in other markets, but the risk gains can basically compensate for the risk losses so that economic risks can be automatically prevented; on the other hand, the enterprise can compare selling prices in different markets and factors of different origin, and quickly adjust its business strategies to improve operating conditions and minimize the risks brought by exchange rate fluctuations.

(2) Financial diversification.

Financial diversification, namely investment diversification and financing diversification, refers to enterprises in different national financial markets, in a variety of currencies to seek capital sources and destinations. In this way, when some foreign currencies depreciate and others appreciate, the foreign exchange risks of enterprises can offset each other. At the same time, enterprises can adjust the assets and liabilities of various currencies according to the exchange rate changes, which makes it easier to realize the matching combination of funds and realize the risk compensation.

In terms of investment, enterprises can choose a variety of currencies to invest, and choose different types of securities with different maturities in the same currency to invest. According to the market forecast, they can constantly adjust the investment objects, increase returns, and achieve the purpose of reducing risks.

In terms of financing, taking into account the changing trend of exchange rate and interest rate, enterprises can borrow the currency in a market with a depreciating trend. If the prediction is accurate, enterprises can obtain the profits. They can also borrow in multiple currencies to reduce the risk of exchange rate movements.

III. Foreign exchange risk management of commercial banks

Commercial banks are one of the main bodies of the foreign exchange markets, and foreign exchange business is a major business of commercial banks. Therefore, the foreign exchange risk management of commercial banks is an important part of foreign exchange risk management. Commercial banks earn the bid-ask spread and commission by buying and selling foreign exchange.

If foreign exchange risk occurs in the process of foreign exchange trading, it will directly affect the profits of banks. Therefore, it is necessary for commercial banks to carry out foreign exchange risk management, including foreign exchange position management and foreign exchange assets and liabilities management.

(ⅰ) Foreign exchange position management

Foreign exchange position refers to the amount of foreign exchange held by banks. Banks buy and sell large amounts of foreign exchange each day, and there is a mismatch between buying and selling, that is, buying more than selling (long forex), or selling more than buying (short forex).

Long or short foreign currency is collectively known as open position or exposure position. Exposure positions are subject to exchange rate movements, exposing banks to foreign exchange risks. When a bank takes a long position in a foreign currency, it is exposed to the risk that the currency will depreciate. When a bank takes a short position in a foreign currency, it is exposed to the risk of that currency appreciating. Therefore, banks should pay attention to the management of foreign exchange positions.

1. Quota management of foreign exchange positions

Generally speaking, commercial banks will set different holding limits for different foreign exchange positions (such as spot position or forward position), and there will be restrictions on foreign exchange positions held by different levels of foreign exchange trading personnel.

(1) Prescribed position limits.

The prescribed position limits means that the bank prevents foreign exchange risk by stipulating the limit of foreign exchange position. Commercial banks should consider the following factors when setting the foreign exchange position limits:

Firstly, the position of the bank in the foreign exchange market, that is, whether the bank is a market leader, an active player or an ordinary participant. In the foreign exchange market, big banks and securities firms with large capital scale, high transaction amounts and well-qualified staff have the ability to influence the market exchange rate and become market makers. If the banks want to be market makers, they must trade large amounts; if the banks are just regular participants, the volumes must not be too high.

Secondly, the attitude of the top leadership of the bank to the expected return of foreign exchange business and foreign exchange risk. Currency movements can bring gains as well as losses. In general, it is easier to control risk than to achieve profit goals. Therefore, the higher the expectation of the top leadership for foreign exchange business and the higher the tolerance of foreign exchange risk, the larger the transaction amount can be.

Thirdly, the overall quality of the bank foreign exchange trading staff. The higher the overall quality of the foreign exchange trading staff, the larger the trading limits can be.

Finally, the type of currency to be traded. In general, the more currencies are traded, the larger the number and size of the transaction, the greater the set of transaction limits.

In actual foreign exchange transactions, foreign exchange position limits are generally controlled by foreign-exchange traders.

(2) Establishment of stop-loss limits.

The establishment of stop-loss limits refers to the prevention of foreign exchange risks by setting stop-loss limits on foreign exchange transactions.

The so-called stop-loss limits, is the maximum loss a bank can tolerate due to foreign exchange exposure. When the market exchange rate moves unfavorably, once the loss reaches the stop-loss limits, the trader should immediately close the position to prevent further losses.

The so-called cut position, is a stop-loss measure. It is used to prevent excessive losses when the holding currency exchange rate falls after the establishment of a position.

2. Adjustment of foreign exchange positions

In order to prevent foreign exchange risks, in addition to managing the number of foreign exchange positions, banks can also adjust their foreign exchange exposure positions, minimize their foreign exchange exposure positions, or make the situation of their foreign exchange exposure positions consistent with the trend of exchange rates.

The specific measures for commercial banks to adjust their positions are as follows: banks should try to reduce the risk part, that is, to minimize the difference between long and short foreign exchange positions. For example, banks can balance their buying and selling positions by expanding their business. Banks can also balance buying and selling positions by counter transaction. The so-called counter transaction refers to the spot transaction or the hedging or swap transaction conducted by forwarding transaction in the interbank market in order to balance the long or short position.

(1) Adjustment of the single currency position.

When the bank only has the exposure position of a certain currency, to prevent foreign exchange risk, it only needs to adjust the position of this currency, that is, single currency position adjustment. The adjustment of the single currency position mainly includes the following elements:

① Adjustment of spot position.

For example, the foreign exchange business situation of a bank on a business day is: buy 5 million dollars, sell 3 million dollars, result in this bank appears 2 million dollars long. To protect against foreign exchange exposure, the bank would have to find a way to sell the 2 million dollars to balance its dollar position.

② Comprehensive adjustment of spot position and forward position.

When banks conduct actual foreign exchange transactions, they generally involve forward foreign exchange transactions rather than spot transactions. Therefore, banks will not only have exposure positions in the spot transactions, but also in the forward transactions. At this point, banks need to make comprehensive adjustments to spot and forward positions.

【Example 9-28】 The foreign exchange trading situation of a bank on a certain business day is: spot transaction buys 8 million dollars, sells 5 million dollars, holds 3 million dollars long; forward transaction buys 5 million dollars, sells 9 million dollars, holds 4 million dollars short, and the bank's consolidated position is short 1 million dollars. There are two ways to adjust the above positions:

First, make both the spot position and the forward position zero, i.e., sell 3 million dollars at the spot and buy 4 million dollars at the forward. In this case, if the forward term of the 4 million dollars purchase is the same as that of the original 5 million dollars purchase and 9 million dollars sale, the foreign exchange risk can be completely eliminated. Of course, in actual transactions, it is difficult to completely match forward positions of different foreign exchange maturities, so commercial banks usually adjust their comprehensive positions.

Second, cover the composite position so that the composite position is zero. In view of the above example, the bank has two choices: one is to buy the spot transaction of 1 million dollars, so that the long position of the spot transaction increases to 4 million dollars, and the comprehensive position is zero. Another is to buy 1 million dollars of forward transaction, reducing the short position in the forward trade to 3 million dollars, matching the long position in the spot trade to 3 million dollars, at which point the composite position is zero.

③Comprehensive adjustment of forward position on different delivery dates.

【Example 9-29】 A bank's transactions on February 1 are: the first forward transaction buys 2 million dollars, settles on May 31; the second forward transaction sells 2 million dollars, settles on June 30. Obviously, the bank's forward composite position is zero, but due to the different delivery dates of the two transactions, the bank is still exposed to foreign exchange risk, i.e., the dollar delivered on May 31 is at risk of depreciation, while the dollar delivered on June 30 is at risk of appreciation.

In this regard, the bank can use the swap transaction to prevent the foreign exchange risk, that is, on February 1, the bank sells 2 million dollars, the delivery date is May 31; it also buys 2 million dollars with a delivery date of June 30. It is worth noting that in this case, the amount of buying and selling dollars is equal, but the delivery date is different, and there may be different delivery dates and transaction amounts. In this case, the bank can use swap transactions to prevent part of the risk, and then move it through foreign exchange transactions.

(2) Adjustment of the various currency positions.

When banks have exposure positions of multiple currencies at the same time, in order to prevent foreign exchange risks, it is necessary to combine these positions for adjustment, that is, the adjustment of multiple currency positions. The adjustment of the various currency positions mainly includes the following two aspects:

① Adjusting positions in various currencies separately. Banks convert mainly through transactions between the currencies in which they have exposure positions and the dollars. For example, a bank has long euros and short pounds at the same time. When adjusting its position, the bank will first convert long euros into dollars, and at the same time replenish short pounds with dollars, and convert the exposure positions of euros and pounds into the exposure positions of dollars, and then eliminate the exposure positions of dollars through transactions between dollars and local currencies.

② Adjusting composite positions, which allow exposure positions in various currencies to exist simultaneously, adjust only composite positions so that risks from various currencies cancel each other out. For example, when a bank holds a short position in the Swiss francs, it can buy a similar amount of the British pounds and, when the exchange rate moves, offset the losses or gains of the Swiss francs with the gains or losses of the long British pounds position.

(ii) Foreign exchange assets and liabilities management

Foreign exchange risks brought about by banks' proprietary foreign exchange transactions and foreign exchange transactions on behalf of clients can be prevented through foreign exchange position management. However, foreign exchange risks brought by foreign exchange deposit and loan business and investment business of banks need to be prevented through foreign exchange assets and liabilities management. Foreign exchange assets and liabilities management mainly includes the following contents:

1. Adjust the currency of assets and liabilities

Banks should try to diversify their funding and investment, that is, lending as much currency as they can borrow; the currency can be raised when the loan is due, the same currency will be paid when the fund is due. As far as possible, the borrowing and payment of the currency will not need to be converted through foreign exchange transactions.

2. Adjust the maturity of assets and liabilities

Among the assets and liabilities in the same currency, try to make the assets that mature at any time in the future offset the liabilities that mature, and try to make the maturity of deposits and loans the same or close.

3. Adjust the number of deposits and loans

The number of foreign exchange deposits and loans that match the interest rate and maturity in the same currency shall be equal. When the market interest rate rises, the number of loans at the floating rate shall be larger than the number of deposits at the floating rate, or the amount of loans at the fixed rate shall be smaller than the number of deposits at the fixed rate. When the market interest rate falls, the floating rate loan is smaller than the floating rate deposit, or the fixed rate loan is larger than the fixed rate deposit.

4. Adjust the interest rate of deposits and loans

The deposit and loan interest paid in foreign currency is also part of the risk, and the level of interest depends on the level of interest rate, so the level of deposit and loan interest rate directly affects the level of foreign exchange risk the banks face. The general practice is to lower the interest rate of foreign exchange deposits absorbed by hard currency and raise the interest rate of foreign exchange loans issued by soft currency.

Task 3   Foreign Exchange Control

I. Overview of foreign exchange control

(i) The meaning of foreign exchange control

Foreign exchange control, also known as foreign exchange management, refers to the intervention of a government in the foreign exchange market, source and use of foreign exchange funds, exchange rate and foreign exchange trading by various laws and regulations in order to balance international payments, maintain the stability of exchange rate level, concentrate foreign exchange funds and distribute them according to policy needs.

Foreign exchange control is a government use of foreign exchange receipts and payments, clearing and restrictive measures, such as mainly by law, and the provisions on foreign exchange management and intervention of the event. The goal is to maintain its balance of payments, limited capital inflows and outflows, maintain exchange rate stability, ensure the effective use of foreign exchange, ensure the orderly operation of the financial markets.

(ii) The reasons for foreign exchange control

Foreign exchange control is the product of capitalism development to a certain stage, it is closely related to the capitalist economic crisis and different stages of economic development.

Before the outbreak of the World War I, capitalist countries generally implemented the gold standard system, gold could be freely exported and imported, countries did not take any foreign exchange control measures. After the outbreak of the World War I, the international gold standard system was on the verge of collapse. By the end of the World War I, countries began to resume economic production. In order to promote economic development and expand foreign trade, countries gradually lifted foreign exchange control. From 1929 to 1933, a serious economic crisis broke out in capitalist countries, international balance of payments continued to deteriorate, the collapse of the international gold standard system, in order to cope with the fierce market competition, western countries had adopted trade protection policies, and re-implemented foreign exchange control.

During the World War II, the major participating countries further strengthened foreign exchange control in order to cope with the huge war costs. After the end of the World War II, western countries continued to implement strict foreign exchange control in order to recover their economies.

In the 1950s, the economy of Western European countries slowly recovered, foreign trade continued to expand, international balance of payments improved, countries began to gradually relax foreign exchange control. Since the 1970s, the good balance of payments situation of Western European countries made them further relax foreign exchange control, some countries even cancelled foreign exchange control. Since the 1980s, western countries had accelerated the pace of foreign exchange control relaxation, while developed countries had generally relaxed foreign exchange control. At the same time, with the rapid economic development of developing countries, foreign exchange control had also appeared a trend of relaxation.

From the evolution of foreign exchange control, we can find that foreign exchange control is closely related to the capitalist economic crisis, and the degree of relaxation of foreign exchange control is related to a country's balance of payments and economic development level.

Case Analysis 9-3

Man was seized on suspicion of illegally carrying 400,000 euros in cash

Police in Alicante, Spain, arrested a man at El Altet airport on suspicion of illegally carrying a large amount of cash without declaring it, Ouhua reported. Hundreds of thousands of euros in cash were seized from his checked luggage.

The man was trying to board a flight from El Altet airport to the Austrian capital Vienna with one piece of hand luggage and a larger checked piece of luggage. Security at the airport found two bags of paper wrapped in metal paper in his checked luggage, which were all filled with new euro notes.

A total of 393,000 euros was found hidden in his checked luggage. Police later found another 4,000 euros in his carry-on luggage. Taken together, the total is close to 400,000 euros.

Although the man was travelling to Austria, which is also part of EU countries, EU residents are legally allowed to take no more than 100,000 euros in cash without declaring it, even when travelling between member states. All the money was confiscated and the man had to explain himself to the Bank of Spain before he could get it back.

Source: Anonymity. Man was seized on suspicion of illegally carrying 400,000 euros in cash [EB/OL]. [2013-03-28]. http: //roll.sohu.com/20130328/n370754075.shtml.

Thinking and discussion:

1. Why the cash was confiscated from the man in this case?

2. What rules did the man break?

II. Subject and object of foreign exchange control

（ⅰ）Subject of foreign exchange control

The subject of foreign exchange control, that is, the implementation of foreign exchange control agencies. At present, all countries in the world implement foreign exchange control by the central bank authorized by the government or the establishment of special institutions as the implementation of foreign exchange control institutions. In the United Kingdom, for example, foreign exchange control functions are exercised by the Bank of England. China has set up a special foreign exchange control agency, the State Administration of Foreign Exchange, which exercises the functions of national foreign exchange control.

（ⅱ）Object of foreign exchange control

The object of foreign exchange control is the target of foreign exchange control. Generally speaking, foreign exchange control can be divided into five levels: person, goods, region, industry and country.

（1）Control over persons, including legal persons and natural persons. Legal persons and natural persons can be divided into resident and non - resident according to their place of residence or place of business. Generally speaking, as the foreign exchange income and expenditure of resident has a great impact on the international balance of payments, the control is stricter, and the control is relatively loose for non-resident.

（2）Control over goods, refers to the control over different forms of foreign exchange, including foreign currency, foreign currency payment vouchers, foreign currency negotiable securities and precious metals. In addition, the control of the export and import of domestic currency also belongs to the control of goods.

（3）Control over regions, refers to the implementation of different foreign exchange control policies for different regions of a country. Generally speaking, the control of export processing zones, bonded zones, special economic zones and so on is relatively loose, while the control of other areas is stricter.

（4）Control over industries, means that the state implements different foreign exchange control policies for different import and export enterprises according to industrial policies. This is a regulation method adopted by some newly industrialized countries in Latin America, which strictly controls traditional export industries while implementing relatively preferential policies for high technology and heavy industry exports. More preferential policies are adopted for the import of daily necessities, while relatively strict policies are adopted for the import of daily luxuries. The foreign exchange retention system implemented in China is a typical industry differential policy.

（5）Control over countries, refers to the adoption of different control policies in different countries and regions.

III. Methods and measures for foreign exchange control

Foreign exchange control mainly includes quantity control and price control. Quantity control refers to the limitation of the number of foreign exchange transactions, usually by means of import and export settlement of foreign exchange, foreign exchange rationing, import license, etc. Price control mainly refers to the adoption of a complex exchange rate system and the way of overvaluation of local currency.

Countries with foreign exchange control usually take certain measures on trade and non-trade foreign exchange payments, capital export and import, and exchange rates.

(ⅰ) Methods and measures for trade foreign exchange control

Foreign trade accounts for the largest proportion of a country's international balance of payments, so the control of foreign trade balance is an important part of the whole foreign exchange control. Trade foreign exchange control mainly includes import foreign exchange control and export foreign exchange control.

Generally speaking, countries under foreign exchange control will first implement import control, and import enterprises must apply to the foreign exchange control department for approval before they can purchase foreign exchange. Countries with foreign exchange control on exports usually require that the foreign exchange earned by exporting enterprises must be sold to designated banks. In order to expand export, many countries have implemented a series of preferential policies on export such as taxation, credit and exchange rate, and at the same time, imposed export quantity restrictions on some domestic commodities that are in short supply. Other countries have reached agreements with relevant countries to impose export limits on certain products.

(ⅱ) Methods and measures for non-trade foreign exchange control

All foreign exchange receipts and expenditures except trade, capital export and import belong to non-trade receipts and expenditures, which mainly aim to concentrate non-trade foreign exchange receipts and limit non-trade foreign exchange expenditures.

The scope of non-trade foreign exchange receipts and expenditures is wide, mainly including transportation cost, insurance cost, commission, dividend, interest, patent fee, license fee, special royalty fee, technical labor fee, copyright fee, author fee, scholarship, overseas student fee, overseas institution fee, travel fee and so on. Among them, trade-related expenses are generally handled in accordance with the way of foreign exchange control, while other non-trade foreign exchange receipts and expenditures need to be reported to designated banks or approved.

(ⅲ) Methods and measures for capital export and import control

Generally speaking, each country can implement different degrees of control to capital export and import. Capital export control refers to the control over the purchase of foreign exchange for capital export, the repatriation of domestic currency, investment profits and dividends, and the export of securities and funds. Capital import control refers to the control over the inflow of foreign capital and the purchase of domestic securities by non-residents. Comparatively, developing countries attach great importance to the management of capital export and import, but the degree of control is different. Developed countries are less prone to exchange controls.

(iv) Management of exchange rates

Many countries manage their exchange rates directly to improve their balance of payments and stabilize their exchange rates. The exchange rates can be managed in the following two ways:

1. Legal exchange rate system

Legal exchange rate system refers to a system in which foreign exchange control agencies regulate and adjust foreign exchange rates in a legal form and set the prices for foreign exchange receipts and payments in accordance with a country's macroeconomic policies and international balance of payments.

2. Complex exchange rate system

Complex exchange rate system refers to a system in which a country simultaneously implements two or more exchange rates. The complex exchange rate system is the main means of adjusting the balance of payments deficit of relatively backward countries. It is worth noting that as a foreign exchange control policy, multiple exchange rates are artificially and actively formulated and implemented by foreign exchange control agencies to achieve the desired purpose, which is different from the actual multiple exchange rate phenomenon in the economy. The common forms of the complex exchange rate system are the dual exchange rate system and the multiple exchange rate system.

(1) Dual exchange rate system.

Dual exchange rate system refers to the coexistence of the official exchange rate and the market exchange rate in order to encourage or restrict certain economic activities. For example, most goods that are encouraged to be exported are allowed to be sold at a higher market exchange rate upon receipt of foreign exchange to boost exporters' income. For most goods subject to import restrictions, importers are required to purchase all or part of the required foreign exchange from the free market at a higher price to increase their costs. For goods in short supply that are encouraged to be imported, importers are allowed to purchase foreign exchange at official exchange rates to reduce import costs. For a few commodities that are restricted from export, exporters are required to sell the foreign exchange earned to designated banks at official exchange rates to reduce their export earnings.

(2) Multiple exchange rate system.

Multiple exchange rate system, that is, a mixture of different exchange rates at the same time, is for different preferential or restricted exchange rates under different forms of the trading system. For example, for exporters, internationally competitive goods are settled at a low exchange rate; goods with weak international competitiveness are settled at a high exchange rate.

Extended Reading 9-2

How to achieve both foreign exchange control and RMB internationalization?

The future outlook of the RMB is worth paying attention to in a world of great changes.

On October 21, Zhou Xiaochuan, vice chairman of Boao Forum for Asia, president of China Finance Society, honorary president of Tsinghua University PBC School of Finance, elaborated his views on the opportunities of RMB internationalization and the preparations that need to be made.

When talking about the recent continued strength of the RMB, Zhou Xiaochuan pointed out that there is no need to pay too much attention to the recent trend of the RMB value and index, which includes the impact of epidemic management, economic growth disparity and the chain reaction of people's doubts about the US dollar. As China implements the floating exchange rate system, the situation of purchasing RMB assets will change with the fluctuation of the RMB exchange rate against the US dollar, but this is not the most critical factor of RMB internationalization.

According to Zhou Xiaochuan, what is really good for RMB internationalization is that:

First, against the backdrop of obvious protectionism around the world, China has continued to follow the path of opening up the real economy and has stepped up opening-up measures, including the construction of more free trade zones, free ports and new port zones.

Second, the domestic financial market has gradually broken through various barriers and the protectionism, such as the launch of the Shanghai-Hong Kong Stock Connect, Shenzhen-Hong Kong Stock Connect and Bond Connect.

Third, in recent years, some psychological barriers have been broken, and the worries over symbolic barriers such as the "break 7" exchange rate and the "over 3 trillion US dollars" foreign exchange reserve are gradually easing.

The opening of currency should serve the opening of the real economy, so to achieve a high level of the open economy, the currency must be in line with the trend, Zhou Xiaochuan stressed.

Zhou Xiaochuan said, more clarity is needed on the idea of both controlling foreign exchange and internationalizing the RMB. We try to have the best of different things, and we find that some things just don't work together.

In the coming period, we need to make greater determination to make the RMB much more freely usable and to minimize controls under the capital account, he said, this involves research, thinking, changes in the policy system and emergency preparedness.

In this context, Zhou Xiaochuan proposed several key ideas:

First, in the process of promoting RMB internationalization and capital account convertibility, a major tradeoff point is to analyze the advantages and disadvantages, and make clear which needs to be combined and which can only be chosen. There is no need to over rely on "control" orientation, and the psychological distrust or even fear of market price should not be generated. The analysis and research should be further in-depth.

Second, on capital flows. Capital flows are often seen as impacting developing countries in the current international economic order, so there is always discussion and even debate about which controls to keep in place. But in fact, when it comes to capital flows, apart from economic and currency factors, the more important is confidence, which can reduce many abnormal flows.

Third, in the process of moving towards an open economy, the effect of foreign exchange control needs to be assessed.

In addition, Zhou Xiaochuan pointed out that further capital account convertibility does not mean 100 percent liberalization. There are global anti-money laundering and anti-terrorism financing requirements, and many financial transactions and remittances are restricted. Besides, after the global financial crisis in 2008, the International Monetary Fund (IMF) revised its views on cross-border capital flows and adopted new policy guidance on capital flow management in emergency situations.

As the RMB becomes more freely used, we need to study what needs to be regulated and what does not need to be regulated for short-term investment products and individual derivative products, so as to usher in a higher level of the open economy, Zhou Xiaochuan said.

In addition to the universal theme, Zhou Xiaochuan also mentioned the content of Chinese characteristics. He said that China is a big country with more than 1.4 billion people, the world's second largest economy and the largest trading nation. In making decisions, China mainly relies on step by step, gradually acquiring experience through pilot programs and then copying and applying it.

Furthermore, some policies in the past encountered the dual-track problem in their extensive application, which requires that the merger process should deal with the system, mechanism, price, interest and other factors. For example, in the stock market, there are A shares, B shares, H shares and red chips. The actual asset contents in different shells are the same, but the prices are different.

In his opinion, it is understandable that the prices of products with different rights of the same share differ greatly, but the obvious price difference of products with the same share and the same rights may be mainly caused by currency inconvertibility and other reasons, and these problems need to be solved in the future.

Source: Cao J N. How to achieve both foreign exchange control and RMB internationalization? Zhou Xiaochuan proposed three key points [EB/OL]. [2020-10-23]. https://www.thepaper.cn/newsDetail_forward_9694853.

IV. Impact of foreign exchange control

The beneficial effect of foreign exchange control lies in that the foreign exchange control authorities achieve the goals of balancing international payments, stabilizing the exchange rate, limiting foreign exchange and stabilizing domestic prices through certain control policies. However, when foreign exchange control comes into play, there will also be some adverse effects, mainly reflected in the following aspects:

(i) Affecting the sound development of international trade and the process of opening up

Foreign exchange control impedes the formation of a free multilateral settlement system and impedes the normal operation of international trade and capital flows. For developing countries, overvalued currency exchange rate and restriction of foreign exchange supply and demand will discourage exporters ' enthusiasm to earn foreign exchange, while foreign exchange shortage will affect the country's import trade. Restrictions on capital export and return of an investment will discourage foreign investors from investing in the country. The experience of many countries has proved that in order to improve the vicious circle among the balance of payments deficit, insufficient foreign exchange reserves, foreign exchange control, low level of opening to the outside world and slow economic development, it is necessary to find a way out by gradual abolishment of foreign exchange control.

(ii) Distorted exchange rate and inefficient resource allocation

In foreign exchange control, government measures that set official exchange rates or restrict the buying and selling of foreign currency can cause exchange rates to deviate from the equilibrium exchange rate of the market, that is, exchange rate distortion. For developing countries, exchange rate distortion often manifests themselves in the form of excessively high exchange rates for the local currency. This may be due to a higher official rate for the local currency set by the government, or it may be the result of government restrictions on the supply and demand of foreign exchange. Such distorted exchange rate can affect the rational allocation of resources. Firstly, it can affect the agriculture sector in developing countries. The government may also restrict the supply and demand of foreign exchange. World agricultural prices are low because of the high subsidies generally provided by developed countries for agricultural exports. In turn, overvaluation of the local currency exchange rate will further reduce the local currency price of imported agricultural products, resulting in lower prices for domestic agricultural products in developing countries, seriously affecting the agricultural development of developing countries. Secondly, overvaluation of the local currency exchange rate will have a negative impact on the export and import substitution industries. The main reason is that overvaluation of the local currency exchange rate raises the local currency prices of domestic exporters and depresses the local currency prices of imported goods. Finally, on a global scale, exchange rate is one of the price signals that guides international capital flows. The distortion of exchange rate makes it difficult for people to judge the correct direction of investment.

(iii) Occurrence of black market transaction in foreign exchange

Black market transaction in foreign exchange has been spawned by the low foreign exchange quotations set by the government. When the scale of the black market transaction in foreign exchange is large, it becomes necessary for the government to open up the foreign exchange transfer market so that a legal two-track exchange rate emerges in the country. At the same time, in order to purchase foreign exchange at a lower official price, certain individuals or enterprises may pay bribes to officials who have the right to ration foreign exchange, contributing to bad culture.

For the long-term development of the world economy, there is a trend for countries to gradually abolish foreign exchange control, but the process is very long. Countries around the world, especially developing countries, should consider how to make the best use of the positive effects of foreign exchange control and avoid or reduce the negative effects.

Mini Case

Read the following news, choose one of the cases to look at online for more information and analyse what rules does it violate? And why?

According to the website of the SAFE, since 2018, the State Administration of Foreign Exchange (SAFE) has closely focused on the three tasks of serving the real economy, preventing and controlling financial risks, and deepening financial reform, to strengthen the supervision of the foreign exchange market, investigate and deal with all kinds of foreign exchange violations in accordance with the law, and crackdown on false and deceptive transactions. According to the relevant provisions of the Disclosure of Government Information Regulations of the People's Republic of China, some of the typical cases of irregularities are notified as follows (excerpts):

Case 1: Bank of Communications Xiamen Qianpu Sub-branch in relation to illegal re-export trade

From January to August 2016, Bank of Communications Xiamen Qianpu Sub-branch failed to exercise due diligence to examine the authenticity of the re-export trade as required by the regulations, and irregularly handled the re-export trade payment business when the enterprises submitted false bills of lading.

The above-mentioned act of the bank violates Article 12 of the Foreign Exchange Control Regulations of the People's Republic of China. In accordance with Article 47 of the Foreign Exchange Control Regulations of the People's Republic of China, the bank was fined RMB 6 million and suspended from public foreign exchange sales for three months and ordered the senior management and other directly responsible persons to be held accountable.

Case 2: Bank of China Putian Branch's irregularity in handling personal foreign exchange business

From January 2016 to April 2017, Bank of China Putian Branch handled the sale and payment of foreign exchange and withdrawal of foreign currency notes for individuals.

The bank's behavior violates Article 7 and Article 34 of the Individual Foreign Exchange Administration Measures. In accordance with the provisions of Article 47 and Article 48 of the Foreign Exchange Control Regulations of the People's Republic of China, a fine of RMB 700,000 was imposed.

Case 3: Dinpay Company foreign exchange evasion cases

From January 2016 to October 2017, Dinpay Company processed cross-border foreign exchange payments based on false logistics information for a total amount of USD 15,588,000.

The act violates Article 12 of the Foreign Exchange Control Regulations of the People's Republic of China, and constitutes an act of foreign exchange evasion, which seriously disrupts the order of the foreign exchange market. The foreign exchange market order is seriously disturbed, and the nature is bad. According to Article 39 of the Foreign Exchange Control Regulations of the People's Republic of China, a fine of RMB 15,308,000 was imposed.

Case 4: Alipay Corporation violates foreign exchange management regulations

From January 2014 to May 2016, Alipay Corporation exceeded the approved scope of the cross-border foreign exchange payment business and incorrectly declared its balance of payments.

The act violates Article 6 of the Cross-border Foreign Exchange Payment Business of Payment Institutions Pilot Guidance and Article 7 of the Balance of Payments Statistic Declaration Measures. In accordance with Article 48 of the Foreign Exchange Control Regulations of the People's Republic of China, a fine of RMB 600,000 was imposed.

Case 5: Zhao from Hebei Province splits and evades the foreign exchange

From January 2016 to December 2017, in order to achieve the purpose of illegally transferring assets abroad, Zhao used the annual foreign exchange purchase quota of himself and 55 others to split his personal assets and purchase foreign exchange and remit them to an offshore account illegally. The total amount of funds transferred was USD 2,453,100.

The act violates Article 7 of the Individual Foreign Exchange Administration Measures, and constitutes an act of foreign exchange evasion. According to the Foreign Exchange Control Regulations of the People's Republic of China, a fine of RMB 1.16 million was imposed.

Source: WANG Q Y. The typical cases of irregularities are notified by the State Administration of Foreign Exchange [EB/OL]. [2018-07-24]. http://finance.china.com.cn/news/20180724/4709011.shtml.

Mind Map

Project Training

I. Single-choice questions

1. The uncertainty of foreign exchange risk refers to（   ）.

A. foreign exchange risk may or may not occur

B. foreign exchange risk to the holder or user of foreign exchange may be losses or may be profits

C. to a party is brought to the loss, to another party is bound to bring a profit

D. foreign exchange rate may rise, may also fall

2. The timing structure of an accounts receivable or payable in a foreign currency has a direct impact on the magnitude of foreign exchange risk. The longer the time period, the （   ） the foreign exchange risk.

A. greater   B. less   C. no effect   D. impossible to judge

3. The importer enters into a forward foreign exchange contract with the bank in order to（   ）.

A. prevent the losses caused by the rise of foreign exchange rates

B. prevent the losses caused by the fall in foreign exchange rates

C. bring the gains because of the foreign exchange rates rise

D. obtain the gains arising from the fall in foreign exchange rates

4. A foreign trade company signs an export contract worth USD 100,000 on 1 September

and the date of receipt is set at 20 November. The foreign exchange risk faced by the company during this period belongs to (   ) .

    A. time risk   B. economic risk

    C. transaction risk   D. conversion risk

5. The creation of a reverse flow in the same currency, in the same amount and for the same period of time as the existence of the risk, the directional flow of funds is (   ) .

    A. early receipt and payment   B. hedging

    C. balancing   D. pairing

II. Multiple-choice questions

1. Components of foreign exchange risk include (   ) .

    A. local currency   B. foreign currency   C. time   D. exchange rate

2. In the following examples, which are no foreign exchange risk (   ) .

    A. Collection in local currency

    B. Inflow and outflow of foreign currency in the same currency, the same amount and the same time

    C. Payment in local currency

    D. Outflow of the same foreign currency at different times with the same amount

3. Soft and hard currencies are negatively correlated as they fall and rise. The rational combination can reduce exchange rate risk. The main ways to do this are (   ) .

    A. Half soft and half hard currencies   B. More soft or more hard currencies

    C. Between soft and hard currencies   D. Arbitrary

4. The methods used by companies to prevent foreign exchange risk are (   ) .

    A. Choosing the currency of the contract   B. Using a "basket" of currencies

    C. Swap transactions   D. Forward transactions

    E. Option transactions

5. Foreign exchange options are classified as (   ) according to whether the time of exercise of the option is flexible.

    A. call options   B. put options

    C. European options   D. American options

    E. buyer's options

6. The objectives of foreign exchange control are (   ) .

    A. Maintain the country's balance of payments

    B. Restrict capital inflows and outflows

    C. Keep exchange rate stable

    D. Ensure the effective use of foreign exchange

    E. Ensure the orderly operation of the financial market

III. Judgment questions

1. Foreign exchange risk does not only mean the risk of loss, it can also be the risk of

profit.   (   )

2. With an appropriate foreign exchange risk management approach, companies can completely eliminate exchange rate risk.   (   )

3. Foreign exchange control only occurs in developing countries, developed countries do not have foreign exchange control.   (   )

4. Denominated in local currency, there is no foreign exchange risk at any time, but may be exposed to inflation risk.   (   )

5. Importers and exporters can reduce exchange rate losses by "taking soft currencies and paying hard currencies".   (   )

IV. Practical questions

An American company is preparing to import a shipment of goods from France on 1 July, valued at 1 million euros, for payment on 31 December of that year. Assume that the futures price of the euro on 1 July is EUR 1=USD 1.1380. How can the company use the euro futures to protect itself against foreign exchange risk?

Project Ten
International Monetary System

Learning Objectives

Knowledge Objectives:

Grasp the meaning of the international monetary system; understand the essence and function of the international monetary system; understand the causes and characteristics of the evolution of the international monetary system.

Competence Objectives:

Analyze the role and impact of RMB internationalization and the causes of changes in the international monetary system.

Operation Objectives:

Express the specific content of the Triffin Dilemma (Triffin Paradox) in professional language; collect and analyze the trend of changes in the international monetary system in the future.

Course Introduction

The emergence of Libra will change the international monetary system and adjust the world financial pattern

The generation of the Libra concept is bringing unprecedented shock to the world. Recently, the United States House of Representatives held two consecutive hearings to enquire questions about Facebook's Libra project.

Although Facebook claims to hope that Libra is a payment tool and will not compete with sovereign currency, from the perspective of Libra's attributes, it is not just a payment tool but has the function of digital currency. It can be predicted that once the Libra project is promoted, it will profoundly change the current international monetary system, which will be subversive.

The emergence of Libra will profoundly change the international monetary system and adjust the world financial pattern:

1. It will intensify currency competition. Once Libra is widely used, it will become an international reserve currency. Libra may challenge the existing monetary system, especially the world monetary status of the US dollar. Therefore, Libra's monetary road will not be smooth and it will inevitably face the encirclement and suppression of US dollar vested interest groups, which has really opened the prelude to the war between sovereign currency and digital currency. There is a fundamental difference between the United States president's prompt response to Facebook's plan and the United States government's lack of confidence in it.

2. It will comprehensively change the social credit system. The monetary system is based on credit, and the emergence of digital currency is precisely due to the indiscriminate issuance of national currency leading to inflation and public distrust. Once Libra succeeds, it is likely to cause a chain reaction, leading to the change of the credit system, the operation mode of the financial system and capital market will be fundamentally changed.

3. It will be the test of monetary regulation. If Libra can become a currency, even under the system of full reserve, the change of Libra supply will lead to the fluctuation of the global money market, and there is a problem of coordination between different currencies. As a currency issuer, Facebook will become the same important institution as the Federal Reserve and the European Central Bank. Libra's lending rate will become an important benchmark of the interest rate system. Once the full reserve system is liberalized, Facebook may become the global "online reserve" and test the monetary regulation of various countries.

The domestic financial community has also realized this fact that the impact of Libra is huge and unknown. Zhou Xiaochuan, Zhu Min and other experts have pointed out the subversion and feasibility of Libra. China's global leading position in mobile payment is facing the subversion of Libra. The expanding influence of RMB in the international currency may also stop suddenly because of Libra. The central bank should actively participate in the reform of digital currency, accelerate the research and launch of China's digital currency to gain a place in the global digital currency.

Source: LUO Z X. The emergence of Libra will change the international monetary system and adjust the world financial pattern [EB/OL]. [2019-07-20]. http: //www. sixi.com/news_detail.aspx?nid=9839.

Thinking and discussion:

1. Find out what Libra is, and how it was born through the Internet.

2. What is the international monetary system? What does it include?

Task 1   Overview of the International Monetary System

I. Definition of the international monetary system

The international monetary system is a general term for the principles, measures and organizational forms established by governments to play the role of the world currency in the international context in order to meet the needs of international trade and international payment.

The international monetary system is a central issue in the field of international finance. The "system" here is translated from English, also known as the international monetary regulation. Since the currencies of various countries are issued by various sovereign countries and international economic transactions are carried out transnationally, an international monetary system is needed to coordinate and regulate the economic transactions of various countries, so as to ensure and promote the smooth progress of international trade and international payment.

The core of the international monetary system is the international exchange rate system. For the sake of national economic development and safeguarding common interests, countries often reach a consensus on the arrangement of currency exchange rate and regulate the change of exchange rate worldwide in accordance with more reasonable principles. Therefore, a common exchange rate system is formed.

II. Concept of the international monetary system

A robust international monetary system should be able to promote the smooth progress of international trade and international capital, so as to promote the development of the whole international economy. The international monetary system generally includes the following main contents:

(i) Determination of key currency and exchange rate system

The key currency is the currency that acts as the basic value conversion tool in the international monetary system. Since countries use different currencies, the exchange ratios between currencies, the adjustment of exchange rates and the composition of international reserves can be determined only when the key currency is identified. In different historical stages of the development of the international monetary system, gold and pound have played the role of key currency. At present, the US dollar is the most widely used and accounts for the largest proportion of foreign exchange reserves in the world. It is the most important international currency. Countries generally take the US dollar as the key currency. However, some African countries regard the pound as a key currency for historical reasons.

What rules should be followed to determine and maintain the exchange rate between a country's currency and other currencies, and maintain the stability of the exchange rate, so as to effectively prevent the competitive depreciation of the exchange rate between currencies of various countries. Since the change of exchange rate can directly affect the redistribution of economic interests among countries, the formation of a more stable international exchange rate arrangement for all countries is the core issue to be solved by the international monetary system. At the same time, governments also stipulate how to determine and maintain the exchange rate between a country's currency and other currencies, the basis for determining the currency exchange rate, the boundary of currency exchange rate fluctuation, the adjustment of the currency exchange rate, the measures taken to maintain the currency exchange rate, whether to adopt diversified exchange rates for the same currency, whether a country's currency can become a freely convertible currency and what exchange rate system to adopt.

(ii) Determination of international reserve assets

What currency should a government use to maintain its trade surplus and creditor's rights and to maintain people's confidence in the reserve currency while ensuring international payment and meeting international solvency.

In order to balance the international payment, a country needs to have a certain number of international reserves. Preserving a certain amount of international reserve assets and their composition, which are generally accepted by all countries in the world, is an important part of the international monetary system. In addition, there are many important elements of the international monetary system such as which currency should be adopted as the international payment currency; how to determine the central reserve currency in a specific period to maintain the operation of the whole reserve system; how to choose the reserve assets of countries all over the world to meet the requirements of various economic transactions.

(iii) Determination of balance of payments and its adjustment mechanism

An effective balance of payments adjustment mechanism can enable all countries to bear the adjustment responsibility of balance of payments imbalance fairly and reasonably, and minimize the cost of adjustment. The balance of payments adjustment mechanism can help countries with an unbalanced balance of payments to adjust and promote balanced economic development and world economic stability.

One of the main contents of the international monetary system is to effectively help and promote countries with serious balance of payments imbalances to adjust through various measures so that they can fairly assume the responsibilities and obligations of the balance of payments adjustment on an international scale. Since the financial and monetary policies implemented by various countries will have an impact on the economies of countries and even the whole world, how to coordinate the financial and monetary policies of various countries related to international financial activities and formulate a number of rules, practices and systems recognized and observed by members through international financial institutions, and establish the structure and form of international monetary cooperation also constitutes an important part of the international monetary system.

In addition, there are many factors affecting the international monetary system. In the settlement of claims and debts between countries, what settlement methods should be adopted and whether restrictions (i. e., foreign exchange control) should be imposed are also the contents of the international monetary system. A country's external claims and debts should be settled immediately; free multilateral settlement should be implemented in the international settlement; or regular settlement and limited bilateral settlement should be implemented.

In order to make international payments, governments of all countries should determine whether their currencies can be freely convertible into the currencies of any other country; whether there are all or part restrictions on external payments, or no restrictions at all, including the provisions on the control of current accounts, capital and financial accounts and the principles of international settlement; whether the flow and transfer of gold and foreign exchange are restricted and cannot flow freely; whether it can only flow freely within a certain region or completely free must be clearly stipulated by the state.

III. Types and functions of the international monetary system

(i) Types of the international monetary system

Determining the type of a monetary system can be divided according to the form of international reserve assets and the degree of monetary cooperation.

1. Classification according to the standard of the form of international reserve assets

Accordingly, the international monetary system can be divided into the gold standard and the credit standard.

(1) The gold standard system.

According to the role of gold as an international reserve asset and international currency, the gold standard system can be divided into gold specie standard system, gold bullion standard system and gold exchange standard system. From the 19th century to the outbreak of the World War I, the international monetary system was the gold specie standard. From the World War I to the outbreak of the economic crisis in the 1930s, the international monetary system was the gold bullion standard. And then to the end of the World War II and the Bretton Woods System from 1944 to 1973 was the gold exchange standard.

(2) The credit standard system.

The credit standard system is a monetary system adopted by countries all over the world after the outbreak of the economic crisis and the collapse of the gold standard in the 1930s. The prevailing international monetary system since 1976 is the credit standard system.

2. Classification according to the standard of monetary cooperation degree

The international monetary system can be divided into two categories: single currency system and multi-currency system.

The international gold standard (also known as the era of sterling standard) and the Bretton Woods System (also known as the era of dollar standard) all implement a single monetary system in which the currency of a country acts as the international currency. Since the implementation of the credit standard system, especially the birth of the euro, the international monetary system has entered the era of a multi-currency system.

(ii) Functions of the international monetary system

The international monetary system in different historical periods has its background and plays an important role.

(1) The adjustment mechanism of the balance of payments and the adjustment policies that can be observed by all countries are determined, which provide a basis for all countries to correct the imbalance of the balance of payments.

(2) A relatively stable exchange rate mechanism has been established, which largely prevents unfair currency competition.

(3) Diversified reserve assets have been created, providing sufficient liquidity for the development of the international economy, and at the same time resisting regional or global financial crises.

(4) Promote the coordination of national economic policies. Within the framework of a unified international monetary system, all countries should abide by certain common norms, and any behavior that benefits themselves at the expense of others will be subject to international criticism. Therefore, the economic policies of all countries can be coordinated and understood to a certain extent.

The international financial system has its defects. Therefore, the international financial system still needs to be reformed and seeking development on this basis.

Task 2　　　Evolution of the International Monetary System

The international monetary system is evolving with the development of history. Different stages of the international monetary system mean that when countries achieve internal and external balance, they should follow different guidelines on the basic issues of international currency. The development of the international monetary system reflects the changes made to these norms to adapt to different historical conditions.

In terms of time sequence, the international monetary system can be roughly divided into three stages: the International Gold Standard stage, the Bretton Woods System stage and the current Jamaica Monetary System stage.

The evolution of the international monetary system is summarized in Table 10-1.

Table 10-1　Summary of the evolution of the international monetary system

International Monetary System	Year
International Gold Standard	From 1880 to 1914
	From 1918 to 1939 （recovery period）
Bretton Woods System	From 1944 to 1973
Transitional Period of Floating Exchange Rate System	From 1973 to 1976
Jamaica Monetary System	From 1976 to present

Source: Comprehensively compiled based on relevant data.

I. International Gold Standard

（i）Formation of the international gold standard

Animation micro-lesson 10-1

International monetary system
and its evolution

The world's first international monetary system was the international gold standard, which was formed around the end of 1880 and ended in 1914 with the outbreak of the World War I. The international gold standard is a system in which gold is the standard currency.

Under the international gold standard, in addition to gold coins, there are banknotes that can be converted into gold and a small number of other metal coins in the currency in circulation, but only gold coins can fully perform all the functions of money, namely value scale, means of circulation, storage, payment and world currencies.

The international gold standard is widely adopted by all countries.

（ii）Characteristics of the international gold standard

The international gold standard is a relatively stable and sound monetary system, which has the following three characteristics:

1. Fixed exchange rate system

Under the international gold standard, the currencies of all countries have their specified gold content. The ratio of pure gold contained in the standard currencies of all countries is called mint parity, which is the material basis of currency exchange rates of all countries.

Due to the relationship between foreign exchange supply and demand, the real exchange rate in the foreign exchange market fluctuates around the mint parity, but there is a limit to the fluctuation of exchange rate, which is the gold delivery point. The mint parity plus the gold delivery fee is the gold export point, which is the maximum limit for the increase of exchange rate. The mint parity minus the gold delivery fee is the gold input point, which is the minimum limit for the decline of exchange rate. Because the gold delivery point limits the change range of exchange rate, the fluctuation range of exchange rate is small and basically stable.

Under the international gold standard, the currency value is relatively stable and the production cost is easy to calculate, which promotes the circulation of goods and the expansion of credit. The scale of production and fixed investment will not fluctuate due to the change of currency value, thus promoting the development of the commodity economy.

2. Automatic adjustment of balance of payments

Under the international gold standard, the international payments of capitalist countries are adjusted spontaneously, because the imbalance of international payments will cause the flow of gold. The flow of gold will increase the bank reserves of gold importing countries and reduce the bank reserves of gold exporting countries. The change of bank reserves will cause the change of money quantity, which will lead to changes in domestic prices and incomes of trading countries, and finally correct the imbalance of international payments and stop the flow of gold. It will not happen in any country that the international gold standard cannot be maintained due to the depletion of gold reserves.

Specifically, when a country has a balance of payments deficit, the supply of foreign exchange is less than the demand, and the foreign exchange rate rises. When the exchange rate rises beyond the gold delivery point, it will cause the outflow of gold, reduce the amount of gold prepared by banks, and thus reduce the currency issuance. Therefore, the financial market is tight and the interest rate of short-term funds rises. When the domestic interest rate is higher than the foreign interest rate, arbitrage activities will occur to promote the inward flow of short-term funds. The rise of the interest rate of short-term funds will also promote the increase of the interest rate of long-term funds and cause the inward flow of long-term funds. If a country has a balance of payments surplus, the opposite will happen. This kind of capital flow can improve the balance of payments and stabilize the international financial market in a short term.

3. National economic policies coordination mechanism

Countries that implement the international gold standard regard external balance (i.e., international balance of payments and exchange rate stability) as the primary objective of their economic policies, while placing domestic equilibrium prices, employment, and stable growth of national income in a secondary position. Therefore, the international gold standard also makes it possible for the major capitalist countries to coordinate their economic policies.

Teaching video 10-1

Learn more about the international gold standard

(iii) Advantages and disadvantages of the international gold standard

The international gold standard has the following advantages and disadvantages:

1.Advantages

When the international gold standard prevailed, it was in the heyday of capitalist free competition. Domestic and international politics were relatively stable and the economy developed rapidly. At that time, the world's manufactured goods came from Britain. The trade deficit of other countries could be made up by British loan funds, and the balance of payments could be basically balanced. Under such favorable conditions, the international gold standard was implemented, and the fixed exchange rate it brought was very beneficial to the development of trade and investment among countries.

2.Disadvantages

The international gold standard itself also has some defects. The automatic adjustment mechanism of the international gold standard is not as perfect as theoretically stated, and its function is limited by many factors. These defects are reflected in the following aspects:

(1) During the more than 30 years of implementing the international gold standard, gold did not flow frequently among countries. When a country has a trade deficit, it does not have to export gold. It can use foreign loans (mainly British loans) to cover the deficit. Similarly, a country with surplus can also use the capital output to reduce the surplus, and it does not have to export gold. Therefore, it is difficult to correct the trade imbalance through the opposite changes in the money supply and price of both sides.

(2) The automatic adjustment mechanism of the international gold standard must change the import and export trade through the change of price level between countries, so as to cause the flow of gold between the two countries, balance the international balance of payments and stabilize the exchange rate. In fact, during the gold standard period, the price change trend of major capitalist countries was quite consistent, and there was no phenomenon of gold flow caused by the price change.

(3) The normal operation of the international gold standard is based on the fact that all governments comply with the basic requirements of the gold standard and do not intervene in the economy. However, at the end of the gold standard, the central banks or monetary authorities of various countries did not allow the gold standard to play an automatic regulatory role but often tried to offset the impact of gold flow on the domestic money supply. When gold flowed into the country, the monetary authority would take measures to curb the increase of money supply in order to stabilize prices; vice versa. Therefore, it is difficult to realize the automatic adjustment mechanism of the international gold standard. In fact, under the capitalist system, the contradictions among countries make it impossible for the international gold standard to automatically adjust to achieve the balance of payments.

(iv) Evolution of the international gold standard

With the deepening of capitalist contradictions, the factors undermining the stability of the international monetary system are also increasing. By the end of 1913, Britain, the United States, France, Germany and Russia had two-thirds of the world's gold stock. Most of the gold was occupied by a few countries, which weakened the foundation of the monetary system of other countries. In order to prepare for war, some countries issued a large number of bank bonds with a sharp increase in government expenditure. As a result, it is becoming more and more difficult to exchange banknotes for gold, which undermines the principle of free convertibility.

In the period of economic crisis, commodity export decreased and capital flight was serious, resulting in a large outflow of gold. Countries had restricted the flow of gold, and gold could not be transferred freely internationally. Due to the gradual destruction of some necessary conditions for maintaining the gold standard, the stability of the international monetary system lost its guarantee.

1. Gold specie standard system

The traditional and most typical gold standard refers to the gold specie standard. Many scholars believe that the gold specie standard period is the "golden period" of world economic development, and some even believe that the gold standard should be rebuilt.

Under the gold specie standard system, gold (as an important means of payment) has the following characteristics:

(1) Gold specifies the value represented by money – each monetary unit has a legal gold content, and the price ratio of national currencies is determined by its gold content.

(2) Gold coins can be freely minted. Anyone can freely hand over the gold to the state mint to be minted into gold coins. Since gold coins can be minted freely, the face value of gold coins can be consistent with the value of the gold contained in them, and the number of gold coins can spontaneously meet the needs in circulation.

(3) Gold coin is a currency with unlimited legal compensation and has the right to unlimited means of payment.

(4) The currency reserve of each country is gold, and gold is also used in international settlement. Gold can be freely imported and exported. Because gold coins can be freely convertible, various value symbols (such as metal coins and banknotes) can stably represent a certain amount of gold for circulation, so as to maintain the stability of currency value and avoid inflation. Since gold can circulate freely among countries, it ensures the relative stability of the foreign exchange market and the unity of the international financial market.

2. Gold bullion standard system

After the outbreak of the World War I, countries stopped cashing bank certificates and banned the export of gold. During the war, countries implemented a free-floating exchange rate system, the exchange rate fluctuated violently, and the stability of the international monetary system no longer existed. After the end of the World War I, countries were unable to restore the gold specie standard.

In 1925, Britain first implemented the gold bullion standard system. Then, France, Italy and other countries also successively implemented the gold bullion standard system. Gold bullion standard system is a monetary system with gold as reserve and value symbol with legal gold content as means of circulation.

Under the gold bullion standard system, the gold content of money is still specified, but gold is only used as the reserve for currency issuance and concentrated in the central bank. Gold coins are no longer minted and circulated. The currency gold in circulation is replaced by value symbols such as banknotes. Banknotes can be exchanged for gold according to the gold content in a certain amount, and the central bank is responsible for the import and export of gold. Also, private export of gold is prohibited.

Although the gold bullion standard system still stipulates the gold content of money and takes gold as the reserve, the free casting and circulation of gold coins and the free import and export of gold have been banned. The exchange of value symbols with gold has also been restricted. At this time, it is difficult for gold to automatically adjust money supply and demand and stabilize the exchange rate. Therefore, the gold bullion standard system is actually an incomplete gold standard system.

3. Gold exchange standard system

The gold exchange standard system, also known as the virtual gold standard system, is a monetary system in which the foreign exchange assets deposited in gold bullion standard or gold specie standard countries are used as reserves and the paper money with legal gold content is used as the means of circulation.

Before the World War I, many colonial countries had implemented this monetary system. After the World War I, some capitalist countries that were unable to restore the gold specie standard but did not adopt the gold bullion standard, and then implemented the gold exchange standard.

The international gold exchange standard, which was reluctantly restored by countries after the World War I, finally collapsed in the world economic crisis in 1929 and the international financial crisis in 1931.

Due to the impact of the economic crisis, Britain's balance of payments has been in trouble. In the international financial crisis of 1931, countries exchanged gold with Britain one after another, which made it difficult for Britain to cope with. Finally, Britain was forced to terminate the implementation of the gold standard in September 1931.

Some countries associated with the pound also abandoned the gold exchange standard one after another. Then, in March 1933, the United States had to stop exchanging gold and prohibit the export of gold, so as to abandon the gold standard. In the 1930s, the collapse of the international gold exchange standard was the first crisis of the monetary system in the capitalist world. After the complete collapse of the international gold standard system, the international monetary system was in chaos in the 1930s, and the normal international monetary order was destroyed. At that time, the three main international currencies, namely sterling, US dollar and franc, formed opposing currency groups - sterling group, US dollar group and franc group. The exchange rate between currencies of various countries had become a floating exchange rate again. There were strict exchange controls among various currency groups, and currencies could not be freely convertible.

In terms of the balance of payments adjustment, countries had also adopted various means. In order to solve the serious domestic unemployment, countries had fought a large exchange rate war and competed to devalue their currencies and to expand exports and curb imports. Moreover, various trade protectionist measures and foreign exchange control methods were also very popular, which had seriously hindered international trade. The international capital flows had almost come to a standstill.

In September 1936, Britain, the United States and France reached the so - called "Trilateral Monetary Agreement" in order to restore and stabilize the international monetary order. The agreement promised to make every effort to maintain the exchange rate at the time of the establishment of the agreement, and reduce exchange rate fluctuations and work together to maintain the stability of monetary relations. In October 1936, Britain, the United States and France signed the "Trilateral Gold Agreement" on the free exchange of gold among the three countries.

However, the international monetary system was still full of contradictions and conflicts. Later, as the imperialist countries were busy preparing for war and purchasing arms, resulting in the outflow of gold, the "Trilateral Monetary Agreement" was destroyed. However, the agreement has achieved some results in stopping foreign exchange dumping and created certain conditions for the establishment of the international monetary system in the future.

II. Bretton Woods System

(i) Formation of the Bretton Woods System

At the end of the World War II, the governments of the United States and Britain conceived and designed the post-war international monetary system out of consideration of their interests, and proposed the "White Plan" and the "Keynes Plan" respectively.

The "White Plan", named after an official of the United States Treasury Department, was put forward in April 1943. Its full name is the "United Nations Foreign Exchange Stabilization Program". The main content of the plan is to establish an international monetary stabilization fund institution, and countries must contribute funds to establish a foreign exchange stabilization fund. The right of each country to speak and vote depends on its share of contributions to IMF. IMF proposes an international monetary unit "unita", which contains the gold equivalent to 10 US dollars. IMF adopts a fixed exchange rate, and the exchange rates of currencies of various countries cannot be changed arbitrarily without the consent of IMF institutions. The main task of IMF is to stabilize the exchange rate, provide the short-term credit and balance the balance of payments. The fund office is located in the country with the largest share. The "White Plan" reflects the attempt of the United States to manipulate and control funds to gain dominance in international finance.

The "Keynes Plan" was put forward by the British economist Keynes. In fact, it is a "scheme of international settlement alliance". The main content is to establish a worldwide central bank and international settlement alliance. The share of countries in it is calculated by the average amount of import and export trade in the three years before the World War II. The content of this plan is obviously beneficial to Britain.

After three months of discussion, the United States and Britain finally reached an agreement. On this basis, in July 1944, the United Nations International Monetary and Financial Conference was held in Bretton Woods, New Hampshire, the United States, with the participation of four countries, including the United States and other three countries. The conference adopted the International Monetary Fund Agreement and the International Bank for Reconstruction and Development Agreement based on the "White Plan", and announced the international monetary system after the World War II: the Bretton Woods System.

(ii) Characteristics of the Bretton Woods System

The Bretton Woods System has the following characteristics:

1. Pegging for currencies

(1) The double pegging system.

The US dollar is pegged to gold. The US dollar is thus called the anchor currency to which other currencies are pegged. The United States monetary authority promises to convert the US dollar possessed by other monetary authorities into gold at the mint parity of 35 US dollars to one ounce of gold.

Therefore, the system establishes the peg between the US dollar and gold, and the peg of other national currencies to the US dollar. Other national currencies are indirectly pegged to gold, because their US dollar reserves could be converted into gold at mint parity.

(2) Adjustable fixed exchange rate.

The International Monetary Fund Agreement stipulates that the exchange rates of currencies of various countries against the US dollar can only fluctuate within the range of 1% above and 1% below the statutory exchange rate. If the market exchange rate exceeds the fluctuation range of 1% of the legal exchange rate, governments have the obligation to intervene in the foreign exchange market to maintain the stability of the exchange rate. Any change in the member's statutory exchange rate by more than 1% must be approved by the International Monetary Fund. The exchange rate system of the Bretton Woods System is called the "adjustable pegged exchange rate system".

2. Convertibility of national currencies and principles of international payment and settlement

The principle of free convertibility of currencies of all countries is: any member shall exchange the national currency accumulated by other members in current account transactions. If the other party is the currency of current account payment, it shall exchange back the national currency. Considering the actual situation of various countries, the International Monetary Fund Agreement also puts forward the provisions of "transition period" and the principles of international payment and settlement. Members shall not impose restrictions on the payment or liquidation of the current account of the balance of payments without the consent of the IMF.

3. Determination of international reserve assets

The provisions on currency parity in the International Monetary Fund Agreement put the US dollar in the position of "equivalent" to gold, making the US dollar the most important international reserve currency in the foreign exchange reserves of all countries.

4. Balance of payments adjustment

25% of IMF members' shares are paid in gold or currencies convertible into gold, and the rest are paid in their currencies. When a member has a balance of payments deficit, it can purchase (i.e., borrow) a certain amount of foreign exchange from the IMF in its currency according to the specified procedures and repay the loan by buying back its currency within a specified time. The larger the share subscribed by members, the more loans they get. Loans are limited to members to cover the balance of payments deficits (current account payments).

5. Establishment of the International Monetary Fund

The establishment of a permanent international financial institution, the International Monetary Fund, is a major feature of the Bretton Woods System. The International Monetary Fund Agreement defines the purpose of the International Monetary Fund: to establish the institutions of the International Monetary Fund and promote international monetary cooperation; to promote the balanced development of international trade and investment, improve the employment and real income level of members, expand production capacity, promote exchange rate stability, maintain normal exchange relation and avoid competitive currency devaluation; to establish a multilateral payment system and try to eliminate foreign exchange control; to provide financial accommodation for members and correct the imbalance of balance of payments and to reduce or prevent the expansion of balance of payments deficit or surplus.

Teaching video 10-2

Learn more about the Bretton
Woods System

(iii) Advantages and disadvantages of the Bretton Woods System

The advantages and disadvantages of the Bretton Woods System are:

1. Advantages

The double pegging of the Bretton Woods System made the US dollar equivalent to gold, and the currencies of various countries could only be pegged to gold through the US dollar, thus establishing the central position of the US dollar in the international monetary system.

Therefore, the international monetary system after the World War II was actually the US dollar standard. The establishment and operation of the Bretton Woods System played a positive role in the development of international trade and the world economy after the World War II.

(1) The fixed exchange rate has stabilized the international financial order.

The Bretton Woods System established the principle of double pegging between the US dollar and gold, between the currencies of various countries and the US dollar, and implemented an adjustable pegged exchange rate system. The fluctuation of the exchange rate was strictly restricted, so the currency exchange rate remained relatively stable. The establishment of the Bretton Woods System ended the turbulence and chaos in the international monetary and financial field, and made the international financial relations enter a relatively stable period. It was very beneficial to the international commodity flow and international capital flow and created good external conditions for the stable development of the world economy.

(2) The US dollar has played the role of the world currency.

The US dollar has become the main international valuation unit, means of payment and international reserve currency, making up for the lack of international clearing capacity, which solves the problem of international reserve shortage caused by insufficient gold supply to a certain extent, improves the global purchasing power and promotes international trade and transnational investment.

(3) There are two ways to adjust the imbalance of balance of payments.

Under the Bretton Woods System, there were two ways to adjust the imbalance of the balance of payments: the short-term imbalance was solved by the credit funds provided by the International Monetary Fund, and the long-term imbalance was resolved through exchange rate parity.

(4) International monetary institutions play an important role.

International monetary institutions such as the International Monetary Fund and the World Bank provide various types of short-term loans and medium and long-term loans to some industrial countries, especially some developing countries, to monitor the changes in exchange rates, alleviate the members' balance of payments difficulties to a certain extent, and enable their foreign trade and economic development to proceed normally. This is conducive to the stable growth of the world economy.

2. Disadvantages

The Bretton Woods System was a relatively successful example of international monetary cooperation after the war. It provided favorable conditions for stabilizing international finance and expanding international trade, but the system still had the following defects:

(1) The privileged status of the US dollar.

The special status of the US dollar has led to the important impact of the United States monetary policy on the economies of various countries. As the US dollar is the main reserve asset and enjoys the reputation of "paper gold", the United States can use the US dollar to make a direct foreign investment, buy foreign enterprises, or use the US dollar to make up for the balance of payments deficit (this phenomenon is called "seigniorage tax", that is, the currency-issuing country can obtain net income through currency transfer), and the currency exchange rates of various countries are pegged to the US dollar. As a result, the currencies of various countries are dependent on the US dollar, and every move of the United States monetary and financial authorities will affect the whole world financial field, resulting in the instability of the world financial system.

(2) The Triffin Dilemma (Triffin Paradox).

In 1960, Robert Triffin, an American economist, put forward in his book "Gold and the Dollar Crisis: the Future of Convertibility" that the Bretton Woods System, an international monetary system, has its own insurmountable contradiction in design structure—since the US dollar is pegged to gold and the currencies of

Animation micro-lesson 10-2

Triffin Dilemma

other countries are pegged to the US dollar, although the US dollar has gained the status of the international core currency, in order to develop international trade, countries must use the US dollar as the settlement and reserve currency, which will lead to the continuous precipitation of currency flowing out of the United States overseas, and there will be a long-term trade deficit for the United States. However, the premise of international currency is to maintain the stability and strength of the US dollar, which requires the United States to be a long-term trade surplus country. These two requirements contradict each other, so it is a paradox. We call this contradiction between the growth of international reserves and confidence in the reserve currency the "Triffin Paradox". If the United States maintains the balance of payments and stabilizes the US dollar, it will block the source of international reserves and lead to insufficient international solvency, which is another irreconcilable contradiction.

(3) The exchange rate mechanism lacks flexibility and the balance of payments adjustment mechanism fails.

The Bretton Woods System overemphasizes the stability of the exchange rate. Countries cannot use the change of exchange rate to adjust the balance of international payments. They can only passively implement foreign exchange control or give up the policy goal of stabilizing the domestic economy. The former will inevitably hinder the development of trade, while the latter violates the principle of stabilizing and developing the own economy. Both of them are undesirable. It can be seen that the inflexible exchange rate mechanism is not conducive to the stable economic development of all countries.

Since the 1950s, the above defects had constantly shaken the foundation of the Bretton Woods System, and finally fell into collapse in the 1970s.

(iv) Evolution of the Bretton Woods System

After the World War II, the economic strength of the United States increased unprecedentedly.

In 1949, the United States had 71.2% of the world's gold reserves at that time. However, Western Europe and Japan, which were traumatized by the war, needed a lot of dollars for economic development. However, because they could not be satisfied through the export of goods and services, a general shortage of dollars was formed.

In the early 1950s, the United States launched the war of aggression against Korea, turning the balance of payments from surplus to deficit, so the gold reserves began to drain.

The first dollar crisis broke out in 1960, the second dollar crisis broke out in 1968, and a new dollar crisis broke out in 1971. On August 15, 1971, the United States government announced the implementation of the "new economic policy". One of its contents was to stop fulfilling the obligation of exchanging the US dollar for gold, cut off the direct peg between the US dollar and gold, and fundamentally shook the Bretton Woods System.

After the US dollar stopped trading against gold, it caused extreme chaos in the international financial market. The "Smithsonian Agreement" was adopted by the "Group of Ten" in February 1971. Its main content is that the US dollar depreciated by 7.89%, the official price of gold rose to $38 per ounce, the exchange rates of major currencies in western countries were adjusted accordingly. It is stipulated that the fluctuation range of exchange rates should not exceed 2.25% of the average price of currencies. Since then, the balance of payments of the United States had not improved. In late January 1973, a new dollar crisis broke out in the international financial market. The US dollar was forced to depreciate again by 10%, and the official price of gold rose to $42.22.

After the second depreciation of the US dollar, in order to maintain their own economic interests, western countries have abandoned fixed exchange rates and implemented floating exchange rates. The overall floating of currencies of various countries has completely lost the status of the central currency of the US dollar, which marks the complete collapse of the international monetary system centered on the US dollar.

Case Analysis 10-1

"Bretton Woods: 75 years later" conference was held in Paris, the participants opposed trade protectionism

"Bretton Woods: 75 years later" conference was held in Paris, and the participants opposed trade protectionism.

2019 marked the 75th anniversary of the Bretton Woods conference. On July 16 local time, a high-level conference called "Bretton Woods: 75 years later" was held in Paris, France.

At the meeting, representatives and experts from many countries expressed their views on international cooperation, multilateralism and future global economic governance. Participants opposed trade protectionism and called for multilateral cooperation to change the hegemonic status of the US dollar.

The meeting was hosted by the Central Bank of France and attended by government representatives of the United States, Britain, France and other countries, some central bank governors, experts and scholars. In his welcoming speech, Francois Villeroy de Galhau, the governor of the Central Bank of France once again stressed the important role of the World Trade Organization and multilateralism in dealing with international trade issues.

Francois Villeroy de Galhau, the governor of the Central Bank of France, pointed out that the new multilateralism must play an important role in three aspects. The first was trade. The G20 unanimously agreed on the need to strengthen the functions of the World Trade

Organization. The World Trade Organization should continue to strengthen trade freedom, especially in the field of services. In this regard, it has lagged behind…

Source: Excerpt from CCTV website on July 17, 2019.

Thinking and discussion:

1. What happened at the Bretton Woods conference in 1944?

2. How is the US dollar hegemony related to trade protectionism?

III. Jamaica Monetary System

(ⅰ) Formation of the Jamaica Monetary System

In the early 1960s, due to the continuous large trade surplus, the Federal Republic of Germany revalued the mark currency, it was even publicly criticized by the International Monetary Fund.

Together with the International Monetary Fund Constitution (Second Amendment), the interim committee of the international monetary system of the International Monetary Fund held a meeting in Kingston, Jamaica, in 1976 and reached the Jamaica Agreement, which officially ended the Bretton Woods System and formally formed a new pattern of international monetary relations.

1. Increasing members' fund shares

According to the provisions of the agreement, the fund shares of members increased from 29.2 billion SDRs to 39 billion SDRs, an increase of 3.6%. The proportion of fund shares of each member has also been adjusted. Among them, the proportion of oil-exporting countries has increased, the proportion of other developing countries has remained basically unchanged, but the share proportion of the United States has decreased.

2. Legalization of exchange rate floating

The Jamaica Agreement formally confirmed the legalization of the floating exchange rate system. Members could choose their own exchange rate system (in fact, they recognized the coexistence of fixed exchange rate system and floating exchange rate system), but their exchange rate policies should be negotiated with and supervised by IMF. IMF coordinated the economic policies of its members, promoted financial stability and narrowed the range of exchange rate fluctuations. The floating exchange rate system should gradually restore the fixed exchange rate system. When conditions were met, the International Monetary Fund could implement a stable but adjustable fixed exchange rate system.

3. Reduced the role of gold in the international monetary system

The Jamaica Agreement made a decision to gradually withdraw gold from the international currency. It abolished all gold clauses in the original agreement and stipulated that gold would no longer be used as the standard for the valuation of currencies of various countries. It also abolished the official price of gold so members could buy and sell gold in the market. The obligations to settle creditor's rights and debts with gold among members and between members and IMF were cancelled. Some of the IMF gold holdings were sold, some returned to the paying members at the official price, and the rest at their discretion.

4. Special drawing rights are stipulated as the main international reserve assets

The main contents of enhancing the role of special drawing rights were to improve the international reserve status of special drawing rights, expand its scope of use in the operations of the International Monetary Fund, and revise the relevant provisions of special drawing rights in due time.

The Jamaica Agreement stipulated that the special drawing rights could be used as a standard for the valuation of national currencies. It could also be used by relevant countries to pay off their debts to IMF, and could also be used for borrowing.

5. Expand financing for developing countries

Teaching video 10-3

Learn more about the Jamaica Monetary System

The Jamaica Monetary System established a trust fund to provide assistance to the least developed developing countries on preferential terms to help solve the balance of payments problems; to expand the amount of IMF credit loans and increase the number of "export fluctuation compensation loans" of IMF.

(ii) Features of the Jamaica Monetary System

The Jamaica Monetary System has inherited and strengthened the International Monetary Fund under the Bretton Woods System and abandoned the double pegging system.

The Jamaica Monetary System mainly has the following characteristics:

1. Diversification of reserve currencies

Under the Bretton Woods System, the international reserve structure is single and the status of the US dollar is very prominent.

Under the Jamaica Monetary System, international reserves are diversified. Although the US dollar is still the dominant international currency, the status of the US dollar has been significantly weakened, and the monopoly of foreign exchange reserves by the US dollar no longer exists. With the economic recovery and development of the two countries, the German mark and the Japanese yen stand out and become important international reserve currencies.

At present, the international reserve currency has become increasingly diversified, and the proportion of the euro in the international reserve has increased. Gold remains the most stable means of value and the ultimate means of international settlement. In addition to gold and major national currencies, there are the special drawing rights.

2. Diversification of exchange rate arrangements

Under the Jamaica Monetary System, the floating exchange rate system coexists with the fixed exchange rate system. A variety of exchange rate arrangement systems dominated by floating exchange rates can more flexibly adapt to the changeable situation of the world economic situation and the needs of the economic policies of major reserve currency countries. Generally speaking, most developed industrial countries adopt separate floating or joint floating, but some also adopt pegging to their own currency basket.

Most developing countries are pegged to an international currency or currency basket. Different exchange rate systems have their advantages and disadvantages. The floating exchange rate system can provide greater activity space and independence for domestic economic policies, while the fixed exchange rate system reduces the exchange rate risk that domestic enterprises may face and facilitates production and accounting. Countries can weigh the advantages and disadvantages according to a series of relevant factors such as their own economic strength, openness and economic structure.

3. Regulating balance of payments through various channels

(1) Domestic economic policy.

As an organic part of a country's macro-economy, the balance of payments must be affected by other factors. A country usually uses domestic economic policies to change domestic demand and supply, so as to eliminate the imbalance of balance of payments. For example, in the case of capital account deficit, we can raise interest rate and reduce currency issuance, so as to attract foreign capital inflows and make up the gap. It should be noted that when using fiscal or monetary policy to adjust external equilibrium, it is often limited by the Meade Conflict. While realizing the balance of payments, it sacrifices other policy objectives, such as economic growth and fiscal balance. Therefore, internal policy should be coordinated with the exchange rate policy.

(2) Exchange rate policy.

Under the floating exchange rate system or the adjustable pegged exchange rate system, the exchange rate is an important tool to adjust the balance of payments. Its principle is: when the current account deficit, the local currency tends to fall. If the local currency falls, the foreign trade competitiveness will increase, so the export increases, the import decreases, and the economic account deficit may decrease or disappear. On the contrary, in the current account surplus, the value of the local currency rises, which enhances the competitiveness of import and export commodities, thus reducing the current account surplus. However, in the actual economic operation, the regulatory role of the exchange rate is restricted by the "Marshall-Lerner Condition" and the "J-curve Effect", and its function is often disappointing.

(3) International financing.

Under the Bretton Woods System, the international financing function is mainly completed by the International Monetary Fund. Under the Jamaica Monetary System, the International Monetary Fund provides loans to deficit countries through governments and commercial banks.

In particular, with the outbreak of the oil crisis and the rapid development of the European money market, countries have gradually turned to the European money market, using the market's more favorable loan conditions to finance funds and adjust the surplus and deficit in the balance of payments.

（4）International coordination.

Functions of international coordination mainly include: through the International Monetary Fund, governments of all countries jointly maintain the stability and prosperity of the international financial situation through consultation.

The G7 Summit has its function, seven western countries reached consensus through many meetings and jointly intervened in the international financial market many times, subjectively for their own interests, but objectively promoted the stability and development of the international finance and economy.

（iii）Advantages and disadvantages of the Jamaica Monetary System

The advantages and disadvantages of the Jamaica Monetary System are very prominent.

1. Advantages

（1）The diversified reserve structure gets rid of the rigid relationship between currencies under the Bretton Woods System, providing a variety of settlement currencies for the international economy and solving the contradiction between the supply and demand of reserve currencies to a great extent.

（2）Diversified exchange rate arrangements adapt to the diversified economies of various countries with different levels of development, which provide flexibility and independence for countries to maintain economic stability and development and help maintain the continuity and stability of domestic economic policies.

（3）Multiple channels go hand in hand to make the adjustment of the balance of payments more effective and timelier.

2. Disadvantages

（1）Under the diversified international reserves, countries that issue reserve currencies still enjoy various benefits such as "seigniorage tax". At the same time, under the diversified international reserves, the lack of a unified and stable monetary standard may lead to international financial instability.

（2）Exchange rates fluctuate. The instability of the exchange rate system increases the foreign exchange risk, which inhibits international trade and investment activities to a certain extent. For developing countries, this negative impact is particularly prominent.

（3）The balance of payments adjustment mechanism is not perfect. Various existing exchange rate channels have their own limitations. The Jamaica Monetary System has not eliminated the global balance of payments imbalance.

（iv）Evolution of the Jamaica Monetary System

If the international financial crisis is accidental and partial under the Bretton Woods System, the international financial crisis is regular, comprehensive and far-reaching under the Jamaica Monetary System.

After the floating exchange rate was widely implemented in 1573, the fluctuation of currency exchange rate and gold price in the western foreign exchange market often occurred with small crises and major crises from time to time. In October 1978, the exchange rate of the US dollar against other major western currencies fell to an all-time low, causing turbulence in the whole western monetary and financial market, which was the famous western monetary crisis from 1977 to 1978.

Due to the disintegration of the gold exchange standard, credit currencies have greatly increased in both types and amounts. Credit currencies account for more than 90% of the currency circulation in the west. There are many kinds of checks, payment vouchers and credit cards, while cash accounts for only a few percent of the currency in some countries. The growth of money supply and deposit is much higher than that of industrial production, and the development of the national economy depends more and more on credit. In short, the existing international monetary system is generally considered to be a transitional and imperfect system, which needs to be thoroughly reformed.

Task 3   Reform of the International Monetary System

Economic globalization is the inevitable trend of productivity development and scientific and technological progress. It is also the extension of production socialization to internationalization. Under the condition of the open economy, the international monetary system is playing a more and more important role. The international monetary system is a series of institutional arrangements to maintain global financial stability and promote world economic development. It is an important factor affecting the security and stability of the global economic and financial system. A reasonable and effective international monetary system can promote global financial stability and world economic growth. It is an important condition for the sustained, stable and healthy operation of the global economy.

I. Overview of the reform of the international monetary system

(i) The reform of the international monetary system is imperative

Since the financial crisis in Southeast Asia and Mexico in the 1990s, the international community has put forward various plans for reforming the international monetary system. In the face of the current American financial crisis, some experts have proposed to reshape the Bretton Woods System and reposition the International Monetary Fund.

The worldwide financial crisis caused by the subprime mortgage crisis in the United States in 2007 triggered the thinking of various countries on the current monetary system:

(1) The hegemony of the US dollar has contributed to the development of the financial crisis. After the financial crisis, it is generally believed that the dominant position of the US dollar in the international monetary system established by the Bretton Woods System has contributed to the excessive debt and consumption of the United States, which in turn contributed to the development of the financial crisis.

(2) The EU expects to improve the status of the euro in the international monetary system through reform. Based on this strategy, in November 2008, the French President Nicolas Sarkozy repeatedly stressed the need to reform the current international monetary system dominated by the US dollar.

(3) Under the existing US dollar reserve currency system, China and other large foreign exchange reserve countries faced the risk of US dollar depreciation. Therefore, these countries hoped to establish and improve the international reserve currency system.

The international monetary system dominated by the US dollar has played a positive role in the recovery and development of the world economy after the war. However, with the rise of emerging economies such as China and the development of global economic multi-polarization, the current international monetary system could no longer adapt to the profound changes in the world economic pattern. At the same time, the shift of the United States to "anti-globalization" and the abuse of US dollar hegemony have played an increasingly negative role in the recovery and development of the global economy after the international financial crisis. Therefore, it is imperative to reform the international monetary system.

Firstly, the globalization of the world economy has not brought about the globalization of the international monetary system. The current international monetary system continues the "center-periphery" pattern of developed and developing countries and fails to reflect the new changes in the world economic pattern. In 2017, the US dollar accounted for 63% of the global reserve currency, much higher than the US share of global GDP (24%). International financial risks and responsibilities are concentrated in a few countries that issue international currencies, forming a situation in which large countries use the issuance right of reserve currencies to kidnap the global economy.

When the reserve currency-issuing country faces the inconsistency between domestic policy needs and international responsibility requirements, the reserve currency-issuing country often gives priority to meeting domestic policy needs and ignores or despises international responsibility based on its own interests. The policy effects of reserve currency-issuing countries may have negative spillover effects in the world, increasing uncertainty and risk to other countries.

Secondly, the formation and outbreak of the international financial crisis have the international monetary and international monetary system factors. In the process of the financial crisis, there are basically phenomena such as sharp depreciation of exchange rate and imbalance of balance of payments adjustment mechanism. With the high development of the financial derivatives market, the relationship between international currencies is becoming closer, and the harm caused by the unstable international monetary system is becoming greater. The outbreak of the international financial crisis has further exposed the defects of the current international monetary system. The reform of the international monetary system requires a more balanced consideration of the balanced, mutually beneficial and win-win relationship among developed countries, developing countries and emerging markets all over the world.

Thirdly, the importance of the reform of the international monetary system has become the consensus of the international community. The unbalanced and unstable development of the international monetary system is an important factor in the global economic imbalance. In order to effectively safeguard the world economic, trade and financial structure, reforming the international monetary system has become an important basis for promoting the stable development of the global economy and finance, and it is also an important part of improving the global economic governance system. The current global economic governance system is dominated by developed countries, which is unreasonable, unfair and unequal, and pays insufficient attention to the interests of developing countries.

Therefore, reforming the international monetary system and enhancing the representation and voice of emerging market countries and developing countries are important directions and contents for improving global economic governance. As the largest developing country, China should promote countries to strengthen macroeconomic policy coordination, reform the international monetary and financial system, actively participate in the reform of the global governance system, promote the development of the international order in a more just and reasonable direction, and especially play its due role in building a stable and risk-resistant international monetary system.

(ii) Reform objectives of the international monetary system

From the overall development trend, the long-term goal of the international monetary system is to create a unified world currency that does not rely on gold or a single country. This is the inevitable trend of the development of the international monetary system. However, it is still far from achieving this goal, which requires several stages of development, and depends on the high integration of the global economy and the formation of a strong and unified political and economic consortium in the international context. Although this goal is far away, the process of change has begun. The emergence of the "Special Drawing Right (SDR)" and "European Currency Unit (ECU)" founded by the International Monetary Fund in the 1970s broke the pattern of the United States dollar dominating the world. The former is undoubtedly the rudiment of a unified world currency that is neither separated from the gold standard nor attached to the economic strength of a single country, while the latter is the development stage of international and regional currencies that must be experienced in the formation of a unified world currency.

After 30 years of development, ECU has evolved into a new international currency. The emergence of the euro indicates that the international monetary system has evolved into a new historical stage – the establishment of international and regional currencies and the coexistence of several international and regional currencies. As an international and regional currency, the future development path of the euro may be bumpy, but its birth is undoubtedly a milestone in the development history of the international monetary system. However, it is still too early to create a unified world currency that does not depend on gold or a strong country. A unified world currency needs to be issued on the basis of a highly integrated world economy, a unified world government and a global central bank. Obviously, this is a very distant goal. The development law of economic globalization and the operation law of the relative independence of national economies of various countries will affect and interact with each other for a long period.

(iii) Development trend of the international monetary system

The current international monetary system faces dilemmas or even more difficult choices on key issues such as exchange rate system, capital account opening and international reserve currency. Any choice is not perfect. In the future, it will be a competitive international monetary system arrangement with multiple choices.

1. Variability

There are no one - size - fits - all options for exchange rate regimes and capital flow management. The floating exchange rate system and the free flow of capital have been regarded as the standard by reform promoters in various countries. However, with the evolution of the economic and financial situation and the repeated baptism of the economic and financial crisis, many economies especially developing economies, have begun to feel the disadvantages of this choice. They have constantly revised the original reform path in practice to find their own development path.

In fact, the differences in economic structure and market development of various countries have always existed, and different economic objectives and problems appear in different periods. It is difficult for invariable institutional arrangements and management ideas to play a positive role all the time. From the perspective of developed economies, the formulation of economic and financial related policies does not consider its greater spillover. For example, the introduction of quantitative easing monetary policy has greatly increased the risk of free capital flow and the exchange rate volatility under the floating exchange rate system. Developing and emerging economies need to fully consider the changes in the international environment, the operation of the domestic economy, the depth of the financial market, the ability and level of market managers and participants and to summarize historical experience, actively respond to practical challenges and prevent external impact risks.

For example, after the Asian financial crisis, relevant economies have generally increased reserve accumulation, which is equivalent to abandoning the principle of non - intervention of the free-floating exchange rate system. After the international financial crisis, many emerging economies and even some developed economies have strengthened the management of cross-border capital flows, which also reflects the need to deal with the changes in the international financial market.

2. Diversification

The Bretton Woods System is a rule based on arrangement of the international monetary system. The Jamaica Monetary System is an open and inclusive system without system, that is, rules and constraints. On the one hand, the choice of exchange rate systems and the management of cross-border capital flows of various countries have long been unlikely to appear and try to seek unified standards and regulations. Facts have proved that the system suitable for its own economic and financial development status and development stage is the best system, and the management measures conducive to domestic economic and financial stability are effective measures. On the other hand, the current strength comparison among countries means that the international monetary system dominated by the US dollar cannot undergo disruptive changes in the short term, and the reform of the international monetary system cannot go too fast. In the 1960s, the establishment and introduction of the gold treasury and the special drawing right were complementary to the insufficient international solvency under the US dollar standard. In the early 1970s, after the decoupling of the US dollar from gold, the international reserve currency system had entered an era of diversification.

3. Flexibility

As for what currency to choose as the currency for pricing, settlement and investment, including whether to promote the local currency to the international market and whether to choose the super sovereign currency or virtual currency as the international currency, all countries have autonomy, but any choice must compete with the existing international currency and the survival of the fittest in the market.

Although the voice and representation of emerging markets in the existing international monetary system are still insufficient, the reform of the international monetary system has been put on the agenda of the reform of the global governance framework. For example, the economic policy supervision of the International Monetary Fund has expanded from exchange rate policy to the whole macroeconomic policy, and from the supervision of developing countries to all countries, especially important countries in the global system. The Financial Stability Forum, the Basel Committee, the International Securities Regulatory Commission and other institutions have put forward many suggestions to improve and strengthen financial supervision from their respective fields. Monetary cooperation at various levels has been established worldwide. In 2010, the World Bank adopted a reform plan to transfer 3.13 percentage points of voting rights to developing countries. At the same time, the International Monetary Fund is also trying to promote share reform.

II. European monetary integration

(i) The birth of the European Union and the euro

➤ Before the 20th century, the idea of European unity had emerged. Historically, Europe had also become a community of destiny in the form of empires or national alliances at certain times.

➤ In 1948, Netherlands, Belgium and Luxembourg formed a customs union, mainly to exempt tariffs and open free trade in raw materials and commodities.

➤ After the World War II, in September 1946, the British Prime Minister Winston Churchill proposed the establishment of the "United States of Europe".

➤ In 1949, the European Commission was established as the first Pan-European organization.

➤ In May 1950, in view of the fact that coal and steel products were necessary raw materials for military weapons, the French Foreign Minister Robert Schumann proposed the European Coal and Steel Community Plan (i.e., Schumann Plan), which aims to restrain Germany.

➤ On April 18, 1951, France, Italy, Belgium, Netherlands, Luxembourg and Germany jointly signed the 50-year Treaty on Establishment of the European Coal and Steel Community (also known as the Treaty of Paris). In 1952, the European Coal and Steel Community was established. While taking over the management power of Ruhr District and canceling some industrial production restrictions in Germany, cooperating to promote the production and sales of coal and steel.

➤ On June 1, 1955, the six foreign ministers of the European Coal and Steel Community held a meeting in Messina, Italy and proposed to extend the principles of the coal and steel community to other economic fields and establish a common market.

➤ On March 25, 1957, the six heads of state and foreign ministers of the European Coal and Steel Community signed the Treaty on European Economic Community and the Treaty on European Atomic Energy Community in Rome. Later generations called these two treaties the Treaty of Rome.

➤ On January 1, 1958, the Treaty of Rome officially entered into force and the European Economic Community was officially established. It aims to create a common market, eliminate tariffs among members and promote the free flow of labor, goods, funds and services among members. On the same day, the European Investment Bank was established and officially opened in 1959 with its head office in Luxembourg.

➤ On April 8, 1965, Germany, France, Italy, Netherlands, Belgium and Luxembourg signed the Treaty of Brussels and decided to unify the European Coal and Steel Community, the European Atomic Energy Community and the European Economic Community, collectively referred to as the "European Community", which was the predecessor of the European Union.

➤ On July 1, 1987, the European Single Act came into force.

➤ On December 11, 1991, the Maastricht Summit of European Community adopted and initialed the Treaty on European Economic and Monetary Union and the Treaty of Political Union, collectively referred to as the Treaty on European Union, namely the Treaty of

Maastricht.

➤ On February 7, 1992, the twelve foreign ministers and finance ministers of the European Community officially signed the Treaty of Maastricht in Maastricht, a small town in the Netherlands, establishing a council, committee and parliament, and gradually transforming the joint development of regional economy into the development of regional political and economic integration.

➤ On November 1, 1993, the Treaty of Maastricht officially entered into force, the European Union was officially established, and the three European communities were incorporated into the European Union.

➤ On March 30, 1994, the accession negotiations of Austria, Sweden, Finland and Norway were completed. All countries held referendums, and all countries except Norway passed the proposal to join the European Union. However, Norway joined the European Economic Area with EFTA members such as Iceland and Liechtenstein on January 1, 1994.

➤ On January 1, 1994, the European Economic and Monetary Union established the European Monetary Authority.

➤ In January 1998, the European Central Bank was established.

➤ On January 1, 1999, the EU officially launched the euro. Since then, the euro has been officially used in 11 countries, including Austria, Belgium, France, Germany, Finland, Netherlands, Luxembourg, Ireland, Italy, Portugal and Spain. The 11 countries implemented a unified monetary policy, which is the responsibility of the European Central Bank.

➤ At zero o'clock on January 1, 2002, the euro officially circulated.

➤ In July 2002, the euro became the only legal currency in the euro area.

➤ By the end of 2018, the euro was used by nineteen EU countries. In addition, the euro was also the currency of six non-EU countries (regions), namely Monaco, San Marino, Vatican, Andorra, Montenegro and Kosovo.

(Knowledge Link 10-1)

European Central Bank

The European Central Bank (ECB), established on June 1, 1998, headquartered in Frankfurt, the German financial center, is the central bank of the euro area established in accordance with the provisions of the Maastricht Treaty in 1992. It is the maker, implementer and supervisor of the common monetary policy.

The European Central Bank is the product of European economic integration. It is the first central bank in the world to manage supranational currencies. It is also a financial institution established to adapt to the issuance and flow of the euro. The responsibilities and structure of the European Central Bank are modeled on the German Federal Bank, independent of EU institutions and governments. The main task of the European Central Bank is to maintain the purchasing power of the euro and maintain price stability in the euro area.

The European Central Bank manages leading interest rates, currency reserves and issuance, and formulates European monetary policy. Although the power of monetary policy in the eurozone is centralized, the specific implementation is still the responsibility of the central banks of eurozone member states. The central banks of the eurozone still retain their foreign exchange reserves, and the reserves of the European Central Bank are provided by the central banks of member states according to their proportion of population and GDP in the eurozone.

The Governing Council of the European Central Bank is the highest decision-making body responsible for setting interest rates and implementing monetary policies. It is composed of six executive board members and central bank governors of eurozone member states, who meet regularly every month. With the establishment of the European Banking Union, the European Central Bank has been entrusted with the function of supervising major banks in the EU and has performed this function together with the competent authorities of member states from November 2014.

Source: According to the network data and amended.

(ii) European Monetary System

The European Monetary System mainly consists of three components: one is the European Monetary Unit (ECU), the other is the European Monetary Cooperation Fund (EMCF), and the third is the Exchange Rate Mechanism (ERM).

1. European Monetary Unit

The European Monetary Unit is similar to the special drawing right. Its value is the weighted average value of the currencies of member states of the European Community. The weight of each currency is determined according to the proportion of the country's intra-trade in the European Community and the scale of the country's gross national product.

The value of the European Monetary Unit calculated in this way is relatively stable, and the calculation method also determines that the German mark, the French franc and the British pound are the three most important currencies, of which the German mark accounts for the largest proportion. Therefore, the rise or fall of the mark exchange rate often has a decisive impact on the rise and fall of the European Monetary Unit.

The creation of the European Monetary Unit is the biggest difference between the European Monetary System and the Joint Floating, and its issuance has a specific procedure.

The main functions of the European Monetary Unit are as follows: as the standard of the European stable exchange rate mechanism; as a reference index for determining the deviation of the currency exchange rate of member states from the central exchange rate; as an official means of clearing and credit among the member states and a means of intervention in the foreign exchange markets.

2. European Monetary Cooperation Fund

In order to ensure the normal operation of the European Monetary System, the European Community established the European Monetary Cooperation Fund in April 1973, concentrating 20% of the gold reserves and US dollar reserves of member states as preparation for the issuance of the European Monetary Unit.

The main role of the European Monetary Cooperation Fund is to provide corresponding loans to members to help them adjust their balance of payments and intervene in the foreign exchange market, so as to ensure the stability of the European exchange rate mechanism.

The types of loans provided by the European Monetary Cooperation Fund to members vary according to their terms. Loans with a minimum term of less than 45 days (including 45 days) are only provided to countries participating in the stable exchange rate mechanism. Short-term loans of less than 9 months are used to help members overcome short-term balance of payments imbalance. The term of a medium-term loan is 2 to 5 years, which is used to help members solve structural balance of payments problems.

The European Community usually attaches certain conditions when providing loans to its members.

3. Exchange Rate Mechanism

The Exchange Rate Mechanism within the European Monetary System is not completely fixed, and there is a volatile range of currency exchange rates among members.

Each member's currency sets a central exchange rate with the European Monetary Unit (ECU), which fluctuates up and down in the market by plus or minus 2.25%, and 6% for the pound. Since the mark used to be the strongest currency in the European Monetary System and one of the most important trading currencies in the international foreign exchange market, people often take the fluctuation of the exchange rate between the currencies of the members of the European Monetary System and the mark as the symbol of central bank intervention.

(iii) The challenge of the euro to the current international monetary system

The birth of the euro has boosted the economic strength and political status of the EU, and provided a successful example for the financial cooperation of other economic organizations.

The diversification of exchange rate system arrangements, the non-monetization of gold and the difficulty of international policy coordination are the important reasons why the Jamaica Monetary System is called "non-system".

The euro will directly challenge this "non-system" with its stable exchange rate, cross-border coordination and unified central bank.

Moreover, the unified euro will be a creation of a cross-border credit standard currency that can be used for unofficial settlement for the first time in human history. Its birth and development will provide valuable experience for the creation of a unified world currency in the future, and will also play an exemplary role in the monetary integration of other regional economic cooperation organizations.

Many scholars have predicted that the final unification of the world currency will be based on several regional international currencies, and perform its function of the world currency in a wide range of international coordination and institutional framework. We believe that in the future, the monetary reform process of the International Monetary Fund will intersect with the development process of international monetary integration in the region, and finally create a perfect world currency. Although this process is long, it may be the trend of the evolution of the international monetary system in the future.

III. Internationalization of RMB

Economist Thomas Friedman once said, "the earth is round, but the world is flat." The modern society with deep globalization is an interactive whole.

RMB is destined to carry a certain historical mission and play an increasingly important role on the stage of the world economy.

(i) Connotation of RMB internationalization

It is generally believed that a country's currency must have at least three basic functions to become an international currency: settlement function, investment function and reserve function. Among them, the settlement function is a necessary condition rather than a sufficient condition for currency internationalization.

The internationalization of RMB means that RMB is widely recognized and accepted in the international market and plays the functions of valuation unit, exchange medium and value storage, that is, it becomes an international settlement currency, investment currency and reserve currency.

The essential meaning of RMB internationalization should include the following three aspects: (1) RMB cash enjoys a certain degree of circulation abroad, and transactions settled in RMB in international trade should reach a certain proportion. (2) Financial products denominated in RMB have become investment instruments of major international financial institutions, including the central bank, and the scale of the financial market denominated in RMB has been expanding. (3) Most countries in the world accept RMB as their reserve currency. This is a common standard for measuring the internationalization of currencies, including the RMB. The latter two points are the most important.

(ii) RMB internationalization process

RMB was born on December 1, 1948. Before the reform and opening up in the late 1970s, under the highly centralized foreign exchange management system, RMB was almost only responsible for the single role of the domestic currency. In principle, it was neither allowed to carry out the country nor to use RMB for the valuation and settlement of foreign trade, investment and financing and other activities.

With the deepening of reform and opening up, China's foreign personnel exchanges are becoming more and more frequent, including individuals who travel abroad and visit relatives, as well as a large number of foreign businessmen who travel between Hong Kong, Macao, Taiwan regions of China. At the same time, China's national conditions are special, with tens of millions of overseas Chinese and ethnic Chinese distributed overseas, the reform and opening up has strengthened the ties between residents at home and abroad.

In order to meet the needs of the rising amount of cash used in the market, the government adaptively adjusted the RMB cross-border policy and relaxed the restrictions on individuals carrying RMB into and out of the country. In February 1993, it was stipulated that the RMB limit for Chinese citizens and foreigners to enter and leave the country was 6,000 yuan per person; and the places where the small amount of trade was allowed to be opened shall be determined according to the actual situation of the border city. In January 2005, the standard of carrying RMB cash at entry and exit was further raised to 20,000 yuan.

After the floating exchange rate was widely implemented in 1973, the fluctuation of currency exchange rate and gold price in the Western foreign exchange market often occurred. China has a large surplus in foreign trade and a large amount of capital inflow, which means holding a large number of foreign exchange reserves. If the foreign exchange is unstable, China's economic security will be difficult to maintain. When RMB becomes an international reserve currency and international trade can be paid in RMB, we do not need to hold a large number of foreign exchange reserves, and the impact of exchange rate changes in other countries on China will be reduced.

In March 2003, the State Administration of Foreign Exchange (SAFE) issued a document clearly stipulating that the domestic institutions can use RMB as the pricing currency when signing import and export contracts, but the currency for actual external delivery is still converted into equivalent foreign exchange according to the bank quotation on that day for receipt, payment and settlement.

In September 2003, the SAFE issued a document again, allowing RMB pricing and settlement and handling import and export verification and cancellation in border trade, allowing overseas trade institutions to open special accounts for RMB border trade settlement in banks in China's border areas and handle the receipt and payment of funds under border trade settlement. At the same time, banks in border areas are encouraged to establish agency bank relations with commercial banks in border areas of neighboring countries. Direct bank settlement channels will be opened, and the exchange rate of RMB against the currencies of neighboring countries can be added.

In June 2007, the first RMB bond landed in Hong Kong, China.

In December 2008, China and Russia negotiated to use the domestic currency for settlement in trade. China and Korea signed a ￥ 180 billion currency swap agreement.

In July 2009, the pilot of RMB settlement for cross - border trade was officially launched.

In September 2011, Nigeria planned to invest 10% of its foreign exchange reserves in RMB. Chile, Thailand, Brazil and Venezuela planned to include RMB in central bank reserves.

In December 2011, the relevant rules of the pilot program of RMB qualified foreign institutional investors were released.

In October 2012, the direct quotation of JPY/RMB was opened.

In June 2013, China and Britain signed a £ 20 billion bilateral local currency swap agreement.

In October 2013, China and the EU signed a ¥ 350 billion currency swap agreement.

In June 2015, the People's Bank of China issued the 2015 Report on RMB Internationalization for the first time.

On December 1, 2015, RMB officially joined the SDR, and the SDR currency basket was correspondingly expanded to five currencies: US dollar, Euro, RMB, Japanese yen and British pound. The weight of RMB in the SDR currency basket is 10.92%, and the weights of US dollar, Euro, Japanese yen and British pound are 41.73%, 30.93%, 8.33% and 8.09% respectively. So far, this is undoubtedly a new starting point for RMB and China's financial market to move towards the international stage.

According to the statistics of SWIFT, in December 2016, RMB became the sixth-largest payment currency in the world, with a market share of 1.68%.

On October 1, 2016, RMB was officially included in the International Monetary Fund special drawing right (SDR) currency basket, which is an important milestone in the internationalization of RMB.

(iii) Advantages and disadvantages of RMB internationalization

1. Advantages of RMB internationalization

(1) Increase in international seigniorage revenue.

Under the modern monetary system, seigniorage is not a tax under the tax system but refers to the difference between the face value of money obtained by the issuer by virtue of its privilege of issuing money and the issuing cost, which is the income brought by currency issuance.

When a country's currency becomes an international currency, it can obtain rich seigniorage income. Similarly, international seigniorage revenue is the biggest benefit after the internationalization of RMB. Seigniorage can be levied from other countries by issuing international currency, and this benefit is cost-free.

Therefore, if RMB becomes an international valuation and payment currency, or even a reserve currency, China will receive high seigniorage tax. The international seigniorage revenue brought by the internationalization of RMB will become an important source of China's fiscal revenue.

（2）Save foreign exchange reserves and avoid exchange rate risks.

At present, China's foreign exchange reserves are highly concentrated in US dollar assets. Whether the value of US treasury bonds falls or the US dollar exchange rate depreciates sharply, China's foreign exchange reserves will shrink sharply. Realizing the internationalization of RMB can make RMB become one of the main currencies of international settlement. It is both a valuation currency and a reserve currency. Reducing foreign exchange reserves can alleviate the problem of excess liquidity caused by excessive foreign exchange reserves to a certain extent and contribute to internal and external balance. At the same time, the rapid development of foreign trade makes foreign trade enterprises hold a large number of foreign currency claims and debts, which will produce huge risks due to the fluctuation of the foreign currency exchange rate, and which will have an adverse impact on the production and operation of enterprises.

After the internationalization of RMB, the loss of wealth caused by the use of foreign currencies can be reduced, foreign trade and investment can be carried out in domestic currency, and enterprises can effectively avoid exchange rate risks, reduce trade costs, and promote and expand China's foreign trade.

（3）Optimize the world monetary structure.

After the World War II, the US dollar became the overlord of the global currency and accounted for a large proportion of the global foreign exchange reserves. Among them, it accounts for more than 60% in the global foreign exchange reserves and more than 70% in the foreign exchange reserves of developed countries. The internationalization of RMB can disperse the risks of national reserves in currency and strive for rights for developing countries. The choice of adding RMB to the reserves of various countries will greatly help to stabilize the wealth held and reduce the helplessness in the face of the shrinking wealth caused by the sharp depreciation of the US dollar.

（4）Boost financial innovation and development.

At present, there are many problems in China's financial market. Financial innovation lags behind the real economy, and the problem of insufficient innovation is prominent. In contrast, in the developed countries in Europe and America, their financial markets continue to innovate, with various financial derivatives and structured products emerging endlessly, and their financial systems are relatively sound and perfect. These are closely related to the huge voice of the US dollar and the euro in the world. The internationalization of RMB can promote the continuous improvement of China's finance and the continuous renewal of financial derivatives, which is conducive to dispersing and reducing risks, enhancing market liquidity, enriching market investment varieties and increasing investment.

（5）Enhance the voice of politics and economy.

The internationalization of RMB is neither optional nor greedy for foreign countries. This is a necessary strategic step for China's economic development at this stage, whether in terms of economic development or national strategy and geopolitics.

2. Disadvantages of RMB internationalization

(1) The difficulty of macro-control has increased.

At present, the central bank can relatively effectively regulate market liquidity and a series of asset and investment problems related to liquidity by collecting and releasing money. Once the RMB is internationalized, the central bank will face more complex monetary demand due to international demand when formulating monetary policy. The monetary operation idea will change from a top-down linear system in China to a network system linked with the central banks all over the world.

Due to the defects of the market mechanism itself and the lag of various market signal detection, it will become a technical problem to determine the money supply. After the internationalization of RMB, a certain amount of RMB will circulate in the international financial market and increase with the improvement of the internationalization of RMB, which will weaken the control ability of the central bank over domestic RMB and affect the implementation effect of domestic macro-control policies.

(2) Weakening of monetary policy autonomy.

The sharp increase of international financial transactions makes it more difficult for central banks of various countries to deal with. As a result, relevant countries have to give up the benefits of financial globalization and control capital flows through the implementation of capital account control. Countries with floating exchange rates and free capital flows are at a disadvantage in using the world's savings resources. A country's implementation of a floating exchange rate system can control short-term interest rates, but currency internationalization makes the impact of exchange rate on interest rates more obvious, and the change of interest rates is more sensitive to the impact from the change of exchange rates. After currency internationalization, if the real exchange rate of the local currency deviates from the nominal exchange rate, or the spot exchange rate and interest rate deviate from the expected exchange rate and interest rate, it will give international investors the opportunity to arbitrage and stimulate the flow of short - term speculative capital.

(3) The impact of international speculative capital on China's financial market has increased.

After the internationalization of RMB, the relationship between China's economy and the world economy is bound to be closer. Any disturbance in the international financial market may have an impact on China's financial market. Whether it is the Asian financial crisis or the international financial crisis that has not yet dissipated, China's relatively stable economy and finance benefit from its relatively closed economic and financial markets and strict control of the foreign exchange. Once the financial market is opened up, a large amount of external "hot money" is bound to flow in. Therefore, after the internationalization of RMB, it is likely to become a transmission tool of the financial crisis and reduce the ability of China's economy and financial market to resist risks.

(4) Greater money demand and exchange rate fluctuation.

After becoming an international currency, RMB will be stored and used by many countries. Once the preference of foreign money demand changes, it will lead to the fluctuation of domestic money supply and demand, resulting in the fluctuation of the exchange rate.

(5) Export enterprises face challenges.

At present, China has become the world's largest exporter. Over the years of reform and opening up, the rapid economic development has benefited from high exports. At the same time, the internationalization of RMB will further increase the pressure of RMB appreciation. After the appreciation of RMB, in order to maintain the same RMB price, the current price of China's export products expressed in US dollar will increase, which will weaken its price competitiveness. If the US dollar price of export products remains unchanged, it is bound to squeeze the profit space of export enterprises, which will inevitably have an impact on export enterprises.

Mini Case

"Currency" is a 10 - episode large - scale documentary produced by CCTV. This documentary introduces the origin of money, the development of money, the rise of money, the disaster of money and the future of money.

This documentary comprehensively and deeply combs the relationship between money and political, economic, cultural and social operation order, and interprets money in an open, popular and vivid way.

Please watch the ninth episode of the documentary "Currency" - "Across Borders" and answer:

(1) Talk about the emergence time and development context of several major international currencies in the world.

(2) Try to summarize the conditions for the evolution of national currency into international currency.

(3) Think about how to realize the real internationalization of RMB from the perspective of globalization?

Mind Map

```
                              Definition of the international monetary system
         Overview of the International   Concept of the international monetary system
              Monetary System           Types and functions of the international monetary system

                              International Gold Standard
International      Evolution of the International   Bretton Woods System
Monetary System       Monetary System           Jamaica Monetary System

                              Overview of the reform of the international monetary system
         Reform of the International   European monetary integration
              Monetary System           Internationalization of RMB
```

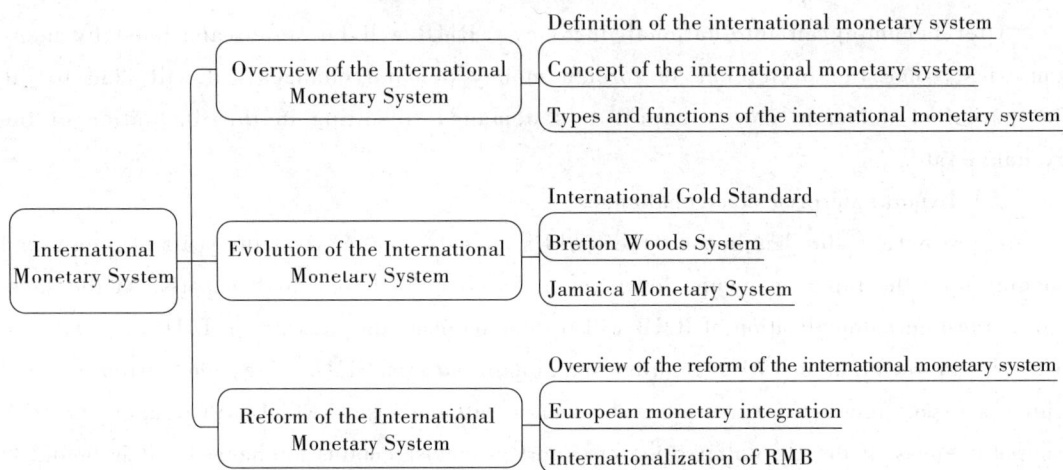

Project Training

I. Single-choice questions

1. The international monetary system entered the era of the floating exchange rate, which began in the (   ).

A. International Gold Standard   B. Bretton Woods System

C. Jamaica Monetary System   D. after the birth of the euro

2. The basic conditions for maintaining the operation of the Bretton Woods System do not include (   ).

A. The United States balance of payments maintained a surplus and the external value of the US dollar remained stable

B. Countries around the world have sufficient and balanced gold reserves to maintain full exchange for gold

C. The United States has sufficient gold reserves to maintain the limited convertibility of the US dollar against gold

D. The price of gold remained at the official level

3. One of the basic contradictions mentioned in Triffin Dilemma is (   ).

A. The contradiction between maintaining the exchange rate of the US dollar and the balance of payments of the United States

B. The contradiction between maintaining the price ratio between the US dollar and gold and maintaining the exchange rate between the US dollar and the currencies of various countries

C. The contradiction between the US dollar and gold and the currencies of various countries and the US dollar

D. The contradiction between floating exchange rate and controlled exchange rate

4. The first international monetary system in history was (   ) .

A. International Gold Standard   B. International Gold Exchange Standard

C. Bretton Woods System   D. Post Bretton Woods System

5. The start-up time of the euro is (   ) .

A. January 2002   B. January 1999   C. October 2000   D. March 2002

II. Multiple-choice questions

1. The contents of the international monetary system include (   ) .

A. Determination of key currencies and exchange rate regime

B. Determination of international reserve assets

C. Determination of the balance of payments and its adjustment mechanism

D. What kind of settlement method should be adopted when settling claims and debts between countries

E. Restrictions imposed (i.e., exchange controls)

2. Which of the following statement about the International Monetary Fund are correct (   ) .

A. It is a professional institution of the United Nations system with its headquarters in Washington

B. As one of the founding countries of the organization, China has always maintained the legal seat of the organization

C. It is an enterprise financial institution composed of members' shares, and the fund shares of members constitute its main source of funds

D. The term of ordinary drawing rights shall not exceed 5 years, and the maximum amount of loans shall be 100% of the shares paid by members

3. The advantages of RMB internationalization are (   ) .

A. Increase in international seigniorage revenue

B. Save foreign exchange reserves and avoid exchange rate risks

C. Optimize the world monetary structure

D. Boost financial innovation and development

E. Enhance political and economic voice

4. Under the Bretton Woods System, which of the following statement are correct (   ) .

A. Gold is pegged to the dollar

B. National currencies are pegged to the US dollar

C. National currencies are directly pegged to gold

D. Currencies are indirectly pegged to gold

5. The international monetary system are characterized by （　　）.

A. Coexistence of multiple exchange rate systems

B. Basically the US dollar is the central international currency

C. Coexistence of multiple central international currencies

D. It is generally pegged to an international central currency

III. Judgment questions

1. According to the standard of the form of international reserve assets, the international monetary system can be divided into gold standard and credit standard. There are two types of the standard system.　　　　　　　　　　　　　　　　　　　　　　　　　　　　（　　）

2. The key currency is the currency that acts as the basic value conversion tool in the international monetary system.　　　　　　　　　　　　　　　　　　　　　　　　（　　）

3. The first international monetary system in the world is the International Silver Standard System.　　　　　　　　　　　　　　　　　　　　　　　　　　　　　　　　　（　　）

4. The International Monetary Fund was established during the period of Jamaica Monetary System.　　　　　　　　　　　　　　　　　　　　　　　　　　　　　　　　　　（　　）

5. The euro was born in 1999.　　　　　　　　　　　　　　　　　　　　　　（　　）

IV. Practical questions

Collect information through the Internet, books and other materials, understand the latest progress of RMB internationalization, and analyze the advantages and disadvantages of RMB internationalization.

References

［1］ CHEN Y L. International Finance ［M］. 6th Edition. Beijing: China Renmin University Press, 2019.

［2］ WANG X G. International Finance ［M］. 5th Edition. Beijing: Tsinghua University Press, 2019.

［3］ JIANG B K. New Edition of International Finance ［M］. 6th Edition. Shanghai: Fudan University Press, 2018.

［4］ LIU S E, ZHAO X Y. International Finance and Practice ［M］. 2nd Edition. Beijing: Tsinghua University Press, 2018.

［5］ SUN L Z. International Finance ［M］. 4th Edition. Beijing: Higher Education Press, 2019.

［6］ LI M. International Finance Practice ［M］. 3rd Edition. Beijing: China Financial Publishing Press, 2019.

［7］ ZHANG Z Y, JI J X. International Finance Practice ［M］. 2nd Edition. Beijing: University of International Business and Economics Press, 2017.

［8］ LI J Y, LOU Y J. International Finance Practice ［M］. 3rd Edition. Dalian: Dongbei University of Finance and Economics Press, 2021.

［9］ LIU Y C, CAO H. International Finance Practice ［M］. 6th Edition. Dalian: Dongbei University of Finance and Economics Press, 2021.

［10］ HE Z R. Principles of International Finance ［M］. 3rd Edition. Chengdu: Southwestern University of Finance and Economics Press, 2015.

［11］ WANG Z H. International Financial Practice ［M］. 2nd Edition. Beijing: University of International Business and Economics Press, 2015.

［12］ FU H L. Theory and Practice of International Trade ［M］. 5th Edition. Beijing: University of International Business and Economics Press, 2018.

［13］ CHENG Z W. International Trade Settlement and Financing ［M］. 4th Edition. Beijing: China Renmin University Press, 2016.

［14］ YAO J. International Settlement Practice ［M］. Beijing: China Renmin University Press, 2018.

［15］ XU N. International Settlement ［M］. Beijing: China Renmin University Press, 2014.

[16] LIU J B. Principle and Practice of Foreign Exchange Trading [M]. 2nd Edition. Beijing: People's Posts and Telecommunications Press, 2016.

[17] ZHANG Y P. Financial Derivatives [M]. 5th Edition. Beijing: Capital University of Economics and Business Press, 2018.

[18] REN J X. New International Trade Theory and Practice [M]. 2nd Edition. Beijing: Peking University Press, 2016.

[19] International Monetary Fund. Balance of Payments and International Investment Position Manual [M]. 6th Edition. Beijing: China Financial Press, 2012.

[20] Department of Balance of Payments, State Administration of Foreign Exchange. Interpretation of the New Standard for Balance of Payments Statistics [M]. Beijing: China Economic Press, 2015.

[21] International Monetary Fund website, https: //www.imf.org/zh/home.

[22] State Administration of Foreign Exchange website, https: //www.safe.gov.cn/.

[23] China Foreign Exchange Trade System website, http: //www.chinamoney.com.cn/chi nese/index.html.

[24] World Gold Council website, https: //www.gold.org/.

[25] Chinese Financial News website, https: //www.financialnews.com.cn/.